T0350462

Open Information Management:
Applications of Interconnectivity and Collaboration

Samuli Niiranen
Tampere University of Technology, Finland

Jari Yli–Hietanen
Tampere University of Technology, Finland

Artur Lugmayr
Tampere University of Technology, Finland

INFORMATION SCIENCE REFERENCE

Hershey · New York

Director of Editorial Content: Kristin Klinger
Senior Managing Editor: Jamie Snavely
Managing Editor: Jeff Ash
Assistant Managing Editor: Carole Coulson
Typesetter: Amanda Appicello
Cover Design: Lisa Tosheff
Printed at: Yurchak Printing Inc.

Published in the United States of America by
        Information Science Reference (an imprint of IGI Global)
        701 E. Chocolate Avenue, Suite 200
        Hershey PA 17033
        Tel: 717-533-8845
        Fax: 717-533-8661
        E-mail: cust@igi-global.com
        Web site: http://www.igi-global.com/reference

and in the United Kingdom by
        Information Science Reference (an imprint of IGI Global)
        3 Henrietta Street
        Covent Garden
        London WC2E 8LU
        Tel: 44 20 7240 0856
        Fax: 44 20 7379 0609
        Web site: http://www.eurospanbookstore.com

Library of Congress Cataloging-in-Publication Data

Open information management : applications of interconnectivity and collaboration / Samuli Niiranen, Jari Yli-Hietanen, and Artur Lugmayr, editors.
        p. cm.
  Includes bibliographical references and index.
  Summary: "This book provides a practical-level reference discussing the impact of emerging trends in information technology toward solutions capable of managing information within operational environments"--Provided by publisher. ISBN 978-1-60566-246-6 (hardcover) -- ISBN 978-1-60566-247-3 (ebook) 1. Information technology--Management. 2. Information resources management. 3. Management information systems. I. Niiranen, Samuli. II. Yli-Hietanen, Jari, 1970- III. Lugmayr, Artur. HD30.2.O637 2009
  658.4'038--dc22
                                    2008052165

British Cataloguing in Publication Data
A Cataloguing in Publication record for this book is available from the British Library.

Table of Contents

Detailed Table of Contents

Chapter I
Open Formats, Open Information and Future Trends in Software Engineering.................................... 1
Teemu Saarelainen, Kymenlaakso University of Applied Sciences, Finland

The amount of information surrounding us is ever increasing. Usable information is our most valuable asset both in professional and personal lives. Authors are constantly struggling to find the information needed in our various every day situations. Search engines have given us the tools to cope with the problem so far, but what lies ahead? This chapter describes some of the current trends of information management in software systems and discusses the aspects of using natural language, open formats and open source software in the field of software engineering while keeping in mind the needs of our future society.

Chapter II
Engineering Information into Open Documents.. 9
Chia-Chu Chiang, University of Arkansas at Little Rock, USA

Documents are perfectly suited for information exchange via the Internet. In order to insure that there are no misunderstandings, information embedded in a document needs to be precise and unambiguous. Having a (de facto) standard data model and conceptual information model insures that the involved parties will agree on what the information means. XML (eXtensible Markup Language) has become the de facto standard format for representing information in documents for document exchange. Many techniques have been proposed to create XML documents, including the validation and transformation of XML documents. However, very little is discussed when it comes to extracting information from non-XML documents and engineering the information into XML documents. The extraction process can be a highly labor intensive task if it is done manually. The use of automated tools would make the process more efficient. In this chapter, the authors will briefly survey document engineering techniques for XML documents. Then, they will present two techniques to extract data from Windows documents into XML documents. These two techniques have been successfully applied in two industrial projects. They believe that techniques that automate the extraction of data from non-XML documents into XML formats will definitely enhance the use of XML documents.

This chapter presents a look at the decision-making methods used by real-life, collegial, high-achieving, technical teams and organizations. One may argue that the type of technical team that is being considered is not critical. When a group of individuals come together to examine and solve a tough technical challenge the synergy created in reaching a conclusion is usually quite astounding. As the authors will explore in this chapter, many researchers have come to the conclusion that the manner in which those teams make decisions is one factor that affects the achievement level of the team. It is then reasonable to suggest that an organization's achievement level is related to the decision-making method of its technical teams. This chapter contains a review of the published literature on team decision-making. In keeping with the practical-level theme of this book, also discussed are the results of a unique study of 31, intact, real-life, technical teams. The teams operated in open, unbounded environments. The resulting theory that emerged from the data was that a collegial, technical, team's selection of the majority-rule method may be an indicator that the team will reach a high-achievement level. The preceding is important because contemporary work organizations may not be obtaining the maximal benefits from their work teams if they attempt to "force" teams to implement other types of decision-making methods.

The purpose of this chapter is to discuss the relationship between three entities: hierarchical organization, information management, and human collaboration. This relationship is composed of two parts: the first part is the relationship between the hierarchical organization and information management where the role of the hierarchical organization to facilitate the information management processes is discussed. The second part is the relationship between information management and human collaboration where the role of information management to improve human collaboration in problem solving is discussed. The information management processes are illustrated through an information management life cycle model. This model has three major stages: active, semi-active, and inactive stages and has three major phases: creation, searching and utilization phases. The creation phase includes: information creation and using, information authoring and modifying and information organization and indexing. The searching phase includes: information storage and retrieving and information exchange. The utilization phase includes: information accessing and filtering processes. The arguments about the role of hierarchical organization in information management and human collaboration are also discussed. The authors showed that the hierarchical organization acts as a facilitator for common information management processes which are required in team collaboration such as: information gathering, organization, retrieving, filtering, exchange, integration or fusion, display and visualization. Human collaboration models are discussed with emphasis on the team collaboration structural model which has four unique but interdependent stages of team collaboration. These stages are: team knowledge construction, collaborative team problem solving, team consensus, and product evaluation and revision. Each stage has four levels: meta-cognition process which guides the overall problem solving process, the information processing tasks which is required by the team to complete each collaboration stage, the knowledge required to support the information processing tasks and the communication mechanisms for knowledge building and information processing. They focused on the role of information management to improve human collaboration across the four collaboration stages of the team collaboration structural model. They showed that the hierarchical organization is more efficient for information management processes and team collaboration rather that other alternative organizations such as flat, linear and network organizations.

Christine B. Glaser, University of Surrey, CCSR, I-Lab, UK
Amy Tan, University of Surrey, CCSR, I-Lab, UK
Ahmet M. Kondoz, University of Surrey, CCSR, I-Lab, UK

Managing information collaboratively in an open and unbounded environment without an information management application influenced and challenged the users actions and cognitive abilities, hence collaborative information management behaviour (CIMB). This issue motivated the auhtors to investigate distributed synchronous CIMB to deduce criteria for the design of an intelligent information management application that supports interconnectivity and human collaboration in such an environment. They developed a model to understand CIMB based on qualitative and quantitative findings, which emerged from four video recordings. These findings revealed that CIMB manifests itself in five behavioural stages: Initiation, Identification, Formulation, Structuring and Decision Making. Thus, an application for open information management should support human-to-computer and human-to-human interaction, should facilitate the behavioural stages users went during an information selection task and should sustain cognitive abilities. This chapter proposes the design for such an application, which supports users actions and cognitive abilities required to manage information collaboratively in an open and unbounded environment.

Lobna Hsairi, SOIE: Institut Supérieur de Gestion de Tunis, Tunisie
Khaled Ghédira, SOIE: Institut Supérieur de Gestion de Tunis, Tunisie
Adel M. Alimi, REGIM: Ecole Nationale d'Ingénieurs de Sfax, Tunisie
Abdellatif BenAbdelhafid, CERENE-SILI: Université du Havre, France

In the age of information proliferation, openness, open information management, interconnectivity, collaboration and communication advances, extended enterprises must be up to date to the new strategic, economic and organizational structures. Consequently, intelligent software based on agent technology emerges to improve system design, and to increase enterprise competitive position as well. The competitiveness is based on the information management, cooperation, collaboration and interconnectivity. Thus, within these interconnectivity and cooperation, conflicts may arise. The automated negotiation plays a key role to look for a common agreement. Argumentation theory has become an important topic in the field of Multi Agent Systems and especially in the negotiation problem. In this chapter, first, the proposed model MAIS-E2 (Multi Agent Information System for an Extended Enterprise) is presented. Then an argumentation based negotiation framework: Relationship-Role and Interest Based Negotiation

(R2 IBN) framework is presented, and within this framework, the authors focused mainly on, argument generation module via inference rules and argument selection module via fuzzy logic.

Chapter VII

Pauli Brattico, University of Jyväskylä, Finland
Mikko Määttä, University of Helsinki, Finland

Automatic natural language processing captures a lion's share of the attention in open information management. In one way or another, many applications have to deal with natural language input. In this chapter the authors investigate the problem of natural language parsing from the perspective of biolinguistics. They argue that the human mind succeeds in the parsing task without the help of language-specific rules of parsing and language-specific rules of grammar. Instead, there is a universal parser incorporating a universal grammar. The main argument comes from language acquisition: Children cannot learn language specific parsing rules by rule induction due to the complexity of unconstrained inductive learning. They suggest that the universal parser presents a manageable solution to the problem of automatic natural language processing when compared with parsers tinkered for specific purposes. A model for a completely language independent parser is presented, taking a recent minimalist theory as a starting point.

Chapter VIII

Sune Lehmann, Northeastern University, USA & Harvard University, USA

A network structure of nodes and links is an informative way to study information systems. The network representation is valuable because it encodes the structure of the data. This chapter reviews recent advances in the field of network science with an emphasis on describing the structure of information networks. The authors argue that bipartite networks constitute an important class of networks, and they describe a method for detecting overlapping communities in bipartite networks. They discuss the relevance of network communities to the future of organizing and understanding large datasets.

Chapter IX

Juha Kesseli, Tampere University of Technology, Finland
Andre S. Ribeiro, Tampere University of Technology, Finland
Matti Nykter, Tampere University of Technology, Finland

In this chapter the authors study the propagation and processing of information in dynamical systems. Various information management systems can be represented as dynamical systems of interconnected information processing units. Here they focus mostly on genetic regulatory networks that are information processing systems that process and propagate information stored in genome. Boolean networks are used as a dynamical model of regulation, and different ways of parameterizing the dynamical behavior are studied. What are called critical networks are in particular under study, since they have been hypothesized as being the most effective under evolutionary pressure. Critical networks are also present in man-made systems, such as the Internet, and provide a candidate application area for findings on the theory of dynamical networks in this chapter. They present approaches of annealed approximation and find that avalanche size distribution data supports criticality of regulatory networks. Based on Shannon information, they then find that a mutual information measure quantifying the coordination of pairwise element activity is maximized at criticality. An approach of algorithmic complexity, the normalized compression distance (NCD), is shown to be applicable to both dynamical and topological features of regulatory networks. NCD can also be seen to enable further utilization of measurement data to estimate information propagation and processing in biological networks.

Chapter X

In the context of the prodigious growth of network-based information services, messaging and edutainment, the authors introduce new tools that enable information management through the use of efficient multimodal interaction using natural language and speech processing. These tools allow the system to respond to close-to natural language queries by means of pattern matching. A new approach which gives the system the ability to learn new utterances of natural language queries from the user is presented. This automatic learning process is initiated when the system encounters an unknown command. This alleviates the burden of users learning a fixed grammar. Furthermore, this enables the system to better respond to spontaneous queries. This work investigates how an information system can benefit from the use of conversational agents to drastically decrease the cognition load of the user. For this purpose, Automated Service Agents and Artificial Intelligence Markup Language (AIML) are used to provide naturalness to the dialogs between users and machines.

Chapter XI

The purpose of this chapter is to introduce tools for automatic audio management. The authors present applications which are already available for the users and describe the algorithms and methods behind these applications and their performance. They also discuss the concept of metadata, which is an important prerequisite for modern distributed personal content applications. The variety of automatic audio management tools is wide-ranging. This chapter covers audio segmentation and classification, query by example of audio, music retrieval and recommendation, and speech management, which the authors consider as being the most important aspects of audio information management. Computational complexity is one major concern in the present era of personal mobile devices and large multimedia collections available on the Internet. Therefore they also introduce clustering and indexing techniques which are developed for faster access in large databases.

Due to the advancement of hardware technologies and mobile communication systems, the mobile devices are transforming into multimedia devices capable of consuming multimedia data. The mobile multimedia devices having the 3G/4G mobile communication interfaces have created the ubiquitous multimedia applications paradigm. The ubiquitous multimedia advocates that adaptable media contents should be available to users any time and any where. These ubiquitous multimedia applications have promising business potentials. The ubiquitous multimedia applications create an infrastructure for multimedia information management, where contents can be managed with interconnection and collaboration between users. The personalized ubiquitous multimedia (PUM) is a subset of ubiquitous multimedia applications, where users can create, store, share and re-use the personalized heterogeneous media contents using mobile multimedia devices. Hence, PUM is an example of interconnected and collaborative multimedia content management system. This chapter illustrates the evolution of Computer-Phone and the concept of PUM. An integrated architecture is described aiming to deploy the PUM applications. The integrated architecture is composed of mobile agent systems (MAS) and a specialized mobile distributed file system. A set of advantages of the integrated architecture is described.

Chapter XIII

Human computer interaction (HCI) challenges in highly dynamic computing environments can be solved by tailoring the access and use of services to user preferences. In this era of emerging standards for open and collaborative computing environments, the major challenge that is being addressed in this chapter is how personalisation information can be managed in order to support cross-service personalisation. The authors' investigation of state-of-the-art work in personalisation and context-aware computing found that user preferences are assumed to be static across different context descriptions whilst in reality some user preferences are transient and vary with changes in context. Furthermore, the assumed preference models do not give an intuitive interpretation of a preference and lack user expressiveness. This chapter presents a user preference model for dynamic computing environments, based on an intuitive quantitative preference measure and a strict partial order preference representation, to address these issues. The authors present an approach for mining context-based user preferences and its evaluation in a synthetic M-Commerce environment. The authors also show how the data needed for mining context-based preferences is gathered and managed in a Grid infrastructure for mobile devices.

Chapter XIV

Efficient and effective knowledge management plays an increasingly important role in knowledge intensive organizations. The research project DYONIPOS focuses on detecting the knowledge needs of knowledge workers and automatically providing this required knowledge just in time. The prototype DYONIPOS generates new knowledge out of artifacts, while avoiding additional work and violations of the knowledge worker's privacy. The knowledge is made accessible through semantic linkage of the relevant information from existing repositories. In addition DYONIPOS creates an individual and an organizational knowledge data base to achieve the knowledge. This chapter is structured as follows: the introduction section describes the current knowledge management approach and the new approach with use of the DYONIPOS prototype. The background section addresses the relation between the applied approach and the challenge in e-government, summarizes the aims of the research project DYONIPOS and delivers also insight into the topic knowledge management by describing and criticizing the "SECI-model" according to Ikujiro Nonaka and Hirotaka Takeuchi. After this the research project DYONIPOS, the semantic and knowledge discovery technologies used are presented as well as the use case project DYONIPOS showing the results of the first and the second test and screenshots of the updated DYONI-POS application. The chapter concludes with presentation of the benefits and the technical advantages of the prototype DYONIPOS.

Chapter XV

In this chapter the open-source based collaboration model of Finnish Wikipedia is examined from the perspective of user culture, which is the fundamental basis of Wikipedia's project management. The concept of user culture in a mediated collaboration project is introduced and the user culture of Finnish Wikipedia is analyzed in terms of this concept. Also the concept of user-system-relation is presented and the relation between users and the socio-technical system of Wikipedia is examined. This analysis considers the crucial factors in the process of building a trusting relation between the user and the Wikipedia system. From the perspective of user-system-relation, the relationship of trust between the user and the system is much more important than the trust relations between individual users. This chapter explains the role of user culture and user culture design in a collaborative Web community and considers the nature of a trusting user-system-relation. Examination of one functional example of open information management gives understanding of management tools for open peer-collaboration in general.

Chapter XVI

The use of information management tools in open and unbounded operational environments demands an efficient and robust communication infrastructure in order to allow the appropriate transmission of large amount of information and the collaboration among several humans located in geographically distant places, in different organizations, and usually involving several network administrative domains. In order to provide such efficient communication infrastructure, mechanisms for data network management must be used. However, traditional network management models do not provide the required support to the management of such networks. In this context, an alternative distributed network management model must be employed to the efficient management of the communication infrastructure required to support these information management tools. This chapter presents the use of peer-to-peer (P2P) technologies as support for the management of such networks. It presents a P2P-based distributed network management model and a network management environment that follows this model. The functionalities required for the environment are discussed, including its features, potentialities, and drawbacks.

Chapter XVII

The problem of server performance in a contemporary, rapidly developed and multi-discipline environment is examined. Multiple requests in a very short period of time increase the number of connections and push the server to the limit. Nowadays servers' ability to work semi autonomously, in regards to the decision of the appropriate query plan and the provision of the effective data location, plays a significant role for the query and network performance. For autonomous server operations many of the offered services need to be self-managed. Data sources' administration during the execution of the query plan becomes of primary interest especially for the starting query server. The proposed server grouping process, server's scale up capabilities and the application of Data Mining concepts in a wireless environment can contribute a lot to the optimization of the query plan and also increase server independence. Various methods of distributed data exploration and exploitation that support server's semi-autonomous operational behavior are developed. Simulation results are provided. This work covers a significant part of cooperative domains in the area of information management and can offer integrated solutions very attractive to the mobile users.

Chapter XVIII

This chapter discusses the role of open health information management to develop a novel, adaptable mixed-platform for supporting health care informational needs. This platform enables clients (patient users) requiring healthcare to enter an unstructured but detailed account of their day-to-day health informational requirements that may be structured into a lifetime electronic health record. It illustrates the discussion with an operational model for a pilot project that can help to explore the potential of a collaborative network of patient and health professional users to support the provision of healthcare services, helping to effectively engage patient users with their own healthcare. Such a solution has the potential to allow both patient and health professional users to produce useful materials, to contribute toward improved social health outcomes in terms of health education and primary disease prevention, and to address both pre-treatment and post-treatment phases of illness that are often neglected in the context of overburdened support services.

Chapter XIX

The global interconnected information space offers unprecedented ways of accessing and analyzing information. New infringements of the rights of individuals to privacy, personality and personal autonomy may be a consequence presenting possible legal and ethical issues for developers and users of open information systems. Awareness of these issues will assist the use, engineering and regulation of open information systems with minimal infringement of those rights.

Preface

BACKGROUND

The wireless music box has no imaginable commercial value. Who would pay for a message sent to nobody in particular?
– David Sarnoff's associates in response to his urgings for investment in the radio in the 1920s

This apocryphal quote from the early days of broadcasting is a favorite in the marketing slide shows of technology company executives as they attempt to persuade suspicious audiences about the potential of their innovation.

Ironically, the skepticism of the ubiquitous associates is actually more relevant than ever today, with the advent of personalized advertising pioneered by the search engine Google. As search-based marketing eats to the revenues of mass media advertising, who indeed will anymore pay for messages sent to nobody in particular? Private broadcasting relies almost exclusively on advertising as a business model. Without advertising, there will be no consumer mass media as we currently know it. This reorganization in advertising is directly coupled to the ongoing collapse of the commonly shared media experience seen famously in the trend towards the consumption of Internet-provided content. The future of media content will be shaped by the individual.

The trend towards the segment size of one is not isolated to consumer media. Economically feasible mass-customization of goods has been the golden calf of the manufacturing industry for quite some time. Personalized healthcare is a hot topic in the medical community. More and more people are coming to the realization that actual learning is a deeply personal process which formal education can only support.

The key tenet is personalization. The reader may notice a dichotomy between personalized experiences and products and the means currently deployed for producing them. Mass-customization equals complexity equals hierarchy. Diversity in outcome requires hierarchy in organization. Although we seek individual experiences as consumers, as units of work hours we experience anything but the promotion of such values.

The underlying complexity of modern society is something we cannot escape from. Reality seems ambiguous, yet man has the ability to function as an independent, decision making agent within it and be in complex interaction with the environment. Automation in both physical production and information management has made work less repetitive and more productive, yet the large hierarchies and centralization persist in complex human activities.

Can the link between complexity and centralization be broken with the help of suitable information management tools? We will look into this question by first presenting a brief overview on the history of information management.

TRIBES, COLLABORATION AND SPOKEN LANGUAGE

Stanley Kubrick's 1968 film "2001: A Space Odyssey" begins famously with an artist's fictive look at how our ancestors first stumbled upon technology in the form of a weapon of war[a] giving one tribe a physical advantage over others. Considering technology, The Greek word *technologia* has the ancient meaning of being the "systematic treatment of an art". The primitive apes of Kubrick's fiction demonstrated technological ability as they and their descendants eventually developed the means to analyze an art or a skill at an abstract level and to transform this analysis into knowledge efficiently shared with others and maintained over generations. Systematic treatment is analysis, abstraction and persistence.

How did the technological man come about? Proponents of evolutionary psychology, Steven Pinker being perhaps the most famous example[b], argue that the mental evolution of primates towards the sentient, technological man was pushed forward by the environments faced by early hunter-gatherers. The result, Homo Sapiens, is the ultimate hunter-gatherer, a social animal who's mental and physical skills are tuned at co-operation and collaboration at the small scale of hunting parties.

A key physical ability which separates the technological man from other species is the ability to use language for abstract analysis of the environment and rich communication of knowledge. Language is a necessary precursor of technology, the systematic treatment of an art of skill. For the hunter-gatherer spoken natural language enabled efficient co-operation at the scale of small hunting parties and a tribal social organization. This evolutionary adaptation is still with us. It is evident in the native proficiency man exhibits in processing and storing information in matters and situations analogous in scale to the life style of our pre-historic ancestors.

How is this proficiency evident in everyday life? To illustrate this we consider two medical professionals who share a common intellectual background and have shared experiences in work settings. The following is an example[c] of a succinct communication between two physicians in patient handoff situation:

"50ish yo M with COPD – stable"

Despite the small amount of space this fragment takes, it conveys a multitude of information on the condition of the patient.

Considering the efficiency of human-to-human communication via natural language, a direct, iterative conversation between two or more similarly grounded participants is the apex of natural knowledge exchange. For example, in a teaching hospital patient encounter a medical student and an attending physician are involved in a complex knowledge exchange situation. Inquisitive conversations between the student, the physician, and the patient, direct visual and other observations made of the patient, comments by a nurse and a plethora of quiet signals coupled together represent a rich collection of knowledge, which the student efficiently is able to assimilate to enhance his medical skills.

Linguists have long recognized the power of natural conversations and small-scale collaboration as a knowledge exchange medium. The concept of a common ground[d] has been introduced by the community to denote the shared educational, professional and cultural background critical for fluent collaboration between human actors. A common ground increases communication efficiency ("fewer words needed to convey and idea") and supports innovation ("faster common filtering of unworkable ideas") in a collaboration context.

Construction and architecture are professional occupations where the power of common ground can be nicely illustrated. Mark, a contractor, wants George, an architect specialized in New England Colonial architecture, to come up with a design for a housing unit with well-known general specifications.

"George? It's Mark from Rockport, how ya doing?"

"Hi Mark, What can I do for you?"

"I'm looking at building a 3 bedroom Salt Box house in ...
Could you come up with preliminary plans for the unit?"

"Sure Mark. I think I know what you are looking for. I'll get back to you shortly..."

Using the simple term "Salt Box" Mark can efficiently convey a complex meaning to George as both understand at a deep level the concept in the context of designing and constructing a new housing unit. Building on this, iterative conversations can be seen as massively connected knowledge accumulation and sharing processes in the sense that they draw information and inferences from all the previous experiences of the involved persons.

Of course, underlying this deep understanding is the information processing and management capability of the human mind not yet understood by modern science. Steven Pinker argues, in layman's terms, for a computational theory of mind in his book How the Mind Works (Pinker, 1999). His main thesis is that the mind can be understood as a computational unit with a modular structure having sub-units specialized for different cognitive tasks[e].

In summa, humans are equipped with a native set of information management tools enabling efficient collaboration at the small-scale level. The tribal form of organization is adaptive, decentralized and self-organizing to a large extent. Most importantly, our ability to share knowledge through the use of language, a reflection of our cognitive capability, enables us to develop technology further increasing the efficiency of our endeavors.

HIERARCHIES, AGRICULTURE AND WRITTEN LANGUAGE

The Fertile Crescent of the Middle East - a term first coined by the American archeologist James Henry Breasted and encompassing principally parts of modern Egypt, Israel, and Iraq - has the earliest Neolithic farming communities known to archeology. There are many theories as to what pushed the hunter-gatherer communities of the Middle East towards the adoption of agriculture. The common explanations include climate changes making the hunter-gatherer lifestyle untenable and difficulties in maintaining subsistence under an increasing population growth rate[f].

Whatever the underlying causes, it is commonly accepted that the introduction of agriculture brought a radical change to the lifestyle of a hunter-gatherer. The decentralized organizational structure of smallish tribes and hunting-parties gave away to forms predating the modern state. The populations became less mobile through the establishment of permanent settlements around arable land, a more complex and hierarchical social organization began to develop while the development of technology accelerated. The emergence of complexity in human societies, as we currently understand the term, coincided with an increasing population density and the beginning of urban settlement patterns. This was facilitated by the surplus of food created by advancing agriculture.

The societal transformation set in motion by agriculture gradually but consistently created a need to move forward in information management. This was due to the increasing amounts of diverse information created related to the management of large, complex communities. The universal answer to this historical case of information overflow was the emergence of information management technology; written language and documentation in the abstract sense of the word.

The history of written language begins in the Fertile Crescent, specifically in the Southern Mesopotamian civilization of Sumer. Samples of the Sumerian cuneiform script, some dating back to the 4th millennium B.C.E., survive to this day as clay tablets. Incidentally, almost all of the surviving early tablets contain texts related to general administration, accounting, and trade. The native human capacity for information management was not enough to enumerate and process all the transactions related to a sedentary society. As organizations grew bigger in size, face-to-face communication and co-operation was no longer possible and written documentation was needed to convey messages, and thus facilitate a bi-directional flow of information, between different levels of a hierarchical organization.

Systems of writing are logographic, syllabic or alphabetic in nature with the first written languages being logographic. In alphabetic systems letters are combined to words to represent a principally unbounded number of concepts. Natural written language is highly context-dependent where the specific meaning of words or their aggregates depends on the context they appear in. The example below illustrated the context-dependency of natural language as interpreted by humans.

Whasnigotn DC is the cpaatil ctiy of the USA.

Despite the fact that most of the words in the sentence are scrambled, except for the first and last letters of each word, from the standard form, the interpretation of the sentence is still easy for a human reader thanks to the associative powers of our cognitive system.

Going back to organizational forms, ad-hoc organizations emerge naturally among small groups sharing a motivation to strive towards a shared goal such as basic survival in a hunter-gatherer society. The organization is self-regulatory with dynamically changing roles and responsibilities. Spoken language and face-to-face conversations are the primary knowledge sharing mechanism. The actors of this dynamic network of collaboration share a deep understanding of the intricate meanings of the pieces of information related to goal at hand with the help of their cognitive abilities. Human actors have the ability to process information in a complexly connected and principally unbounded, open case space.

However, as noted earlier, the evolving use of written language provided a mechanism to enable division of labor in large organizations. In a hierarchical organization the basic paradigm is that few top-level decision makers feed executive directives through a layered network of people as these directives a broken down into smaller and smaller directives. Simultaneously, a reporting mechanism pushes information from the lower organization levels up to the key decision makers. Written language is the primary technology to convey directives and reporting within such an organization.

The use of written language and documentation to convey and store the large mass of information created by advancing agricultural, and later on industrial, societies represented a fundamental break from innate information management. Although documents are written in natural language with in principle unbounded expressivity, they fail to fully reflect the context as directly experienced by a human actor. When we document something, we almost always lose a part of the original information. Documentation is a lossing process. Perhaps the loss is a part of its context of which we are not even conscious at the time of the documentation. With documentation, the worst case is that relevant information is lost into a sea of unrelated data without meaning and context. A shared common ground between content compilers and consumers is paramount for a successful communication.

With this in mind, it can be argued that while written language and documentation was a necessary tool in the management of complexity its limitations manifest in the need to have hierarchically complex organizations to manage large-scale and complex activities. The development of society caught up with our evolution very early on.

MODERNITY, AUTOMATION AND NETWORKS

The Sumerian cuneiform script was but the beginning of a long journey in the development of information management technology. Diverse forms of written language emerged around the world with characteristics of the spoken languages they originally developed to represent. Many distinct forms of written language have since disappeared from common use while some partially survive as artifacts in other languages.

Beginning in the Mediterranean more than 3,000 years ago, a series of historical developments led to the almost universal adoption enjoyed today by the Latin script of the Romans. The Roman Empire carried the Latin language and its script to all reaches of the region becoming the *lingua franca* of the day. Later on, Latin was the common language in education and religion throughout the Middle Ages in Western Europe.

Western Europe also witnessed the initial adoption of the printing press in the mass production of written texts, a revolutionary invention which, beginning from the 15th century, made knowledge an accessible commodity within its cultural sphere. The printing press automated the replication of written text and provided significant benefits in terms of speed, accuracy and cost when compared to manual transcribing. The underlying development of materials technology, specifically in paper production and metallurgy, continuously increased the efficiency of printing technology.

The science, religion and philosophy of the Renaissance, Reformation and Enlightenment spread with the help of this automated information replication technology. At the same time, the Latin script was carried around the globe with the Age of Exploration establishing its primacy continuing to this day. The development of technology saw an unprecedented acceleration partly thanks to efficient means available for information dissemination provided by the printing press.

The confluence of these and other related developments was a driving force behind the development of technology leading into the emergence of modern industry beginning in the 17th century. Apart from being the birth place of the steam machine, a key innovation in the development of modern industry, Britain was the forerunner of industrialization. Iron and textile works, industrial scale shipbuilding and basic chemical industry began to appear first in Britain and later on in continental Europe, Northern America and Japan beginning in the 18th and continuing into the 19th and 20th centuries.

Looking at the developments in information technology coinciding with and contributing to the industrial revolution and later stages of modernity, one can notice three coinciding trends: the emergence of formalization, automation and complexity.

The use of exact, formal instructions to support automation goes back to 18th century France and the textile industry of the era: operating instructions, stored on punch cards, for reproducing a pattern on cloth were first introduced with the development of semi-automated looms[g]. Unlike humans manually operating looms, the semi-automated loom relies on exact, formal operating instructions for operation. The introduction of a single fault in the set of instructions is likely to render the entire system nonfunctional. Similarly, the introduction of a change in the pattern to be reproduced requires overall recoding of the processing instructions. This is in contrast to a human operator who has the capability to adapt to operate under a principally unbounded set of fault conditions and can immediately start reproducing another pattern on the cloth if previously known to him or her. Despite these limitations, industrial automation technology has provided a basis for the enormous increase in productivity experienced after the onset of the industrial revolution. The control of a typical industrial process, say a process for synthesizing ammonia in chemical industry, is a bounded and static automation problem which can relatively easily be formalized into a set of exact instructions for controlling the process.

Expanding from industrial automation, the potential of computationally universal computers, first successfully implemented in the mid 20th century, in information management automation and developments such as the introduction of character encoding for representing the Latin script in these computers prompted the emergence of the electronic document. To provide for automation in the management of textual information made widespread by the printing press, use of elaborate structure began to emerge. Free-text, natural language documentation is not conducive to automation as the currently available computational tools do not provide for the context awareness and associative capabilities required for interpreting a natural language composition reliably. Natural language understanding remains a fundamentally unsolved problem in computational linguistics and artificial intelligence. Giving formal structure to information helps to make it computable. An example on the use of a formal structure is a move from the use of hand-written, free-text order slips to an automated system wherein predicted content of the slip is formulated as labeled fields with atomic content. The result is a move from free-text compositions towards multiple-choice questions.

However, unlike the bounded industrial automation process, information management in the sphere of complex human collaboration has a principally unbounded, constantly evolving and open case space as reflected by the expressive power of natural language. It became evident early on in the history of knowledge and software engineering that the use of formal structure in the context of these complex domains and continuous automation represents a significant challenge. Many domains of information management are so complex, medicine and health care being a well-known example, that elaborate formalization of all the information related to field is in itself a monumental task. This problem is further aggravated by the fact that domain knowledge is constantly evolving and becoming more complex. This results in an elaborate maintenance process with ever-growing complexity. Also, almost every information management system in use today which handles tasks related to human collaboration contains the possibility to augment structural information with free text, i.e. the ubiquitous comment field. This relaxation reduces computability but is usually necessary for gathering all the relevant information. There is clear trade-off between conventional use of structure, automation and completeness.

When these challenges in knowledge engineering, e.g. in the formation of domain ontologies, are considered together with the fact that information management systems are conventionally tightly and complexly coupled to the use of a specific structure for representing information to be processed the maintenance problem grows even more complex. For example, augmenting a complex structure with an extra field representing a container for a new piece of related information can result in a surprisingly complex re-engineering process. Information management systems typically combine structured information in complex ways to provide for automated processing, e.g. in the form of aggregation and reporting.

Much effort has been put into speeding up the knowledge and systems engineering processes in information management automation. Much of the software engineering research of the last 50 years has concentrated on finding ways to more efficiently transform continuously evolving user needs into usable and updateable systems (e.g., via the use of a formal modeling such as the Unified Modeling Language or UML). A recent craze in knowledge engineering is research into the development and use of hierarchical domain ontologies for content annotation under the umbrella of Semantic Web. Despite these efforts an argument can be made that information management systems in many domains have yet to fulfill many of the early promises.

OPEN INFORMATION MANAGEMENT

Is there any direction where we could look for guidance? The World Wide Web is an excellent demonstrator on the power of conceptually simple but massive linkage created and maintained in a decentralized and open fashion[h]. Linkage is to documents what roads are to cities. The associative power of even a simple linkage can be seen the way it supports the search and sorting of documents. For example, the PageRank algorithm of the Google search engine sorts Web documents according to the number of incoming links. The argument is that a higher number of incoming links from other web sites is associated with the relevance of the match to the initiator of the search. The unprecedented success of the search engine speaks for the power of this approach although the underlying technology has progressed far beyond the original algorithm[i]. It is now commonly agreed that the most efficient current way to organize and make available information in the complex and diverse environment of the Web is the semi-automated process employed by the search engines. A key component in the utility of search engines is ability of users to initiate search actions using natural language fragments (i.e., search terms) which is the common language of the users and the Web documents they search for.

The goal of this book is to give a practical-level reference on an emerging trend in information technology towards solutions capable of managing information within open, principally unbounded, operational environments. These developments – evident in many contemporary areas of research including artificial intelligence, network science, natural language processing, and ubiquitous media – are projected to bring about a new breed of tools for the management of information going beyond the conventional paradigms. The emergence of search-driven information management, as discussed above, is one initial illustration of this trend. Open information management[j] will potentially provide ways to automate and decentralize tasks in the sphere of complex human collaboration which has a constantly evolving and principally open case space. On a more general level, this technology will provide consumers access to experiences and products with unprecedented levels of personalization. The explored aspects include:

- Mechanisms for flexible information representation and exchange including the use of open formats and standards in information technology.
- Organizational forms and related information technologies including tools for decentralized and distributed collaboration contexts.
- Modern theory and tools of natural language processing and computational linguistics including those inspired by Noam Chomsky's Minimalist Program.
- Networks and linkages in biological systems and human communities as an inspiration for evolving artificial information management systems.
- Natural human-computer interaction including developments in multimedia, automated audio technology and ubiquitous computation.
- Personalization and context-sensitivity including related knowledge management tools and physical architectures.
- User-driven, decentralized content creation including cultural and trust issues.
- Viewpoints from ICT infrastructure development including networking solutions for distributed computation and decentralized collaboration and content creation.
- Connections to different concrete human activities including medicine and law.

REFERENCES

Barabási, A-L. (2002). *Linked: How Everything Is Connected to Everything Else and What It Means.* Cambridge, MA: Perseus Publishing.

Bellwood, P. (2004). *First Farmers: The Origins of Agricultural Societies.* Malden, MA: Blackwell Publishers.

Clark, H. (1996). *Using language.* Cambridge, UK: Cambridge University Press.

McGrath, S. (2000). *XML processing with Python.* Prentice Hall.

Pinker, S. (1999). *How the Mind Works.* New York, NY: W.W. Norton & Company.

Solet, D., Norvell, J., Rutan, G., & Frankel, R. Lost in Translation: Challenges and Opportunities in Physician-to-Physician Communication During Patient Handoffs. *Academic Medicine, 80*(12), 1094-1099.

ENDNOTES

[a]   A bone to attack other apes with.

[b]   For a look into evolutionary psychology in the context of a theory of mind see (Pinker, 1999).

[c]   From (Salet, 2005).

[d]   See (Clark, 1996).

[e]   Underlying the computational paradigm is the mind's ability to relate basically everything to everything within a relation network of concepts constantly incremented by input from the sensory system and coupled to various abstraction and decision making processes.

[f]   Peter Bellwood analyzes the origins of agriculture societies in (Bellwood, 2004).

[g]   The semi-automated loom was not a general purpose (i.e., Turing complete) computer, which essentially means having the ability to perform any computational task. Strictly speaking, Turing completeness requires the availability of an infinitely expandable storage, a physical impossibility. A relaxation is conventionally made to include machines which would be Turing complete if they had, using Turing's terminology, an unlimited tape length. The first known computationally universal design, as proven much later, was the analytical engine of Charles Babbage from 1837. The first actual implementation of such a machine was Konrad Zuse's electronic computer Z3 from 1941.

[h]   Albert-László Barabási discusses the structure and nature of the Web and other scale-free networks in (Barabási, 2002).

[i]   For example, user preference information (i.e., which links are clicked most often with a certain search term) is surely used to enhance search result ranking.

[j]   According to one definition of open information management from computer science (McGrath, 2000) it means "managing information so that it is open to processing by any program, not just the program that created it". We use the term in a broader meaning while also covering this goal.

Chapter I
Open Formats, Open Information and Future Trends in Software Engineering

Teemu Saarelainen
Kymenlaakso University of Applied Sciences, Finland

ABSTRACT

The amount of information surrounding us is ever increasing. Usable information is our most valuable asset both in our professional and personal lives. People are constantly struggling to find the information needed in various every day situations. Search engines have given us the tools to cope with the problem so far, but what lies ahead? This chapter describes some of the current trends in information management in software systems and discusses the aspects of using natural language, open formats and open source software in the field of software engineering while keeping in mind the needs of our future society.

INTRODUCTION

This chapter concentrates on the concept of open information management with a software engineering point of view. The significance of finding valid information in our every day lives is becoming more and more important, which has influenced the field of software engineering probably more than any other area of research and development. The purpose of the chapter is to give the reader some background on the development of open formats as well as discuss some of the advances made in web technology and search engines that affect our way of using the internet and accessing information. Interoperability and data portability aspects are also covered and their importance in the software definition and design phases are examined. Some conclusions are drawn based on the current state of open information management in software systems and future trends are briefly discussed.

BACKGROUND

We live in a world full of information, some of which is totally useless, some has a meaning, some is important and some is absolutely vital for us. In order to use this massive amount of information and find the bits we need, we must have the means to filter out certain parts effectively. In the world of internet the answer today is Google. We simply 'google'[a] everything using search criteria described in our own natural language. Interaction with practically any other human being across the globe is a reality and networking with other people using social web applications is a natural part of our lives. How do these systems work? What gives them the ability to grasp users and be so effective? In our everyday lives, we don't give much thought to the inner mechanics of search engines or social web sites – we expect those systems to 'just work', but for computer scientists it's a field of endless research and development.

Before search engines became so effective in the very late 1990's and after the millennium, we used to find the information we needed using internet-directories, which sorted different web-pages and sites into different subdirectories and categories. This system relied totally on the creator of the web site or page having the particular content and the maintainer of the directory to have the correct information in the correct category. In practice, this proved to be an inflexible, limited and difficult system to use, and resulted in outdated directories with outdated information. The solution to the problem was search engines, which at first used simple keywords and a database of indexed documents. Now, the creator of a web page no longer had to report his/her new content into a directory, but instead the search engine crawled through millions and millions of web pages and automatically indexed them according to their content. No keywords are required and we can take advantage of natural language. What data can be exploited in these intelligent systems?

The growing trends in computing today are open information and open software systems. There is a certain amount of ideology behind this, but it doesn't mean that everything related to software is free in the future, which is a common misconception. In practice, open information access is still rarely available for us and the cause often is in the data itself or in the software. To aid in these efforts, open data formats have been suggested and adopted in software systems and organizations more and more. Data exchange between applications is required in many fields, which gives rise to standardized xml-based formats.

Open source software is another hot topic and the concept has even changed the business models of traditional software companies. European countries have traditionally led the development and adoption of open source software. The Finnish government, for instance, has given a statement which says that in all new software acquisitions for the government, open source systems should be preferred and interoperability taken into account.

In software engineering, the processes and best practices are open for everyone to use for their own needs. Thus, using the best current knowledge and the development of even better methods is possible for anyone. Even though making specifications is quite formal and writing program code is governed by strict rules, the most important tool in the documentation is natural language. Model-driven-architecture is a reality and program code can be generated from UML-models, and vice-versa. So, why is it that we still cannot use natural language to construct programs?

Computers only handle data in bits. The rules of the Turing machine govern computers even today. Computer scientists and programmers have managed to build systems that somehow understand natural language as inputs. Nevertheless, a totally new level of abstraction is needed in order to develop a system which could be programmed using something similar to our own natural language.

From Internet-Directories to Search Engines

When world-wide-web pages started to become increasingly popular in the mid 1990's, people started to struggle in finding pages that interested them. One couldn't simply memorize and type in http-addresses into a browser, and bookmarking one's favorite pages became more and more difficult. The first solution that alleviated this was the launch of internet-directories like Yahoo! (http://www.yahoo.com), which started in 1994 and is one of the oldest directories. The idea of these directories was – and still is – to organize web sites into categories and subcategories by their content. To certain extent this worked quite well and people began using the directories as a place to find usable information and web sites.

One of the problems with these directories was that someone had to insert new web sites and categorize them properly in order for the directory to work. This system relied totally on the creator of the web site or page having the particular content and the maintainer of the directory having the correct information in the correct category. At the time, there were no tools that could do this automatically and most of the directories had a system which enabled a user to insert new sites into the directory. Often this required a user registration by name and e-mail address, which consequently helped to diminish the misuse of the system. Nevertheless, internet-directories suffered from the huge workload which was needed from the human editors who organized the material. In practice, this proved to be an inflexible, limited and difficult system to use, and resulted in outdated directories with outdated information. Consequently, Yahoo! switched to crawler-based listings in 2002.

One of the most popular directories today is the Open Directory Project (ODP, http://www.dmoz.org), which has over 4 million pages listed and organized into over 590 000 categories. The ODP uses volunteer editors, which clearly reflects the ideology and social aspect of today's internet. It is hosted and administered by Netscape Communication Corporation and was founded on the premise that directories with small staffs can not scale to the growth of the Web, and still maintain a quality, current directory. (Open Directory Project, 2008)

In the late 1990's search engines started to appear on the internet and their popularity gradually began to grow as the databases and query results of the search engine providers improved. Obviously, there were several companies that wanted to have the best search engine with most users, and the key factor in this at the time was the size of the database of indexed documents. Revenues for the search engine companies come from advertising and the more users a search engine has the more advertisers it will have. The battle for the biggest search engine was finally won by Google, which had 8 billion pages indexed in November 2004, while its biggest rival at the time, MSN, had only 5 billion pages. Nowadays, Google is the 'de facto' search engine and has widened its portfolio to cover other application areas as well. (Search Engine History, 2008)

Why did search engines become so popular and why exactly did Google prevail? Well, for one thing it probably had the most relevant results mainly due to its page rank-algorithm. Google also had, and probably still has, the most simplistic user interface. Basically, the reasons are the same as in any application – usability and usefulness. The user interface of a search engine is simple and the results appear in under a second – everyone knows how to use it and the user experience is outstanding. It's merely an impossible idea to use the web without a search engine. Recently, search engines have also invaded desktops since the amount of data in our personal computers has also grown exponentially and a simple find utility that searches by filename only is not that practical anymore. Operating systems usually have their own utilities for searching, but these are often cumbersome and quite inefficient. Nowadays, there are over a dozen desktop search engines and most of them are freely available (Goebel Group: Desktop Search Tools Matrix, 2008).

Excursion: Search Technology

Web search engines have their roots in the early 1990's in simple programs that existed on the internet before the web servers and web pages. The basic parts of a search engine include a crawler (or bot), an index and a frontend for making queries (Scime, 2004). The crawler's task is to literally 'crawl' through the web and collect data for the index. The index (or catalog) holds records of web page addresses and either a small part or their whole contents. Usually the information includes metadata, such as key words from titles, headings or special tags. When a user enters a search request into the query field, the search engine actually finds the corresponding data from its index and not the current web.[b]

The basic method for a search engine to perform queries is to match the entered keywords with the database and sort the results according to some relevancy measure. Recently, more efforts have been put to natural language search algorithms used by search engines such as Lexxe (Lexxe Search Engine, 2008) and Hakia (Hakia Search Engine Beta, 2008). These novel search algorithms use semantics and analyze the structure and grammar of the search phrase prior to performing queries. The possibilities of natural language search engines are much richer than traditional keyword based engines, but the technology has not yet matured to such a level that they could handle complicated natural language queries. It has also been argued whether or not it is even feasible to use such complex methods for web search queries, where people are used to making queries by entering just a few simple keywords. There has also been some discussion about the way in which different web pages are ranked within the search results of current search engines. Nevertheless, advances in search technology and natural language processing are important for many reasons – for a long time the ultimate goal for scientists has been to implement a system with which one could have a natural conversation.

INFORMATION EXCHANGE IN SOFTWARE SYSTEMS

The key to success in any area nowadays is information. Especially in business, information flow is vital and the role of the information technology department in organizations has changed over the years. Accessibility, availability and security have become the most important factors from the perspective of different stakeholders.

Over the years, companies have invested a lot of resources in document management software (DMS), which usually require the user to give particular properties for the document. Information can then be searched by keywords, persons, dates and other metadata. DMS is a much more efficient way of storing and retrieving relevant documents than simple tree structures or directories. However, the query results in a DMS depend heavily on the metadata that has been entered by the users, which can be inaccurate.

There are plenty of other systems for managing information and resources, such as enterprise resource planning (ERP) and customer relationship management (CRM) systems. At the moment, integrating the various solutions within organizations seems to be the most problematic issue. The main reason for this is the lack of information exchange possibilities. To solve this problem, software engineers who define new software and analyze the requirements should take open interfaces and data accessibility

Figure 1. Information exchange between different applications without integration (upper) and interoperability taken into account with interfaces and database design (lower)

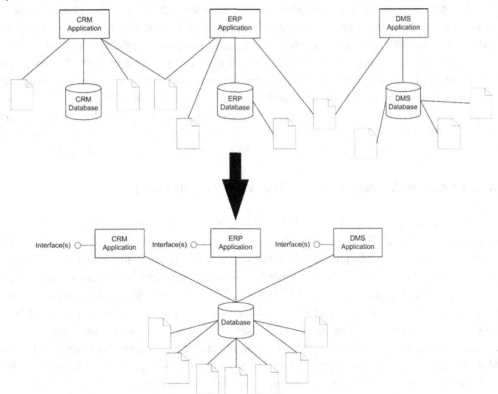

seriously into account when designing new systems. If integration possibilities are not considered or are left out in the requirements' definition phase, it is much more difficult and more expensive to add them later on in a software project.

In Figure 1 a common problem in application integration is presented (upper part) along with a solution (lower part), which takes into account data interchange and interoperability using a shared database and interfaces. Nowadays, design patterns are quite mature and source code as well as software architectures can be reused efficiently, so it no longer adds that much workload to design and implement these interfaces. Rather, it is a matter of having such a mindset which considers the matters of integration and interfaces early enough in the software project.

Data Formats

Historically, digital data used by commercial applications has been stored in proprietary binary formats, which could only be read only by certain software programs – usually made by the same company. If another company wanted to read or use the same proprietary format it had to reverse engineer the file format, which can be considered illegal, or buy a license from the company that owned the format. Usually, competing software companies did not want to reveal their file format structures, so the licensing fees were set quite high, making it unfeasible to acquire licenses for the needed formats. This of course efficiently rendered real competition quite impossible.

Recently, open formats have risen to alleviate the situation. An open format is a published specification for storing data, which can be used and implemented by anyone (Openformats.org: Open vs. proprietary formats, 2008). Open file formats are usually based on standardization work carried out by several international organizations. What is different in open file formats is the fact that their data presentation model is publicly available. This guarantees interoperability among different applications and software vendors. The most notable open formats are probably (X)HTML, XML, PDF and PNG. Lately, open document formats for word processing, which are based on XML have appeared (ECMA International: Office Open XML Overview, 2008). However, it should be kept in mind that there may also be other issues, such as efficiency, that affect the choice between different formats.

Open Information Management in Software Engineering

In software engineering the use of (relational) databases to store information is a natural approach for almost any application area. But even more important is to have access to that information from different applications. In (McGrath, 2000), Goldfarb defines open information management as follows: "Open Information Management" (OIM) means managing information so that it is open to processing by any program, not just the program that created it. That extends even to application programs not conceived of at the time the information was created." Goldfarb gives quite a good definition for OIM because it is not restricted by assumptions and merely addresses information access by applications.

However, in practice we use different types of applications and information can also be stored in several different ways. One particular division in information storage types can be made between databases and documents. In databases, information is stored independently of the presentation form, whereas in documents, presentation style matters and data are bound inside the document.

"OIM is based on the principle of data independence: data should be stored in computers in non-proprietary, genuinely standardized representations. And that applies even when the data is the content of a document. Its representation should distinguish the innate information from the proprietary codes of document processing programs and the artifacts of particular presentation styles. Business data bases—which rigorously separate the real data from the input forms and output reports—achieved data independence decades ago. But documents, unlike business data, have historically been created in the context of a particular output presentation style. So for document data, independence was largely unachievable until recently." (McGrath, 2000)

By means of open information management we are enabling and empowering applications to use and interchange information. For the software business there has been a noticeable change in recent years due to open formats and standardization work. Some companies have battled against open formats and tried to keep their data presentation formats proprietary. One reason for this has been to protect their products against competition. But this, as Goldfarb says, has been regrettable: "That is doubly unfortunate. It is unfortunate because documents are a far more significant repository of humanity's information. And documents can contain significantly richer information structures than data bases." (McGrath, 2000)

FUTURE TRENDS

One of the most interesting trends on the internet is the field of web based applications that are used within a web browser. These applications are spreading and replacing their traditional desktop counterparts with an increasing rate. Some of the rationale behind browser applications lies in ease of deployment, cross platform support, familiarity of the user interface and client security. Since the application is stored centrally in one place, updates are guaranteed and there is no risk of running an outdated version.

Of course web applications have existed for some time now, but it hasn't been until recently that they have had modern visual and user interface components, which really has made them quite impressive and enabled them to rival native applications. Thus far, AJAX (Asynchronous JavaScript And XML) has been the most viable option for implementing responsive and user friendly applications, but new technologies have lately appeared. For example, Microsoft is offering its WPF/E (Windows Presentation Foundation/Everywhere) and Adobe has Flex, which is an open source framework. Each of these is targeted to their own audience.

Since web applications naturally have a potential user base of millions and millions of users, it's only logical that social web applications trying to grasp as many users as possible must take user requirements seriously into account. The revenues for these social applications (e.g. Facebook, MySpace, YouTube) come from advertising, which usually works by a pay per click principle, so they cannot afford losing their users and thus application developers try to listen to their wishes. In this respect, it can be seen that more and more it's the users who decide the features and even the purpose of software. User demographics and behavior can be collected quite easily within a web application, which means that users are getting personalized applications without the need for manual customization. This is currently utilized in placing advertisements, but can also be adopted in the automatic modification of the user interface.

CONCLUSION

The amount of information in the world is far beyond anyone's comprehension and different databases have become absolutely necessary for our every day lives. Open formats are gradually gaining ground in software systems and interoperability has become more and more important. Access to vital information must be assured in applications that are critical for businesses, which means that requirements engineering and application design must take open interfaces and information management into account. The users are the most valuable asset and they must be listened to carefully when building applications – whether it be a social web application or a native desktop application or some other software program.

REFERENCES

ECMA International: Office Open XML Overview (2008). Retrieved September 1, 2008, from http://www.ecma-international.org/news/TC45_current_work/OpenXML%20White%20Paper.pdf

Goebel Group: Desktop Search Tools Matrix (2008). Retrieved September 1, 2008, from http://www.goebelgroup.com/desktopmatrix.htm

google. (2008). In Merriam-Webster Online Dictionary. Retrieved September 1, 2008, from http://www.merriam-webster.com/dictionary/google

Lexxe Search Engine (2008). Retrieved September 1, 2008, from http://www.lexxe.com

Hakia Search Engine Beta (2008). Retrieved September 1, 2008, from http://hakia.com/

McGrath, S. (2000). *XML processing with Python*. Prentice Hall.

Openformats.org: Open vs. proprietary formats (2008). Retrieved September 1, 2008, from http://www.openformats.org/

Scime, A. (2004). *Web Mining: Applications and Techniques*. Idea Group Publishing.

Search Engine History (2008). Retrieved September 1, 2008, from http://www.searchenginehistory.com/

The Open Directory Project (2008). Retrieved September 1, 2008, from http://www.dmoz.org

ENDNOTES

[a]   The Merriam-Webster Online Dictionary defines the term *google* as follows: to use the Google search engine to obtain information about (as a person) on the World Wide Web.

[b]   This sometimes lead to 'linkrot', which means that the actual content on the web does not match the content in the index and hence the search results may lead a user to irrelevant pages.

Chapter II
Engineering Information into Open Documents

Chia-Chu Chiang
University of Arkansas at Little Rock, USA

ABSTRACT

Documents are perfectly suited for information exchange via the Internet. In order to insure that there are no misunderstandings, information embedded in a document needs to be precise and unambiguous. Having a (de facto) standard data model and conceptual information model insures that the involved parties will agree on what the information means. XML (eXtensible Markup Language) has become the de facto standard format for representing information in documents for document exchange. Many techniques have been proposed to create XML documents, including the validation and transformation of XML documents. However, very little is discussed when it comes to extracting information from non-XML documents and engineering the information into XML documents. The extraction process can be a highly labor intensive task if it is done manually. The use of automated tools would make the process more efficient. In this chapter, the author will briefly survey document engineering techniques for XML documents. Then, the author will present two techniques to extract data from Windows documents into XML documents. These two techniques have been successfully applied in two industrial projects. He believes that techniques that automate the extraction of data from non-XML documents into XML formats will definitely enhance the use of XML documents.

INTRODUCTION

Due to the availability of electronic devices and networking systems today, the use of information has shifted mainly to the use of computer-based information systems to collect, store, process, and retrieve information from the Internet. Organizations including companies, governments, and individuals mainly conduct business functions through the exchanging of documents that carry information via the Internet. A document can therefore be viewed as an electronic file created by a computer application that contains meaningful data.

We can agree that nowadays, we are overwhelmed by the huge volume of information in the documents created every day. Unfortunately, the information stored in the documents is not always represented in the same format; currently, there exists a multitude of incompatible document types. Thus, we are required to use different software tools to access different document types for the information we need. The root of this problem lies in the fact that documents and their corresponding tools have inseparable relationships where each tool creates different representations of documents, and many of the representations are proprietary. Not only do incompatible document types create a problem when accessing documents, but incompatible conceptual data models also describe the problem of aggregating and comparing information in different documents even when they are of the same type. Both the document type and conceptual data model must be defined by the organizations if they wish to agree on the meaning of their documents.

In this chapter, we are particularly interested in techniques that can engineer information into open documents in XML. When we use the term "open documents", we are referring to the documents that are created using a de facto standard document type, such as XML. Although there exists more than one standard for document types, we are not resolving the issues of incompatible standards in this chapter. Existing techniques for processing XML documents will be discussed. Several conferences such as ACM, SIGMOD, and DocEng provide excellent resources for the techniques that will be discussed. A survey (Forward & Lethbridge, 2002) presents the relevance of documentation, tools, and technologies. Afterwards, we will present two techniques used to extract information from non-XML documents into XML documents. Finally, we discuss issues and future trends and conclude the chapter.

The chapter is organized as follows: The background section briefly introduces XML syntax and semantics. This section also presents engineering techniques for XML documents. Some techniques support the syntax and semantics of XML documents. Some techniques target the transformations of XML documents into other document types. In the next section, we will present two techniques that emphasize the creation of XML documents from non-XML documents. We observe that many commercial companies have provided software tools to automate this process. Unfortunately, the technical details of these tools are usually not released to the public. The techniques presented in this section will allow users to convert entire documents to XML and also allow users to extract data of interest to XML. The future trends section will discuss the issues of document engineering and the potential solutions. Finally, the chapter is summarized in the conclusion section.

BACKGROUND

Glushko and McGrath (2005) define documents in a general notion as follows,

"Document in a technology-neutral way as a purposeful and self-contained collection of information."

Organizations should think of documents in an abstract and technology-neutral way. Documents should be flexibly exchanged via the Internet without concern as to how the documents are to be sent via the Internet. Documents should also be considered as a self-contained package of related information that can effectively organize business functions for use by other organizations. In addition, the interfaces between organizations used to process documents should be kept as minimal and simple as possible. More importantly, software tools should be able to enable quick and efficient means for documentation. One way to create such documents on the Internet is through the use of XML that is a universal, text-based, and self-describing data format. Almost every organization has computers and software tools to process XML.

XML Basics

XML recommended by W3C (XML, 2008) is used to structure, store, and transport data in a standardized and text-based format. It has become a language used to represent information in electronic documents for information exchange via the Internet. The book written by Benz and Durant (2003) provides a detailed discussion on XML. The following XML document shows how XML structures represent a name:

```
<name>
<firstname> Doe </firstname>
<middlename> </middlename>
<lastname> John </lastname>
</name>
```

The name above is quite self-descriptive. A name consists of first name, middle name and last name. The values are embedded in tags defined by organizations. Having XML as a document type provides the following advantages for information exchange,

- XML supports for extensibility. For domain specific content, tags can be easily introduced into XML documents. For example, we can easily add a set of tags into the above document without affecting the other tags.

   ```
   <address> 2801 South University Avenue </address>
   <city> Little Rock </city>
   <state> Arkansas </state>
   <zip> 72204 </zip>
   <country> USA </country>
   ```

- XML supports for information encapsulation. The ability to separate tags and their contents allows the contents to be changed without modifying the tags. The contents can even be left blank in a pair of tags.
- XML supports for information interoperability. Incompatible document types cause documents to be difficult to interpret. The Internet itself does not resolve the issue of incompatible document types. XML serves as a common standard for syntax, structure, and semantics for software tools that process documents.

- XML supports for unambiguous structured data. XML schemas define the contents of the document using the data types, the constraints of the contents, and the relationship between the contents. The schemas ensure that the contents of XML documents are interpreted without ambiguities.
- XML supports for automated information processing. A set of available tools allows XML documents to be created from non-XML information and vise versa. For instance, XML documents are created by extracting information from announcements in the Internet, a database, or a legacy application. Web pages are also created automatically by converting XML information into HTML tags. In the next section, several techniques are discussed to present the use of XML for document creation, definition, aggregation, and validation.

Conflicts in XML Documents

One basic requirement for document exchange states that the information to be exchanged needs to be semantically equivalent. Glushko and McGrath (2005) present a list of problems when XML is used to describe documents with content conflicts, encoding conflicts, structural conflicts, and semantic conflicts. To resolve these conflicts caused by syntax, Glushko and McGrath suggest that we can rigorously redefine the language and the grammar of the language to prevent the conflicts. For semantic conflicts, we must ensure the meaningful communication of information. For example, the creation of name tags needs to be examined to ensure the semantics of the document components. Content conflicts can be prevented by implementing more granularity of structure in the component types and the constraints placed on the content. Most importantly, the contextual use of documents must be defined and document interfaces must be kept as stable as possible between organizations.

Document Engineering Techniques for XML

Researchers have proposed a variety of techniques to support the engineering of documents in XML ranging from the validation of XML documents to the transformation of XML documents into other document types to the development of the framework of document engineering. Glushko and McGrath (2005) propose a document engineering approach to consolidate different techniques to help create models of documents and processes that support implementation from reuse. The document engineering approach starts with an analysis of the requirements for modeling documents that support business processes in an effective manner. The analysis locates the information and helps the user understand the intent and usage of the information. With the requirements in place, the rest of the software development activities such as design, implementation, and testing are similar to those found when implementing other software applications.

Techniques Based on Syntax Analysis

Grammar-based techniques (Chuang & Lin, 2004; Gançarski & Henriques, 2003; Hardy & Brailsford, 2002; Kuikka et al., 2002; Kuo et al., 2003) ensure that the syntax of XML documents is precise and unambiguous against the rules specified in grammars. A structure of XML documents can be defined in a language grammar, namely CFG (Context Free Grammar). A CFG $= (\Sigma, N, S, P)$ consists of a finite set of terminals, Σ, a finite set of non-terminals, N, a start symbol, S, and a set of production rules, P (Aho et al., 2008). Terminals are the basic building symbols from which strings are formed. Non-terminals are syntactic variables that impose a hierarchical structure on the language. Productions are the rules that specify how a set of strings is generated from the terminals and non-terminals. The start symbol is a non-terminal for the beginning derivation of strings. A CFG can be used to structure a document into a set of hierarchical document components (objects) such as chapters, appendices, headings, paragraphs, footnotes, and figures. A derivation begins with the start symbol and continues the replacement of non-terminals until all the non-terminals are replaced by the terminals. A parse tree in a graphical representation can be accurately created from a derivation. The root node of the tree is labeled by the start symbol, the leaves are labeled by terminals, and each interior node is labeled by a non-terminal. CFG can be extended by allowing the right-hand side to be a regular expression. Document type definitions (DTDs) and XML schemas are examples of an extended CFG. XML DTDs and schemas can both be used to define tags and attributes. However, DTDs only allow the string values to be placed within tags and assigned to attributes. The XML schemas allow a set of simple data types, such as strings and integers, to be placed in a document's slots. Complex data types and the restrictions on values can also be defined using regular expressions (Zeigler & Hammonds, 2007).

Structural based approaches use grammars not only to define the contents and the structures of XML documents for the validation of XML documents but also to automate a transformation from a structure in a grammar to another structure in another grammar. Hardy and Brailsford (2002) present an approach for structural transformations between XML and PDF. They then use XML to describe structures of PDF in the Mars project (Hardy, 2007). Gançarski & Henriques (2003) develop an interactive system to retrieve information from XML documents represented by attribute grammars. Kuo, Wang, and Shih (2003) develop a syntax-based editor to assist users when constructing valid XML documents. Some work on XML transformation (Blouin & Beaudoux, 2007; Boukottaya & Vanoirbeek, 2005; Kurtev & Berg, 2003) is based on XML schema. DTD (Chuang & Lin, 2004) is also used as a vehicle for XML transformation. XML schemas and DTDs can be used to describe the structure of XML in which both can be represented in a formal grammar. Pugin and Ingold (2007) use DTD and XML schemas to conduct type checking in XML in addition to a syntax check.

DOM (Document Object Model) (DOM, 2000) and SAX (Simple API for XML) (Brownell, 2002) both provide simple access to data in XML documents through a set of application programming interfaces (APIs) that support the integration of XML data with applications. This greatly improves the efficiency when coding so that programmers do not have to write code to analyze the document into some data structures and perform retrieval operations on the structures in order to obtain the data of interest. The concerns of writing tedious code can be ignored by the programmers. Chen and Tompa (2003) improve the performance of DOM.

Techniques Based on Semantic Analysis

The techniques that handle XML transformations mostly depend on the structural rules to determine if the possibility of conversion of components into another type is possible. Unfortunately, one-to-one mapping based on the syntax rules does not guarantee that the results will be semantically equivalent. If we convert a XML document into another one, there is a possibility that we create semantic conflicts in it such as functional dependency conflicts, vocabulary conflicts, and contextual conflicts (Glushko & McGrath, 2005). Nevertheless, semantic conflicts can be effectively resolved as long as the context of use is rigorously defined and agreed on by the organizations.

Vocabulary conflicts are also concerns when we interpret XML documents. Choosing and inserting name tags into XML documents is often a problematic task (Iyengar & Malyankarm, 2002). In many cases, each participating organization wants to have their name tags in their own languages. Even in the same language, the same name tags may have different meanings to different organizations. The vocabulary including name tags has to be rigorously defined. Possible solutions for vocabulary conflicts are presented including controlled vocabularies, a closed set of defining terms, and formal ontologies (Glushko & McGrath, 2005). A controlled vocabulary can be regarded as a dictionary. Every name must come from the dictionary. A closed set of defining terms is also a controlled vocabulary. With domain semantics, a closed set of names can be defined for that particular domain to minimize size. Formal ontologies provide richer semantics and more formal mechanisms for assigning metadata and classifications to names. Renear et al. (2002) present their project, attempting to develop the semantics of XML vocabulary. Kuo et al. (2005) present a form-based user interface for applications used to prescribe vocabularies automatically. A case study of vocabulary development can be referenced in (Malyankar, 2002).

Ontologies (Alexiev et al., 2005; Fensel, 2005; Gomez-Perez et al., 2004) have been researched to assure the common understanding of XML documents in semantics. Ontologies are logical languages that can be used to define a common vocabulary of terms and axiomatic relations for a subject area. Zeigler and Hammonds (2007) introduce pragmatics into ontologies for information exchange. Their approach to data engineering provides an effective means of XML document exchanges to ensure the agreement on syntax, semantics, and pragmatics of information and its use.

TEXT EXTRACTION TO XML

Existing published techniques of document engineering mostly emphasize the creation of XML documents from scratch, but very few cover the technical solutions on the conversion of XML documents from non-XML documents. Although several existing commercial tools provide technical solutions to help convert a non-XML document to the XML, unfortunately, the technical details of the tools are usually proprietary and unpublished. In this section, we will focus on the extraction of the data of interest from non-XML documents into XML. The extraction techniques are classified into two categories: one for formatted document and the other for unformatted. Formatted documents like tables have data written in a repeated pattern. As long as we know the position of the data of interest, we can easily extract the data from the pattern. If no pattern can be found, the document is unformatted such as text in a natural language. Basically, these techniques focus on natural language understanding and analysis (Weiss et al., 2005). We have much experience when it comes to developing techniques for text extraction from formatted documents (Ray et al., 2005) and unformatted ones (Ford et al., 2004; Ford et al., 2005).

Text Extraction from Formatted Documents

The first technique we are going to present is one that allows a user to select the data of interest from formatted documents on Windows and extract the data into XML (Ray et al., 2005). A user, of course, is also allowed to extract data from the entire document to XML (Ray et al., 2005). One benefit of using this tool is that organizations can extract data from documents in a proprietary document type. A typical example of this case occurs during the extraction of data from Windows documents. Without knowing the structures of the document, there is no way of locating the data of interest in the documents for extraction. Even when the structures are known, some problems still exist. For example, only a portion of the data of interest needs to be extracted from a document. It would be very time consuming to manually locate the data of interest and extract them out of the document. A tool that can extract the data automatically is needed to save time and effort. We implemented a tool to perform this task.

The tool starts by opening any document on Windows using the corresponding software. The document is sent to a virtual printer for printing. Since the printer is virtual, the print job will be held in the print queue. The tool then removes the print job from the queue and displays the image of the print job on the screen. A user can then draw a box around the data of interest for extraction into a XML file. The tool would not be efficient if a document contains inconsistent formats because the tool requires the user to locate the data for extraction as needed throughout the entire document. Nevertheless, the tool becomes very effective if the document's content has consistent formats, such as bank statements. For example, the name and address of each customer in the document can be selected and automatically extracted into XML by the tool as long as the positions of the name and address are located in the first bank statement. Address verification can then be further conducted in XML documents. The tool also provides an additional function allowing the bar code to be inserted into XML documents corresponding to the zip code. Finally, the XML document is converted back to a print job for printing.

In summary, if a user is going to print a bank statement for each customer, the only thing that he/she is required to do is to click the print button. The tool will help the user verify the customer data in the bank statements and print them out. The user just walks to the printer and receives the bank statements. The tool also provides additional functions for mailing purposes. The names and addresses of the customers can be extracted as mailing labels with bar codes. We have completed the tool for Windows documents. A company is using this tool to provide mailing services for its customers. We continue to do research on text extraction from PDF documents. The ultimate goal of this research is to extract data from existing documents in different document types to XML documents. Once we have XML documents, the techniques widely covered in literature can then be applied for other purposes.

Text Extraction from Unformatted Documents

The second technique we are going to present in this section is one that allows a user to select the data of interest from unformatted documents on Windows and extract the data into XML. For example, we developed a technique to extract personal information from online Web pages (Ford et al., 2004; Ford et al., 2005). A list of the web sites corresponding to the subject matter is semi-automatically chosen using criteria such as availability, relevance, and importance of web sites. The tool constantly downloads web pages including the hyper links to other pages and saves them into text files. The tool also keeps a copy of all visited pages for preventing repeatedly accessing the same web pages. A set of patterns is used to locate the data of interest embedded in phrases, sentences, or paragraphs such as names, phone numbers, and addresses. Patterns are formulated based on domains such as marriage, obituary, etc. The patterns are therefore very domain oriented. A parsing technique is then used to extract the data of interest and construct tree representations of the data in terms of the found patterns. Other techniques for mining texts from unformatted documents can be referenced in (Weiss et al., 2005).

The extracted data are then grouped into records where the quality of the records is evaluated against a Trusted Index. However, it is very often the case that both the extracted data records and the records stored in the Trusted Index are incomplete and exhibit some degree of variation in both content and format. Therefore, the tool assigns a confidence level to each record indicating the match level and implied confidence that the record is the one that matches the actual record stored in the Trusted Index. The results of the extracted data with the confidence levels are then used to augment datasets in the Trusted Index used in production.

FUTURE TRENDS

Apparently, there is an increasing demand to overcome the plethora of proprietary document types for interoperability. The lack of integration, of incompatible document types, overwhelms us with varieties of documents that make it difficult to manage them all. The best solution is to have a unified approach to create, access, and validate the documents. The open document architecture (ODA) was developed in the mid-1980s for the interchanging of documents including texts and images (Fandert et al., 1992). The International Organization for Standardization has recently published the open document format (ODF) as an official standard (Cheng, 2006; ISO, 2006). As long as organizations decide to follow the standard, the organizations will agree on the interpretation of the documents. However, more research needs to be done on the re-engineering of non-standard documents into standard form.

CONCLUSION

XML has been widely adopted as a means to store data in digital documents for exchange. Several techniques have been presented to help create and process documents in XML. These techniques include XML editing, XML validation, XML transformations, and XML tracking. Most of them mainly focus on XML creations. Many vendors are also advertising their tools that assist in the creation of XML documents from non-XML documents. Unfortunately, we are not given the technical details of these proprietary tools including how these tools are developed and how effective they are. Nevertheless, in this chapter we presented our experience in developing tools for text extraction into XML documents from non-XML documents. One tool was presented to extract data from formatted documents into XML documents. Data of interest was extracted, validated, and written into XML documents. Another tool was presented to extract data of interest from unformatted documents. The data was extracted into XML and validated against a master database. Many techniques have been researched and presented to improve text extraction from unformatted documents. However, very few technical details are published in industry literature on how a user can extract data of interest from proprietary documents. A technique presented in this chapter provides us an alternative solution without having to know the formats of the proprietary documents.

REFERENCES

Aho, A., Lam, M., Sethi, R., & Ullman, J. (2008). *Compilers – principles, techniques, & tools*. (2nd ed.). Boston, Massachusetts: Addison Wesley.

Alexiev, V., Breu, M., Bruijn, J., Fensel, D., Lara, R., & Lausen, H. (2005). *Information integration with ontologies*. Hoboken, New Jersey: John Wiley.

Benz, B., & Durant, J. (2003). *XML programming.* New York, New York: Wiley.

Blouin, A., & Beaudoux, O. (2007). In P. King & S. Simske (Ed.), *Proceedings of the 2007 ACM Symposium on Document Engineering Conference* (pp. 219-221). New York, New York: ACM.

Boukottaya, A., & Vanoirbeek, C. (2005). Schema matching for transforming structured documents. In P. King (Ed.), *Proceedings of the 2005 ACM Symposium on Document Engineering Conference* (pp. 101-110). New York, New York: ACM.

Brownell, D. (2002). *SAX2.* Sebastopol, California: O'reilly.

Chen, H., & Tompa, F. (2003). Set-at-a-time access to XML through DOM. In C. Roisin, E. Munson, & C. Vanoirbrrk (Ed.), *Proceedings of the 2003 ACM Symposium on Document Engineering Conference* (pp. 171-174). New York, New York: ACM.

Cheng, J. (2006). *Open document format published as ISO standard.* Retrieved July 10, 2008, from http://arstechnica.com/news.ars/post/20061204-8349.html

Chuang, T. R., & Lin, J. L. (2004). On modular transformation of structural content. In Jean-Yves Vlon-Dury (Ed.), *Proceedings of the 2004 ACM Symposium on Document Engineering Conference* (pp. 201-210). New York, New York: ACM.

DOM. (2000). Document Object Model (DOM) Level 2 Core Specification. W3C Recommendation. Retrieved October 4, 2008, from http://www.w3.org/TR/2000/REC-DOM-Level-2-Core-20001113/DOM2-Core.pdf

Fandert, H., Fischer, K., & Kämper, J. (1992). The open document architecture: from standardization to the market. *IBM Systems Journal, 31*(4), 728-754.

Fensel, D. (2005). *Ontologies: a silver bullet for knowledge management and electronic commerce.* New York, New York: Springer.

Ford, C. W., Chiang, C.-C., Wu, H., Chilka, R. R., & Talburt, J. (2004). Confidence on approximate query in large datasets. In P. K. Srimani (Ed.), *Proceedings of the IEEE International Conference on Information Technology Coding and Computing* (pp. 480-484). Los Alamitos, California: IEEE.

Ford, C. W., Chiang, C.-C., Wu, H., Chilka, R. R., & Talburt, J. (2005). Text data mining: a case study. In H. S. Selvaraj & P. K. Srimani (Ed.), *Proceedings of the IEEE International Conference on Information Technology Coding and Computing* (pp. 122-127). Los Alamitos, California: IEEE.

Forward, A., & Lethbridge, T. (2002). The relevance of software documentation, tools and technologies: a survey. In E. Munson, R. Furuta, & J. Maletic (Ed.), *Proceedings of the 2002 ACM Symposium on Document Engineering Conference* (pp. 26-33). New York, New York: ACM.

Gançarski, A., & Henriques, P. (2003). Interactive information retrieval from XML documents represented by attribute grammars. In C. Roisin, E. Munson, & C. Vanoirbrrk (Ed.), *Proceedings of the 2003 ACM Symposium on Document Engineering Conference* (pp. 171-174). New York, New York: ACM.

Glushko, R., & McGrath T. (2005). *Document engineering: analyzing and designing documents for business informatics & Web services.* Cambridge, Massachusetts: The MIT Press.

Gomez-Perez, A., Corcho, O., & Fernandez-Lopez, M. (2004). *Ontological engineering.* New York, New York: Springer.

Hardy, M., & Brailsford, D. (2002). Mapping and displaying structural transformations between XML and PDF. In E. Munson, R. Furuta, & J. Maletic (Ed.), *Proceedings of the 2002 ACM Symposium on Document Engineering Conference* (pp. 95-102). New York, New York: ACM.

Hardy, M. (2007). The Mars project – PDF in XML. In Peter King & Steven Simske (Ed.), *Proceedings of the 2007 ACM Symposium on Document Engineering Conference* (pp. 161-170). New York, New York: ACM.

ISO, (2006). *Information technology—open document format for office applications (OpenDocument) v1.0. ISO/IEC 26300:2006,* Retrieved July 10, 2008, from http://www.iso.org/iso/iso_catalogue/catalogue_tc/catalogue_detail.htm?csnumber=43485

Iyengar R. K., & Malyankar, R. M. (2002). A method for automating text markup. In *Proceedings of the 2002 Annual National Conference on Digital Government Research* (pp. 1-6). New York, New York: ACM.

Kuikka, E., Leinonen, P., & Penttonen, M. (2002). Towards automating of document structure transformations. In E. Munson, R. Furuta, & J. Maletic (Ed.), *Proceedings of the 2002 ACM Symposium on Document Engineering Conference* (pp. 103-110). New York, New York: ACM.

Kuo, Y. S., Wang, J., & Shih, N. C. (2003). In C. Roisin, E. Munson & C. Vanoirbrrk (Ed.), *Proceedings of the 2003 ACM Symposium on Document Engineering Conference* (pp. 222-224). New York, New York: ACM.

Kuo, Y. S., Shih, N. C., Tseng, L., & Hu, H.-C. (2005). In P. King (Ed.), *Proceedings of the 2005 ACM Symposium on Document Engineering Conference* (pp. 58-60). New York, New York: ACM.

Kurtev, I., & Berg, K. (2003). Model driven architecture based XML processing. In C. Roisin, E. Munson & C. Vanoirbrrk (Ed.), *Proceedings of the 2003 ACM Symposium on Document Engineering Conference* (pp. 246-248). New York, New York: ACM.

Malyankar, R. (2002). Vocabulary development for markup languages – a case study with maritime information. *Proceedings of the 11th International Conference on World Wide Web* (pp. 674-685). New York, New York: ACM.

Pugin, C., & Ingold, R. (2007). Combination of transformation and schema languages described by a complete formal semantics. In P. King & S. Simske (Ed.), *Proceedings of the 2007 ACM Symposium on Document Engineering Conference* (pp. 222-224). New York, New York: ACM.

Ray, R., Chiang, C.-C., & Melescue, J. (2005). Text extraction on Windows-based documents. *Proceedings of the IEEE Eighteenth International Conference on Systems Engineering* (pp. 205-210). Los Alamitos, California: IEEE.

Renear, A., Dubin, D., Sperberg-McQueen, C. M., & Huitfeldt, C. (2002). In E. Munson, R. Furuta, & J. Maletic (Ed.), *Proceedings of the 2002 ACM Symposium on Document Engineering Conference* (pp. 119-126). New York, New York: ACM.

Weiss, S. M., Indurkhya, N., Zhang, T., & Damerau, F. J. (2005). *Text mining: predictive methods for analyzing unstructured information*. New York, New York: Springer.

XML. (2008). Extensible Markup Language (XML) 1.0, 4th Ed., World Wide Web Consortium. W3C Recommendation. Retrieved June 18, 2008, from http://www.w3.org/TR/REC-xml

Zeigler B. P., & Hammonds P. E. (2007). *Modeling and simulation-based data engineering*. Boston, Massachusetts: Elsevier Academic Press.

Chapter III
Decision–Making as a Facilitator of High–Achievement in Non–Hierarchical Technical Environments

Dwayne Rosenburgh
The George Washington University, USA

ABSTRACT

This chapter presents a look at the decision-making methods used by real-life, collegial, high-achieving, technical teams and organizations. One may argue that the type of technical team that is being considered is not critical. When a group of individuals come together to examine and solve a tough technical challenge the synergy created in reaching a conclusion is usually quite astounding. As the author will explore in this chapter, many researchers have come to the conclusion that the manner in which those teams make decisions is one factor that affects the achievement level of the team. It is then reasonable to suggest that an organization's achievement level is related to the decision-making method of its technical teams. This chapter contains a review of the published literature on team decision-making. In keeping with the practical-level theme of this book, also discussed are the results of a unique study of 31, intact, real-life, technical teams. The teams operated in open, unbounded environments. The resulting theory that emerged from the data was that a collegial, technical, team's selection of the majority-rule method may be an indicator that the team will reach a high-achievement level. The preceding is important because contemporary work organizations may not be obtaining the maximal benefits from their work teams if they attempt to "force" teams to implement other types of decision-making methods.

INTRODUCTION

The purpose of this chapter will be to provide an insight into, and description of, the decision-making method of flat-structured (i.e., collegial), technical organizations. This chapter will provide a basis for exploring how a technical organization's structure and decision-making method are related to its level of achievement. In this chapter, we examine an organization via its teams that are operating in open and unbounded environments. Since collegial, or ad hoc, or self-managed, teams (and their surrounding organizations) may be more competitive when compared to large hierarchical enterprises, understanding how these micro-enterprises reach their levels of achievement should be of interest to those who are affiliated with cross-disciplinary research.

The underlying premise for this chapter is that a team's decision-making process affects the team's level of achievement. The preceding is a reasonable assumption, in light of the research that has been done in this area (e.g., Russo & Schoemaker, 1990; Watson et al., 1991; Yeaple, 1992; Safoutin & Thurston, 1993; Barrick et al., 1998; Katzenbach & Smith, 1999).

The word **team** will be used frequently in this chapter. However, do not let that term mislead you. The concepts and principles apply to larger **organizations**. That is especially true if one considers that most technology-based organizations are a collection of technical teams. Therefore, we will be loose with the terms teams and organizations; often using them interchangeably. It should be readily apparent when one moniker is not a suitable substitute for the other. For example, if a reference is made to research that was done using ten teams, then this is not the same thing as saying that the research was done using ten organizations; all of the teams could have been from a single organization.

The objectives of this chapter are to provide:

- Insight into how flat-structured high-achieving technical organizations view decision-making.
- Insight into how high-achieving technical organizations select and implement their decision method.
- Identifiers of when a technical organization may be headed towards high-achievement levels.
- Strengths and weaknesses of various decision methods as they apply to flat-structured technical organizations.

BACKGROUND

At this point, it is probably helpful to define what is meant by a decision-making method, and for that matter, a team. The decision-making methods (advocacy, autocratic, consensus, inquiry, and majority-rule) discussed in this chapter, and defined below, were selected because they are frequently used by teams, and they are frequently studied by researchers that do team research.

In devil's **advocacy**, a team member champions a less accepted view or alternative for the sake of argument; helping to ensure that all alternatives are equally discussed. Devil's advocacy often prevents a team from discarding, or overlooking, excellent ideas.

An **autocratic** decision-making method is one where an individual, or possibly a small group of individuals, is the team's decision-maker. The decision-maker may or may not seek advice and recommendations from other team members.

A dictionary[a] definition for **consensus** is:

1a: *general agreement: UNANIMITY* **b**: *the judgment arrived at by most of those concerned* **2**: *group solidarity in sentiment and belief*

It is not as easy to define a **consensus-method**. In defining consensus decision-making methods, Hornsby et al. (1994) list three techniques—the traditional consensus approach, the nominal group technique, and the Delphi technique. In this research, there was no distinction made between the techniques. Hereafter, the term consensus-method refers to the procedure of listening to, and understanding everyone's ideas and opinions, discussing the pros and cons of the alternatives, and having everyone actively support the decision in thoughts, words, and actions. Therefore, it is possible for a single individual to block a consensus. This is consistent with the definition of consensus used by other researchers (Laufer et al. 1999; Katzenbach & Smith 1999).

Dialectical **inquiry** may take several forms. Usually, it follows either the Socratic method of doubting and questioning, or the Hegelian method of developing a thesis, an antithesis, and synthesis. Regardless of the form, dialectical inquiry uses systematic reasoning, exposition, or argument that juxtaposes contradictory ideas and attempts to resolve their conflict. (Schweiger et al. 1986; Hornsby et al. 1994).

The **majority-rule** method provides all team members with a "vote" to determine the team's decision. In the simple majority-rule method, the alternative that receives the highest number of individual votes becomes the team's choice. In a weighted majority-rule method, the alternatives are evaluated against a, team derived, set of selection criteria. The selection criteria are established before details of the alternatives are known (to prevent establishing criteria that may be purposefully biased towards or against a particular alternative). Subsequently, the criteria are assigned various weights, according to the team's preferences. The alternative with the highest score, rather than the one with the most votes, becomes the team's choice.

The word **team** is used, as defined by Katzenbach & Smith (1999), to refer to a "small number of people with complementary skills who are committed to a common purpose, performance goals, and approach for which they hold themselves mutually accountable". This definition is consistent with the definition of "team" used by other researchers, such as Hollenbeck et al. (1995), Cohen & Bailey (1997), and Kepner & Tregoe (1997). The important point to emphasize is that there is a difference between a team and a workgroup. A workgroup can be defined as an assemblage of people working together. The commitment to a common purpose, and to performance goals, along with mutual accountability turns a workgroup into a team.

The use of flat-structured, self-managed teams has become popular since the last quarter of the 20th century. The literature that is relevant to team decision-making in collegial environments is found in a wide variety of publications. The literature is voluminous and multifarious, making a comprehensive review a difficult task. This review focuses on the literature that explores the methods that teams use and how those methods relate to team achievement.

The following broad survey and review of the relevant literature in the field of multi-agent decision-making presents some historical foundational research of group and team decision-making (Arrow 1963; Hackman & Morris 1975). Hackman and Morris focused mainly on the qualitative aspects of group decision-making. Arrow's emphasis was on the quantitative aspects of decision-making. What can be cumulatively drawn from the qualitative and quantitative foundations is that understanding how teams and groups select and implement their decision method and process is important; however, there is not an adequate understanding of the collegial, team decision-making method (Hackman & Morris 1975).

Nearly all of the research studies on the effectiveness of group decision-making found that decision-making methods other than consensus resulted in higher achievement levels and better decisions (Farris & Sage 1975; Hackman & Morris 1975; Stasser & Titus 1985; Schweiger et al. 1986; Russo & Schoemaker 1990; Dias 1990; Gruenfeld et al. 1996; Popick & Sheard 1996; Cohen & Bailey 1997; Gross & Brodt 2001; Yager 2001). A smaller number of studies found that a consensus decision-making method yielded higher achievement than non-consensus-methods (Watson et al. 1991; Crow 1994; Yeatts & Hyten 1998).

Several researchers did studies on the metadecisions and interactions of groups (Hackman & Morris 1975; Castore & Murnighan 1978; Bettenhausen & Murnighan 1985; Driskell & Salas 1991; Katzenbach & Smith 1998). Those studies provide a framework for identifying group decision methods.

SELECTED STUDIES OF DECISION-MAKING IN TEAM ENVIRONMENTS

Following is a summary of selected contributions to the theory of team decision-making, and how decision-making relates to team achievement levels. Field studies and experiments which examined the potential linkage of achievement and a team's decision-making method were of particular interest. Some non-experimental studies by widely published researchers are also presented. Examples of experimental and non-experimental studies include Schweiger (1986) and Katzenbach & Smith (1999), respectively; both works document factors relating to decision-making and achievement in team environments.

Arrow

In 1951, Arrow showed that, generally, it is not possible to reach a true consensus when there are at least two people and three alternatives to be considered (Arrow 1963). Arrow's work initiated much of the research into how best to amalgamate the, often conflicting, preference patterns (i.e., choices) of the members of a group (or society) to arrive at a compromise preference pattern for the group as a whole. As interpreted by Arrow, this became a question of "combining" individual choices to generate a single choice for the group composed of those individuals. In other words, Arrow's theorem accepted individual preferences as input, and provided the group's preference as output.

This *possibility theorem* became known as Arrow's Impossibility Theorem. In establishing his theorem, Arrow proposed five conditions:

- **Condition 1:** There are least two individuals; and the number of alternatives is greater than two.
- **Condition 2:** (positive association of individual and group preferences) If alternative *A* is preferred to *B* for a given set of individual preferences, that preference is maintained when the set is modified in *A's* favor.
- **Condition 3:** (independence of irrelevant alternatives) If the group prefers *A* over *B,* and some of the individual preferences between alternatives <u>other than</u> *A* and *B* are modified, but the individual preferences between *A* and *B* remain unchanged, then the original group preference for *A* over *B* is maintained.

- **Condition 4:** (citizen's sovereignty) For each pair of alternatives *A* and *B*, there is some set of individual orderings such that the group prefers *A* to *B*.
- **Condition 5:** (non-dictatorship) There is no individual with the property that whenever he or she prefers *A* to *B*, the group does likewise, regardless of the preferences of other individuals.

One can argue that the above axioms are reasonable and not too restrictive. Condition 2 states that in a situation where the group prefers *A* over *B*, if some of the members maintains or increase their enthusiasm for *A* via some other alternative(s) and none of the members lessen their enthusiasm for *A* via any other alternative, then the group maintains its preference for *A* over *B*.

Condition 3 says that a group's preference of *A* over *B* should depend only on how individuals rank *A* and *B*, and not on how individuals rank some irrelevant alternative (*C*) relative to *A* and *B*. Satisfying Condition 3 requires that the group selects *A* as long as the majority of the members prefer *A* to all other projects.

Condition 4 simply states that the collective opinions of the group have some relevance to the group decision. Thus, for any pair of alternatives *A* and *B*, there is some set of individual preferences which could lead to a group preference of *A* over *B*. If Condition 4 were not true, then the group would not have the power to establish preferences between all of the alternatives.

Condition 5 states that there is no dictator in the group; that is, there is no individual whose preference between *A* and *B* will dominate the group decision even if all other members of the group have the opposite preference structure.

Arrow's impossibility theorem states that Conditions 1, 2, 3, 4, and 5 are not logically consistent. That is, there is not a group decision process or method that possesses the properties demanded by all of these conditions. In other words, if a function satisfies Conditions 1 – 4, then condition 5 cannot hold.

Arrow provided a basis for an evaluation of choice and decision-making. In his research, Arrow established several apparently reasonable conditions for the method of group decision-making (or social choice); these require that a decision be responsive to the desires of individuals and that, among any given set of possible alternatives, a decision depends only on the preferences of the individuals among the members of that set. He then showed that the complete set of conditions cannot be met. Arrow's theorem can provide the basis for determining which type of decision method a team used. This can be achieved by analyzing the data obtained from observing a team or organization and determining which of Arrow's conditions apply. As an example, it is reasonable to assume that a consensus-method should satisfy Conditions 1, 2, 4, and 5. If the data shows that a team's decision method included satisfying Condition 3, then the team did not use a consensus-method – this is true even if the team members indicate that they used a consensus-method. The reason for this is that Condition 3 fails to take into consideration the strength of support that the team members have for one alternative relative to another. If the team did not take into consideration "strength of support", then their method is probably best described by some other moniker, since discussions of support are part of the consensus-method (Laufer et al. 1999).

After Arrow published his research, other researchers sought to resolve the logical inconsistency of Arrow's five conditions. Notable was the work of Farris & Sage (1975), their work is summarized below.

Farris and Sage

Farris & Sage (1975) surveyed the problem of group decision-making from the standpoint of finding a social welfare function to amalgamate the preference structures of individuals into a preference structure for the group. They found that the method of majority-rules can satisfy all of Arrow's conditions if Condition 1 is modified to require two alternatives. This is a special case, however, since a condition such as independence of irrelevant alternatives (Arrow's Condition 3) is not a problem when there are fewer than three alternatives.

In group decision-making, a *worth assessment* approach is a method for determining individual preferences among alternatives described by multiple attributes (Farris & Sage 1975). Steps in the worth assessment procedure are:

1. Listing criteria;
2. Constructing an hierarchy;
3. Determining branch weights;
4. Selecting performance measures and confidence weights;
5. Assigning worth scores; and
6. Determining the preference ordering.

Farris and Sage determined that a group worth assessment approach, which included the method of majority decision and confidence indicators, imposed the minimum amount of restrictions on individual preference orderings. Fewer restrictions on the ordering of individual preferences allowed groups to consider a more complete set of alternatives and information.

Farris and Sage built on the work of Arrow (1951), and Luce & Raiffa (1957), and showed that for groups, a purely majority-rules decision method does not *consistently* yield a best or correct decision. However, according to the researchers, a decision-making process that uses a combination of methods (e.g., worth assessment approach and majority decision) can yield decisions that are, consistently, the best – by allowing more alternatives to be considered. Farris and Sage's research indicated that in limited use, majority-rule can lead to better decisions.

About the same time that Farris and Sage were examining quantitative aspects of group decision-making, Hackman & Morris (1975) were doing research into the qualitative aspects of group decision-making. Their ground-breaking research is reviewed below.

Hackman and Morris

Hackman & Morris (1975) stated "...we still know very little about why some groups are more effective than others. We know even less about what to do to improve the performance of a given group..." They suggested that the key to understanding the "group effectiveness problem" is to be found in the on-going interaction process which takes place among group members. One key challenge noted in their report was to identify those aspects of a group's process that contribute to differences in group effectiveness (or achievement). However, they stated that research that directly relates characteristics of group process to performance (or achievement) outcomes is scarce.

Hackman and Morris found that group members seldom discussed strategic issues, even when it was clear that such discussion would enhance their performance. This makes it difficult to document some processes or methods, such as the decision-making method, because members themselves are often not aware of their processes and methods. The researchers also reported that performance is likely to increase when the members owned their processes, because the problems of a group are highly idio-syncratic, hinging on rather unique coincidences of people, tasks, and situations. (Those findings also were supported by research done by Bartlett (1991)). One finding of particular was that the performance of a group can be affected by the strategies that members use. Hackman and Morris also reported that regardless of the decision method, individuals whose preferences are in closer accord with a group's decision will be supportive of that decision. The two preceding findings supported the results reported by Farris & Sage (1975).

The research by Hackman and Morris, and Farris and Sage, in the mid-1970's, was followed by a considerable amount of research centered on team and group decision-making in the late 1970's. Castore & Murnighan (1978) were amongst the first researchers to examine the efficacy of different decision-making methods in group settings.

Castore and Murnighan

Castore & Murnighan (1978) examined four different decision methods used by groups:

1. Majority-rule with parliamentary voting;
2. Discussion to majority agreement;
3. Executive choice; and
4. Unanimity.

The researchers used 40, five-person groups in their study. The group members were 200 volunteers enrolled in an introductory psychology class. All participants appeared in response to an advertisement which promised a free record album and credit toward a course requirement for participating in the study. It was made clear to all participants prior to their volunteering that the exact album they would receive would depend in large part upon the decisions reached by their particular group. Castore and Murnighan were interested in how a group's decision-making method affected both the decision and support for the decision.

The task for the groups was chosen to simulate conditions that exist when individuals must reconcile conflicting preferences to reach a group decision. This task required the group members to rank order a set of five record albums using the decision method assigned to their group. All groups were given as much time as they required to arrive at this group ranking.

Groups in the majority-rule with parliamentary voting condition were told to begin by choosing any pair of alternatives and, after any discussion desired, to vote between them. The winning alternative (that one obtaining at least three out of the five votes) was to be paired with one of the remaining alternatives and the procedure would be repeated. Sequential pairings of this nature were continued until one of the alternatives remained as the group's first choice. The remaining alternatives were to be similarly selected, until the second, third, fourth, and fifth choices had been determined. Groups in the discussion to majority agreement condition were simply told to reach a decision about the ranking of the alternatives in which at least a majority of the members concurred. Groups in the unanimity condition were told that they should discuss their preferences until they all agreed upon the ranking. One member from each of the groups in the executive choice condition was randomly designated, by the experimenter, as the "decision-maker" (i.e., executive) for his or her group. The other group members were told that they could present arguments in favor of their own personal preferences, but that the decision-maker would make the final decision for the group.

Castore and Murnighan found that merely having individuals present their views and having them share equally in the decision-making is not sufficient to ensure that all of the participants will be equally favorable toward and supportive of a group decision. The effectiveness of a decision method is moderated by both the overall diversity of group member pre-decision preferences and by the relative congruence between an individual's preferences and his group's decision. Overall, the most effective decision-making method (in terms of support generated) appeared to be one which would not reveal the exact nature of the group members preferences to each other, while giving each equal control over the actual decision-making. Castore and Murnighan stated that such a method would seem to be rarely attainable in practice, because most parties to a decision are aware (or become aware) of the nature of the other participant's preferences. (If this observation is accurate, the question that needs to be answered is, "what is the method that teams use in practice?")

The findings reported by Castore and Murnighan validated the work done by Arrow (1963), Farris & Sage (1975), and Hackman & Morris (1975). The only drawbacks to Castore and Murnighan's work are that their groups were not teams, as is defined in this chapter, and that the groups were ad-hoc. (This is a common "problem" in group research, as noted by Naudé et al. (1997)). While Castore and Murnighan did not specifically indicate which method may be the most effective, their results indicate that a method similar to a private vote may be preferred over a method that includes open discussion.

Later, Murnighan teamed with Bettenhausen to do a grounded theory research on decision-making groups. Their research is summarized below.

Bettenhausen and Murnighan

Bettenhausen & Murnighan (1985) did research on the emergence of norms in decision-making groups. The researchers studied 19 groups; each group was required to make 48 separate decisions. The group members role-played representatives of one of five different engineering departments that were competing for federal research funds. Bettenhausen and Murnighan collected and analyzed both qualitative and quantitative data. The qualitative analysis led to their propositions; the quantitative analysis substantiated the qualitative interpretations. The researchers used observations of decision-making groups to infer behavior and construct propositions that were subjected to quantitative tests.

According to Bettenhausen and Murnighan, the identification of behaviors, especially implicit behaviors, is a difficult methodological issue. They cautioned that the (qualitative) propositions are a model; and the (quantitative) data do not substantiate the model, but indicate that the propositions have some empirical foundation.

During the mid-1980's, the idea of using consensus in decision-making was gaining in popularity. However, Stasser & Titus' (1985) research on information sharing and discussion in group decision-making began to lay foundations for questioning the role of consensus and for focusing on majority-rule. Their work is described below.

Stasser and Titus

Stasser & Titus (1985) did research on information sharing in group decision-making. Their main area of interest was to investigate how the sharing of information, via discussion, affected the decision of a group. This was accomplished by comparing the initial individual preferences with the subsequent group's preference. The 30 groups were comprised of 120 university students who read descriptions of three hypothetical candidates for student body president and then met in four-person groups to decide which candidate was best suited for the position.

The profile of Candidate A contained more positive and fewer neutral attributes than the profiles of Candidates B and C. The valences (positive, neutral, or negative) of profile attributes were determined via pre-experimental ratings. Thus, Candidate A was the best candidate in the sense that his profile contained more of the consensually valued attributes of a student body president. Therefore, the challenge for the groups was to select the correct candidate using information from their individually assigned candidate profiles, which were not complete. However, unknown to the participants, the distribution of information across a group's members was designed so that a group, collectively, had all of the information and could recreate the complete candidate profiles during discussion. Stasser and Titus stated that one goal of discussion is to achieve consensus among the group's members. However, they noted that discussion was rarely a systematic and balanced exploration of the relevant issues surrounding the alternatives. On the contrary, it was often thematic and consensus confirming; that is, discussions tended to focus on particular issues and supported an existing or emergent consensus.

According to Stasser and Titus' results, a "plurality-supported wins" rule accounts for most group decisions; that is, an alternative with at least a plurality of initial support is likely to be the group's decision. Such a process suggests that discussion rarely has an effect on a group's decision. Therefore, it would appear that a consensus-method is not essential for a group to reach consensus. Stasser and Titus stated that their findings supported the conclusion that groups deciding issues of social preference are likely to follow a majority-rules method.

Similar to Stasser and Titus, Schweiger, William, & Ragan's (1986) research, which is summarized below, did not support the growing consensus that consentaneous decision-making would produce better outcomes.

Schweiger, William, and Ragan

Schweiger et al. (1986) examined the quality[b] of recommendations and assumptions made by groups that used a consensus-method and groups that used non-consensus-methods (e.g., dialectical inquiry or devil's advocacy). They were interested in comparing the effectiveness of decision methods. They found that the non-consensus-methods led to higher quality decisions than did the consensus-method. In summarizing their results, the researchers wrote, "...the evidence provided in this study clearly suggests that it (consensus) is inferior to both dialectical inquiry and devil's advocacy with respect to the overall quality of the assumptions and recommendations made." (Schweiger et al. 1986).

Like many researchers in group decision-making, Schweiger et al. used ad-hoc groups in a laboratory setting, vice real-life teams. Their research was constructed so that the groups could produce correct decisions or recommendations. Issues such as group buy-in and strength of support were not significant factors. In addition to the strong statement in the preceding paragraph, they found that active, heated, and intense debates between and among the group members resulted in the group discovering and inventing entirely new alternatives. These findings should be of interest to anyone involved in getting high-achievement from teams in technical environments.

Unlike the previous four groups of researchers, Russo & Schoemaker (1990) did their research by studying genuine groups – not ad hoc groups in laboratory settings. The researchers were amongst the first to study real teams and to de-emphasize the use of teams in laboratory settings. Their research, which is summarized below, suggested that conflict was beneficial to decision-making.

Russo and Schoemaker

Drawing on almost 20 years of experience as researchers at the University of Chicago's Center for Decision Research, Russo & Schoemaker (1990) compiled their findings and published their guide for "decision-making in the real world". They introduced the term, "metadecision", to define the activity of making choices about the decision method. Russo and Schoemaker contend that an intelligent meta-decision—deciding how to decide—is probably more important in group decisions than in individual decision-making. While an individual who has started in the wrong direction can turn around and go back to square zero easily, a group that realizes it is moving in the wrong direction will have a tougher time undoing agreements and expectations among members in order to change course. The groups that Russo and Schoemaker used were, almost exclusively, genuine groups involved in making various types of decisions.

Russo and Schoemaker, like Schweiger et al. (1986), found that cognitive conflict and devil's advocacy created better results than a consensus-method. Russo and Schoemaker expressed the view that a consensus-method is likely to cause a group to converge too rapidly to conclusion. They stated that in important decisions, groups must avoid the dangers of conformity and overconfidence. According to the researchers, "Probably the biggest barrier to outstanding group decision-making is the misconception that 'conflict is bad'". They claimed that conflict (among ideas) is necessary and valuable if a group decision-making method is going to accomplish more than simple groupthink.

The research done Russo and Schoemaker begins to create a decision-making framework that may be applicable to high-achievement groups. The starting point for their framework is a metadecision. It seems clear that their framework includes a decision method that promotes cognitive conflict and hinders a consensus-method.

A contemporary of Russo and Schoemaker was Dias (1990); he, too, did research using real-life teams. Dias, study on an engineering team, which is described below, was mainly focused on the team's structure. Dias' results showed that a team does not always have to have open, direct communication in order to be successful.

Dias

Dias (1990) did a study on an engineering research project team whose objective was to help engineers find the most cost-effective structural form for a given elevated-tank or ground-reservoir capacity. The project manager was on a peer level with many coworkers but hierarchically below others. This combination of conditions resulted in the evolution of a circular organizational structure, which reflected a high degree of informal interaction, as opposed to an apical position of a project director. The project manager functioned as a facilitator – being responsible for the flow of information. Dias stated, "This allowed the other team members to concentrate on their specific tasks and reduced wasted time arising out of delays in communication". While a circular organizational structure is not the same as a horizontal structure, it is more closely related than the typical pyramidal structure.

Most of Dias' study focused on structure. His interest was in investigating how a team with a circular structure would accomplish its goals. However, one observation that Dias noted was that brainstorming sessions within the team were the valuable foundation for the group's processes. According to Dias, "The brainstorming sessions...resulted in consensus of design assumptions and parameters..." Dias' findings showed that consensus can be reached without using a consensus-method, and that direct communication amongst team members may not always be necessary for a team to reach a high-achievement level.

By the early 1990's, it was becoming apparent that there was some discrepancy between the theory and the practice of team decision-making. In addition to researchers (such as the previous two research groups) suggesting that teams in laboratory settings may behave differently from real-life teams, Driskell & Salas (1991) questioned whether organizational theory could be appropriately applied to teams.

Driskell and Salas

Driskell & Salas (1991) did research on four groups that were required to make decisions under stressful conditions. The researchers used 78 students at a US Navy technical school. Driskell and Salas stated that previous research suggested that organizations respond to stress with a centralization of authority so that decision-making becomes concentrated in the higher levels of an organizational hierarchy. They extended that hypothesis to the small-group level, and examined the effects of stress on group status and decision-making. The subjects performed their group decision-making tasks under either normal or acute stress conditions. Acute stress was defined as an interaction that (a) threatens the individual's physical or psychological well-being and (b) increases individual responsibility for successful task performance.

The threat aspect was introduced by informing the subjects that they would perform the group task under simulated conditions of a tear-gas drill. No tear-gas actually was used; therefore, the anticipatory threat of the tear-gas constituted the stress manipulation. Additionally, each subject was told that only *their* final score (of several tasks) would count as the team score. This served to increase individual responsibility for task outcome; if an individual failed, then the team failed.

According to the conventional, centralization-of-authority hypothesis, in stressful situations high status group members should become more rejecting of others' input as they increasingly make decisions on their own. The results presented by Driskell and Salas suggested an increased receptivity under stress, whereby high status members became *more* likely to accept the contributions and input of other group members in decision-making. The significance of Driskell and Salas' findings is that they suggest that applying some hypotheses and theories from the organizational literature may not be appropriate to small groups. According to the researchers, hypotheses and theories, based on organizational research, that contend to describe team decision-making may not be accurate. Driskell and Salas' results help to support the importance of doing research on real-life teams.

Real-life teams are exactly what Watson, Michaelsen, & Sharp (1991) studied; their research is summarized below. The researchers did a significant longitudinal study that emphasized the importance and values of studying real-life teams, as opposed to laboratory groups. Their research indicated that when a team used a consensus decision-making method, the team usually made better decisions. However, their research did not indicate that teams preferred a consentaneous method.

Watson, Michaelsen, and Sharp

Watson et al. (1991) noted, "Nowhere in the literature is there a greater disparity between management practice and the results of the vast majority of empirical research than is the case with the relative effectiveness of individual versus group decision-making." The researchers stated the view that, in organizational settings, groups will consistently produce better decisions than those of their most knowledgeable member is close to achieving the status of conventional wisdom. However, they also noted that empirical evidence does not support the superiority of group decisions over those of a group's most knowledgeable member. They agreed with previous researchers (e.g., see Hackman & Morris 1975) that the primary reason for the discrepancy is the artificial nature of the groups, tasks, and settings in which previous research was conducted. According to the researchers, other than case studies contrasting effective and ineffective groups (e.g., see Hackman 1990), only a handful of studies that empirically examined group decision-making effectiveness have used real-life groups.

The researchers created 50 groups, from 272 graduate students enrolled in an organizational behavior course. Group membership was permanent throughout the four-month semester. Therefore, the groups could be considered real-life teams; as opposed to the more common laboratory team that may exist for only a day or two. The primary objective of their study was to examine the extent to which increased experience in working in a group would affect group versus individual problem solving. This was accomplished by examining group behavior and achievement at three different points in time. The phenomena that the researchers addressed were: 1) What changes occurred in the effectiveness of group decision-making as the amount of time working in the group increased; and 2) What changes occurred in how member input was used in group decision-making as the amount of time working in the group increased.

The results from Watson et al.'s longitudinal study "…strongly support the value of group-consensus decision-making…" Their results showed that groups are highly likely to make better decisions than their most knowledgeable member is, and that any "top scorer" became less important to the group's success as time progressed. Another result from Watson et al. was that groups should be able to combine members' knowledge and produce higher quality decisions than would be possible from any individual member working alone or from any combination of individual inputs.

Watson et al. provided a strong argument for using real-life teams to do empirical research in decision-making. They claimed that their results supported the value of consensus decision-making; unfortunately, they did not provide details of the method. In addition, their results showed that consensus decision-making had value, not that it was preferred or most often used by groups. Similar to Driskell & Salas (1991), and Hansen et al. (1996), Watson et al. also called into question the results of some earlier decision-making studies[c].

Watson et al. were not the only researchers in the 1990's that were proponents of consentaneous decision-making. Crow (1994), whose results are summarized below, studied decision-making on empowered teams that had a flat structure. Crow was a proponent of consensus decision-making. However, he observed that implementing a consentaneous decision-making method is difficult and time consuming.

Crow

One of the widely published consultants on integrated product development teams and consensus decision-making is Kenneth Crow (1994). He stated, "Consensus is a decision-making process that fully utilizes the resources of a group. It is more difficult and time consuming to reach than a democratic vote or an autocratic decision." Crow also contended that in order "to respond to an increasingly dynamic and challenging environment, manufacturers are implementing integrated product development (IPD) concepts to reduce design cycle time and improve product value." Those concepts include a flat team structure, with the team empowered to make and implement decisions.

Similar to the findings reported later by other researchers (Popick & Sheard (1996) and Grossman (1997)), Crow recognized the seemingly inherent difficulty that technical groups tend to have with implementing a consensus-method. Crow stated that, "A consensus decision represents a reasonable decision that all members of the group can accept. It is not necessarily the optimal decision for each member."

Crow's findings suggested that organizations may not have been getting the most benefit from their integrated, empowered teams. Additionally, he suggested that decision-making via a consensus-method would be a benefit to teams, such as an IPT or IPD team. However, Crow's statement that a consensus decision represents a reasonable and acceptable decision, not necessarily an optimal one, appears to be the antithesis of reaching a high-achievement level.

Similar to Crow, Popick & Sheard (1996) observed that many teams were not successful using a consensus-method due to the inherent difficulties of the method. Popick and Sheard spent several years studying real-life teams. Like most other researchers, these two researchers did not address which decision-making method real-life teams selected on their own. Their research is described below.

Popick and Sheard

In publishing their findings, which resulted from several years of working with real-world teams (i.e., IPTs), Popick & Sheard (1996) noted that many teams are not successful using a consensus-method. Most of their research resulted from working with scientific and engineering teams at Loral Federal Systems, and the Johns Hopkins University Applied Physics Laboratory. They highlighted four reasons for the lack of success in using a consensus-method on IPTs. The first reason was that the people who make up the IPTs have had little or no experience with consensus decision-making. They have experience with decision-making by a majority or by an individual, but not with consensus. Popick and Sheard observed that many of the team members that they worked with did not understand that a consensus team decision will not be optimal for each individual but must be workable. They concluded, "As a result, an individual may believe that it is right to refuse to agree to a decision".

The second reason cited was that people outside the IPT have overruled IPT decisions. According to Popick and Sheard, either this is because the team has made decisions outside their responsibility domain, or it is because others do not accept the team's empowerment. They said, "Many times when we delved into this, we found the team was not properly set up; there was no clear understanding of the team's purpose and domain". They suggested that when an IPT's decision is overruled, it has a paralyzing effect on the IPT, creating a cynicism that there is just lip service to the IPT approach. Both the team and the program leadership must understand and agree upon the team's decision-making boundary.

The third reason cited by the researchers was that some IPTs try to make every decision by consensus. Some decisions need to be made by an individual, some by small groups, and others by consensus. Popick and Sheard's position was that decisions should be limited to the smallest group that they affect within the IPT. They wrote, "We found that IPTs can usually agree on which decisions the IPT leader, sub-team, or members can make quickly and which require consensus of the IPT members".

Popick and Sheard stated the fourth problem developed when important decisions were made by edict or by a small group of individuals. They wrote, "This sends the message that consensus is not a real decision-making mechanism. For consensus decision-making to succeed, it must be embraced and used by the leadership, otherwise it will never be generally accepted by the teams and the program". Popick and Sheard found that teams performed best when they used a combination of decision-making methods to support a consensus and incorporate multidisciplinary views.

Popick and Sheard's ethnography reflected that some real-life IPTs have efficiency and high-achievement when several decision-making methods are used. They also suggested that there is a difference between using a consensus-method and using a method that support a consensus. Some of the teams that Popick and Sheard observed and worked with were using (or attempting to use) a consensus-method – due to a directive or a strong suggestion. Others used different (unidentified) methods – perhaps also due to a directive or strong suggestion. Popick and Sheard's research did not focus on which method, or methods, a team would choose on its own. Additionally, they did not provide detailed descriptions of any decision-making methods other than consensus. Also, Popick and Sheard noted that usually, consensus yielded "workable" decisions. It is not intuitive that merely workable decisions will lead to high-achievement.

Similar to Popick and Sheard, Gruenfeld, Mannix, Williams, & Neale (1996) also studied collegial groups; their results are summarized below. They reported that groups who selected an advocacy approach to decision-making usually reached a correct solution to a problem relatively quickly.

Gruenfeld, Mannix, Williams, and Neale

Gruenfeld et al. (1996) did research on decision-making methods in collegial groups. The focus of their research was the relationship of a group's composition and its performance (i.e., achievement). Specifically, they were interested in how group member familiarity and information distribution affected the decision-making method and subsequent performance. The groups were to solve a murder mystery (i.e., make a correct decision); therefore, effectiveness was a straightforward measure. The researchers used 71 three-person groups—Executive MBA students at two Midwestern business schools. In their research, they asked groups to evaluate their own achievement. The results suggested that a group's perception of its own behavior reflected its actual achievement.

Gruenfeld et al. also reported that in group decision-making, a devil's advocate can reduce the incidence of groupthink by surfacing faulty assumptions and disconfirming evidence. Similarly, a vocal deviate who proposes unusual and even incorrect solutions during problem solving can lead groups to generate more arguments, apply more strategies, detect solutions that are more novel, use multiple perspectives simultaneously, and generally outperform groups without this type of influence.

Gruenfeld et al. exemplified the trends towards recognizing that having all members of a team actively supporting the team's decision may not lead to high-achievement. Cohen & Bailey (1997) published a review of 130 studies on teams; their work is summarized below. They stated that the published literature, from 1990 to 1996 supported the value of conflict over concurrence and support. Cohen and Bailey also highlighted that additional field research was needed on the relationship of decision-making to group outcomes.

Cohen and Bailey

Cohen & Bailey (1997) did a comprehensive review of the research on teams and groups in organizational settings published from January 1990 to April 1996. They categorized effectiveness into three major dimensions according to the team's impact on: (1) performance (i.e., achievement) effectiveness assessed in terms of quantity and quality of outputs, (2) member attitudes, and (3) behavioral outcomes. Examples of performance effectiveness include efficiency, customer satisfaction, and innovation. Examples of attitudinal measures include employee satisfaction and commitment. Examples of behavioral measures include absenteeism and turnover. Some of the relevant and "key learnings (*sic*)" they reported were:

1. The performance and attitudinal benefits from self-directed work teams are superior to those from parallel (hierarchical) teams.

2. Autonomy is associated with higher performance for work teams (the typical, well-defined, stable team), but not project teams (time-limited, multidiscipline, one-time output team). Some theorists have made arguments for the self-management of project teams; however, that does not fit the empirical evidence.

3. The factors most associated with success vary based on who is rating the team's performance. Team members tend to rate performance based on internal processes, such as collaboration and resolution of conflict. Managers, tend to rate performance based on external factors, such as group communication with external agents. Cohen and Bailey asserted that although objective measures should be sought if what we are interested in is how well the group is achieving quantitative goals, in many instances, we are interested in the perceptions of effectiveness from key stakeholders.

4. Functional diversity was not found to be related to internal team processes on project teams. Additional field work and research is needed to relate internal processes, such as communication and decision-making dynamics, to outcomes.

Additionally, Cohen and Bailey found that for groups performing non-routine tasks, conflict, in some cases, is beneficial. They reported that conflict appeared to promote critical evaluation of problems and options, while simultaneously reducing thoughtless agreement (i.e., groupthink).

The review done by Cohen and Bailey is significant because it amalgamated almost 130 studies in which the dependent variables are concerned with various dimensions of effectiveness. However, their research did not focus on any particular method.

Cohen and Bailey were not the only ones who thought that more research was needed on team decision-making and team achievement. Yeatts & Hyten (1998) published the results of their research on flat-structured teams, decision-making, and achievement. Their work is summarized below.

Yeatts and Hyten

Yeatts & Hyten (1998) presented data from their three-year National Science Foundation study of the performance (and achievement) of self-managed work teams. They found that the decision-making method was an important team characteristic that affected team achievement. According to the researchers, the decision-making method of high-achievement teams included giving extra weight to the opinions of those team members who had the most talent with regard to the particular problem being solved. On low-performing teams, some team members were found to dominate team decision-making, even when other team members had more talent with regard to the particular subject being considered.

In a high-performing nursing home team, they found that the decision-making method most often used was to seek a consensus among the team members before a decision was chosen. The researchers reported that using a consensus-method appeared to heighten team member commitment to the decision reached, but it also frustrated team members because decisions were not made in a "timely fashion".

A low-performing government team studied by Yeatts and Hyten used a different decision-making method – majority-rule. Yeatts and Hyten also stated that majority-rule appeared to be used most often by teams that had received no formal training in team decision-making. Without training, the team members appeared less likely to be aware of any other method for making a decision.

Despite the in-depth research done by Yeatts and Hyten, their observations and comments on decision-making methods were limited to the few aforementioned examples. The results reported by Yeatts and Hyten are similar to the results reported by Herrera-Videma et al. (2002), however neither group of researchers studied multiple technical teams in research environments.

While the work of Yeatts and Hyten was limited to a few teams, Katzenbach & Smith (1999) studied many real-life teams in various environments (as did Klein (1999)). A summary of Katzenbach and Smith's work is presented below.

Katzenbach and Smith

In 1993, Katzenbach and Smith published a summary of their combined 55 years of team research. They stated that although there are no rules, best practices, or secret formulas that ensure high-performance outcomes, high-performing teams provide a terrific model for any potential team to study. Katzenbach and Smith were strong proponents of the view that performance and decision-making are linked. For example, they stated, "...teams can make no greater mistake than to try to solve problems without relating them to performance" (Katzenbach & Smith 1999). According to the researchers, interpersonal conflicts, and numerous side-bar conversations about personal styles and biases, causes a team to become diverted from its performance goals. This, in turn, leads to placing undue importance on decisions that are not related to the team's performance objectives.

At the end of the 20th century, Katzenbach and Smith established a standard for defining teams and performance. One of the first reports on teams and decision-making of the 21st century was by Gross & Brodt (2001). Their results indicated that advocacy and inquiry should be used by teams in order to have high-achievement; their results are summarized below.

Gross and Brodt

Gross & Brodt (2001) reported on how decision-making can be affected by non-cognitive consensus. They reported that in new cross-functional teams focused on product development or organizational redesign, the decision method often includes an assumption or perception of consensus.

According to Gross and Brodt, "getting people to reduce reliance on their own judgments and seek out contrary evidence can improve decision-making greatly." They went on to state that "it is helpful to have group members hold one another accountable." The researchers advocated that in decision-making, the team members should adopt different perspectives and accept them as being valid. Adopting different perspectives is one of the most effective ways of counteracting projection. In general, groups are more likely to uncover important information if they discuss facts rather than opinions.

In summary, Gross and Brodt asserted that groups should reach a consensus in decision-making via methods that resemble Devil's Advocacy and Dialectical Inquiry. Engaging in a consensus-method and discussing one's personal views was not seen to be beneficial to decision-making effectiveness. This is consistent with the findings reported by Schweiger et al. (1986).

While the results of Gross and Brodt seemed to take one back to 1986, Yager (2001) also revisited earlier times—the 1950's. Yager, whose work is described below, reported that optimizing a group's preference should result in the group selecting the best alternative. Again, it is interesting to note that a group preference achieved by consensus is usually not an optimal preference.

Yager

Yager (2001) built upon the work of Arrow (1963), and Luce & Raiffa (1957) in his theoretical research on group decision-making and preference modeling. He specifically focused on multi-agent groups where the agents (or team members) represent competing interests. According to Yager, in multi-agent (i.e., group) decision-making, the best selected action of a group is one that optimizes the group preference. However, Yager cautions that each member's real objective is not the maximization of the group function, but the maximization of his or her own preference function. In other words, since each member provides a preference function to the group decision process, a member can possibly bias the process to enhance their chances of obtaining their most preferred alternative.

A group decision mechanism consists of a process (or method) for selecting one of the alternatives based upon the preferences of the individuals making up the group. Yager imposed two conditions that should be present if the group is free from manipulation. The first condition is impartiality. Impartiality means that the decision method is nondiscriminatory – all participants are treated the same way. The second condition is Pareto optimality. Pareto optimality requires that any alternative that is the first choice of all participants also be the first choice of the group.

Glass and Grosz

In 2003, Glass and Grosz wrote that in team decision-making, "...an intermediate level of social consciousness yields better results in certain circumstances than an extreme commitment." Similar to the findings of other researchers, which have been highlighted in this literature review, Glass and Grosz suggests that the high level of commitment that is needed for a consensus may be counterproductive. The researchers were interested in how individuals work collaboratively to attain mutual goals. They stated that in order to make a socially conscious decision, individuals "...must be able to make decisions about actions and intentions in the context of commitments to group activities." They measured the level of achievement of teams via determining the "income" of the teams. Glass and Grosz did not use genuine teams; however, they did determine that in their experiments increased levels of commitment did not lead to higher team achievement.

Kocher, Strauß, and Sutter

Kocher et al. (2004) published results on the preferences of individuals to make decisions on their own, or to make decisions as part of a team. The researchers noted that little is known about the decision-making preferences of individuals and teams. They found this to be troubling since, according to them, "...teams have become important vehicles for identifying high-quality solutions to emerging organizational problems." Kocher et al. used laboratory settings because, in their view, this allowed for more control over the decision-making situation. However, they did note that field studies have the obvious advantage of a more natural environment. The researchers used a "beauty-contest" game for the teams and individuals. The participants were 90 students, recruited from introductory level classes at the University of Innsbruck. Kocher et al. reported that regardless of whether a person chose to make decisions individually or as part of team, there was a high degree of satisfaction for the preferred selection. The researchers also noted that most people (around 60%) preferred to make decisions as part of team because there was the expectation that a team decision would be a better, and more profitable, decision.

Kocher et al. suggested that when an individual volunteers to be part of a team, the individual is likely to embrace the concept of team decision-making. Also, the individual is likely to have an expectation that the team will reach a high-achievement level.

Finally, in this literature review is the results of a recent study that focused on majority-rule and consensus. The research is summarized below.

Chappell, McGregor, and Vermilyea

In 2004, Chappell et al. published results of a study on the aggregation of preferences within the (US) Federal Reserve's Federal Open Market Committee (FOMC). While the FOMC is not entirely flat-structured – it does have a formal Chair – there is little hierarchy on the committee. In their study, the researchers noted that a consentaneous decision-making method usually increases the influence of a leader. In contrast, a majority-rule method makes it more likely that other members will challenge proposals offered by an agenda-setting Chair. This finding is important because one of the reasons for having a group decision is to limit the power or influence of any single individual. The research done by Chappell et al. suggests that majority-rule leads to more cognitive conflict than does consensus. As noted by other researchers in this literature review, cognitive conflict usually leads to higher team achievement. It appears that the research done by Chappell et al. is in concordance with the findings of most other researchers that study team decision-making – usually debate and conflict on a team yields better decisions.

NON-HIERARCHIAL DECISION-MAKING

A main reason for the trend towards using collegial teams is that organizational structures began to change in the early 1990's (Nahavandi & Aranda 1994; Druckman et al. 1997). According to the Institute of Electrical and Electronics Engineers (IEEE), "Competition in rapidly changing markets, downsizing and distributed decision-making are transforming many organizations' management structures. Hierarchical and directive management structures are breaking down in the new horizontal world of self-managed teams and project-oriented companies..." (Stelluto 2002). This type of organizational flatness and participative environment is common in technical organizations (Bartlett 1991; Sattler & Sohoni 1999; Sosa et al. 2002).

It is widely acknowledged that decision-making is a major factor in the success of a team (Russo & Schoemaker 1990; Watson et al. 1991; Yeaple 1992; Safoutin & Thurston 1993; Katzenbach & Smith 1999; IPT n.d.). In addition, some researchers have asserted that a team's decisions and its performance are directly linked – "Team performance levels, however, ultimately require the *team* to be decisive..." (Katzenbach & Smith 1999). If the preceding views are accurate, then gaining insight into a team's decision-making method should provide additional insight into what makes a team successful and reach its level of achievement.

In the following discussion, decision *models* such as rational decision-making (Kepner & Tregoe 1997) and the recognition-primed decision (RPD) model (Klein 1999) are not considered a decision-making *method*. In the RPD model:

- The decision-maker typically searches for the first workable option they can find, not necessarily the best option.

- The focus is on assessing the situation and judging it by its familiarity, not on comparing options.
- Options are generated and evaluated individually and independently. There is no comparing the pros and cons of alternatives.
- The emphasis is on being ready to act, rather than being paralyzed until all the evaluations have been completed.

Rational decision-making:

- Is usually time consuming and resource-intensive. Therefore, it is usually too slow for a fast-moving project.
- Requires compliance with a result that *appears* rational, but based on other criteria is clearly not the right one.
- Depends heavily on reliable information (which is often difficult to obtain).

Decision models such as the aforementioned types are effective when a decision-maker is to select from a set of known alternatives, or when a desired outcome has been previously experienced or can be easily imagined. They have not been shown to be effective, or commonly used, when a desired outcome is new, unique, or, as is the case for RPD, not well defined (Klein 1999).

In 2001, researchers reported, "work teams are becoming very big business", and organizations are increasingly relying on teams to accomplish their missions (Offermann & Spiros 2001). By the year 2006, it was self-evident that work teams were big business. According to the Committee on Techniques for the Enhancement of Human Performance, the Commission on Behavioral and Social Sciences and Education, and the (US) National Research Council, "...to compete effectively in a turbulent, global marketplace,... organizations have to be highly flexible. Decisions must be made quickly and consistently, and then perhaps changed in a matter of months if not days" (Druckman et al. 1997). Druckman et al. go on to say that, "Research is needed...to gain a better understanding of these trends and how ongoing they are likely to be." All of the above suggests there is a growing need for rapid decision-making and adaptability, and there is a need to understand the method that modern teams use in making decisions.

"When real teams meet to discuss and make decisions, they tend to focus entirely on performance, particularly on those issues that cut to the heart of the team's basic purpose and goals ... In addition, the decisions that emerge are team decisions, for which everyone feels a strong sense of mutual accountability." (Katzenbach & Smith 1999). The above quote suggests a linkage between a team's decisions, or decision-making, and a team's performance. Many other researchers (Schweiger et al. 1986; Libby et al. 1987; Watson et al. 1991; Nahavandi & Aranda 1994; Gruenfeld et al. 1996; Laufer et al. 1999; Garvin & Roberto 2003) have noted a connection between a team's performance (and achievement) and its decision-making method.

There are many decision-making methods (e.g., majority-rule, advocacy, autocratic, inquiry, consensus, etc.); presumably, each has strengths and weaknesses. In real-life situations, combinations of methods may be needed.

Now, we look at the decision methods used by some high-achieving technical teams. In research conducted in 2004 – 2005, a systematic approach that used quantitative and qualitative methods, and field research to identify, categorize, and analyze a team's self-selected decision-making method was used by this chapter's author. The approach employed in that research used qualitative procedures that are found in *grounded theory* development, then subjected the results to quantitative (i.e., statistical) methods to determine if the qualitative results had an empirical basis. A team's decision-making method was identified by a combination of direct observation, and the perspectives of the team members, and by applying economic theory (i.e., Arrow's Impossibility Theorem). A team's achievement level was determined by querying the team members and the team's external sponsor (or the problem owner) after the team had completed its assignment.

The research used 31 real-life, flat-structured, technical teams in a US DoD research environment. The solutions that these teams were pursuing, typically, were to some of the most difficult and important defense related problems of the US Government (USG). A team's success or failure could have a direct impact on the national security of the USG. An exemplar problem, which these teams addressed, was to develop a set of features, or protocols that can be added to a network or computer's operating system that will allow a network to remain almost fully functional while it is under a continuous and aggressive attack by a sophisticated attacker (or attackers).

Typically during the selection of team participants, a panel of selection officials interviewed and examined the candidate's technical background, the candidate's previous significant technical accomplishments, judged the candidate's willingness to be "a team player", and judged the candidate's creative thinking ability. Usually, around one-third of the volunteer candidate pool was selected for team membership. Therefore, the environment for the teams, and the team selection criteria were such that there was a high probability that the teams would become high-achieving. Thirty of the teams met the pre-existing requirements to be labeled as high-achieving.

One result of the research suggests that these high-achieving teams are biased towards selecting a majority-rule method for solving problems where there are no standard solutions. A second result of the research indicated that discussion and cognitive conflict are common for the teams. However, the teams are not likely to attempt to get full support and buy-in from all of the team members. The teams usually discovered their best solution via examining alternatives from multiple perspectives and by establishing a utility function to guide the final selection. The team's final selection was most often determined by a majority-rule method.

The preceding suggests that teams that reach a high-achievement level are likely to have members who can explore and debate the pros and cons associated with an alternative, who can continue to contribute to the team's activities when his or her preferences have not been fully explored (a great deal of tact and sensitivity is not common), and who can work in an environment where achieving the (perceived) best or correct solution is not strongly related to team member support. The preceding leads to the induced theory that the selection of a majority-rule decision-making method by a collegial, technical, team may be an indicator that the team will reach a high-achievement level.

We now arrive at an interesting dichotomy. Referring back to the literature review, we see that some research suggests that full buy-in and support by everyone is important to arriving at the best decisions. Other research suggests that full buy-in and support by everyone involved in the decision-making process is not important, and may yield sub-optimal decisions. The research outlined above, which used 31 teams, suggests that latter of the two preceding views may be more accurate.

FUTURE TRENDS

Almost all research on teams and their decision-making have been done using groups that were not true teams, in laboratory environments. Those results, as is suggested by several of the researchers, which were highlighted in the Literature Review, may not directly apply to real-life teams or organizations in their true environments. Therefore, more research is needed on intact teams working in their normal environments.

In recent years, interest has been growing in Six Sigma, which we did not discuss in this chapter. However, it may be worthwhile to investigate if high-achieving self-managed teams that are using rapid and innovative decision-making can fit into a Six Sigma environment.

CONCLUSION

In this chapter we have seen that many of today's technical organizations are using flat-structured, empowered teams to solve difficult problems and make decisions. The research on such teams and organizations is somewhat divided when attempts are made to describe how the higher achieving groups make decisions. However, the preponderance of evidence suggests that the teams usually discovered their best solution via examining alternatives from multiple perspectives and by establishing a utility function to guide the final selection. The team's final selection was most often determined by a majority-rule method.

This chapter suggests that teams that reach a high-achievement level are likely to have members who can explore and debate the pros and cons associated with an alternative, who can continue to contribute to the team's activities when his or her preferences have not been fully explored (a great deal of tact and sensitivity is not common), and who can work in an environment where achieving the (perceived) best or correct solution is not strongly related to team member support. The preceding leads to the induced theory that the selection of a majority-rule decision-making method by a collegial, technical, team may be an indicator that the team will reach a high-achievement level.

If an organization is comprised of teams that are high-achieving, then one would expect that the organization should be, at least close to, high-achieving.

REFERENCES

Arrow, K. J. (1963). *Social Choice and Individual Values.* 2nd ed. New Haven: Yale University Press. Original edition, (1951), New York: John Wiley & Sons.

Barrick, M. R., et al. (1998). Relating Member Ability and Personality to Work-Team Processes and Team Effectiveness, *Journal of Applied Psychology*, (3), 377-391.

Bartlett, R. O. (1991). *An Evaluation of Participative Management: Effects of Group Decision Making on Productivity and Job Satisfaction in a Satellite Ground Station.* Doctoral dissertation, George Washington University.

Bettenhausen, K., & Murnighan, J. K. (1985). The Emergence of Norms in Competitive Decision-Making Groups, *Administrative Science Quarterly*, (30), 350-372.

Castore, C. H., & Murnighan, J. K. (1978). Determinants of Support for Group Decisions, *Organizational Behavior and Human Performance*, (22), 75-92.

Chappell, H. W., Jr., McGregor, R., & Vermilyea, T. (2004). Majority Rule, Consensus Building, and the Power of the Chairman: Arthur Burns and the FOMC. *Journal of Money, Credit & Banking*, *36*, 407-422.

Cohen, S. G., & Bailey, D. E. (1997). What Makes Teams Work: Group Effectiveness Research from the Shop Floor to the Executive Suite. *Journal of Management*, (3), 239-290.

Crow, K. A. (1994). *Building Effective Product Development Teams / Integrated Product Teams*. Palos Verdes, CA: DRM Associates. Retrieved November 10, 2001, from http://www.npd-solutions.com/pdt.html.

Dias, W. P. S. (1990). Circular Organizational Structure for Project Teams, *Journal of Management in Engineering*, *6*(4), 471-478.

Driskell, J. E., & Salas E. (1991). Group Decision Making Under Stress. *Journal of Applied Psychology*, *76*(3), 473-478.

Druckman, D., Singer, J. E., & Cott, H. V. (Eds.). (1997). *Enhancing Organizational Performance*. Washington, D.C.: National Academy Press.

Farris, D. R., & Sage, A. P. (1975). Introduction and Survey of Group Decision Making with Applications to Worth Assessment. *IEEE Transactions on Systems, Man, and Cybernetics*, SMC-5*(3), 346-358.

Garvin, D. A., & Roberto, M. A. (2003). What You Don't Know About Making Decisions. *IEEE Engineering Management Review*, *31*(2), 3-9.

Glass, A., & Grosz, B. J. (2003). Socially Conscious Decision-Making. In *Journal of Autonomous Agents and Multi-Agent Systems*, Special Issue. The Netherlands: Springer.

Gross, R. L., & Brodt, S. E. (2001). How Assumptions of Consensus Undermine Decision-Making. *Sloan Management Review*, *42*(2), 86-94.

Grossman, S. (1997). Turning Technical Groups into High-Performance Teams. *IEEE Engineering Management Review*, *25*(4), 32-34.

Gruenfeld, D. H., et al. (1996). Group Composition and Decision Making: How Member Familiarity and Information Distribution Affect Process and Performance. *Organizational Behavior and Human Decision Processes*, *67*(1), 1-15.

Hackman, J. R. (Ed.). (1990). *Groups That Work (and Those That Don't)*. San Francisco: Jossey-Bass.

Hackman, J. R., & Morris, C. G. (1975). *Group Tasks, Group Interaction Process, and Group Performance Effectiveness: A Review and Proposed Integration*. (US Office of Naval Research, Organizational Effectiveness Research Program, Contract No. N00014-67A-0097-0026, photocopy), (pp.45-95).

Hansen, K. L., & Tatum, C.B. (1996). How Strategies Happen: A Decision-Making Framework. *Journal of Management in Engineering, 12*(1), 40-48.

Herrera-Viedma, E., Herrera, F., & Chiclana, F. (2002). A Consensus Model for Multiperson Decision Making With Different Preference Structures. *IEEE Transactions on Systems, Man and Cybernetics—Part A: Systems and Humans, 32*(3), 394-402.

Hollenbeck, J. R., et al. (1995). Multilevel Theory of Team Decision Making: Decision Performance in Teams Incorporating Distributed Expertise. *Journal of Applied Psychology, 80*(2), 292-316.

Hornsby, J. S., Smith, B. N., & Gupta, J. N. D. (1994). The Impact of Decision-making methods on Job Evaluation Outcomes: A Look at Three Consensus Approaches. *Group & Organization Management, 19*(1), 112-128.

Integrated Product Teams (IPT). (n.d.). Retrieved November 10, 2001 from http://www.dsmc.dsm.mil/jdam/contents/ipt.htm.

Katzenbach, J. R., & Smith, D. K. (1999). *The Wisdom of Teams.* New York: HarperCollins.

Kepner, C. H., & Tregoe, B. B. (1997). *The New Rational Manager: an updated edition for a new world.* Princeton: Princeton Research Press.

Klein, G. (1999). *Sources of Power: How People Make Decisions.* Cambridge: The MIT Press.

Kocher, M., Strauß, S., & Sutter, M. (2004). Individual or team decision-making – Causes and consequences of self-selection. In *Discussion Papers on Strategic Interaction.* Jena, Germany: Max Planck Institute of Economics.

Laufer, A., Woodward, H., & Howell, G. (1999). Managing the Decision-Making Process During Project Planning. *Journal of Management in Engineering, 15*(2), 79-84.

Libby, R., Trotman, K. T., & Zimmer, I. (1987). Member Variation, Recognition of Expertise, and Group Performance. *Journal of Applied Psychology, 72*(1), 81-87.

Luce, R. D., & Raiffa, H. (1957). *Games and Decisions.* New York: John Wiley & Sons.

Nahavandi, A., & Aranda, E. (1994). Restructuring Teams for the Re-engineered Organization. *Academy of Management Executive, 8*(4), 58-68.

Offermann, L. R., & Spiros, R. K. (2001). The Science and Practice of Team Development: Improving the Lin. *Academy of Management Journal, 44*(2), 1-17.

Popick, P. R., & Sheard, S. A. (1996). *Ten Lessons Learned from Implementing Integrated Product Teams.* Retrieved November 9, 2001 from http://www.stsc.hill.af.mil/crosstalk/frames.asp?uri=1996/07/tenlesso.asp.

Russo, J. E., & Schoemaker, P. J. (1990). Decision *Traps: the ten barriers to brilliant decision-making and how to overcome them.* New York: Simon & Schuster, Fireside.

Safoutin, M. J., & Thurston, D. L. (1993). A Communications-based Technique for Interdisciplinary Design Team Management. *IEEE Transactions on Engineering Management, 40*(4), 360-372.

Sattler, L., & Sohoni, V. (1999). Participative Management: An Empirical Study of the Semiconductor Manufacturing Industry. *IEEE Transactions on Engineering Management, 46*(4), 387-396.

Schweiger, D. M., William, W. R., & Ragan, J. W. (1986). Group Approaches for Improving Strategic Decision Making: a comparative analysis of dialectical inquiry, devil's advocacy, and consensus. *Academy of Management Journal, 29*(1), 51-71.

Sosa, M. E., et al. (2002). Factors That Influence Technical Communication in Distributed Product Development: An Empirical Study in the Telecommunications Industry. *IEEE Transactions on Engineering Management, 49*(1), 45-58.

Stasser, G., & Titus, W. (1985). Pooling of Unshared Information in Group Decision Making: Biased Information Sampling During Discussion. *Journal of Personality and Social Psychology, 48*(6), 1467-1478.

Stelluto, G. C. (2002). Continuous Learning - Get the Jump on Getting a Job. *The Institute, 26*(4), 1.

Watson, W., Michaelsen, L. K., & Sharp, W. (1991). Member Competence, Group Interaction, and Group Decision-making: A Longitudinal Study. *Journal of Applied Psychology, 76*(6), 803-809.

Yager, R. R. (2001). Penalizing Strategic Preference Manipulation in Multi-Agent Decision Making. *IEEE Transactions on Fuzzy Systems, 9*(3), 393-403.

Yeaple, R. N. (1992). Why Are Small R&D Organizations More Productive? *IEEE Transactions on Engineering Management, 39*(4), 332-346.

Yeatts, D. E., & Hyten, C. (1998). *High-Performing Self-Managed Work Teams: A Comparison of Theory to Practice.* Thousand Oaks, CA: Sage Publications.

ENDNOTES

[a] *Merriam-Webster's Collegiate® Dictionary*, 10th ed. (2001), s.v. "consensus".

[b] The quality was determined by an independent panel of subject matter experts judging both validity and importance.

[c] E.g.: Hall, J. & Williams, M.S. (1970). Group dynamics training and improved decision-making, *Journal of Applied Behavioral Science*, (6), 27-32.
Rohrbaugh, J. (1979). Improving the quality of group judgement: Social judgement analysis and the Delphi technique, *Organizational Behavior and Human Performance*, (33), 112-124.
Burleson, B.R., Levine, B.J. Levine, & Samter, W. (1984). Decision-making procedure and decision quality, *Human Communication Research*, (10), 557-574.

Chapter IV
Hierarchical Organization as a Facilitator of Information Management in Human Collaboration

Khaled Ahmed Nagaty

Ain Shams University, Faculty of Computers & Information Sciences, Cairo, Egypt

ABSTRACT

The purpose of this chapter is to discuss the relationship between three entities: hierarchical organization, information management and human collaboration. This relationship is composed of two parts: the first part is the relationship between the hierarchical organization and information management where the role of the hierarchical organization to facilitate the information management processes is discussed. The second part is the relationship between information management and human collaboration where the role of information management to improve human collaboration in problem solving is discussed. The information management processes are illustrated through an information management life cycle model. This model has three major stages: active, semi-active and inactive stages and has three major phases: creation, searching and utilization phases. The creation phase includes: information creation and using, information authoring and modifying and information organization and indexing. The searching phase includes: information storage and retrieving and information exchange. The utilization phase includes: information accessing and filtering processes. The arguments about the role of hierarchical organization in information management and human collaboration are also discussed. The author showed that the hierarchical organization acts as a facilitator for common information management processes which are required in team collaboration such as: information gathering, organization, retrieving, filtering, exchange, integration or fusion, display and visualization. Human collaboration models are discussed with emphasis on the team collaboration structural model which has four unique but interdependent stages of team collaboration. These stages are: team knowledge construction, collaborative team problem solving, team consensus, and product evaluation and revision. Each stage has four levels: meta-cognition process which guides the overall problem solving process, the information processing tasks which is required by the team to complete each collaboration stage, the knowledge required to support the information processing tasks and the communication mechanisms for knowledge building and information processing. The author focused on the role of information management to improve human collaboration across the four collaboration stages of the team collaboration structural model. He showed that the hierarchical organization is more efficient for information management processes and team collaboration rather than other alternative organizations such as flat, linear and network organizations.

INTRODUCTION

It is widely observed that human collaboration is the true competitive advantage for the new era. Merriam Webster's dictionary defines collaboration as working jointly with others or together especially in an intellectual endeavor. Collaboration is seen as a good work practice because it should, by definition, involve share workload, multiple perspectives provided by diverse expertise, enhance creativity, innovation, and higher product reliability, creation of knowledge and information access and exchange. Collaboration and teamwork are closely coupled activities in which team members work together to produce a product, solve a problem or carry out an action (David N., 2002). Effective partnerships improve human interactions to create more efficient and effective collaboration where partners in human collaboration attempt to reach shared understanding or common ground (Scott, Mark, XiaoQi, & J. Geoffrey, 2008)). Common ground refers to the set of mutual knowledge, shared beliefs and assumptions that collaborators have. This process of establishing shared understanding or grounding involves communication using a large amount of information. According to Schrage (1995) people's collaborative efforts with different skills are required to create innovative solutions and products.

To better understand and improve the effectiveness of team collaboration there is a need to better understand cognitive processes employed when collaborating to solve high stakes problems that may be characterized with time compression, supported by uncertain and open source information. This can be achieved by studying the process by which team members may interpret data to develop information, build shared understanding that informs decisions, and collaborate to ensure that information and knowledge are shared in support of synchronized action to take decisions. Cognitive collaboration models based on information management help collaborators to attain common situational awareness among multidisciplinary, distributed team members engaged in collaboration for issue resolution or decision making. It examines the cognitive aspects of joint analysis or problem solving for the purpose of attaining shared understanding sufficient to achieve situational awareness for decision making or creation of a product (Office of Naval Research, 2008). Information management processes such as collection, retrieval, exchange, fusion and display of information help to attain shared understanding of a situation at both the individual and team levels. The shared understanding of a situation is affected by the type of collaboration environment which can be one of the following:

1. **Distributed environment:** Which is an open standard agent-based infrastructure of communications, information processing, decision support, knowledge processing and resource management

services which can be configured to enable information sharing to support team collaboration (William, 2003). It interconnects remotely and temporally participants, computational resources and databases to seamlessly interoperate, gracefully enter and exit the collaboration for the purpose of developing a product or other action related to decision support in the organization (William, 1997). A distributed collaborative environment supports both single individuals and collaborating groups by managing and distributing virtual workspaces (Vance & William, 1997). These virtual workspaces contain the necessary information visualization and resource management tools each user needs to contribute to decisions throughout the life cycle.

2. **Asynchronous environment:** Which is a distributed collaboration team where members and components can be at any location and they can connect from any computer with a view independent from the connection point. No component is responsible of coordinating other components and no component is the only holder of specific information. Members of a group decide freely which actions to perform, which resources and services provide and when will be connected or disconnected. A group has a capability to continue operating with some malfunctioning or not available component. Replication of objects, resources or services can be used to improve availability and quality of service. It allows information exchange where information belonging to a group such as events, objects, and presence of information....etc. can be used by several applications. It maintains information security by a selective and limited access to the shared information and by identity authentication of information user (Joan, Leandro, & Thanasis, 2004).

3. **Culturally diverse:** Culture is obviously a source of variance in the human behavior. Therefore, a culturally heterogeneous group would be expected to display types of behavior and interactions that are different from those displayed by a culturally homogeneous group. The impact of cultural heterogeneity on group performance might ultimately result in performance outcomes that are different from those generated by a culturally homogeneous group (Imad, Souren, Peter, & Priya, 2002). Teams composed of members with homogeneous backgrounds find collaboration to be much easier than heterogeneous teams; however, heterogeneous teams eventually make decisions that are of higher quality than those of homogeneous teams.

4. **Heterogeneous knowledge:** Knowledge can be derived from different information resources such as text, maps, images and videos. Integration of these resources using knowledge management will facilitate a single query traversing transparently all knowledge repositories and related databases, regardless of their physical location. Knowledge management hierarchical organization consists of a number of layers including: knowledge portal, raw data, data transformation, knowledge discovery repository, and knowledge entry and analysis tools (Sokol, 2002). A knowledge portal is used as a convenient starting point for team members to begin their quest to enter, find and access knowledge.

5. **Unique roles:** Assigning separate roles to team members increases the scope of group collaboration. Boredom is reduced by differentiating the roles of individuals. Also, accountability can be determined by how well a team member performs particular roles.

6. **Rotating team members:** In order to use team's limited time most efficiently and to improve collaboration and participation by all members, many teams assign roles that can be rotated among the members. Rotation may be by volunteering, alphabetical order assignment, or any other agreed upon by the group (Maryland Coalition for Inclusive Education, 1999).

7. **Common organization:** Which may be hierarchical or flat, a hierarchical organization is structured in a way such that every entity in the organization, except one, is subordinate to a single other entity.

Flat organizations emphasize a decentralized approach to management that encourages well trained employees involvement in making decisions rather than supervised by many layers of management and to become more productive. The purpose of this structure is to create independent small businesses or enterprises that can rapidly respond to customers' needs or changes in the business environment where comments and feedback information reach all personnel involved in decisions more quickly. Supervisor tends to have a more personal relationship with his or her employees with few or no intervening middle management. (Gemmy, 2002). In hierarchical organization it is important to improve how collaborators interact on the highest, medium and low levels. Such human collaboration largely depends on how people manage information, relationships and define their goals and expectations. At lower management, people share information in small groups through informal communications and social relationships. At middle management, actors design and use processes and systems to convert informal information into codified and structured information in order to routinize repeated behaviors, transactions and information processing sequences. At upper management, highly codified and regularized information flows are produced through the enactment of property rights, laws, regulations, contracts and other overarching formal rule systems. Due to the interactions among these three levels, when information flow changes at one level the other two levels are typically affected (Fountain, 2007). User requests within working groups can be organized into a hierarchy that represents an increasingly specialized range of information topics as a query goes down the hierarchy (Wensheng; Vellaikal,; Son, 2001). It establishes a logical flow of collaboration stream between interest groups. After the problem has been identified the team must decide which steps to use in solving the problem. Planning activities provide coherency, coordination and efficiency it involves dividing the problem into sub-problems. The work may be decomposed so that team members can easily work independently, or may be partitioned into interdependent tasks. Team members may work in different locations great distances apart, such as in online collaboration, or work in the same building such as in distributed collaboration. People in such collaboration environments can often meet together, or work separately, with each member in the group performing his task at his convenience and rarely engaging in synchronous conversations with others (David N., 2002). Governments seeking to share intelligence information often create hierarchical relationships to manage risks that partners will defect (James, 2007). Hierarchy organization reassures that subordinate partners will comply with their agreement to cooperate in three ways (Williamson, 1985):

1. Hierarchy gives the dominant power the right to interpret the agreement, which minimizes the subordinate's opportunities to exploit ambiguities and unexpected developments.
2. Hierarchy allows the dominant party to create and maintain oversight mechanisms to ensure the subordinate's compliance with the terms of their intelligence sharing agreement.
3. The acceptance of a hierarchy relationship by a subordinate partner implies that it gives the dominant power the right to legitimately punish the defective party without the right to retaliate.

Hierarchical organizations are most useful to participants when there are substantial benefits from cooperation. Hierarchy makes it easier for participants to capture joint benefits of information sharing which increases with the frequency the participants exchange information and the range of issues their agreement includes (James,2007). Information plays an important role in people or government interaction within their hierarchical organization. Information is one of the chief inputs of each working group activity and it is vitally important to be stored, indexed and accessed effectively. Information is a knowledge derived from study, experience or instructions. It comes in a wide variety of types, for example it could be email messages, blogs, wikis, rules or instructions, photographs, documents, presentations, databases, charts, graphs, plans, audio files, video files or an order in an online transaction processing system. The extent of collected and generated information and its technical nature is important in the process of organizing, exchanging and providing equitable access to information. Information management is essentially required for the management requirements of internally produced or externally collected information. The main concern of an efficient information management system is to provide the right information to the right people at the right time. In doing so, it is important to understand current practices related to information management. It is concerned with every thing that happens to information during its life time, this include gathering information from heterogeneous resources and transform them into a unified form for the user to issue a single query that can be transparently traverse all knowledge repositories, facilitate information retrieval, display information in an easy to understand form, facilitate information exchange to help collaborators attaining a shared understanding and maintaining information security. Information management life cycle models break the life cycle of information that moves through into phases and identifying the most pertinent issues that influence how information should be managed during each phase (JISC Infonet Service, 2007). This will help work teams to identify information volumes and growth rates, its strength, any gaps and will help to organize where they are starting from. Team members in collaboration should represent a mix of information practitioner communities such as information management, records management, web management, libraries, knowledge management and information technology as well as the technical units of the organization. In the light of this, our objectives are to answer the following questions:

1.   As information is hierarchically structured in nature, it is interesting to discus how hierarchical organization facilitates information management processes?
2.   Why the hierarchical organization is better than other alternative organizations such as flat, linear and network organizations for information management?
3.   As human collaboration depends on information it is interesting to discus how information management improves human collaboration?

This chapter provides the answer for these questions.

BACKGROUND

The relationship between hierarchical organizations and information management and its impact on human collaboration can be represented using a composite abstract relationship which can be depicted using Figure 1. In the next subsections, we will define each part of this relationship and discus its importance.

Information Management

Information is one of the most vital, strategic assets of any organization. Information may be formal or informal; formal information includes statistical and management reports while informal information

Figure 1. Composite abstract relationship

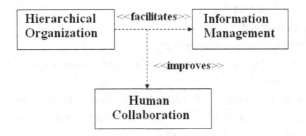

includes team discussions, experience, education, common sense, intuition and knowledge of organization's internal and external environments. Properly organized and maintained records and information -in either paper or electronic formats- is vital to enterprises of all sizes and types whether business is done locally or globally. Reliable, complete, timely, accurate, up-to-date and can be integrated information is required in order for managers to make well-informed management decisions in their organizations and to determine whether the organization is meeting its objectives, whether resources are being used efficiently and appropriately, and ultimately whether the organization is on the right path to achieve its goals. Otherwise, managers will not able to make decisions at the right time that ensure the beneficiary of their organizations.

Information management programs are typically tied to organizational objectives such as improving performance, gaining competitive advantages, innovation, developmental processes, and the general development of collaborative practices. Therefore, an organization requires the ability to identify, organize, maintain and access required information by everyone who needs it, in a timely manner, and then properly disposing it in accordance to appropriate rules. That is the reason why an organization needs an efficient information life cycle management. An information life cycle management can be defined as a combination of processes and technologies that determines how information flows through an organization. It can also be defined as a policy based approach to managing the flow of an information system's data through its life cycle from creation and initial storage to the time when it becomes obsolete and is deleted. (Roger R., Gareth F., & David S. ,2006). Information is organized according to specified policies:

1. As a rule, newer information and more frequently accessed information, is stored on faster, but more expensive storage media, while less critical information is stored on cheaper, but slower media.
2. Hierarchical storage management represents different types of storage media such as redundant array of independent disks systems, optical storage, or tapes. Each type representing a different level of cost and speed of retrieval when access is needed. The information technology manager can establish and state guide lines for how often different kinds of files are to be copied to a backup storage device.

Before we discus the information life cycle management model there are some principles and requirements that should be considered while an organization is setting its information management policy and guidelines. These principles are (British Columbia Province, 2003):

1. Information is created and managed in a way that ensures completeness, reliability and authenticity.
2. Information is identified and retrieved.
3. Information can be exchanged.
4. Information is maintained and stored securely.
5. Information is retained long enough to meet all organization's requirements, and permanent, archival values are identified.
6. Information is disposed of securely according to retention schedules, policies and procedures.
7. Information should be managed as an asset rather than a liability and development and establishing the channels through which information can flow.

The requirements for an efficient information life cycle management are:

1. Long term and short term information needs should be determined and schedule its records accordingly.
2. The context of electronic records such as the nature of the software, hardware, links to records in other formats ... etc is required.
3. An organization should determine the final disposition of its information.
4. All information records should be identified, classified according to their function and their retention period is established.
5. Improving information flow through explicit communication between individuals and external groups.

Information Life Cycle Management Model

Information may be accessed at three stages: before, during or after information related activities. Some people argue that there is a life cycle to information use starting with capture or creation, moving on to use and reuse with the ultimate goal of enriching an organization's or work team capability. Conversely, some people would state that such a life cycle view is too linear in nature and reflects an information centric view.

There are several models to describe the information life cycle. Figure 2 shows an information life cycle management model (Borgman, Bates, Cloonan, Efthimiadis, Gilliland-Swetland, Kafai, Leazer, & Maddox, 1996) which has three major stages:

1. The active stage which includes information creation, authoring and modification, organization and indexing. If the life time of an information topic is extended or an information topic is created through data mining, this information topic is transferred to the active stage.
2. The semi-active stage which includes storing, retrieval and distribution of information.
3. The inactive stage which includes information disposal and discarding. Less frequently accessed records may be considered for relocation to an inactive stage until they have their assigned retention period.

The model has three major phases:

1. **Creation phase which includes the following information processes:**
   a. **Creation and using:** It deals with topics from their point of origination. This could include their creation by a member of an organization at varying levels or receipt of information from external sources using gathering tools. It includes sensors, correspondence, forms, reports, drawings, computer input / output or other resources.
   b. **Authoring and modifying:** Where information is produced or modified internally.
   c. **Organization and indexing:** In a manner that allows rapid and effective access for both individuals and work groups for knowledge building and understanding. It is actually the process of arranging information in a predetermined sequence and creating a system to manage it for its useful existence within an organization. Failure to establish an effective method for information organization makes its retrieval and use nearly impossible.
   Information in this phase is in the active stage.

2. **Searching phase which includes the following information processes:**
   a. **Storing and retrieving:** Efficient structures are required for storing information across an organization, to make it easy to overcome the semantic heterogeneity between information resources and keep it over time. Retrieving is the process of responding to requests, retrieval from files and providing access to authorized users to have access to the information. Information is tracked by the use of tracking information to ensure it is returned or available to others who may need access to it.
   b. **Distribution or exchange:** Which is the process of managing the information once it has been created or received. This includes both internal and external distribution, as produced information becomes a topic of a transaction with others.
   In this phase, information is in semi-active stage.

3. **Utilization phase:** It includes information accessing and filtering. Information can be accessed by some particular users or agents from a larger information source or stream of information while filters acts as mediators between the information sources and their end users.
   Information in this phase is in the active stage.

However, we suggest adding to this model the fusion or integration of information process which is the merging of information from different resources with different conceptual, contextual and typographical representations. This process is included in the utilization phase and information will be in the active stage. An organization must ensure the identification and preservation of permanently valuable records and the destruction of all other records in a timely, secure and environmentally sound manner (British Columbia Province, 2003). If the information has met all of its need and is no longer considered to be valuable, it should be disposed of by means appropriate for the content. This may include ensuring that others cannot obtain access to outdated or obsolete information as well as measures for protection privacy and confidentiality. Less frequently accessed information is assigned to an inactive stage until they have met their assigned retention period. Retention periods are based on retention schedule, business needs, and potential historic, intrinsic or enduring value of information. Retention schedule is based on research of the regulatory, statutory and legal requirements for management of information for the industry in which the organization operates. Retention periods may be indefinite, 25 years or longer for information that is identified to have a continuing value. This information should be efficiently archived using persistent identifiers for the items to ensure it's persistently accessible for the length of time they are retained (Warwick, Colin, & Julie, 2001). Policies and procedures must be established for the periodic conversion and migration of information stored electronically to ensure it remains accessible for its required retention periods.

Hierarchical Organization

The hierarchical organization is made up of organizational units it refers to how people and tasks are grouped together. The hierarchy includes an artificial organizational entity called a root at the top. All other organizational entities are descendents of this root. Under the root all nodes of the hierarchy do not need to have fixed semantics. This means that you can construct your hierarchy using a mix of sub-organizations and units. One of the major strengths of a hierarchical structure is that people are familiar with it. From universities to companies to government, people can find a hierarchical structure used to facilitate the workflow of the organization (Indratmo, & Julita ,2008).

All information is hierarchy in one way or another, without links between random facts we have no method to expand our understanding of a subject. Hierarchy helps users understand an information collection better where information items relating to one another can be logically structured, and their

Figure 2. Information life cycle model (Borgman, Bates, Cloonan, Efthimiadis, Gilliland-Swetland, Kafai, Leazer, & Maddox, 1996. Used with permission)

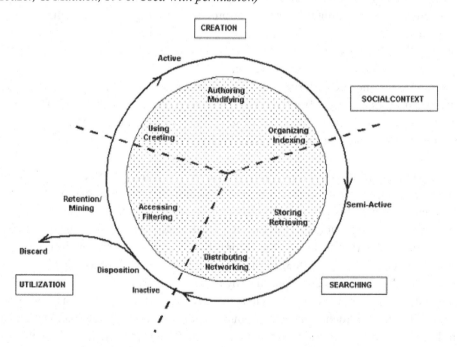

NOTE: The outer ring indicates the life cycle stages (active, semi-active, and inactive) for a given type of information artifact (such a s business records, artworks, documents, or scientific data). The stages are superimposed on six types of information uses or processes (shaded circle). The cycle has three major phases: information creation, searching, and utilization. The alignment of the cycle stages with the steps of infomration handling and process phases may vary according to the particular social or institutional context.

relationships are explicitly captured. So, people tend to organize information items based on the task relating to the items (Barreau, 1995; Kwasnik, 1989, 1991). For example, we can't learn about a new topic, without grouping together what we know about that topic in a hierarchical structure which provides a means to find relevant information. Organizing information items hierarchically is an intuitive and familiar process it is currently the predominant way to organize information items where a node in a tree represents an information item or collection of items. A hierarchical structure facilitates information search and retrieval by enabling users to reduce a search space and to eliminate any ambiguity of a term which can refer to different contexts (Indratmo, & Julita, 2008). Therefore, hierarchies are a useful meta-index to large collections of related but individually self-contained articles or information. Good examples are that people deal with a hierarchy classification scheme while looking for books in libraries or information topics in an encyclopedia, or in statutes or laws of a nation or region. Many software systems such as file systems and email clients use the hierarchical organization and allow users to create folders and subfolders to organize files to facilitate information classification, management and retrieval. Hierarchies can act as a task manager where nodes reflect the command and control relationship between them. Parent nodes send tasking information and control commands to their child nodes. Depending on the situation, complex tasks are decomposed into subtasks distributed among child nodes. Nodes routinely update their parents with feedback information such as the results of their operation, reports on failures or success, updates on their capability status. The practice of using hierarchies as an aid to task management leads to the idea of structure reuse where users can use a copy of the hierarchy structure of a project if they have another project with similar tasks (Boardman, Spence, & Sasse, 2003; Jones, Phuwanartnilrak, Gill, & Bruce, 2005). Figure 3 shows the hierarchical organization of a project structure where goals are set at the top and the project is divided into tasks. These tasks are assigned to work teams where subtasks are divided between participants who are engaged in an activity towards common objective. They have their own goals, actions, knowledge, organizational rules and structure. However, they cooperate with each other to facilitate achieving common objective.

Despite the advantages of the hierarchical structures (Lansdale, 1988; Mander, Salomon, Wong, 1992; Ravasio, 2004; Karger, & Jones, 2006; Whittaker, & Sidner, 1996; Malone, Yates, & Benjamin, 1987; Lopez, 2002) argue that a hierarchical structure has some drawbacks:

Figure 3. Hierarchical organization of a project

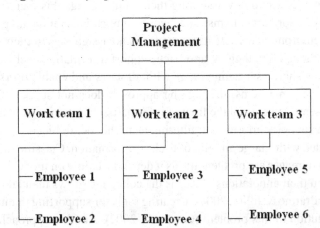

1. The traditional hierarchical topologies frequently used by companies and organizations, are poorly designed in terms of efficiency. As the information is an appropriate measurement of centrality, this kind of topology is so attractive for leaders, because it helps the individual aim of monopolizing as much information as possible within the network. The global influence each actor has within the network is completely determined by the hierarchical level occupied (Almendral, A., López, L., Mendes, F., & Sanjuán, 2003). We will address this disadvantage later in this chapter.

2. Creating a hierarchy and classifying information accordingly is a heavy weight cognitive activity. This difficulty especially applies to knowledge workers such as analysts and researchers, who have unstructured and dynamic tasks who have to deal with ever changing work contexts and sometimes consider filing documents unimportant (Kidd, 1994). When adding an information item to a hierarchical organization, it is put into a class that is appropriate at that time. When goals and work contexts change the created hierarchies may become outdated and require a lot of time and efforts to re-organize. Furthermore, since knowledge workers handle multiple tasks concurrently, they may find information which can be put under more than one collection in the hierarchy, making it even more difficult to choose in which collection they should put them (Indratmo, & Julita ,2008). Although, people can overcome this problem by creating multiple copies of a document, they tend to put a document into a single collection only.

3. Relevant information can be gathered from different sources using different information gathering tools each of which maintains its own hierarchical organization, being unable to collect this information into a single hierarchy is known to be information fragmentation. Information fragmentation leads to repeated efforts to organize different types of information items (Bergman, Beyth-Marom, & Nachmias, 2006; Boardman, Spence, & Sasse, 2003). Consequently, users have to consult various storage locations to retrieve needed information, and it is hard to maintain consistency in overlapping hierarchies.

4. Other organization structures are available and some are gaining popularity especially on the web:

    1. **Flat organization:** It has recently gained popularity where tags or attributes are assigned to information items. These tags are used to group or retrieve the information items, providing associative access to the items (Dourish, Edwards, LaMarca, & Salisbury, 1999; Gifford, 1991; Gopal, & Manber, 1999). This approach is known as tagging. The tagging approach provides flexibility in organizing information items where we can put information items under more than one collection by assigning them multiple tags this facilitates the grouping and regrouping of information items. The favorite applications for the tagging approach remains in the web environment where users manage and assign tags to their shared collections on the web. Although, the tagging approach support information exchange on the web where these systems share user defined tags with all users and enable users to find other people who share the same items, the tagging approach does not support feedback information which is essential to control the flow of information between organization staff at different levels nor it supports information filtering as in the hierarchical organization where a user can be flooded with a large amount of useless information. Classification of documents such as videos and images are problematic as it depends mainly on manual annotations and users may differ in their annotations. Also, as the collection grows manual annotation becomes a problem (Indratmo & Julita, 2008). Creating tools for supporting manual annotations is one possible solution to this problem (Gemmell, 2002). Another approach to annotating infor-

mation items is by using context analysis (Soules, & Gagner, 2003). The tagging approach does not support information security because it makes the information available to all users. Consistency is guaranteed with the hierarchical organization while it is a major problem with the tagging approach due to the freedom to associate multiple tags with an information item. This inconsistency prevents users from retrieving all relevant items in a collection at once. The hierarchical organization can support an efficient retrieval process by decomposing the retrieval process hierarchically into successive steps each of which involves decisions about only a few major alternatives. This is not available for the tagging approach which depends mainly on the flat organization.

2. **Linear organization:** In this organization information items are arranged in a list on certain order, the location of an item in the list is determined according to a particular attribute used to compare the item with other items. Alphabetical, frequency of use, priority, contextual and temporal information are among the attributes used to sort a collection of information. A sorted list of information items significantly helps the users adding new information item to the list and significantly improves the retrieval process. However, when a sorted list becomes too long it becomes difficult to manage where traversing the list to find a specific item is not easy. The hierarchical organization is used to decompose a list into sub-lists containing only subsets of the sorted information in the main list. Another weakness of a linear organization is that it shows only a single dimension of information. When a collection is sorted alphabetically, the chronological order is lost and vice versa. Moreover, unlike a hierarchical structure, a linear structure does not capture semantic relationships between information items explicitly. To overcome this limitation of the linear organization users generally integrate the linear organization with hierarchical organization instead of replacing it (Indratmo, & Julita, 2008).

3. **Network organization:** It is a generalized case of hierarchical organization, where information items can be linked to one another arbitrarily without any constraints. In recent years studies have shown that networks also show a hierarchical organization where vertices are divided into groups that are further divided into sub groups and so on. In many cases these groups are found to correspond to known functional units. The knowledge of hierarchical structure can be used to predict missing connections in partly known networks with high accuracy, and for more general network structures than competing techniques (Aaron, C., Cristopher, M. & Newman, M. ,May 2008). Aaron (2008) suggests that hierarchy is a central organizing principle of a complex networks, capable of offering insight into many network phenomena. One of the major drawbacks of network organization is that it is less structured than other organizational structures this makes it inefficient to get an overview of the information and to navigating the network in a search of an information item.

4. Shrideep, Geoffrey & Harshawardhan (in press) argued that organizing information topics hierarchically has some disadvantages which include:

   1. A parent topic has no control over either breadth, depth or the number of child topics within the topic hierarchy.
   2. The topic string itself reveals the hierarchy of the topics. It is thus possible to launch denial of service attacks by simply flooding the system with messages to topics within the hierarchy.

3. Since no one really owns topics or enforces hierarchies, it is generally quite difficult to discover the structure of the topic hierarchy. This also results in the inability to enforce who would be authorized to discover such information.

We will also address Shrideeps's argument later in this chapter.

To overcome the limitations of the hierarchical structures (Dourish, Edwards, LaMarca, & Salisbury, 1999; Karger & Quan, 2004) extended the notion of a hierarchical structure as follows:

1. An information item can belong to multiple collections.
2. The concept of flexible collections allows users to put different types of information items such as group relevant files, email messages, appointments and web bookmarks together with other types of information into a single collection.

In this way, information organization is abstracted from the applications that produce and manage the items and users can organize their items in a more logical and meaningful way (Kaptelinin, 2003). This principle reduces the need to maintain multiple hierarchies in various information gathering tools, alleviating fragmentation on a desktop (Indratmo, & Julita, 2008). Robin & Theodosis (1997) proposed the approach of fuzzy decision tree algorithms, to maintain a large number of classes where an information item can belong to more than one collection with different degrees of membership while minimizing the time for making the final decision by a series of small local decisions. In fact, very often it takes only $O(log\ n)$ time to reach one of the n possible classes, since a tree of n leaves usually has depth of $log\ n$.

Human Collaboration

Improving communications tools for people in all areas of an organization encourage collaboration which help to save time, reduce duplication of work, and speed decisions that could translate to more benefits. Collaboration introduces the concept of individuals coming together to create something new, commonly a new process (Anne, 2008). By definition, collaboration is the interaction between team members with the intent of creating a shared understanding that none had previously possessed or could have come to on their own (Scharge, 1995). Alberts, Garstka, Hayes, & Signori (2001) define collaboration as actors actively sharing data, information, knowledge, perceptions, or concepts when they are working together toward a common purpose and how they might achieve that purpose efficiently or effectively. Andriessen (2003) describe the term collaborative work as the situations where two or more people act together to achieve a common goal, but the actual extent of togetherness can vary substantially. When people work together toward a joint goal, they can accomplish something larger, greater, and with more impact than something done in isolation. The social need for collaboration can be seen as a consequence of two phenomena:

1. The world is becoming increasingly complex,
2. This complexity requires that people cultivate specialties and then collaborate.

There must not only be trust and integrity as a foundation, but the parties need to understand the perspectives of the other collaborators' self interests. This understanding suggests a greater depth of involvement between collaborators. It is not only exchanging information but developing a sense of situation awareness of the other parties such as what motivates them, and what they need out of working together (Anne S., 2008). It is the mental aspects of joint problem solving for the purpose of achieving a shared understanding, making a group decision, or creating intellectual products such as situation assessments, courses of action, plans, analyses, recommendations or carry out a joint action.

Effective collaboration refers to the exchange of information, critical discussion, and insight within the team. Teams must process information both individually and collectively (Ickes, & Gonzalez, 1994). Once the team members start to interact, they use transitive memory to share and critique information among the team members (Wegner, 1987; Wegner, 1995). Some degree of information exchange must occur in order for the team to operate successfully (Hinsz, Tinadle, & Vollrath 1997). To help team collaboration, information exchange is a focal point which can be done by giving team members secure access to company information through the organization's website or Intranet. According to (Hinton, Botelho, & Suchman 1998) there are three collaborative principles for effective collaboration:

1. Building and maintaining relationships is an active process requiring attention and effort.
2. One must strive to understand the perspective of others and one's own to be an effective partner.
3. Shared decision making is the ultimate hallmark of partnership, enhancing motivation and consolidating mutual commitment.

These principles are consistent with (Weaver, & Farrell, 1997) use of the acronym TARGET to describe the characteristics of collaboration and partnerships. These characteristics include: Truth, Accountability, Respect, Growth, Empowerment and Trust. TARGET components can be used to measure the effectiveness of collaborative relationships, regardless of whether these relationships are between individuals and groups, administrators and employees or interdisciplinary colleagues. Human collaborations are characterized with three features which are (Blake, & Cabri, 2003):

1. **Negotiation:** It uses information exchange to reach shared situation awareness between collaborators.
2. **Rules:** By defining rules we control collaborators' behaviors. Rules can be mandatory such as constraints or expected such as norms.
3. **Roles:** The main advantage of a role based approach is the separation of concerns, but it leads also to flexibility, dynamism, reuse of solutions, context dependency. Many roles oriented objectives can be naturally described with a hierarchical organization.

These three features are very important in open and dynamic environments, such as the Internet, where team members in online collaboration interact in order to collaborate. Some argue that many individuals and organizations are currently experiencing a growing need to search for alternative ways of working together. Herbst (1976) suggests that the traditional hierarchical model of organization, based upon the principles of vertical control and a single, uniform type of superior-subordinate relationship can no longer cope with the demands of our complex and rapidly changing society. McGregor (1957) argues that this model also ties workers to limiting jobs which do not utilize their capabilities, discourages the acceptance of responsibility, encourages passivity, and has eliminated meaning from work. People who are dissatisfied with working together under the hierarchical model are saying that managers above them in the hierarchy make their decisions without regard for the effect they had on the lives of people below them. However, we argue that the hierarchical organization provides a seamless environment for collecting, indexing and disseminating the information produced to the correct users at the right amount of detail. A good manager in a hierarchical organization encourages his subordinates to become positive, to accept responsibility and to like the work they do. He should have the capabilities to recognize and utilize his employees' capabilities to the best. A good manager should effectively engage with his employees in setting, implementing and uptake of objectives, decisions and outputs. This can be achieved by running forums and meetings to display information, presenting and discussing alternative solutions so subordinates feel that they are partners in taking these decisions. Some people suggest that flat organization is a good alternative for the hierarchical organization. However, this argument is generally possible only for small businesses or enterprises but when they reach a critical size they cannot keep completely flat manger-to-staff organization and they must transfer to traditional hierarchical organization otherwise they may affect productivity. Certain financial responsibilities may also require a more conventional structure such as the hierarchical organization. In collaborative distributed computing which is a form of an online collaboration, some researches argue that there is no need for hierarchical organization in online collaboration where colleagues communicate with each other using emails and collecting information from different resources, this makes information items scattered on many different collaboration tools such as emails, file systems and web sites. However, each of these tools has its own hierarchical organization and there is a need to integrate them into a single hierarchical organization. In online collaboration, a large project needs to be divided hierarchically into smaller tasks that are sent out over the internet to be completed on personal computers. The technical challenge is to slice a project into thousands of tiny pieces that can be completed independently and then to reassemble them. Many people all over the world participate voluntarily in such large projects, as collaborative distributed computing only works if many people participate, the social problem is how to find all those widely spread collaborators and persuade them to participate (Holohan, 2005).

THE COMPOSITE ABSTRACT RELATIONSHIP

In this section we will discuss in details the composite abstract relationship between the hierarchical organization, information management and human collaboration. We start with the first part of this relationship which is between hierarchical organization and information management. In the next subsections, we will first discuss the issues, controversies and problems that face information management within an organization and then we discus how hierarchical organization facilitates information management processes.

Issues, Controversies and Problems

All organization and enterprises, regardless of the internal and external environments in which they operate, need enormous amount of information. Management and operations within organizations and enterprises suffer from inefficient and ineffective information management processes, they do not benefit from their relevant and reliable information available from their information resources. In many organizations there is a great number of different information resources managed in different ways. They have no organized special libraries, information centers or services of any kind and also suffer from lack of well trained librarians and information professionals. Scholars have long been concerned with the impact of information management on the functioning of an organization. Some of this research has focused within the firm, and has considered whether greater computerization leads to increased or decreased centralization of decision making and standardization of work processes (Leavitt, & Whisler, 1958; Attwell, & Rule, 1984; Zuboff, 1988). Others have focused on the boundary of the firm, analyzing whether greater diffusion of information technology makes it more or less attractive to distribute organization's activity across a network of markets rather than within a hierarchy.

Locating, retrieving, integrating, processing and disseminating information are activities of great importance for the successful functioning of organizations. The key issue facing information integration or fusion within an organization is locating and understanding both the information to be fused and the semantic relationships between information resources. Efficient structures are required for storing the meta-data across an enterprise, to make it easy to overcome the semantic heterogeneity between information resources and keep it over time. Lacking of efficient structures to store, retrieve and process information to fulfill the organization's demand of information is a major problem. Some organizations implement the flat, linear or network structures to store and retrieve information. Some scholars argue that network organization provides a better environment for information exchange while other scholars argue that better information management can be performed using hierarchical structures. Network organizations are characterized by their fully distributed control that is no supervision is available, the keep of minimal amount of global information, cooperation among the network is loose and autonomous communication prevails. These characteristics of network organizations make them not favored for both information management and human collaboration. Better monitoring can be valuable within hierarchies which make them more attractive than networks for organizations. Hierarchical structures are favored for information filtering, retrieval and classification while in network organizations it is very hard to navigate the network searching for an information item. However, for the hierarchical organizations, difficulties remain in organizing and maintaining the hierarchical structure with growing size of the repository. Lopez (2002) argued that, the higher the position on the hierarchy, the larger the amount of information that can be handled. Lopez considered this a very interesting conclusion because it shows that the topology of this kind of organization benefits the nodes located in the upper levels of the hierarchy, allowing them to receive more information than all other nodes located under them. This means that the hierarchical structure guarantees that in terms of information, the efficiency of the relationships always improves when moving up in the tree. Thus, considering that all actors invest the same effort in relating with the others, the position on the hierarchy determines the amount of information that can be managed. The hierarchical organization provides the higher levels with high information centrality and improves their dominance of information. They can have the power to intercept, manipulate and obscure information. However, we do not consider the conclusions of Lopez as drawbacks for the hierarchical organization because they comply with the requirements of secure information exchange especially when relates to information of defense, intelligence, homeland security missions and financial responsibilities while basic information is made available to each actor in the hierarchy. In regard to the above problems, a key issue arises about the relationship between information management and the hierarchical organization, which is the question of "how does hierarchical organization facilitates information production, retrieval, fusion, display and diffusion"?

Solutions and Recommendations

In this section, we will discuss how the hierarchical organization addresses the problems and issues facing information management processes in work teams or organizations whether they are private or public. Information technology provides us with tools such as the multi agent technology and distributed computing technology to deal with these problems. A distributed multi agent system for collaborative information management and sharing was presented in (Chen, Wolfe, & Wragg, 2000) where collaborative agents help users access, manage, share and exchange information. The system has three types of collaborative agents:

1. Personal agents help their owners to find information to current needs.
2. Matchmaker agents designed to establish connections between users with similar interests and expertise.
3. System's agents to provide needed services for users to share and learn information from one another on the World Wide Web.

This system provides tools and utilities for users to manage their information repositories with dynamic organization and virtual views. Collaboration between users is aided by easy exchange utilities as well as automated information exchange. Contents of repository are kept in object oriented storage to facilitate information exchange. Flexible hierarchical display is integrated with indexed query search to support effective information access. Automatic indexing methods are employed to support user queries and communication between agents.

In the next sub sections we will focus in more details on how hierarchical organization facilitates information management processes. According to the information life cycle model in Figure 2, the information management processes are:

1. Information gathering.
2. Information organization.
3. Information feedback.
4. Information retrieval.
5. Information exchange and security.
6. Information filtering
7. Information fusion.
8. Information display and visualization.
9. Information disposition.

Information Gathering

Information can be created through the interaction between the organization and its internal and external environments. Internally, information can be produced while solving old and new problems through data collection, statistics and researches. Information comes through many different types of records, forms, monthly summaries, official reports and special studies which are prepared by staff at different levels and in different departments. Externally, the organization can interact with its external environment through sensors, emails, information gathering agents, interviews, surveys or web sites. While new information is continuously developed, organizations play an important role in identifying and organizing this information. Managers at different hierarchical levels must continually acquire and assimilate this information to affect the functioning of their organization.

A bottom up approach is considered very helpful for gathering, structuring and organizing information from one or more sources of expertise and its transfer to the knowledge base. Information is gathered at the lower level of the hierarchy using different gathering techniques which can vary based on the source and type of information as well as the intended use. Types of information and how they will be collected and reported, who will collect it, to what upper management level it will be submitted, how it will be used, and the level of details needed should be made clear to all members of the work team to ensure an appropriate flow of information in the correct sequence and the team knows how the information system functions. Questionnaire is a manual knowledge acquisition technique into which users write short answers to open questions or leave the questions blank. Observation technique is a time consuming technique, needs skill and is difficult to observe and analyze what was observed. Interview technique avoid many problems of questionnaire but it is hard to set up specially in structured interview where there must be a predefined structure and there is no flexibility in acquiring knowledge from an expert (Shouman, Abou-Ali, Mostafa, 2008). Records, reports, statistics and forms should be examined to see if they supply the required information to the upper management. In many cases, the upper management may need information that is not available from the reports submitted routinely. Special survey and research methods can be used to obtain this type of information. The team should be involved with an expert in the design and implementation of these special investigations as well as in the analysis and interpretation of the results. When improving, changing or creating some of the forms team members should be involved in these processes. Making sure that the design of the form facilitates recording and tabulating information accurately because time is wasted in filling bad designed forms as a large amount of information is lost and the form will be illegible. Some problems may occur during information collection, the team involved in the collection process should identify the source of these problems and how to eliminate them. In statistical signal processing, algorithms and studies utilizing sensor networks for detection and tracking are based on hierarchical organization that uses layers of clusters (Manjeshwar, & Agrawal, 2001; Zhao, Shin & Reich, 2002). Clustering is one of the commonly used methods to organize communications in large networks (Heinzelman, Chandrakasan, & Balakrishnan, 2000; Subramanian, & Katz, 2000). Hierarchical organization facilitates the transfer of information between clusters in different layers. Nodes send their information to the cluster heads via a single hop or multi hops depending o the size of the cluster. The cluster head can perform data aggregation and processing then relay the data to either a higher layer cluster head or the sink. Communications within each cluster are of the one-to-many type, that is data flows from each sensor to the cluster heads where they can be processed, compressed, aggregated and relayed (Enrique, Duarte, & Mingyan, 2003). During the collection of information from web sites over the internet routing of this information is an essential process. Hierarchical source routing has proven to perform well for information routing, compared to the global routing strategy which imposes no hierarchy such as distance vector and link state algorithms, while utilizing less storage and communication overheads (Awerbuch, Du, & Shavittb 2000). Hierarchical routing was suggested in (Castineyra, Chiappa, & Steenstrup 1996). In this approach, a network is grouped into hierarchy of nodes at various levels. Each node at a high level reports information for underneath topology to other interested nodes. Also, each node receives reported routing information from nodes in other domains and exchanges them information to other lower level nodes. As a result, each node needs only to maintain partial information about the entire network. Requirement on routing information storage at each node is substantially reduced. Sensory cortex is also arranged in a hierarchical organization, with information flowing from low level areas, which are closely tied to direct sensory input, to higher level areas, which are tied more to other cortical areas as opposed to sensory input. Neurons at lower level areas tend to have small receptive fields are tuned to localized features of sensory input, and thus tend to rapidly fluctuate in their activity in response to time varying sensory input. By contrast, neurons at higher levels have large receptive fields are tuned to more global abstract properties of the sensory world such as object identity, and are thus more invariant with respect to fluctuations in the raw sensory input (Redwood, 2007).

Information Organization

Information organization refers primarily to the logical arrangement of information topics in a file system. Nowadays, there is a wealth of information resources available for direct and easy access on the user's desktop. However, finding appropriate information has become a significant problem for many users. Organized information spaces are easier to search. Once relevant information is found, pointers to it must be locally organized and stored in a manner that allows rapid and effective access for both individuals and workgroups. The most important factors for an effective information organization are:

1.   The rapid access to an information topic or number of topics which are related to each other.
2.   The adding, modification, or deletion of information topics.
3.   Efficiency of storage and retrieval of information topics.
4.   Ensuring integrity between information topics.

Current personal information organizing schemes on the World Wide Web are mostly limited to bookmarks which also called hot lists or favorites. Bookmarks provide an easy way to organize Unified Resource Locators (URLs) in a hierarchical manner and to attach personal comments to them. Although clearly superior to unstructured lists, hierarchical folder organization forces users to think in terms of a neatly decomposable structure consisting of disjoint clusters of related URLs (Chen, Wolfe, & Wragg, 2000).

The hierarchical relationship between information topics is used to organize them in a hierarchical organization where the parent and child topics are determined. In this organization, authorizing to access a parent topic automatically implies authorizing to access child topics. However, the converse is not true accessing a child topic does not imply accessing to any of the parent topics. To address the problems associated with using the hierarchical organization to organize information topics Shrideep, Geoffrey & Harshawardhan (to appear) noted in their framework that the creation request of a root topic should include information about:

1.   Whether it allows hosting child topics, if so what is the maximum depth that is the maximum level including the level of that topic?
2.   What is the maximum width that is the total number of immediate child nodes that any topic within the topic sub-tree can have?
3.   Which would be the parent topic of the topic under consideration?
4.   The topic creation request should also include information about entities that are authorized, or barred from either registering child topics or discovering the topic hierarchy.

To register an information child topic the immediate parent for that topic is determined and a check is made to verify that adding this topic to that parent will not violate any of the constraints specified by the parent such as the maximum depth or maximum width. If a violation to these constraints is discovered then the adding process will fail. If there is no violation occurs then the hierarchical tree is updated to reflect the addition of that child topic. The life time of a child topic is determined by the life time of its parent. When a parent topic expires, all child topics also expire. The expiration time associated with a child topic never exceeds that of any of the parent nodes within its topic hierarchy. A topic collection is a tree based structure which is used to manage the information topics that comprise the collection. A collection may itself be composed of multiple collections. The constituent topics and collections may be added, removed or reorganized within the collection's structure. Additionally, a given topic or collection may be part of multiple collection concurrently. Figure 4 shows an example of collections tree where *T* stands for an information topic and *C* stands for a collection of topics.

Information Feedback

Feedback is a process by which effective performance is reinforced and less than desirable performance is corrected. Feedback should be information that highlights the relationship between what is expected and what has been accomplished after the work is performed or the action is taken. Feedback highlights the notion of temporal order, hierarchical organization and the necessary relation between its components. Mutual interaction occurs because the interacting processes are linked to each other the interaction is not an event but a process (Hector, to appear).

Hierarchical organization facilitates information feedback through a cyclic bottom up and top down operations where the top element in the hierarchy has control over lower elements. For example, our bodies are built in a hierarchical organization where the brain is its top element which controls the functions of all other body organs. By using the bottom up process the brain receives feedback information from the spinal chord which is in turn receives feedback information from body organs. The brain

Figure 4. A collection tree

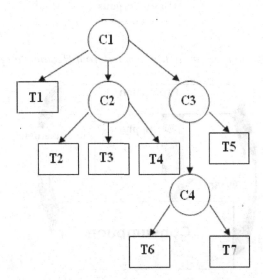

analyses this information and by using top down process it sends command signals to the spinal chord which in turn sends it to body organs to perform a specific action (Hector, to appear). Figure 5 shows the relationship between the brain and body organs.

The relationship between production and consumption is another example of hierarchical organization. By using the bottom up process the producer receives feedback information about demands on its products. The producer then analyses the information and makes decision to whether increase or decrease advertisements and supply to the market. Figure 6 shows the production – consumption hierarchy.

The relationship between employees and supervisors also follows the hierarchical organization where supervisors are encouraged to gather data regarding employees' performance at a systematic manner throughout the year. The performance feedback records are guides that can be used by supervisors, to assist their employees to enhance their skills and expertise to improve results. By using the top down process supervisors should communicate to employees to explain what is expected of them, define satisfactory criteria for those expectations. Then by using the bottom up process supervisors then evaluate the performance on an ongoing basis. Also, the relationship between departments and top management follows the hierarchical organization where the performance feedback statistics and reports are guides to the general director to evaluate the performance of each department. Expectations and guides should

Figure 5. Brain-body organs hierarchy (as adapted from Hector, to appear)

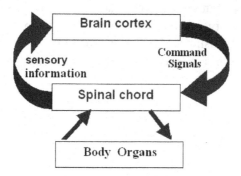

Figure 6. Production-consumption hierarchy (as adapted from Hector , to appear)

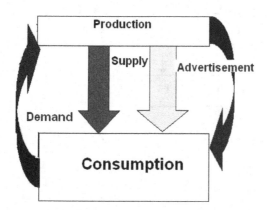

be provided to each department. Figure 7 shows the supervisor-employees and department–top management hierarchy. In this hierarchal organization there is a hierarchy of levels (Top Management (General Director) / Middle Management (Supervisor)/ Low Management (Employees)) that interact with each other in continual processes of mutual and hierarchical feedback. Together, bottom-to-top and top-to-bottom actions constitute a cycle, a continuously operating feedback.

Artificial neural networks are another example of how the hierarchical organization facilitates information feedback to improve performance. Artificial neural networks consist of neurons which are organized hierarchically into successive layers; each neuron in a layer is fully connected with all other neurons in the upper layer. The hierarchical organization facilitates the flow of feed forward information and the back propagation of feedback information between layers to enhance network learning which in return increases its recognition rate. The running of the network consists of two passes: the forward pass and the backward pass. In the feed forward pass information flows from the input layer to the output layer to adjust the weights between neurons. Then outputs are calculated and the feedback information which is also called error is calculated at the output units. In the backward pass feedback information, which is the calculated error, is back propagated from the output layer to the input layer to correct the weights of the network connections between neurons of these layers. This process is performed iteratively to minimize the back propagated error and to increase the network performance. Figure 8 shows an artificial neural network model.

Information Fusion

Applications might require information fusion from a handful of information sources to literally hundreds of sources. The information could be (Simoff, & Maher, 1998):

1. Structured data files such as stored in database management systems or specific applications such as data warehousing, enterprise resource planning, scheduling, payroll, finance and accounting.

Figure 7. Supervisor-employees & department-top management hierarchy

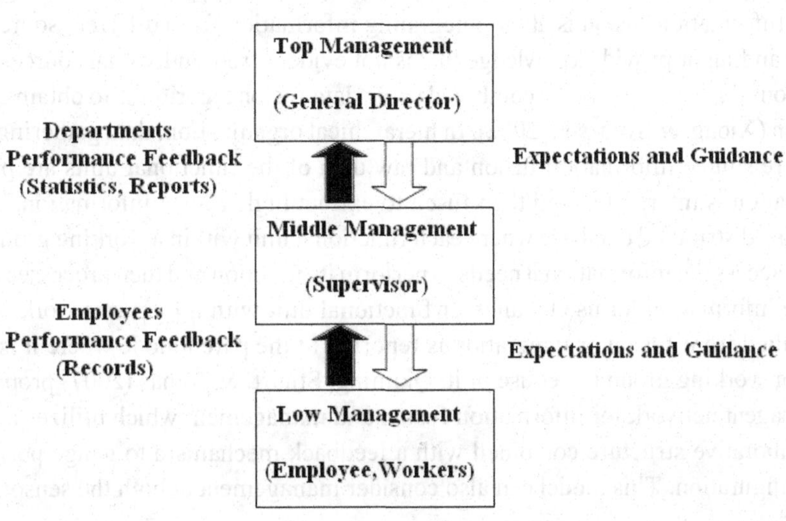

Figure 8. Artificial neural network model

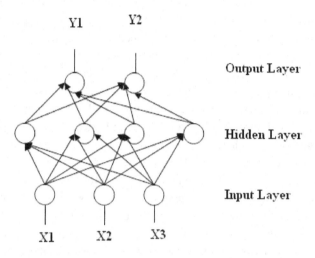

2.   Semi-structured data files such as HyperText Markup Language (HTML), eXtensible Markup Language (XML), or Standardized General Markup Language (SGML) files.
3.   Unstructured text data files, such as contracts, specifications, catalogs, change orders, requests for information, field reports, and meetings.
4.   Unstructured graph files stored in binary format such as 2D and 3D drawings.
5.   Unstructured multimedia files such as pictures, audio, and video files.

The main goal of using the hierarchical organization in information fusion is to increase the fidelity and availability of information within the organization. Since a single source of data can generally perceive limited partial information about the problem, multiple similar or dissimilar data sources can provide sufficient local pictures with different focus and from different view points in an integrated manner (Zhou L.,2007). Information fusion is about integrating information from different sources in order to facilitate understanding or provide knowledge that is not evident from individual sources. Information from heterogeneous data sources can be combined using data fusion algorithms to obtain clearer picture about the problem (Xiong, & Svensson, 2002). In hierarchical organization, data gathering occurs at the lowest level where simple information fusion and raw data of the functional units are produced. The resulting information is interpreted and then fused to extract higher level information. This could be achieved through a distributed database where each functional unit within a working group maintains a local database to access the information it needs to perform its function and then processes and transmits its best available information for use by another functional unit within the same working group. The information resulted from fusion or integration is reported to the parent node where it is available for any other child or working group to get use of it. Qiuming, Stuart, & Tomas (2007) proposed a hierarchical collective agent network for information fusion and management which utilizes a sophisticated multi-agent collaborative structure combined with a feedback mechanism to gauge performance and drive system configuration. This model can also consider management at both the sensor level and the higher system level of the total platform capability and its mission. The hierarchical collective agent network possesses the properties that agents are grouped in layers which organized hierarchically. Agents within each layer are weakly connected while agents between layers are strongly connected. The control and coordination of the agents at each layer are carried out through the agents at the higher layer. Weakly connected means that interactions between the agents are mainly data communications only, no control function takes place, while strongly connected means that agents on the two ends of the link have both data exchange and control relations. Figure 9 shows the hierarchical collective agent network of agent collaboration. In the hierarchical organization the collective nature of agent relation simplifies the functional design of the agent interactions and enhances the security and efficiency of the information processing, an advantage over the web-like and grid-like topologies. Also, it relieves the burden of intensive data exchange between fellow agents in star like topology by limiting agent communication to vertical layers of the assembly only.

The hierarchical collective agent organization thus strikes a balance between the centralized control and distributed computation by allowing distributive agent operation within layers of the hierarchy and enforcing centralized control between the layers of the hierarchy, thus creating a federated agents integration structure. The hierarchical structure of the model facilitates the on-site analyses of the collected data and extraction of information that is useful for the control agent to coordinate the actions of the distributed agents or agent groups (Qiuming, Stuart, & Tomas, 2007). In problem decomposition, the hierarchical organization simplifies a large problem by dividing it into well defined sub-problems, which are again divided into sub-problems recursively until a trivial solution can be calculated at a lower level. Afterwards the solutions of the sub-problems are passed to the higher level to fuse or integrate together and reach a solution to the main problem. This strategy can be applied as is to achieve recursive problem decomposition. As the smaller tasks are usually independent of one another, the tasks can be calculated in parallel, this reduces significantly the time complexity required to solve the main problem. Parallel sorting algorithms often use hierarchical recursive decomposition. The hierarchical organization also facilitates the integration between different models which helps in information fusion. A hierarchical hybrid Bayesian network consists of a Bayesian networks model at the top layer serving as a fusion center, several Hidden Markov Models at the bottom layer belonging to several agencies serving as information filters, they process the raw information and provide soft evidence to the corresponding Bayesian network

Figure 9. Hierarchical collective agent network of agent collaboration (as adapted from Qiuming, Stuart, & Tomas, 2007)

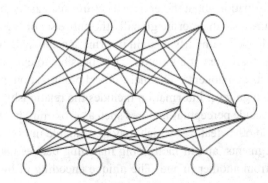

node where the Bayesian network is maintained by another agency. Raw information is represented by transactions and information entities to be integrated are modeled as random variables. Each random variable has certain states with probabilities assigned to them (Haiying, Jeffrey, Satnam, Krishna, & Peter, 2006). Figure 10 shows the hierarchical hybrid Bayesian network for information fusion.

Also, the hierarchical organization facilitates the use of ontology for information fusion. Fig.11 shows a hierarchical model for gathering provenance information from different sources for decision making (Fred, 2006). Ontology is used at the top layer for information fusion. At the lower layer information is gathered from different resources such as images, maps and texts which are then transferred to the middle layer the Resource Description Framework (RDF). RDF is an infrastructure that enables encoding, exchange, and reuse of structured metadata. It uses XML (eXtensible Markup Language) as a common syntax for the exchange and processing of metadata.

The main requirements for all information fusion or integration models are that the information to be fused or integrated must have a well defined measure of uncertainty and confidentiality and that the information fusion process must ensure that the databases maintained by all functional units after fusion remain consistent. Information consistency is necessary to get rid of redundant information which has a disastrous effect on information fusion. Information consistency can be maintained using the hierarchical organization while it is not possible in network organization, web-like or grid organizations.

Information Retrieval

An efficient retrieval process can be achieved using a top down approach of successive refinements to narrow the domain of search in geometrically successive fashion. This is accomplished by decomposing the retrieval process hierarchically into successive steps each of which involves decisions about only a few major alternatives, in such a way that decisions at earlier steps facilitate more detailed decisions at later steps (Eylon, & Reif, 1979). This suggests the hierarchical organization for information retrieval tasks, where knowledge is subdivided into knowledge units related in such a way that a few information items in any unit are elaborated by further description through subordinate knowledge units. Figure 12 shows a classification tree to classify a person into either a purchaser or non-purchaser class.

As more information becomes available the search space narrows as we go down the hierarchy. This elaborates that the hierarchical organization of knowledge facilitates information retrieval using a top down approach.

For an efficient and rapid retrieval of images hierarchical organization facilitates the matching of image segments from different scenes. The primary advantage of using the hierarchical organization in scene representation is that image information is represented in a structured manner. The top node of the structure contains information about the entire structure, such as its total size, average intensity or amplitude, and other features which describe globally the entire set of segments which makes up the structure. Lower level branch nodes similarly contain information about all nodes subordinate to them. Thus, by examining only the top layers of a structure, it is possible to extract a great deal of information about the structure and its components. The hierarchical organization explicitly encodes valuable high level information. This high level information includes the relationships between the segmented regions in an image which include perceptual features such as proximity between segments, similarity of intensity or amplitude, and other features which may be valuable in both characterizing the nature of a structured cluster of segments, and in facilitating matching between sets of segments from one image to sets of segments from another image. The unique encoding of hierarchical data structures

Figure 10. Hierarchical hybrid Bayesian network for information fusion (as adapted from Haiying, Jeffrey, Satnam, Krishna, & Peter, 2006)

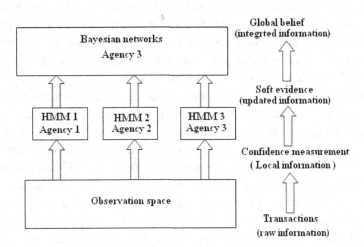

Figure 11. Gathering provenance information during decision making (as adapted from Fred, 2006)

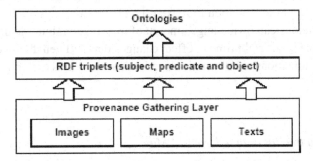

facilitates rapid identification of significant and/or strongly differentiated areas of interest in each image (Allanna, Robert, & Craig, 1989). Information retrieval search engines can get more accurately and organized results if the search terms are organized in hierarchical structure which is called the query tree. By providing an order in which web pages are searched or retrieved by following a specific path the search engine can quickly narrow down the search space and obtain the desired data. An example of such search engine is the World Wide Web based Information Retrieval and Extraction system WIRE mentioned in (Aggarwal, Hung, Weiyi, 1998). WIRE permits users to provide examples and patterns that help in the search and information extraction. The examples and patterns are associated with the search terms of the query tree. They are hierarchically organized into a paradigm tree that is similar in structure to the query tree.

With growing size of the World Wide Web and becoming a prevalent source of information in scientific researches and everyday life, bookmarks strategies are widely used to relocate sites of interest that allow the user to create a personalized Uniform Resource Locator (URL) repository, which facilitates easy and fast access to relevant information (Abrams, Baecker, & Chignell, 1998). Traditionally, these repositories are stored on the client side and can be organized in a hierarchical folder structure via the browser interface. Recently, server side mechanisms like the so called "Social Book marking" have gained popularity (Hammond, Hannay, Lund, & Scott, 2005). Hierarchies are the primary organizing principle for many document classification systems. Cataloging systems (OCLC, 1993) uses a classification hierarchy to facilitate browsing and searching it has been implemented and currently runs with over 50,000 book records. The system's interface allows the hierarchy to be displayed and traversed easily. A search query is applied to documents in a document repository where documents are organized into a hierarchy. A search engine searches the hierarchy to return documents which match a query term either directly or indirectly. It organizes the query term into individual sub-terms and matches the sub-terms against documents returning only those documents which indirectly match the entire search query term and directly match at least one of the query sub-terms. The Dewey classification system which is probably the most widely used international classification system is the purest hierarchy of the major library classification systems (Robert B., 1994). A study was designed to investigate forms of human internal knowledge organization that facilitate the recall of information or its use for complex problem solving tasks. A hierarchical organization model was specified and designed to facilitate selective information retrieval constructed by successive elaborations of a few top level ideas most important for a specific task domain. Subjects with such a hierarchical organization performed appreciably better compared to subjects with a single level organization of the same knowledge (Eylon, & Reif, 1979).

Gaining access to the right information to make critical decisions can often be more difficult than it first appears. Organizations can own a huge amount of information, but one often find it difficult to get this to the right people in the right time to effect changes that will benefit the organization. A common problem facing organizations is information overload, as the levels of explicit knowledge become

Figure 12. Classification tree (as adapted from XLMiner, 2007)

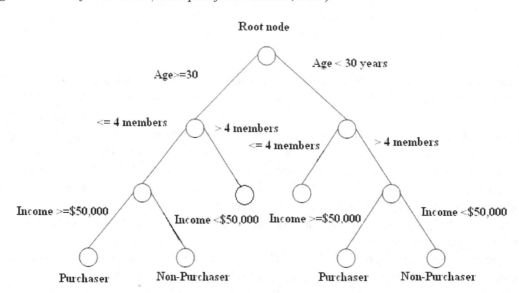

so overwhelming that they cannot be appropriately filtered. Information overload refers to the state of having too much information to make a decision or remain informed about a topic. It is often referred to in conjunction with various forms of computer mediated communication such as emails and web sites. Research shows that many members of organizations may receive regular reports but often they are not tailored to their needs, pertinent to them or in helpful formats. As more and more people in the organization need to make decisions based on accurate and up-to-date information, they need to receive important information but do not want to be flooded with unimportant information. The general causes of information overload include:

1. An increasing rate of information production.
2. Too much useless information.
3. Information can be easily duplicated and deployed over the internet.
4. Information can be received through multiple channels such as telephone, emails and instant messaging.
5. Large amount of stored information to mine through.
6. Contradictions and inaccuracies in available information.
7. A lack of methods for information filtering.

Email remains a major source of information overload, although people should be delighted with the growing use of e-mail attachments in the form of lengthy reports, presentations and media files, they struggle to keep up with the rate of incoming messages. In a world increasingly filled with a flood of information and with users strained for available time, filters will assume an important role in the acquisition of information (Rajeev R., Snehasis M., Michael B., & Nila P., 1997). Filtering out unsolicited commercial messages, help users to keep up with their important messages. Information filters are programs that select and prioritize information according to the instructions, needs, or customs of a given user. Keeping efficient indexes of historic information also facilitates information filtering where indexes are usually based on hierarchical organizations. These indexes prevent users from creating new files and generating new reports which might exist and therefore reduce the problem of information overloading and inefficiencies in the storage of information. A hierarchical multi-agent system based on the model of beliefs, desires and intentions for retrieving information from heterogeneous databases is used for fast retrievals of heterogeneous distributed information over different data sources. A model for information filtering to solve the information overload problem on the web was presented by (Li, Zhang & Swan, 2000). The model hierarchically describes the user information need into two levels: profiles on category level and Boolean queries on document level. To efficiently estimate the relevance between the user information need and documents, the user information need is treated as a rough set on the space of documents. The rough set decision theory is used to classify the new documents according to the user information need. In return for this, the new documents are derived into three parts: positive region, boundary region, and negative region. This approach was shown to be effective in solving the information overload problem. The web search engine WWW based Information Retrieval and Extraction system (WIRE) mentioned in (Aggarwal, Hung, Weiyi, 1998) has a sophisticated filter mechanism, the filter conditions which could be local, global or structural are organized in a hierarchy called the restriction tree. Also the queries of WIRE are tree structured. WIRE provides an order in which web pages are to be searched and filters out undesired information to further improve retrieval accuracy.

Information Exchange and Security

Information exchange, distribution or diffusion is the timely collection, exchange and distribution of information to the work team. This information needs to be delivered in the right format and at the right time to the right place to ensure that informed team decisions can be made. Information diffusion can take place through formal or informal mechanisms. Information technology's exchanges capabilities make it easier and less costly communicate the required large volumes of information across organization boundaries (Malone, Yates, & Benjamin, 1987; Clemons, Reddi, & Row, 1993). Management decisions can largely influence the flow of information within the organization. As the hierarchical organization reflects the position each actor occupies in the organization, it reflects authority relationship among actors, showing that there exist a close connection between the hierarchical level of an actor and the information it receives, benefiting the hierarchical levels in terms of information transfer. Therefore, managers should manage the process of information diffusion within an overall strategy to achieve the organization's goals.

In information exchange multi agent based model each data exchange node serves as a basic organization which can send and receive information automatically and store the information. The model has a hierarchical organization of multi-agents which cooperate to realize the exchange and the integration of information. Multi agent coordinating information exchange model adopts the tier-based configuration which is composed of three basic organizations namely the Information Processing Center Basic Organization which serves as the root node. This root node has two subordinates Information Processing Sub-Node 1 Basic Organization and Information Processing Sub-Node 2 Basic Organization. Each of these subordinates has also a hierarchical organization of multi agents which contains agents to send, receive, evaluate and manage information. Figure 13 shows the architecture of the coordinating information exchange model. Figure 14 shows Information Processing Sub-Node Basic Organization. Figure 15 shows Information Processing Center Basic Organization (Xing-kai, & Yan-zhang, 2006).

Huang, Shian-Shyong, & Wu, Haung, Shian-Shyong, & Zhang (1999) proposed a knowledge sharing and collaboration system hierarchical model based on internet called the "Internet Knowledge Based" system. It facilitates collaboration and sharing knowledge between web-based knowledge systems. This model is composed of three hierarchical layers namely, the Data Exchange layer, Collaboration layer and Knowledge-based Application layer. Data Exchange layer solves the problem of how to represent and manipulate knowledge.

Collaboration layer devotes to collaboration between servers over internet. Knowledge-based Application layer defines the user interface for knowledge processing over internet such as information searching, decision support application and data mining. Data exchange between the Internet Knowledge Based Webs is in XML format, knowledge can be shared between heterogeneous knowledge bases, and knowledge can be remotely manipulated. Collaboration between Internet Knowledge Based systems is supported through collaboration agents to resources a user wants. Also, the Internet Knowledge Based system can support information retrieval and browse. Information security is a critical point in the field of information exchange where hierarchies are an important concept in information protection systems. Integrity, confidentiality, authenticity and traceability have to be guaranteed for transferred information (Kunis, Rünger, &Schwind, 2007). The uses of hierarchies in the security domain of computer information systems include access hierarchies, levels of abstraction in security kernels, multi-level security and user hierarchies among others. Security levels are organized into a hierarchical order in the multi-level security that prevents downward information flow from a high security level to a low security level (Gollmann, 1999). Basic information which is easy to obtain is located at the bottom and the higher order need located at the top. At the very bottom of the hierarchy is open information which is not secure at all, it is how most enterprises, financial institutions and government agencies share information. The next level is basic point-to-point encryption for a specific data stream, which must be set up and torn down on a case-by-case basis. The third layer is network encryption, which provides secure information exchange on a broad level (CipherOptics,2008). Figure 16 shows the security levels of information exchange hierarchy. A user hierarchy is defined as a network structure of users arranged in the order of their authority in the organization. Figure 17 shows a user hierarchy. An arc between two users indicates that one is the supervisor of the other. An information protection system should be able to store, verify, and guard such a user with rigorous discipline. In Figure 17 for instance, the protection system should grant the request of user c to read a file of user e since user c is superior to user e. On the other hand, the system should deny a similar request for user b to read file of user c because user b is a sibling of user c and does not possess such access rights.

Figure 13. Architecture of the coordinating information exchange model (as adapted from Xing-kai, & Yan-zhang, 2006)

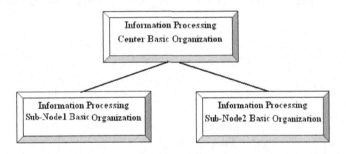

Figure 14. Information processing sub-node basic organization (as adapted from Xing-kai, & Yan-zhang, 2006)

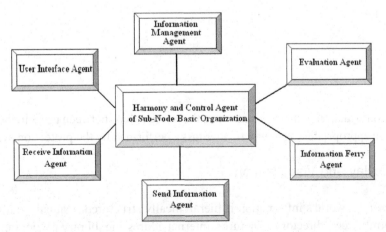

Figure 15. Information processing center basic organization (as adapted from Xing-kai, & Yan-zhang, 2006)

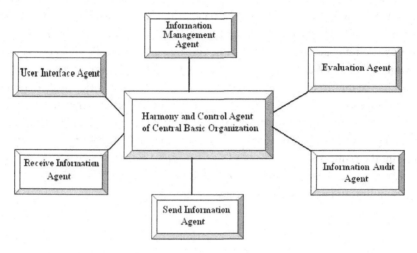

Figure 16. Security levels of information exchange hierarchy(as adapted from CipherOptics, 2008)

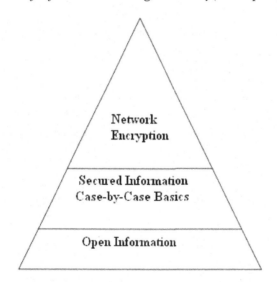

In effect, the confirmation of the arcs and hence the relationships between users in the hierarchy will help determine the appropriateness of any further tasks performed by the protection system.

Information Display and Visualization

A large quantity of the world's information is hierarchically structured: manuals, outlines, corporate organizations, family trees, directory structures, internet addressing, library cataloging, and computer

Figure 17. A users hierarchy

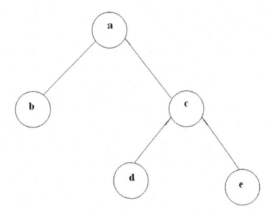

programs....etc. Most people come to understand the content and organization of these structures easily if they are small, but have great difficulty if the structures are large (Brian, & Shneiderman, 1991). To display hierarchical information traditional methods are classified into: listings, outlines and tree diagrams. It is difficult for people to extract information from large hierarchical information structures using these methods as the navigation of the structures is a great burden and content information is often hidden within individual nodes (Kim, Brian, & Robert, 1987). The tree map visualization technique was proposed by (Brian, & Shneiderman, 1991). Tree mapping is a method for displaying tree-structured data using nested rectangles. Hierarchical information structures contain two kinds of information: structural information associated with the hierarchy and content information associated with each node. Tree maps are able to depict both the structure and content of the hierarchy. This approach is best suited to hierarchies in which the content of the leaf nodes and the structure of the hierarchy are of primary importance, and the content information associated with internal nodes is largely derived from their children.

The Tree map visualization method maps hierarchical information to a rectangular 2-D display in a space-filling manner, where 100% of the designated display space is utilized. Interactive control allows users to specify the presentation of both structural as depth bounds....etc. and content display properties such as color mappings information. With the Tree-map method, sections of the hierarchy containing more important information can be allocated more display space while portions of the hierarchy which are less important to the specific task at hand can be allocated less space (George, 1986; Tyson, & Scott, 1990). This tree map approach was successfully applied to computer directories, sales data, business decision making (Asahi, Turo, & Shneiderman, 1995) and web browsing but user take 10-20 minutes to accommodate to complex tree maps (Mitchell, Day, & Hirschman, 1995; Mukherjea, Foley, & Hudson, 1995). Figure 18 shows tree map visualization for a representation tree.

In case of multi-dimensional data, stacked display techniques are tailored to present data partitioned in a hierarchical organization. Data dimensions to be used for partitioning the data are building the hierarchy have to be selected appropriately. The basic idea is to embed one coordinate system inside another coordinate system, i.e. two attributes from the coordinate system and two other attributes are

Figure 18. Tree map visualization for a representation tree (as adapted from Re'mi, 2002)

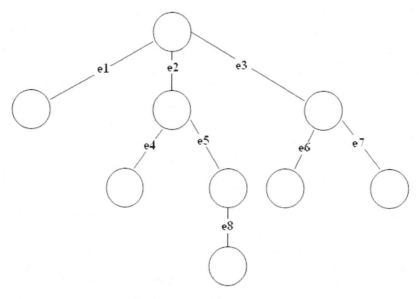

(a) A node-link representation tree

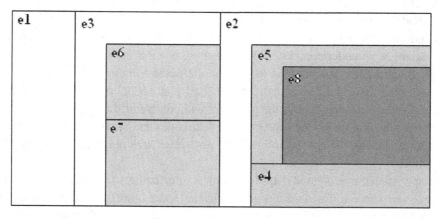

(b) The corresponding treemap

embedded into the outer coordinate system and so on. The display is generated by dividing the outmost level coordinate system into rectangular cells and within the cells the next two attributes are used to span the second level coordinate system. This process may be repeated more than one time. The usefulness of the resulting visualization largely depends on the data distribution of the outer coordinates and therefore the dimensions which are used for defining the outer coordinate system have to be selected carefully (Keim, 2002). Figures 19 and 20 display the population of the United states circa 2000 as a

Figure 19. Stacked bar showing United States population for states and regions (Corbet 2003. Used with permission)

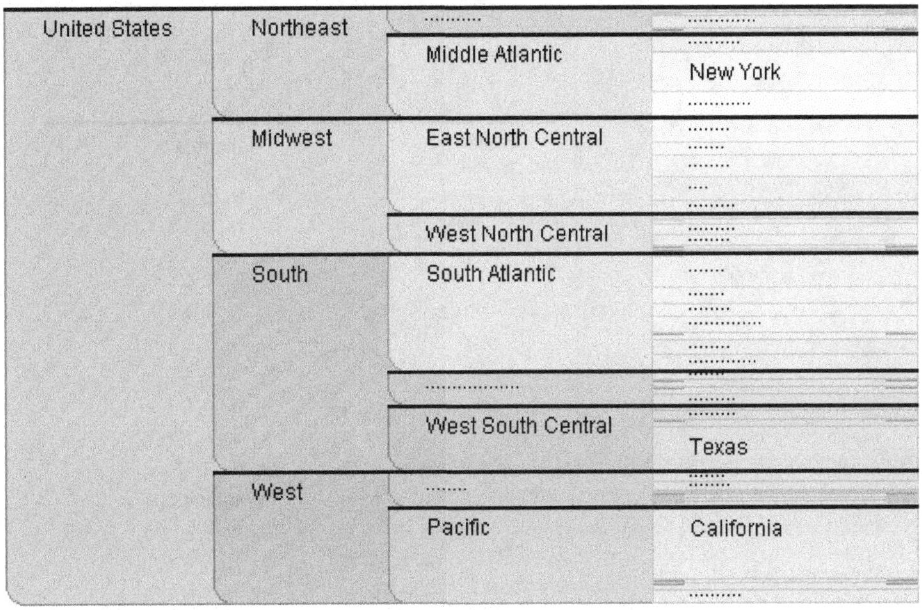

stacked bar chart. Height represents population, boxes represent regions and states. By clicking on the West, would scale the data so that the West filled the available height. In this view, it is apparent that California is more populous than the entire Mountain region.

In case of visualizing the World Wide Web information, one difficulty is representing the quantity of information and its distribution within a set of linked documents. This information along with the type of document such as text, image, audio,....etc. can be helpful on deciding whether a web site may be interesting or useful without spending a great deal of time browsing the deep structure of the site. Nation, Plaisant, Marchionini, Komlodi (1997) developed a tool called WebToc to visualize web sites using a hierarchical table of contents browser it consists of two parts: the parser and the viewer. The parser starts with a web page and follows all the local links generating a hierarchical representation of the documents local to the site. The viewer displays this information as a table of contents for the site using a standard web browser by following the links included in the documents and treating each new set of links as another level of the hierarchy. The lines of text in the web browser each represent a link to a document which may be another web page or a multi-media file such as an image or audio file. In addition, to the lines of text, each local document is represented by a colored line with a length corresponding to the size of the file. The color of the line represents the type of file such as text, image or audio. When a document contains links to other documents, the lines representing the documents it includes can be collapsed into a thicker size bar that shows the total size of the document it references. Each size bar has a shadow under it. The size of the shadow indicates the number of items subordinate to the document it represents. This gives a visual cue to let the user distinguish quickly between items with a few subordinate links or many links. Figure 21 shows a representation of the HCIL Web site using a hierarchical organization which clearly indicates that the largest number of documents is included

Figure 20. Stacked bar focused on the Western United States (Corbett, 2003. Used with permission)

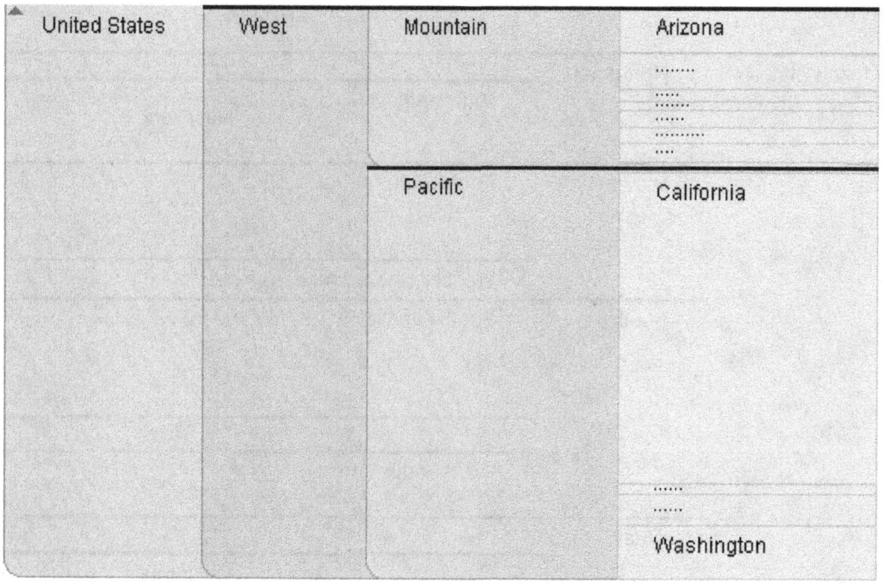

in the Students: Graduate and Undergraduate branch. The message in the status area at the bottom of the browser indicates the actual number of items and size for that branch.

Information Disposition

It is the practice of handling information that is less frequently accessed or has met its assigned retention periods. The information disposition process enables an organization to dispose information which no longer has operational value, either by permitting their destruction or by requiring their transfer to library and archives or by agreeing to their alienation from the control of the organization. Information organization process is used to store this information into libraries or archives.

HUMAN COLLABORATION AND INFORMATION MANAGEMENT

In the previous section we discussed the issues, controversies, and problems facing information management processes within organizations and work teams, and how the hierarchical organization facilitates information management processes to solve these problems better than any other alternative organizations. In this section, we discuss the issues, controversies and problems facing human collaboration and we will show how information management improves the role of collaborators within their work teams.

Figure 21. Representation of the HCIL Web site in hierarchical organization (as adapted from Nation, Plaisant, Marchionini, Komlodi, 1997)

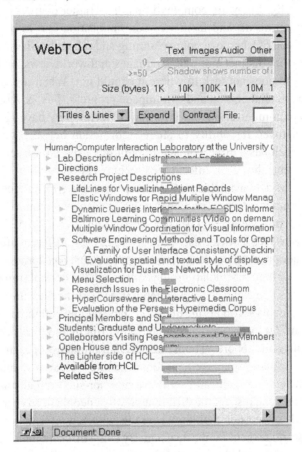

Issues, Controversies and Problems

Two groups of problems are identified: problems of coordination, misinformation and misunderstandings and problems of cultural differences and information security. Greater coordination problems are associated with size, distance, interdependence and scientific competition. Problems of culture and security are associated with size, distance, scientific competition, and commercialization. Email use is associated with reporting fewer coordination problems, but not fewer problems of culture and security, while neither phone use nor face-to-face meetings significantly reduces problems. Group cohesion has an impact on collaboration problems. It is measured in terms of tie strength and consistency with social network theory. A collaboration rich in strong ties will report fewer problems with coordination and misunderstandings. Similarly, groups with many strong ties that are with high cohesion should have fewer problems of trust, security, and cultural differences (Walsh, & Maloney, 2007). Information flow requires links between team members; some argue that loosely linked networks allowing new information to flow (Burt, 1992; Podolny, & Baron, 1997). Others argue that strongly linked networks facilitate information flow especially if they are complex in nature. Higher degrees of group cohesion increase group adherence to group norms and facilitates communication and information flow. Work teams have to decide on a division of labor, overcome planning and scheduling issues, monitor and coordinate progress, possibly deal with distinct cultures, languages and worldviews, and ensure that information flows where it should and does not leak to where it should not. When not carefully controlled, these processes create strain in collaboration and can impede progress (Fox, & Faver, 1984).

Recent advances in communication and information technology have changed the face of human collaboration. They improved the ability to share information between team members at different organizational levels which has a direct impact on building a shared awareness and decision making. Despite these improvements, however, information technology is not without its problems. Because of the tremendous amount of data available, collaboration teams are often faced with information overload. Much of that information comes from open sources such as the internet. As a result, knowledge uncertainty becomes a primary concern (Warner, Letsky, & Cowen, 2005; Warner, Letsky, & Cowen, 2004). On the World Wide Web a novice user finds a difficulty to differentiate between useful and useless information. A major problem is documenting every change has done and tracking every revision needs some consistency or they risk violating rules or loosing the critical trail of work that was part of a work plan. Other problems that can face team collaboration are time pressure and dynamic information. Therefore, our key issue in this section is the question "how human collaboration can be improved using information management"? Information management within the hierarchical organization can help human collaboration by honoring and supporting both integrity and autonomy of each individual. It helps people to communicate well. Information management causes people to have trust, mutual respect, co-creation, empowerment and sufficient communication within a superior-subordinate relationship. Also, decisions can be made in a sense that can respect the different views of people in an organization. Surveys help in using the consensus style of decision making where the collected information are analyzed and moved to upper management to guide them for the decision. By using information management we believe that collaboration is using in a principled way some objective criteria or objective standards to decide what method to use to make decision. There are times when it is appropriate to gather information from the whole group when it's affected, there are times when it's appropriate to delegate and then taking some feedback information when people are going to call you on it.

Solutions and Recommendations

Due to the big advances in information technology as we experience nowadays we can show that the hierarchical organization with its effect on information management processes can significantly improve human collaboration.

In this section, we will discuss the impact of information management processes on human collaboration models. Firstly, we will discus the primary processes that might occur in each collaboration process and then we will discus the effect of information management on the performance of human collaboration models. As suggested by Bolstad, & Endsley, (2005) the primary processes for team collaboration include:

1. **Planning and scheduling:** Planning in hierarchical organization proceeds by decomposing tasks recursively into smaller and smaller subtasks, until primitive tasks which can be performed directly using the planning operators, are reached. For each task, the planner chooses an applicable method, instantiates it to decompose the task into subtasks, and then chooses and instantiates other methods to decompose the subtask even further. If the constraints on the subtasks or the interactions among them prevent the plan from being feasible, the planning system will backtrack and try other methods. The Hierarchical Task Network (HTN) planning method is conceived of as a useful method for web service composition as well as task planning, and several works on the web service composition have been attempted with HTN (Nau., Au, Ilghami, Kuter, Murdoek, Wu, & Yaman, 2003). Many task-oriented objectives can be naturally described with a hierarchical structure. The purpose of a hierarchical task network planner is to produce a sequence of actions that perform some activity or task. Different decompositions of a task are independent so the designer of a method does not have to know how further decompositions it will go. The description of a planning domain includes a set of planning operators and methods, each of which is a prescription of how to decompose a task into its subtasks or smaller tasks. The description of a planning problem contains an initial state as in classical planning and instead of a goal formula there is a partially ordered set of tasks to accomplish. Methods by decomposing tasks recursively into smaller and smaller subtasks, until primitive tasks which can be performed directly using the planning operators are reached. For each task, the planner chooses an applicable method, instantiates it to decompose the task into subtasks, and then chooses instantiates other methods to decompose the subtasks even further. If the constraints on the subtasks or the interactions among them prevent the plan from being feasible, the planning system will backtrack and try other methods. Staff scheduling, also known as workforce allocation, creates schedules that provide the best possible coverage and meet employee preferences (Tiehua Z.; Gruver, W..; Smith, M., 1999). Scheduling assigns a task for each team member for each day and gives information about when a task might be implemented. Scheduling algorithms based on artificial intelligence techniques and algorithms generate an ordered list of activities. A model of the tasks to be scheduled is first generated which describes the possible set of activities, the constraints between those activities, and the resources required for each activity. Several algorithms such as "Automated Scheduling and Planning Environment" (ASPEN) have been implemented for generating initial schedules from the requests, and repairing existing schedules with conflicts. These algorithms are generic and can be used on any given model. The scheduler determines the conflicts in an input schedule of requests and loops through all of the conflicts, trying to resolve each by performing a schedule modification. A conflict in the schedule is simply a violation of one of the resource, state, or temporal constraints defined in the model. The modifications it can perform include moving, adding, and deleting activities (Paul, Kam, & Gregory, 1998).

2. **Tracking information:** Is a type of information that includes identifying information which is distinguishable from the produced information. It is used to track the information as it flows between team members at each stage of the collaboration process or between individuals at different levels of the hierarchical organization. Tracking information can be used to make a complete trace of the processes that contributed to a topic of information's pedigree. Recording such a trace of all the processes upon which information depends may be useful for a variety of reasons, e.g., explaining how results were obtained, vetting results from unknown, untrusted, or unreliable processes, and selecting follow-on tasks to perform (Christopher, William, Paulo, Deborah, David, & Richard, 2005).

3. **Brainstorming:** Helps a team to create a list of tasks when planning for a project, analyzing potential problems and finding creative solutions. It allows for group discussions between team members rather than the opinion of a single person to discus problems, finding possible solutions, choosing the most feasible solution, identifying the most appropriate methods to achieve the goals of a project, and finding the most efficient means and strategies for problem solving and tasks implementation. The results can be uploaded to the team's web site allowing non-member individuals to review and propose amendments. This will help to explore hidden potentials of the project and find numerous possible solutions to the assigned tasks.

4. **Document processing:** A document is a bounded physical representation of information designed with the capacity and intent to communicate. A document may record symbolic, diagrammatic or sensory representational information. To create a document is to edit by collecting and representing information. Conventionally, a document is understood as ink marks on a paper, containing information. Increasingly, documents are also understood as digital documents such as e-mails and reports generated by word processors (Michael, 1997), they are digital artifacts caused by digital encoding of information. The document started as a pending or draft document created by a team member. The supervisor would then approve or reject the document. Once approved, the document is made available in the working development library for other users with security rights. If rejected, the document stayed as pending and was not published for the group to see. Raphael,. Gudula, & Michael (2007) introduced a flexible, adaptable document management system for e-governments to face the challenges of increasing efficiency and quality while decreasing the processing time. This system is based on hierarchical process folders and information security levels. A hierarchical process folder mainly consists of files that belong to a government process and includes all documents processed during process execution. The folder grows during execution and contains all versions of changed, existing, and added documents. This means that the model of hierarchical process folders can be deployed to exchange process folders in whole or in part between authorities to support the execution of distributed hierarchical government processes. With large document processing systems in e-governments the hierarchical design is necessary because parts of the processes are executed on external systems. Instead of copying the overall process to all involved systems only the needed small parts that should be executed have to be available.

5. **Information gathering and retrieval processing:** Possible mechanisms for collecting and sharing of information are manual filing, electronic databases, collaboration software, and management information systems (Anticlue, 2006). Effective information gathering is the most important process an effective team requires. Good quality information marks out the context in which the team operates, creates the information patterns from which ideas emerge, and provides the criteria by which ideas are screened and assessed (MindTools ,2008). Information types that are involved in human collaboration include:
   1. Verbal (Speech) information.
   2. Textual information.
   3. Spatial/graphical information - such as maps or drawings
   4. Emotional information - including fatigue, workload, competence, and anxiety which are often important in team collaboration activities
   5. Photographic information.
   6. Video information.

Effective team members gather two main types of information (MindTools, 2008):

a. **Background information:** This information is made up of the countless facts, trends and opinions that team members encounter and the observations they make on a daily basis. The higher the quality of background information gathered the more accurate their view of the world will be, and the better their judgment and common sense. Background information on the environment the team working in can be gathered using:
   1. Reading newspapers and magazines.
   2. Reading websites.
   3. Talking to people.
b. **Task-related information:** The amount of information required depends on the scale of the decision, the time available, and the consequences of getting it wrong. Talking to experts, knowledgeable people and reading related magazines and brochures in the field are important tools for gathering related information.

6. **Information distribution:** Team collaboration must be characterized by open, timely, and reliable information exchange. The main objective of information distribution is to make sure that the right information is available to the right people at the right time. Information distribution executes the communication plan and responds to the unexpected requests for information. The distribution mechanism can affect the information's usefulness because if it is not timely or comprehended, then it shouldn't have been communicated. Methods of information distribution can be portals, collaborative work management tools, web conferencing, web publishing, and if all this technology is not available, manual filing systems and hard copy distribution are used (Anticlue, 2006). Team members achieving fully integrated collaborative team through information distribution early in the project process are most likely to achieve the desired outcomes: fast, efficient, effective, and cost-bound buildings (CURT, 2004). Such collaboration transfers the bulk of analysis, design, and decision-making earlier in the design process, thus giving the collaborators a good chance for making good decisions. One of the products of information distribution is the information feed-back that catches the project status, issues and progress reports. This information can be used to modify or improve future project performance.

7. **Shared awareness:** Awareness usually refers to the information about the activities of other team members (Dourish, & Belloti, 1992; Gutwin, & Greenberg, 2000; Matsuura, Fujino, Okada, & Matsushita, 1996). Awareness is useful in linking different components of the collaborative system including team members. There are many types of awareness information include:
   a. Activity awareness, which is information about the related activities of other team members. During real-time collaboration, this may simply mean knowing what actions others are taking at any given moment.
   b. Availability awareness, which is information about the physical availability of people and their willingness to social interaction or informal encounters (Tollmar, Sandor, & Schemer, 1996).
   c. Process awareness, which is often found in workflow management systems, where the tasks are usually well defined and represented by a series of sub-tasks. Workflow systems generally assert more control in information flow and the order in which tasks are completed (Prinz, Rodden, Syri, Trevor, & Modeling, 1996).
   d. Perspective awareness, which is not only information about background, beliefs and knowledge, but also information on how particular actions emerged. (Boland, Schwartz, & Tenkasi, 1992; Gutwin, & Greenberg, 2000).

e.   Environmental awareness, which focuses on events occurring outside of the immediate workspace that may have implications over group activities (Fussell, Kraut, Lerch, Scherlis, McNally, & Cadiz, 1998).

To develop shared awareness between team members Bolstad. & Endsley (2005) provided a taxonomy of collaboration tools for information sharing such as face-to-face, video conferencing, audio conferencing, telephone, networked radio, chat/instant messaging, white board, file transfer, program sharing, email, groupware, bulletin board, management information systems and domain specific tools as shared awareness requires integrating information from multiple sources.

HUMAN COLLABORATION MODELS

Several models of team collaboration have been proposed (Orasanu, & Salas, 1992; McNeese, Rentsch, & Perusich, 2000; Cooke, 2005). In this section we will discus some of these models:

a.   Schrage M. (1995) identifies three stages of collaboration
   1.   **The first stage:** Individuals work independently, interacting only at a basic level by sharing information to meet their own specific needs.
   2.   **The second stage:** Individuals engaged in information exchange because of common interests, but not with the intent of achieving a common goal.
   3.   **The third stage:** Individuals work as a team to achieve a common goal by sharing information and, as a result, gain new insights. This is the highest level of collaboration and the focus of most collaboration technology.
b.   A research group identified three distinct stages of collaboration (Ancona, & David, 1990):
   1.   **The creation stage:** Team members meet together to learn about each other and come to agreement about how to proceed. Tasks centered on exploring the problem, possible solutions, and available knowledge and resources. Team members' attention was focused outward, on research activities and networking, and inward, on team building and role clarification (HermanMiller, 2002). Information sharing facilitates team learning while information gathering, retrieval, fusion and exchange facilitate exploring the possible solutions.
   2.   **The intense development stage:** Team members involved in intense interaction, although the team was still drawing on external resources as needed.
   3.   **The diffusion stage:** The team worked to transfer ownership and commitment to others in the organization. The diffusion phase requires members to stay in contact and commitment while being in touch with other outside the team. Focus turned outward, as team bonds began to loosen and individual members were drawn off into other projects (HermanMiller, 2002)
c.   Gutwin & Greenberg (2000) have developed a conceptual framework, the mechanics of collaboration. Their framework suggests that there are two major types of work involved in collaboration: teamwork or the work of working together and task work or the work that carries the task. These types of works imply two main types of activities namely: communication and coordination from which four categories of mechanics are derived:
   1.   **Explicit communication:** It is considered to be fundamental to collaboration, it is essential for identifying the information needs. The purpose of communication is to exchange in-

formation at its best to assure all intended receivers can use the distribution methodology (Anticlue,2006). Four types of communication are involved: spoken, written, gesture and electronic. Electronic communication tools send messages; files, information or documents between people hence facilitate the exchange of information. The team collaborates on a regular basis using communication tools to discuss emerging insights, share feedback information and provide cross-component collaboration.

2. **Information gathering about the group and the activity:** Information gathering must take place for information acquisition. Team members engaged in a new project for an organization might access information resources to learn lessons from similar projects, access relevant information during project implementation to find solutions for problems, and access relevant information afterwards for advice on after-project actions and review activities. Besides retrieving formal information individuals have to gather information from experts on an ad hoc basis. Information gathered from experts is rich in content and suitable for the problem being addressed and suited for people who addressing it. However, you can not capture an expert's insights and experience for future use which results in problems when the expert becomes unavailable or a new solution is required for a new issue. More recently social computing tools such as blogs and wikis have developed to provide a more unstructured, self-governing approach to the transfer, capture and creation of information through the development of new forms of community. These tools face challenges in filtering meaningful re-usable and intelligible information and ensuring that their content is transmissible through diverse channels, platforms and forums. Social computing is defined as any type of computing application that serves as an intermediary or a focus for a social relation, shifting importance away from traditional technologies such as e-mail (Schuler, 1994). Social computing tools can be used in the creation of new information and the transfer of existing ones within collaborative environments such working groups, organizations or community.

3. **Management of shared access or how information accessed and used:** Information access is different from information exchange because team members may have access to information without exchange it. When information is available on an intranet or, in other words, when access to information is established, this is not a guarantee that information exchange will occur. Management of information sources involves management of different types of resources namely, shared repositories, internal, external, primary and secondary information sources, ensuring the information flow in an organization and ensuring access of team members to relevant information. Management of shared access is critical to ensure the distribution of information through the group and to guarantee that the information distribution remains dynamic and oriented toward the needs of specific groups of information users.

4. Transfer of objects and tools between team members to make sure that the task is divided, or roles are switched so that they can achieve the task. This implies two activities: handoff (when an object or tool is transferred) and deposit (when a resource is put in a particular place to retrieve it later) (Bouthillier, & Shearer, 2003).

d. A team collaboration model proposed by Warner, Letsky, & Cowen (2004) focuses on macrocognition and based on information management processes it provides a better context to evaluate collaboration tools, because there is empirical support for their collaboration stages. The model has four unique interdependent stages of team collaboration. Each stage has its own requirements for work tools and environmental support; what helps at one point in the team's life cycle can hinder at another. These four stages are:

1. Team knowledge base construction.
2. Collaborative team problem solving.
3. Team consensus.
4. Outcome evaluation and revision.

Before we discuss in details each of these stages, we want to know what the inputs for that model are.

Model Inputs

The inputs represent general information that is required before team collaboration. This information includes (Warner, Letsky, & Cowen, 2004):

1. A description of the problem to be solved.
2. Team member expertise.
3. Organization structure.
4. Team members' roles and responsibilities.
5. Projected events or future information.
6. Resources available.
7. Supporting collaboration technology.
8. Information certainty.

First Stage

Which is the team knowledge base construction where team members begins by identifying the relevant domain of information required, setting up the communication environment necessary to address the problem, selecting team members and manager, and developing individual and team task knowledge. As mentioned previously, team members should represent a mix of information practitioner communities (e.g., information management, records management, web management, libraries, knowledge management and IT), culturally diverse, having heterogeneous knowledge as well as the technical units of the organization.

This stage has three processes (Warner, Letsky, & Cowen, 2004):

a. **Meta-cognitive process:** Teams with the needed communications connectivity can collaborate effectively if individual team members know what they need to know to develop member's understanding of the elements, relations and conditions that compose the problem. Teams whose members lack this knowledge are prone to various kinds of predictable collaboration problems. Knowledge is central to collaboration and teamwork (Wegner, 1987).

b. **Information processing tasks:** Human collaboration depends on collecting and exchange information to identify the problem to be solved and to understand the problem task. Researchers have sought to understand the potential relationships between information and team performance (Larson, & Christensen, 1993; Grant, 2000). Team members typically tend to proactively seek new information to achieve their joint goals. Some psychological studies about high performing teams have identified the ability to proactively offer information needed by team members as one of the key characteristics of effective team work (Dickinson, & McIntyre, 1997; McIntyre, &Salas, 1995; McIntyre, 1995). Proactive information delivery occurs more frequently when human teams need to filter and fuse an overwhelming amount of information and to make critical decisions under time pressure. Because of the large amount of information available, collaboration teams are often faced with information overload. Much of that information comes from open sources such as the internet. As a result, information uncertainty becomes a primary concern. In addition, some information such as government intelligence is dynamic in nature, and is, therefore, constantly changing. In this case, continually monitoring the flow of information to ensure accurate and timely mission planning and execution becomes mandatory (Warner, Letsky, & Cowen, 2004;Warner, Wroblewski, & Elizabeth, 2004). For instance, applications for dynamic domains often require a large number of intelligent agents and human agents to form a team to cooperate effectively in information gathering, information fusion and information delivery for making better group decisions. Information fusion is used to combine information from different sources in order to facilitate their integration. The collected information may contain a huge amount of useless information which must be removed before it can be verified and stored. Information filtering is used to remove information outliers and construct the team's knowledge base.

c.   **Knowledge required:** Knowledge and understandings are usually distributed among members of a team. Everybody does not need to know everything for a team to be effective. But every team member does need to know how to get the knowledge he or she needs to develop his or her individual knowledge to carry out the task, e.g. the knowledge to support "task work". The team has to establish a combined representation of the team's knowledge of the task, which is the knowledge required for the team members to work together effectively; e.g., the knowledge to support "teamwork." (David N., 2002).

Communication Mechanism for Knowledge Building and Information Processing

For the team to build the required knowledge base needed the team will use the following information management processes (Warner, Letsky, & Cowen, 2004):

a.   Information gathering
b.   Information retrieval
c.   Information fusion or integration
d.   Information organization
e.   Information display and visualization
f.   Information filtering

Specific Communication Mechanisms Between Team Members

These mechanisms include (Warner, Letsky, & Cowen, 2004):

1.   **Presenting individual information:** An individual can use tables to present his information. Tables display key information usually numbers and can form a summary of information, or they

may be a starting point for a negotiation. Percentages, rather than actual numbers, are used to compare between different information groups. Diagrams are a common graphical way of presenting information. Processes and ideas can often be summarized more effectively in diagrammatic form than in words.

2. **Discussing individual and team generated information and possible solutions:** These discussions lead to share ideas and reference documents, stimulate valuable peer-to-peer discussion among decision makers. Create a positive collaboration culture in which team members present their thoughts and gather opinions on how to progress their thinking and in turn improve solutions.

3. **Negotiating perspectives:** Team members should get more accurate information about the problem, tasks and the proposed solutions before negotiation to allow them to make choices and decisions. Transparent and accurate information flow between negotiators of the team elevates the effectiveness of team production such as team assessments, plans and solutions. Also, negotiation creates explicit rules for operations and routines for management and hence has a direct impact on team collaboration. Team performance is expected to benefit from negotiation.

4. **Questioning:** Questions are designed to support monitoring tests of the proposed solutions, so that teams can spot opportunities to engage in collaborative critical thinking and avoid needless debates.

5. **Agreement:** An agreement between team works will deepen their information exchange on a confidential basis, enables them to accessing documents, formalizes and strengthens the ongoing collaboration between them. An agreement represents a valuable coordination of the roles of team members to better perform their responsibilities. In case of exchanging confidential information, a receiving team should maintain the security of this information using a reasonable standard of protection, and no less than the standard of protection taken to protect his own confidential information, and will use such confidential information solely for the purposes of implementing his assigned tasks in the collaboration agreement. When confidential information is no longer required for purposes of a collaboration agreement and continued use of confidential information is not provided for another collaboration agreement, each receiving team should return or dispose of any tangible records of confidential information.

6. **Disagreement:** Team leaders and members use disagreement within the group as an indicator for conflicting interpretations should be resolved, that the relevancy and accuracy of assumptions and paradigms should be tested, and that uniquely held information should be shared. Disagreements are pointers to uncertainty in the assessments and plans the team generates. Proficient teams use disagreement as an indicator when they monitor the need to engage in collaborative critical thought (Jared, & Kathleen, 2003).

The following collaboration capabilities are required to facilitate the team using the above mechanisms during this stage are (Warner, Letsky, & Cowen, 2004):

1. **Explicit communication:** Explicit communication can significantly multiply the capabilities and effectiveness of team works. It requires explicit signaling and reception of the communicated information. It refers to the things we say or write, often messages intended to influence the behavior of others (Robert ,2007)

2. **Information exchange:** Team members should be able to exchange information freely with other team members either upon request or spontaneously. This exchange should produce any available information that may be relevant to an analysis or investigation of the problem and other relevant information and the persons or work teams involved. Information exchanged between individuals should be used only for the specific purpose for which the information was sought or provided.

3. **Conventions for information exchange:** Exchange information with the others should be on the basis of reciprocity or mutual agreement and consistent with procedures understood by the requested and requesting party. A party requesting information should disclose, to the party that will process the request, at a minimum the reason for the request, the purpose for which the information will be used and enough information to enable the receiving party to determine whether the request complies with its domestic law. Information exchanged between parties may be used only for the specific purpose for which the information was sought or provided.

The requesting party may not transfer information shared by a disclosing party to a third party, nor make use of the information in an administrative, investigative, prosecutorial, or judicial purpose without the prior consent of the party that disclosed the information (Egmont Group, 2001).

Second Stage

Which is the collaborative team problem solving where the majority of collaboration occurs among team members. This stage also includes three processes (Warner, Letsky, & Cowen, 2004):

a. **Meta-cognitive process:** Where the team develops a mental representation of how to solve the problem. This stage includes three related mental process:
    1. Selective encoding where information filtering process is used to revise the collected information to eliminate more irrelevant information.
    2. Selective combination where information fusion process is used to put together elements of the problem or the task.
    3. Selective comparison where data mining processes can discover non-obvious relationship between new information and information acquired in the past. Using information exchange the team gains more complete understanding of task elements, goals or overlooked information.
b. **Information processing tasks:** The information-processing model developed by (Bouthillier & Shearer, 2003) suggests a number of activities that would require collaboration and, by definition, information retrieval and exchange.
c. **Knowledge required:**
    Five types of knowledge are required at this stage (Warner, Letsky, & Cowen ,2004):
    1. Team member has to develop his or her individual knowledge through accessing relative information in the knowledge base. Information filtering facilitates accessing relative information. Information fusion helps a team member integrates between retrieved information from multiple knowledge bases.
    2. The team as a whole has to develop team's knowledge of the task through information exchange and distribution and integration.

3. The team needs to develop shared understanding of the problem to be solved or the task to be completed. Shared understating is achieved through the communication of large amount of information and a set of shared information, information visualization, shared beliefs, joint agreements of the facts, perspectives and assumptions that collaborators have.

4. Collaborative knowledge: is an informal type of information which results from team discussions, brainstorming, information exchange and integration, information display and visualization processes which could result in new information which deepens team understanding of the problem and agreement of the facts. The produced informal information should be codified and structured to facilitate information processing sequences.

5. Domain experts are another type of informal information which is needed by team members to complete their task. Interviews, questionnaires and surveys are helpful to collect this type of information. Emailing an expert can be used on ad hoc bases.

Communication Mechanism for Knowledge Building and Information Processing:

In this stage the team will use some or all of the communications mechanisms discussed later to perform knowledge building. The following collaboration capabilities are required to facilitate the team using the above mechanisms during this stage are (Warner, Letsky, & Cowen, 2004):

1. **Agent-based structural collaboration model:** Is a loosely-coupled network of several, autonomous and interacting software agents which are problem solvers that work together to solve some problems being above their individual capabilities. The sum of several interacting agents' capabilities in a multi-agent system exceeds the sum of its individual parts (BileK, & Hartmann, 2003). The adaptation of agent technologies to the specific needs and requirements of collaborative work implicitly requires the decomposition of the entire problem solving process into adequate, domain-specific interacting agents.

2. **Information retrieval, fusion and presentation:** The team uses the information retrieval, fusion and visualization processes to reach a shared understanding about the problem at hand which helps the team to build its knowledge base.

3. **Critical thinking and negotiation:** If team members sense uncertainty and the stakes are high they engage in critical thinking about their assessments and plans by negotiating their understanding of the situation at hand, refining their knowledge, and adapting their decision making and planning to the problems at hand. Identify sources of uncertainty (i.e., gaps, untested assumptions, and conflicting interpretations), and reduce or shift that uncertainty   disseminate information, testing assumptions, and forming contingency plans before taking action. Negotiation occurs through explicit communication and the reliance on shared information, shared interpretations of information patterns, and standardized responses to those patterns(Jared, & Kathleen, 2003).

4. **Knowledge retrieval among team members:** Perceived interdependent information sharing, information retrieval within a team's knowledge network and perceptions of knowledge interdependence affect members' satisfaction with the team's overall performance (Palazzolo, & Clark, 2007). Information sharing between team members enhances existing collaborative processes, introduces more efficient and effective collaborative processes and removes redundant processes.

5. **Identification of team differences:** The aim of team identification is to encourage dissimilar individuals to behave according to team norms and conventions, in order to gain acceptance in the

team (Branscombe, Ellemers, Spears, & Doosje,1999) and to mitigate the negative effects of diversity. At the team level diversity refers to the amount of variance in demographic e.g. age, gender, professional background characteristics or values. Research into dissimilarity provides insight into an individual's experience of being different from other team members, and how these differences affect their individual behaviors and attitudes (Chattopadhyay, 1999; Jackson, Brett, Sessa, Cooper, Julin, & Peyronnin, 1991; O'Reilly, Caldwell, & Barnett, 1989; Tsui, Egan, & O'Reilly, 1992). Mary (2007) posed the following questions about conflicts within team members: how frequently team members disagree about the content of the team's decisions. How frequently were there disagreements about the ideas generated by the team? How often were there differences of opinion in the team? How often did people in your group disagree regarding the group's decisions cohesion? The answers to these questions provide a picture of the team cohesion or dissimilarity.

6. **Joint information visualization:** Is a collaboration visualization using the visualization techniques in order to display shared information between team members; information from different resources is fused together and joint visualization helps to combine all this information for interpretation it is indispensable to share visualization results (Suzuki, Matsumoto, & Sai, 2004).

7. **Hidden knowledge elicitation:** Much expert knowledge is implicit and difficult to articulate and express directly. In order to address the problems of implicit and hidden knowledge, the knowledge engineering community has borrowed techniques from experimental psychology, designed to access internal mental structures. These techniques, termed indirect knowledge elicitation techniques which are: repertory grid analysis, multi-dimensional scaling, and hierarchical clustering. These techniques are used in situations where it is difficult for the expert to articulate their knowledge in response to direct questions (Hudlicka, 1996).

Third Stage

Is team consensus and begins after the problem has been identified and team members exchange ideas to clarify issues and have several solution alternatives to the problem. The main objective of team consensus is to reach consensus to decide which steps to use to achieve team agreement of the common output. This stage has also three processes (Warner, Letsky, & Cowen, 2004):

a. **Meta-cognitive process:** Includes team keep tracking of what they have done, what they are currently doing and what need to be done in the future.

b. **Information processing tasks:** Team negotiation is performed through the information presentation of solution alternatives and exchange comments and beliefs in order for the team to achieve agreement of the common output and to develop a unified team mental model.

c. **Knowledge Requirement:** Two types of knowledge are required to achieve convergence of the team's mental model and successful negotiation of solution alternatives:

   1. **Shared understanding:** It is a shared knowledge base required for cooperative problem solving which contains knowledge of a problem or domain that is common to team collaborators. The knowledge contained in the shared knowledge base does not have to be explicitly communicated.

   2. **Collaborative knowledge:** It is an informal type of information which results from team discussions, brainstorming, information exchange and integration, information display and visualization processes which could result in new information which clarifies and deepens

team understanding of the several solution alternatives to the problem. The produced informal information should be codified and structured to facilitate information processing sequences.

Communication Mechanism for Knowledge Building and Information Processing

In this stage the team will use some or all the communication mechanisms mentioned earlier in this chapter. The following collaboration capabilities are required to facilitate the team using the above mechanisms (Warner, Letsky, & Cowen, 2004):

1. **Visual representation of the team's mental model:** Mental models vary somewhat, but are generally viewed as organized and integrated memory structures used to comprehend a given phenomenon (Johnson-Liard, 1983). Regardless of the exact nature of a mental model, visual representations play a crucial role in shaping and communicating mental models. Researchers suggest that, because diagrams are external and often analogical representations of information presented in the text, they may facilitate the development of mental models associated with the content of that text. Visualization support negotiators' convergence of perceptions of reality and has positive socio-emotional consequences in terms of increasing cohesiveness. As a result groups with visualization support reach consensus more easily and are more satisfied with the process (Roderick, Tom, Peter, Marius, & Adrie, 2002).

2. **Agent based identification of team differences:** Team members in general differ in their skills and in the way they perceive the external environment. One of the key assets of based identification of team differences is that agents simulate as faithfully as possible, all that is known or inferred about the behavior of human collaborators and their actions in collaborating sessions with their suitability to adapt themselves to any individual's particular skills, knowledge and personal characteristics. This adaptability can be only reached through a proper human collaborator modeling by every collaborator agent. The basic view underlying the agent-based identification team differences is that agents are embedded in a social frame that regulates their behavior. This social frame, called role space, is composed of roles which are available to the agents and through which an agent can try to achieve individual and joint objectives either alone or in collaboration with other agents. An agent may own several roles and a role may be owned by several agents at the same time. Roles serve as a means for specifying desired behavior and for achieving behavioral predictability, but not as a means for making sure that agents do never exhibit unexpected and undesirable behavior. In particular, roles do not fully constrain individual behavior, but leave room for individuality (Gerhard, Matthias, Michael, & Felix, 2004). With that, system designer can explicitly specify the limits within which human collaborators simulated by collaborator agents are supposed to act and to predict the expected differences between human collaborators.

    1. **Joint information visualization:** Is a collaborative visualization using the visualization techniques in order to discus experimental results or simulation results of alternative solutions in the joint research between remote locations; information from different resources is fused together and joint visualization helps to combine all this information for interpretation, it is also indispensable at this stage to share visualization results (Suzuki, Matsumoto, & Sai, 2004).

2. **Infrastructure for negotiation:** The infrastructure supporting negotiation between collaborators within work teams requires combining different technologies, such as software engineering techniques, middleware-level coordination facilities and multi-agent systems support.

Fourth Stage

It is outcome evaluation and revision which is the final stage of collaboration. The main objective is to analyze, test and validate the agreement upon team solution against the goal requirements and exit criteria. Included in this stage is an iteration loop for deriving other solutions for the problem if necessary.

This stage has also three processes (Warner, Letsky, & Cowen, 2004):

a. **Meta-cognitive process:** This process involves comparing problem solution against the goals. Information display and visualization is important in this stage to present the solution against the goals. Also, information exchange is required to negotiate these results.

b. **Information processing task:** In this process the team analyses and revises the problem solution if necessary. Information retrieval, exchange and visualization processes are required.

c. **Knowledge required:** Two types of knowledge are required:

   1. **Goal requirements:** Goals for a desired system are often not clear at the outset they must be extracted from diverse sources of information. It is important to gather as much information as possible in order to obtain a broad understanding of the domain, organization, process and system. A team must have the ability to store, share and display this information for the purpose of identifying, organizing and classifying goals. It is unreasonable to expect to produce a complete set of goals for a system from only one information source. Fusion or integration of various information sources produce a more complete set of goals especially if they incorporate the analysis of both the current and desired system. Goal information must ultimately be translated into requirements specification. A requirement places a condition on the achievement of a goal. A precondition must exist for the achievement of a goal to be possible. The post-condition characterizes the state of the system once the goal is completed. These are done by consolidating the goal information into a set of goal schemas. Goal schemas specify the relationships between goals and agents in terms of events that cause a change of state. Agents are the entities or processes that seek to achieve goals within an organization or system based on the implicit responsibility that they must assume for the achievement of certain goals (Annie, 1996).

   2. **Exit criteria for viable solutions:** Are the criteria or requirements which must met to complete a specific process. When testing the product of a proposed solution, a set of test specifications are created to test these products to ensure that it meets minimum acceptable operational specifications. This test specification will state the minimum criteria necessary for the testing process to be considered complete and the products are of acceptable quality.

Model Output

The output of the model reflects the type of product from team collaboration process. The product type will vary depending on the problem domain addressed by the team.

The product types are (Warner, Letsky, & Cowen, 2004):

1. **Selected course of action:** Shared understanding among team members with regard to the impact, importance, and quality of relevant information items such sensor outputs, text documents, images, messages and Web pages is a critical element in the selection of an effective course of action (Michael B., & Robert A., 2005). It is important to decide what the minimum information that needs to be exchanged for shared understanding to occur, how do we capture that information an how should it best be displayed or visualized.

2. **Recommendations:** Are team suggestions given to the users to help them solving a problem or to implement a proposed solution.

3. **Situation awareness:** Is an important element to support responses and decision making to problems. Decision making for a complex situation often needs a team to work cooperatively to get consensus assessment for the situation. Team situation assessment is characterized including information sharing, opinion integration and consensus situation assessment generation. In the meantime, various uncertainties are involved in team situation assessment during information collection and awareness generation. Also, the collaboration between team members may be across distances and need web-based technology to facilitate it (Jie, Guangquan, & Fengjie, 2008).

4. **Risk assessment:** Is the ability and motivation to look ahead and to handle risks before they become problems. Provide feedback information both internal and external to the project on the risk activities, current risks and emerging risks. Identifying changes and group risks, quantity impact, probability, and time frame and set program priorities to arrive at a joint understanding of what is important. Processing risk information into decision-making information to determine what is important to the project, to set priorities, and to allocate resources. Communication occurs formally as well as informally.

5. **Product or tool:** A team work may recommend a product or tool to solve a problem or to implement a proposed solution.

6. **Opinion:** Team members often want to exchange opinion on their files or on the project as a whole. Email is one way to do this.

7. **Guidelines:** These guidelines are intended to assist and guide members in the workplace in relation to specific issues. They specify requirements to implement a recommended solution on a specific problem. Guidelines are also intended to complement the development of local workplace policies and protocols on professional issues. Draft guidelines are developed by the work team and subjected to internal comment and review by team members, and then they are submitted to the team leader for approval before becoming available to the upper management.

FUTURE TRENDS

IBM predicted five future trends that will increase demand for the fast growing unified communications market and reshape the way businesses and workers communicate and collaborate worldwide.

These five future trends as stated by IBM are (Bill, 2008):

1. The collaborative virtual workplace will become the rule where teams can communicate, collaborate, and share information, regardless of their geographic location. Social networking tools and virtual world meeting experiences will simulate the feeling on being there in-person. Work models will be changed to encourage work at home to reduce travel.

2. Instant messaging and other real time collaboration tools will become the norm. As the email became a necessity instant messaging will be the preferred method of business interaction. Skype is a good example of a tool for instant messaging and voice over IP.

3. Interoperability and open standards will destroy the barriers between business and public domains and force unified communications providers to embrace interoperability. This will help businesses and persons to better find appropriate resources thus removing inefficiencies from business processes and daily lives.

4. Companies will tend to deep integrate with business processes and line-of business applications where they can realize the greatest benefit. For example, Skype makes efforts to integrate its product with other software applications such as Microsoft Outlook or Mozilla FireFox, where users can use an integrated toolbar to locate the sender of an e-mail or a person whose Skype ID is mentioned on the web (Ned, 2008).

5. New meeting models will emerge and the definition of meetings will be radically changed and become increasingly ad hoc and instantaneous based on context and need. Virtual reality technology will deeply impact online meeting experiences to deliver more life-like experiences to next generation collaborators who will operate efficiently in the familiar environment.

Currently there is no generalized model of human collaboration that combines the various collaborative services and provides a common language and framework for those seeking to better understand and expand the collaborative aspects of any given field of human endeavor. Such model would provide a body of knowledge for those developing collaborative software and other design based enterprises to draw on. The generalized model should include both qualitatively and quantitatively the team social behavior such as motivation, the way people interact, emotional information and issues of cultural change and a willingness to share and collaborate with colleagues which is not included in the current team collaboration models, despite it has a significant effect on human collaboration with team work. The field of human collaboration is now mature and a standardization of its metrics is required. A standardized collaborative index to evaluate the quality of team collaboration at each of its stages is required. We propose a metric called the collaboration coefficient to measure the degree of collaboration between working groups. This coefficient ranges from 0 (no collaboration) that is team members are working in isolation all the time to 1 (full collaboration) that is team members are working in collaboration all the time. This measure is simple:

$$\text{Collaboration coefficient } (CC) = \frac{\text{Total time spent in collaboration}}{\text{Total time of the project}}$$

For example, if a work team is composed of three members say i, j and k then the collaborative coefficient is measured as follows:

$$CC = \frac{T_{ij} + T_{jk} + T_{ki} + T_{ijk}}{T} \tag{1}$$

$$T = T_{ij} + T_{jk} + T_{ki} + T_{ijk} + T_{i} + T_{j} + T_{k} \tag{2}$$

$$T_{ij}, T_{jk}, T_{ki}, T_{ijk} < T$$

Where T_{ij}: time spent in collaboration between i and j.

T_{ik}: time spent in collaboration between i and k.

T_{jk}: time spent in collaboration between j and k.

T_{ijk}: time spent in collaboration between i, j and k.

T_i, T_j, T_k: time spent by members i, j and k working in isolation respectively.

T: time spent to complete the whole project.

Our measure differs from that mentioned by (Ajiferuke, 1988) in that our collaboration coefficient depends mainly on time as a factor for measuring collaboration while that used by Ajiferuke depends mainly on the number of collaborators in a project. We believe that a combination between the two measures will give a more realistic value for collaboration. It is important to discuss if there is an optimum collaboration size for how many collaborators working together? If so, what is this size? This metric is also a measure for the complexity of the potential division of labor and communication channels (March, & Simon, 1958), as well as the difficulty of monitoring team members; information security becomes particularly problematic as collaboration size increases (Baker, & Faulkner, 1993). We believe that if the number of collaborators exceeds the optimum number then some of the team members can be nonproductive or impeding. A standardized metric to measure the degree of group cohesion is important in team collaboration. As the group becomes more diverse, it becomes increasingly difficult to count on shared understandings to solve problems as they occur (Rothschild-Whitt, 1979). It is important to develop guidelines for selecting the right team members, providing the right kind of training, and selecting the right types of collaboration tools to improve team collaboration.

CONCLUSION

In this chapter we have showed that the hierarchical organization is more efficient for the management of information processes rather than other alternative organizations such as flat, linear and network organizations. We also showed that using the hierarchical organization facilitates information retrieval through the efficient classification of information topics.

The hierarchical organization is efficient in information gathering, and it is the best for both information routing and large scale networks. The problem of information overload is efficiently reduced through building information filters and bookmarks that are organized hierarchically. In information organization hierarchical bookmarks facilitate organizing the information on the World Wide Web also people are familiar with the hierarchical organization and can easily understand the hierarchical relationships between information topics. The hierarchical organization makes adding, modification or deletion of information topics efficient and guarantees their integrity and consistency. We showed the hierarchical organization facilitates information feedback through a cyclic bottom-up and top-down operations through examples from our daily life and from the field of artificial intelligence where the performance of artificial neural networks increases if it is organized hierarchically and applied the feed forward back propagation learning algorithm. In information fusion the hierarchical organization increases the fidelity and availability of information within the organization. In problem decomposition the hierarchical organization simplifies a large problem by dividing it into well defined sub-problems which are solved at the lower level and the solution is reassembled at the higher levels. Also, hierarchical organization facilitates information exchange across the hierarchical levels of the organization and across the Internet using multi-agent based systems. In information visualization we showed the hierarchical organization is very effective in displaying hierarchical information, Web pages and multidimensional information organized hierarchically. In human collaboration, we showed that information management improved the interaction between team members at the four collaborative stages of the cognitive collaboration information based model. In the first stage the team collects and exchange information to identify the problem to be solved and to understand the problem task. In the second stage the team needs information filtering, fusion or integration and data mining processes to develop a mental representation of how to solve the problem. Each team member has to develop his or her knowledge through accessing relative information. The team as a whole has to develop its knowledge and reach a shared understanding through information exchange. In the third stage the team is trying to reach a consensus about a solution therefore they need to exchange ideas and display information. Two types of knowledge are required in this stage which is shared understanding and collaborative knowledge. The fourth stage is outcome evaluation and revision, two knowledge types are required which are goal requirements and exit criteria for viable solutions.

REFERENCES

Aaron, C., Cristopher, M., & Newman, M. (May 2008), Hierarchical structure and the prediction of missing links in networks. *Nature, 453*, 98-101.

Abrams, D., Baecker, R., & Chignell, M. (1998). Information archiving with bookmarks: personal web space construction and organization. *Proceedings of the SIGCHI Conference on Human Factors in Computing Systems* (pp. 41-48). ACM Press/Addison-Wesley Publishing Co., New York, NY, USA.

Aggarwal, S., Hung, F., & Weiyi, M. (25-28 August 1998). WIRE-a WWW-based information retrieval and extraction system. *Proceedings of Ninth International Workshop on Database and Expert Systems Applications,* (pp. 887 - 892).

Ajiferuke, L., Burrel, Q., & Tague, J. (1988). Collaborative Coefficient: A Single Measure of the Degree of Collaboration in Research. *Scientometrics, 14,* 421-433.

Alberts, D., Garstka, J. Hayes, R., & Signori, D. (2001). *Understanding Information Age Warfare.* Command and Control Research Program. Washington DC.

Allanna, J., Tullahoma, M., Robert, M., & Craig, T. (March 27-31, 1989). A hierarchical data structure representation for fusing multi-sensor information. *SPIE Technical symposia on Aerospace Sensing* Orlando, FA.

Almendral, A., López, L., Mendes, F., & Sanjuán, F. (2003). Modeling Of Complex Systems: Seventh Granada Lectures. *AIP Conference Proceedings, 661,* 253-253.

Ancona, D., & David, C. (1990), Information Technology and Work Groups: The Case of New Product Teams. *Intellectual Teamwork: social and technological foundations of cooperative work,* (pp. 173-190).

Andriessen, & Erik, J. (2003). *Working with groupware: understanding and evaluating collaboration technology.* London: Springer.

Anne S. (2008). *Collaboration for Victims'. National Victim Assistance Academy Textbook.* Retrieved 5 November 2008 from http://www.ojp.usdoj.gov/ovc/assist/nvaa2000/academy/chap19.htm

Annie I. (1996). Goal-Based Requirements Analysis. *IEEE Proceedings of ICRE* '96 (pp. 136-144).

Anticlue (2006). *Information Distribution.* Retrieved 5 November 2008 from http://www.anticlue.net/archives/000804.htm

Asahi, T. Turo,D. & Sheiderman, B.i,(December 1995). Using treemaps to visualize the analytic hierarchy process. *Information Systems Research, 6*(4), 357-375.

Attewell, P., & Rule, J. (1984). Computing and Organizations: What We Know and What We Don't Know. *Communications of the ACM, 27*(12), 128-136. 4.

Awerbuch, B., Du Y., & Shavittb, Y. (2000). The effect of network hierarchy structure on performance of ATM PNNI hierarchical routing. *Computer Communications, 23*(10), 980-986.

Baker, W., & Faulkner, R. (1993). The social organization of a conspiracy. *American Sociological Review, 58*(6), 837-860.

Barreau, D. (1995). Context as a Factor in Personal Information Management Systems. *Journal of the American Society for Information Science, 46*(5), 327-339.

Bergman, O., Beyth-Marom, R., & Nachmias, R. (2006). The Project Fragmentation Problem in Personal Information Management. *In Proceedings of the SIGCHT conference on human factors in computing systems,* (pp. 271-274).

Bilek, J., & Hartmann, D. (2003). Development of an Agent-based Workbench supporting Collaborative Structural Design. *Proc. of the 20th CIB W78 Conference on Information Technology in Construction* (pp. 39-46).Waiheke Island, New Zealand.

Bill, D. (March 31st 2008). *IBM predicts demise of traditional offices.* Retrieved 24 August 2008 form http://blogs.techrepublic.com.com/wireless/?p=222

Blake, M., & Cabri, G. (June 2003). Agent-based Computing for Enterprise Collaboration. What Agents Can Learn from Human Collaboration? *Proceedings of the WETICE2003: The 2003 Workshops on Enabling Technologies: Infrastructure for Collaborative Enterprises,* (pp. 21-23). IEEE Press.

Boardman, R., Spence, R., & Sasse, M. (2003). Too Many Hierarchies? The Daily Struggle for Control of the Workspace. *In Proceedings of HCI international,* (pp. 16-620)11.

Boland, R., Schwartz, G., & Tenkasi, R. (November 1992). Sharing perspectives in distributed decision making. *In Proceedings of CSCW '92*, Toronto Canada, ACM Press, (pp. 306-313).

Bolstad, C., & Endsley, R. (2005). Choosing Team Collaboration Tools: Lessons from Disaster Recovery Efforts. *Ergonomics in Design, 13*, 7-14.

Borgman, C., Bates M., Cloonan, M., Efthimiadis, E., Gilliland-Swetland, Kafai, A., Leazer, Y. G. L. & Maddox, A. (1996). Social Aspects of Digital Libraries. Final Report to the National Science Foundation; Computer. Information Science, and Engineering Directorate; Division of Information, Robotics, and Intelligent Systems; Information Technology and Organizations Program. Retrieved 15 July 2008, from http://is.gseis.ucla.edu/research/dl/index.html.

Bouthillier, F., & Shearer, K. (2003). Assessing Collaborative Tools from an Information-Processing Perspective: Identification of Value-Added Processes. *Proceedings of the Twelfth IEEE International Workshops on Enabling Technologies: Infrastructure for Collaborative Enterprises (WETICE'03)*

Branscombe, N., Ellemers, N., Spears, R., & Doosje, B. (1999). The context and content of social identity threat. In N. Ellemers, R. Spears, & B. Doosje (Eds.), *Social identity: Context, commitment,content* (pp. 35-58). Oxford, UK: Blackwell Science.

Brian, J., & Shneiderman, B. (22-25 October 1991). Tree-maps: a space-filling approach to the visualization of hierarchical information structures (pp. 284-291). *Proceedings of IEEE Conference on Visualization Publication*

British Columbia Province (10 October 2003). Records Management in the system development life cycle. Retrieved 2 November 2008, from http://*www.cio.gov.bc.ca/other/daf/recmgmt_sdlc_v1-6.pdf*

Burt, R. (1992). *Structural Holes*. Cambridge, MA: Harvard Press.

Castineyra, I., Chiappa, J., & Steenstrup, M. (February 1996). The nimrod routing architecture, Internet Draft, Nimrod Working Group.

Chattopadhyay, P. (1999). Beyond direct and symmetrical effects: The influence of demographic dissimilarity on organizational citizenship behavior. *Academy of Management Journal, 42*, 273-287.

Chen, J., Wolfe, S., & Wragg, S. (2000). A Distributed Multi-Agent System for Collaborative Information Management and Sharing. *In 9th International Conference on Information and Knowledge Management (CIKM-00)* MacLean, VA.

Christopher, W., William, M., Paulo, S., Deborah, L., David, F., & Richard, F. (2005). Tracking Information Extraction from Intelligence Documents. *International Conference on Intelligence Analysis,* McLean, VA.

CipherOptics (2008). Secure information sharing. Retrieved 13 November 2008 from http://www.cipheroptics.com/securitysolutions/secure-information-sharing.html

Clemons, E., Reddi, S., & Row, M. (1993). The impact of information technology on the organization of economic activity: The "move to the middle" hypothesis. *Journal of Management Information Systems: Jmis, 10*(2), 9-35.

Cooke, N. (January 2005). *Measuring collaborative cognition.* Collaboration and knowledge management workshop proceedings, San Diego, CA.

Corbett, J. (2003). *Size Trees: augmenting hierarchies to aid size comparisons between   categories and   individuals.* Retrieved 25 July, 2008, from http://www.pictographer.com/sizetree/index.html

CURT (2004). *Collaboration, Integrated Information, and the Project Lifecycle in Building Design, Construction and Operation.* Retrieved 6 November 2004 from *www.eua.com/pdf/resources/integrated_project/Construction_Users_Round_Table.pdf*

David N. (2002). *A Cognitive Description of Collaboration and Coordination to Help Teams Identify and Fix Problems.* Retreived 13 November 2008 from http://www.stormingmedia.us/authors/Noble__David.html

Dickinson, T., & McIntyre, R. (1997). A conceptual framework for teamwork measurement. In M. T. Brannick, E. Salas, & C. Prince (Eds.), *Team performance assessment and measurement: theory, methods and applications,* (pp. 19-44), Hillsdale, NJ:Erlbaum.

Dourish, P., Edwards, W., LaMarca, A., & Salisbury, M. (1999). Presto: An Experimental   Architecture for Fluid Interactive Document Spaces. *ACM Transactions on Computer-Human Interaction, 6(2),* 133-161).

Dourish, P., & Bellotti, V. (November 1992). Awareness and coordination in shared workspace. In *Proceedings of CSCW '92* (pp. 107-114), Toronto Canada: ACM Press.

Egmont Group (2001). *Principles for Information Exchange between Financial Intelligence Units for Money Laundering and Terrorism Financing Case.* Retrieved July 25, 2008, from http://www.egmontgroup.org/princ_info_exchange.pdf .

Enrique, J., Duarte M., & Mingyan L. (15 November 2003).   Data-gathering wireless sensor networks: organization and capacity. *Computer Networks 43(4),* 519-537.

Eylon, B., & Reif, F. (April 8-12, 1979). *Effects of Internal Knowledge Organization on Task Performance.* Paper presented at the Annual Meeting of the American Educational Research Association 63rd, San Francisco, California.

Zhao, F., Shin J., & Reich J., (March 2002). Information-driven dynamic sensor collaboration for tracking applications. *IEEE Signal Processing Magazine, 19(2),* pp.61-72.

Fountain, J. (August 2007). Challenges to Organizational Change:Multi-Level Integrated Information Structures (MIIS). *Paper presented at the annual meeting of the American Political Science Association, Hyatt Regency Chicago and the Sheraton Chicago Hotel and Towers, Chicago, IL* Online <APPLICATION/PDF> Retrieved 15 August 2008 from http://www.allacademic.com/meta/p210129_index.html

Fox, M., & Faver, C. (1984). Independence and cooperation in research. *Journal of Higher Education, 55(3),* 347-359.

Fred, F. (2006). *An Ontology-Driven Model for the Efficient Use of Provenance Information.* Retrieved 15 July, 2008, from http://www.personal.psu.edu/facultv/f/u/fuf1/publications/fonseca NCSA.pdf.

Fussell, S., Kraut, R., Lerch, F., Scherlis, W., McNally, M., & Cadiz, J. (November 1998). Coordination, overload and team performance: Effects of team communication strategies. *In Proceedings of CSC W '98* (pp. 275-284). Seattle, WA: ACM Press.

Gemmell, J., Bell, G., Lueder, R., Drucker, S., & Wong, C. (2002). MyLifeBits: Fulfilling the Memex Vision. *In Proceedings of the 10th ACM international conference on multimedia* (pp. 235-238).

Gemmy, A. (2002). *Supervision.* Retrieved 6 October 2008 from http://ollie.dcccd.edu/MGMT1374/book_intro.html

George, W. (1986). Generalized fisheye views *In Pro- Factors in Computing Systems, Visualizing Complex Information Spaces*, (pp. 16-23).

Gerhard, W., Matthias, N., Michael, R., & Felix, F. (2004). Specifying the Intertwining of Cooperation and Autonomy in Agent-based Systems. *International Journal of Computer and Information Science, 5*(2):73-88.

Gifford, D., Jouvelot, P., Sheldon, M., & OToole, J. (1991). Semantic File Systems. *In Proceedings of the 13th ACM symposium on operating systems principles,* (pp. 16-25).

Gollmann, D. (1999). *Computer Security.* Chichester, England: John Wiley & Sons.

Gopal, B., & Manber, U. (1999). Integrating Content-Based Access Mechanisms with Hierarchical File Systems. *In Proceedings of the 3rd symposium on operating systems design and implementation* (pp.265-278).

Grant, J. (2000). Proactive behavior in organization. *Journal of management, 26*(3), 435-462.

Gutwin, C., & Greenberg, S. (June 14-16 2000). The Mechanics of Collaboration: developing low cost usability evaluation methods for shared workspaces. *IEEE 9th international workshop on enabling technologies: infrastructure for collaborative enterprises*, NIST, Gaithersburg, MD USA.

Haiying, T., Jeffrey, A., Satnam, S., Krishna, R., & Peter, W. (November 2006). Information Integration via Hierarchical and Hybrid Bayesian Networks, Systems, Man and Cybernetics, Part A. *IEEE Transactions on 36*(6), 1257-1268.

Hammond, T., Hannay, T., Lund, B., & Scott, J. (April 2005). Social book marking tools (I) – A General Review. *D-Lib Magazine 11*(4).

Hector, S. (to appear). Biotic Feedback: Priority and supremacy in Nature, science and Society. *Part of the series Bios and the Cybernetics of creative system, special issue for cybernetics and semiotics edited by Hector Sabelli.*

Heinzelman, W., Chandrakasan, A., & Balakrishnan, H. (2000). Energy-efficient communication protocol for wireless microsensor network. *In Hawaii International Conference on System Sciences* (HICCS), Maui, HI.

Herbst, P. (1976). *Alternatives to Hierarchies.* Leiden, the Netherlands: H. E. Stenfer Kroese.

Herman, M. (2002). Making Teamwork Work. Retrieved 6 November 2008 from *www.hermanmiller. com/hm/content/research_summaries/pdfs/wp_Collaborative_Settings.pdf*

Hinsz, V., Tindale, R., & Vollrath, D. (1997). The emerging conceptualization of groups as information processors. *Psychological Bulletin, 121*(1), 43-64.

Hinton-Walker, P., Botelho, R., & Suchman, A., (1998). Partnerships, power and process: An introduction. In A. Suchman, R. Botelho & P. Hinton-Walker (Eds.), *Partnerships in healthcare: Transforming relationship process,* (pp. 3-9). Rochester, NY: University of Rochester Press.

Holohan, A. (2005). Collaboration Online: The Example of Distributed Computing. *Journal of Computer-Mediated Communication.*

Hudlicka, E. (1996). Requirements elicitation with indirect knowledge elicitation techniques: comparison of three methods (15-18 April 1996). *Proceedings of the Second International Conference on Requirements Engineering,* (pp. 4-11).

Ickes, W., & Gonzalez, R. (1994). Social cognition and social cognition: From the subjective to the inter-subjective. *Small Group Research, 25*, 294-315.

Imad, S., Souren P., Peter Jr., & Priya S. (2003). The Collaborative Conflict Management Style and Cultural Diversity in DGSS Supported Fuzzy Tasks: An Experimental Investigation. *Proceedings of the 36th Hawaii y International Conference on System Sciences (HICSS'03).*

Indratmo, & Julita V. (2008). A Review of Organizational Structures of Personal Information Management. *Journal of Digital Information, 9*(26).

Jackson, S., Brett, J., Sessa, V., Cooper, D., Julin, J., & Peyronnin, K. (1991). Some differences make a difference: Individual dissimilarity and group heterogeneity as correlates of recruitment, promotions, and turnover. *Journal of Applied Psychology, 76*, 675-689.

James, W. (2007). Defection and Hierarchy in International Intelligence Sharing. *Journal of Public. Policy., 27,* 151-181.

Jared, F., & Kathleen, P. (June 17-19, 2003). Collaborative Critical Thinking. *8th International Command and Control Research and Technology Symposium.* National Defense University, Washington, DC.

Jie, L., Guangquan, Z., & Fengjie, W. (January, 2008). Team Situation Awareness Using Web Based Fuzzy Group Decision Support Systems. *International Journal of Computational Intelligence Systems, 1*(1) 50-59.

JISC Infonet Service (2007). *Manage the information lifecycle.* Retrieved 5 November 2008 from www.jiscinfonet.ac.uk/infokits/information-lifecycle

Joan, M., Leandro N., & Thanasis, D. (2004). Extending the Scope of Asynchronous Collaboration: a Matter of Being Autonomous and Self-sufficient. *Proceedings of the 13th IEEE International Workshops on Enabling Technologies: Infrastructure for Collaborative Enterprises (WET ICE'04).*

Johnson-Laird, P. (1983). *Mental models: toward a cognitive science of language, inference, and consciousness.* Harvard University Press, Cambridge, MA.

Jones, W., Phuwanartnilrak, A., Gill, R., & Bruce, H. (2005). Don't Take My Folders Away! Organizing Personal Information to Get Things Done. *In CHI '05 extended abstracts on human factors in computing systems,* (pp. 1505-1508).

Kaptelinin, V. (2003). UMEA: Translating Interaction Histories into Project Contexts. *In Proceedings of the SIGCHI conference on human factors in computing systems*, (pp. 353-360).

Karger, D., & Jones, W. (2006). Data Unification in Personal Information Management. *Communications of the ACM, 49*(1), 77-82.

Karger, D., & Quan, D. (2004). Collections: Flexible, Essential Tools for Information Management. In CHI '04 extended abstracts on human factors in computing systems, (pp. 1159-1162).

Keim, D. (January - March 2002). Information Visualization and Visual Data Mining. *IEEE Transactions on Visualization and Computer Graphics, 7*(1), 100-107.

Kidd, A. (1994). The Marks are on the Knowledge Worker. *In Proceedings of the SIGCHI conference on human factors in computing systems,* (pp. 186-191).

Kim, J., Brian, C., & Robert, C. (1987). Assaying and isolating individual differences in searching a hierarchical file system. Human, Factors, 29(3),(pp.349-359).

Kunis, R. Rünger, G., & Schwind M. (2007). A Model for Document Management in e-Government Systems Based on Hierarchical Process Folders. *The Electronic Journal of e-Government, 5*(2), 191 – 204.

Kwasnik, B. (1991). The Importance of Factors that are not Document Attributes in the Organisation of Personal Documents. *Journal of Documentation, 47*(4), 389-398.

Kwasnik, B. (1989). How a Personal Document's Intended Use or Purpose Affects Its Classification in an Office. *In Proceedings of the 12th annual international ACM SIGIR conference on research and development in information retrieval,* (pp. 207-,210).

Lansdale, M. (1988). The Psychology of Personal Information Management. *Applied Ergonomics, 19*(1), 55-66

Larson, J., & Christensen, C. (1993). Groups a problem-solving units: Toward a new, meaning of social cognition. *British Journal of Social Psychology,* (pp. 5-30).

Leavitt, H., & Whisler, T. (1958). Management in the 1980s. *Harvard Business Review, 36*, 41-48.

Li, Y., Zhang, C., & Swan, J. (2000). An Information Filtering Model on the Web and its Application in Job Agent. *Knowledge-Based Systems, 13*(5), 285-296.

Lopez, L., Jose, F., & Miguel, A. (15 December 2002). Hierarchical social networks and information flow. *Physica A: Statistical Mechanics and its Applications, 316*(1-4), 695-708.

Malone, T., Yates, W., & Benjamin, R. (1987). Electronic Markets and Electronic Hierarchies. *Communications of the ACM, 30*(6), 484-497.

Mander, R., Salomon, G., & Wong, Y. (1992). A 'Pile' .Metaphor for Supporting Casual Organization of Information. In Proceedings of the SIGCHI conference on human factors in computing systems, (pp. 627-634).

Manjeshwar A., & Agrawal, D. (2001). Teen: a routing protocol for enhanced efficiency in wireless sensor networks. *International Workshop on Parallel and Distributed Computing Issues in Wireless*

Networks and Mobile Computing in Conjunction with the International Parallel and Distributed Processing Symposium (IPDPS), San Francisco, CA.

March, J., & Simon, H. (1958). *Organizations.* New York: Wiley.

Mary, R. (2007). Collective Team Identification in Temporary Teams. *Proceedings of the 40th Hawaii International Conference on System Sciences.*

Maryland Coalition for Inclusive Education (1999). Collaborative Teams Structures for Success. Retrieved on 11 November http://www.mcie.org/docs/publications/Collaborative%20teams.doc

Matsuura, N., Fujino, G., Okada, K., & Matsushita, Y. (1996). A tele- communication environment to support awareness for informal interaction. In D. Shapiro, M. Tauber & R. Traunmuller (Eds.), *The Design of Computer Supported Cooperative Work and Groupware Systems.* Amesterdam: Elsevier Science B.V.

McGregor, D. (1957, April 9). The Human Side of Enterprise. *Proceedings of the Fifth Anniversary Convocation of the School of Industrial Management.*

McIntyre, R., & Salas, E. (1995). Measuring and managing for team performance: emerging principles from complex environments. In R. Guzzo and E. Salas, (Eds.), *Team effectiveness and decision making in organizations* (pp. 149-203). San Francisco: Jossey-Bass.

McNeese, M., Rentsch, J., & Perusich, K. (2000). Modeling, Measuring and Mediating Teamwork: The Use of Fuzzy Cognitive Maps and Team Member Schema Similarity to Enhance BMC3I Decision Making. *IEEE International Conference on Systems, Man and Cybernetics,* (pp. 1081-1086). NY: Institute of Electrical and Electronic Engineers.

Michael, B. (Sept. 1997). What is a 'document'? *Journal of the American Society for Information Science, 48*(9), 804-809.

Michael B., & Robert A. (2005). Improving Collaboration in Command and Control Environments: Creating and Exchanging Iconic Tags of Key Information. *CCRTS 2005.* Retrieved 6 November from www.dodccrp.org/events/10th_ICCRTS/CD/papers/057.pdf

MindTools (2008). *Information Gathering.* Retrieved 6 November 2008 from http://www.mindtools.com/pages/article/newLDR_03.htm

Mitchell, R., Day, D., & Hirschman, L. (1995). Fishing for information on the internet. *Proc. IEEE Information Visualisation '95,* (pp. 105-111).

Mukherjea, S., Foley, J., & Hudson, S., (1995), Visualizing complex hypermedia networks through multiple hierarchical views. *Proc. ACM CHI95 Conference: Human Factors in Computing Systems,* (pp. 331-335) + color plate.

Nation, D., Plaisant, C., Marchionini, G., Komlodi, A. (June 12, 1997). Visualizing Websites Using A Hierarchical Table Of Contents Browser: WebToc, *Proceedings of Designing for the Web: Practices and Reflections,* (13 pages). Denver.

Nau, D., Au, T., Ilghami, O., Kuter, U., Murdoek, J., Wu, D., & Yaman F. (2003): *SHOP2: An HTN Planning System. J. Artifical intelligence Research, 20*(12), 379-404.

Ned, F. (2008). *Encyclopedia of E-collaboration.* Published by Idea Group (IGI).

OCLC (1993). *Electronic Dewey.* Dublin OH, 1 Forrest Press.

Office of Naval Research (2008). *Human Performance: Collaboration and Knowledge Interoperability.* Retrieved 5 November 2008 from http://www.onr.navy.mil/sci_tech/34/341/hp_ckm.asp

Orasanu, J., & Salas, E. (1992). Team Decision Making in Complex Environments. In G. Klein, J. Orasanu, & R. Calderwood (Eds.), *Decision Making in Action: Models and Methods.* Norwood, NJ: Ablex Publishing Corp.

O'Reilly, C., Caldwell, D., & Barnett, W. (1989). Work group demography, social integration, and turnover. *Administrative Science Quarterly, 34*, 21-37.

Palazzolo, E., & Clark, M. (2007). Knowledge Interdependence and Information Retrieval Affects on Performance Satisfaction in Transactive Memory Teams. *Paper presented at the annual meeting of the International Communication Association, TBA, San Francisco, CA* Online <APPLICATION/PDF> Retrieved 20 August 2008 from http://www.allacademic.com/meta/p172543_index.html

Paul, G., Kam, S., & Gregory, K (May 1998). Tharp. Mars Pathfinder mission Internet-based operations using WITS. *In Proceedings IEEE International Conference on Robotics and Automation,* Leuven, Belgium (pp. 284-291).

Podolny, J., & Baron, J. (1997). Resources and relationships. *American Sociological Review, 62*(5), 673-693.

Prinz, W., Rodden, T., Syri, A., & Trevor, J. (1996). Cooperative work settings with active workspaces. In D. Shapiro, M. Tauber, & R. Traunmuller (Eds.), *The Design of Computer Supported Cooperative Work and Groupware System.* Amsterdam, The Netherlands: Elsevier Science B. V.

Qiuming, Z., Stuart, L., & Tomas, N. (July 2007). Hierarchical Collective Agent Network (HCAN) for efficient fusion and management of multiple networked sensors. *Information Fusion* 8(3), 266-280.

Rajeev R., Snehasis M., Michael B., & Nila P. (9-12 September 1997). D-SIFTER: A Collaborative Information Classifier. *International Conference on Information, Communications and Signal Processing (ICICS '97)* Singapore.

Raphael, K., Gudula, R., & Michael, S. (2007). A Model for Document Management in e-Government Systems Based on Hierarchical Process Folders. *Electronic Journal of e-Government, 5*(2), 191-204.

Ravasio, P., Schar, S., & Krueger, H. (2004). In Pursuit of Desktop Evolution: User Problems and Practices with Modern Desktop Systems. *ACM Transactions on Computer-Human Interaction, 11*(2), 156-180.

Redwood Center for Theoretical Neuroscience (2007). *Hierarchical Organization, feedback and generative models.* Retrieved July 18, 2008, from http://redwwod.berkely.edu/wiki/Mission_Research.

Re'mi, C. (2002). Treemaps for Search-Tree Visualization. *The seventh Computer Olympiad Computer-Games Workshop Proceedings* Uiterwijk, J.W.h.M., Maastrich.

Robert, A. (2007). *Implicit & Explicit communication.* Retrieved 6 November 2008 from http://ezinearticles.com/?Implicit-and-Explicit-Communication&id=464406

Robert, B. (1994). *Navigating and Searching in Hierarchical Digital Library Catalogs Information Filtering.* Retrieved 5 November 2008 from *www.csdl.tamu.edu/DL94/paper/allen.html*

Robin, L., & Theodosios, P. (January 1997). Fuzzy Decision Tree Algorithms. *IEEE Transaction on Systems, Man, & Cybernetics, SMC-7*(1), 28-35.

Roderick, I., Tom, P., Peter, N., Marius, H., & Adrie, CM. (Summer 2002). Multiparty Negotiation Support: The Role of Visualization's Influence on the Development of Shared Mental Models. *Journal of Management Information Systems, 19*(1), 129-150.

Roger R., Gareth F., & David S. (2006). *Data Lifecycles: Managing Data for Strategic Advantage.* Wiley Publishing

Rothschild-Whitt, J. (1979). The collectivist organization. *American Sociological Review, 44*(4), 509-527.

Schrage, M. (1995). No More Teams! *Mastering the Dynamics of Creative collaboration*, Doubleday, as cited in P.A. Dargan.

Schuler, D. (1994) Social computing, *Communications of the ACM, 37*(1), 28–29.

Scott, A. Mark, B., Xiao Qi, C., & Geoffrey, J. (2008). Human-Robot Collaboration: A Literature Review and Augmented Reality Approach in Design. *International Journal of Advanced Robotic Systems, 5*(1), 1-18.

Shouman, M., Abou-Ali, G., & Mostafa, A. (2008). A Hybrid Model for Knowledge Acquisition Using Hierarchical Cluster Analysis. *International Arab* Conference *of e-Technology.*

Shrideep, P., Geoffrey, F., & Harshawardhan, G. (to appear). On the Secure Creation, Organization and Discovery of topics in Distributed Publish/Subscribe Systems. *International Journal of High Performance Computing and Networking (IJHPCN).* Special issue of extended versions of the six best papers at the ACM/IEEE GRID Workshop in Seattle, W.A.

Simoff, S., & Maher, M. (1998). Ontology-based multi media data mining for design information retrieval. *In Proceedings of Computing in Civil Engineering* ASCE, Reston, VA, (pp. 212-223).

Sokol, L. (2002). Creating knowledge from heterogeneous data stove pipes. *Proceedings of the Fifth International Conference on Information Fusion 2*, 1162 - 1167

Soules, C., & Ganger, G. (2003). Why Can't I Find My Files? New Methods for Automating Attribute Assignment. *In Proceedings of the 9ᵗʰ workshop on hot topics in operating systems,* (pp.115-120).

Subramanian, L., & Katz, R. (2000). An architecture for building self-configurable systems. *In IEEE/ACM Workshop on Mobile Ad Hoc Networking and Computing (MobiHoc)*, Boston, MA.

Suzuki, Y., Matsumoto, N., & Sai, K. (29-30 January 2004). Collaborative visualization for supporting joint researches. *In ITBL project Creating, Connecting and Collaborating through Computing,* (187).

Tiehua, Z., Gruver, W., & Smith, M. (1999). Team scheduling by genetic search. *Proceedings of the Second International Conference on Intelligent Processing and Manufacturing of Materials (IPMM apos, 99), 2,* 839 – 844.

Tollmar, K., Sandor, O., & Schemer, A. (November 1996). Supporting social awareness Work: Design and experience. *In Proceedings of CSCW'96* (pp. 298-307). Cambridge MA: ACM Press.

Tsui, A., Egan, T., & O'Reilly, C. (1992). Being different: Relational demography and organizational attachment. *Administrative Science Quraterly, 37,* 549-579.

Tyson, R., & Scott, E. (May 1990). *Viewing large graphs.* (Tech. Rep. No. 90). University of Arizona.

Vance, M., & William, K. (June 1997). Collaborative Virtual Prototyping. *Joint Avionics Weapon Software Support and Simulation Conference Proceedings.*

Walsh, J., & Maloney, N. (2007). Collaboration Structure, Communication Media and Problems in Scientific Work Teams. *Journal of Computer Mediated Communication, 12*(2), 19.

Warner, N., Letsky, M., & Cowen, M. (September 2005). *Cognitive model of team collaboration: macrocognitive focus.* Paper presented at the 49th Annual Meeting of the Human Factors and Ergonomics Society. Orlando.

Warner, N., Letsky, M., & Cowen, M. (November 2004). *Structural Model of Team Collaboration, Office of Naval Research, Human Systems Department,* Arlington, VA. Retrieved on 5 November 2006 from *www.au.af.mil/au/awc/awcgate/navy/model_of_team_collab.doc*

Warner, N., Wroblewski, W., & Elizabeth, M. (January 2004*). Achieving Collaborative Knowledge in Asynchronous Collaboration. Collaboration and knowledge Management Workshop Proceedings. Office of Naval Research, Human Systems Department,* Arlington, VA.

Warwick, C., Colin, W., & Julie, W. (18-19 June 2001). Archiving the Web: The Pandora Archive at the National Library Of Australia. *Preserving the Present for the Future Web Archiving Conference.* Copenhagen.

Weaver, R., & Farrell, J. (1997). *Managers as facilitators.* San Francisco: Barrett-Koehler.

Wegner, D. (1995). A computer network model of human transactive memory. *Social Cognition, 13,* 319-339.

Wegner, D. (1987). Transactive memory: A contemporary analysis of the group mind. In B. Mullen & G. R. Goethals (Eds.), *Theories of* group *behavior* (pp. 185-208). New York: Springer – Verlag,.

Wensheng, Z., Vellaikal, A., & Son D. (2001). Cooperative content analysis agents for online multimedia indexingand filtering. *The Proceedings of the Third International Symposium on Cooperative Database Systems for Advanced Applications, CODAS 2001,* (pp. 118 – 122).

Whittaker, S., & Sidner, C. (1996). Email Overload: Exploring Personal Information Management of Email. *In Proceedings of the SIGCHI Conference on Human Factors in Computing Systems,* (pp. 276-283).

William, K. (2003). *Distributed Collaborative Environments for Decision Support.* Retrieved 5 July 2008, from http://www.modelingandsimulation.org/text/McQuay.html

William, K. (1997). Put a Virtual Prototype on Your Desktop. *Program Manager Magazine,* (pp. 94-99).

Williamson, O. (1985). *The Economic Implications of Capitalism: Firms, Markets, and Relational Contracting.* New York: Free Press.

Wu, G., Huang, Y., Shian-Shyong, T., & Zhang, F. (1999). A knowledge sharing and collaboration system model based on Internet. *IEEE International Conference on Systems, Man, and Cybernetics, 2,* 148-152.

XLMiner (2007). *Classification Tree.* Retrieved on 23 November 2008, from http://www.resample.com/xlminer/help/Ctree/ClassificationTree_intro.htm.

Xing-kai, Y., & Yan-zhang, W. (2006). A New Information Exchange Model Based on the Multi-agent. *Proceedings of the 2006 IEEE/WIC/ACM International Conference on Web Intelligence and Intelligent Agent Technology.*

Xiong, N., & Svensson, P. (June 2002). Multi-sensor management for information fusion: issues and approaches. *Information Fusion, 3*(2), 163-186.

Zhao, F., Shin, J., & Reich, J., (March 2002). Information-driven dynamic sensor collaboration for tracking applications. *IEEE Signal Processing Magazine, 19*(2), pp.61-72.

Zhou, L. (2007). Research of Data Processing in Mine Safty Monitoring System Based on Multisensor Information Fusion. *The Eighth International Conference on Electronic Measurement and Instruments ICEMI'2007*

Zuboff, S. (1988). *In the Age of the Smart Machine: The Future of Work and Power.* New York: Basic Books.

KEY TERMS

Distributed Collaboration: It is a form of online collaboration where team members work in an asynchronous environment.

Flat Organization: It is an organizational structure with few or no middle management between staff and managers thus bringing top management in direct contact with staff and customers.

Hierarchical Organization: It is a pyramid like organization where the top node is called the root under which there are one or more subordinates. The higher level nodes have domination and superiority over the lower nodes.

Human Collaboration: It is the process of working together, especially in a joint intellectual effort.

Information Classification: It is the process of arranging information topics in a hierarchical organization that are related by parent-child relationships.

Information Creation: It is a process that includes collecting data from observation, experts, sensors and data analysis results.

Information Filtering: It is the process of finding the most interesting and valuable information so people can avoid the problem of information overload.

Information Flow: Is the transfer of information between team members in a collaboration process or between individuals at different levels of a hierarchical organization in a communication process.

Information Fusion: is integrating information from different sources in order to facilitate understanding or provide knowledge that is not evident from individual sources.

Information Gathering: It is the process of collecting as much information as possible about a problem through problem analysis and search activities in information sources.

Information Management: It is the discipline for collecting, organizing, filtering, retrieving, distributing of information with a goal of efficient management.

Information Organization: It is the logical arrangement of information topics in a file system.

Information Processing: It is the process of gathering, organizing, storing, retrieving and using of information.

Information Retrieval: It is the process of searching information topics within documents, in relational databases and on the World Wide Web.

Information Visualization: It is the process of converting data into a geometric or graphic representation to create visual images that aid in understanding complex information.

Knowledge Building: It is the process of creating new knowledge.

Knowledge Management: It is the discipline used by organizations for gathering, organizing, sharing, and analyzing what it knows.

Meta-Cognitive Process: It refers to individual awareness of what he needs to know to develop his understanding of the elements, relations and conditions that compose the problem.

Network Organization: It is an organization structure where every node is connected to any other nodes arbitrarily without any constraints.

Online Collaboration: Team members working in different locations at great distances apart.

Team Collaboration: It is the process in which team members working together, sharing information and ideas and negotiating in attempt to reach a shared understanding of a situation.

Chapter V
An Intelligent Information Management Tool for Complex Distributed Human Collaboration

Christine B. Glaser
University of Surrey, CCSR, I-Lab, UK

Amy Tan
University of Surrey, CCSR, I-Lab, UK

Ahmet M. Kondoz
University of Surrey, CCSR, I-Lab, UK

ABSTRACT

Managing information collaboratively in an open and unbounded environment without an information management application influenced and challenged the users actions and cognitive abilities, hence collaborative information management behaviour (CIMB). This issue motivated us to investigate distributed synchronous CIMB to deduce criteria for the design of an intelligent information management application that supports interconnectivity and human collaboration in such an environment. The authors developed a model to understand CIMB based on qualitative and quantitative findings, which emerged from four video recordings. These findings revealed that CIMB manifests itself in five behavioural stages: Initiation, Identification, Formulation, Structuring and Decision Making. Thus, an application for open information management should support human-to-computer and human-to-human interaction, should facilitate the behavioural stages users went during an information selection task and should sustain cognitive abilities. This chapter proposes the design for such an application, which supports user's actions and cognitive abilities required to manage information collaboratively in an open and unbounded environment.

INTRODUCTION

Information management behaviour (IMB) describes activities a person carries out when identifying his or her own needs for information, searching for information and using or transferring information (Wilson, 1999). Wilson's definition clearly points at individual information management behaviour, with which many researchers are concerned (Wilson, 1981, 1999; Kuhltau, 1991; Butcher & Rowley, 1998). These actions can be understood as sources for the design of an information management application useful in an open and unbounded environment (Yli-Hietanen & Niiranen, 2008). In order to study actions related to information management and further applying these findings for the design of an application a model has to be developed that considers collaborative information management behaviour and aspects of interconnectivity. Existing models of information management behaviour in information science research focus on the actual initiation of individual information seeking and information retrieving behaviour (Butcher & Rowley, 1998; Kuhltau, 1991; Wilson, 1981, 1999) although research has also revealed that people in organizations conduct most of their work as a collective (Foster, 2006; Reddy & Jansen, 2008). Thus, the need for a model that considers collaborative information management behaviour (CIMB) and interconnectivity of users is clearly warranted, which has been addressed recently by Hansen & Jaervelin (2004), Hyldegård & Ingwersen (2007), and Reddy & Jansen (2008). These studies focused on collaborative information management behaviour of co-located groups or asynchronous teams.

In regard to the growing interest of companies to save travel costs and time, human collaboration in an open and unbounded environment is becoming more important. Subsequently, understanding the complexity of human collaboration in a distributed synchronous environment and developing applications that support interconnectivity and collaboration is all the more relevant (Yli-Hietanen & Nirranen, 2008). Therefore, the investigation of distributed synchronous groups managing information collaboratively in an open and unbounded environment, specifically over a shared digital workspace and video has not yet been addressed by researchers of information science.

In order to address this need we conducted a small-group experiment with four two-person remote teams performing an information selection task without an application to manage the information. To increase the task complexity users had to play different roles, the parties of authority and protagonist. At this point we define collaborative information management behaviour in the context of our experiment from a sociological point of view as any perception, cognition, and action (Hogg and Vaughan, 2005) that is carried out by a user over a shared digital workspace and video that causes a reaction and influences the other users' perception, cognition and action at the same time. Managing information without an application and interacting over a shared digital workspace with video was found to affect users actions and reactions carried out to manage information collaboratively, so did the existence of the two roles, as users had different information needs and interests.

Based on these insights the objectives of this chapter are

- To determine the actions and reactions users carried out over a shared digital workspace and video to manage information collaboratively.
- To identify the collaborative information management behaviour these actions and reactions encompass and their applicability for the design of an information management application which supports interconnectivity and collaboration.

- To identify the relationship between collaborative information management behaviour and cognitive abilities in order to develop a model for CIMB
- To determine factors that hinder or support users during an information selection task in order to deduce criteria for the design of an intelligent information management tool and
- To propose an interface that meets our criteria and supports interconnectivity and collaboration.

The four video recordings emerged from the experiment have been studied by means of grounded theory and analysed using different qualitative methods, qualitative behavioural video analysis and qualitative content analysis. We corroborated our findings from both analyses using qualitative comparative behavioural analysis. Finally, we quantified our results from qualitative comparative behavioural analysis in order to define the structure for our model. Form our model we deduced design criteria that an intelligent information management application (tool) should inhibit in an open and unbounded environment.

This chapter consists of four sections starting with a discussion of existing theoretical concepts and models for information management behaviour and their applicability for the development of our model. Followed by the methodology including: qualitative behavioural video analysis, qualitative content analysis and qualitative comparative behavioural analysis and quantitative analysis of frequency. Two examples are given that demonstrate our analytical procedure. The third section focuses on the development of our model based on the findings of qualitative comparative behavioural analysis and quantitative analysis of frequency and includes a discussion of the model in relation to the theoretical background given in the beginning of this chapter. The last section is concerned with the deduced design criteria an intelligent information management tool should inhibit and proposes an interface for an intelligent information management tool used in an open and unbounded environment. Each section concludes with a summary. We conclude our main insights in relation to our research questions and outline limitations. Finally, future trends are given.

BACKGROUND

Our theoretical framework is a template for analysing and understanding collaborative information management behaviour (CIMB) that will lead us to conceptualise results and assumptions in order to develop a model for CIMB, thus to deduce criteria for the design of an intelligent information management tool. Our model for CIMB is based on conceptual frameworks, models and theoretical propositions of information management behaviour by Wilson, (1999), Hyldegard and Ingwersen (2007), Spink (2000), Kuhlthau, (1991), Reddy and Jansen (2008), Hansen and Jaervelin (2004) and Xie (2000). The concepts by Wilson, 1999; Kuhlthau, 1991; Spink, 1997, and Xie (2000) investigated individual information management behaviour while Hyldegard and Ingwersen (2007), Reddy and Jansen (2008), and Hansen and Jaervelin (2004) considered collaborative information management behaviour and focused on co-located groups and teams. Concepts of individual information management behaviour can help us to understand collaborative information management behaviour. Wilson (1981, 1996) was one of the first scholars who developed a model for information-seeking behaviour and defined information management behaviour (IMB) as activities a person carries out when identifying his or her own needs for information, searching for information and using or transferring information (Wilson, 1999). Hyldegard and Ingwersen (2007) applied Kuhlthaus's model of individual information-seeking behaviour to examine co-located collaborative information management behaviour and found that her model is sensitive to group processes. Reddy and Jansen (2008) and Hansen and Jaervelin (2004) were interested in the transition from the individual to collaborative information management behaviour and they identified the triggers for this shift. They established that information-seeking is more related to collaborative activities between humans whereas information retrieving is more of a document related task dimension. In the following section we discuss the concepts and models for both individual and collaborative information management behaviour.

Stages of Individual Information Management Behaviour

Kuhlthau's widely accepted model of information-seeking process (ISP) has been found to be of great value to understand the affective and cognitive level of individual information seekers. Her model reflects a phenomenological perspective of information-seeking, illustrated in seven stages: initiation, selection, exploration, formulation, collection, presentation and assessment. An individual seeking for information goes through each stage with certain feelings and thoughts and approaches each stage by carrying out specific actions. Emotions are found to influence the decisions and choices a person makes. They can range from uncertainty, confusion and disappointment to satisfaction, clarity and a sense of accomplishment. These are accompanied with either vague or focused or self-aware thoughts. Actions carried out by these individuals were seeking, discussing, conferring with others, or summarizing. This shows that although Kuhlthau's model focuses on an individual the author has taken the involvement of other people into account. This aspect is crucial for collaboration and contributes to our conceptual framework. Kuhlthau's ISP model does not only concentrate on finding and reproducing information but also on seeking meaning which the author describes as a process of construction. In order to construct meaning one has to coordinate his or her thoughts during the process of information seeking. The strength of this model is the acknowledgement of feelings and thoughts that exist in each stage of the information-seeking process. Both aspects, the existence of information management stages and the accompanying feelings and thoughts will be considered in relation to our experimental findings in order to develop our model. Kuhlthau (1991) describes the sequence of these stages as a linear process as she focuses on individual information-seeking instead of collaborative information management. Her idea of the stages can be useful to analyse and understand an individual users' information management behaviour in distributed collaboration. However, the linear character of this model seems to contradict with the idea of collaboration.

Applying Concepts of Individual IM Behaviour for Collaborative Processes in IM

Hyldegård and Ingwersen (2007) addressed this issue by revisiting Kuhltau's ISP model and applied it for information management behaviour in group-based problem solving. Findings of their study revealed that the ISP model was sensitive to group processes. Group members followed the general stages of information-seeking behaviour and the same cognitive patterns were unveiled as suggested in the ISP-model. They moved from recognizing and uncertainty towards formulating and clarity, which enabled the group members to complete the information management process. However, group members did not adapt their behaviour during the information-seeking process. The key features of this study are that group members were endowed with different cognitive abilities and constantly shifted between an individual level and a group level. This aspect has been of great value to understand collaborative information management behaviour in co-located and distributed environments and thus will be examined in greater detail to develop our model for distributed collaborative information management behaviour. Hyldegård and Ingwersen (2007) focused on co-located information-seeking behaviour while Hansen and Jaervelin's (2005) focused on co-located collaborative information-seeking and -retrieving processes. The latter study revealed that collaborative information processes consist of three task levels: work task, information-seeking task and retrieval task. Each level includes synchronous (human-related) and asynchronous (document-related) activities. Specifically, human-related activities reflect the increased complexity accrued by managing information collaboratively such as task cooperation, sharing information/strategy, and sharing external and internal domain expertise and personal opinions. Interestingly, results showed that the first level (work task) and the third level (retrieval task) contain more document-related activities, whereas the second level, information-seeking task clearly contains a high level of synchronous human-related activities. This aspect showed that an information-seeking task in group-based problem solving requires synchronous collaboration.

Triggers for the Shift Between Individual and Collaborative IM Behaviour

The aspect that information-seeking is highly related to collaborative processes provokes the question of what triggers cause a shift from an individual to collaborative information management behaviour. Reddy and Jansen (2008) found that if the information-seeking problem is simple the individual is able to manage information on his/her own and information-seeking does not require collaboration with colleagues. If the individual realises that seeking for information becomes too complex and additional expertise is needed, collaboration is required. A lack of expertise is therefore one of the triggers leading to a shift from an individual to collaborative information-seeking behaviour. An increased task complexity does not only require extra help, additional information is required and consistent information sources as well as immediate access to information is necessary. At this point we can relate the task complexity to two interaction levels. Firstly, a task performed between a human and a machine is a simple interactional task, whereas a task in collaboration, between humans, entails a complex interactional task. The differentiation of these two levels and its significance for collaborative information management will be considered later in this chapter, see section *Model for CIMB*. The authors have identified a lack of expertise, the need for additional information, fragmented information sources and insufficient access of information as the four triggers for the shift from individual to collaborative information management behaviour. The discovery of these four triggers is fundamental and of special interest for the development of our model. Although, this study strongly contributes to a better understanding of collaborative information management behaviour this model is based on an ethnographical study of health care teams, which have unique characteristics. Team members have different expertise and training which could bias the way they require additional expertise, need more information or can access information. We will reconsider these triggers in relation to our findings in order to address this limitation.

Additionally, we found other factors that seemed to be of great value to enable us to understand and analyse our video recordings in order to formulate our model. These are the concept of feedback, information management strategies, and the significance of cognitive abilities in information management behaviour. Wilson (1996) and Spink (1997) investigated the concept of feedback in information management behaviour from different perspectives. Wilson's revised model of information-seeking behaviour shows the necessity of cognitive feedback loops. Satisfying the information need, processing and using information requires human's reflection on his or her decision why some information sources may be used and others excluded. The necessity of cognitive feedback loops also requires the humans' cognitive ability to recall information in order to reflect this decision this aspect has been neglected by Wilson (1996). Referring to Hansen and Jaervelin (2007) this aspect is crucial as human's cognitive abilities play an important role for the shift from individual to collaborative information management. Clearly, Wilson refers to the cognitive level of individual information-seeking behaviour, while Spink's (1997) focuses on the interaction between a user and an information retrieving system. This study revealed that the process of information searching includes interactive feedback loops. Spink's (1997) shows that feedback in an interactive information retrieving process can be related to different information elements such as the content of information or magnitude judgments about the information or the information relevance. This is a strong point that reflects that interactive information management is a circular process rather than a linear one as suggested by Kuhlthau (1991). However, this study focused on human-system interaction instead of collaboration between humans. Looking at the concept of feedback from a collaborative perspective in a distributed environment may be a challenge as it involves social factors and two levels of interaction human-to-system and human-to-human.

Another interesting study that we found to be highly important to develop our model focused on information-seeking strategies and goals during an information-seeking process (Xie, 2000). The choice of using a certain strategy to manage information collaboratively is of special interest for us as it may influence human-to-human interaction significantly and therefore the collaborative information management behaviour. In regard to Hyldegård and Ingwersen (2007) statement, different group members consist of different cognitive abilities thus, they constantly shift between an individual and collaborative level. We assume that different users inhibit different information management strategies which may have an effect on collaborative information management behaviour. Xie (2000) identified three strategies to achieve information-seeking goals: supplementing, improving and choosing an alternative option. Supplementing is defined as assessing the usefulness of the item in relation to the sub goal and the task goal. Improving the existing strategy and sub goal means that a user modifies his or her interactive intention of the sub goal. Thirdly, the user looks for an alternative information-seeking strategy and replaces the unsuccessful one. The strength of this study lies in the discovery of these three strategy types based on individual information-seeking behaviour.

Summary of Theoretical Framework

The concepts and models discussed above, expanded our understanding for studying collaborative information management behaviour. We highlighted here several aspects that are central for analysing CIMB and will be considered in greater detail in relation to the findings of our study:

1. According to Kuhlthau's ISP model and her stages we will attempt to identify similar stages in our data (video recordings) by means of qualitative comparative behavioural analysis. We will discuss our findings alongside Kuhlthau's aspects in order to formulate concepts for our model for CIMB and define the properties of each concept.

2. The shift between individual and collaborative activities pointed out by Hansen and Jaervelin (2007) is another important aspect we found to be crucial for investigating CIMB. We assume that this phenomenon of transition is related to Kuhlthaus' stages. We will include the shift from

individual to collaborative information management behaviour and its significance for CIMB in our considerations.

3. The investigation of CIMB requires the identification of triggers that cause a shift between individual and collaborative information management behaviour. We will consider Reddy and Jansen's (2008) findings regarding this issue.

4. The concept of interactive feedback loops as investigated by Spink will be set into contrast with findings from qualitative analysis. We infer that collaborative information management requires feedback, which we hope to find in the video recording.

5. According to Hansen and Jaervelin's aspect regarding the importance of cognitive abilities for collaborative information management, we will define what cognitive abilities are needed in distributed, collaborative information management behaviour and how these can be supported.

6. Lastly, the necessity of changing information management strategies to achieve the task goal as emphasized by Xie (2000) will be considered. We infer that changing strategies in collaborative information management is essential to achieve a goal and to foster CIMB.

METHODOLOGICAL APPROACH

Qualitative Data

The data analysed in this study was collected from four video recordings of two-person distributed teams carrying out a collaborative task for a quasi-experiment conducted in June 2007. The two-person distributed teams collaborated over a shared digital workspace with video and were video recorded while performing a route-planning task. Participants had to plan a route for a demonstration during a fictional state visit in Vienna using information based on ten different documents.

The participants were informed that three out of the ten documents were essential for the route planning and had to be selected. The information selection task (IST) required that users collaborated regarding the relevance of information for the overall task. This was also influenced by the fact that participants had to play either the role of police or the head of a demonstrator organization. Having two different roles increased the complexity of the information selection task. In addition to the shared digital documents, each participant had been given specified information appropriate to their roles in the form of paper documents. The shared digital documents consisted of spreadsheets (schedule of state visit), maps (city centre locations of stops), and correspondences (emails) between the police and the demonstration organization. The paper document for the demonstrator contained information about the times of specific stops for speeches by the VIP and how long it would take to walk from one stop to another. The other user (representing the police) had information about the stops and times of the VIP and safety issues. The demonstrator had his or her suggested times, stops and duration for speeches while the police had information about the VIP route. The user assuming the role of the police had to ensure as part of the collaboration that the route of the VIP could not change and were only allowed to overlap o time and route at two stops. After selecting the essential documents the two users had to agree the route for the demonstration. It was designed that each party had information useful to themselves and which was of also of relevance for the party if the two parties were to come to an agreement about the route for the demonstrators.

It is important to mention that the shared digital workspace that each collaborator had access to consisted of two resolution areas; an A3 high resolution area (fovea) which was surrounded by a low resolution area (periphery). The high resolution area is useful to view two A4 documents clearly, whereas documents in the low resolution area appeared blurry and were difficult to read. In order to read information clearly the user had to drag a document into the high resolution area. This forced users to move documents in and out of the fovea in order to be able to seek, read or compare information.

Qualitative Approach and Research Questions

We have chosen to analyse the four video recordings by means of grounded theory. Initial investigation of the material showed that the information selection task using a shared digital workspace influenced the user's collaborative behaviour fundamentally. In this chapter collaborative behaviour is understood as the actions and reactions carried out by the users to interact with the system (human-computer interaction) and to interact with each other (human-to-human interaction) in order to manage information collaboratively. If user A dragged a document into the high resolution area (human-computer interaction), user B automatically had to view then the same information at the same time. This action could have led to a reaction by user B towards the action of user A (human-human interaction). Because of the existence of two different roles with different interests, dragging a document into the high resolution area could have restrained users. Referring to Hansen & Jaervelin (2007) different users have different cognitive abilities to perceive and process information. Therefore, managing information collaboratively in a distributed synchronous environment requires coordinated actions, hence a strategy which will be of an interest to examine in detail. Another issue that emerged was the complexity of the information selection task. Having to select three essential documents also challenged the cognitive abilities of the users to manage information collaboratively. These two issues of carrying out actions and reactions and having different cognitive abilities constitute our research questions:

1. What actions and reactions do users carry out during the information selection task?
   The first research question is concerned with the individual perspective of CIMB. By defining action and reaction types we hope to gain insights of user's behaviour while managing information collaboratively.
2. What kind of CIMB can be derived from nonverbal actions and reactions carried out by a user to manage information collaboratively?
   The second question concentrates on the collaborative perspective of the information selection task and examines the actions and reactions of users during the first fifteen minutes of the distributed synchronous meeting. By answering this question we intend to analyse the collaborative nonverbal information management behaviour during the information selection task.
3. What kind of CIMB can be derived from verbal actions and reactions of a user carried out to manage information collaboratively?
   The third question also focuses on the collaborative perspective of the information selection task. By investigating the collaborative verbal actions and reactions, we hope to expand our understanding for collaborative verbal information management behaviour during the information selection task.
4. How is nonverbal and verbal CIMB related to cognitive abilities and what effect does this relationship have for the information selection task?

By answering this question we hope to deduce theoretical propositions for CIMB in order to describe a model of CIMB.

5.   What factors support or hinder users to manage information collaboratively in a distributed synchronous environment?

The fifth question is concerned with applying the theoretical propositions to formulate criteria for the design of an intelligent information management tool.

Qualitative Method

The first fifteen minutes of each video recording have been found of great value to study collaborative information management behaviour in depth. (In this chapter we use the general term video recordings to describe those fifteen minutes.) Initial observation of the data revealed that users carried out verbal and nonverbal actions and reactions during the information selection task. This finding answered our first research question and was of great importance for our analysis as it induced us to analyse our data with different methods. Firstly, we analysed the four videos by means of qualitative behavioural video analysis in order to determine users' collaborative nonverbal information management behaviour. Secondly, we transcribed the video recordings and analysed verbal actions and reactions using qualitative content analysis in order to identify the collaborative verbal information management behaviour. This method of examining a phenomenon by means of qualitative content analysis has been found to be a valid method in a previous study conducted to identify usability problems of distributed collaboration systems (Glaser et al, 2008). Analysing the same data with different methods was also crucial to substantiate codes and categories, as only two researchers have coded the data.

After analysing video recordings and transcripts separately we corroborated our findings to examine how verbal and nonverbal actions and reactions are related to cognitive abilities and what effect this relationship has for the information selection task by using qualitative comparative behavioural analysis (QCBA). This method allowed us to deduce theoretical propositions and define concepts for CIMB, which have been used to develop a model for CIMB. We also quantified our findings in order to determine the relationship between concepts. Based on this model, we were able to define a set of criteria for the design of an intelligent information management tool.

QUALITATIVE ANALYSIS

Qualitative Behavioural Video Analysis (QBVA)

Qualitative behavioural video analysis (QBVA) allowed us to focus on the collaborative behavioural perspective of users' information management behaviour during distributed synchronous collaboration. We were interested in understanding the collaborative nonverbal information management behaviour during the IST. We identified all nonverbal actions and reactions in the four video recordings and coded and categorized them, e.g. user A dragged a document into the high resolution area. This action of user A has been coded as dragging a document. User B nodded. This action has been coded as feedback. Several codes have been found in all four video recordings and were used for further analysis, see Table 1. These nonverbal actions and reactions (codes) have certain properties. During the coding process we found that users carried out these nonverbal actions either individually or collaboratively, e.g., User A dragged a document (collaborative action) user B read (individual action) and nodded (collaborative action). These properties of actions and reactions revealed that an information selection task performed over a shared digital workspace consists of collaborative nonverbal actions and individual nonverbal actions. Although, an individual nonverbal action carried out in distributed synchronous collaboration does not necessarily indicate collaborative behaviour, this action still contributes to collaborative information management. The individual nonverbal action reading has been categorized as seeking behaviour and found to be essential to manage information collaboratively. Without seeking information users would not have been able to continue the collaborative information management process. All other nonverbal actions and reactions indicated collaborative nonverbal information management behaviour and have been categorized as the behaviour viewing, reviewing, pre-selecting, selecting, and feedback. After coding and categorizing each video we compared codes and categories of all four videos to ensure that these codes are legitimately found in all.

Table 1 represents the codes and categories identified in all four videos. Codes were given for nonverbal individual and collaborative actions and reactions of the users; categories were used to describe the collaborative nonverbal information management behaviour (CIMB nonverbal) that a specific nonverbal action or reaction encompassed.

In the following section we demonstrate by means of two examples of Video 1 how codes and categories have been created. The first example represents the beginning of the distributed meeting and illustrates how users started to manage information collaboratively. The second example describes the collaborative nonverbal information management behaviour while users were reviewing information during the information selection task.

Example 1, (Video 1, 2.32-2.46 (Min.): Action-Reaction)

In Video 1, user A read quietly and asked a question. At the same time user B was reading a paper document and when user A finished his question user B nodded and replied.

Table 1. Codes and categories of QBVA

Codes *Nonverbal Actions and Reactions*	Categories *CIMB nonverbal*
Reading quietly digital document Reading quietly paper document	Seeking
Dragging documents in order to view	Viewing
Pointing at documents (digital or paper) Nodding	Feedback
Dragging multiple documents out of the high resolution area on to the left or right side	Pre-selecting
Dragging specific documents back into the high resolution area	Reviewing
Pointing at specific information in a document in the high resolution area Dragging documents out of the high resolution and leaving them Leaving three documents in the high resolution area	Selecting

Codes and Categories (Example 1, Video 1, 2.32-2.46 (Min.): Action-Reaction)

By reading quietly and asking a question user A performed a nonverbal and a verbal action. We focus on the nonverbal action, reading quietly and coded this action as reading quietly. User B was reading a paper document, which was a nonverbal action that has been coded as reading quietly. The reaction of user B nodding has been coded as feedback. We categorized the action reading quietly as *behaviour seeking* and nodding as the *behaviour feedback*. The codes found in this example are reading quietly and nodding. The categories of these codes were feedback and seeking behaviour.

Example 2 (Video 1, 5.51-6.20 (min.): Action and Reaction)

User B dragged specific documents into the high-resolution area one by one in order to demonstrate what documents they had found so far and agreed on. While user B was dragging the document user A looked down at the workspace and followed the action of user B and nodded occasionally.

Codes and Categories (Example 2, Video 1, 5.51-6.20 (Min.): Action and Reaction)

The nonverbal action of user B dragging specific documents into the high-resolution area has been coded as dragging specific documents. Because users have already pre-selected some documents they were able to drag the preselected documents into the high-resolution to have a closer look. The coded action of dragging specific documents after preselecting them has been categorized as *behaviour reviewing*. The reaction of user B nodding has been coded as nodding and categorized as feedback. This example revealed the codes dragging specific documents and nodding categorized as reviewing behaviour and feedback.

Summary of QVBA

Analysis of all four videos revealed that users performed specific nonverbal collaborative and individual actions and reactions during the first fifteen minutes of the IST. Findings showed that users mainly dragged documents, pointed at documents in the shared digital workspace, read digital or paper documents or pointed at paper documents and nodded. These nonverbal actions and reactions occurring at specific times during the meeting revealed our codes. From our codes we established five categories that represented collaborative verbal information management behaviour during the IST. These five categories occurred several times in the first fifteen minutes of all four video recordings: Seeking information (reading quietly), Viewing information (dragging a document, pointing at documents), Pre-selecting information (pointing at specific information in documents, dragging different documents), reviewing information (dragging specific documents back into the high-resolution area, pointing at specific information in a document in the high-resolution area), Selecting information (dragging documents out of the high-resolution and leaving them, leaving three documents in the high-resolution area) and giving feedback (nodding).

QBVA was useful to define nonverbal actions and reactions and we gained insights regarding the collaborative behaviour these nonverbal actions and reactions reflected. However, during the analysis we found that verbal actions and reactions dominated the distributed synchronous meetings and further analysis of collaborative verbal actions and reactions has been required.

Qualitative Content Analysis

Each video has been transcribed following the rules of conversation analysis and we analysed each transcript by means of qualitative content analysis. We examined each verbal action and reaction. Verbal actions and reactions consisted of several single-word and multiple word phrases that were of importance to study. We coded the phrases in each verbal action and reaction and determined the collaborative meaning of each phrase. After the coding process we deduced the collaborative behaviour of the verbal actions and reactions, which revealed our categories. Categories represent the collaborative verbal information management behaviour. Table 2 illustrates all the codes and categories found in the four transcripts.

In the following section we illustrate the coding and categorizing process of the transcripts by means of the two examples of Video 1 that were analysed in the previous section, Transcript 1, verbal actions 3-4, line 004-005 and verbal actions 23-26, line 035-040.

Example 1 (Transcript 1, Verbal Action and Reaction 3-4, Line 004-005)

A: "So, do you want to discuss each document one by one?"
B: "I think it's better, yeah, * let's start then."

Codes and Categories (Example 1, Transcript 1, Berbal Action and Reaction 3-4, Line 004-005)
The first verbal action shows two interesting phrases. The first phrase "So, do you want to discuss" shows user A expressing his desire to collaborate. This phrase has been coded as pointing out a problem (something has to be discussed). We coded this phrase as pointing out a problem. The second phrase

Table 2. Codes and categories of QCA

Codes	Categories
Suggesting a strategy, solution, decision Asking a question Pointing out a problem	Suggesting
Specifying document type Telling the other user where to put documents Referring to specific information in emails, Referring to specific information in maps Referring to specific information in schedules Referring to specific information in paper document	Specifying
Comparing information of different digital documents Comparing information of digital and paper documents	Comparing
Enumerating selected documents Specifying the enumerated documents Enumerating information in selected documents	Interpreting
Assessing relevance of information	Assessing
Agreeing or disagreeing as a response towards a verbal action of the other user (e.g. suggesting a strategy, pointing out a problem, comparing information, etc.)	Giving Feedback

"each document one by one" implied that user A found that there is more than one document and that managing a large amount of information is best handled by using a strategy of going through each document one at a time. This second phrase has been coded as suggesting a strategy. Pointing out a problem and suggesting a strategy has been categorized as the collaborative verbal behaviour suggesting.

The second utterance of user B contains three phrases that are important to analyse. The first phrase "I think it's better" indicates that user B has also encountered the same problem of having a large amount of information that has to be managed. We coded this first phrase as agreeing towards the codes pointing out a problem. The second, one-word phrase "Yeah" emphasizes the agreement of user B and the suggestion of using this particular strategy of user A. We coded this second phrase of the verbal action as agreeing towards the code suggesting a strategy. The third phrase "Let's start then" refers to the users' readiness to start the information selection task and we coded this behaviour as agreeing to collaborate. All three phrases have been categorized as the collaborative verbal behaviour giving feedback in order to collaborate.

Example 1 of transcript 1 revealed the codes suggesting a strategy, pointing out a problem, and agreeing towards the verbal action of a user. The categories that emerged were suggesting and feedback.

Example 2 (Transcript 1, Verbal Action and Reaction 23-25, Line 035-040)

B: "So we have got the two maps, the two routes…"
A: "Okay."
B: "…and the schedules for the demonstration and one for the state visit. I think we need to keep both of them."
A: "Yeah."

Codes and Categories (Example 2, Transcript 1, Verbal Action and Reaction 23-25, line 035-040)

The first verbal action is interrupted and consists of five phrases. The first phrase "So we have got the two maps" of user B indicates that different documents have been found and specified, this has been coded as enumerating selected documents. The phrase "the two maps" has been coded as specifying enumerated documents. The second part of the phrase "two routes" refers to specific information in the two maps and has been coded as specifying information in enumerated documents. Both phrases have been categorized as the collaborative verbal behavior interpreting.

The interrupting utterance of user A has been coded as agreeing and implied that user A has also specified the documents as maps and the information in the documents as routes. Agreeing has been categorized as feedback.

User B continues his specification. The third phrase of the verbal action "the two schedules" has been coded as enumerating selected documents. The fourth phrase "for the demonstration and one for the state visit" points at specific information in the specified documents. Specifying enumerated documents has been categorized as interpreting. The fifth phrase "I think we need to keep both", also refers to the collaborative verbal behavior interpreting.

The phrase of user A shows that user A understood user B. We coded this verbal action as agreeing and categorized it as feedback.

Example 2 revealed the codes specifying document types, referring to specified information in a document, and agreeing. These codes revealed the categories feedback and interpreting.

Summary of QCA

Qualitative content analysis of all four transcripts revealed that verbal actions and reactions consisted of phrases that reflected the collaborative verbal information management behaviour. The phrases contained in a verbal action or reaction, have been coded and the collaborative behavioural meaning of the verbal actions and reactions of a user have been deduced in order to categorize them. Six categories that describe collaborative verbal information management behaviour have been found: suggesting, specifying, comparing, interpreting, assessing and giving feedback to someone. These findings answered our third research question concerned with the collaborative verbal information management behaviour.

QCA was useful to analyse the verbal actions and reactions, hence human-to-human interaction. Our findings showed that verbal behaviour is crucial to manage information collaboratively over a shared digital workspace although users could see the same information at the same time. In order to manage the information collaboratively the existence of the shared digital workspace was of great importance and CIMB was reflected in both, nonverbal and verbal actions and reactions. Analysing nonverbal actions by means of QCA has been found to be difficult, which QBVA was useful for.

Qualitative Comparative Behavioural Analysis (QCBA)

In order to compensate for the shortcomings of each approach, we corroborated the outcomes from QBVA and QCA by using qualitative comparative behavioural analysis. We compared the categories of video recordings with the categories of the transcripts in order to determine similarities and differences between them and to deduce patterns between outcomes of each video recording with the matching transcript.

Comparing Categories

For the comparison of categories we focused on all the categories found in both videos and transcripts. We compared the categorised nonverbal actions and reactions from the video recordings with categorised verbal actions and reactions of the transcripts. Comparison of the categories revealed that specific categorized nonverbal actions and reactions occur before specific categorized verbal actions and reactions, e.g. the category seeking information from the video recordings has always been found to occur before the category suggesting from the transcripts.

We revisit our example 1 of video 1 used for QBVA and QCA. Comparing the collaborative nonverbal behaviour of user A (seeking) with the same part of transcript 1, showed that suggesting a strategy by asking a question took place before seeking for information. The collaborative nonverbal behaviour of user B has also been categorized as seeking. The reaction of user B nodding and agreeing has been categorized as the collaborative behaviour feedback in the video recording and giving feedback in the transcript. This example indicates that user A and user B approached the information selection task in a similar way, both were seeking for information, and both had the cognitive ability to acquire knowledge. Seeking for information has been identified as preverbal construing (Kelly, 1955/1991). Table 3 illustrates the cognitive abilities of the users and the accompanying cognitive process.

By seeking for information user A acquired knowledge and learned about a problem. After user A had learned something he was able to express his thought by suggesting a strategy.

In our second example of video 1 we found that the collaborative nonverbal behaviour of user B reviewing documents by dragging them one by one into the high-resolution area has been followed by the collaborative verbal behaviour interpreting. By interpreting information user B created meaning of the reviewed information. This cognitive ability of creating meaning refers to the cognitive process of comprehension.

We deduce that cognitive processes have functional significance for the behaviour of the users (Kuhl & Atkinson, 1986; Matthews et al, 2004) and can be understood as the link between nonverbal and verbal action and reactions carried out during the IST. Collaborative nonverbal behaviour enabled users to process information cognitively and the collaborative verbal behaviour decoded the cognitive process. Table 4 illustrates which categories of the video recordings matched categories of the transcripts and which cognitive abilities were needed.

Having compared and linked the categories of the video recordings with the categories of the transcripts allowed us to deduce theoretical proposition. The collaborative nonverbal information behaviours of seeking, viewing, pre-selecting, reviewing and selecting matched the collaborative verbal information behaviour of suggesting and giving feedback, specifying and giving feedback, comparing and giving feedback, interpreting and giving feedback. Assessing and giving feedback occurred repeatedly together during the IST.

Firstly, users sought for information, acquired knowledge (cognitive process of learning) and verbally suggested something. After that both users viewed the documents, categorized the document type (cognitive process of recognizing) and specified the document type. This nonverbal and verbal behaviour enabled them to pre-select documents, associate information (cognitive process of analysing) and verbally compare information. After they had pre-selected some documents they reviewed the pre-selected documents, created contextual meaning (cognitive process of comprehension) and verbally interpreted the information. Finally, users selected a certain document or information in the document that seemed to be useful, drew conclusions (cognitive process of judging) and verbally assessed the relevance of the documents.

Drawing on these findings we deduce that collaborative information management behaviour consists of collaborative nonverbal information behaviour (which enable users to process information cognitively) and collaborative verbal information behaviour (which decodes the users' cognitive processes by expressing verbally). Collaborative nonverbal behaviour plus with the cognitive ability plus the collaborative verbal behaviour has been grouped as a theoretical concept that describes a specific behavioural stage of the users during an information selection task (IST). Five concepts have been developed, see Table 5: *Initiation, Identification, Formulation, Structuring* and *Decision Making*.

After defining all the concepts that emerged from our data we realised that the concepts occurred repeatedly in a video recording. The occurrence of the five concepts in each video recording can be

Table 3. Cognitive abilities of users and accompanying cognitive processes

Cognitive ability of user	Cognitive process of
Acquiring knowledge	Learning
Categorizing information	Recognizing
Associating information	Analysing
Creating meaning	Comprehension
Drawing conclusions	Decision Making

Table 4. Cognitive abilities link categories of video with categories of transcripts

Categories of Videos		Categories of Transcript
CIMB nonverbal	**Cognitive ability**	**CIMB verbal**
Seeking information	Acquiring knowledge	Suggesting something Giving feedback
Viewing information	Categorizing information	Specifying something Giving feedback
Pre-selecting information	Associating information	Comparing something Giving feedback
Reviewing information	Creating meaning	Interpreting something Giving feedback
Selecting information	Drawing conclusions	Assessing something Giving feedback

visualized as a sequence, e.g. IN-ID-FO-ST DM-ID-DM- IN-ID- ... -ST-DM (sequence of video 1, for abbreviations of concepts, see Table 5)

We compared the sequence of each video with the sequences of one other video and found that at the beginning of each meeting the concept *Initiation* occurred. *Initiation* can be also found several times in a sequence during the whole video and every time it occurred it was always followed by *Identification*. *Decision Making* always occurred before *Initiation* during the IST and as the last concept of a sequence and also occurred between the concepts, *Identification, Formulation* and *Structuring*. This finding gave us reason to distinguish between *Final Decision Making* and *in-between Decision Making*. The concept *in-between Decision Making* always occurred before *Initiation* and throughout a sequence. The concept *Final Decision Making* took place in the end of the information selection task. We inferred that *Initiation* and the concept *Final Decision Making* symbolise a start and an end point of a sequence, hence the start and the end point of the information selection task. After understanding how users start and finish the information selection task, we analysed the sequence of each video and found that *Initiation, Identification, Formulation, Structuring and Decision Making (in-between)* several times during the information selection task. This indicates a cyclical character of the concepts in a sequence.

The temporal position of these concepts in a sequence was difficult to define. Therefore, we quantified our results and conducted an analysis of frequency in order to analyse the order of the concepts in a sequence.

Quantifying Results of QCBA: Quantitative Analysis of Frequency

This analysis states the number of occurrences of each concept before or after the current concept of interest, e.g. *Initiation* occurs 24 times before *Identification*. Figure 1 illustrates the frequency of each concept to every other concept identified by QCBA in all four video recordings. The arrows symbolise the occurrence of each concept before or after one other concept. Bold arrows imply that the current concept of interest occurs frequently before one other concept in contrast to thin arrows, which represent the occurrence of the current concept to one other concept as less frequently. The number above the arrow indicates that the current concept of interest occurred before one other concept. The number under the arrow shows the occurrence of the current concept of interest after one other concept. Arrows

Table 5. Five concepts of CIMB during an information selection task

Concept	CIMB nonverbal	Cognitive Ability	CIMB verbal
Initiation (IN)	Seeking information	Acquiring knowledge	Suggesting Giving feedback
Identification (ID)	Viewing information	Categorizing	Specifying Giving feedback
Formulation (FO)	Pre-selecting information	Associating	Comparing Giving feedback
Structuring (ST)	Reviewing information	Creating meaning	Interpreting Giving feedback
Decision Making (DM)	Selecting information	Drawing conclusions	Assessing Giving feedback

are either one-directional or bi-directional. A one-directional arrow illustrates that the current concept of interest only occurred either before or after on other concept. A bi-directional arrow means that the current concept of interest occurred before and after one other concept. The number 0 implies that the current concept of interest neither occurred before and or after one other concept.

Initiation occurred 24 times but only before *Identification* and did not take place before or after the concepts *Formulation, Structuring* or *Final Decision Making*. But, *Initiation* has been found to occur 23 times after *in-between Decision Making*. This finding substantiates our assumption that the character of the concepts representing CIMB is cyclical.

Identification has been counted 24 times after *Initiation* but never before *Initiation*. *Identification* occurred 23 times before *Formulation* and 5 times after *Formulation*. *Identification* took place 3 times before and 4 times after *Structuring* and 7 times before *in-between Decision Making* and 6 times after *in-between Decision Making*. *Identification* has not been found before *Final Decision Making*. Due to the frequent occurrence of *Identification* before *Formulation* and after *Initiation* the position of *Identification* is between these two concepts.

Formulation never occurred before and or after *Initiation*. The concept *Formulation* took place 5 times before *Identification,* 23 times after *Identification,* 24 times before *Structuring* and 3 times after *Structuring*. *Formulation* has also been found to occur 11 times before and 3 times after *in-between Decision Making* but not before *Final Decision Making*. This finding gives reason to assume that *Formulation* is located between the concepts *Identification* and *Structuring*.

Structuring has never been found before and or after *Initiation* nor *Final Decision Making*. *Structuring* occurred 4 times before and 3 times after *Identification*. The occurrence of the concept *Structuring* before *Formulation* was less frequent with 8 times compared to after *Formulation,* 25 times. *Structuring* before *in-between Decision Making* has been counted 21 times and after *in-between Decision Making* 3 times. We deduced that the concept *Structuring* is positioned before the concept *in-between Decision Making* and after *Formulation*.

The concept *in-between Decision Making* has been found to occur 23 times before *Initiation* and 7 times before *Identification* and 6 times after *Identification*. *In-between Decision Making* took place 11 times before and 4 times after *Formulation* and 3 times before and 11 times after *Structuring*. Therefore, the position of the concept *in-between Decision Making* is before *Initiation* and after *Structuring*. The concept *Final Decision Making* has been counted four times after *Structuring*. Therefore the concept *Final Decision Making* only occurred once in a sequence after the concept *Structuring* and never before and or after the concepts *Initiation, Identification* or *Formulation*. *Final Decision Making* symbolises the end of the information selection task.

Summary of QCBA

QCBA revealed that different approaches QBVA, QCA and quantitative analysis of frequency were needed to create a comprehensive picture of collaborative information management behaviour during the IST in a distributed synchronized environment. QVBA was useful to analyse collaborative nonverbal behaviour, whereas QCA was helpful to study the collaborative verbal behaviour. Combining these findings allowed us to answer our fourth research question regarding how collaborative nonverbal and

Figure 1. Analysis of frequency of all four video recordings: Concepts before and after one other concept

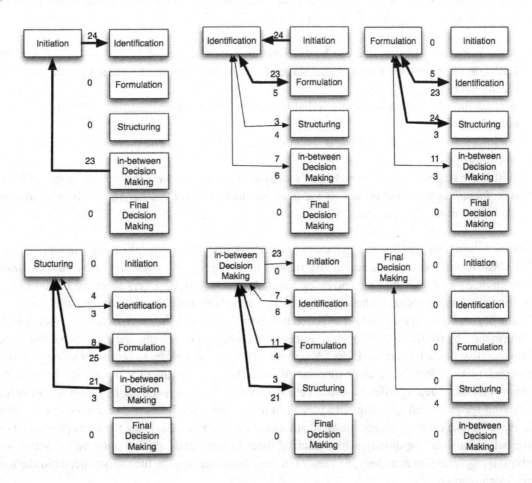

verbal behaviour of the users is related to cognitive abilities of the users and what effect this relation has for the CIMB during the IST. The cognitive abilities required during the IST are acquiring knowledge (cognitive process of learning), categorizing information (cognitive process of recognising), associating information (cognitive process of analysing), creating meaning of information (cognitive process of comprehension) and drawing conclusions (cognitive process of judging). These represent the link between collaborative nonverbal behaviour and the collaborative verbal behaviour during the information selection task. Based on these findings five concepts have been established and each concept describes a stage of CIMB users went through during the information selection task: *Initiation, Identification, Formulation, Structuring* and *(in-between or Final) Decision Making.*

By quantifying the results we located the position of each concept and derived that *Initiation* symbolises the start point of an IST and *Final Decision Making* the end point of the IST. Quantitative findings also revealed that the character of the concepts describing CIMB is cyclical and concepts occur in a common order within the information selection task *Initiation, Identification, Formulation, Structuring* and *in-between Decision Making.*

MODEL for CIMB

Based on the findings of qualitative and quantitative analysis we will discuss the following findings in details to develop our model for CIMB, also see Figure 2:

1. An information selection task can be described in a sequence. A sequence consists of concepts. Each concept represents a behavioural stage of collaborative information management behaviour during the IST.
2. A stage includes collaborative nonverbal behaviour, cognitive abilities and collaborative verbal behaviour.
3. An information selection task starts with the stage *Initiation* and ends with the stage *Final Decision Making.*
4. Within the stages of *Initiation* and *Final Decision Making* users went through the stages of *Initiation, Identification, Formulation, Structuring* and *(in-between) Decision Making* in order to finish the information selection task.

Figure 2 illustrates the CIMB of two users (user A and user B) performing an information selection task. CIMB of an information selection task implies five behavioural stages: *Initiation, Identification, Formulation, Structuring* and *(in-between or Final) Decision Making.* Users enter these stages at the same time and continue together because they carry out collaborative actions and reactions.

In the beginning of an information selection task both users are in the stage *Initiation.* User A seeks for information by reading a document, acquires knowledge and learns that there is a large amount of information that has to be managed. User A verbally expresses himself by suggesting a strategy of how to approach this problem. At the same time user B reads the same document as it has been dragged into the high-resolution area in order to read it clearly and user B gives feedback by nodding and agreeing. Giving feedback and agreeing with user A indicates that user B has also encountered the same information management problem, the large amount of data. Within this stage the users performed the nonverbal actions reading quietly, which enabled them to learn and to carry out a verbal action and reaction. By agreeing on a strategy, to view each document one by one, the users proceed to the next stage, *Identification.*

Identification means that user A and user B view the documents together by applying the strategy they agreed on. Viewing each document by dragging one by one into the high-resolution area allows users to recognize information. Users, either user A or user B verbalise the recognized information by specifying the document as a map, a schedule or an email.

In the third stage, *Formulation,* pre-selection of the documents takes place. After users specify the document type they pre-select, analyse and verbally compare information. Comparing includes information of document-related information or task-related information. The former has been found when user A compares details of map 1 with details of map 2. Comparing task-related information is understood as comparing the map 1 with the requirements of the task. This stage of *Formulation* is of great importance because users know that the information selection task requires them to select three out of ten documents, therefore pre-selecting and analysing information is necessary to continue the information selection process. By analysing information users examine the information methodologi-cally and pick out specific documents or information. *Formulation* is related to the goal of meeting the task requirements.

The next stage is *Structuring.* In this stage users review the pre-selected documents, which enable them to create contextual meaning of the information for their purpose. This stage has been found to be related to the roles users perform during the IST. The goal is to gain information appropriate for the specific role. Comprehension is verbally expressed by interpreting.

After interpreting, users enter the stage *in-between/final Decision Making* by selecting the analysed documents and drawing conclusions. The cognitive process of judging information has been found to happen in relation to other documents or the overall task. Users verbalise their judgments in form of verbally assessing them, e.g. User B: "I think we should keep both of them" (Video 1). User A gives feedback by reminding user B about the task requirements, e.g., User A: "We have four documents but we are supposed to have just three" (Video 1). In order to select the three out of the four documents they already have selected, users continue by re-entering one of the stages *Initiation, Identification, Formulation or Structuring* again.

This behaviour of re-entering a different stage (continuing backwards) can occur any time during the information selection task. Users can also start a new cycle, beginning with *Initiation*, and loop. The example given above when user A reminded user B of how many they should actually select, forced them to re-enter the stage *Formulation*. Users finish the information selection task when they have found the three documents and made a final decision together, *Final Decision Making*.

Discussion of the Five Stages

The five stages have been found to be important in different ways to complete the information selec-tions task. *Initiation* is inevitably during the information selection task as it helps the users to orient themselves. *Identification* is necessary to categorize documents, which helps users to collaborate over the shared digital workspace because they have established names for the document together, e.g. the large map, the inner city map.

Formulation is a stage where users pre-select, recognize and specify information. This requires the cognitive ability to categorize the information. Users had problems doing this, which was expressed in their verbal actions and reactions. Kuhlthau (1991) emphasized that it is in this stage that feelings of uncertainty can hinder individuals and that they have to recreate meaning to diminish uncertainty in order to increase confidence, which boosts their impetus to move on in the information management

Figure 2. Model for CIMB during an information selection task

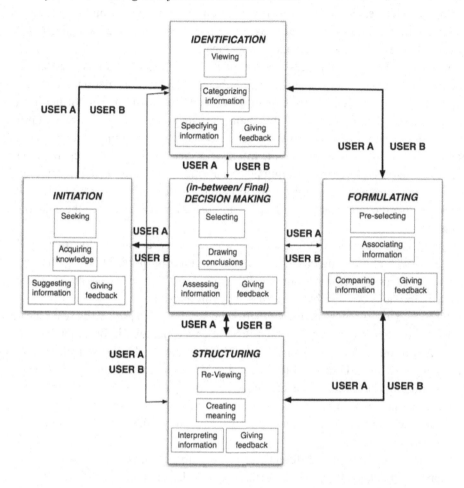

process. Analysis of our transcripts reflected the verbal expression of uncertainty clearly and by pre-selecting, recognizing and specifying information users could overcome this problem, *Formulation*. If users could not overcome the problem they stopped during the stage *Formulation* and changed their strategy. Instead, they selected a different document they have viewed before and judged its usefulness for their interest, *in-between Decision Making*. After that they reviewed documents they have pre-selected before and interpreted them, *Structuring*. Continuing this way has been found to hinder users in selecting the three essential documents because users needed more time. This shows that the stage *Structuring* represents a turning point during an information selection task. Although, users could share the same documents and verbalize their thoughts, they are also able to create different contextual meaning. The video recordings showed that participants had problems following their colleagues during this stage. We interpreted this behaviour as a lack of the creation of situational meaning and found that in order to manage information effectively a user must communicate his or her cognitive awareness clearly. Users achieved cognitive awareness by repeating what they referred to. Reviewing and interpreting multiple information sources also challenged the users' cognitive abilities (Hyldegård & Ingwersen, 2007, Vakkari, 2003) because the users could only remember fragments of information, which prevented them from making judgments on the relevance of the information in relation to the task. Consequently, users continued backwards to accomplish the goal. This behaviour has been identified as indecision of the user (Karamuftuoglu, 1998). Indecision of a subject describes the relation of a document to an inquirer (user or community) that cannot be determined at the time of the interaction. A high number of documents resulted in users' cognitive fragmentation of information sources and forced users to re-enter certain stages. Reddy & Jansen (2008) identified fragmented information sources as one of the triggers responsible for the shift from individual to collaborative information management behaviour. Indecision due to fragmented information has been found to lead to the use of a different strategy. Users decided to choose an alternative information management strategy (Xie, 2000). Finding the right strategy enables users to continue, to assess the relevance of the information and to make absolute judgments, and to come to a final decision (Sperber and Wilson, 1986).

Summary of Model for CIMB

Our model for CIMB derived from qualitative and quantitative findings revealed that performing an information selection task is a cyclical and dynamic process, which is reflected in the users CIMB. Five stages describe CIMB during an IST: *Initiation, Identification, Formulation, Structuring and Decision Making (final and in-between).* These stages can be compared with Kuhlthau's (1991) stages during an information-seeking task. Users start an IST in the stage *Initiation* and finish the task with the stage *Final Decision Making.* Within the task users go through the stages *Initiation, Identification, Formulation, Structuring and in-between Decision Making).* The stages also represent the user's progress during the IST. The stages *Formulation* and *Structuring* have been found to be crucial for an IST, as the cognitive abilities of users can be challenged. Because users have different cognitive abilities, users can also create different contextual meaning, which influences the ongoing process. The fragmentation of information sources has also been found to have an effect on CIMB as it can lead to indecision and to the change of information management strategies.

AN INTELLIGENT INFORMATION MANAGEMENT TOOL

Criteria for the Design of an IMtool

The discussion of the model revealed that cognitive demands on users are high in distributed synchronous meetings during an information selection task. Having an intelligent information management tool to reduce users' mental load would help them focus their attention on accomplishing the task. From our model we derived three main criteria to design an intelligent collaborative information management tool (IMtool), which answered our fourth research question:

1. The IMtool should facilitate and encourage both levels of interaction, human-computer interaction and human-to-human interaction by visualising the users progress of both levels during the information selection task.

2. The IMtool should support the users in each stage during the information selection task, specifically nonverbal actions, by visualising information structured, e.g. viewing documents, pre-selecting documents, etc.

3. The IMtool should support the cognitive abilities such as acquiring knowledge, information, categorizing information, associating information, creating meaning of information and drawing conclusions of information by visualising the cognitive processes of each user, e.g. recognizing information, analysing information, etc.

These criteria correlate with design rules outlined by Bailey (1989) and Keyes & Krull (1992) who pointed out that a well-designed interface should have a level of information structure, a level of specification and visual consistency.

A level of information structure includes organization and simplification of the information. This is achieved by grouping documents of the same type (Bailey, 1989), e.g. all documents that contain timetables are in the beginning of a document list. The users can focus their attention and orient themselves. A level of information structure would support the stages *Initiation* and *Identification*, hence the cognitive processes of learning and recognizing, which meets our first and third criteria.

Simplification of the information includes labelling the information (Bailey, 1989). A descriptive title or familiar document name and a picture of the document assists the user to memorize information. The user can associate documents before reading them in detail. The level of specification refers to functions that allow the user to specify the meta-information and interpret the information in the document. This would be achieved by providing functions of categorizing, annotating, assessing its relevance or adding comments (Bailey, 1989). The level of specification refers to all three criteria. It would enhance the stages *Identification, Formulation, Structuring and Decision Making,* hence support the cognitive processes of recognizing, analysing, comprehension and judging. It would also facilitate both levels of interaction because users can record their verbal and nonverbal actions by using functions of categorizing, adding comments or keywords etc.

Visual consistency is concerned with the layout of the interface. The layout should be neither chaotic nor overwhelming (Keyes & Krull, 1992), so that users can retrieve information easily, which would support the all cognitive processes. This rule refers to our third criteria.

Proposed Interface for an IMtool: *InfoManager*

Based on these design rules we conceptualised a tool that meets our criteria and called it *InfoManager*. Figure 3 illustrates such an interface.

Instead of being overwhelmed with documents displayed in the shared digital workspace, users open the *InfoManager* window. A menu list at the top and minimum of two columns appear. In order to support the first stage of an information selection task, *Initiation* (which includes the nonverbal behaviour seeking and requires the cognitive ability of acquiring knowledge), the column on the left contains the documents in form of a list. Users can orient themselves, seek for information and acquire knowledge.

After users have sought for information they have the possibility to view and pre-select, review and select information, which the second and subsequent column, the user-column is meant for. This refers to the stages *Identification, Formulation, Structuring* and *Decision Making*. The user-column is a personalized column that can be used individually or collaboratively. Individually, as users would be able to use the IMtool to prepare themselves for a distributed synchronous meeting, or as users want to view information individually in the beginning of such a meeting.

The user-column should help to manage information either individually or collaboratively. If the participants in our experiment would have had such a tool they could have used either one user-column together or a user-column each. If users want their own user-column they can enter the name on the top of the column. Having separate user-columns meets the users personal preferences to seek, view, pre-select, review and select information at the time it supports cognitive awareness because the other user can see who is annotating what kind of information. This would be of great importance if more than two users manage information collaboratively distributed and synchronously.

The user-column used individually or collaboratively contains certain functions (see Figure 3) that should facilitate users in the stage of *Formulation, Structuring* and *Decision Making*. By clicking the *categorize* button user(s) can categorize information. Next to the button *categorize* a window opens and the user(s) can type the identified category, e.g. email of police. This enables users to view and categorize information individually and collaboratively. Adding *keywords* allows the users to specify and recall the information and helps users to remember the content, e.g., what was important in this document. The window next to the button *annotated* informs the user and the other party that this document has been viewed and changes have been made. If the window next to button *annotated* shows the word "Open" it means that the user(s) are currently working on this specific document. If the window next to button *annotated* shows the word "annotated" it means that the user(s) have annotated this document but do not work on it anymore. Commenting on a document can be achieved by clicking the button *comments*. The user(s) enter their thoughts (interpretations, uncertainties, etc.) individually or collaboratively about the information in the comment box. If "yes" appears alongside the *comment* button; it indicates that the comment box contains comments. To assess the relevance of a document a *relevance* button is provided. By clicking on the button a window with numbers (1 for low importance to 10 for high importance) allows the user(s) to score the relevance of the meta-information and document content. If users decided to manage information individually they can carry out the same actions simultaneously and can also follow the proceedings of the other party. In contrast, if users decided to manage information collaboratively the user-column should support the users cognitive abilities and help users to verbalise their thoughts, hence facilitate human-to-human interaction.

The menu list contains several standard functions. *File* allows users to save the project, close the project, adding new documents and an export function. Users can export whole projects or parts of the project (comments, annotations etc,) as emails or convert them into word documents or pdf or place them as images in a power point presentation. *Edit* contains copy, paste, cut and a function for deleting a document. *Tools* provide a formatting palette. The last but most important one for managing information collaboratively is *Users*. This function includes comparing information, selecting documents, adding new user or deleting a user. Comparing information offers two possibilities for the users and is meant to support users who work with separate user-columns: the user can either compare his or her own annotations between documents (individual comparing) or the user can choose to compare his or her document annotations with the document annotations of the other user (collaborative comparing). The *InfoManager* opens the selected documents and shows similarities such as highlighted sections, similar comments or relevance scores.

Figure 3. InfoManager, an intelligent information management tool

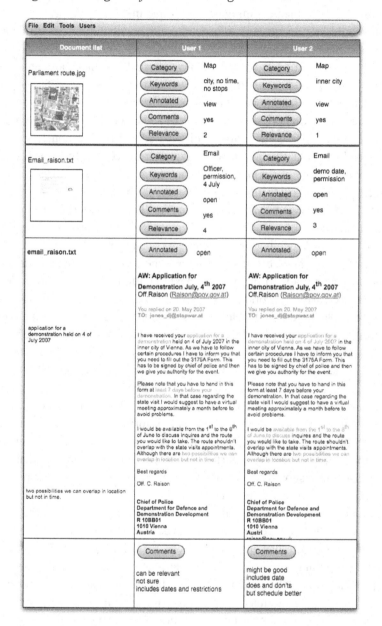

Summary of Intelligent IMtool

The developed IMtool, called the *InfoManager* has been designed to assist the behavioural stages, thus CIMB users went during an information selection task in a distributed synchronous environment. The intelligence of the *InfoManager* is manifested in its flexibility to serve users information management behaviour, either individually or collaboratively. The functions of the IMtool should support human-to-human interaction, and facilitate the cognitive abilities needed in each stage during an information selection task. Moreover, it should allow users to manage information individually and at the same time encourage users to manage information collaboratively. Being able to manage several documents of several users is a desired function, as it would allow the user to manage information as in a co-located environment, where several users manage information face-to-face.

FUTURE TRENDS

The aim of this chapter was to contribute to existing research and theories on individual information management behaviour and single-user design approaches by developing a model for CIMB and proposing an interface for an intelligent IMtool. However, we recognize that our findings are based on two-user interaction and that distributed synchronized meetings can consist of more than two users. This has been considered in the design of our IMtool. Therefore, further research is required to firstly, test the usability of our proposed IMtool for two or more users and secondly, to validate our model for more than two users. We suggest conducting experiments with more than two users and to conduct experiments with more than two users in different constellations using the proposed IMtool. Collecting data of real-time distributed synchronous meetings would be ideal.

The concept of the IMtool has been designed as an application implemented in a specific collaborative technology such as the Virtual Collaboration Desk. However, it would be of an interest if users could also access or even use this application on other systems to manage information remotely. Referring to the idea of open information management (Yli-Hietanen & Niiranen, 2008) users should not be restricted in having to use a specific collaboration tool to use this application. Specifically, the usage of the IMtool to prepare for a distributed synchronous meeting, e.g. A user preparing documents could automatically connect relevant and work in progress documents with the IMtool. At the same time the IMtool could update the list of documents necessary for the meeting. This update could be sent automatically as a message to the other team members, which would help them to manage new information quicker. These functions emphasize the idea of open, boundless information management applications and would support interconnectivity and collaboration.

CONCLUSION

This chapter has addressed the recent interest in information sciences to understand CIMB (Foster, 2006; Hansen & Jaervelin, 2008; Reddy & Jansen, 2008). We attempted to provide a model to understand distributed synchronous CIMB during an information selection task from sociological and psychological points of view and to derive criteria useful to design an intelligent information management tool. By investigating distributed synchronous CIMB from a sociological and psychological user-oriented approach we considered individual information management behaviour and single-user interaction as well as collaborative information management behaviour and dual-user interaction during an information selection task.

Our model and the derived criteria were based on five research questions, which have been answered by findings of qualitative and quantitative analyses. Initial observation of the data revealed that CIMB during an information selection task contains both verbal and nonverbal actions and reactions carried out by the user in order to manage information collaboratively. This finding answered our first research question. This distinction between nonverbal and verbal actions and reactions required different methods. We investigated nonverbal actions and reactions by means of qualitative behavioural video analysis. Findings of this analysis revealed six forms of nonverbal CIMB that occur during the information selection task, which answered our second research question: seeking, viewing, pre-selecting, reviewing selecting and feedback. Verbal actions and reactions have been studied by means of qualitative content analysis. Findings of QCA highlighted five forms of verbal CIMB, which answered our third research question: suggesting, specifying, comparing, interpreting and assessing. Both approaches were useful in analyses and revealed a comprehensive picture of CIMB. Qualitative comparative behavioural analysis was used to compare findings of both approaches and revealed collaborative nonverbal information management behaviour enabled users to process information cognitively and collaborative verbal information management behaviour can be understood as encoding these cognitive processes. The link between verbal CIMB and nonverbal CIMB is the cognitive ability of the users to process and encode information, which answered our fourth research question. Encoding these cognitive processes by verbalizing their thoughts enabled users to interact and manage information collaboratively. Cognitive abilities enable users to shift from individual to collaborative information management behaviour (Hansen & Jaervelin's, 2004). Five concepts have been established and each concept illustrates this shift from collaborative (nonverbal actions and reactions) to individual (cognitive abilities) to collaborative information management behaviour (verbal actions and reactions): *Initiation, Identification, Formulation, Structuring and Decision Making.*

We quantified our results from QCBA and determined the position of each concept during the information selections task. Quantitative findings showed that each concept represented a specific behavioural stage during the information selection task and revealed that concepts occur in a common order. Based on these findings we created our model for CIMB. Both users started the information selection task in the stage *Initiation* and finished the information selection task with the stage *Final Decision Making.* Within these two stages users went through the stages *Initiation, Identification, Formulation, Structuring* and *in-between Decision Making* several times. They remained in these stages for the same time and re-entered stages several times during the information selection task. Moving back and forwards between stages reflected the users' cognitive feedback loops during the process of managing information collaboratively (Spink, 1997; Wilson, 1996) and indicates that an IST is a cyclical and dynamic process, which is reflected in users CIMB. Re-entering stages also implies that an IST challenges the users cognitive abilities needed to manage information collaboratively. Because different users have different cognitive abilities the progress can be influenced which leads to indecision and the change of information management strategies. Our stages that represent CIMB can be compared with the stages of Kuhlthau's model for individual information seeking (Kuhlthau, 1991). However, our model is cyclical and dynamic instead of linear and illustrates collaborative information management behaviour in distributed synchronous collaboration during an information selection task which includes seeking and retrieving behaviour.

Based on our model we derived three criteria for the design of an intelligent information management tool (IMtool), which answered our fifth research question. The IMtool should facilitate and encourage both levels of interaction, human-computer interaction and human-to-human interaction by visualising the users progress of both levels during the information selection task. The IMtool should support the users in each stage during the information selection task, specifically nonverbal actions, by visualising information in an order, e.g. viewing documents, pre-selecting documents, etc. The IMtool should sustain the cognitive abilities such as acquiring knowledge, categorizing information, associating information, creating meaning of information and drawing conclusions of information by visualising the cognitive processes of each user, e.g. recognizing information, analysing information, etc.

These criteria indicate that the design of an intelligent IMtool should consider a level of structure, a level of specification and visual consistency in order to support two users during an information selection task in a distributed synchronous environment (Bailey, 1989; Keyes & Krull, 1992). The hypothetical design of our IMtool, called the *InfoManager* meets our criteria. The proposed functions of the *InfoManager* emphasize the cyclical, dynamic and complex character of human collaboration in a distributed synchronous environment.

In conclusion, our model expanded our understanding for distributed synchronous CIMB of two-person remote teams and our findings further substantiated existing literature and theoretical propositions. However, the development of our model, thus the design for an intelligent IMtool is based on video recordings and experiment data instead of real-life data. Our model only considers two users at a time during an information selection task, instead of multiple users and did not consider affective factors as recommended by Kuhlthau (1991).

REFERENCES

Bailey, R. W. (1989). *Human Performance Engineering Using Human Factors/Ergonomics to Achieve Computer System Usability*. New Jersey, USA: AT&T   Bell Laboratories.

Butcher, D., & Rowley, J. (1998). The 7'Rs of Information Management. *Managing information, 5*(2), 5-7.

Case, D. O. (2006). Information Behaviour. *Annual Review of Information Science and Technology, 40*, 293-327.

Charmaz, K. (2006). *Constructing Grounded Theory. A practical Guide Through Qualitative Analysis*. Wiltshire, GB: Sage Publications.

Chen, J.R., Shawn, R.W., Wragg, S. D. (2000)A Distributed Multi-Agent System for Collaborative Information Management and Sharing. *Proceedings of the ninth international conference of information and knowledge management* (pp. 382-388). Nov. 06-11, Virginia, USA.

Dias, C. (2001). Corporate Portals: A Literature Review of a new Concept in information Management. *International Journal of Information Management, 21,* 269-287.

Foster, J. (2006). Collaborative Information Seeking and Retrieval. *Annual Review of Information Science and Technology, 40*, 329-356.

Hansen, P., & Jaervelin, K. (2005). Collaborative Information Retrieval in an Information-intensive Domain. *Information Processing and Management, 41,* 1101-1119.

Hogg, M. A., & Vaughan, G. M. (2005) *Social Psychology*. Gosport, UK: Pearson Education Limited.

Hyldegard, J., & Ingwersen, P. (2007). Task Complexity and Information Behaviour in Group Based Problem Solving. *Information Research, 12*(4), Retrieved May 21, 2008, from http://InformationR. net/ir/12-4/colis/colis27.html.

Ingwersen, P. (1996). Cognitive Perspectives of Information Retrieval Interaction: Elements of a Cognitive IR Theory. *Journal of Documentation, 12*(1), 1-18.

Karamuftuoglu, M. (1998). Collaborative information retrieval: towards a social informatics view of IR interaction. *Journal of American Society for Information Sciences, 49*(12), 1070-1080.

Keyes, E., Krull, R. (1992). User Information Processing and Online Visual Structure. *Proceedings of the 10th annual international conference on System Documentation.* (pp.121-128), Ontario, USA.

Kelly, G. A. (1955). *The Psychology of Personal Constructs.* NY: Norton.

Kelly, G. A. (1991). *The Psychology of Personal Constructs.* London: Routledge.

Kuhl, J., & Atkinson, J. W. (1986). *Motivation, Thought, and Action.* NY: Praeger Publishers.

Kuhlthau, C. (1991). Inside the Search Process: Information Seeking from the User's Perspective. *Journal of American Society for Information Sciences, 42*(5), 361-371.

Malone, T. W., & Crowston, K. (1994). The interdisciplinary study of coordination. *ACM Computing Surveys, 26*(1),87-118.

Matthews, G., Davies D. R., Westerman, S. J., & Stammers, R. B. (2004). *Human Performance, Cognition, Stress and individual differences.* NY: Psychology Press.

Reddy, M. C., & Jansen, B. J. (2008). A Model for Understanding Collaborative Information Behaviour in Context: A Study of Two Healthcare Teams. *Information Processing and Management, 44,* 256-273.

Simnett, R. (1996). The Effect of Information Selection, Information Processing and Task Complexity on Predictive Accuracy of Auditors. *Accounting, Organizations and Society. 21*(7/8), 699-719.

Spink, A. (1997). Study of Interactive Feedback during Mediated Information Retrieval. *Journal of the American Society for information science, 48*(5), 382-394.

Strauss, A., & Corbin, J. (1998). *Basics of Qualitative Research. Techniques and Procedures for Developing Grounded Theory.* California, USA: Sage Publications.

Talja, S. (2002). Information Sharing in Academic Communities: Types and Levels of Collaboration in Information Seeking and Use. *New Review of Information Behaviour Research. 3(3),* 143-160.

Taylor, A., & Farrell, S. (1992). Information Management in Context. *Aslib Proceedings, 44*(9), 319-322.

Vakkari, P. (1999). Task Complexity, Problem Structure and Information Action: Integrating Studies of Information Seeking and Retrieval. *Information Processing and Management, 35,* 819-837.

Wilson, T. D. (1981). On User Studies and Information Needs. *Journal of Documentation, 37*(1), 3-15.

Wilson, T. D., & Walsh C. (1996). *Information behaviour: an interdisciplinary perspective. Sheffield:* University of Sheffield Department of Information Studies.

Wilson, T. D. (1999). Models in Information Behaviour Research. *Journal of Documentation. 55*(3), 249-270.

Xie, H. I. (2000). Shifts of Interactive Intentions and Information-Seeking Strategies in Interactive Information Retrieval. *Journal of American Society for Information Science. 51*(9), 841-857.

Yil-Hietanen, J., & Niiranen, S. (2008). Towards Open Information Management in Health Care. *The Open Medical Informatics Journal, 2*(1), 42-48.

Chapter VI
R²–IBN:
Argumentation Based Negotiation Framework for MAIS–E² Model

Lobna Hsairi
SOIE: Institut Supérieur de Gestion de Tunis, Tunisie

Khaled Ghédira
SOIE: Institut Supérieur de Gestion de Tunis, Tunisie

Adel M. Alimi
REGIM: Ecole Nationale d'Ingénieurs de Sfax, Tunisie

Abdellatif BenAbdelhafid
CERENE-SILI: Université du Havre, France

ABSTRACT

*In the age of information proliferation, openness, open information management, **interconnectivity**, **collaboration** and communication advances, **extended enterprise**s must be up to date to the new strategic, economic and organizational structures. Consequently, intelligent software based on **agent** technology emerges to improve system design, and to increase enterprise competitive position as well. The competitiveness is based on the information management, **cooperation**, **collaboration** and **interconnectivity**. Thus, within these **interconnectivity** and **cooperation**, conflicts may arise. The automated negotiation plays a key role to look for a common agreement. Argumentation theory has become an important topic in the field of **Multi-Agent Systems** and especially in the negotiation problem. In this chapter, first, the proposed model **MAIS-E²** (Multi-**Agent** Information System for an **Extended Enterprise**) is presented. Then an **argumentation based negotiation** framework: Relationship-Role and Interest Based **Negotiation** (**R²-IBN**) framework is presented, and within this framework, the authors focused mainly on, argument generation module via inference rules and argument selection module via **fuzzy logic**.*

INTRODUCTION

Nowadays, a number of new concepts have been proposed, e.g., Virtual Organization, Supply Chain Management, Virtual and **Extended Enterprise**, etc (Tsung-Yi , 2008; Martinez, Fouletier, Park & Favrel, 2001). An **extended enterprise** is the **cooperation, collaboration** and **interconnectivity** of legally independent enterprises, institutions, or individuals. The **extended enterprise** will be characterized by intensively concurrent engineering based on open information both in management and technologies such as digitalization, computer network, and artificial intelligence (Tsung-Yi, 2008). The intelligent software **agent** technology provides a natural way to overcome such problems (Martinez, Fouletier, Park & Favrel, 2001). **Agents** help to capture individual interests, local decision making using incomplete information, autonomy, responsiveness, robustness, modular and distributed. A **Multi-Agent System (MAS)**, as a society of autonomous **agents**, is an inherently open and distributed system. It is made up of a group of **agents** combined with each other to solve a common problem cooperatively. In addition, **negotiation** is a key form of interaction in systems composed of multiple autonomous **agents** (Bench-Capon & Dunne, 2007). The automated **negotiation** plays a key role in sharing information and resources to look for a common agreement. The research literature proves that **Argumentation Based Negotiation (ABN)** is an effective means of resolving conflicts in **MAS** (Bench-Capon & Dunne, 2007; Hsairi, Ghédira, Alimi & Ben Abdelhafid, 2008). Besides, the **fuzzy logic** of Zadeh (1965) opens new horizons in the vast world of information analysis and treatment. One of the present tendencies in the **fuzzy** modeling is generating models that take into consideration two fundamental conditions at the same time: interpretability (which is the description capacity of the modeled systems behavior) precision and fidelity of model towards the original system (Casillas, Cordòn, Herrera & Magdalena, 2003).

In this chapter, in the first place, we present our research efforts in developing a **MAS** architecture named **Multi-Agent** Information Systems for an **Extended Enterprise (MAIS-E²)**. Then, we define the Relationship-Role and Interest Based **Negotiation (R²-IBN)** framework. R²-IBN framework is an extension of an existing one namely IBN (Rahwan, Sonenberg & Dignum, 2004). In this chapter, we present mainly the extensions made in two modules: the argument generation module via inference rules and argument selection module via **fuzzy** rules based system as an intelligent method in order to better estimate the desirability degree of the argument to send.

The remainder of this chapter is structured as follows: the *background* section describes **extended enterprises**, reviews **negotiation** approaches and related works. The *MAIS-E²: An Intelligent Model Toward An Inter-Enterprise Cooperation* section presents our research efforts and experiences in developing a **multi-agent** model for an **Extended Enterprise**. The *R²-IBN: Argumentation Framework* section describes our proposed **argumentation based negotiation** framework. *Future Trends* section presents emerging tendencies. Finally, in the *conclusion* section remarks and perspectives are given.

BACKGROUND

In this section, we first describe **extended enterprises**, then, we review **negotiation** approaches and finally, we review related works.

Extended Enterprises

The term **extended enterprise**, which is generally attributed to Mowshowitz (Mowshowitz, 1986), characterizes such an organization of future enterprises. The term obtained its current importance for business economics from Davidow and Malone's landmark book (Davidow & Malone, 1992). An **extended enterprise** is a **cooperation** of legally independent enterprises, institutions, or individuals, which provide a service on the basis of a common understanding of business. The cooperating units mainly contribute their core competency, whilst sharing skills, costs, and access to each others market. To external partners they act, however, as a single corporation. The corporation refuses an institution-alisation, e.g., by central offices; instead, the **cooperation** is managed by using information and communication technologies (Fischer, Muller & Pischel 1996).

Negotiation Approaches

A variety of automated **negotiation** approaches have been studied in the literature. The major families are:

Game-Theoretic Approaches

Game theory offers a very powerful tool for studying and engineering strategic interaction among self-interested computational **agents** in general (Von Neumann & Morgenstern, 1944), and to automated **negotiation** in particular. But, there are many drawbacks associated with its use in such **negotiation**:

- Game theory assumes that it is possible to characterize **agent**'s preferences with respect to possible outcomes.
- Game theory often assumes perfect computational rationality.

Heuristic-Based Approaches

In heuristic-based approaches, **agent** designers relax some of the assumptions of game theory, particularly regarding unbounded rationality. But, they still have a number of drawbacks (Jennings, Faratin, Lomuscio , Parsons, Sierra & Wooldridge, 2001).

- The models often lead to the outcomes which are sub-optimal because they adopt an approximate notion of rationality.
- It is very difficult to predict precisely how the system and the constituent **agents** will behave.

These two approaches are centered around the trading of proposals. However, they have the following main limitations:

- The only feedback that can be made to a proposal is a counter-proposal or an acceptance or withdrawal;
- It is hard to change the set of issues under **negotiation** in the course of a **negotiation**.

In such case alternative techniques would be needed.

Argument-Based Approaches

The aim of an **Argumentation Based Negotiation** (**ABN**) is to remove the above limitations. The basic idea behind the **ABN** approach is to allow additional information called argument, to be exchanged, over and above proposals (Jennings, Faratin, Lomuscio, Parsons, Sierra & Wooldridge, 2001). An argument is a piece of information presented by the pair <Premises, Conclusion> and have a degree of desirability. It is attached to the exchanged proposals during **negotiation**. It is also used to improve the **negotiation** by introducing flexibility via the introduction of new information, which is taken into consideration in the **negotiation** space. Thus, this information provides a means of changing the **negotiation** space itself.

Related Works

A number of researchers attempted to play **agent** technology to industrial enterprise integration. Thus, we can distinguish, an **Agent**-Based Intelligent Manufacturing for the 21st Century (Qiao & Zhu, 1999) and a supply web co-ordination by an **agent** based trading network with integrated logistic services (Kovac & Paganelli, 2003). With these different efforts, researchers take into consideration the integration problem according to different levels. Our research efforts are different from the others. We take into consideration the communication level and the exchange of information and knowledge. In fact, communication takes place between multiple entities but in this chapter we focus only on the reasoning mechanism of just one peer.

Moreover, other researchers proposed many formal frameworks based on **ABN** for automated **negotiation**. These efforts take into consideration different aspects. We can distinguish works that deal with protocols (McBurney, Parsons, Van Eijk & Amgoud, 2002), abductive reasoning (Sadri, Toni & Torroni, 2001), devising and formalizing rebutting and undercutting arguments (Parsons, Sierra & Jennings, 1998; Amgoud & Cayrol, 2002), and catering epistemic and motivational reasoning (Rahwan, 2004). Our approach is different from these models since they tend to focus on the product of argumentation. Our approach aims at catering in the same framework the main modules of argumentation: Evaluation, Generation and Selection. The whole framework is considered to be appropriate to industrial domain and especially to the **extended enterprise** case.

MAIS-E²: AN INTELLIGENT MODEL TOWARD AN INTER-ENTERPRISE COOPERATION

Multi-Agent Information System for an **Extended Enterprise** (**MAIS-E²**) model is proposed in order to have an integrated logistic system for the **extended enterprise** case. **MAIS-E²** is a collection of intelligent **agent** agencies with specialized expertises which interact, cooperate and collaborate to carry out common objectives.

The remainder of this section is as follow: first sub-section presents the system design and the second sub-section describes the **MAIS-E²** functioning.

System Design

The **extended enterprise** is "a set of partner *agents* that share the complementary, similar or dissimilar resources and competencies and *cooperate* together to maximize shared objectives". Two ideas emerge from this definition: *cooperation* and *agent* technology. The **cooperation** between these partner **agents** is a diagonal **cooperation** accomplished with the intermediate of an agency of "Mediator" **agents**. Also, we distinguish four types of **agents** in our proposed model **MAIS-E²**:

* "Enterprise" **agents**: composed by the different kinds of enterprises which constitute the **extended enterprise** such as partners, competitors, suppliers etc.
* "Mediator" **agents**: assume the **cooperation** between different "Enterprise" **agents**.
* "Specialist" **agents**: that can be planning, information, logistic **agents** etc.
* Personal assistant: represents the user in the **agent** network. It behaves to support the user during his work and interaction with the system.

In this work, we consider the **extended enterprise** like a society of intelligent **agents** that cooperate to satisfy a common objective. The architecture of **MAIS-E²** model is shown in figure 1.a and detailed in (Hsairi, Ghédira, Alimi & Ben Abdelhafid, 2006).

In this stage, we are interested in the functioning of **cooperation** between "Enterprise" **agent**s by the intermediate of "Mediator" **agents** agency as depicted in figure 1.b.

The **MAIS-E²** model rely on the existence of the distributed "Mediator" **agents** agency that assume binding between all partners in the **extended enterprise**. This primordial role consists of assuming and managing the Inter-enterprise Cooperative Information System. The "Mediator" **agent** agency consists in the key element for the **MAIS-E²** model functioning and inter-enterprise **cooperation**.

MAIS-E² Functioning

We define the inter-enterprise **cooperation** like: a situation where two or multiple partner **agents**, under the aegis of contracts, which have in common some resources and means for problems resolution in order to accomplish one or multiple activities in common. These **agents** communicate and collaborate between them in order to coordinate their tasks. Within this **cooperation**, as defined by Ferber (1995), the partners are also getting to:

* Collaborate;
* Coordinate their tasks and roles;
* Resolve conflicts.

Thus, it is important to define the conceptual elements of a "Mediator" **agent**.

Mediator Agent Architecture

As shown in figure 1.a and described before, we can distinguish four types of **agents**: Enterprise, Specialist, Personal assistant and Mediator.

An "Enterprise" **agent** covers a set of **agents** composed of: Mediator, Specialists, and Personal Assistant **agents**. These **agents** represent also the enterprise as a whole to the **MAIS-E²** model.

The Mediator **agent** architecture, that belongs to the proposed model are shown in figure 2. This architecture is based on a set of modules and a local database, which contains all relevant information about the **agent** behaviors.

The descriptions of the main modules that compose the Mediator **agent** architecture are as follow:

- Decision-making module: this module controls all the activities of the **agent**. The decision-making process consists of analyzing available information and applicatting decision mechanisms.
- Knowledge Base module: the local database stores all knowledge about **agent** behaviors and the community where the **agent** belongs.
- Local control and monitoring module: this module intends to control and monitor the operational execution of the **agent**.
- Perception processor: this module intends to perceive the external and internal environment.

The above modules constitute the knowledge processing unit for the Mediator **agent**.

- Behavior evaluation and the simulation expert display the **agent**'s behavior.
- Communication module: this module deals with the need to standardize the interaction between distributed **agents** and to define a language of communication. Within this module we notice the encapsulation of the **cooperation** module. This module manages the **cooperation** with the **agents** belonging to the model, while requesting **cooperation** for other **agents**, collecting responses, and sending them to the decision-making module. **Cooperation** module is divided to three sub-modules as defined by Ferber (1995): **collaboration**, coordination and conflicts resolution modules; these modules refer to the three levels of **cooperation**, which are the main roles of Mediator **agent**.

In this stage, we focus on the conflict resolution part of **cooperation**. Furthermore, the **extended enterprise** environment is characterized by: openness, heterogeneity, dynamicity etc. These charac-

*Figure 1. a. **MAIS-E²** organizational model. b. "Mediator" **agent** agency*

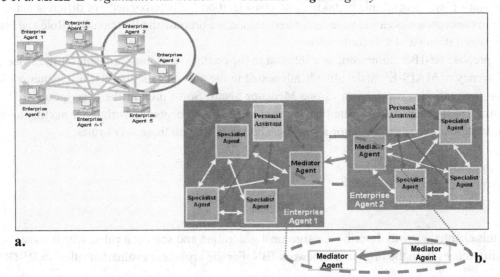

*Figure 2. Mediator **agent** architecture*

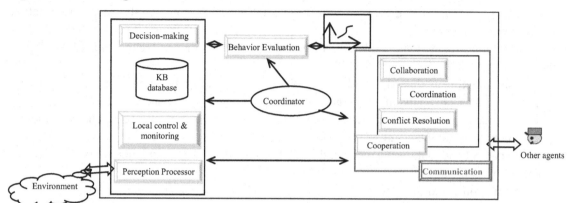

teristics make the conflict resolution process more and more difficult. As a solution we use automated **negotiation**. In fact, designing **negotiation** mechanisms aim at satisfying a number of features: simplicity, efficiency, distribution, symmetry, stability and flexibility (Rahwan, 2004). Thus, in the **extended enterprise** case study the "Flexibility" feature plays a crucial role by taking into consideration the heterogeneity of different actors. For this reason, we adopt the **Argumentation Based Negotiation** approach, and we propose the **R²-IBN** framework detailed in the following section.

R²-IBN: ARGUMENTATION FRAMEWORK

R²-IBN: Relationship-Role and Interest Based **Negotiation** framework is an extension of an existing one which is IBN proposed by Rahwan (2004). IBN uses mental attitudes: beliefs, desires, goals and planning rules as the primitives upon which argumentation are based (Rahwan, Pasquier, Sonenberg & Dignum, 2007). Being in the context of the **extended enterprise**, concepts like **agent** roles and relationships play a crucial role by taking into consideration the heterogeneity of different actors. For that, such concepts are essential to be integrated. Hence, we propose the Relationship-Role and Interest Based **Negotiation** (**R²-IBN**) framework.

We propose **R²-IBN** framework as a solution to the conflict resolution problem for the "Mediator" **agent** agency of **MAIS-E²** model already advocated in the previous section. In this chapter, we focus only on the reasoning mechanism of one Mediator **agent**. So to present the description of **R²-IBN** framework, it is crucial to advocate that in order to be able to negotiate with other **agents**, based on argumentation approach, a Mediator **agent** must be provided with three set of rules:

- Argument evaluation rules
- Argument generation rules
- Argument selection rules

In this chapter, we will describe the argument generation and selection rules, which constitute the main differences from the original framework IBN. For the argument evaluation rules, in **R²-IBN** we proceed in the same way as in IBN via three distinct parts of evaluation: one for reasoning about beliefs, another for arguing about what desires should be pursued and a third, for arguing about the best plan to intend in order to achieve these desires. We made some extensions by taking into consideration: the roles of the **agents** and their relationships in the reasoning mechanism of a Mediator **agent**.

Before detailing the generation and selection rules, it is important to introduce the definition of the proposed extensions: Role and relationship (advocated by the confidence level attributed to the peers).

Let $\mathcal{L}$ be a propositional language with $\wedge$ for conjunction, $\rightarrow$ for implication and $\neg$ for negation. Let $\vdash$ denote classical inference.

Role

An **agent** role is defined by a set of **agent** capabilities (We differentiate between the capabilities of communication: request, tell, confirm, etc. and the capabilities of task achievement. In this definition of **agent** role we mean by the capabilities of task achievement, the role of the **agent** in the **extended enterprise** case).

$$RolAg = \{Cap_1, ..., Cap_i, ... Cap_n\}$$

The addition and/or deletion of **agent**'s capabilities can generate an evolution of the **agent**'s role. The Mediator **agent** has its basic capabilities defined as

$$B_{Cap} = \{(Cap_i, cap_i), i = 1, ..., n\}$$

Where Cap_i is a propositional formula of **L** and cap_i its degree of certainty.

In addition to that, it has the capabilities of their partners defined as:

$$B_{ACap} = \left\{\left(A_j, \left(Cap_i^{A_j}, cap_i^{A_j}\right)\right), i = 1, ..., n; j = 1, ..., m\right\}$$

Where A_j is an **agent**, $Cap_i^{A_j}$ is a propositional formula of **L** and $cap_i^{A_j}$ its degree of certainty.

Confidence Based Relationship

Soh (2004) define five Confidence parameters:

- The helpfulness of the peer: the satisfaction degree of requests to the peer.
- The reliance of the peer on the **agent** in terms of the ratio of receiving requests from the peer among all peers.
- The tardiness degree: the communication delay between the **agent** and the peer.
- The hesitation degree: how readily the peer is to agree with a request.
- The availability degree of capability: whether the peer possesses the desired capability to solve task.

Following this list of parameters and according to their applicability to the **extended enterprise** characteristics, we can define an **agent**'s confidence parameters as follows:

$Conf_{Para}$ = *{helpfulness, reliance, tardiness degree, hesitation degree, availability degree}*.

We define the confidence base as follows:

B_{Conf}= {(A_j, $Conf^{A_j}$), j=1,..., n}

Where $Conf^{A_j}$: the confidence value attributed to the **agent** A_j.
The confidence value is defined by the function (1):

$Conf:$ $A \times Aj \rightarrow [0, 1]$

$$Conf^{A_j} = W_R * \mathrm{Re}\,put_{A_j} + W_C * \frac{\sum_{k=1}^{nb\_ParaConf} \left(Conf^k_{A_j} \right)}{nb\_ParaConf} \tag{1}$$

Where:

- Aj : an **agent**.
- $\mathrm{Re}\,put_{A_j} \in [0,1]$: The reputation value (value made by indirect interaction) of **agent** Aj passed by partner **agents** (for the first meeting).
- $Conf^k_{A_j} \in [0,1]$: The confidence value (value made by direct interaction) attributed to **agent** Aj for the k parameter ($k \in Conf_{Para}$).
- *nb_ParaConf*: The number of confidence parameters used.
- $W_R \in [0,1]$: The weight attributed to reputation.
- $W_C \in [0,1]$: The weight attributed to confidence (direct interaction).

Since, the reputation and direct confidence values have not the same impact on the total confidence value ($Conf^{A_j}$), we propose to handle this difference by assigning different weights W_R and W_C to $\mathrm{Re}\,put_{A_j}$ and $nb\_ParaConf$ $\left(\frac{\sum_{k=1}^{} \left(Conf^k_{A_j} \right)}{nb\_ParaConf} \right)$ respectively, such as $W_R + W_C = 1$ and $W_R < W_C$. We also attributed to the $\mathrm{Re}\,put_{A_j}$ a minor value via the weight W_R because the reputation given by other peers is not always reliable and we attribute to the direct interaction a major value via the weight W_C since it is an experience made by the **agent** itself.

Argument Generation Rules

The argument generation process consists in generating candidate arguments, by a Mediator **agent**, to be presented to a **negotiation** counterpart (another Mediator **agent**). An argument is constituted by the following pair <Premises, Conclusion>. The premises are constituted by believes, desires of the proponent and capabilities of the opponent. So, the **agent** role, via a set of its capabilities, is taken into account when generating arguments.

The argument generation process takes shape in the deductive reasoning context. We also need inference rules to infer from knowledge base. For that, we adopt the basic rules of reasoning used in classical logic: the Modus Ponens for forward reasoning and the Modus Tollens for backwards reasoning, whose symbolic expressions are:

Modus Ponens $P \rightarrow Q, P \vdash Q$.

Modus Tollens $\quad P \rightarrow Q, \neg Q \vdash \neg P$.

Argument Selection Rules

The Mediator **agent** may generate several arguments for any specific situation; and only one argument should be used for each step of the **negotiation**. The key features that determine what argument to send are the following: utility of the proposal to the proponent ("Mediator" **agent**); the confidence degree (which describes the degree of trust that the proponent puts in the opponent and it is calculated and updated using function (1). In the experimental setting, $W_R = 0.2$ and $W_C = 0.8$); and the capability degree of the opponent in the specific task (according to the proponent belief). Since these characteristics are generally imperfect and uncertain. We propose a **fuzzy** rule based system as an intelligent method in order to better estimate the desirability degree of the argument to send (Jang, 1997). Thus our **fuzzy** controller parameters are as follows:

Inputs Parameters

- Confidence degree: {Low, Medium and High}.
- Capability degree: {Low; Medium and High}.
- Proposal utility: {Low and High}.

Output Parameter

- Argument desirability degree: {Weak and Strong}.

All parameters are defined by trapezoidal membership functions illustrated by figure 3.

The rule base model is built by combination of inputs and output parameters. So, rules of the following form are encoded into our "Mediator" **Agent**

- **Rule1:** IF Confidence is low AND Capability is high AND Utility of the proposal is high THEN send an Argument with high degree of desirability.
- **Rule2:** IF Confidence is high AND Capability is high AND Utility of the proposal is low THEN send an Argument with low degree of desirability.

For inference process, Mamdani (Max-Min) (Jang, 1997) inference method is used. The Center of Gravity (COG) method is used for defuzzification to determine the output value: The argument desirability degree.

Experimental Evaluation

The experiments aim to postulate about the efficiency: **negotiation** cycle and argument exchanged numbers to reach agreement. For that, at this stage of work, we restrict the **negotiation** to two Mediator **Agents** in harbor application, the set of the argument that can be uttered between 0 and 10 and the **negotiation** cycle per proposal between 1 and 10. A simulation run involves 1000 separate **negotiation** encounters. These encounters are paired between Mediator **agents** using the same argument selection mechanism; **R²-IBN** Fuzzy: using our mechanism, Ramchurn Fuzzy: using Ramchurn mechanism (follow a Rhetoric Approach) (Ramchurn, Jennings & Sierra, 2003); Ramping: using Kraus mechanism (use different kinds of arguments: appeals, rewards and threats) (Kraus, Sycara, & Evenchik, 1998); Random: choosing any available argument at random and Non-arguing: not using arguments. The simulation was repeated 20 times.

From figure 4 we can deduce that **R²-IBN Fuzzy** mechanism fares better than the other ones. The better performance of **R²-IBN fuzzy** selection mechanism is mainly provided by using **fuzzy** rules. Thus, the **agent** has more meaningful means in selecting its arguments than the other **agents** and hence does better. In addition, in its **fuzzy** rules, **R²-IBN** Mediator **agent** takes into consideration the certainty degree of the capability of the opponent and the confidence value attributed to this opponent. This mechanism, improves the estimation of the desirability degree of the argument to be send which leads to optimize the **negotiation** cycle and argument exchanged numbers.

FUTURE TRENDS

Enterprises which are distributed in space and/or which are composed of a joint venture of legally different units have been recently called **extended enterprises**. The choice of intelligent software **agent** technology provides a natural way to design such systems because the intrinsic features of **MAS** cor-

Figure 3. Membership functions: Confidence, capability, proposal utility and argument desirability respectively

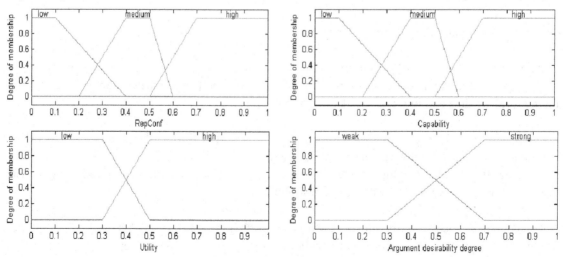

respond to those to be preserved in the hoped **extended enterprise**. Autonomy, heterogeneity, openness, **cooperation**, **collaboration**, dynamicity, **interconnectivity**, commitment, open information management etc. are all at the heart of our reflection.

MAIS-E², provides the **cooperation** and the **collaboration** of different actors in the **extended enterprise**. **R²-IBN** framework, grounded in a specific theory of argumentation, provides a flexible **negotiation** mechanism for **MAIS-E²** model. However, this work opens many horizons. First, the main current trend consists of defining a dynamic **negotiation** protocol to provide **interconnectivity** between two or more Mediator **agents**. Then, conceiving an ontology to allow Mediator **agents** to communicate despite having semantic and understanding problems, consist of an important future trend. Finally, the real world applications provide meaningful means for the applicability of the proposed model and framework.

CONCLUSION

The choice of intelligent software **agent** provides a natural way to design **extended enterprises** because the intrinsic features of **MAS** correspond to those to be preserved in the hoped **extended enterprises**. **MAIS-E²**, provides the **cooperation** of different actors in **extended enterprises**. In addition to that, the analysis of **cooperation** leads to the problem of conflict resolution. For that, **ABN** is an effective means of solving conflicts in **MAS**. In this way, we have already defined **R²-IBN** framework. **R²-IBN** argument selection mechanism has more meaningful means in selecting its arguments. However, it is still difficult to evaluate the number of arguments and cycles to reach agreement between more than two Mediator **agents**. In addition, each one can use its own selection mechanism. The future research goals consist of: making deep experimental evaluation of the argument selection process, extending the **negotiation** between more than two Mediator **agents**, conceiving an ontology to allow Mediator **Agents** to communicate despite having semantic and understanding problems and the instantiation of the **R²-IBN** for harbor application, that was considered as an **extended enterprise**.

Figure 4. Number of arguments and cycles to reach agreement

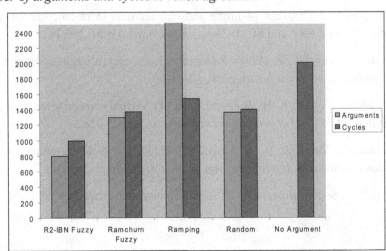

REFERENCES

Amgoud, L., & Cayrol, C. (2002). A reasoning model based on the production of acceptable arguments. *Annals of Mathematics and Artifcial Intelligence, 34*(1.3), 197-215.

Bench-Capon T. J. M., & Dunne P. E. (2007). Argumentation in Artificial Intelligence. *Artificial Intelligence, 171*(10–15), 619-641.

Casillas J., Cordòn O., Herrera F., & Magdalena L. (2003). Interpretability issues in fuzzy modeling. Vol. 128, *Studies in fuzziness and soft computing*, Springer, Berlin Heidelberg NewYork.

Davidow, W. H, & Malone, M. S. (1992). *The virtual Corporation: Structuring and Revitalizing the Corporation for the 21ˢᵗ Century.* New York, Harper Collins.

Ferber, J. (1995). *Les systèmes Multi-Agents Vers une intelligence collective.* Paris: Edition InterEditions.

Fischer, K., Muller, J. P., & Pischel, M. (1996). A pragmatic BDI architecture. In M. Wooldridge, J. P. Muller, & M. Tambe, (Ed.), *Intelligent Agents II: Agent Theories, Architectures and Languages, LNAI 1037.* Berlin: Springer.

Hsairi, L, Ghédira, K., Alimi, M. A., & Ben Abdelhafid, A. (2006, October). *Resolution of Conflicts via Argument Based Negotiation: Extended Enterprise Case.* Paper presented In: IEEE/SSSM06, (pp. 828-833), Université de Technologie de Troyes, IEEE Press, France.

Hsairi, L, Ghédira, K., Alimi, M. A., & Ben Abdelhafid, A. (2008, September). *R²-IBN: Argumentation Based Negotiation Framework for the Extended Enterprise.* Paper presented In HAIS'08, 3rd International workshop on Hybrid Artificial Intelligence systems, LNAI 5271, (pp. 533-542), Springer-Verlag Berlin Heidelberg, Burgos, Espagne.

Jang, J. (1997). IN P. Hall (Ed.), *Neuro-Fuzzy and Soft Computing.*

Jennings N. R., Faratin P., Lomuscio A. R., Parsons S., Sierra C., & Wooldridge M. J. (2001). Automated negotiation: prospects, methods and challenges. *IJG of Decision and Negotiation, 10*, 199-215.

Kovac, G. L., & Paganelli, P. (2003). A planning and management infrastructure for large, complex, distributed projects—beyond ERP and SCM. *Computer in Industry, 51*, 165-183.

Kraus, S., Sycara, K., & Evenchik, A. (1998). Reaching agreements through argumentation: A logical model and implementation. *Artificial Intelligence, 104*, 1-69.

Martinez, M. T., Fouletier, P., Park, K. H., & Favrel, J. (2001). Virtual enterprise-organisation, evolution and control. *International Journal of production economics, 74*, 225-238.

McBurney, P., Parsons S., Van Eijk, R., & Amgoud, L. (2002). A dialogue-game protocol for agent purchase negotiations. *Journal of Autonomous Agents and Multi-Agent Systems.*

Mowshowitz, A. (1986). Social dimensions of office automation. *Advances in Computers, 25*, 335-404.

Parsons S., Sierra C., & Jennings N. (1998). Agents that reason and negotiate by arguing. *Journal of Logic and Computation, 8*(3), 261-292.

Qiao B., & Zhu J. (1999). *Agent-Based Intelligent Manufacturing System for the 21ˢᵗ Century.* From www.shaping-thefuture.de/pdf_www/152_paper.pdf.

Rahwan I., Sonenberg L., & Dignum F. (2004). On interest-based negotiation. *Advances in Agent Communication, vol. 2922 of LNAI,* (pp. 383-401). Springer Verlag, Germany.

Rahwan, I. (2004). *Interest-based Negotiation in Multi-Agent Systems.* Unpublished doctoral dissertation, Department of Information Systems, University of Melbourne, Melbourne, Australia.

Rahwan, I., Pasquier, P., Sonenberg, L., & Dignum, F. (2007). *On the Benefits of Exploiting Underlying Goals in Argument-based Negotiation.* Paper presented In: Proceedings of 22ⁿᵈ Conference on Artificial Intelligence (AAAI). AAAI Press, California, USA.

Ramchurn S., Jennings N. R., & Sierra C. (2003). *Persuasive negotiation for autonomous agents: a rhetorical approach.* Paper presented in IJCAI Workshop on Computational Models of Natural Argument, pp. 9-17. AAAI Press.

Sadri F., Toni F., & Torroni P. (2001). Dialogue for negotiation: agent varieties and dialogue sequences. In John-Jules Meyer & Milind Tambe, (Ed.), *Intelligent Agent Series VIII: Proceedings of the 8th International Workshop on Agent Theories, Architectures, and Languages.*

Soh, L., & Li, X. (2004). *Adaptive, Confidence-based Mult-iagent Negotiation Strategy.* Paper presented in: AAMAS'04, New York, USA.

Tsung-Yi, C. (2008). Knowledge sharing in virtual enterprises via an ontology-based access control approach. *Computer in industry, 59,* 502-519.

Von Neumann, J., & Morgenstern, O. (1944). The Theory of Games and Economic Behaviour. *Princeton University Press.*

Zadeh, L. A. (1965). Fuzzy sets. *Inform Control, 8,* 338-358.

Chapter VII
Natural Language Parsing:
Perspectives from Contemporary Biolinguistics

Pauli Brattico
University of Jyväskylä, Finland

Mikko Määttä
University of Helsinki, Finland

ABSTRACT

Automatic natural language processing captures a lion's share of the attention in open information management. In one way or another, many applications have to deal with natural language input. In this chapter the authors investigate the problem of natural language parsing from the perspective of biolinguistics. They argue that the human mind succeeds in the parsing task without the help of language-specific rules of parsing and language-specific rules of grammar. Instead, there is a universal parser incorporating a universal grammar. The main argument comes from language acquisition: Children cannot learn language specific parsing rules by rule induction due to the complexity of unconstrained inductive learning. They suggest that the universal parser presents a manageable solution to the problem of automatic natural language processing when compared with parsers tinkered for specific purposes. A model for a completely language independent parser is presented, taking a recent minimalist theory as a starting point.

INTRODUCTION

Natural language parsing constitutes a skill that has been the target of automatization since the emergence of modern digital computers. Open information management environments are no exception. Whatever the intended application, the undertaking is nontrivial due to several features of natural languages, such as ambiguities and phonologically empty elements. A specialized scientific literature and parsing technology has thus emerged to tackle various aspects of this problem (Aho & Ullman, 1972). Some parsing algorithms supply parse trees for any context-free language; others work with a more restricted set of grammars or language fragments and could be conceived as special purpose algorithms or instances of "shallow" (quick and dirty) parsing (Abney, 1996; Argamon et al., 1998; Ramshaw & Marcus, 1995).

In this chapter we adopt a supplementary perspective to the problem of parsing, that of biolinguistics. Biolinguistics takes the human ability to use language to be a specialized faculty of the brain. The aim of this chapter is to explore the implications of this view for the study of (automatic) natural language parsing. More specifically, we argue for the existence of a completely language independent and universal (innately given) parser that is part of the language faculty and describe some of the properties this universal parser ought to have. The core of the parser is based on the minimalist theory of grammar (Chomsky, 1995), while we suggest that the problem of computational complexity is dealt with an unsupervised extraction of templates for partial parse trees corresponding to skill automatization.

BACKGROUND

In linguistics, as in the field of parsing technologies mentioned above, there are basically two different perspectives one can assume. First, one can concentrate on the detailed description of a specific language. There are around 6000 languages spoken around the world, each with its own intricate rules of construction, vocabulary, and stylistic rules (Comrie, 2001; Greenberg, 1963). Each individual grammar can be further dissolved into several interacting levels, such as semantics, syntax, morphology, morphosyntax, phonology and phonetics. It is thus possible to develop specialized grammatical systems, specialized scientific techniques, and nomenclature for the description of different languages and their subcomponents. The first attempts in this direction were made already two thousand years ago, as in the case of Panini's grammar for Sanskrit. Moreover, such descriptions can achieve considerable precision due to the fact that the different levels of human language consist of smaller units that are put together according to well-defined, combinatorial rules.

Some 50 years ago linguists studying natural language grammars began to pursue a different track. Instead of developing new technologies and methods for the description of individual languages and their subcomponents, they studied the method 2-4-year old children use in order to break the code of their own native language. It is well-known that this happens effortlessly, without much linguistic input or cognitive sophistication, and in effect in a couple of years (Chomsky, 1969; Graffi, 2001; Marcus, 1993; Moro, 2008; Pinker, 1994). When the problem is set this way, it becomes feasible to find out the cognitive representational apparatus that the child uses when acquiring and using her own language(s).

One could entertain the possibility that the child acquires her native language merely by paying sufficient attention and drawing inferences. It is obvious that since languages differ from each other, some learning must be going on (Yang, 2002). Under this scheme, the child uses a primitive representational system sufficiently rich to express the rules of possible languages and then tries to formulate the rules of the target language based on the linguistic and extra-linguistic input. Since it is known that children learn languages without being explicitly taught, rule formulation must be based on an inductive logic, or rule induction. Rule induction allows the child to generalize beyond what she has perceived in the past. It is sometimes assumed that rule induction is implemented by general cognitive skills, such as pattern recognition, statistical inference or analogical reasoning (Bates & Elman, 1996; Deacon, 1997;

Saffran et al., 1996; Tomasello, 2003). This scheme is by no means restricted to a description of language learning by children. One could harness such a model for pragmatic purposes, for instance, by developing algorithms that are able to extract statistical regularities from linguistic data (Abney, 1996; Argamon et al., 1998; Ramshaw & Marcus, 1995).

The problem with this approach is that rule induction is useless in all but the most trivial cases. An infinite number of hypothetical rules exist that are consistent with any finite dataset (Gold, 1967; Goodman, 1955). Second, natural languages are so complex that a whole scientific enterprise has emerged to find out how they work, with no end currently in sight if judged by the amount of controversy that still exists in the field. This is not surprising, given that the phenomenon itself arises from what is perhaps the most complex system known, the human brain (Brattico, 2008). Third, even if the search space is constrained, rule induction leads easily to an astronomical search. Learning is an abysmally complex task (Judd, 1990, 1996; Valiant, 1984). Fourth, there is very little evidence that the child actually uses the kind of trial-and-error procedure characteristic of rule induction. For these reasons among others, linguists gave up the idea that each child induces the rules of her language with a general learning algorithm. It is assumed that the search space must be strongly constrained *a priori* (Chomsky, 1959, 1975; Komarova & Nowak, 2003; Nowak et al., 2001, 2002; Vapnik, 1995; Wexler & Culicover, 1980; Yang, 2002). These *a priori* constraints are called a *Universal Grammar* (UG). It follows from this that each individual language should be amenable to an analysis in terms of the UG, since each natural language must occupy a position in the set of possible languages strongly constrained by the UG. Universal Grammar provides a more constrained framework for the description of individual languages.

It is sometimes asserted that statistical learning algorithms can escape *a priori* constraints (Tomasello, 2003). Often this appears not to be true: for any statistical learning algorithm that works at least remotely well in some range of data, it can easily be pointed out that they work only within a tightly constrained set of hypotheses (Geman et al., 1992), sometimes so constrained that it can be shown that they are not able to learn the properties of natural languages (Fodor & Pylyshyn, 1988; Pinker & Prince, 1988). Certainly, one may be interested in some special fragment of language in the first place; it nevertheless remains the case that such models too make the assumption that learning is constrained *a priori*, hence that there is a universal grammar (Nowak et al., 2001, 2002).

It could be suggested that the acquisition is accelerated by extra-linguistic data. The child is, after all, an interactive player in a world containing visual and auditory information beyond her primary linguistic data. What must be a bewildering array of sensory stimulation is always stimulating the child's nervous system while provably affecting its growth and patterning. However, as far as current understanding goes, this extra-linguistic data does not provide clues about most of the rules of grammar. Parents don't teach the rules of grammar to their children for two obvious reasons: they do not know the rules themselves, and even when they do, children do not pay any attention. The rules are certainly not written anywhere, and there is no representation of them in any format in the child's proximal environment. If extra-linguistic data is used in the acquisition task at all, it must be used by making inferences; but then the search space must be restricted *a priori*.

After the problem of language acquisition was seen in this light, it became obvious that there is a tension between the need to constrain acquisition and the diversity among existing natural languages. For instance, we "want to give an accurate account of the phenomena of English, Hindi, etc." which easily leads us to "postulate complex mechanisms with varied grammatical constructions, with different properties internal to the language and certainly across languages" (Chomsky, 2000, p. 12). No doubt the same is true of the parsing industry. Yet because of the problem of language acquisition "the conclusion about the variety and complexity of languages cannot be correct"; instead, "languages must somehow be extremely simple and very much like one another; otherwise, you couldn't acquire any of them" (Chomsky, 2000, p. 13). This insight directed linguistic efforts into a formulation of a theory of UG such that all languages would look similar in terms of their grammatical rules.

The tension between describing languages and their acquisition was resolved successfully during the 80's when the principles and parameters model crystallized (Chomsky, 1981, 1988). According to this model, all languages are based on the same grammatical principles. However, these principles are parameterized so that each principle may have two or perhaps three variations. Since there are several principles, many of which allow parameterization, combinatorial possibilities emerge which explain some amount of the observed variety between languages around the world (Baker, 2003). For instance, assuming that each universal principle contains a parameter with two possibilities, n principles generate 2^n grammars. The search space for the child remains finite, as the only thing she needs to do apart from memorizing the words and other singular facts is to find the correct settings for the parameters. Furthermore, it is possible to imagine that parameter setting is triggered reliably by easily detectable features in the linguistic input.

Although it must be mentioned here that in recent years the principles and parameters model itself has been subjected to considerable empirical criticism, the general conclusion has been that an even tighter set of possible grammars and a more constrained acquisition process is needed (Yang, 2002). Let us assume that this model or something similar is a correct description of what is going on in the acquisition of grammars, and turn to parsing.

NATURAL LANGUAGE PARSING

Issues, Controversies, Problems

Learning to parse is analogous to acquiring a language on several fronts. In the case of grammars, there is a tension between the diversity among existing natural languages and the desire to constrain learning to a minimum. We want to argue that parsing is subject to the same tension. To illustrate, consider two languages that differ from each other in some respects, Finnish and English. Finnish has a rich morphosyntactic encoding for several grammatical roles (subject, object, etc.) with a relatively free word order (Vainikka, 1989; Vilkuna, 1989, 2000), whereas in English word order is relatively fixed but morphosyntax is impoverished. Now consider the following two (simplistic and unrealistic) heuristic parsing strategies:

Parsing Strategy A: Encode grammatical roles (e.g., subject, object) on the basis of morphosyntax, but ignore word order

Parsing Strategy B: Encode grammatical roles on the basis of word order.

Parsing Strategy A works well for Finnish, in which the parser needs to ignore a portion of word order variation in order to arrive at the correct assignment of grammatical roles. The strategy fails for English, since in English word order cannot be ignored in this way. Strategy B works better in English, but fails for Finnish in which the inspection of word order leads the parser astray. Similar differences can be easily imagined concerning many features that are relevant for parsing, such as finding the head of a phrase and detecting the right edge of a relative clause. It could then be suggested that Finnish and English require opposite heuristic parsing strategies in this (and many other) respects. This leads to the conclusion that each language must use a unique set of parsing rules. The existence of these rules is needed to explain, for example, how fast real-time parsing of complex sentences is possible.

It is perhaps not wrong to say that a significant portion of the natural language parsing industry works under the assumption that the task can only be achieved through special-purpose algorithms, each tinkered for one language, often only for a fragment of one language. For instance, Lin's (2001) Minipar is based on the earlier principles-based parser Principar (Lin, 1993, 1994). In Minipar the problem of complexity is avoided by implementing the grammar, as well as the parser, as a network. However, although the grammatical rules implemented in the network are designed following the minimalist program, the network representing the grammatical rules is not language-independent, i.e. the network designed for English is not as such applicable to any other language.

If we look at language acquisition from the viewpoint of the child trying to acquire her native language, it becomes difficult to accept the fact that parsers would differ from each other in terms of the grammatical and parsing rules they use. Suppose that the child must learn to parse her target language by constructing a database of special-purpose rules, starting without any constraints whatsoever. This situation does not differ in any fundamental way from grammatical rule induction, which, as shown above, has been shown to be impossible without substantial constraints. It is equally impossible to induce the rules of parsing; it makes no difference for the problem of learning whether one is inferring the rules for parsing or the rules for grammar. In addition to the universal grammar, there must be a *universal parsing algorithm* which restricts the range of possible parsing rules and which can thus reliably parse any language, perhaps entirely without language-specific rules. In this paper, we call any parsing algorithm that uses neither language-specific rules of grammar nor language-specific rules of parsing a 'completely language independent parser'. It is important to note that with this term we denote a parser that does not use language-specific *rules*; it may still use language-specific singular facts, such as a list of words.

Additional considerations support the idea that there has to be a completely language independent parser. It seems, in fact, that the ability to parse is already required to learn both the grammar of the language and the language specific heuristic parsing strategies. With respect to acquiring the grammar, the child cannot acquire the parameters or other aspects that must be captured from the input if reliable parsing is not available. To decide, for example, whether or not a grammatical subject in a finite sentence is mandatory in a language, the child must be able to parse the incoming sentences correctly.

On the other hand, the learning of language specific parsing rules also already requires a parser. Consider the child who does not initially know whether to apply the Parsing Strategy A or B above. Suppose she is learning Finnish and assumes Parsing Strategy B. She will fail to parse most of the Finnish sentences correctly, as she assumes that word order is tied to grammatical roles. Yet the child cannot know whether the problem is due to a mistake in the parsing strategy or a mistake in the grammar, and the acquisition task becomes more complex. In fact, what the child seems to need in order to decide between strategy A and strategy B is an independent parser which assigns the grammatical roles correctly. When the child has the correct parses for the sentences available, she can decide which heuristic strategy to use. But it seems that for this to be possible, there has to be a parser which does not utilize any specific parsing strategies that could lead the child astray.

The idea that there are universal parsing rules is not new. It constitutes a starting point for psycholinguistic parsing research as well. While psycholinguists are not primarily interested in constructing fully working parsing algorithms, their approach illuminates the type of approach that emerges if the above guidelines are adopted. Consider one example, the *argument-over-adjunct attachment preference* (Gibson, 1991; Pritchett, 1992). This principle says that during the online parsing process, a parsing is preferred where the incoming words are attached to the existing structure as an argument rather than as an adjunct. Clearly, the principle is not meant as a rule that applies only to some languages; instead, it characterizes the way the human mind works. On the other hand, if there was a language in which an adjunct interpretation is preferred, then this proposal for a universal parsing principle would not work since the child would need to infer – without the help of neither a fully working grammar nor a fully working parser – that in this or that language adjuncts are preferred over arguments, or vice versa.

For another example, Gibson (1998) proposed a particularly convincing treatment of parsing efficiency, arguing that what makes a given expression difficult to parse is the number and distance of dependencies that the hearer must keep simultaneously in mind. This constitutes the basic idea of the Dependency Locality Theory. Again, the theory is not tied to a particular language but applies cross-linguistically. A third example from psycholinguistics is the principle of simplicity in parsing advocated by Gorrell (1995). According to this principle, only the minimal amount of new structure is added to the phrase structure representation when a new word from the input is processed. If, for example, a verb is followed by a noun phrase, this noun phrase is analyzed by default to be the object of the verb and not the subject of an object clause. For one last example, Pritchett (1992) has suggested an account that unifies parsing and grammar. The parser is based on the "Theta Principle", which was included in the Minimalist Program by Chomsky (1995). The theta principle requires that every argument (e.g. DP or PP) is associated with a thematic role. Furthermore, every thematic role is associated with an argument. Recent models of parsing based on the theta principle are proposed by Mulders (2002) and Sadeh-Leicht (2007). All these rules are, and have to be, universal, since it is not possible for the child to learn them reliably by rule induction.

More generally, in biolinguistics it has been assumed that the human language faculty uses a parsing algorithm that is both "invariant" and "unlearned" (Chomsky, 1995, p. 170). But the question of how to combine an "invariant" and "unlearned" parsing algorithm with the great deal of observed variation between and within languages remains to date without a definite answer.

We would like to approach the problem of parsing from this vantage point. We begin by sharpening the issue by laying down certain (somewhat idealized) requirements for grammar and parsing; we then sketch some initial thoughts on how to meet them. The ideas presented below are part of an ongoing effort to build a computational universal parsing algorithm: they are partly programmatic, partly detailed. Some reference to empirical and computational parsing literature is made to support the arguments, but otherwise we can only regard some of these ideas as preliminary.

The first requirement is that insofar as we aim to constrain the theories of parsing by language acquisition, we are adopting a perspective whereby the term "parser" refers to something that has reality in the human mind/brain. According to a fairly typical usage, this is taken to mean a biologically endowed component in the human brain. On the other hand, this psychologically or biologically realistic usage does not mean that we should abandon the idea of writing an explicit and testable universal parsing algorithm. We believe that in the long run it would be fruitful to simulate the way the human brain parses languages.

The second assumption concerning the universal parsing algorithm is that we are aiming for an algorithm that does not need any language-specific rules. In reality, it is possible that there are some such rules, but it makes sense first to pursue a solution that has none. It follows from this that the universal parsing algorithm cannot be a "completely language independent parser" in the widely used sense of an algorithm that still requires language-specific rules of grammar as its input. We nevertheless allow the parser to have a finite memory for language-specific encyclopedic, singular facts. Ideally, these facts should be such that the child could also acquire them easily from the linguistic input.

It is perhaps important to sharpen the above assumption in the following way. The main motivation for the completely language independent parsing algorithm as discussed here concerns the problem of language acquisition. This difficulty is above all a problem of rule induction, not memorization of singular facts. Yet insofar as there are parsing rules which are universal and apply to any natural language, no special problem arises. The problem arises only when the rules are language specific, therefore learned by rule induction.

The third assumption is that the parser should work reliably in the case of any natural language, but there is no need to parse artificial languages, ungrammatical expressions, or any other types of input that do not constitute a natural language. An important implication of the exclusion of other kinds of input is that we can embed the universal grammar into the parser. For reasons that will be spelled out presently, we take the recent minimalist model of the universal grammar (Chomsky, 1995, 2001, 2005, 2007) as our starting point. We will also work with a particularly strong form of UG embedding, in which the parser is logically dependent on the UG. If the principles of UG change, parsing changes as well; but not vice versa. This assumption is a commonplace in parsing technology, but controversial when proposed as a model of psychologically realistic parsing. We nevertheless believe, and later argue, that this is a sound path to follow.

Taken together, the second and third assumptions suggest a rough model of the completely language independent parser. It should contain, at minimum, three components: (1) universal rules of grammar (possibly with parameters), (2) universal rules of parsing (possibly with parameters) and (3) language-specific singular facts, the latter acquired by observation and memorization. Since we aim to embed the Universal Grammar into the parser, we define the universal parser as a conjunction of components 1 and 2. Component (3) fine-tunes the parser for a particular language. This component is acquired from experience, so that the learning algorithm is part of the universal parser. All three components are at least necessary for successful parsing. In this article, we do not touch on the issue of whether the parser has parameters or something analogous: the null hypothesis is that it does not.

The fourth assumption is that languages do vary at their surface. The term surface is here used to refer to concrete expressions or raw text, linear strings of words, preferably with no abstract features, labels or hierarchical structure assigned. A realistic language learner has access to other types of input as well, but even when such input is taken into account, the fact that languages vary at their surface level remains uncontested. Note that it is logically possible to think of all languages sharing their surface properties, much like logical languages or programming languages, this is just factually not the case.

A central problem for characterizing the completely language independent parser of the human language faculty is that the variation between languages at their surface is in conflict with the fact that there must be a completely language independent parsing algorithm or parsing faculty that is able to handle any language without the child inducing language-specific parsing rules. This in effect seems to us to be the same "flat contradiction" (Chomsky, 2000) that guided research to the direction of the principles and parameters model some twenty or thirty years ago.

Let us point out once more that we do not think that the completely language independent parser consists solely of a statistical learning algorithm or other general learning device. The parser is posited here in order to prevent any type of rule induction or learning, not to instantiate it. However, by this we do not wish to argue that stochastic processes are irrelevant to realistic natural language parsing; as discussed at the end of this article, stochastic processes do and presumably must play a role in successful parsing. But they are not the solution to the problem of rule induction.

We think that these four assumptions generate a challenging framework, perhaps even a "flat contradiction". We know that one language produces different surface expressions than another language, yet we cannot allow any language-specific rules in our parser to deal with such differences. In the case of grammar, this contradiction was solved by abstraction and idealization. Thankfully it was found that the wide variety of grammatical constructions in different languages do share a unifying set of simple principles, if looked from an abstract point of view. In the case of the parser, the situation is perhaps more difficult due to the fact that the parser cannot idealize from the linguistic surface variation; rather, it must be able to work directly with every bit of the surface complexity of any natural language in the world.

Solutions and Recommendations

Suppose an engineer is planning the construction of a complex electric grid for a city. Each city has a unique geographical layout and other unique properties. The engineer can thus work with each city's particular set of problems as if it would be independent of the rest, designing heuristic rules and principles for each city and finally implementing the grid accordingly. A well-known alternative is to use computational search through the space of possible solutions in order to arrive at something that fills some reasonable criterion of goodness. A universal grid optimizing algorithm would be a reasonable choice, because the search rules could encapsulate some amount of mechanical flexibility, an ability to look for and evaluate alternatives.

In natural language parsing (universal or not), some form of search is inevitable (Barton et al., 1987; Earley, 1970; Kaplan, 1973; Kay, 1986; Younger, 1967). We would like to suggest in this article that something very similar to the universal grid planning algorithm is at work when the child attempts to parse her native language: given some linguistic input, the child combines universal grammar with a constrained search algorithm. More specifically, given the earlier assumption that the child has the universal grammar and a list of singular language specific facts at her disposal, we take a string of words as input and perform a bottom-up search for grammatical trees consistent with that string. This gives us the set of possible parse trees. The algorithm handles surface variation in the same way as an optimization algorithm can see through variations in the differently constituted cities. We will also propose that the results of the search are stored for later use. We will proceed by first describing the search, and then the storage issue.

It is important to point out that by issuing search, we are betting on the fact that it would allow us to eliminate all forms of language-specific parsing heuristics. Thus, although search in some form or another is inevitable in parsing, we are proposing that when combined with the universal grammar, we should eventually get rid of all language specific rules.

During the last ten years or so, the idea of using bottom-up search as a part of the universal grammar has been explored at an in-depth level (Chomsky, 1995; Kitahara, 1997). This development was not triggered by problems of parsing specifically, but by the empirical findings which suggest that several operations of the universal grammar are optimal. Search makes it possible to compare various constructions in terms of the number and length of the computational steps required to generate them. Here we borrow the results, nomenclature and technology from this approach, called the Minimalist Program (MP), and apply it to the problem of parsing. If this proves to be successful, we can integrate the grammatical competence and the parser closely together (e.g. Phillips, 1996).

Let us say that the search begins from an array of words called a 'lexical vector' (a lexical array with linear order). We conceive the lexical vector to be a vector of morphemes. Word boundaries and linear order is encoded as well. For instance, the sentence *John loves Mary* is encoded by the vector < John, love-Tense, Mary >. A search is issued which goes through all possible binary trees that can be constructed out of these elements. The search is called a 'grammatical derivation'. Each step which combines two elements, either something from the vector or from the current derivation, is called 'Merge' (Chomsky, 1995; Kitahara, 1997). All legitimate results which exhaust the whole lexical vector are considered to be acceptable parse trees for the given input. Whether a given tree is "legitimate" is determined by the UG and the language-specific facts. In the minimalist grammar, legitimacy is determined at the interfaces by checking whether the construction satisfies independently motivated semantic and phonetic constraints. We call constructions which satisfy these interface properties UG-compliant constructions.

There are several independent reasons for adopting the derivational parser. Even when we restrict ourselves to single languages, the real parser must be able to recover from many types of inconsistencies of real linguistic communication. Real speakers repeat words, change their order, begin new phrases in the middle of others, misspeak words, keep long pauses and so forth. A derivational parser can recover from these errors and construct the correct grammatical structure by issuing constrained search. Furthermore, as soon as we allow derivation into the model of grammatical competence, it becomes available for parsing as well. In fact, we see here the remote possibility for the unification of parsing and grammar, perhaps akin to Phillips (1996), Reinhart (2006) and Weinberg (1999). According to these authors, if the grammar can build representations by issuing derivations, the parser can do the same in real-time with no penalty for the simplicity of the theory. Further, it is precisely in the case of parsing that the power of derivations becomes rather striking, as it offers the kind of flexibility that the processing of variable linguistic input seems to require.

The following problem emerges as soon as this alternative is pursued seriously. We gave up language-specific grammars and language-specific parsers due to the complexity of rule induction. The present solution seems to bring complex search back again. Indeed, the construction of all binary trees out of a given lexical vector is too complex a task for any practical or realistic purposes.

Fortunately, the problem of computational complexity is not a problem about search *per se*. It is a problem about unconstrained search. Given the UG we can filter out derivations locally which we know are unable to produce legitimate outputs. For instance, determiners are never combined with verbal elements. The illegitimacy of such combinations is detected by inspecting the local determiner-verb configuration, provided that no further step in the derivation can reconfigure these elements. This kind of reconfiguration is disallowed in several recent models of UG, in which grammatical displacement (permutation of grammatical elements during the derivation) is implemented in terms of copying (Chomsky, 2001, 2007). Copying leaves the original element in place, hence if the original combination is illegitimate, it will remain so at all later stages of the derivation. Consequently, we can filter out derivations locally by relying on the UG. When we take into consideration all the following universal constraints, the search space can be diminished considerably:

After Merge(X, Y) = YP, derivation is cancelled locally if:

1. YP does not have a coherent semantic interpretation,
2. XY constitutes a word-internal morpheme combination that does not exist in the input,
3. XY constitutes a word-internal morpheme combination that is not allowed by the UG.

Filters (1-3) are possible by virtue of the fact that elements are copied when they are moved; hence these constitute a parsing-related argument in favor of copying instead of moving. Additional filters are available if an element is valued case (e.g. nominative, accusative) or phi-features (gender, person, number) and the valued case and phi-features do not match the features the particular element has in the input. Also, distribution of morphemes from the same input word to different words during the derivation is not allowed. Such information is not always locally available, however.

Merge by itself creates a complex derivational search space, but the complexity is further increased by copying. Suppose that at each step the grammatical derivation can either Merge a new element from the lexicon into the existing tree ("external Merge"), or probe an element from within an already existing construction, then copy and merge it at the top of the same construction ("internal Merge"). The option of allowing both external Merge and internal Merge to apply at any point increases the search space: under some assumptions the search space becomes infinite. A better solution is to let external Merge operate freely, but use internal Merge only when necessary. In several versions of the minimalist theory, internal Merge is triggered when the construction contains some feature, called the probe, that requires the execution of internal Merge (Chomsky, 1995, 2008). Under this model, internal Merge becomes like a grammatical reflex that is executed immediately as the need arises, but never creates new possibilities for grammatical search.

Practical computational implementations of the above ideas suggest that constraining the search by the principles of UG is unlikely to solve the problem of complexity in its entirety. The derivations are too complex even for trivial looking inputs. Practical applications of this system have shown that the upper limit for the number of elements (morphemes, functional heads) in the derivation is 15. Beyond this number the derivation becomes too complex. This is unfortunate, as it shows the parsing of a simple embedded relative clause to be impossible in practice. It is furthermore easy to see that no local filtering is able to complete the job, since the lexical vector itself can be arbitrarily long. We need some way to break the lexical vector into parts, each of which is parsed individually and later integrated.

One possible solution, pursued in recent work, is to derive expressions in grammatical packages called phases (Chomsky, 2008). An example of a phase is the complementizer phrase, referring to finite sentences such as *who Mary saw* in *The man who Mary saw slept*. One rationale for assuming phases is empirical: certain phrases look like closed packages in terms of their grammatical behavior. They constitute islands to various grammatical operations. Another reason is the reduction of computational burden, as explained above. This model could work for parsing if we could find an algorithm that dissects any given expression reliably into correct phases without assuming parse trees as given. The latter condition is important to keep in mind, since no such condition is required of the theory of grammatical competence where the phase model was first invented. If we model competence, phases can be easily set up since full information about the phrase structure is available. We can simply decide on empirical and theoretical grounds where to put the phases (e.g., at C, and v*). This is not the case with the parser. The parser does not have a complete phrase-structure tree available; rather, it must *find one*. Therefore, for the phase-model to work in conjunction with parsing it must be able to find phases from the lexical vector without any other information about the structure of the lexical vector. One of the early results of our experimentation with a derivational parser was that we found no such algorithm.

Specifically, a phase-seeking algorithm would need some way to detect the beginning and the endpoint of each phase from each lexical vector, but there seem to be no unambiguous surface cues to signal these junctures. Put differently, it is far from trivial to infer which strings of words constitute complete phrases. It is not a good idea to apply search for this task, since the scheme was invented to reduce search, not to increase it. The problem of determining the boundaries of phases is made worse by the fact that words may often be displaced from their original positions, as in interrogatives where in many languages the *wh*-element is moved to the left periphery of the sentence from its base position (*who did Mary believe John wanted to see (who)*). Because of these problems, it looks as if the phase-seeking algorithm would have to presuppose parsing, rather than constitute it.

Brattico (2008) addresses the problem of computational complexity in the case of cognitive processing. He defines three positions one might take in solving this matter. According to the first, called 'shallow reductionism', our cognitive processes reduce to computational principles which are both fast and constituted by very little information in terms of the algorithmic information theory. Most approaches make this assumption in one way or another, even though there is very little empirical evidence supporting it. Quite the contrary, the fact that most such models end up being computationally complex suggests that the assumption is wrong (Brattico, 2008; Fodor, 1983, 2000; Pylyshyn, 1986). In the case of parsing, for instance, it is well-known that the problem is too complex to allow such a simple solution.

At the other end of the continuum lies what Brattico calls 'nonreductionism'. In this case computational principles are constituted by irreducible information, pure randomness in the worst case. This stance is called 'nonreductionism' because it implies that there are no unifying regularities, rules or deeper generalizations: the phenomenon is constituted by a mountain of information that cannot be reduced away. We do not want to assume that parsing is based on irreducible noise, so we reject this possibility as a basis for modeling parsing. Certainly, however, the universe is full of systems which are constituted by pure entropy, so this assumption might have some range of applications in biology and could have some relevance in parsing, too. Between these two alternatives exists a compromise option, 'deep reductionism', which assumes that the phenomenon allows for a simple description only if we tolerate computations. In other words, insofar as we aim for computational efficiency, the description requires a lot of information. Deep reductionism in turn is based on the notion of logical depth (Bennett, 1988). Intuitively, if a system is deep in this sense, then extracting its hidden regularities takes a lot of time.

The hypothesis we adopt here is that the parsing of natural languages represents a case of deep reductionism. Parsing has a simple and deep logic, implemented by the rules of UG together with search. But this logic is destined to be computationally costly. In order to speed up the processing, we need to find a way to turn computation into information. One clue to how this might happen is provided by the way children acquire their languages. Children are not able to parse complex sentences at once; instead, they start with simple sentences and make their way towards the more complex ones gradually. Thus, suppose that a set of lexical vectors is ordered along some complexity measure to form a *training set*. The simplest expressions, such as individual words or two-word expressions might then be simple enough to be parsed with search. This corresponds to a cognitive process in which the child is trying to find a way to map the input with his or her preexisting grammatical template (UG). Let us assume that after each successful parse, the child stores the result into a table-lookup memory containing the input vector and the parse trees. We call such entry a 'grammatical schema'. The child is now able to access previously successful derivations when deriving new expressions. If the training set is ordered in terms of complexity, it is possible that the child will eventually reach adult competence: any new complex expression can be seen as containing parts that have been derived in the past, hence these parts do not need to be derived but only retrieved from memory. This could damp down computational complexity with the expense of storage capacity. We propose that in addition to the principles of UG, the parser uses this kind of memorization and chunking as a way to reduce the computational burden.

This model can be characterized as a completely language independent parser that extracts templates from its input for partial parser trees. The parser then needs a model of template matching that is able to match the templates in the memory with the substrings in the input. The search strategy implemented in the parser tries to maximize the coverage of the input string with the schemas. This way the number of constituents that are passed to the analyzer is minimized and the first analysis requires the least amount of processing. In addition, the most comprehensive schemas are tried first. In practical applications, it is also possible to use frequency information and e.g. information about the co-occurence of schemas in the search for applicable schemas. The schema implementation by itself does not restrict the type of statistical information that can be selected for enriching the schemas.

Acquisition of schemata does not require rule induction: schemata are memorized after a successful derivation has occurred. Minimally, each schema contains a lexical vector paired with all UG-compliant phrase-structure representations that can be, or were actually, derived from the array. This list consti-tutes a significant portion of the component (3) above, singular language-specific facts that the parser consults during the parsing process. Without schemas, the parser is able to parse if given unlimited time; with schemas, its ability to parse is a function of the training set. This moves us towards the goal of making the most frequent linguistic structures efficient, while the rest (e.g. garden-path sentences) still lead to more complex strategies. This is in agreement with what is known about realistic parsing (Jurafsky, 1996; MacDonald et al., 1994; Trueswell & Tanenhaus, 1994).

An important advantage of the schema model is that it is not limited to a particular syntactic descrip-tion or labeling of syntactic constituents: any constituent can be a schema. The statistical approaches previously used for detection of constituents, such as automatic chunking, are often restricted to certain types of phrases. This is not the case with schemas: if the schema-parser fails to match e.g. a full DP, it may instead match one or several subparts of that DP. This kind of flexibility makes the parser more robust when it encounters novel syntactic structures.

However, a model in which the grammatical schemas pair concrete input strings into a list of deriva-tions is clearly still insufficient. This is due to the productivity and systematicity of natural languages. Suppose, for instance, that we introduce a new word into the language. All lexical vectors containing that word would lack a corresponding schema in the memory, no matter what the training set. The learner would need to build a separate schema for all grammatical constructions combined with all words in the language. Thus, increasing the size of the lexicon by one would slow down all parsing processes involving a lexical vector containing that word. To remedy this problem, we assume that the schemata contain grammatical structures but no lexical content. Thus, input vectors such as *a small boy* and *the big girl* both invoke the same schema Determiner-Adjective-Noun, to which lexical content is inserted during the parsing process.

In addition to potentially solving the problem of computational complexity, the schema model provides a way to resolve the tension between the observation that different languages seem to require separate heuristic parsing strategies and the requirement for a universal parser. In the context of this model, there really are no language specific parsing rules or strategies that would need to be learned, so there is no tension, either. Language specificity is achieved by the gradual accumulation of language specific schemata, which are not, to repeat, induced but rather stored in a mechanical way.

Another noteworthy point concerns automatization. It is well-known from the literature on expertise that the acquisition of new skills proceeds via certain well-established routes, the final phase being a state where the person has automatized or chunked the relevant information into a table-lookup memory that allows him or her to maintain performance even when conscious processing is allocated elsewhere. The present proposal not only implements automatization but shows why it is necessary.

In reality children do not master their native language(s) at once. On the contrary, while children do not make that many mistakes in acquisition, they begin to practice with relatively simple expressions and proceed to the complex ones via a highly predictable route (Bickerton, 1990, 1995; Crain & Lillo-Martin, 1999; Guasti, 2002). The first expressions are single words, then come the two-word expressions with a limited amount of morphology, and then gradually the length of utterances increases and grammatical devices such as relative clauses, passives, complementizers, auxiliaries, and others emerge. The child seems to be building some kind of a database of linguistic routines, while the building is constrained by complexity. The idea that parsing involves search explains why complexity is a relevant variable in language acquisition.

One additional argument that speaks in favor of the schema-parser is that by embedding the UG logically within the parser, we are able to avoid several problems which arise if the UG is not embedded in this way. Suppose that the parser and the universal grammar are two distinct components. The universal grammar defines the possible and impossible linguistic phrase structures for language L, while the parser is supposed to assign one or several of these phrase structures to a given input. How does the parser know which phrase structures are possible in language L? The universal grammar being a distinct component, the parser has no way of knowing unless it duplicates the entire contents of the UG. Yet the odds are against the possibility that our brains contain two separate components so that one embodies within itself an identical copy of the other. For note that for the parser and UG to work in tandem, the parser would have to know the contents of the UG *exactly*, an approximation would lead the parser astray. Since it is unavoidable that the child needs an UG, it is only natural to assume that the parser depends on the UG. The idea that the parser is based on the grammar also seems to be a common assumption in studies of language acquisition. Several authors assume that the parsing that takes place during language acquisition is based either on the grammar that the child has acquired so far (e.g. Meisel, 2000) or on one or several of the grammars that are allowed by the UG (e.g. Valian, 1990).

The final point we wish to make relates to realistic parsing. It is well-known that real speakers and hearers are often not able to parse sentences that are grammatical. Some sentences are simply too difficult to parse (*the horse the boy the man saw raced fell*), others lead the parser onto a wrong path and require reanalysis (*the horse raced past the barn fell*). It has been argued that language is to a significant extent "unusable", making available expressions that are never used. Automatization and chunking offer one way to model this behavior. First, several schemas can often be matched with a given input string. Since we work under the assumption that such schemas should reduce the computational burden, we would not like to assume that all possible combinations of matching schemas with a given input are tried out, either serially or in parallel. Instead, the schemas must be prioritized based on frequency of previous use and other factors. Such prioritization will lead the parser astray at least in some cases, triggering reanalysis that could be modeled as an explicit search. As is well-known from the psycholinguistic literature on parsing, this is not far from what happens in reality.

FUTURE TRENDS

The work presented here calls attention to some issues emerging in the field of natural language processing. As has been suggested in the previous sections, the view that parsing can be done only by special purpose algorithms tinkered separately for each language or part of a language is untenable if we take language acquisition into account. Perhaps it would be worthwhile to consider the possibility that the problem of natural language parsing will not be solved by special-purpose algorithms, since nature seems not have solved the problem in this manner. More efforts could be directed to finding the general principles of the parsing mechanism, taking advantage of research done in biolinguistics over the past 50 years. The search-plus-schemata model introduced in the previous section provides a possible starting point for future research in this direction.

CONCLUSION

In this chapter we have argued that the child can induce neither the rules of grammar nor the rules of parsing. There has to be a universal grammar that works in tandem with a universal parsing algorithm, which together allow the child to reach a full command of her native language(s). But languages differ from each other, meaning that it makes little sense to think of this in terms of rigid parsing rules. We then argued that there is one well-known solution for situations like these, namely computational search that provides flexibility at the expense of computation. Similarly, provided a universal grammar the child can try to work through the input she gets by finding out which configurations of the incoming words satisfy the principles of the UG, and then interpret the input accordingly. Intuitively, the child is plotting linguistic surface variation with more structured, universal and rigid interpretations provided by the UG. This solution has the drawback that such search is immensely complex; the rules of the UG, taken alone, don't restrict the search space sufficiently. In addition, since the input can be arbitrarily long, one must in any case break it into independent units that are parsed separately. We found no way to use the phase theory of Chomsky (2001) for this purpose, as phase boundaries seem difficult to detect from a lexical vector. The alternative is to train the parser with simple expressions first, let it store the results into a memory, and then retrieve them when an identical or similar input is confronted again. This amounts to the deep reductionism in the sense of Brattico (2008).

This model fits well with empirical facts about language acquisition and general cognition, as was demonstrated at the end of the section 'Solutions and recommendations'. In addition, the model provides a new perspective to automatic natural language processing. We would like to believe that together these observations imply that the model presented in this chapter is worth exploring further.

ACKNOWLEDGMENT

This research project was supported financially by the Finnish Funding Agency for Technology and Innovation (Tekes) for the second author. We would like to thank Saara Huhmarniemi (University of Helsinki) and Jukka Purma (University of Helsinki) for their contribution to the development of the ideas presented in this chapter. The second author would also like to thank the staff and students at the Institute of Cognitive Science, University of Osnabrück, Germany, for their comments.

REFERENCES

Abney, S. (1996). Partial parsing via finite-state cascades. *Natural Language Engineering, 2*(4), 337–344.

Aho, A. V., & Ullman, J. D. (1972). *The Theory of Parsing, Translation, and Compiling, Vol. 1*. Englewood Cliffs, NJ: Prentice-Hall.

Argamon, S., Dagan, I., & Krymolowski, Y. (1998). A memory-based approach to learning shallow natural language patterns. In *COLING/ACL-98* (pp. 67–73). Montreal: ACL.

Baker, M. (2003). *The Atoms of Language: The Mind's Hidden Rules of Grammar*. New York: Basic Books.

Barton, Jr., G. E., Berwick, R. C., and Ristad, E. S. (1987). *Computational Complexity and Natural Language*. Cambridge, MA: MIT Press.

Bates, E., & Elman, J. (1996). Learning rediscovered. *Science, 274*, 1849-50.

Bennett, C. H. (1988). Logical depth and physical complexity. In R. Herken (Ed.), *The Universal Turing Machine; A Half-Century Survey*. Oxford: Oxford University Press.

Bickerton, D. (1990). *Language & Species*. Chicago: University of Chicago Press.

Bickerton, D. (1995). *Language and Human Behavior*. Seattle: Washington University Press.

Brattico, P. (2008). Shallow reductionism and the problem of complexity in psychology. *Theory & Psychology, 18*, 483-504.

Chomsky, N. (1959). Review of Verbal Behavior by B.F. Skinner. *Language, 35*, 26-57.

Chomsky, N. (1969). *Aspects of the theory of syntax*. Cambridge, MA: MIT Press.

Chomsky, N. (1975). *Reflections on Language*. New York: Pantheon.

Chomsky, N. (1981). *Lectures on Government and Binding. The Pisa Lectures*. The Hague: Mouton.

Chomsky, N. (1988). *Language and Problems of Knowledge. The Managua Lectures*. Cambridge, MA: MIT Press.

Chomsky, N. (1995). *The Minimalist Program*. Cambridge, MA: MIT Press.

Chomsky, N. (2000). *The Architecture of Language*. Oxford: Oxford University Press.

Chomsky, N. (2001). Derivation by Phase. In M. Kenstowicz (Ed.), *Ken Hale: A Life in Language* (pp. 1-52). Cambridge, MA: MIT Press.

Chomsky, N. (2005). Three factors in language design. *Linguistic Inquiry, 36*, 1-22.

Chomsky, N. (2007). Approaching UG from below, ms, MIT.

Chomsky, N. (2008). On Phases. In R. Freidin, C. P. Otero & M. L. Zubizarreta (Eds.), *Foundational Issues in Linguistic Theory. Essays in Honor of Jean-Roger Vergnaud*. Cambridge, MA: MIT Press.

Comrie, B. (2001). Languages of the World. In M. Aronoff & J. Rees-Miller (Eds.), *The Handbook of Linguistics*. Cornwall: Blackwell.

Crain, S., & Lillo-Martin, D. (1999). *An Introduction to Linguistic Theory and Language Acquisition*. Oxford: Blackwell.

Deacon, T. (1997). *Symbolic Species. The Co-evolution of Language and the Brain*. New York & London: Norton.

Earley, J. (1970). An efficient context-free parsing algorithm. *Communications of the ACM, 6*(8), 451-455.

Fodor, J. (1983). *The Modularity of the Mind*. Cambridge, MA: MIT Press.

Fodor, J. (2000). *The mind doesn't work that way: The scope and limits of computational psychology*. Cambridge, MA: MIT Press.

Fodor, J., & Pylyshyn, Z. (1988). Connectionism and cognitive architecture. *Cognition, 28*(1-2), 3-71.

Geman, S., Bienenstock, E., & Doursat, R. (1992). Neural networks and the bias/variance dilemma. *Neural Computation, 4*, 1-58.

Gibson, E. (1991). *A computational theory of human language processing: Memory, limitations and processing breakdown*. Doctoral dissertation, Carnegie Mellon University, Pittsburgh, PA.

Gibson, E. (1998). Linguistic complexity: Locality of syntactic dependencies. *Cognition, 68*, 1-76.

Gold, E. M. (1967). Language identification in the limit. *Information and Control, 10*, 447-474.

Goodman, N. (1955). *Fact, Fiction, and Forecast*. Cambridge, MA: Harvard University Press.

Gorrell, P. (1995). *Syntax and parsing*. Cambridge: Cambridge University Press.

Graffi, F. (2001). *Two Hundred Years of Syntax: A Critical Survey*. Amsterdam: Benjamins.

Greenberg, J. H. (Ed.). (1963). *Universals of Language*. Cambridge, MA: MIT Press.

Guasti, M. T. (2002). *Language Acquisition: The Growth of Grammar*. Cambridge, MA: MIT Press.

Judd, J. S. (1990). *Neural network design and the complexity of learning*. Cambridge, MA: MIT Press.

Judd, S. J. (1996). Complexity of learning. In P. Smolensky, M. C. Mozer & D. E. Rumelhart (Eds.), *Mathematical perspectives on neural networks*. New Jersey: Erlbaum.

Jurafsky, D. (1996). A probabilistic model of lexical and syntactic access and disambiguation. *Cognitive Science, 20*, 137-194.

Kaplan, R. M. (1973). A general syntactic processor. In E. Rustin (Ed.), *Natural Language Processing* (pp. 193-241). New York: Algorithmics Press.

Kay, M. (1986). Algorithm schemata and data structures in syntactic processing. In B. J. Grosz, K. S. Jones & B. L. Webber (Eds.), *Readings in natural language processing* (pp. 35–70). San Francisco, CA: Morgan Kaufmann Publishers.

Kitahara, H. (1997). *Elementary Operations and Optimal Derivations.* Cambridge, MA: MIT Press.

Komarova, N. L., & Nowak, M. A. (2003). Language, Learning and Evolution. In M. H. Christiansen & S. Kirby (Eds.), *Language Evolution.* Oxford: Oxford University Press.

Lin, D. (1993). Principle-based Parsing without Overgeneration. *Proceedings of ACL 93. Columbus, Ohio* (pp. 11-120).

Lin, D. (1994). PRINCIPAR: An Efficient, Broad-coverage, Principle-based Parser. *Proceedings of COLING 94. Kyoto, Japan* (pp. 482-488).

Lin, D. (2001). LaTaT: Language and Text Analysis Tools. *Proceedings of the Human Language Technology Conference.*

MacDonald, M. E., Pearlmutter, N., & Seidenberg, M. (1994). The lexical nature of syntactic ambiguity resolution. *Psychological Review, 101*, 678-703.

Marcus, G. F. (1993). Negative evidence in language acquisition. *Cognition, 46*, 53-83.

Meisel, J. M. (2000). Parameters in Acquisition. In P. Fletcher (Ed.), *The handbook of child language* (pp. 10-35). Oxford: Blackwell.

Moro, A. (2008). *The Boundaries of Babel: The brain and the enigma of impossible languages.* Cambridge, MA: MIT Press.

Mulders, I. (2002). *Transparent parsing: head-driven processing of verb-final structures.* Doctoral dissertation, Utrecht University, LOT dissertation series.

Nowak, M. A., Komarova, N. L., & Niyogi, P. (2001). Evolution of Universal Grammar. *Science, 291*, 114–118.

Nowak, M. A., Komarova, N. L., & Niyogi, P. (2002). Computational and evolutionary aspects of language. *Nature, 417*, 611–617.

Phillips, C. (1996). *Order and structure.* Doctoral dissertation, MIT.

Pinker, S. (1994). *The Language Instinct.* London: Penguin Books.

Pinker, S., & Prince, A. (1988). On language and connectionism: Analysis of a Parallel Distributed Processing model of language acquisition. *Cognition, 28*, 73-193.

Pritchett, B. (1992). *Grammatical competence and parsing preference.* Cambridge, MA: MIT Press.

Pylyshyn, Z. (Ed.). (1986). *The robot's dilemma: the frame problem in artificial intelligence.* Norwood: Ablex.

Ramshaw, L. A., & Marcus, M. P. (1995). Text chunking using transformation-based learning. In *Proceedings of the Third Annual Workshop on Very Large Corpora* (pp. 82–94).

Reinhart, T. (2006). *Interface Strategies: Optimal and Costly Computations.* Cambridge, MA: MIT Press.

Sadeh-Leicht, O. (2007). *The Psychological Reality of Grammar: The Theta Principle in Parsing Performance*. Doctoral dissertation, Utrecht University, LOT dissertation series.

Saffran, J. R., Aslin, R. N., & Newport, E. L. (1996). Statistical learning by 8-month old infants. *Science, 274*, 1926-1928.

Tomasello, M. (2003). *Constructing a language: A Usage-Based Theory of Language Acquisition*. Cambridge, MA: Harvard University Press.

Trueswell, J. C., & Tanenhaus, M. (1994). Towards a lexicalist framework for constraint based syntactic ambiguity resolution. In C. Clifton, L. Frazier & K. Rayner (Eds.), *Perspectives on sentence processing*. Hillsdale, NJ: Lawrence Erlbaum.

Vainikka, A. (1989). *Deriving Syntactic Representations in Finnish*. Doctoral dissertation, University of Massachusetts, Amherst.

Valian, V. (1990). Logical and psychological constraints on the acquisition of syntax. In L. Frazier & J. De Villiers (Eds.), *Language Processing and Language Acquisition* (pp. 119-145). Dordrecht: Kluwer Academic Publishers.

Valiant, L. G. (1984). A theory of learnable. *Communications of the ACM, 27*, 1134-1142.

Vapnik, V. (1995). *The Nature of Statistical Learning Theory*. Berlin: Springer.

Vilkuna, M. (1989). *Free word order in Finnish. Its syntax and discourse functions*. Helsinki: SKS.

Vilkuna, M. (2000). *Suomen lauseopin perusteet*. Helsinki: Edita.

Weinberg, A. (1999). A Minimalist Theory of Human Sentence Processing. In S. D. Epstein & N. Hornstein (Eds.), *Working Minimalism* (pp. 283-316). Cambridge, MA: MIT Press.

Wexler, K., & Culicover, P. (1980). *Formal Principles of Language Acquisition*. Cambridge, MA: MIT Press.

Yang, C. (2002). *Knowledge and Learning in Natural Learning*. Oxford: Oxford University Press.

Younger, D. H. (1967). Recognition and parsing of context-free languages in time n^3. *Information and Control, 10*, 189–208.

Chapter VIII
Structures in Complex Bipartite Networks

Sune Lehmann
Northeastern University, USA & Harvard University, USA

ABSTRACT

A network structure of nodes and links is an informative way to study information systems. The network representation is valuable because it encodes the structure of the data. This chapter reviews recent advances in the field of network science with an emphasis on describing the structure of information networks. The author argues that bipartite networks constitute an important class of networks, and describes a method for detecting overlapping communities in bipartite networks. The author discusses the relevance of network communities to the future of organizing and understanding large datasets.

INTRODUCTION

In 1990, Tim Berners-Lee implemented the first successful communication between an HTTP client and server (CERN, 2008). Since then, the growth of the World Wide Web has been exponential. In 2008, the search engine Google increased their index to contain more than one trillion distinct pages (Alpert & Hajaj, 2008). In addition to the pages on the World Wide Web, there exists a rich ecology of servers with content that is not accessible to the search engines. This *deep web* is estimated to be orders of magnitude larger than the World Wide Web (Barker, 2004). Fifteen years ago, data was scarce and valuable, and acquisition of relevant datasets was one of the main challenges for academia and businesses alike. Today, the challenge is to filter, segment, and make sense of the prodigious amounts of available data.

Below, we take advantage of the fact that much of the data described above is *linked*. The pages of the World Wide Web are connected via hyperlinks. The Internet is the physical manifestation of the World Wide Web; this system, where routers and servers are the nodes and the physical connections between them are the links, forms a network that spans the globe. The databases that store the exa-bytes of information available to each user of the World Wide Web can be viewed as complex networks. Further, since information networks are often related (e.g. the internet acts as substrate for the world wide web), the various networks interact and influence the growth and structure of each other. The power of utilizing a network representation - of nodes and links - to describe complicated systems is that it allows us to investigate the underlying *structure* of large datasets. As it turns out, the self-organized networks described here possess structure on every level from small motifs involving only a few nodes and links through a meso-level of communities and modules that are all combined in a global organization.

In this chapter we discuss the structure of information networks. In the first part, different types of self-organized structure in complex networks are described, with a particular focus on network communities. The following part takes root in the fact that many information networks belong to a specific class of networks, called *bipartite* networks. In a bipartite network the nodes can be divided into two non-overlapping sets, where links must have one endpoint in each of the two node sets. In much of the previous work regarding complex networks, the bipartite nature of complex networks has been neglected. Here, we show that one discards important information by neglecting bipartite information. We then suggest a novel procedure for detecting communities that works directly on bipartite network data. The final part of the chapter discusses future trends in network science.

BACKGROUND

The science of networks is a relatively new field with roots in sociology, biology, mathematics, and physics. Physicists began thinking about the Laws of Networks around the same time as large databases became available via the Internet. Their way of thinking about networks was inspired by great advances in the field of non-equilibrium thermodynamics, made in the 1970's and 1980's. On the molecular level, nature tends to be uniform. Matter is made up from a huge number of particles that all behave accord-

Figure 1. Degree distributions. Panel (a) shows a Poisson distribution with mean $>>1$ (in this regime, the Poisson distribution tends towards the Normal distribution). In random networks, node degrees are distributed according to the Poisson/Normal distribution. Panel (b) displays a power-law distribution; many real-world networks have power-law degree distributions. When plotted on log-log axes, a power-law distribution forms a straight line.

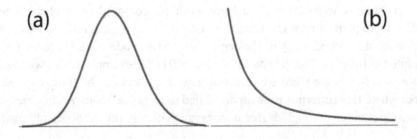

ing to the same, simple set of rules. Knowledge of these rules allows us to predict the macroscopic properties of matter based on the collective statistics of the myriads of particles. Due to the success of statistical physics in analyzing the states of matter and especially the transitions between states, it was a natural assumption to think that similar, simple laws govern the behavior of individual nodes; that the macroscopic properties of networks can be analyzed using the principles of statistical physics. Physicists began to investigate networks with the assumption that networks can be understood as collections of many particles (nodes) that interact (connect/link) according to simple rules.

Therefore, in terms of both chronology and structural complexity, random networks are the starting point for network science. Random networks are designed to possess no structure. A random network is entirely defined by a number of nodes n, and the probability p that a link exists between each pair of nodes. The view that most networks are essentially random was challenged in 1999, when it was discovered that the distribution of links per node (degree) for many real networks is different from what is expected in random networks (Barabási & Albert, 1999). In random networks, node degrees are distributed according to the Poisson distribution, which tends towards the normal distribution when n is large, see Figure 1 (a). However, in many real networks, degrees are distributed according to a power-law distribution. Power-law distributions entail a much higher probability of extreme events than the normal distribution. Human height, for example, is distributed according to a normal distribution – had height been distributed according to a power-law, we would have a finite (but small) probability of running into individuals that were thousands of meters tall. In the context of networks, the power-law implies that individual nodes are *not* similar, see Figure 1 (b). The first important discovery of structure in complex networks, replaced the homogeneity of random networks with the heterogeneity of power-law networks.

Another problem with random networks as a model for social networks, is the fact that real social networks display a property called clustering. Loosely speaking, clustering describes the propensity of a person's friends to also be friends with each other. In a more technical formulation, social networks tend to have a much higher fraction of triangles than random networks. Watts and Strogatz (1998) define the clustering coefficient c_i of node i in an undirected network, as the actual number of links between node i's neighbors divided by the maximum number of links that could exist between them, that is, $c_i = 2 t_i/(k_i(k_i-1))$. Here, k_i is the degree of node i; the actual number of links between the neighbors, (or, equivalently, the number of triangles) that i participates in is denoted t_i, and $k_i (k_i-1)/2$ is the maximum number of *possible* links between node i's neighbors. The network clustering coefficient C, is the average of all node clustering coefficients, $C = (1/n) \Sigma_i c_i$. Random networks display almost no clustering, since no part of the definition of random networks encourages the formation of triangles. It turns out that for random networks with $p < 1$, $C_{rand} = O(n^{-1})$ (Watts and Strogatz, 1998), which is significantly lower than C found in of most real world networks.

The discovery of power-laws and the clustering coefficient was, however, only the beginning of discovery of structure in real world networks (Caldarelli, 2007; Dorogovtsev., Goltsev & Mendes, in press; Newman, Barabasi & Watts, 2006). The degree is simply counting the number of neighbors for a single node. What about pairs of nodes? It turns out that when we consider *pairs of nodes*, the question of who links to whom depends strongly on the degrees of the two nodes (Maslov & Sneppen, 2002). In the case of the internet (Maslov, Sneppen & Zaliznyak, 2004), for example, nodes with similar degree tend to link to each other, while there are relatively few links between high-degree and low-degree nodes. Networks where this pattern is present, are called *assortative networks*. In other networks the opposite relationship is common: high degree nodes systematically link to nodes of low degree – this is the case in the networks of molecular biology (Maslov & Sneppen, 2002). Such *disassortativity* decreases the likelihood of 'cross talk' between functional modules inside the cell and increases overall robustness. Two networks with the same power-law degree-distribution, can still possess very different degree-correlations.

The degree distribution and (dis)assortativity are global statistics calculated on the basis of the properties of single nodes and pairs of nodes, respectively. The next step was to consider structures that include several nodes, essentially generalizing the idea of the clustering coefficient. We call a small set of nodes and their connections a *motif*. In real networks, a few select motifs are expressed with a much higher frequency than one would expect in a random network (Milo et. al., 2002), while most other motifs either occur with the same frequency as they would in a random network or are actively suppressed. Each type of network (information, technological, biological, social, etc.) has its own characteristic set of motifs. This is because motifs are small, functional units important to the function the network was designed or evolved to perform – they are the building blocks of complex networks (Milo et. al., 2002).

NETWORK COMMUNITIES

On the mesoscopic level between the global and local, the structural unit is network communities (Danon, Duch, Diaz-Guilera & Arenas, 2005; Fortunato & Castellano, in press). Loosely speaking, a community is a densely connected subset of nodes that is only sparsely linked to the remaining network. Modular structure introduces another important heterogeneity in complex networks. Each module may possess its own particular statistics; some modules may have many internal connections, internal degree distribution, motifs, etc; while other modules may have completely different structural properties. When there is large variation among communities, global values for statistical measures can be misleading (Newman, 2006). There is currently no standard method for detecting modules in complex networks (Fortunato & Castellano, in press). A widely used class of community detection algorithms is based on optimization of a quantity called *modularity* (Newman & Girvan, 2004). The modularity is proportional to the difference between the number of edges within communities and the expected number of such

Figure 2. Complete graphs, cliques. If all pairs of nodes of a graph are connected, the graph is said to be complete. A complete graph is also called a clique. This image displays cliques comprised of k = 1, 2, 3, 4, 5, 6 nodes.

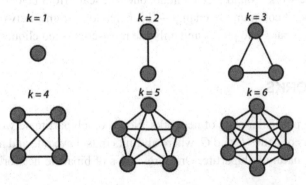

Figure 3. An example of cliques, overlap and clique-adjacency. The figure displays two k-clique communities for k = 3. The k-clique definition allows for overlap between communities. The green and blue communities share one node; the communities are said to be overlapping.

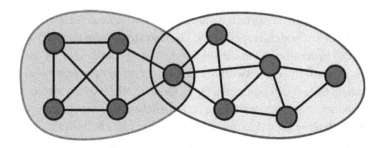

edges. Other community detection methods are inspired by information theory (Rosvall & Bergstrom, 2007), local methods, (Bagrow & Bollt, 2005) message passing (Frey & Dueck, 2007), or Bayesian principles (Hofman & Wiggins, 2008). Here, we focus on a recent approach that views communities as composed of sets of adjacent motifs called *cliques* (Palla, Derényi, Farkas & Vicsek, 2005)

In its simplest form, the k-clique algorithm utilizes a certain type of motifs in undirected network - called *cliques* - to detect communities in unweighted and undirected complex networks. A k-clique is a complete subgraph consisting of k nodes; see Figure 2 for more details. A *community of k-cliques* is defined as the union of all k-cliques that can be reached from each other through a series of adjacent k-cliques; in this context adjacency is defined as sharing at least k - 1 nodes. A k-clique may be a subgraph of a larger clique. Figure 3 shows a simple example of two k-clique communities. One exciting feature of this algorithm, which is evident from Figure 3, is that the algorithm allows for overlap between communities. We know from experience that in a social network, individuals are members of many different communities; family, friends, work, hobbies, etc., and assigning a person to just one of these communities is too simplistic - the concept of overlapping communities is not limited to social networks, but extends to most real world networks. This includes biological and technological networks. For example, tagging computer files is usually superior to storing files in a folders structure, precisely because a file may need more than one tag (community membership).

Note that once the full set of cliques is located, we must determine an optimal value of k. Tuning this parameter enables a better understanding of the behavior of the network in different levels of detail. If the interest lies in the network around a given node, one can scan (from below) through a range of k's and observe how that node's communities change—this behavior is highly network dependent. For high values of k, the network breaks into pieces and only the most-connected cliques remain.

BIPARTITE NETWORKS

Bipartite networks are a particular class of networks. Nodes of a bipartite network can be divided into two non-overlapping sets of nodes D and G, where all links must have one end node in each set. Many real-world networks are naturally bipartite. One large class of bipartite networks is known as affiliation/collaboration networks. This type of bipartite network arises when a set of agents are affiliated with groups, or when individuals work together to create a product. A link is formed when a particular agent is affiliated with a specific group, or when two or more individuals collaborate to create a product. One example of an affiliation network is the paper-author scientific collaboration network, where the two node sets consist of papers and authors, respectively (Newman, 2001a; Newman, 2001b). Another example is the movie-actor network, where the network edges connect an actor to the films he/she has made (cf. www.imdb.com). Since affiliation networks arise whenever people collaborate, many of the Web 2.0 sites on the World Wide Web are also bipartite networks. When users collaborate to create pages in Wikipedia, for example, they form a bipartite network of editors and wiki-pages, where a link arises when an editor edits a page. Another example is the movie-recommendation network (cf. www. netflix.com) that links users to the movies they have watched, or the song-listener network that link music listeners to the music they play on their computer (Lambiotte & Ausloos, 2005). A different type of data that is inherently bipartite are the networks we obtain from collections of documents (webpages, emails, dictionary entries, etc.), where one type of node is documents and the other type is words: A link occurs when a specific word is present in a document (Hofmann, 1999).

It is now clear why we state that these networks are *naturally* bipartite – there is no way that a movie can be an actor in another movie or that a scientific paper can write a scientific paper. Links can only exist between the two sets. An example of a network that is *not* inherently bipartite (but almost bipartite) is the human sexual network, with men and women constituting the two node sets and links are formed when two individual interact sexually. In this case links are formed mostly between men and women, but there is no absolute constraint.

ONE-MODE PROJECTIONS

A bipartite network has a bipartite $(n_D \times n_G)$ adjacency matrix E, where n_D and n_G are the number of nodes in each set. This matrix is constructed such that $E_{ij} = 1$ if there is a link between i and j and $E_{ij} = 0$

Figure 4. A small example of a bipartite network. A bipartite network can be divided into two non-overlapping sets of nodes D and G, where all links must have one end node in each set.

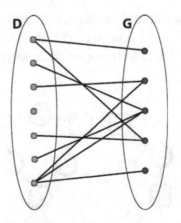

otherwise. Any bipartite network can be transformed into two unipartite networks, one network consisting of just the nodes D set and one network consisting of the nodes in G. These one-mode projections are typically obtained by calculating the two symmetric, weighted matrices $A_D = EE^T$ and $A_G = E^T E$. The diagonal elements A_{ii} of these matrices contain the number of links connected to node i in the bipartite network, and the off-diagonal elements A_{ij} contain information on how many nodes i and j share in the complementary set. A practical example of such a projection is when we project the movie-actor network onto the actors and create a network consisting only of actors, where two actors are linked if they have acted in a film together. Such projections implicitly preceded most of the previous work on bipartite network data.

However, important information is lost when we perform a projection onto one set of nodes. This is clear from the fact that, in general, we cannot reconstruct E from A_D and A_G. Let us study in more detail what information is lost. The root of the problem is that the one-mode adjacency matrices only contain two-point correlations. Given two nodes, i and j, in one of the sets, the corresponding adjacency matrix informs us how many nodes these two share in the complementary set. Given a third node k, we also know the number of nodes that are shared by i,k and j,k in the complementary set, but we have no information about the nodes from the complementary set that i, j, k connect to in common: The same set of nodes could be shared by i, j, k, or the nodes in the complementary set could be shared in a pairwise manner, but not among all three. These considerations may, of course, be generalized to sets of nodes larger than three.

In Figure 5 we display two simple bipartite networks that illustrate this problem. The network described in Figure 5 (a) shows an example, where all nodes in D nodes are linked to a single node in the G set. We can relate this example to the movie-actor network, where this would be the case when three actors work together in a single film. In Figure 5(b) a different bipartite network is displayed. In this case, the D nodes are connected in a pairwise manner via G set. Relating this problem to the previous example, the movie-actor network, the situation in Figure 5 (b) is the case when three actors have all been in films together, but with two common actors per film; *the three movies in G could be far apart in time and space.* Therefore the significance of this network motif is very different from the significance of the motif displayed in Figure 5 (a). However, when we project these two networks onto the D nodes, the two networks are identical. Important qualifying information about the nodes shared in the complementary set is not carried over in the one-mode projections of the network.

Figure 5. Two example bipartite networks with identical one-mode projections. In case (a), the square nodes D = {a,b,c} all link to a single circular node in G = {1}. In the second case the D nodes are linked to G = {1,2,3} in a pairwise manner. The projection onto the D nodes is a triangle in both cases.

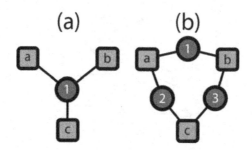

Biclique Communities

The biclique community definition is based on the assumption that communities are 'built' from a number complete subgraphs that tend to share many of their nodes. Six simple complete bipartite graphs are displayed in Figure 6. More formally, we define a $K_{a,b}$ clique as a complete subgraph with a nodes in the D node set and b nodes in the G node set. A $K_{a,b}$ clique can be identical to a maximal complete subgraph or it can exist on a subset of the nodes of a maximal complete subgraph. Extending from Palla et. al. (2005), we now define a $K_{a,b}$ clique community as the union of all $K_{a,b}$ cliques that can be reached from each other through a series of *adjacent* $K_{a,b}$ cliques. We define two $K_{a,b}$ cliques to be adjacent if their overlap is at least a $K_{a-1,b-1}$ biclique. Another way of saying this is that the two cliques must share at least $a-1$ upper vertices and $b-1$ lower vertices (see Figure 7). The biclique method described here is a related to coclustering (Dhillon, 2001; Ding, Zhang, Li & Holbrook, 2006; Reiss, Baliga & Bonneau, 2006). We have developed a tool, *BCFinder*, to detect and visualize biclique communities in real data; BCFinder may be freely downloaded (Lehmann, Schwartz & Hansen, 2007).

The biclique method inherits all of the advantages of the *k*-clique algorithm. Both algorithms are conceptually simple, and contrary to many other community detection methods cited here, they allow for node overlap between communities. Another shared feature is the ability to easily vary the resolution at which the communities are observed, by adjusting the clique size *k*. In the case of the bicliques, nodes from the *D* set can overlap with other nodes from the *D* set and similarly for the *G* set (We will discuss this further below). It is possible to relate the biclique communities in the full bipartite network to *k*-clique communities in the one mode projections. In general, a $K_{a,b}$ community implies:

i.   An *a*-clique community Δ in the projection onto the *D* nodes.
ii. A *b*-clique community Γ in the projection onto the *G* nodes.
iii. Further, to qualify for membership in the community Δ, a node must have a bipartite link to a node in Γ and vice versa.

Figure 6. Bicliques. Here, node-set D is represented by square nodes and G is represented by circular nodes. A biclique is a fully connected subgraph of a bipartite network. Since there are two types of node, the bipartite cliques have two indices $K_{a,b}$.

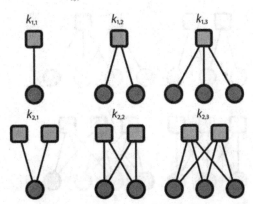

The connection to *k*-clique communities illustrates why the bipartite information is important. The biclique method provides a *context* for the detected communities. In the movie-actor network, a list of actors is always accompanied by a list of films. It is immediately clear why the actors in a group belong together—we know the movies that they share; this presence of context is an important help in understanding the detected communities. In this sense, the bi-community information is more valuable than what we obtained by finding structure in the two unipartite projections separately, because the bipartite communities provide specific (bipartite) links between the communities that we can detect in each the two node sets.

We now illustrate the idea of context via an example. Figure 8 shows the algorithm applied to a real network, the network of authors and scientific papers in condensed matter physics from 1996 to medio 2006. Panel (a) shows a $K_{3,5}$-clique community of 4 authors and 11 papers; this community is a group of scientists studying econo-physics. Panel (b) shows another $K_{3,5}$-clique community. This community consists of 5 authors and 7 papers. The topic of this second community is phase transitions in liquids. A key point is that the author Stanley (highlighted in yellow) is a member of both communities. The division into biclique communities make it immediately clear that it is important that communities are allowed to overlap: Based on the bipartite links, there is no doubt that Stanley is a full fledged member of both communities. In fact, the authors Stanley and Amaral from panel (a) are also members of a third $K_{3,5}$ community studying various biological time series (Lehmann, Schwartz & Hansen, 2008). However, we also understand why the communities are distinct: they regard different subjects. The presence of context (a list of authors are complemented by a list of papers and vice versa) highly enriches our understanding of the communities.

COMMUNITY NETWORK

Based on the biclique communities, it is possible to construct a *community network*. In this meta-network, each biclique community is a node and two community-nodes are linked they have overlapping nodes in

Figure 7. Biclique adjacency. Node-set D *is represented by square nodes and* G *by circular nodes. We define two* $K_{a,b}$ *cliques to be adjacent if they share at least a* $K_{a-1,b-1}$-*clique. The shaded region illustrates the biclique overlap.*

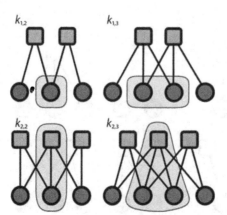

Figure 8. Network of authors and scientific papers in condensed matter physics from the arXiv database (http://www.arxiv.org/) (years: 1996–2006). In these plots authors are represented by the dark blue nodes and papers are represented by light grey nodes. Panel (a) shows a $K_{3,5}$-clique community of 4 authors and 11 papers; this community is a group of scientists studying econo-physics. The bottom panel shows another $K_{3,5}$-clique community, this time consisting of 5 authors and 7 papers. The topic of this second community is phase transitions in liquids. One author (Stanley) is a member of both communities. The division into biclique communities underlines the importance of node overlap: Based on the bipartite linkages, there is no doubt that Stanley is a full member of both communities. However, it is also immediately clear why the communities are distinct: they regard different subjects. The presence of context (a list of authors are complemented by a list of papers and vice versa) highly enriches our understanding of the communities. Both panels are based on screenshots from BCFinder (Lehmann, Schwartz & Hansen, 2007).

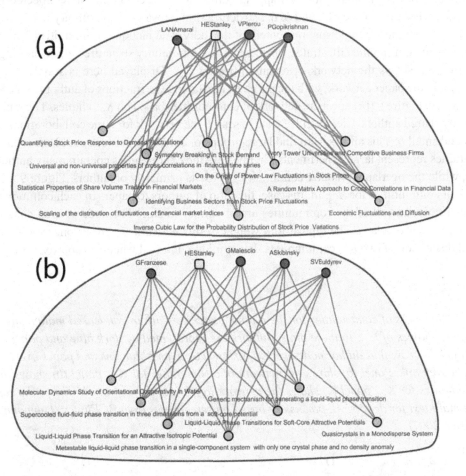

common. Nodes from each partition of the bipartite network are allowed to overlap, so the community network has two types of links (*D*-links and *G*-links). The number of overlapping nodes is encoded as the link weights. Communities can have different sizes and we represent this information by scaling the community-node-sizes according to the total number of members of each community. Finally, it is important to know the ratio of *D* nodes to *G* nodes inside each community. One way of visualizing this information is to color each node (e.g., as a pie chart). The network of communities displays the organization of the entire network, how the parts connect to form the entire network. Figure 9 shows community networks for the previously mentioned condensed matter physics dataset.

What is the expected behavior of the network of communities for different choices of $K_{a,b}$? In the case of $K_{1,1}$ (cf. Figure 9 (a)) the network of communities is simply one large node displaying the fraction of *D* and *G* nodes. When we increase the value of *a* and *b* in $K_{a,b}$, this node breaks into smaller pieces. Since the network is modular with overlapping communities, we find an interconnected network of communities. For any choice of *a* and *b*, the structure of the resulting community network provides a useful way to estimate the information content of the individual biclique communities. This is because the network of communities illustrates what aspects of community structure we are probing.

Figure 9 (a) shows the network of communities for $K_{1,2}$. Displayed here is simply the connected component in the paper network, with the pie chart displaying the fractions of authors and papers in the total network. Figure 9 (b) shows the network of communities based on $K_{8,2}$ cliques. The emphasis here is on many shared authors. Clearly, if we wish to search the network for large collaborations, we choose large *a* and small *b*: This allows us to find large groups of collaborators (one could speculate that these communities represent large experiments); in this case the communities contain many authors and few papers, while the overlap with other communities consists primarily of authors. Figure 9 (c) shows the network of communities for $K_{3,5}$. In this case, the ratio of authors to papers in each community mirrors the global ratio, and all of the communities are of similar in size. The node overlap consists of both author and paper overlaps. The typical link weight in this network is zero or one. See Figure 8 for a detailed discussion of two $K_{3,5}$ communities. In the middle interval when *a* is approximately same size

Figure 9. Networks of communities for the author-paper network in condensed matter physics shown for various choices of $K_{a,b}$. In these plots, authors are represented by dark blue and papers are represented by light gray; thus author node overlap is shown as a dark blue link and paper overlap is shown as a light grey link. Panel (a) shows the network of communities for $K_{1,2}$, panel (b) shows the network of communities for $K_{8,2}$, panel (c) shows the network for $K_{3,5}$, and panel (d) describes the case of $K_{2,12}$. See the main text for details. All panels are based on screenshots from BCFinder (Lehmann, Schwartz & Hansen, 2007).

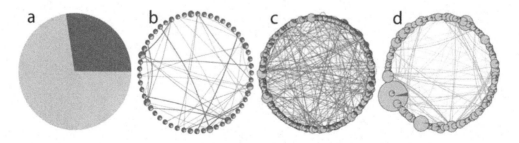

as b, we find balanced groups of medium size that overlap each other both with papers and authors. If a network is highly modular (as is the case for the author-paper network), the size of overlap is typically very small, but in dense, more homogeneous networks, the overlaps can constitute a significant fraction of the nodes in each community. Finally, Figure 9 (d) shows the network of communities for $K_{2,12}$. Here, the emphasis is on many shared papers, so all communities contain a larger fraction of papers than authors (the nodes are mostly light grey). Similarly, the majority of links are paper links; the typical weight is small, between zero and two, but a few heavy links also exist. The vast majority of links are dark blue indicating author overlap between the communities. Thus, if we wish to detect groups of longtime collaborators, we choose small a and large b. The largest community in Figure 9 (d) has 12 authors and 290 papers, but such a large collaboration is the exception rather than the rule; most communities contain longstanding collaborations among 2–4 authors who have written between 20 and 60 papers together. This threshold probes a complementary aspect of the bipartite network compared to the $K_{8,2}$ communities. The considerations above are specific to the author-paper network in condensed matter physics, but a similar analysis may be performed on any bipartite network.

FUTURE TRENDS

Current online design trends are geared towards enhancing information sharing and collaboration among Internet users. This fact makes it clear that bipartite network analysis will continue to play an important role in the future of information management. Collaborative websites (e.g. Wikipedia) naturally result in bipartite network structures of links between editors and webpages. Such collaborative websites are the models for the websites of tomorrow. Another important collaborative trend is collective tagging and classification. An example of this trend is the photo sharing site Flikr (http://www.flickr.com/), where each user is able to attach a tag to his/her own photos, however, the ability to tag content is becoming a more and more common feature of many websites. The combined effort of many users tagging online content is a large bipartite network of objects and their tags. Communities in a tagging-network can be thought of as 'meta-tags', created based on the network structure induced by many local tagging decisions. It is interesting to study the organization and relationships of the global structures that arise from many such local decisions.

CONCLUSION

We have argued that naturally occurring networks have a high amount of structural complexity. This complexity is not a result of design, but rather a result of the network growing slowly, formed by many decisions on the level of individual nodes. Knowledge of the network structure is of great importance when designing new technologies, both in the case of hardware and software. We have shown that bipartite networks are an important class of complex networks, which are likely to be found to be even more important in the future. Finally, we have described a method for detecting overlapping communities in bipartite networks and we expect this method be of practical importance in the study of real world bipartite networks.

ACKNOWLEDGMENT

Thanks to Jim Bagrow for valuable discussions and comments, and to Lars Kai Hansen and Martin Schwartz for their contributions. The work was supported by the Danish Natural Science Research Council. In addition, the work was supported by the James S. McDonnell Foundation 21st Century Initiative in Studying Complex Systems, the National Science Foundation within the DDDAS (Contract No. CNS-0540348), ITR (Contract No. DMR-0426737), and Grant No. IIS-0513650 programs, as well as by the U.S. Office of Naval Research Award Contract No. N00014-07-C and the NAP Project sponsored by the National Office for Research and Technology (Contract No. KCKHA005).

REFERENCES

Alpert, J., & Hajaj, N. We knew the web was big. *The Official Google Blog.* Retrieved August 10, 2008, from http://googleblog.blogspot.com/2008/07/we-knew-web-was-big.html

Barabási, A-.L., & Albert, R. (1999). Emergence of Scaling in Random Networks. *Science, 286,* 509-512.

Barker, J. Invisible Web: What it is, Why it exists, How to find it, and Its inherent ambiguity *UC Berkeley - Teaching Library Internet Workshops.* Retrieved August 10, 2008 from http://www.lib.berkeley.edu/TeachingLib/Guides/Internet/InvisibleWeb.html

Bagrow, J., & Bollt, E. (2005). Local method for detecting communities. *Physical Review E, 72,* 046108.

Caldarelli, G. (2007). *Scale-Free Networks: Complex Webs in Nature and Technology.* New York, NY. Oxford University Press.

CERN. The website of the world's first-ever web server. Retrieved August 10, 2008, from http://info.cern.ch/

Danon, L., Duch, J., Diaz-Guilera, A., & Arenas, A. (2005). Comparing community structure identification. *Journal of Statistical Mechanics: Theory and Experiment,* 09, P09008.

Dhillon, I. S. (2001). Co-clustering documents and words using bipartite spectral graph partitioning. In *Proceedings of the seventh ACM SIGKDD international conference on Knowledge discovery and data mining* (pp. 269-274). ACM, New York.

Ding, C., Zhang, Y., Li, T., & Holbrook, S. R. (2006). Biclustering Protein Complex Interactions with a Biclique Finding Algorithm. In *Proceedings of the Sixth IEEE International Conference on Data Mining* (p. 178-187). IEEE Computer Society Washington, DC, USA.

Dorogovtsev, S. N., Goltsev, A. V. & Mendes, J. F. F. (in press). Critical phenomena in complex networks. *Reviews of Modern Physics.*

Fortunato, S., & Castellano, C. (in press). Community Structure in Graphs. *Encyclopedia of Complexity and Systems Science.*

Frey, B.J. & Dueck, D. (2007). Clustering by Passing Messages between Data Points. *Science, 315*, 972-976.

Hofman, J. M., & Wiggins, C. H. (2008). A Bayesian Approach to Network Modularity. *Physical Review Letters, 100*, 258701.

Hofmann, T. (1999). Probabilistic latent semantic indexing. In *Proceedings of the 22nd Annual ACM SIGIR Conference on Research and Development in Information Retrieval,* (pp. 50-57). New York: ACM.

Lambiotte, R., & Ausloos, M. (2005). Uncovering collective listening habits and music genres in bipartite networks. *Physical Review E, 72*, 066107.

Lehmann, S., Schwartz, M., & Hansen, L. K. *BCfinder.* Retrieved December 12, 2007 from http://www2. imm.dtu.dk/~mhs/bcfinder/

Lehmann, S., Schwartz, M., & Hansen, L.K. (2008). Biclique communities. *Physical Review E, 78*, 016108.

Maslov, S., & Sneppen, K. (2002). Specificity and Stability in Topology of Protein Networks. *Science, 296*, 910-913.

Maslov, S. & Sneppen, K., & Zaliznyak, A. (2004). Detection of topological patterns in complex networks: correlation profile of the internet. *Physica A, 333*, 529.

Milo, R., Shen-Orr, S., Itzkovitz, S., Kashtan, N., Chklovskii, D., & Alon, U. (2002) Network Motifs: Simple Building Blocks of Complex Networks. *Science, 298*, 824-827.

Newman, M. E. J. (2001a). Scientific collaboration networks. I. Network construction and fundamental results. *Physical Review E, 64*, 016131.

Newman, M.E.J. (2001b). Scientific collaboration networks. II. Shortest paths, weighted networks, and centrality. *Physical Review E, 64*, 016132.

Newman, M. E. J. (2006). Modularity and community structure in networks. *Proceedings of the National Academy of Sciences, 103*, 8577-8582,

Newman, M. E. J., & Girvan, M. (2004). Finding and evaluating community structure in networks. *Physical Review E, 69*, 026113.

Newman, M. E. J., Barabasi, A.-L., & Watts, D. J. (2006). *The Structure and Dynamics of Networks: (Princeton Studies in Complexity).* Princeton, NJ. Princeton University Press.

Palla, G., Derényi, I., Farkas, I., & Vicsek, T. (2005). Uncovering the overlapping community structure of complex networks in nature and society. *Nature, 435*, 814-818.

Reiss, D. J., Baliga, N. S., & Bonneau, R. (2006). Integrated biclustering of heterogeneous genome-wide datasets for the inference of global regulatory networks. *BMC Bioinformatics, 7*, 280.

Rosvall, M., & Bergstrom, C. T. (2007). An information-theoretic framework for resolving community structure in complex networks. *Proceedings of the National Academy of Sciences, 104*, 7327-7331.

Watts, D. J., & Strogatz, S. H. (1998). Collective dynamics of "small-world" networks. *Nature, 393*, 440.

Chapter IX
Measuring Information Propagation and Processing in Biological Systems

Juha Kesseli
Tampere University of Technology, Finland

Andre S. Ribeiro
Tampere University of Technology, Finland

Matti Nykter
Tampere University of Technology, Finland

ABSTRACT

In this chapter the authors study the propagation and processing of information in dynamical systems. Various information management systems can be represented as dynamical systems of interconnected information processing units. Here they focus mostly on genetic regulatory networks that are information processing systems that process and propagate information stored in genome. Boolean networks are used as a dynamical model of regulation, and different ways of parameterizing the dynamical behavior are studied. What are called critical networks are in particular under study, since they have been hypothesized as being the most effective under evolutionary pressure. Critical networks are also present in man-made systems, such as the Internet, and provide a candidate application area for findings on the theory of dynamical networks in this chapter. The authors present approaches of annealed approximation and find that avalanche size distribution data supports criticality of regulatory networks. Based on Shannon information, they then find that a mutual information measure quantifying the coordination of pairwise element activity is maximized at criticality. An approach of algorithmic complexity, the normalized compression distance (NCD), is shown to be applicable to both dynamical and topological features of regulatory networks. NCD can also be seen to enable further utilization of measurement data to estimate information propagation and processing in biological networks.

INTRODUCTION

Information propagation and flow are key aspects in understanding how systems interact and function. Various information management systems can be represented as dynamical systems where information processing units (nodes) are connected with links (edges) that represent information transfer. Here we present recent results that provide insight into the general properties of this kind of systems. We focus our discussion on the context of important class of systems, namely the **genetic regulatory networks** that can, at very high level, be modeled as **Boolean networks** (Kauffman, 1993). **Genetic regulatory networks** process and propagate digital information stored in genome and orchestrate a specific response to various external stimuli (inputs) (Hood & Galas, 2003). What makes this class of systems the most interesting is that regulatory networks have evolved over millions of years. Thus, it can be argued that through natural selection and self organization only the most robust and evolvable network structures remain today. Understanding the information processing principles that are present in **genetic regulatory networks** can help us to engineer man made information processing systems that are extremely robust and take advantage of the insights that biological systems have gained over the years of evolution.

The dynamical behavior of large, complex networks of interacting elements is generally difficult to understand in detail. The existence of multiple influences on each element can give rise to exceedingly complicated dynamics even in deterministic systems. A paradigmatic case is the network of genes within a cell, where the interactions correspond to transcriptional and post-transcriptional regulatory mechanisms. The expression of a single gene may be subject to regulation by itself and up to 20 proteins expressed by other genes, and the network of such interactions has a complicated structure, including positive and negative feedback loops and nontrivial combinatorial logic.

The **genetic regulatory networks** may be compared with e.g. Internet traffic, which has been seen to exhibit critical dynamics (Fukuda et al., 2000; Valverde & Sole, 2002). This suggests that Internet as a self-organizing system may optimize information transfer. Internet provides an example of a man-made system of information management and processing, and thus, any insights into information processing in critical networks may have consequences in terms of information management as well. A large part of what we present in this book chapter may be seen as general in the sense that many of the precise characteristics of the network can be abstracted away, and the principles of dynamical behavior still hold.

The structure of this chapter is as follows. First, we present some background of information in **genetic regulatory networks**, our main object of study. In addition, the **Boolean network** model utilized as a simple approximation of **genetic networks** is presented. Our main aim in this chapter is to uncover general features of information processing in cells, and for this purpose, different measures related to global dynamics of the system are suggested. Each of the measures is able to capture an aspect of dynamical information processing in the cells. **Criticality** of cellular dynamics is taken to be the main focus of attention and each of the measures utilized is, in turn, shown to shed some light on this question.

After the background information, we begin by outlining the principles of basic **annealed approximation**. This is a technique that can be used as a first-order approximation of global dynamics. Its main drawback is that the analysis cannot take into account topological details of the networks under study. The findings presented utilizing branching process models give some support to the hypothesis that cells might have critical dynamics. Next, we discuss an application of Shannon's information theory to **genetic regulatory network** models. **Pairwise mutual information** between states of network nodes is utilized as a dynamical measure of coordination between nodes. It is observed that critical networks maximizes this measure, thus making **pairwise mutual information** an interesting tool for characterizing global dynamics.

Finally, we utilize the algorithmic theory of complexity to study both the structural and dynamical aspects of information in regulatory networks. In terms of the flow of dynamical information in particular, new and powerful measurements are shown to characterize information propagation based on microarray measurement data. In the conclusions, we summarize the significance of findings thus obtained.

BACKGROUND

Approaching Information in Biology

Biological systems continuously propagate and process information from various sources to react to changes in their environment or aspects of their internal state. Although the channels used to propagate such information are reasonably known, the quantification of the dynamical information content in biological systems remains a challenge and the significance of the observed phenomena is still poorly understood.

Classical definitions of information content cannot directly capture all aspects of organisms behavior, since biological systems cannot be uniquely separated into agents transmitting or receiving information with a set of predefined symbols. Instead, new meanings are constantly given by evolution to existing signals that change their role in the system. However, within a context of a selected abstraction level, progress can be made with available tools and definitions. That is our goal in this chapter as well. We present some recent approaches that tackle these problems in gene regulatory networks (GRNs) using, as models of GRNs, **Boolean Networks** (BN), commonly used as simple models of large-scale complex dynamical systems (Kauffman, 1969; Kauffman, 1993).

Boolean Networks as Models of Complex Dynamical Systems

The theory of the dynamics of complex networks such as gene regulatory networks began with the study of the simplest model systems capable to exhibit complex behaviors: Random **Boolean Networks** (**RBNs**).

A **Boolean network** (BN) is a directed graph with N nodes. Nodes represent elements of the system and graph arcs represent interactions between the elements. Each node is assigned a binary output value and a Boolean function, whose inputs are defined by the graph connections. Let $s_i(t) \in \{0,1\}$, $i = 1, ..., N$, where N is the number of nodes in the network, be the state of i:th node in a **Boolean network** at time t. The state of this node at time $t + 1$ is determined by the states of nodes $j_1, j_2, ..., j_{k_i}$ at time t as

$$s_i(t+1) = f_i(s_{j_1}(t), s_{j_2}(t), ..., s_{j_{k_i}}(t)), \tag{1}$$

where

$$f_i : \{0,1\}^{k_i} \rightarrow \{0,1\}$$

is a Boolean function of k_i variables. A binary vector

$$s(t) = (s_1(t),...,s_N(t))$$

is the state of the network at time t. In a synchronous BN all nodes are updated simultaneously as the system transitions from state $s(t)$ to state $s(t + 1)$ (Kauffman, 1993).

Random **Boolean networks** (**RBNs**) are networks in which each node has exactly K inputs that are selected randomly. The update rules are chosen with bias, such that for an update rule f $E[f(x)] = b$ for any input x and for any $x \neq y$, $f(x)$ and $f(y)$ are selected independently. In addition to this narrow sense of the word, random **Boolean networks** can also be used to describe networks generated with some other selected distribution or pattern of update rules, for example. These assumptions of randomness permit analytical insights of the behavior of large networks. **RBNs** were used as the first model of GRN (Kauffman, 1969). Each node is a gene, and is assigned a Boolean function from the set of possible Boolean functions of k variables.

By running the network over several time steps starting from an initial state, a trajectory through the network's state space can be observed (referred to as a "time series"). Over time, the system follows a trajectory that ends on a state cycle attractor. In general, a **RBN** has many such attractors. It should be noted that this model can directly be generalized to a larger alphabet by defining $s_i(t) \in \{0,...,L-1\}$ and $f_i : \{0,...,L-1\}^{k_i} \rightarrow \{0,...,L-1\}$, where L is the size of the alphabet.

Dynamical Regime of Boolean Networks

One important feature of **RBNs** is that their dynamics can be classified as ordered, disordered, or critical. During the simulation of a **RBN** some nodes will become "frozen", meaning that they will no longer change their state, while other will remain dynamic, meaning that there state will periodically change from one state to the other. The fractions of frozen and dynamic nodes depend on the network dynamical regime.

In "ordered" **RBNs**, the fraction of nodes that remain dynamical after a transient period vanishes like $1/N$ as the system size N goes to infinity; almost all of the nodes become "frozen" on an output value (0 or 1) that does not depend on the initial state of the network. In this regime the system is highly stable against transient **perturbations** of individual nodes, meaning that externally imposing a change in one node state will not cause significant changes in the other nodes states. In "disordered" (or "chaotic") **RBNs**, the number of dynamical, or "unfrozen" nodes scales like N and the system is unstable to many transient **perturbations**, meaning that a **perturbation** will spread through many nodes.

Here we consider ensembles of **RBNs** parameterized by the average indegree K (i.e, average number of inputs to the nodes in the network), and the bias p (i.e., the fraction of inputs states that lead to an output with value "1") in the choice of Boolean rules. The indegree distribution is Poissonian with mean K and at each node the rule is constructed by assigning the output for each possible set of input values to be 1 with probability p, with each set treated independently. If $p = 0.5$, the rule distribution is said to be unbiased. For a given bias, the critical connectivity, K_c, is equal to (Derrida & Pomeau, 1986):

$$K_c = [2p(1-p)]^{-1}. \tag{2}$$

For $K < K_c$ the ensemble of **RBNs** is in the ordered regime; for $K > K_c$, the disordered regime. For $K = K_c$, the ensemble exhibits critical scaling of the number of unfrozen nodes; e.g., the number of unfrozen nodes scales like $N^{2/3}$. The order-disorder transition in **RBN**s has been characterized by several quantities, including fractions of unfrozen nodes, convergence or divergence in state space, and attractor lengths (Aldana-Gonzalez, Coppersmith & Kadanoff, 2003). In section 4 we present the **annealed approximation** used for the derivation of the mentioned critical connectivity.

Measures of Information

Here some fundamental results of information theory and interesting new developments are discussed. The presented results will form basic tools that allow us to study biological systems through the concepts of information content and processing.

There are two commonly used definitions for information, Shannon information (Shannon, 1948) and Kolmogorov complexity (Chaitin, 1969; Kolmogorov, 1965; Solomonoff, 1964). Both theories provide a measure of information using the same unit: a bit. A natural interpretation of information is the length of the description of an object in bits. Here we discuss the fundamental differences between these two theories and give definitions for information. In addition, we discuss how information can be used to measure the similarity of two objects.

Shannon Information

In Shannon information theory the amount of information is measured by entropy. For a discrete random event x with k possible outcomes, the entropy H is given as

$$H = \sum_{i=1}^{k} p_i I_i = -\sum_{i=1}^{k} p_i \log p_i, \tag{3}$$

where p_i is the probability of an event x_i to occur (Cover & Thomas, 1991). Quantity $I_i = -\log p_i$ is the information content of an event x_i. Natural interpretation for entropy is that it is the expected number of bits that are needed to encode the outcomes of a random event x. It can be observed that entropy is maximized when the probabilities of all events are equal, that is $p_i = \hat{p}, \forall i \in 1,...,k$ (Cover & Thomas, 1991).

As indicated earlier, Shannon information measures information of a distribution. Thus, it is based on the underlying distribution of the observed random variable realizations. The distribution can be obtained based on assumptions about the data generation process or it can be estimated from the data. Thus, to utilize Shannon information, the alphabet of the data source needs to be fixed and there needs to be a model for the origin of the data.

Shannon information is the basis of the mutual information approach presented in section 5. In this approach the average **pairwise mutual information** between the nodes of the system is considered, and it is found that this dynamical observable is maximized at **criticality**. Although our presentation focuses on this use of Shannon information, alternative definitions may be formulated based on Shannon information as well. For example, basin entropy has been defined by looking at the entropy of the distribution describing the division of state space into different attractor basins (Krawitz & Shmulevich, 2007a; Krawitz & Shmulevich, 2007b). Compared with basin entropy, **pairwise mutual information** has the benefit of being much simpler to estimate from data or from a model network.

Kolmogorov Complexity

Unlike Shannon information, Kolmogorov complexity or algorithmic information is not based on statistical properties, but on the information content of the object itself (Li et al, 1997). Thus, Kolmogorov complexity does not consider the origin of an object. The Kolmogorov complexity $K(x)$ of a finite object x is defined as the length of the shortest binary program which, given no input, outputs x on a universal computer. Thus, it is the minimum amount of information that is needed to generate x. Unfortunately, in practice this quantity is not computable (Li et al, 1997).

While the computation of Kolmogorov complexity is not possible, an upper bound can be estimated using lossless compression (Li et al, 1997). Several real-life compression algorithms, like the Huffman (Huffmann, 1952), Lempel-Ziv (Ziv & Lempel, 1977), and arithmetic coding (Rissanen & Langdon, 1979) have proven to give useful approximations of Kolmogorov complexity in practical applications (Li et al, 1997).

Information Distance

As information is an absolute measure, related to a single object or a distribution, it is not directly suitable for comparing the similarities of two objects. Small or large information alone does not tell much about the similarity of objects. Thus, measures to jointly compare the information content of two objects have been proposed.

With Shannon information a joint entropy between two discrete random variables X and Y is defined as

$$H(X,Y) = -\sum_{x,y} p(x,y) \log p(x,y), \tag{4}$$

where $p(x, y)$ is the probability of observing a pair of events x and y and the sum is computed over all the pairs of x and y (Cover & Thomas, 1991). In a similar manner we can define conditional entropy, that is the entropy of X given Y

$$H(X|Y) = -\sum_{x,y} p(x,y) \log \frac{p(x,y)}{p(y)} = H(X,Y) - H(Y). \tag{5}$$

Mutual information is one of the best known information-based measures of similarity (Cover & Thomas, 1991). It is a measure of how much information can be obtained about random variable X by observing Y. The mutual information of X relative to Y is defined as

$$I(X;Y) = \sum_{x,y} p(x,y) \log \frac{p(x,y)}{p(x)p(y)} \tag{6}$$

and by using the notations of joint and conditional entropy it can be written as

$$I(X;Y) = H(X) - H(X|Y) = H(X) + H(Y) - H(X,Y) \tag{7}$$

Thus, mutual information is simply the sum of entropies of X and Y minus the joint entropy (Cover & Thomas, 1991).

Information-based similarity measures can also be defined based on Kolmogorov complexity. This topic has been studied in recent years with the goal of finding an information measure than can be approximated computationally (Bennett et al, 1998; Li et al, 2004). We denote as $K(x, y)$ the length of the shortest binary program that outputs x and y, and a description how to tell them apart. Analogously to Shannon information, we can define a conditional Kolmogorov complexity $K(x \mid y)$ as the length of the shortest binary program that with a given input y outputs x (Li et al, 1997). Thus, information about y, contained in x can be defined as (Li et al, 2004):

$$I(x;y) = K(y) - K(y \mid x). \tag{8}$$

It can be shown that the relation

$$K(x, y) = K(x) + K(y \mid x) = K(y) + K(x \mid y) \tag{9}$$

holds up to an additive precision (Li et al, 1997). Therefore, there exists a symmetry property $I(y;x) = I(x;y)$, up to an additive precision.

Kolmogorov complexity based similarity measure, or information distance, between two objects is the shortest binary program that computes x from y or vice versa. Thus, information distance can be defined as (Bennett et al, 1998)

$$dID(x, y) = \max(K(y \mid x), K(x \mid y)). \tag{10}$$

This is a measure of absolute information distance between two objects. As the size of an object has a direct impact to the Kolmogorov complexity of the object, we should define a normalized version of the information distance that takes the size of an object into account. A normalized information distance can be defined as (Li et al, 2004)

$$d_{NID}(x, y) = \frac{\max(K(x \mid y), K(y \mid x))}{\max(K(x), K(y))}. \tag{11}$$

While normalized information distance can be motivated solely from the information theory point of view, it has some general properties that make it interesting in other ways. The normalized information distance has been shown to incorporate all effective computable distance metrics including, for example, the Euclidean and Hamming distances. Thus, the normalized information distance can be argued to be a universal measure of similarity.

Normalized Compression Distance

While normalized information distance, like Kolmogorov complexity itself, is not computable, it has been shown that this metric can be approximated by any real-life compression algorithm that fulfills several natural criteria of a *normal compressor C*, see (Cilibrasi & Vitanyi, 2005) for details.

By using a compressor C instead of the Kolmogorov complexity K, we can write Equation 11 in a computable form. After we apply Equation 9, to the the numerator of Equation 11, the numerator can be written as $\max\{K(x, y) - K(y), K(x, y) - K(x)\}$ (Li et al, 2004). For compression convenience we can approximate $K(x, y)$ by the concatenation of these strings: $K(x, y) = K(xy) = K(yx)$ holds up to an additive precision. Using these properties the **normalized compression distance** (**NCD**) can be defined as

$$d_{NCD}(x, y) = \frac{C(xy) - \min(C(x), C(y))}{\max(C(x), C(y))}. \qquad (12)$$

It can be shown that this approximation has the same metric properties as the normalized information distance, up to an additive constant (Li et al, 2004). **NCD** is utilized in section 6 to quantify the information propagation in **Boolean network**s and to characterize their dynamical regime.

ANNEALED APPROXIMATION AND BOOLEAN NETWORKS

In this section, we present the basics of **annealed approximation**, a technique utilized to characterize the dynamics of **Boolean networks**. This is important as a starting point for information propagation considerations, since it has been probably the most significant tool utilized in the context of global dynamics of **Boolean networks**. For example, the development of algorithmic information -based measures of information propagation in Section 3 is based on generalizing the approach presented here with a suitable distance measure, the **NCD**.

Standard Analysis

Annealed approximation in **Boolean networks** was presented as a way to give an analytical derivation for the numerically observed differences in behavior between ordered, critical and chaotic random **Boolean networks** (Derrida & Pomeau, 1986; Derrida & Stauffer, 1986). The approach is probabilistic: expected short-term behavior of networks over a distribution of characteristic states is calculated and this expected value is used to predict the expected long-term behavior of a network taken from the distribution. The distribution of characteristic states can be selected or parametrized in different ways, and depending on this selection different approximations are obtained. It is important to note that distributions of **perturbation** sizes can not be studied with the **annealed approximation** in the form we use it here. Instead, the theory of branching processes can be used for this purpose (Rämö et al, 2006), or percolation probabilities can be computed to study the distributions (Samuelsson & Socolar, 2006).

By an annealed network we mean a **Boolean network** in which the connections in the network are reshuffled after each update. This has the effect of, first of all, breaking up the attractor structure. Secondly, the network nodes in general lose their identity in the sense that two states that are identical up to the ordering of the nodes are, in effect, the same state in an annealed network. The quenched network, in which this annealing is not performed, can have local topological structures that affect the network dynamics. Using **annealed approximation** means that we take the results computed in the annealed model and apply them to quenched random networks. For the purposes of the **annealed approximation** all we have left of the topological properties is contained in the distribution of in-degrees of the nodes in the network.

First, let's consider random **Boolean network**s defined in the narrow sense. In this case, the distribution of characteristic states, i.e. states identical up to a permutation of nodes, can successfully be parametrized by a single value ρ_t. This value is the probability that an arbitrary node is perturbed at time t. The nodes are assumed to be independent. As a result, it was found that the parameter values at the phase transition are given by setting what is now called the average sensitivity to one, $2Kp(1-p) = 1$. If the average sensitivity is less than one, **perturbation**s are predicted to die out on average and the network is called ordered. If $2Kp(1-p) > 1$, the network is chaotic and **perturbation** size will approach a non-zero fixed point.

If this case is extended to cover an arbitrary distribution F of functions in the network the change in **perturbation** size ρ from time t to time $t + 1$ can be described by the iterative map h_1, $\rho_{t+1} = h_1(\rho_t)$ with

$$h_1(\rho_t) = \underset{f \in F}{E}[\frac{1}{2^{K_f}} \sum_{x \in B^{K_f}} \sum_{y \in B^{K_f}} f(x) \oplus f(y)(1-\rho_t)^{K_f - |x \oplus y|}(\rho_t)^{|x \oplus y|}], \tag{13}$$

where $x \otimes y$ denotes the pairwise exclusive or between elements of the two vectors. The fixed point ρ^*, $\rho^* = h_1(\rho^*)$ of this mapping is used to predict the chaoticity of the network. If the fixed point is non-zero, $\rho^* \neq 0$, this means that small enough **perturbation**s will grow on average towards the stable-state value and the network is called chaotic. Information propagation in this state is compromised by sensitivity to noise. Chaotic networks correspond to the case $h_1(0) > 1$. If the network has a fixed point at the origin, $\rho^* = 0$, all **perturbation**s will eventually die out according to this **annealed approximation**. If $h_1(0) < 1$ the network is called ordered and as a limiting case if $h_1(0) = 1$ the network is called critical. In the ordered case, information propagation in the system is not efficient, since any information in the initial state is eventually lost at the level of this approximation.

h_1 is commonly called the **Derrida map** or the Derrida curve of the network, and numerical approximations in particular can be called Derrida plots. In the special case of random **Boolean network**s in the narrow sense, this approximation is sufficient for determining the chaoticity of quenched networks with selected p and K. In the following, alternative forms of **Derrida maps** are presented that enable the study of a wider class of **Boolean networks**. Similar classification of networks based on the fixed points of **perturbation** size is made in the following cases as well.

A General Framework

In (Kesseli et al, 2006) a general form describing the annealed model is given in the form of iterative maps

$$P_{00}(t+1) = \underset{f \in F}{E}[\sum_{x \in B^{K_f}} \sum_{y \in B^{K_f}} (1-f(x))(1-f(y))P(x,y,t)],$$

$$P_{01}(t+1) = \underset{f \in F}{E}[\sum_{x \in B^{K_f}} \sum_{y \in B^{K_f}} (1-f(x))f(y)P(x,y,t)],$$

$$P_{10}(t+1) = \underset{f \in F}{E}[\sum_{x \in B^{K_f}} \sum_{y \in B^{K_f}} f(x)(1-f(y))P(x,y,t)],$$

$$p_{11}(t+1) = \underset{f \in F}{E}[\sum_{x \in B^{K_f}} \sum_{y \in B^{K_f}} f(x)f(y)P(x,y,t)],$$

where

$$P(x,y,t) = p_{00}(t)^{(1-x)^T(1-y)} p_{01}(t)^{(1-x)^T y} p_{10}(t)^{x^T(1-y)} p_{11}(t)^{x^T y}.$$

In this mapping, the **perturbation** is parametrized with probabilities p_{ij} that describe the probability that the state of an arbitrary node has value i without a **perturbation** and value j with **perturbation** applied to the network. This iterative mapping is in effect three-dimensional since the sum of p_{ij} is equal to one. The characteristic states of the network can thus in this approximation be described with three parameters. Different kinds of **Derrida maps** are explicitly derived from this general framework in (Kesseli et al, 2006). The interest in **Derrida maps** is justified despite the three-dimensional nature of the **annealed approximation**, since one-dimensional mappings are simpler to analyze in terms of their fixed point behavior. In addition, applying the three-dimensional map to **perturbation** spreading gives one-dimensional mappings in a natural way.

In addition to the **Derrida maps** describing **perturbation** propagation, an additional iterative map called the bias map is used to describe the evolution of the proportion of ones in the state of a network. With the help of the bias map, versions of the **Derrida map** can be used to capture fixed-point behavior of the annealed model. The bias map can be written as

$$g(b) = \underset{f \in F}{E}[\sum_{x \in B^{K_f}} f(x)P(x \mid b)],$$

where

$$P(x \mid b) = b^{|x|}(1-b)^{K_f - |x|}$$

is the probability for input vector x given that we know probability b for an input to have value 1. This mapping is contained in the iterative maps for p_{ij} and can be obtained from the update equation for p_{11} by setting $p_{01} = p_{10} = 0$. The bias map can be iterated by

$$b_{t+1} = g(b_t).$$

This mapping may have non-trivial fixed point solutions depending on the chosen function distribution (Andrecut & Ali, 2001; Andrecut, 2005; Matache & Heidel, 2004). In (Rämö et al, 2005) a definition is given for stable functions as ones that have a bias map fixed point at zero or one. If that occurs, the network constructed of these functions will necessarily be stable without further study of **Derrida maps** being needed. In annealed models used for biological applications we typically assume for modeling purposes that the bias will reach some fixed point $b^* = g(b^*)$. If we study e.g. **perturbation** propagation we can then use this fixed point of the annealed model to correspond to states on the attractor in the quenched model.

Average Sensitivity

For a function distribution average influence $I(b)$ is

$$I(b) = \underset{f \in F}{E} \left[\frac{1}{K_f} \sum_{i=1}^{K_f} \sum_{x \in B^{K_f}} f(x) \oplus f(x \oplus e_i) P(x \mid b) \right].$$

We define average influence I of function distribution F at bias-map fixed point b^* as

$$I = I(b^*).$$

Average influence I can be considered as the average probability that an arbitrary arc is propagating a **perturbation** at the fixed point state. Influence of variable i is defined as

$$I_i(b) = \sum_{x \in B^{K_f}} f(x) \oplus f(x \oplus e_i) P(x \mid b).$$

The average sensitivity of a Boolean function is the sum of influences $I_i(b)$. The average sensitivity of a function distribution is given by

$$\lambda(b) = \underset{f \in F}{E} \left[\sum_{i=1}^{K_f} \sum_{x \in B^{K_f}} f(x) \oplus f(x \oplus e_i) P(x \mid b) \right].$$

By using the average sensitivity at the bias map fixed point we can define the network's average sensitivity as

$$\lambda = \lambda(b^*).$$

$\lambda(\frac{1}{2})$ has also been used for the purpose, but this can be misleading in cases in which b^* differs significantly from $\frac{1}{2}$ (Shmulevich & Kauffman, 2004). λ is the average amount of nodes that are perturbed one time step after we have flipped the value of a randomly chosen node, given that the network has reached the bias map fixed point before the **perturbation**. In its asymptotical nature $\ln\lambda$ can be considered to correspond to the Lyapunov exponent in the classical theory of chaotic systems, although the analogy should not be stretched too far.

Two Definitions of Derrida Maps

Two **Derrida maps** have been suggested for use in cases where the evolution of state bias needs to be taken into account. We can select the characteristic states so that one state is characterized by its bias b_1 alone and the second state is characterized by the probability ρ of any one of its bits being different from the first state. In this case the **Derrida map** is derived from the general iterative maps in (Kesseli et al, 2006) by setting $b_1 = b^*$ and $b_2 = b^*(1 - \rho) + \rho(1 - b^*)$. $h_2(\rho)$ is obtained as

$$h_2(\rho) = \underset{f \in F}{E}[\sum_{x \in B^{K_f}} \sum_{y \in B^{K_f}} f(x) \oplus f(y)((1-b^*)(1-\rho))^{(1-x)^T(1-y)} \ldots$$

$$(b^*(1-\rho))^{x^T y}(\rho(1-b^*))^{(1-x)^T y}(b^*\rho)^{x^T(1-y)}].$$

This expression can be simplified as

$$h_2(\rho) = \underset{f \in F}{E}[\sum_{k=1}^{K_f} \lambda_k \rho^k (1-\rho)^{K_f - k}], \tag{14}$$

where

$$\lambda_k = \sum_{x \in B^{K_f}} \sum_{y \in P_k} f(x) \oplus f(x \oplus y) P(x \mid b^*)$$

is the average sensitivity of function f over k variables. In this form the map is used to compute $\lambda(b^*)$ and visualize ordered and chaotic regimes for canalizing functions in (Moreira & Amaral, 2005). λ_k is also called the generalized sensitivity in (Bernasconi, 1998).

Alternatively, we can assume that $b_1 = b_2 = b^*$. That is, we only make such **perturbation**s that lead to the same bias for the second annealed network. **Derrida map** $h_3(\rho)$ is now given by

$$h_3(\rho) = \underset{f \in F}{E}[\sum_{x \in B^{K_f}} \sum_{y \in B^{K_f}} f(x) \oplus f(y)(1-b^* - \frac{1}{2}\rho)^{(1-x)^T(1-y)} \ldots \tag{15}$$

$$(b^* - \frac{1}{2}\rho)^{x^T y}(\frac{1}{2}\rho)^{|x \oplus y|}].$$

This map was first introduced in (Kesseli et al, 2005) in a spectral form. Fixed point ρ^* is given correctly by this **Derrida map** because in this fixed point both annealed networks have also reached their bias-map fixed points $b_1 = b_2 = b^*$. However, by using this definition the maximum **perturbation** size that can be drawn is $\min(2b^*, 2 - 2b^*)$.

Since we lose information when we use one-dimensional **Derrida maps** instead of the three-dimensional map from which these maps can be obtained, we should in general use the original map to study the behavior of the system. In any case, the **annealed approximation** in this form is limited in its ability to represent information propagation in networks due to the limitation to average quantities instead of distributions. A crude approximation of the dynamics may, however, be obtained in this form.

Perturbation Avalanches and Criticality

To investigate the distribution of avalanche sizes in the system, a branching process methodology may be used. We assume here, for simplicity, a Poissonian distribution of out-degrees for the nodes with K connections on average,

$$p_o(j) = \frac{K^j}{j!} e^{-K}.$$

This may be obtained, for example, by selecting K random inputs for each node.

Assuming that each arc has the same probability of propagating a **perturbation**, called the influence I, the so called branching distribution may be obtained as (Rämö et al, 2006)

$$q_k = \left(\frac{I}{1-I}\right)^k \sum_{j=k}^{\infty} \binom{j}{k} p_o(j)(i-I)^j.$$

The branching distribution describes the distribution of the number of nodes into which the **perturbation** will propagate starting from a single node. If the nodes in the tree of avalanche are assumed to behave independently, the resulting distribution of tree sizes can be derived in this case as (Rämö et al, 2006)

$$p_n = \frac{(n\lambda)^{n-1}}{n!} e^{-n\lambda}.$$

Utilizing the Stirling's approximation this may be written as

$$p_n \approx \frac{1}{\sqrt{2\pi}} e^{n(1-\lambda)} \lambda^{n-1} n^{-\frac{3}{2}}.$$

In the case of critical networks ($\lambda = 1$) the theoretical distribution of avalanche sizes is seen to approach a power-law distribution $p_n \sim n^{-\frac{3}{2}}$. This heavy tail in the avalanche distributions can therefore be seen as an indicator of critical dynamics of the information processing in the system.

To estimate **criticality** from **perturbation** avalanches we have utilized data from (Hughes et al, 2000), where 300 gene deletions and other experiments were made on yeast and response of 6312 genes measured with microarrays. We have selected 227 experiments hat were performed with single-gene deletions, and a histogram of avalanche sizes in these experiments can be seen in Fig. 1. In this figure, the log-ratios are thresholded with $R = 4$ to compute the avalanche sizes.

Writing out a log-likelihood function based on Eq. 5 assuming independent experiments with sizes n_i, $i = 1,...,M$ results in

$$\ln L(\lambda) = \sum_{i=1}^{M} \left((n_i - 1)\ln(n_i\lambda) - \ln(n_i!) - n_i\lambda\right),$$

from which the maximum likelihood estimator

$$\lambda_1 = 1 - M \left(\sum_{i=1}^{M} n_i \right)^{-1}$$

may be derived. This estimator is limited in that it cannot give correct values in case λ is close to or larger than 1. Alternatively, denoting by m_n the number of avalanches of size n in the data, we may also derive a maximum likelihood estimator based on the histogram of sizes. The probability that there will be m_n avalanches of size n given λ can be written using Eq. 5 as

$$P(m_n \mid \lambda) = \binom{M}{m_n} p_n(\lambda)^{m_n} (1 - p_n(\lambda))^{M - m_n},$$

from which the estimator can be written as

$$\lambda_2 = \arg\max_{\lambda} \sum_{n=1}^{N/2} \left(m_n \ln(p_n(\lambda)) + (M - m_n) \ln(1 - p_n(\lambda)) \right).$$

The values for this estimator may be computed numerically with relative ease. In chaotic finite-size networks there will be a number of large avalanches not modeled by the branching process model, so the upper bound of the sum in the estimator is set to $N/2$. The results shown in Fig. 2 suggest that the values most compatible with the simple avalanche model lie in the range $\lambda \approx 0.85 - 1.0$ for the dataset

Figure 1. A histogram of binned avalanche size data from (Hughes et al, 2000). The dashed line shows the theoretical power-law distribution with slope $-\frac{3}{2}$.

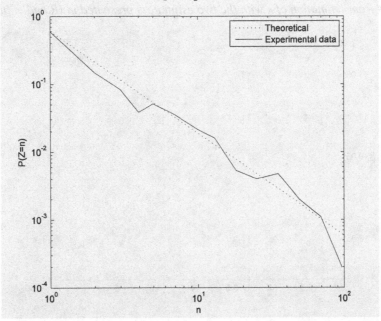

in question. The effect of changing the threshold R can be seen to be clear to both estimators, but utilizing e.g. $R = 4$ like suggested in (Serra et al, 2004) both estimators agree with reasonable accuracy. The results of the branching process approach thus suggest that the dynamics of **genetic regulatory networks** might be critical, although due to the simplified model and limited data utilized the estimation results should be approached carefully. Further work on the avalanche size distributions is required and is currently ongoing.

MUTUAL INFORMATION AND DYNAMICS

The mutual information (Shannon, 1948) between the time series of two elements measures of how well their activities are coordinated. In networks of interacting elements, the average of the mutual information over all pairs $< I >$ is a global measure of how well the system is coordinating its internal dynamics.

Here we study how the average **pairwise mutual information** in random **Boolean network**s (RBNs) varies with the number of connections and the distribution of Boolean rules implemented for each element, assuming that the links in the network are randomly placed. Additionally, we study effects of noise in the transmission of messages on the overall level of coordination of the networks.

Maximization of $< I >$ seems sensible for maximizing the fitness within an ensemble of evolutionarily accessible networks: systems based on high-I networks can orchestrate complex, timed behaviors, possibly allowing robust performance of a wide spectrum of tasks. If so, maximization of $< I >$ within the space of networks accessible via evolution may play an important role in natural selection of real GRNs, and in a broader sense, of any complex system of interacting agents.

We begin by showing, using numerical methods for calculating $< I >$, that in the infinite system size limit there is a discontinuity at parameter values corresponding to critical RBNs and that, for finite

Figure 2. Results from estimation of λ with the two estimators presented in (Rämö et al, 2006)

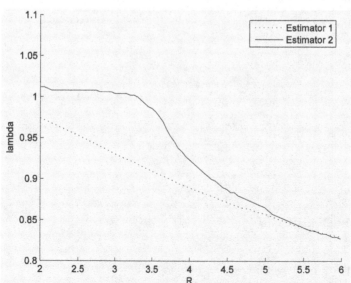

systems, the mutual information is maximum near the critical value (Ribeiro et al, 2006), but slightly in the disordered regime. In the critical regime, the source of high $< I >$ is the indirect correlations between pairs of elements from different long chains with a common starting point. The contribution from pairs that are directly linked is zero for critical networks and peaks well into the disordered regime (Ribeiro et al, 2008). Given the tentative evidence for **criticality** in real GRNs these results may be biologically important.

The results above were obtained assuming absence of noise in signals transmission between the elements of the network. However, in reality, noise plays a relevant role in the dynamics of complex networks, including in gene regulatory networks (Arkin et al, 1998; Ribeiro et al, 2006). Thus, here we also briefly analyze the effects of noise in information propagation efficiency between elements of a network. We show that to cope with noise in transmissions, the network structure requires more redundancy and we estimate the necessary level of redundancy.

Mutual Information as a Measure of the Correlation Between Elements Time Series

The mutual information contained in the time series of two elements gives a measure of how well their activities are coordinated in time. In a large, complex network of interacting elements, I is a global measure of how well the system coordinates the dynamics of its elements. I is defined as follows. Let s_a be a process that generates a 0 with probability p_0 and a 1 with probability p_1. We define the entropy of s_a as

$$H[s_a] \equiv -p_0 \log_2 p_0 - p_1 \log_2 p_1. \tag{16}$$

For a process s_{ab} that generates pairs xy with probabilities p_{xy}, where $x, y \in \{0,1\}$, the joint entropy is defined as

$$H[s_{ab}] \equiv -p_{00} \log_2 p_{00} - p_{01} \log_2 p_{01}$$

$$-p_{10} \log_2 p_{10} - p_{11} \log_2 p_{11}. \tag{17}$$

In case any of the probabilities in the entropy formulas happens to be zero, its contribution to the entropies should be zero as well. Thus, in this context, we assume: $0\log_2 0 = 0$.

Ideally, for a particular RBN, we would simulate the dynamics starting from all possible initial states and observe the time series for infinite time steps. However, the state space of even modestly sized RBNs is prohibitively large to use such approach. Instead, the network is started from a random initial state, and is run for a certain number of time steps. This way one attains an unbiased sample of the network dynamics.

The fraction of steps for which the value of node i is x gives p_x for the process s_i. The value of p_{xy} for the process s_{ij} is given by the fraction of time steps for which node i has value x and on the next time step node j has value y. The mutual information between the time series of the pair ij is then defined as (Ribeiro et al, 2008):

$$I_{ij} = H[s_i] + H[s_j] - H[s_{ij}] \tag{18}$$

With this definition, I_{ij} measures the extent to which information about node i at time t influences node j one time step later, at $t + 1$. Note that the propagation may be indirect; a nonzero I_{ij} can result when i is not an input to j but both are influenced by a common node through previous time steps.

To quantify the efficiency of information propagation through a RBN, we use the average **pairwise mutual information**, defined as:

$$I = N^{-2} \sum_{i,j} I_{ij}. \tag{19}$$

To characterize the efficiency of information propagation in an ensemble of networks we use the average **pairwise mutual information** of the ensemble (Ribeiro et al, 2008), $<I>$, the mean value of I over the members of the ensemble.

In general, since usually the networks' connectivity is relatively low ($K \leq 5$), one does not expect an element to be strongly correlated with more than a few other elements in the network, so the number of pairs ij that contribute significantly to the sum in Eq. (4) is expected to be at most of order N. It is therefore convenient to work with the quantity $I_N \equiv N <I>$, which may approach a nonzero constant in the large N limit. We use the symbol I_∞ to denote the $N \to \infty$ limit of I_N.

Here, we estimate the average mutual information of RBNs in two ways: first we do a mean-field analytical calculation of $<I>$. For this one assumes sparse, tree-like structures. Next, we do numerical calculations of the $<I>$ of quenched networks, meaning we calculate the mutual information of the time series of networks randomly generated whose time series we then simulate for a given time interval.

Average Pairwise Mutual Information in Large Networks: Mean-Field Calculation of I_∞

Two arguments show that I_∞ is zero both in the ordered regime and deep in the disordered regime. First, M_{ij} is zero whenever s_i or s_j generates only 0s or only 1s. In the ordered regime, where almost all nodes remain frozen on the same value on all attractors, the number of nonzero elements M_{ij} remains bounded for large N. Thus $<I>$ must be of order N^{-2} and $I_\infty = 0$ *everywhere in the ordered regime*.

Second, if s_{ij} is the product of two independent processes s_i and s_j, then $M_{ij} = 0$. When the system is highly disordered, where K is very large and the Boolean rules are drawn from uniformly weighted distributions over all possible rules, the correlation between the output of a node and any particular one of its inputs becomes vanishingly small. That is, all pairs of nodes will mostly have independent time series, thus, I_∞ vanishes in the limit of large K.

Given that $I_\infty = 0$ for all network parameters that yield ordered ensembles, one might expect that it rises to a maximum somewhere in the disordered regime before decaying back to zero in the strong disorder limit. However, it was shown that this is not the case (Ribeiro et al, 2008). Fixing the bias parameter p at 1/2 and allowing K to vary, it was found that I_∞ exhibits a jump discontinuity at the critical value $K = 2$, then decays monotonically to zero as K is increased. The conclusion is that among ensembles of unbiased RBNs, average **pairwise mutual information** is maximized for critical ensembles (Ribeiro et al, 2008).

The analytic arguments for these statements are rather complex, and can be seen in (Ribeiro et al, 2008). Here, we present the results of this analysis in Fig. 3 and the results from numerical simulations obtained by averaging over 10^4 instances of networks of sizes up to $N = 1000$ (Fig. 7).

From this data a strong peak near the critical value $K = 2$ is observable, as expected from the analysis. Interestingly, the peak is substantially higher than the size of the jump discontinuity, which may indicate that I_∞ for $K = 2$ is an isolated point larger than $\lim_{K \to 2^+} I_\infty$. Finally, we present numerical results on the variation of I_N with p at fixed K, which again shows a peak for critical parameter values (Fig. 5).

Mean-field calculations are commonly used in the theory of random **Boolean networks**. The most common forms of mean field calculations are within the realm of the so called **annealed approximation**. In the **annealed approximation**, one assumes that the rules and the inputs are randomized at each time step. This approach is sufficient, for example, for calculating the average number of nodes that change value at each time step.

For understanding the propagation of information, a more elaborate mean field model is needed, based on the assumption that the state of a node in a large disordered network is independent of its state at the previous time step, but that its rule remains fixed (Ribeiro et al, 2008).

Additionally, an important feature characterizing the propagation of information in a network is the distribution of local biases. The local bias at a given node is determined by the rule at that node and the local biases of its inputs. When the bias of the output value is stronger than the bias of the inputs, information is lost in transmission through the node.

In the model of RBN used here, each node takes the value 1 with a given probability b, the local bias. In the **annealed approximation** all local biases are equal because the rules and the inputs are redrawn randomly at each time step, so the system is characterized by a single global bias. In the extended mean field model used here and first presented in (Ribeiro et al, 2008), it is considered a distribution of local biases. To determine I_∞, one has to determine the distribution of local biases, b, and then use it to analyze the simple feed forward structures that provide the non-vanishing contributions to I_∞ in the disordered regime.

We now present the main results of the analysis (Ribeiro et al, 2008) of how mutual information propagates in feed-forward structures such as the one shown in Fig. 3.

Mutual Information in Feed-Forward Structures

Given a rule distribution that has a well-defined distribution of local biases, one can calculate the mutual information between pairs of nodes in feed-forward structures that are relevant in the large network limit in the disordered regime. This technique is based on the assumption that the value of a given node at time $t + n$ is statistically independent of the value at time t for $n \neq 0$, in which case the behavior of the inputs to a feed-forward structure can be fully determined from the distribution of local biases.

The most direct contribution to $< I >$ between t and $t + 1$ comes from comparing an input to a node with the output of the same node. Other contributions to $< I >$ come from chains of nodes that share a common starting point. (See Fig. 3.)

From the analysis in (Ribeiro et al, 2008) of these structures it was shown that the critical point occurs at $K = 2$, with ordered networks arising for $K < 2$ and disordered networks for $K > 2$. The results of this meanfield analysis are shown in Fig. 4.

The Large System Limit

The results of the analytical estimation of I_∞ for $K > 2$ and for $\lim_{K \to 2^+} I_\infty$ are shown in Fig. 4. As mentioned this was done using a meanfield analysis (the details of this analysis can be found in (Ribeiro et al, 2008)). The solid line in Fig. 4 shows the result for I_∞. The dashed line shows the contribution to I_∞ that comes from pairs of nodes that are directly linked in the network. It is interesting to note that the direct links alone are not responsible for the peak at **criticality**. Rather, it is the correlations between indirectly linked nodes that produce the effect, and in fact dominate I_∞ for K at and slightly above the critical value.

Because as the network becomes more chaotic (as K increases) the dashed and solid lines converge, one can conclude that the loss of correlation between the long chains is the cause for loss of **criticality** of the network. Also, one can conclude that critical networks are the only ones where such long chains starting from the same node exist. This topological feature (long chains of nodes that start from the same node) is unique to critical networks and is the reason why in this regime mutual information is maximized.

The distribution of local biases plays an important role in determining I_∞. Biases that are significantly different from $b = 1/2$ are important for K that are not deep into the disordered regime, and the

Figure 3. Schematic structure assumed for the mean-field calculation of I_∞. The average indegree of a node in the network is $K = 3$. Black nodes are an example of a directly linked pair. Light grey nodes are an example of a pair that contributes to I_∞ because of a shared influence (i_0). Information from i_0 takes exactly one time step longer (one additional link) to get to the light grey node on the right than to the one on the left. The node labels mark two chains of the type referred to in the text. Hatching indicates frozen nodes.

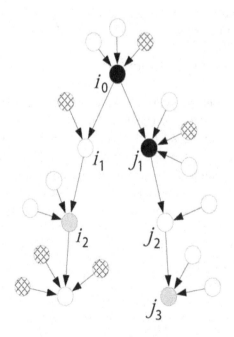

distribution of local biases is highly non-uniform. Dense histograms of biases distributions for various K are shown in Fig. 3. Singularities at $b = 0$ and $b = 1$ occur for K in the range $2 < K < 3.4$, and for all $K > 2$ there is a singularity at $b = 1/2$.

Mean-Field Estimation of the Effects of Noise in the Dynamics

When uncorrelated noise is added to each node at each time step, I_∞ may decrease due to the random errors, but may also increase due to the unfreezing of nodes. Here we present the results of analytical analysis done in (Ribeiro et al, 2008) of the net effect as a function of K. The results are shown in Fig. 6 for the case where each output is inverted with probability ε on each time step. In a following section we will show the results of effects of noise in the mutual information of networks using numerical simulations.

As ε is increased from zero, the peak at which mutual information is maximized shifts to the disordered regime and broadens. The mutual information increase due to random unfreezing is visible on the ordered side ($K < 2$).

In the critical regime where indirect contributions dominate I_∞, however, there is a strong decrease as correlations can no longer be maintained over long chains. This is the main reason for why noise causes a shift in the value of connectivity that maximizes mutual information and is confirmed by the numerical simulations.

Deep in the disordered regime, there is a slight decrease expected due to the added randomness. For $\varepsilon > 0.1$, the maximum of I_∞ shifts back toward $K = 2$. In fact, it can be shown that as ε approaches $1/2$, which corresponds to completely random updating, the I_∞ curve approaches (Ribeiro et al, 2008)

Figure 4. The large system limit I_∞ for $N < I >$ (solid line) and the contribution to I_∞ from direct information transfer through single nodes (dashed line). The empty circles at the discontinuity of I_∞ indicate that we do not know the value of I_∞ for $K = 2$. The size of the sample vectors is $S = 10^4$.

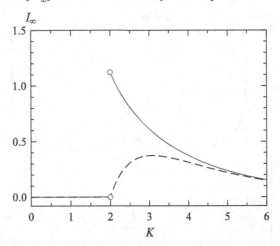

$$I_\infty = \frac{K}{\ln 2} (\frac{1}{2} - \varepsilon)^2 \exp(-K/2).$$

(20)

In this limit, the maximum mutual information occurs at $K = 2$ and the peak height scales like $(1/2 - \varepsilon)^2$.

It is interesting to notice that the fact that the critical K is recovered in the strong noise limit is coincidental, since it does not occur for other choices of Boolean rule distributions.

Finite Size Effects

Numerical simulations on finite networks (Ribeiro et al, 2006) reveal an important feature near the critical value of K that is not analytically accessible using the above techniques because of the difficulty of calculating I_∞ at the critical point. In (Ribeiro et al, 2008) only the limit as K approaches K_c was computed, not the actual value at K_c.) The $< I >$ is now computed by sampling the mutual information from pairs of nodes from many networks.

In collecting numerical results to compare to the I_∞ calculation, there are some subtleties to consider. The calculations are based on correlations that persist for long times in the mean-field model. To observe these, one must disregard transient dynamics and also average over the dynamics of different attractors of each network. The latter average should be done by including data from all the attractors in the calculation of the mutual information, not by calculating separate mutual information calculated for individual attractors. For the results presented here, a satisfactory convergence was observed both for increasing lengths of discarded transients and for increasing numbers of initial conditions per net-

Figure 5. Histograms for the distributions of unfrozen local biases b for $K \to 2_+$ (bold black line), $K = 3$ (bold grey line), and $K = 4$ (thin black line). Bins of width 10^{-4} were used to estimate the probability density from a sequence of 10^6 sample vectors that were drawn after 10^3 steps for convergence. The size of the sample vectors is $S = 10^4$. The combination of a small bin-width and a large sample size enables a clear picture of the strongest singularities.

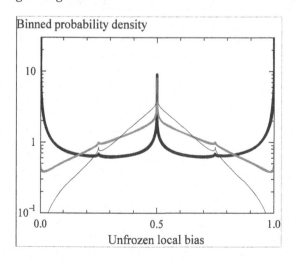

work. Finally, an accurate measurement of the mutual information requires sufficiently long observation times; short observation times lead to systematic overestimates of the mutual information. In the figures below, the size of the spurious contribution due to finite observation times is smaller than the symbols on the graph.

Fig. 7 shows that the peak in I_N extends well above the computed I_∞ value. The figure shows I_N as a function of K for several system sizes N. As N increases, the curve converges toward the infinite N value both in the ordered and disordered regimes. In the vicinity of the critical point, however, the situation is more complicated. The limiting value at **criticality** will likely depend on the order in which the large size and $K \to K_c$ limits are taken.

One can also study I_N as a function of the bias parameter p, while holding K fixed at 4. Fig. 2 shows that I_N is again peaked at the critical point $p = (2 - \sqrt{2})/4$; the qualitative structure of the curves is the same as that for varying K. The calculation of I_∞ for $p \neq 1/2$ requires modifications of the analysis described above that are beyond the scope of this work.

Special Rule Distributions

Up to now, we focused on rule distributions parametrized only by an independent probability p of finding a 1 in a given row of the truth table for any given node (the p-bias). Consideration of other possibilities shows that I_∞ can actually be made as large as desired in networks that are as deep as desired in the disordered regime (Ribeiro et al, 2008). Let λ be the average sensitivity of a node to its inputs; i.e., the average number of nodes that change values when the value of one randomly selected node is flipped. $\lambda = 1$ is one criterion for identifying critical networks (Shmulevich & Kauffman, 2004). For any value of λ in the disordered regime ($\lambda > 1$) and any target value I of I_∞, one can always define a rule distribution that gives a random network characterized by λ and I. To construct the distribution one has to account

Figure 6. The large system limit I_∞ as a function of K for various noise levels ε in the updating. The thin solid line shows I_∞ for networks without noise as displayed in Fig. 2. The other lines represent $\varepsilon = 0.001$ (thick solid line), 0.01 (dashed line), and 0.1 (dotted line). The size of the sample vectors is $S = 10^4$. 10^3–10^6 were drawn after 10^3 steps. Extensive sampling was required close to criticality for $\varepsilon = 0.001$.

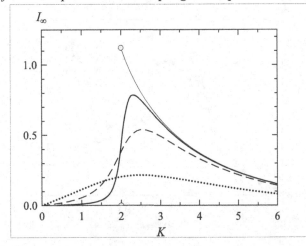

for that long chains of single-input nodes produce large I_∞ and that a small fraction of nodes with many inputs and maximally sensitive rules (multi-input versions of xor) is enough to make λ large.

Consider the following class of random networks. Each node has an indegree k of either 1 or g, with the probability of having g inputs being γ. All $k = 1$ nodes have rules that either copy or invert their input. Each $k = g$ node has one of the two possible truth tables for which flipping any input causes a change in the output. Thus, the Boolean function of each node is the parity function, since it counts whether the number of ones of the inputs states is even or odd. Note that there are no frozen nodes in these networks.

For these networks, we have

$$\lambda =< k >= 1 - \gamma + g\gamma. \tag{21}$$

The network consists of γN nodes with multiple inputs, which can be thought of as the roots of a tree of single-input nodes. If $g^2 \ll \gamma N$, loops in the graph will be rare enough that they will have little effect on the average **pairwise mutual information**. If g and γ are fixed and N is taken to infinity, loops can be neglected in computing I_∞. For a node with $g > 1$, the mutual information between any given input node and the output is zero for the rule distribution under consideration. This is because the bias distribution in networks consisting entirely of maximally sensitive nodes is a delta function at $b = 1/2$. Thus $<I>_k = 0$ for all $\mathbf{k} \neq \{1,1,...,1\}$. For $\mathbf{k} = \{1,1,...,1\}$, one has:

$$I_\infty = \frac{1-\gamma}{\gamma(2-\gamma)}. \tag{22}$$

Figure 7. I_N as a function of K for several different system sizes. For these calculation we use 10^4 networks with 40 runs from different initial states per network and a discarded transient of length 10^4 updates for each run. (For large K, good convergence was obtained for discarded transients of length 10^3.) The sequences of states were recorded for a sample of 10N pairs of nodes in each network. The vertical dashed line indicates the critical value of K.

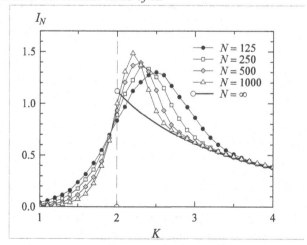

By choosing $\gamma \ll 1$ and $g \gg 1/\gamma$ we can make I_∞ as large as desired while simultaneously making λ as large as desired.

Generalization of this construction to networks with a broader distribution of indegrees and/or rules is possible. High I_∞ occurs deep in the disordered regime when there is a small fraction of nodes of high indegree and high sensitivity and the remaining nodes are sensitive to exactly one input.

Effects of Noise in Information Propagation Between the Elements of a Network

Finally, we present the results of a numerical assessment of the effects of noise in the dynamics (Ribeiro et al, 2006). We show how networks can adapt to the existence of noise in the messages transmitted between its elements. A small increase in connectivity is shown to confer higher robustness, making the network and its elements able to cope with noise such that the information transmitted through the elements is reliable.

Noise is defined as follows. Each time a node state is updated, it will have a probability that it ends up with a state opposite to the state that is dictated by its inputs states and Boolean update rule. That probability value equals the noise, here defined as a quantity whose values range from 0 to 0.5. Note that, given the definition, a noise value of 1 would simply impose the deterministic inversion of all Boolean functions.

In Fig. 9 we show the results of our simulations to study the effect of noise in RBN with average K of 1, 2 and 3. Networks size is 1000 nodes. As noise increases, the elements of the network become more and more uncorrelated (shown with the decrease of I). Yet, for low connectivity values, noise (smaller

Figure 8. I_N as a function of p for several different system sizes. For these calculation we use 10^3 to 10^4 networks with 40 runs from different initial states per network and a discarded transient of length 10^4 updates for each run. The sequences of states were recorded for a sample of 10N pairs of nodes in each network. The vertical dashed line indicates the critical value of p.

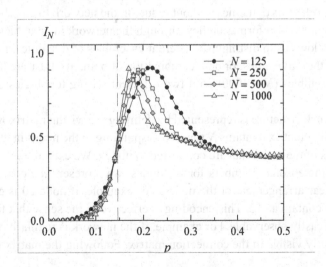

then 0.05) allows "unfreezing" elements, which leads to an increase of I. Above that value, noise increases cause I to decrease, since elements become more and more uncorrelated. The other effect of noise is to shift the connectivity that corresponds to **criticality**. As expected, the loss of certainty in signal transmit can only be compensated by an increase of connectivity.

Thus, as expected, for large N, the value of the connectivity at which mutual information is maximized increases with noise, as shown in Fig. 10. The results are in agreement with the mean-field predictions.

The "extra" connections are necessary to recover **criticality** and thus, maximize mutual information. As noise increases, more connections are needed. Interestingly, the number of connections necessary to cope with noise grows slowly, as seen in the figure. This means that a relatively small increase in connectivity is sufficient to cope with high levels of noise.

ALGORITHMIC INFORMATION

Here we will apply algorithmic information theory to study how information is propagated and stored in complex systems. The use of algorithmic information allows us to consider individual networks as objects without the need of defining underlying distributions for the origin of these networks. By comparing the structures of the networks we can study the similarities of network structures and, for example, study how information flows in the structures as the networks evolve.

Using this framework we also establish connection between structure and dynamics of **Boolean networks**. This connection gives important insight for understanding dynamical systems as the structure directly affects emergent properties such as the ability to process information. In addition, we will propose an information-based order parameter that can be used to quantify the dynamics of any discrete dynamical system. This order parameter also provides insight to the nature in information propagation in dynamical systems.

Information Content and Flow

Making use of the universal information distance as approximated by the **NCD**, we are able to relate the structure of a network to its dynamics without reducing the network to an arbitrary set of features, thus allowing us to capture the information flow through the network in an unbiased (feature-independent) manner. It also allows us to distinguish different ensembles of dynamical networks based solely on their structure, on their dynamics, or on a combination of both. To illustrate this, we generated six **Boolean network** ensembles ($N = 1000$) with two different wiring topologies: random and regular, each with $K = 1$, 2, or 3.

The **Boolean network** structure is represented by defining the wiring matrix W and the truth tables (functions) F. The wiring matrix contains N rows corresponding to the nodes in the network. Each row i contains the numbers of the nodes that are connected to node i. We extend this encoding further such that instead of using the absolute numbers for the nodes, we represent the connections by distances along an arbitrary linear arrangement of the nodes. For example, if node 20 is connected to node 8, then row 20 in W will contain a -12. This encoding is effective in the sense that the regularities in the network structure are easily observable. For example, if the network is regularly wired as in a cellular automaton, this is clearly visible in the connection matrix. Following the matrix representation of the

Figure 9. Average mutual information of the time series, of length 1000, of Boolean networks size 1000. Each data point corresponds to an average over 100 networks.

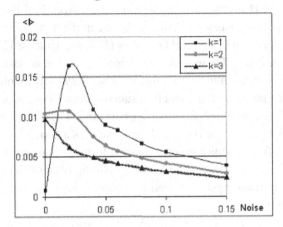

Figure 10. Value of the average connectivity for which mutual information is maximized for increasing levels of noise.

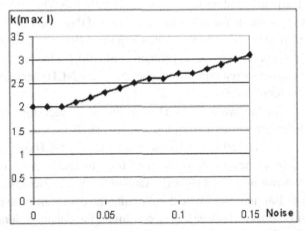

connections, the truth tables F of the Boolean functions are given for each node i. The matrix F defines how the output of the node is obtained using the inputs defined in W.

In comparing the network structures, one distinctive parameter is their size and thus, the size of their respective compressed data structures. For example, using our encoding for the network structure, **Boolean network**s with connectivity $K = 1, 2,$ and 3 could be separated from each other simply by looking at the sizes of W and F. To verify that the proposed method is able to find the information within the network structure and does not merely classify the networks based on their size, we introduce fictitious inputs to make all network representations to be of equal size. A fictitious input is one that does not affect the output of the function. We choose the fictitious input(s) randomly to be one of the existing connections; that is, the same connection is repeated more than once in the network encoding. For our analyses, fictitious inputs have been applied such that all **Boolean network**s are encoded with the same size as $K = 3$ networks. As Figure 11 illustrates, all of the different ensembles considered are clearly distinguishable.

To demonstrate that the **NCD** is able to capture meaningful structural relationships between networks, we applied it to compute the pairwise distances between the metabolic networks of 107 organisms from the Kyoto Encyclopedia of Genes and Genomes (KEGG) database (Kanehisa & Goto, 2000) as explained in (Ma & Zeng, 2003). These networks were encoded in a manner similar to that used with **Boolean networks**. Each reaction in the metabolic network was represented as a node. Each such node has a set of inputs corresponding to the reaction substrates and a set of outputs corresponding to the reaction products, yielding two connection matrices W_{in} and W_{out}. The stoichiometric coefficients for the substrates and products in each of the metabolic reactions are stored as entries in matrices T_{in} and T_{out}. The transformation from a stoichiometric matrix to these matrices is lossless and thus, the stoichiometric matrix could easily be regenerated. This encoding is equivalent to the often used reaction graph representation. Fictitious inputs are used to make all reactions in a given organism to have equal numbers of inputs and outputs.

To build the phylogenetic tree based on the metabolic networks we concatenated all of the above matrices encoding network stoichiometry and used the bzip2 compression algorithm to compute the **NCD**. The resulting phylogenetic tree, generated using the complete linkage method, is shown in Figure 12. The organisms are clearly grouped into the three domains of life. The archaea and eukaryotes both separate into distinct clades based on the information content of their metabolic networks. The bacteria form three distinct clades, with parasitic bacteria encoding more limited metabolic networks separating from the rest, as has been observed previously (Podani et al, 2001). The fact that the phylogenetic tree reproduces the known evolutionary relationships suggests that the **NCD** successfully extracts structural information embedded in complex networks.

To extend this analysis further, we used **NCD** to study the relationship between structural information and dynamical behavior within a common framework. Within each of the above 6 **Boolean network** ensembles, we generated 150 networks and calculated the **NCD** between all pairs of network structures and between their associated dynamic state trajectories. In order obtain comparable data from the dynamics of **Boolean networks** (that is, state-space trajectories) from different ensembles, we performed a burn-in of 100 time steps before collecting the data. This was done in order to ensure that the network is not in a transient state. Based on simulations, using a longer burn-in period did not affect the results. After the burn-in, trajectories were collected for 10 consecutive time steps, and subsequently were used to compute the **NCD** between pairs of trajectories. Using longer time series did not affect the results. This process was repeated for exactly the same networks that were used for comparing network structures.

The relationship between structure and dynamics was visualized by plotting the structure-based **NCD** versus the dynamics-based **NCD** for pairs of networks within each ensemble (Figure 13). All network ensembles were clearly distinguishable based on their structural and dynamical information. Additionally, the critical ensemble ($K = 2$, random wiring) exhibited a distribution that is markedly more elongated along the dynamics axis as compared to the chaotic and ordered ensembles, supporting the view that critical systems exhibit maximal diversity. The wide spread of points for the critical network ensemble in Figure 13 shows that their dynamics range between those of ordered and chaotic ensembles. Indeed, very different network structures can yield both relatively similar and dissimilar dynamics, thereby demonstrating the dynamic diversity exhibited in the critical regime. Thus, the universal information distance provides clear evidence that the most complex relationships between structure and dynamics occur in the critical regime.

Quantifying Information Propagation

Consider two stimuli that transiently place the complex system into two different states. If we can quantify the difference between the information content of these two states, we can then ask how this information difference changes as the system proceeds forward in time. Information loss can occur in two different ways. On the one hand, the successor states of the system may tend to be more similar than their predecessor states, leading to informational convergence. In contrast, the successor states may become more dissimilar, resulting in informational divergence. In the former case, the system forfeits discriminatory sensitivity in that it tends to forget the differences that distinguish different stimuli. In the latter case, robustness is killed because even small differences get amplified, making it difficult or impossible to reliably propagate information over time. In terms of information dynamics, critical behavior represents precisely the point of minimal information loss convergence nor divergence and thus a balance between adaptability and stability.

To quantitatively study this tradeoff, we required a means of measuring the difference in the information content of two different system states so that we could examine whether this information tends to get attenuated or amplified by the dynamical system.

Dynamical behavior of a system can be characterized using an order parameter. For random **Boolean network**s commonly used order parameter is the slope of the **Derrida map** (Derrida & Pomeau, 1986), as discussed in Section 4. Let $\mathbf{s}^{(1)}(t)$ and $\mathbf{s}^{(2)}(t)$ be two states of the system at time t. A normalized Hamming distance between the states is

$$d(t) = \tfrac{1}{n} \sum\nolimits_{i=1}^{N} \left(s_i^{(1)}(t) \oplus s_i^{(2)}(t) \right),$$

where $\oplus$ is XOR operator and N is the number of nodes. The **Derrida map** can be drawn by plotting the expected distance $d(t + \Delta t)$ versus the distance $d(t)$. The expectation here is relative to the distribution over the state space of a particular system or over some ensemble of systems, or both (Shmulevich & Kauffman, 2004). In practice, the state space of a dynamical system can be sampled for constructing an empirical **Derrida map** (Figure 14). If the slope of the **Derrida map** at the origin is greater than 1, then the system can be said to be chaotic; if less than 1, ordered; and if equal to 1, critical.

In addition to the **Derrida map** several other order parameters have been proposed for **Boolean networks**. In the case of random **Boolean network**s these are all equivalent in terms of the phase transition (Luque & Sole, 2000; Flyvbjerg, 1988; Shmulevich & Kauffman, 2004). Order parameters are usually defined in the context of a specific model class. Thus, the definition is dependent on the selected distance metric, in the case of **Derrida map**, the Hamming distance. Making the definition of an order parameter dependent of a model class poses limitations for measuring the behavior. For example, the order parameter can only be used with one type of a model class and thus, the properties of different model classes can not be compared. Furthermore, the purpose of an order parameter is to study the propagation of information through the system. Thus, instead of looking at the propagation of individual bits, it is more justified to study the propagation of information.

We propose a new information-based order parameter for measuring the information propagation through a system. This measure is based on the normalized information distance and thus it can directly be applied to any model class as it makes no assumptions about the model or the alphabet the model is using. We have defined our order parameter analogously to the **Derrida map**. Instead of using the Hamming distance as the measure of similarity, we are using the normalized information distance.

In computational applications **normalized compression distance** can be used as an approximation. Thus, the information-based **Derrida map** is obtained by computing the distances between the states $s^{(1)}(t)$ and $s^{(2)}(t)$ using $d(t) = d_{NCD}(s^{(1)}(t), s^{(2)}(t))$. Examples are shown for Boolean and ternary networks in Figures 15 and 16, respectively.

When compared with the traditional **Derrida map** for random **Boolean network**s, our information based version has an interesting property. For a critical network the curve stays at the diagonal for all the distances, not just close to the origin. With the traditional approach that is based on the Hamming distance the dynamical regime can be characterized only by using very small **perturbation**s, as the order parameter is defined by the slope at the origin. Our information-based version allows us to use **perturbation**s of any size as the same dynamical behavior is observed throughout the curve. This allows us to apply the information based order parameter directly to data, measured from real dynamical systems. For example, when a stimulus is given to a biological system, it is usually not known what the exact response is. Thus, our measure allows the usage of biological data even though the size of the response, or the **perturbation**, is not known. This type of analysis of information propagation is discussed in (Nykter et al, 2008).

Figure 11. The normalized compression distance (NCD) applied to all pairs of networks. The resulting distance matrix was then used to build a dendrogram, using the complete linkage method. Six ensembles of random Boolean networks (K = 1, 2, 3) each with random or regular topology; N = 1000) were used to generate 30 networks from each ensemble.

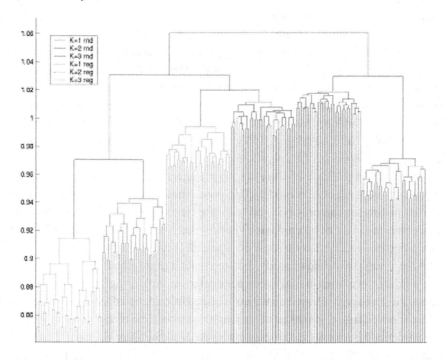

Figure 12. A phylogenetic tree generated using NCD applied to all pairs of metabolic network structures from 107 organisms in KEGG. Bacteria are shown in red, archaea in blue, and eukaryotes in green. Subclasses are labeled on the right. Parasitic bacteria (bottom clade) are separated from the rest as observed earlier.

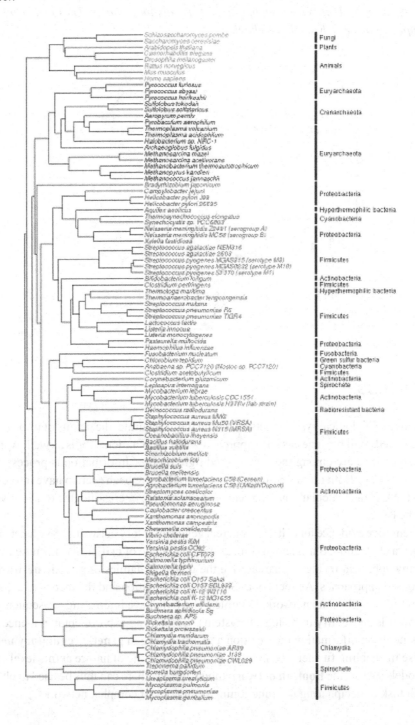

Figure 13. The normalized compression distance (NCD) applied to network structure and dynamics. Six ensembles of random Boolean networks (K = 1, 2, 3 each with random or regular topology; N = 1000) were used to generate 150 networks from each ensemble. NCDs were computed between pairs of networks (both chosen from the same ensemble) based on their structure (x-axis) and their dynamic state trajectories (y-axis). Different ensembles are clearly distinguishable. The critical ensemble is more elongated, implying diverse dynamical behavior.

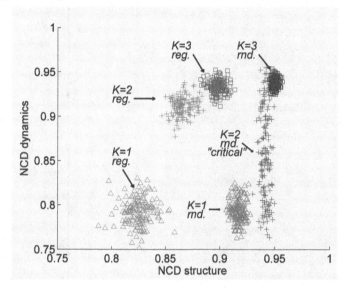

FUTURE TRENDS

As the knowledge of biological systems gets more and more accurate, the details of information processing occurring in cells will become easier to approach with computational tools as well. Approaches such as those presented here are among the first to shed light on how information is processed, at a global level, in living systems. Both mutual information and **NCD** have been seen to have interesting features in this context. **NCD** in particular could be seen as particularly interesting due to its universality as an information measure.

Given the tentative evidence for **criticality** in real gene regulatory networks (Nykter et al, 2008; Rämö et al, 2006; Serra et al, 2004; Shmulevich et al, 2005), the theme of **criticality** discussed in this chapter is central in any approach trying to characterize the global dynamics of **genetic networks**, including information-based approaches. As seen, both Shannon information and the theory of algorithmic complexity can provide insights into network dynamics, and both have interesting consequences for the use of evolving towards **criticality** in biological systems. Combining experimental evidence and theoretical insights, studies on information propagation and processing in **genetic regulatory networks**, have shown promise in enabling further advances in our understanding of nature at this level of abstraction. Simplified models such as the **Boolean network** model utilized here can thus be used to obtain advances in the difficult task of deciphering the functioning of biological complex networks.

CONCLUSION

Above, we have noted some early evidence that eukaryotic cells may be dynamically critical. In terms of quantifying information propagation, we have seen that this corresponds to maximizing the **pairwise mutual information** between the nodes in the RBN model (Section 5). **Perturbation** avalanches, in this case, show a tentative power-law tail as a sign of critical dynamics. Experimental data of avalanches from regulatory networks has been utilized to support the hypothesis of **criticality** (Section 4). Approaches of algorithmic information theory can be applied for the same purpose as well (Section 6).

It is an attractive hypothesis that **genetic regulatory networks** in cells are critical or perhaps slightly in the ordered regime (Kauffman, 1969). Critical networks display an intriguing balance between robust behavior in the presence of random **perturbation**s and flexible switching induced by carefully targeted **perturbation**s. That is, a typical attractor of a critical RBN is stable under the vast majority of small, transient **perturbation**s (flipping one gene to the "wrong" state and then allowing the dynamics to proceed as usual), but there are a few special **perturbation**s that can lead to a transition to a different attractor. This observation forms the conceptual basis for thinking of cell types as attractors of critical networks, since cell types are both homeostatic in general and capable of differentiating when specific signals (**perturbation**s) are delivered.

Recently, some experimental evidence has been shown to support the idea that **genetic regulatory networks** in eukaryotic cells are dynamically critical. In Ref. (Shmulevich et al, 2005), the microarray patterns of gene activities of HeLa cells were analyzed, and the trajectories in a HeLa microarray time-series data characterized using a Lempel-Ziv complexity measure on binarized data. The conclusion was that cells are either ordered or critical, not disordered. In Ref. (Rämö et al, 2006) (Section 4), it was

Figure 14. Derrida map for Boolean networks from ensembles K = 1, 2, 3, 4 with b = 0.5. The slope of the Derrida map at the origin determines the dynamical regime.

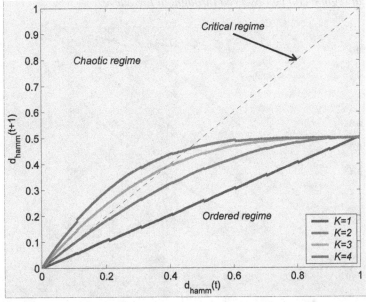

deduced that deletion of genes in critical networks should yield a power law distribution of the number of genes that alter their activities with an exponent of –1.5 and observed data on 240 deletion mutants in yeast showed this same exponent. And in Ref. (Serra et al, 2004), micro-array gene expression data following silencing of a single gene in yeast was analyzed. Again, the data suggests critical dynamics for the gene regulatory network. The approach of Section 6 has been utilized in Ref. (Nykter et al, 2008) to characterize macrophage dynamics as critical. These results suggest that operation at or near **criticality** confers some evolutionary advantage.

Based on the mutual information approach, within the class of RBNs with Poissonian degree statistics and typically studied rule distributions, critical networks provide an optimal capacity for coordinating dynamical behaviors. This type of coordination requires the presence of substantial numbers of dynamical (unfrozen) nodes, the linking of those nodes in a manner that allows long-range propagation of information while limiting interference from multiple propagating signals, and a low error rate. To the extent that evolutionary fitness depends on such coordination and RBN models capture essential features of the organization of **genetic regulatory networks**, critical networks are naturally favored. For these reasons it has been conjectured (Ribeiro et al, 2008) that mutual information is optimized in critical networks for broader classes of networks that include power-law degree distributions and/or additional local structure such as clustering or over-representation of certain small motifs.

A key insight from these studies is that the maximization of average **pairwise mutual information** is achieved in RBNs by allowing long chains of effectively single-input nodes to emerge from the background of frozen nodes and nodes with multiple unfrozen inputs. The correlations induced by these chains are reduced substantially when stochastic effects are included in the update rules, thus destroying the jump discontinuity in I_∞ at the critical point and shifting the curve toward the dashed one in Fig. 4 obtained from direct linkages only. Though the noise modeled here is rather strong, corresponding to

Figure 15. Information-based Derrida map for Boolean networks from ensembles K = 1, 2, 3, 4 with b = 0.5. The dynamical regime can be observed throughout the curve.

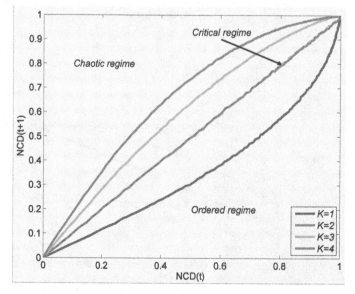

a large fluctuation in the expression of a given gene from its nominally determined value, the direction of the shift in the maximum may be expected to occur in other models.

The behavior of the average **pairwise mutual information** in RBNs with flat rule distributions is nontrivial and somewhat surprising. This is due largely to the fact that the network of unfrozen nodes in nearly critical systems does indeed have long single-input chains. By choosing a rule distribution carefully, however, one can enhance the effect and produce arbitrarily high values of I_∞ even deep in the disordered regime. Whether real biological systems have this option is less clear. The interactions between transcription factors and placement of binding sites required to produce logic with high sensitivity to many inputs appear difficult (though not impossible) to realize with real molecules.

Maximization of **pairwise mutual information** may be a sensible proxy for maximization of fitness within an ensemble of evolutionarily accessible networks: we suggest that systems based on high-$<I>$ networks can orchestrate complex, timed behaviors, possibly allowing robust performance of a wide spectrum of tasks. If so, the maximization of **pairwise mutual information** within the space of networks accessible via, e.g., genome evolution may play an important role in natural selection of real **genetic networks**.

This principle ought to applicable to any network of interacting agents whose goal is to maximize the information flow between all its agents, such as human organizations.

We have found that maximization of **pairwise mutual information** can be achieved deep in the disordered regime by sufficiently non-uniform Boolean rule distributions. However, in the absence of further knowledge, a roughly flat rule distribution remains the simplest choice, and in this case **pairwise mutual information** is maximized for critical networks.

It is also of interest to note that a small increase in the networks' average connectivity is sufficient to cope with high levels of noise. This observation may be of importance for example to understand how gene regulatory networks, which have been shown to be highly stochastic (Arkin et al, 1998; Ribeiro et al, 2006), may cope with its internal and external stochasticity.

Figure 16. Information-based Derrida map for Ternary networks from ensembles K = 1, 1.5, 2, 3, 4 with b = 0.5. The dynamical regime can be observed throughout the curve.

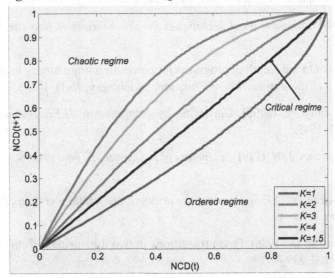

As we have seen, the **Normalized compression distance** -based approach allows studying both the topological and dynamical aspects of Boolean network models. It can be observed that the greatest variation of dynamical behavior is obtained in the critical networks, supporting intuition of the most varied information processing capabilities in this regime.

Another significant feature of NCD results from the form of Derrida curves obtained if the Hamming distance measure in the standard **annealed approximation** is replaced with NCD. The resulting curves depict either convergence or divergence of dynamical trajectories in the system in terms of their informational proximity to one another. This can be interpreted as characterizing the information processing in the system. A particular benefit of the approach is that available data can be utilized more efficiently than with previous annealed approximation approaches of similar nature. This and the fact that NCD can be viewed as a universal information-based distance measure, not in principle dependent on the exact way the states or components of the systems are presented, suggest that replacing more traditional approaches with algorithmic complexity ones might provide useful in other cases as well.

REFERENCES

Aldana-Gonzalez, M., Coppersmith, S., & Kadanoff, L.P. (2003). Boolean dynamics with random couplings. In E. Kaplan, J. E. Marsden, & K. R. Sreenivasan (Eds.), *Perspectives and Problems in Nonlinear Science*. New York: Springer.

Andrecut, M. (2005). Mean field dynamics of random Boolean networks. *Journal of Statistical Mechanics, P02003*.

Andrecut, M., & Ali, K. (2001). Chaos in a simple Boolean network. *International Journal of Modern Physics B, 15*(1), 17–23.

Arkin, A., Ross, J., & McAdams, H. H. (1998). Stochastic Kinetic Analysis of Developmental Pathway Bifurcation in Phage λ -infected *Escheria Coli* Cells. *Genetics, 149*, 1633-1648.

Bennett, C. H., Gacs, P., Li, M., Vitanyi, P. M. B., & Zurek, W. (1998). Information distance. *IEEE Transactions on Information Theory, 44*(4), 1407–1423.

Bernasconi, A. (1998). *Mathematical Techniques for the Analysis of Boolean Functions*. PhD thesis, University of Pisa.

Chaitin, G. J. (1969). On the length of programs for computing finite binary sequences: Statistical considerations. *Journal of the Association of Computer Machinery, 16*(1), 145–159.

Cilibrasi, R., & Vitanyi, P. (2005). Clustering by compression. *IEEE Transactions on Information Theory, 51*(4), 1523–1545.

Cover, T. M., & Thomas, J. A. (1991). *Elements of Information Theory*. Hoboken, New Jersey: Wiley-Interscience.

Derrida, B., & Pomeau, Y. (1986). Random networks of automata: a simple annealed approximation. *Europhysics Letters, 1*, 45–49.

Derrida, B., & Stauffer, D. (1986). Phase transitions in two dimensional Kauffman cellular automata. *Europhysics Letters, 2*, 739–745.

Flyvbjerg, H. (1988). An order parameter for networks of automata. *Journal of Physics A: Mathematical and General, 21*(19), L955–L960.

Fukuda, K., Takayasu, H., & Takayasu, M. (2000). Origin of critical behavior in Ethernet traffic. *Physica A, 287,* 289–301.

Hood, L., & Galas, D. (2003). The digital code of DNA. Nature, *421,* 444-448.

Huffman, D. A. (1952). A method for the construction of minimum-redundancy codes. *Proceedings of the Institute of Radio Engineers, 40,* 1098–1102.

Hughes, T., Marton, M., Jones, A., Robers, C., Stoughton, R., Armour, C. et al. (2000). Functional discovery via a compendium of expression profiles. *Cell, 102,* 109–126.

Kanehisa, M., & Goto, S. (2000). KEGG: Kyoto encyclopedia of genes and genomes. *Nucleic Acids Research, 28*(1), 27–30.

Kauffman, S. A. (1969). Metabolic stability and epigenesis in randomly constructed genetic nets. *Journal of Theoretical Biology, 22,* 437–467.

Kauffman, S. A. (1993). The Origins of Order: Self-organization and selection in evolution. New York: Oxford University Press.

Kesseli, J., Rämö, P., & Yli-Harja, O. (2005). Tracking perturbation in Boolean networks with spectral methods. *Physical Review E, 72,* 026137.

Kesseli, J., Rämö, P., & Yli-Harja, O. (2006). Iterated maps for annealed Boolean networks. *Physical Review E, 74,* 046104.

Kolmogorov, A. N. (1965). Three approaches to the quantitative definition of information. *Problems in Information Transmission, 1*(1), 1–7.

Krawitz, P., & Shmulevich, I. (2007a). Basin Entropy in Boolean Network Ensembles. *Physical Review Letters, 98*(15), 158701.

Krawitz, P., & Shmulevich, I. (2007b). Entropy of complex relevant components in Boolean networks. *Physical Review E, 76,* 036115.

Li, M., Chen, X., Li, X., Ma, B., & Vitanyi, P. (2004). The similarity metric. *IEEE Transactions on Information Theory, 50*(12), 3250–3264.

Li, M., & Vitanyi, P. (1997). *An Introduction to Kolmogorov Complexity and Its Applications.* New York: Springer-Verlag., 2nd edition.

Luque, B., & Sole, R. V. (2000). Lyapunov exponents in random Boolean networks. *Physica A, 284*(1-4), 33–45.

Ma, H.-W., & Zeng, A.-P. (2003). Reconstruction of metabolic networks from genome data and analysis of their global structure for various organisms. *Bioinformatics, 19*(2), 270–277.

Matache, M., & Heidel, J. (2004). A random Boolean network model exhibiting deterministic chaos. *Physical Review E, 69,* 056214.

Moreira, A., & Amaral, L. (2005). Canalizing Kauffman networks: Non-ergodicity and its effect on their critical behavior. *Physical Review Letters, 94,* 218702.

Nykter, M., Price, N. D., Aldana, M., Ramsey, S., Kauffman, S. A., Hood, L., et al. (2008). Gene expression dynamics in the macrophage exhibit criticality. *Proceedings of the National Academy of Sciences USA, 105*(6), 1897–1900.

Podani, J., Oltvai, Z. N., Jeong, H., Tombor, B., Barabási, A.-L., & Szathmáry, E. (2001). Comparable system-level organization of archaea and eukaryotes. *Nature Genetics, 29*(1)5, 4–56.

Rämö, P., Kesseli, J., & Yli-Harja, O. (2005). Stability of functions in gene regulatory networks. *Chaos, 15,* 034101.

Rämö, P., Kesseli, J., & Yli-Harja, O. (2006). Perturbation avalanches and criticality in gene regulatory networks. *Journal of Theoretical Biology, 242,* 164–170.

Ribeiro, A. S., Zhu, R., & Kauffman, S. A. (2006). A General Model for Gene Regulatory Networks with Stochastic Dynamics. *Journal of Computational Biology, 13*(9), 1630-1639.

Ribeiro, A. S., Este, R. A., Lloyd-Price, J., & Kauffman, S. A. (2006). Measuring information propagation and retention in Boolean networks and its implications to a model of human organizations. *WSEAS Trans. on Systems, 12*(5), 2935.

Ribeiro, A. S., Kauffman, S. A., Lloyd-Price, J., Samuelsson, B., & Socolar, J. (2008). Mutual information in Random Boolean models of regulatory networks. *Physical Review E, 77*(1), 011901.

Rissanen, J., & Langdon, G.G. (1979). Arithmetic coding. *IBM Journal of Research and Development, 23,* 149–162.

Samuelsson, B., & Socolar, J. (2006). Exhaustive percolation on random networks. *Physical Review E, 74,* 036113.

Serra, R., Villani, M., & Semeria, A. (2004). Genetic networks models and statistical properties of gene extression data in knock-out experiments. *Journal of Theoretical Biology, 227,* 149–157.

Shannon, C.E. (1948). A mathematical theory of communication. *Bell System Technical Journal, 27*:379–423.

Shmulevich, I., & Kauffman, S.A. (2004). Activities and sensitivities in Boolean network models. *Physical Review Letters, 93*(4), 048701(1–4).

Shmulevich, I., Kauffman, S. A., & Aldana, M. (2005). Eukaryotic cells are dynamically ordered or critical but not chaotic. *Proceedings of the National Academy of Sciences of the USA, 102*(38), 13439–13444.

Solomonoff, R. (1964). A formal theory of inductive inference. *Information and Control, 7,* 1–22.

Valverde, S., & Sole, R. V. (2002). Self-organized critical traffic in parallel computer networks. *Physica A, 312,* 636–648.

Ziv, J., & Lempel, A. (1977). A universal algorithm for sequential data compression. *IEEE Transactions on Information Theory, 23*(3), 337–343.

Chapter X
Natural Human–System Interaction Using Intelligent Conversational Agents

Yacine Benahmed
Université de Moncton, Canada

Sid-Ahmed Selouani
Université de Moncton, Canada

Habib Hamam
Université de Moncton, Canada

ABSTRACT

In the context of the prodigious growth of network-based information services, messaging and edutainment, we introduce new tools that enable information management through the use of efficient multimodal interaction using natural language and speech processing. These tools allow the system to respond to close-to natural language queries by means of pattern matching. A new approach which gives the system the ability to learn new utterances of natural language queries from the user is presented. This automatic learning process is initiated when the system encounters an unknown command. This alleviates the burden of users learning a fixed grammar. Furthermore, this enables the system to better respond to spontaneous queries. This work investigates how an information system can benefit from the use of conversational agents to drastically decrease the cognition load of the user. For this purpose, Automated Service Agents and Artificial Intelligence Markup Language (AIML) are used to provide naturalness to the dialogs between users and machines.

INTRODUCTION

Nowadays, most interfaces incorporating speech interaction fall into three broad categories. The first category includes Command and Control (C&C) interfaces that rely on a fixed task dependant grammar to provide user interaction (Paek, 2007). Their main advantage is their ease of implementation and high command recognition rate. However, their downside is the high cognitive load required to learn and use the system because of its lack of flexibility and lack of uniform command sets. The Universal Speech Interface project tries to fix some of the problems tied to C&C and natural language processing. This is done by providing a general task independent vocabulary for interaction (Nichols, 2007). However, the user is still limited in his choice of utterance since the system is strict on form.

The second category is based on interactive voice response (IVR) that guides users by the means of prompts in order to validate the utterance at every step (Shah, 2007). This style of interaction is mostly used in menu navigation such as that found with phone and cable companies. Its relative lack of efficiency for fast interaction makes it a poor choice for every day use.

Finally, the third category uses natural language processing (NLP) to parse the user's utterance and to determine the goal of the request. This can be done through multiple ways such as semantic and language processing and filtering (Sing, 2006). Hence, to be effective, due to "limitless" vocabulary, this type of interface needs an accurate Automatic Speech Recognition (ASR) system. Another disadvantage of this system is the relatively steep development cost. This is mainly due to the complexity of parsing spontaneous utterances that might not follow conventional grammar.

In this chapter we demonstrate that an effective speech interfaces can be created by following a simple architectural plan, and combining Artificial Intelligence Markup Language (AIML) (ALICE, 2005) for language processing as well as a novel automatic learning framework capable of learning new utterance patterns tied to the current context and to the user profile and preferences.

BACKGROUND

Spoken dialogue constitutes the most natural and powerful means to interact with computers. Systems based on natural spoken dialogue start to appear feasible with the recent improvements in computer engineering and in speech and language processing. Speech-based interfaces increasingly penetrate into environments that can benefit from hands-free and/or eyes-free operation. In the context of the growth of network-based information services, messaging and edutainment, or the demand for personalized real-time services, automatic speech recognition and speech synthesis are highly promising. They are considered as sufficiently mature technologies to allow their inclusion as effective modalities in both telephony and multimodal Human-Computer Interaction (HCI) (Deng & Huang, 2004). Some applications of Internet searching and navigating are currently known; Opera version 9 has a basic voice interface (Opera, 2007). However, its recognition engine is pretty basic and cannot be trained; also, its synthesized voice is robotized. Google provides this kind of functionality through Google Voice Search which is still in a demo state. To use it, a user needs to make a phone call. This is not very convenient for users (Google, 2006). Another application is the one developed by Dr. Meirav Taieb-Maimon and colleagues from Ben-Gurion University of the Negev where car drivers can consult the Internet through voice commands (Sommer, 2005). Lyons et al. (2004) introduced a concept of a dual-purpose speech interaction that provides meaningful input to the computer in order to manage calendar and other communication tools for users. In these applications, the limitation of automatic speech recognition engines is outlined as the main obstacle to the efficiency of the interaction.

One of the main concerns for both companies and research teams is the lack of efficient and affordable natural language based Human-Computer Interfaces. While companies such as Nuance (http://www.

nuance.com/) offer highly efficient speech interfaces, the fact is that its user penetration is limited by its relatively high price. On the other hand, Microsoft® Windows Vista™ offers some control over its operating system via speech recognition, it is still highly command based, and thus limits the naturalness of the interaction and increases the cognitive load. In light of this, we believe that natural language based speech interfaces are a preferred solution. The need to learn numerous commands is eliminated reducing the cognitive load of users (Pietquin, 2004). Moreover, problems might arise for users with disabilities. Indeed, a lack of proper modality can severely hamper their ability to use a computer. It is important to provide them with a means to use a computer that is close in cost/performance to conventional alternatives. An example of these systems could be "Let's Go", a dialogue system designed to allow dialogue experiments to be carried out on the elderly and non-native speakers in order to provide Pittsburgh area bus information (Raux et al., 2003).

Rather than considering the interaction as a series of commands, current approaches involves defining and discussing tasks, exploring ways to perform the tasks, and collaborating to get the communication goal achieved. In order to allow the anticipation of the users' need and to provide answers to the users' goals, the interaction is contextually interpreted with respect to the interactions performed so far. The suitability of dialogue-based interfaces is closely related to the complexity of the tasks to perform. Five levels of task complexity and their corresponding type of interaction systems could be defined (Alen et al., 2001). The first level is a simple framework constituting the basis of actual Graphical User Interfaces (GUIs), the finite-state system that follows a script of user prompts. Such systems are in use today for simple applications such as long-distance dialling by voice, and have been proven very efficient (Hirsch, 2006). The second level of complexity deals with most spoken dialogue systems by using a frame-based approach that interprets the speech to acquire enough information to perform a specific action. In this system the context of application is fixed. For instance, this approach has been used for systems providing information for booking rooms through a tourism service (Caelen, 2003). Because of the simplicity of these domains, it is possible to build very robust language processing systems. The third type of system represents the task by a series of contexts; each represented using the frame-based approach. With multiple contexts, such systems must be able to identify when the user switches contexts (Diaper and Sanger, 2006). In the fourth level of complexity, the tasks are too complicated to be represented as a series of parameterized contexts. In fact, these tasks require the system to maintain an explicit model of possible scenarios. Its dialogue scheme is based on the plan-based approach which starts by modeling the collaborative problem that the system and user engage in. It is done by interactively constructing a plan with the user (Nguyen, 2004). The last and fifth level of complexity involves dynamic agent-based models. These systems use planning, but also procedures that execute and monitor operations in dynamically changing interaction contexts (Chaib-Draa, 2006). These latter systems lead us to propose a new paradigm based on intelligent conversational agents capable of learning from their past dialogue experiences.

Nowadays, one of the hottest topics of HCI research targets the realization of a universal interaction framework. Principal configurations are built on mobile computing systems and are designed to interact with numerous services. The main issues of these configurations are discovery of services and adapted devices to reach these services. Besides this, the composition of modalities and interfaces become feasible (Bouchet, 2004). Discovery is performed by numerous service-oriented standards and communication protocols such as Universal Remote Console Standard URC (Laplant, 2004) Universal Plug and Play UPnP (www.upnp.org), Java/Jini network technology (http://www.sun.com/software/jini/). Modern device selection is fully automated and it is based on context clues and user history. Obviously, wireless technologies such as WiFi, Bluetooth, and Zigbee (IEEE, 2008), play a crucial role in the realization of the universal interaction framework. The ultimate goal is to acquire the ability to control multiple services, with as little *a priori* information as possible about these services and devices. However, current interaction frameworks still offer non-intuitive control schemes and therefore are hard to use. They still require a minimum of skills in computer science to reach fully effective and optimal use.

In order to answer these shortcomings, we designed a system that fully supports the use of ASR and Text-To-Speech (TTS) modules to search and navigate the web: the IVSN (Internet Voice Searching and Navigating) system (Benahmed & Selouani 2006). After extensive testing, we found that the vocal interaction was too strict as it was limited to specific commands. We wanted the system to be able to better respond to natural queries. This would then alleviate the burden of users learning a fixed grammar. Furthermore, this would enable the system to better respond to spontaneous queries.

To reach the flexibility and adaptability of information retrieval and management, we developed a series of evolutionary and user-customizable tools based on natural language multimodal interaction. The evaluation of these systems in real life applications such as e-learning, communications and healthcare, confirm both their suitability and effectiveness. In this chapter, we propose to include ASR and TTS technologies into innovative tools and solutions in order to give users the ability to search and retrieve information using verbal interaction.

PROPOSED ARCHITECTURE

To achieve the goal of providing a natural language interaction based human-computer interface, a general architecture must first be determined. The architecture used in our solutions consists of three independent layers that sit at the core of the system. This provides ample flexibility since modifications to one layer does not affect the other layers. The three layers consist of: automatic speech recognition engine, semantic/pragmatic (utterance) analyser, and command interpreter. Figure 1 depicts this architecture.

The speech recognition engine is the first layer in the user interaction pipe. It receives the user's natural and spontaneous spoken utterances and transforms them into a textual form. Since automatic speech recognition engines are particularly efficient nowadays, it is easy to find a suitable low cost/free engine to use in our system since only the textual output is needed for the rest of the process.

The utterance analyzer represents the brain of the user interaction layer. It receives the recognised text from the automatic speech recognition engine and analyzes it to get an understanding of what the user is trying to accomplish. This is where we think that most of the research effort must be undertaken. Multiple possibilities exist to improve efficacy and flexibility of speech-enabled interfaces by performing processing at this level. It can be as simple as pattern matching, or as complex as a fully knowledge driven artificial intelligence. The main goal of this layer should be to generalise the user request as much as possible. Once the text is parsed, it should send command IDs with parameters to the command interpreter.

The final step in the interaction pipe can be visualised as a case-based process. It receives the command ID and parameters from the utterance analyzer or mouse and keyboard and calls the appropriate system functions. The solutions presented in this chapter are based on this architecture.

Figure 1. Three layer multimodal interaction architecture

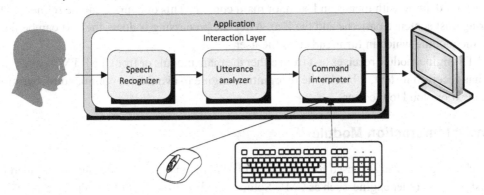

CONVERSATIONAL INFORMATION RETRIEVAL AND MANAGEMENT SYSTEM

A system integrating automatic speech recognition, natural language processing, as well as speech synthesis is designed to allow users to search and navigate both the web and the user's computer freely by vocal interaction. This system includes multiple innovative features. It is able to learn new command patterns from users. Through the use of a feedback system based on an answer/action interface, the system learns the new command and creates an appropriate (and new) XML grammar entry using a finite state graph. It provides a means for users to expand the vocabulary of the recognition engine as well as to have the engine train itself automatically. The system accomplishes its self-training by using a high quality synthetic voice which preferably supports pitch variation (Benahmed and Selouani 2006). The system proceeds with the parsing of the local documents and/or URLs and stores the relevant utterances. With this process, the interactive system can be tailored to the specific activities, the profile and the bookmarks of users.

Another feature of the system is its ability to read out loud the text of web pages by using a Text-to-Speech voice. This can prove quite useful to blind or hard of sight users. It saves them from having to buy or travel with a text-to-brail peripheral or having to use a software magnifier. Moreover, it can be practical for users wishing to have the software read them a web page while doing something else.

As was stated previously, the interaction layer sits at the core of natural speech interaction. Furthermore, since the system consists of a browser, additional modules are needed to achieve the desired functionality. The main module processes the events and messages coming from the interaction layer, browser and TTS engine modules. It sends out text to the TTS engine to notify the user that he/she initiated a certain action. It also tells the browser engine to go to a certain page, or that it has to pass its HTML code to the parser. It can change the grammar according to the users need. Figure 2 shows the general architecture of the application. Furthermore, as can be seen by figure 3, the interface we created is as simple as possible in order to avoid user confusion.

The browser engine module is responsible for fetching and displaying web pages or computer content and folders. It also tells the main module when it is ready to have its text parsed. The HTML parser module is responsible for extracting relevant text from the HTML pages found in the browser engine module. For this task, we came up with a simple yet effective algorithm.

Each container element of the current page is processed, and a word count is made in order to determine if we are dealing with menus and such, or main content. This of course, can be refined and made to check against sentence patterns and the like. After the processing is done, the text can be fed to the TTS engine module which in turn reads it to the user.

The TTS engine module receives text from either the main module or from the HTML parser module. Once it has received its text, it blocks the recognition engine to avoid false command recognition, and reads the text out loud to the user.

Multimodal Interaction Module

The speech recognition engine used for this system is Microsoft®'s free ASR engine included it Windows Vista™. Any other engine, such as CMU Sphinx (Sphinx Project, 2008) could have as easily been used. However we chose it for its ease of implementation, reliable performance, and guarantee that it would come in every computer equipped with Microsoft® Window Vista™.

In the utterance analyzer layer, we considered the use of regular expressions, a regular language, and BNF\EBNF context-free grammars (Aho et al., 2006). We have also investigated some possibilities such as the Automated Service Agent (Colloquis, 2006). However, those systems are commercial and their inclusion in the final product will drastically increase the final cost. On the contrary, our solution aims at providing a system that requires minimal purchase on the part of the end-user by using the open source Artificial Intelligence Markup Language (AIML). This framework is used to design "intelligent" chat bots (ALICE, 2005). It is an XML compliant language. It was designed to create chat bots rapidly and efficiently. Its primary design feature is minimalism. It is essentially a pattern matching system which maps well with Case-Base Reasoning. In AIML botmasters effectively create categories which consist of a pattern, the user input, a template, and the Bots' answer. The AIML parser then tries to

Figure 2. General architecture of the information retrieval system

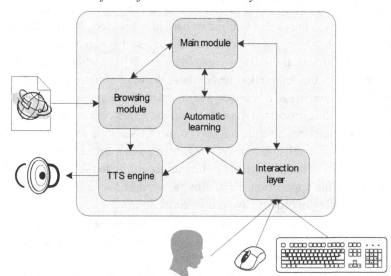

Figure 3. Natural language and speech enabled information retrieval and management system interface

match what the user said to the most likely pattern and outputs the corresponding answer. Additionally, patterns can include wildcards which are especially useful for our application. Moreover, the language supports recursion which enables it to answer based on previous input.

Since the system was programmed in C#, we decided to implement AIML in our system through the use of the open source Program# (Tollervey 2006). In order to cover the broadest set of interaction possibilities, 66 categories relating to searching and navigating were created (see Figure 4). As a rule, the system will always try to match the user input with the AIML grammar before passing it to the fixed Speech Application Programming Interface (SAPI) grammar. Besides this four different XML grammars are built. The first one is used while the application is in search mode; it has basic navigation features and specialized searching features. The second one is used for dictation; it is initiated when the user wants to input keywords. The third one is for spelling; it is used when the dictation mode does not yield good results for searching. It is also used to spell out URLs in the case of navigation mode. The fourth XML grammar is devoted to the full navigation mode; it has a rich vocabulary for navigating the Internet as well as the computer content. The recognized commands are then fed to the main module which accomplishes the corresponding task.

Automatic Learning Agent

To enable the system to learn new searching or navigating commands from the user, an automatic learning framework has been developed. If a user said something that the system does not understand, it would ask the user if he wanted to add that as a new command. Through a feed-back system, which falls in the answer/action interface, the system would learn the new command and create the appropriate AIML entry for it.

Figure 4. Sample AIML patterns

```
<category>
        <pattern>PLEASE SEARCH FOR * </pattern>
        <template>
                SEARCHING FOR <star/>
        </template>
</category>
<!--SEARCH-->
<category>
        <pattern>* SEARCH FOR *</pattern>
        <template>
                        <srai>
                        PLEASE SEARCH FOR <star index="2"/>

                </srai>
        </template>
</category>
```

The basis of the learning system can be represented by a finite state graph as illustrated by Figure 5. State S is the starting state; it is when a user says a command that is not recognized by the system. It then goes to state A. The system repeats what the user said and asks if it got it right. If yes it goes to state B and asks the user to speak the command part of what he said. Then it goes to state C. It asks to confirm (yes or no) if it understood the command. If yes, it goes to the final state Add which adds two entries in the AIML file with appropriate wildcards and template (dependant upon the previous context (searching or navigating)). If the user answers no in state C, it goes back to state B and proceeds until it understood the command part correctly.

There is also another possible branching in state A. If the user answers no to the question, it goes to state E. The system will then ask the user if it was a command. If yes; it goes to State B, if no; it goes to final state Quit.

To illustrate the novelty of the proposed dialog system, the following example shows the automatic learning module in action after an unseen utterance pronounced by the user:

User: Could you look for chicken recipes
System: Did you say "Could you look for chicken recipes"?
User: Yes I did
System: Was it a command for me?
User: Yes
System: Could you please dictate the command part of: "Could you look for chicken recipes"
User: Could you book for
System: Did you say: "Could you book for"?
User: No
User: Could you look for
System: Did you say: "Could you look for"?
User: Yes

Figure 6 shows the creating patterns depending on the previous context and that will be automatically included in the grammar set. Hence, the system learns from its experiments and errors. This behavior mimics the human learning and memorization processes.

Automatic User Profile Building and Training System

Users of the conversational information retrieval system might want to do some research on terms that might not be covered by the recognition engine's vocabulary. To reach this goal, we integrated the Automatic User Profile Building and Training (AUPB&T) system that provides an efficient means for users to expand the vocabulary of their recognition engine as well as to launch automatic training. The system accomplishes its self-training by using a high quality TTS voice which preferably supports pitch variation. The way the system works is as follows: the user specifies the documents and/or URLs that he would like the system to use. Then, the system proceeds with the parsing of the documents and the URLs and stores the text locally. It then adds the words found to its dictionary. Finally, it launches an automatic training session using the documents specified by the user. With this process, the system obtained up to a 6% recognition performance improvement over a baseline system (Benahmed and Selouani 2006).

More Natural Spoken Dialog in Information Retrieval System

In order to evaluate if the interactivity improvement after the implementation of AIML-based framework, we proceeded with informal dialog testing. First, we compare the original search dialog against

Figure 5. Automatic learning finite state graph

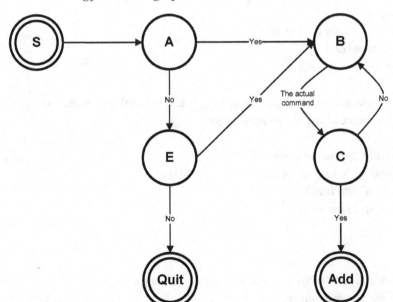

Figure 6. Example of created pattern after the automatic learning process

```
<category>
        <pattern>* could you look for *</pattern>
        <template>
                <srai>PLEASE SEARCH FOR <star
index="2"/> </srai>
        </template>
</category>

<category>
        <pattern> could you look for *</pattern>
        <template>
                <srai>PLEASE SEARCH FOR <star/></srai>
        </template>
</category>
```

the dialog made possible by the implementation of AIML. Second, we compare the original navigation dialog compared against the new navigation dialog. We start with the original searching dialog which unfolds like this:

User: Search for
System: Please dictate your keywords
User: Banana split recipes
System: Banana split recipes
User: Stop
System: Your keywords are banana split recipes
User: Begin searching
System: Searching for banana split recipes
User: Display result number 5
System: displaying result number 5

With the implementation of AIML, the searching dialog can take multiple forms and is primarily limited by the performance of the recognition engine:

User: Could you search for banana split recipes?
System: Searching for banana split recipes
User: I'd like to see the fifth result
System: displaying result number 5

Or:

User: Search for banana split recipes and display the top 20 results
System: Searching for banana split recipes

User: I'd like to see result number 15
System: displaying result number 15

As we can see from those results, the previous system only allowed user interaction in a strictly controlled and sequential manner. However, the new system allows the user to speak more freely and naturally to the system, as instead of speaking five commands, the same result can be accomplished in only two commands.

Now, we evaluate the navigation dialog. On the old system, to navigate to a website a user would have to follow this syntax:

User: Navigate
User: www . u m c s .ca
User: go

With the implementation of AIML the navigation dialog can take multiple forms:

User: I'd like to see the page at w w w . u m c s . c a

Or:

User: go to the page at w w w . u m c s . c a

With the implementation of AIML, we can accomplish the same task with only one command compared to three on the previous system. As we can see from those dialogs, the implementation of AIML served our purpose well. We are able to communicate in a more natural approach. This results in an improved user experience and diminished cognition load. Indeed, the user is not required to learn any specific set of commands. The system is able to both interpret a large array of utterances and adapt to new ones by taking the current context into account.

SOLUTIONS USING ENHANCED MULTIMODAL INTERACTION

Virtual Presentation Assistant

The virtual presentation assistant allows users to create speech-enabled presentations. The user creates his electronic presentation as usual but inserts speech related cues which will be masked from during the presentation. The application then parses those cues during runtime and speaks the content using a high quality text-to-speech voice. The system allows for fully automatic presentation of the content. It also allows for a mixed mode, where the user can control the flow of the presentation using simple voice commands. The full automated presentation involves a virtual conversational agent that can "improvise" like human do when presenting examples, animations or citations or when skipping from one slide to another.

One interesting use is for helping deaf, hard of hearing or people having difficulty speaking the presentation target language. Indeed, it would be both useful for the author of the presentation as well as for the target audience. On one hand, an author can easily produce a written presentation in the target language. Stress would be reduced as the author would not have to worry about mispronunciation and other challenges of the spoken language. Additionally, the target audience would benefit from this. The cognitive load of understanding someone with a strong accent or having difficulty speaking the language would be greatly reduced.

Assistance to Physically Challenged Users

This application successfully maps the functionality of a mouse to voice commands. It has been successfully integrated in a double modality computer interface for learners with reduced mobility. In addition to the conversational agent, the system is able to interpret the user's hand or head gestures. This design allows using simple head movements to perform basic computer mouse operations, such as moving the mouse cursor on a computer screen. Two different infrared sensor layouts are designed to detect and process a user's head or hand movements.

Besides this, the global platform incorporates a complementary system that deals with pathological speech. It aims at improving automatic speech recognition rate and intelligibility of dysarthric speakers. Dysarthria is a disease affecting millions of people over the world. A dysarthric speaker communicates with many difficulties characterized by a poor articulation, bad pronounced phonemes, very slow rate, variable intensity, etc. Hence, this speech is less intelligible than that of non-dysarthric speaker. Figure 7 shows the system we designed to improve verbal interaction through the automatic recognition and synthesis of dysarthric speech. This system is speaker dependant. At recognition level (ASR), the system uses variable Hamming window size for each speaker. We have carried out an intensive set of experiments in order to find the optimal window size giving the best recognition rate (Sidi-Yacoub, 2008). At synthesis level (TTS) the system introduces a new technique to define variable units, a new concatenating algorithm and a new grafting technique to correct the speaker voice and make it more intelligible. The ASR system is build using HTK tools (Speech Group, 2006). Each phoneme is represented by a 5-state Hidden Markov Model with two non-emitting states (1st and 5th state).

Multimodal E-Learning Platform

Web-based learning is rapidly becoming the preferred way to quickly, effectively, and economically create and deliver training or educational content. We have designed systems that use speech technology, to emulate the one-on-one interaction a student can get from a virtual instructor. A web-based learning tool, the Learn IN Context (LINC+) system, designed and used in a real mixed-mode learning context for a computer (C++ language) programming course taught at the Université de Moncton (Canada) is developed (Selouani, 2008). It integrates an Internet Voice Searching and Navigating system that helps learners to search and navigate both the web and their desktop environment through voice commands and dictation. It also incorporates the AUPB&T module which allows users to increase automatic speech recognition performance without having to go through the long and fastidious manual training process. With the addition of a synthesized voice and a facility for speech recognition to the LINC environment, the learner can listen to a voice reading the Web page content as well as by navigating within this learning environment by using his/her own voice instead of using a mouse. After accessing LINC+'s Home page, a simple click allows the user to see a list of courses; another click allows them to choose a course. After this click a login window will be displayed asking the user for a username and a password. The system can recognize two types of users: a professor and a student. Different vocal commands are available depending on the type of user. Users have access to the complete functionalities of the vocal interface, after logging in and choosing a lesson. Figure 8 is labelled with sections from A to F. By clicking on one of the speaker icons, the text displayed in the corresponding section will be read by the TTS agent. Section A contains the Links list (lesson's topics); Section B, the page's header; Section C, the Situation; Section D, the Actions; Section E, the Comments (not indicated); and Section F contains all sections from C to F.

Some words, as the «Introduction» in the Actions section, are light blue, but are hotspots. If the user passes the cursor over this word, a tool tip will appear with a supplementary content in a yellow window (for a concept explanation or the definition of a term). Clicking on the word will cause the content to be read. It is also possible to interact with the site by launching a vocal command. To enable this facility of speech recognition, the user must first click on the microphone icon (on the right in the first yellow field). There are several commands that can be used to navigate within the site. Some of them are only available for the teacher, and some others are only available for the students.

Figure 7. The overall system designed to help dysarthric speakers

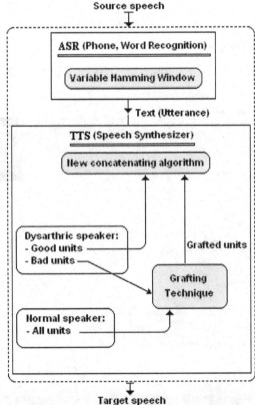

FUTURE TRENDS

The growth of popular computing observed in the last decades is closely related to the development of effective and simple HCI that made computers easy to use by ordinary people. The first mass-produced WIMP (windows, icons, mouse, pointer)-based machine is unanimously recognized as the beginning of the information era. The "democratization" of the so-called popular computing was possible thanks to the WIMP-based interfaces. The HCI continues to play a leading role in the information and communication technology market since a product's success depends on each user's experience with it. Nowadays, most software is interactive. The code related to the interface is more than half of all code of a given application. This confirms that the need to evolve towards a more implicit and proactive interaction with humans is clearly emerged and is unanimously agreed upon. Both applications and services provided through HCI will be based on the analysis of context and knowledge. The user-centered interfaces of the near future will have to cope with highly dynamic environments and changing resources.

The key issue of which modality or combination of modalities to use, as well as the problem of the cognition load, is the focus of many actual research efforts in the field of Human-System interaction (Jorgensen, 2008). In fact, it is important to achieve an effective balance between the three basic elements of interaction, namely modalities, technologies and services. Interaction technologies can drastically enhance the user's ability to access and manage information, but it is vital to match the right tools with both the user and the tasks to be undertaken. New generation of interfaces will gradually replace the current command-based scheme in order to have the computer observing the user and adapting the dialogue to the user's needs based on its inference from analyzing the user's utterances. Then, it

Figure 8. The multimodal e-learning system

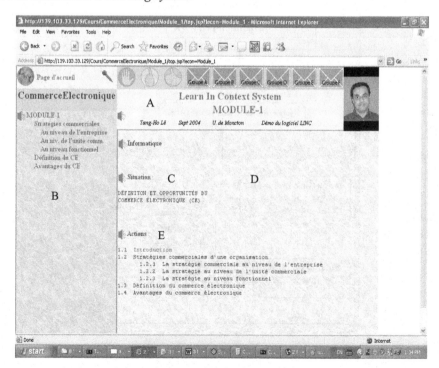

would be interesting to further refine the utterance analyzer presented in this chapter by combining approach using semantics, pragmatics, as well as a knowledge base. A system could be built around such architecture to provide ever more complex functionalities. Several trends indicate that the concept of command-based dialogue existing in current interfaces is outdated. Instead, the information object with semantic structure will be the fundamental unit of information in future computer systems. User-centered interfaces will be based on more flexible information objects that can be easily accessed by their content through the use of intelligent conversational agents. These latter will be the key features of future pervasive computing. Our belief is that these agents will ease the control of the physical world via many speech-enabled sensors and actuators. The next generation of ubiquitous interfaces has to consider situations where devices cooperate and adapt spontaneously and autonomously. Therefore, many technical problems need to be faced in order to cope with pervasive information. Some criticisms say that there has been little progress in interface development since the Mac WIMP, but we believe that a silent evolution (revolution) tends to gain a dazzling speed in order to allow intuitive and natural interaction with machines for widely differing applications. To confirm this trend, we can cite the emergence of new paradigm such as Tangible User Interaction (TUI) that allows exploiting the capabilities of physical objects as rich input devices. Infinite possibilities will then be provided to the users who can use the movements of objects for control and interaction.

CONCLUSION

Motivated by the expressive power of speech as a natural means of intuitive interaction, we have presented, in this chapter, a series of tools and technologies that provide an augmented interaction modality by incorporating speech and natural language processing. Users who do not have the ability or the patience to deal with the manual training process should find these new tools especially attractive, since they do not require sophisticated technical skills or a significant amount of time to learn how to use them effectively. However, incorporating such technologies into real-life environments yields many technological challenges. The systems must be sufficiently robust and flexible in order to cope with environment changes. In some situations, users are faced with the task of reviewing their overall interaction strategy in light of the opportunities provided by these new modalities. Thus, from our viewpoint, universal and robust speech-enabled intelligent agents must be able to provide natural and intuitive means of communication for a wide range of applications and devices. Moreover, the mapping between modalities and services should be dynamic. We are currently working on configurations where the mapping is context sensitive. The service that is associated to a given modality can be determined ad-hoc according to the user's context, rather than being specified by the user or previously fixed.

REFERENCES

Aho, A. V., Sethi, R., & Ullman, J. D. (2006). *Compilers: Principles, Techniques, and Tools*. New York. Addison Wesley, 2nd edition.

Allen, J. F., Byron, D. K., *Dzikovska*, M., Ferguson G., *Galescu, L.,* & Stent, A. (2001). Toward conversational human-computer interaction. *AI Magazine*, (22) 4, (pp. 27-37).

ALICE. (2005). Artificial Intelligence Markup Language (AIML) Version 1.0.1, *AI Foundation*. Retrieved August 23, 2008, from http://alicebot.org/TR/2005/WD-aiml.

Benahmed, Y., & Selouani, S. A. (2006). Robust Self-Training System for Spoken Query Information retrieval using Pitch Range Variations. *Proceedings of IEEE Canadian Conference on Electrical and Computer Engineering* (pp. 949-952). Ottawa, Canada.

Laplant, B., Trewin, S., Zimmermann, G., & Vanderheiden, G. (2004). The Universal Remote Console: a universal access bus for pervasive computing. *Pervasive Computing, IEEE, 3*(1), 76–80.

Bouchet, J., & Nigay, L. (2004). ICARE: A Component-Based Approach for the Design and Development of Multimodal Interfaces. *Extended Abstracts of International conference for human-computer interaction* (pp. 1325-1328). CHI2004: Vienna, Austria.

Caelen, J. (2003). Strategies of Dialogue. *Speech Technology and Human-Computer Dialogue Conference, Editura Academiei Romane* (pp. 27-42). Bucharest, Romania.

COLLOQUIS INC. (2006). Comparing Automated Service Agent (ASA) Systems to Browse-and Search Search-Based Self-Service Solutions, Maximize Self-Service ROI through Savings and Sales. Retrieved August 23, 2008, from http://download.microsoft.com/download/5/8/c/58c709a8-921f-4ae4-ac48-05020a9186c0/ASAvsSearch.pdf

Deng, L., & Huang, X. (2004). Challenges in adopting speech recognition. *Communications of the ACM, 47*(1), 69-75.

GOOGLE Inc. (2006). Google Voice Search. *US patent No 7027987*, Mountain View, CA. available at http://patft.uspto.gov/

Hirsch, H.-G., Dobler, S., Kiessling, A., & Schleifer, R. (2006). Speech recognition by a portable terminal for voice dialing. *European Patent* EP1617635.

IEEE. 2008. Overview on IEEE wireless standards. Retrieved October 8, 2008, from http://standards.ieee.org/wireless/overview.html

Jørgensen, A. H., & Myers, B. A. (2008). User interface history. *In Proceedings of ACM CHI 2008 Conference on Human Factors in Computing Systems* (pp. 2415-2418). Florence, Italy.

Lyons, K., Skeels, C., Starner T., Snoeck, C. M., Wong, B. A., & Ashbrook, D. (2004). Augmenting conversations using dual-purpose speech. *Proceedings of the 17th annual ACM symposium on User Interface Software and Technology* (pp. 237-246). Santa Fe, USA.

Myers, B. A. (2005). Using handhelds for wireless remote control of PCs and appliances. *Interacting with Computers, 17*(3), 251–264.

Diaper, D., & Sanger, C. (2006). Tasks for and tasks in human-computer interaction. *Interacting with Computers, 18*(1), 117–138.

Raux, A., Langner, B., Black, A., & Eskenazi, M. (2003). *LET'S GO: Improving Spoken Dialog Systems for the Elderly and Non-natives, Eurospeech 2003* (pp. 753-756). Geneva, Switzerland.

Chaib-draa, B., Naudet, N., Labrie, M.-A., Bergeron, M., & Pasquier, P. (2006). *DIAGAL: An Agent Communication Language Based on Dialogue Games and Sustained by Social Commitments. Journal of Autonomous Agents and Multi-Agent Systems, 13*(1), 61-93.

Piolle, G., Demazeau, Y., & Caelen, J. (2006). Privacy Management in User-Centred Multi-agent Systems. *In Engineering Societies in the Agent World (ESAW 2006)*, (pp. 354-367). Dublin, Ireland.

Nguyen, H., & Caelen, J. (2004). Multi-session Management in Spoken Dialogue System. *Advances in Artificial Intelligence*, IBERAMIA 2004, Springer editors. (pp. 266-274).

Nichols, J., Chau, D. H., & Myers, B. A. (2007). Demonstrating the viability of automatically generated user interfaces. *Proceedings of the SIGCHI conference on Human factors in computing systems* (pp. 1283-1292).

OPERA Software ASA. (2006). Opera Browser. Retrieved August 23, 2008, from http://www.opera.com/voice.

Paek, T., & Chickering, D. (2007). Improving command and control speech recognition: Using predictive user models for language modeling. *User Modeling and User-Adapted Interaction Journal*, *17*(1), 93-117.

Pietquin, O. (2004). *A Framework for Unsupervised Learning of Dialogue Strategies*. Doctoral dissertation, Presses Universitaires de Louvain, SIMILAR Collection, ISBN 2-930344-63-6.

Selouani, S. A., Tang-Hô, L., Benahmed, Y., & O'Shaughnessy, D. (2008). Speech-enabled tools for augmented Interaction in e-learning applications. *Special issue of International Journal of Distance Education Technologies, 6*(2), 1-20. IGI publishing.

Shah, S. A. A, Ul Asar, A., & Shah, S. W. (2007). Interactive Voice Response with Pattern Recognition Based on Artificial Neural Network Approach. *International conference on Emerging Technologies*, (pp. 249-252). IEEE.

Sidi-Yacoub, M., Selouani, S. A., O'Shaughnessy, D. (2008). Improving Dysarthric Speech Intelligibility through Re-synthesized and Grafted Units. *21ˢᵗ IEEE-Canadian Conference on Electrical and Computer Engineering* (pp. 1523-1526).

Sing, G. O., Wong, K. W., Fung, C. C., & Depickere, A. (2006). Towards a more natural and intelligent interface with embodied conversation agent. *Proceedings of international conference on Game research and development* (pp. 177-183), Perth, Australia.

Sommer A. K. (2005). Israeli research introduces the 'Maestro' - voice-only Internet system for drivers. Retrieved August 23, 2008 from: http://www.israel21c.org/bin/en.jsp?enZone=Technology&enDisplay=view&enPage=BlankPage&enDispWhat=object&enDispWho=Articles%5El1000http://www.israel21c.org

Speech Group. (2006). The HTK Book (Version 3.4), Cambridge University. Retrieved August 23, 2008, from http://htk.eng.cam.ac.uk/docs/docs.shtml.

Sphinx Project. (2008). *The CMU Sphinx Group Open Source Speech Recognition Engines*. Retrieved August 23, 2008 from (http://cmusphinx.sourceforge.net/).

Tollervey, N. H. (2006). Program# - An AIML Chatterbot in C#. Retrieved August 23, 2008 from http://ntoll.org/article/project-an-aiml-chatterbot-in-c. Northamptonshire, United Kingdom.

Chapter XI
Tools for Automatic Audio Management

Marko Helén
Tampere University of Technology, Finland

Tommi Lahti
Nokia Research Center, Finland

Anssi Klapuri
Tampere University of Technology, Finland

ABSTRACT

The purpose of this chapter is to introduce tools for automatic audio management. The authors present applications which are already available for the users and describe the algorithms and methods behind these applications and their performance. They also discuss the concept of metadata, which is an important prerequisite for modern distributed personal content applications. The variety of automatic audio management tools is wide-ranging. This chapter covers audio segmentation and classification, query by example of audio, music retrieval and recommendation, and speech management, which they consider as being the most important aspects of audio information management. Computational complexity is one major concern in the present era of personal mobile devices and large multimedia collections available on the internet. Therefore they also introduce clustering and indexing techniques which are developed for faster access in large databases.

INTRODUCTION

The huge amount of digital multimedia available nowadays has created a growing need for automatic tools to manage all this data. People have their own personal image, video, and audio databases collected for example by mobile phones or digital cameras that are always close at hand. Above all these, there is the internet with an enormous amount of information accessible almost free of charge. Managing all this becomes impossible without the proper tools.

The most typical operations with personal databases are organizing the samples or searching a certain kind of sample from the database. Samples can be organized based on several criteria. In the simplest case, they can be arranged in an alphabetical filename order or in a chronological order using the time stamps of the files. A more challenging way to organize the samples is to do it based on their actual content. For example, it is possible to organize speech samples by the speaker or music by the genre or artist. This is called content based classification (Liu, 2007; Lu, 2002) or clustering (Cai, 2008), and will be covered later in this chapter.

Finding similar samples from a database, referred to as query by example, is an operation where the user wants to find samples that resemble a particular query sample. Again, there are different criteria for similarity, and even in the case of content based similarity, one has to define in which sense similarity is measured. One example is *query by humming* (Lu & Zhang, 2001; Song et al., 2002), which retrieves melodically similar samples to an input humming. Another is *query by beat boxing* (Kapur, 2004), which retrieves rhythmically similar samples to the example.

A common denominator in all automatic content analysis techniques is the need for an accurate similarity measure. A number of different similarity measures have been used in the literature (Kashino et al., 2003; Zhou & Hansen, 2000). The choice between them is made based on the task and the requirements like speed, accuracy, or whether temporal changes should be taken into account. Recently, the distance between probability density functions (pdfs) estimated from frame-wise feature vectors is often used as a similarity measure (Helén & Virtanen, 2007; Hershey & Olsen, 2007). Several pdf-based distance measures will be introduced in this chapter.

An important factor in multimedia information management is the concept of metadata. The term refers to structured data that characterizes the information-containing entities. Metadata may include for example spectral features extracted from an audio signal but also the relations that different samples have with each other like the above-mentioned similarity of samples. Metadata is the base on which the multimedia management applications are built.

In this chapter, we first discuss the challenges in handling metadata and how the metadata is extracted from audio samples. Then, we introduce applications which utilize the metadata to perform certain audio management tasks, and finally discuss the future trends in this field.

BACKGROUND

Trend Towards Distributed Personal Content Applications

Content of the data is what makes it valuable for its owner. Therefore, helping the users to find, organize, and share the data by its content is naturally central for the application design. Traditionally, and looking just a couple of years back, the systems utilizing automatic audio content analysis techniques have been more or less stand-alone applications targeted for professional use. Transcribing broadcast television and radio news, for example, has been studied extensively already over a decade (Cook et al., 1997; Gauvain et al., 2002). Companies have also used various speech recognition applications in their automatic feedback systems.

Along with the various personal portable devices, the data has become more mobile and personal in nature. Therefore research on personalized content management in smart phones has become more popular (Aaltonen, 2007). Many mobile phone manufacturers, for example, have introduced voice dialing features into their products. The amount of contextually rich data like images, audio, and video has grown rapidly. The data is distributed to other devices and shared with other people who use their own devices and applications to see and hear it. All this sets high requirements for the compatibility between applications.

A key concept in handling content rich data items is the metadata, informally defined as "data about data". Metadata is seen as the most promising way to facilitate smart interaction between seemingly independent applications (Aaltonen, 2007; Lehikoinen et al., 2007).

Figure 1 shows a block diagram of a distributed personal content application. In distributed systems data is usually recorded on a personal device and then transferred to an external server that is better able to handle the data sharing duties. The data can also be analyzed on the server. This is advantageous in many ways, since it removes the burden from the often computationally challenged personal devices and it is also easier to plug in new analysis tools or update them on the server side. Older data which may have been erased from the personal device can still be revisited and the existing analysis results can be complemented with new ones.

In automatic content analysis, the feature extraction phase is usually performed first and this is followed by further processing by various content analysis algorithms. Storing the features as metadata removes the need for recalculating them if new tools are later plugged in to the system. Since totally different devices and applications utilize the data, the structure and the semantics of the stored analysis results have to be well specified. This is currently a challenge as the situation with the multimedia metadata standards is immature. However, the increased number of various distributed personal content applications gives hope that a better consensus will be achieved in this matter.

Figure 1. Block diagram of the distributed personal content application

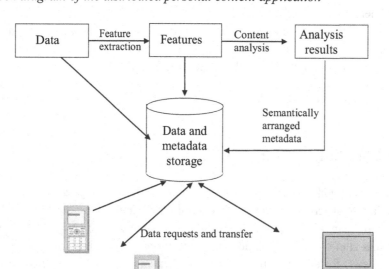

Most of the existing metadata formats have been designed for professional and public use. In distributed personal content applications there are many things that need to be handled as private information. Distributed systems often collect metadata associated with the user, such as usage counts or user locations when they download material from the server. These are clearly private information by default. In ID3v2 format, for example, the metadata is stored in a header before the actual binary data. This has the advantage but also the disadvantage that the metadata always moves along with the data. Metadata handling in distributed application frameworks requires much more than just relying on some particular metadata formats. The World Wide Web Consortium (W3C), for example, is actively developing interoperable technologies for this purpose (www.w3.org).

Users can request data from the server in different ways. If they know exactly what they are looking for, they can request it directly from the server. In this case, metadata does not necessarily need to be involved in any way. However, the metadata can also be downloaded to the user's device along with the actual data and used for various tasks. For audio/video data, for example, there may exist similarity metadata relating the file with other interesting audio/video files and this can be used for recommendation applications (see e.g. www.last.fm). Segmentation information can be useful in finding key frames in video or enable fast editing actions on the data (www.muvee.com). In general, the data can be retrieved based on content criteria, if the user is not able to specify any particular data item directly. Various categorizations and ontologies are often used to help users to find the kind of data they are interested in.

Many popular file formats have been available for storing and transferring the metadata along with the actual data. Some of them are rather general and extensible and not necessarily too tightly associated with any particular data type. On the other hand, e.g. for music audio the situation with metadata tagging has already reached a rather mature level. The ID3v2 metadata format (www.id3.org), for example, has practically become an industrial standard in music business. It is used for augmenting music files with information concerning the song title, author, lyrics, tempo, genre, etc. The semantics of the used metadata tags are also widely agreed upon in the industry and as long as the automatic content analysis methods follow the same conventions there are no big obstacles to make use of it.

Metadata Types for Multimedia

In many cases the purpose of automatically created metadata is to provide support for smart application development. A brief summary of different metadata types relevant for this purpose is provided below, using a music recommendation system as an example application. It should be noted that the above discussion on distributed personal content applications is also applicable here although the scale and the viewpoint is now different.

- **Content metadata.** Content metadata is deduced from the original data and no information outside that is required. Signal analysis methods, for example, can be used for analyzing tempo, loudness, and other musical features from musical content.
- **Context metadata.** Context metadata is information that describes other information related to the data item but which cannot be deduced from the data itself. The location of the user who is listening the music, for example, is context information that describes how and when the music is consumed. It is valuable metadata which can be used for example to steer the recommendations during the day.

- **Relationship metadata.** Relationship metadata describes how the original data item is related to other data items. For example, similarity estimation between song files establishes relationship metadata. Relationships can also be defined across media types.
- **Usage history metadata.** Usage history metadata describes how and when the content is used. In its simplest form, it may accumulate statistics on how often a song is played, for example. Generally, usage history metadata describes how the data is used and thus also tells how important the content is to its users.
- **Community metadata.** The term community metadata refers to a special kind of metadata which establishes relationships between users. Different community relationships may apply in different situations. For example, recommendations during the day may vary based on the people the user is connected with. During the working hours the user may get recommendations from his colleagues but on his spare time he is more connected with friends.

Our focus in the following will be on the content and relationship metadata. The challenges with automatic content analysis tools and with proper handling of produced metadata can be rather wide-ranging as discussed above. There are many important issues that we have not covered here. For those interested, Lehikoinen et.al (2007) presents a more thorough discussion on the subject.

Hardware Limitations

A lot of recordings nowadays are made with portable devices like mobile phones. This sets limitations on the quality of the samples and therefore the algorithms need to be robust for degraded audio quality. Here are some of the challenges that personal audio recordings may introduce:

1. Audio enhancements are typically run on the incoming signal. These enhancements are designed to counter the effects of hardware limitations and adjust the sound so that the quality of speech is maximized in terms of intelligibility and pleasantness. Dynamic compression and discontinuous transmission algorithms tend to suppress the properties of audio signals which could have been used to discriminate signal classes from each other. All these operations are made to favor speech samples at the expense of other audio information.
2. The acoustic components of portable devices are usually not designed to capture high-quality audio. As a consequence, the frequency response is typically strongly distorted and the dynamic range is reduced. The directional microphones of a mobile phone are also optimized to capture speech when the device is held at the talking position.
3. With mobile devices, the recordings are often made on the spur of the moment, which results in poor recording conditions. There is typically wind noise or other sounds in the background and the volume levels are inconsistent, which results in poor signal-to-noise ratio and distortion.

AUDIO MANAGEMENT TOOLS

Various retrieval and classification applications can readily benefit from automatic metadata creation, but there is also a possibility for more innovative applications which utilize the analyzed data from various sources. It should be noted that most of the actual work is usually done at the metadata extraction stage and that the audio management applications show only the tip of the iceberg. In this section we cover several tools which are used in automatic audio management.

Extraction of Audio Features

The first operation that has to be done for an audio sample before any kind of content processing is possible is the extraction of low-level acoustic features. In audio signal processing, the features are typically extracted in short (20-60 ms) frames and they aim at modeling the most relevant information in a compact form. The human auditory system performs frequency analysis (Zwicker & Fastl, 1999, pp. 20-53) which is why certain properties of the spectrum of the sound correlate better with human perception than the time domain signal does. Therefore most of the features parameterize the spectrum of the sound.

Mel-frequency cepstral coefficients (MFCCs) are by far the most widely used feature in audio content analysis (Tokuda et al. 1994). They represent the spectral energy distribution of an audio signal and are calculated as follows. First, the signal within an analysis frame is discrete Fourier transformed (DFT) and spectral power is estimated within approximately 40 subbands that are uniformly distributed on the Mel-frequency scale that mimics the near-logarithmic frequency resolution of the human auditory system. The vector of subband powers is then log-compressed and discrete cosine transformed. The resulting transform coefficients are called MFCCs and approximately ten lowest-order coefficients are typically used as features.

Other features used in audio processing include for example short-time energy, zero-crossing rate, crest factor, and spectral flux. Zero-crossing rate is defined as the number of times the time-domain signal changes its sign within an analysis window, and it correlates with the perceived brightness of the audio signal. Crest factor is defined as the peak-to-average ratio of the power envelope of the time domain signal, and spectral flux is calculated as the squared Euclidean distance of the frame-to-frame difference of magnitude spectra.

Some music-specific acoustic features will be introduced later in Section 5.1. For a more extensive introduction to audio features, see (Peeters, 2004). Matlab implementations of many of these features are available in the MIR toolbox of the University of Jyväskylä (Lartillot & Toiviainen, 2007).

Similarity Estimation Between Audio Samples

One of the most important types of audio metadata is the similarity estimate between two samples. However, when estimating the similarity of two audio samples, a fundamental problem arises: the loose definition of audio similarity. If only one example is given, it is impossible to know what kind of properties the user is searching for. In the case of two speech samples, for example, the similarity can be judged by the speaker identity, by the topic of the speech, or by any sounds in the background.

A solution to the above problem is to provide the retrieval application some additional information about the properties that the user is interested in. Query by humming applications, for example, retrieve pieces which are melodically similar to the input humming or whistling, but should not be affected by the rhythmic content of the target pieces. In a general query-by-example application, the similarity is defined by the features used to represent the input signals. The features can model for example the frequency content or the dynamics of the audio signals.

In order to estimate similarity, we need to calculate the distance between samples, which is actually a measure of dissimilarity. There are numerous different distance measures suitable for different tasks.

Usually, the distance is calculated based on the feature distributions. Traditional distance measures utilize some statistical measures (mean, covariance, etc.) of the continuous valued features. Examples of such measures are Mahalanobis distance defined as

$$D_{Mah}(f,g) = (\mu_f - \mu_g)^T \Sigma^{-1} (\mu_f - \mu_g)$$

and Bhattacharyya distance

$$D_{Bha}(f,g) = \frac{1}{4}(\mu_f - \mu_g)^T (\Sigma_f + \Sigma_g)^{-1} (\mu_f - \mu_g) + \frac{1}{2}\ln\frac{\left|\dfrac{\Sigma_f + \Sigma_g}{2}\right|}{\sqrt{|\Sigma_f||\Sigma_g|}},$$

where f and g are Gaussian components with means μ_f and μ_g and covariances Σ_f and Σ_g, respectively. Covariance matrix Σ is estimated across all samples. If the covariances are the same, Bhattacharyya distance simplifies to Mahalanobis distance up to a constant summation term, and furthermore, if the covariances are identity matrices, both distances simplify to Euclidean distance.

The Bayesian information criterion (BIC) has also been used as a distance measure, especially in the segmentation and classification of speech material (Zhou & Hansen, 2000). The BIC difference between two Gaussian models is given by

$$D_{BIC}(A,B) = (N_A + N_B)\log(|\Sigma|) - N_A\log(|\Sigma_A|) - N_B\log(|\Sigma_B|) - \frac{1}{2}\lambda(d + \frac{1}{2}d(d+1))\log(N_A + N_B),$$

where N_A and N_B are the numbers of observations in sequence A and B respectively. Σ, Σ_A, and Σ_B are the covariance matrices of all observations, sequence A, and sequence B, respectively. λ is a penalty factor which compensates for the small sample sizes and d is the number of dimensions.

Lately, the use of pdf-based distance measures has become very popular. Helén and Virtanen (2007) derived a closed form solution for Euclidean distance between Gaussian mixture models (GMMs). Hershey et al. (2007) and Goldberger et al. (2003) proposed approximations for Kullback-Leibler divergence between GMMs. Virtanen and Helén (2007) proposed using the likelihood ratio test between GMMs or hidden Markov models (HMMs) for audio similarity. These will be discussed later in this chapter.

Audio Classification and Segmentation

Supervised classification can be used to classify signals into predefined classes, such as speech, music, and environmental sounds. Speech can be further classified by the gender of the speaker or the emotion of the speech, music can be classified by the artist or genre, and so on. Supervised classification in general has been widely studied and audio classifiers typically employ some of the standard techniques, including especially GMMs, HMMs, neural networks, and support vector machines. Applications of supervised classification include e.g. highlight extraction for spotting exciting scenes from movies or sport events. These applications usually require pre-trained acoustic models of the matching sounds, such as explosions, laugher, or screaming.

Audio Segmentation

Segmentation is an operation, where a long audio sample is subdivided into shorter segments. The most common way of doing this is to examine the original audio sample in short (for example one second) time windows. The frames are then classified into predefined audio classes using supervised classification, and finally, consecutive frames belonging to a same class are merged into acoustically homogenous segments.

Lu et al. (2002) proposed a segmentation and classification algorithm which operates in several consecutive phases. First, they segmented the input audio stream into speech and non-speech segments using k-nearest-neighbor classifier and linear spectral pairs vector quantization. As features they used zero-crossing rate, short-time energy ratio, and spectral flux. Secondly, silence segments were detected from the non-speech segments. A segment was classified as silence if its short-time energy and zero-crossing rate were lower than a manually set threshold. Thirdly, music was discriminated from environmental sounds using band periodicity, spectral flux, and noise frame ratio. Decisions were made simply by checking the value of each feature and comparing them to pre-defined thresholds.

After the segmentation and classification is completed, there is typically some kind of post processing stage, which further reduces the misclassifications. For example Lu et al. (2002) smoothed the segmentation using three rules. First, audio types do not change too frequently. Second, if there is only a one-second segment of some audio type, it is changed to the same as the previous segment. Third, silence is an exception and can occur also as one-second segments. Furthermore, Lu et al. also proposed an unsupervised speaker segmentation algorithm, which required no prior knowledge about the number or the identity of the speakers in a sample. The system had the precision of 96.5 % for speech/music/environmental sounds. For the speaker change detection and segmentation the recall was 89.9 % and precision 83.7 %. Precision and recall are often used as performance measures and are defined as

$$recall = \frac{number\ of\ correctly\ retrieved\ samples}{number\ of\ relevant\ samples}$$

$$precision = \frac{number\ of\ correctly\ retrieved\ samples}{number\ of\ retrieved\ samples}$$

Highlight Extraction

Highlight extraction refers to an application which finds interesting parts from a video stream. The input could be for example a movie from which the user wants to find certain scenes like a car-chase or a gunplay. In these cases, one could use the visual content, but video analysis is typically much more expensive computationally than audio analysis. In many cases, the audio content actually gives better clues about the semantics of the scene than the visual content. In a soccer game, for example, the crowd cheering is easier to recognize than the ball going into the goal. Chen et al. (2003) used both audio and visual features to extract goal events from a soccer game.

The main challenge in highlight extraction is to narrow the gap between low-level audio features and the semantic content of the video. Chu et al. (2005) achieved this using a hierarchical approach. They extracted certain audio events from an action movie, and based on these, they detected the semantic content of the scenes. Audio events like gunshot and explosion were used to detect gunplay scenes, and events like engine noise and car-braking to detect car-chase scenes. They used both GMM and HMM models for the semantic context detection. In gunplay detection both models performed equally well, but as expected, in car-chase detection the HMM based approach gave better results. This is because the state-transition matrix of the HMM represents the temporal evolution of the scene and is therefore more adequate to model the complex semantic content of the event.

Query by Example

A query by example system allows the user to present his query in the form of an example signal which describes the type of content the user is searching for. The system then retrieves signals which, according to the algorithms used, are closest match to the example. Since typically only one audio example is provided to the system it is impossible to know exactly what properties in the example signal are interesting to the user. However, perceptually motivated generic audio features, such as MFCCs, have proven to give quite good results in this task (Helén & Virtanen, 2007).

The structure of a typical query by example system is presented in Fig. 2. First, the features are extracted from each database item and from the query signal. Second, the distance from each database signal to the example is calculated. Finally, the database samples which have the shortest distance to the example signal are retrieved to the user.

For retrieving the results there are basically two approaches: ε-range query and k-nearest neighbor (k-NN) query. In ε-range query, there is a fixed threshold ε which defines a hypersphere around the example signal in the feature space. All the signals in the database located inside this hypersphere are retrieved to the user. The advantage of this approach is that similar samples can be retrieved to the user as soon as they are found, even though the search is still underway. The drawback is that finding the proper threshold is not straightforward and may require going through the whole database. Kashino et al. (2003) suggested using the value $\varepsilon = \mu + \sigma c$, where μ and σ are the mean and standard deviation of all distances between samples in the training data, and c is an empirically set threshold.

In k-NN query, the k samples which have the shortest distance to the example are retrieved to the user. The advantage here is that the user always finds the same amount of samples regardless of the content of the database. A drawback is that the whole database has to be gone through before any results can be retrieved.

Figure 2. Overview of a query by example system

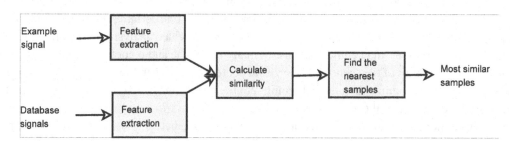

Distance Measures Between PDFs

Virtanen and Helén (2007-2) tested different distance measures in the query by example task. In particular, they studied pdf-based distance measures: cross-likelihood ratio test, Euclidean distance, and Kullback-Leibler (KL) divergence (see the reference for definitions). As a reference they used Mahalanobis distance, compression based distance, and KL divergence between single Gaussians. The pdf-based measures were found to outperform the reference methods.

We studied Goldberger's approximation of KL divergence using the same database and experimental setup as in (Virtanen & Helén, 2007-2). The database contained 1332 10-second samples from 17 classes. Table 1 gives the precision error rates for different distance measures in the query by example task. It can be seen that all the methods perform quite well. However, the cross-likelihood-ratio test and Goldberger's approximation of KL divergence are the most accurate in query by example with this test database.

Parameter-Free Query-by-Example Method

Helén and Virtanen (2007-1) proposed a query by example method which was based on perceptual audio coding and compression. Specific to this method is that explicit feature extraction is avoided entirely. The original audio signals are first coded using some, preferably low bit rate, perceptual audio codec like MP3. The resulting bit streams are then compressed using some lossless compressor, for example gzip or bzip. The same compression is also performed for a file which is the concatenation of the two MP3 files. Finally, the similarity is determined from the compression ratios of these two cases: the higher the compression ratio of the concatenated file, the more similar the samples are. This is due to the similar codewords which appear in the perceptually coded files.

Cilibrasi and Vitányi (2005) proposed the normalized compression distance (NCD)

$$NCD(x, y) = \frac{C(xy) - \min(C(x), C(y))}{\max(C(x), C(y))},$$

where $C(x)$ and $C(y)$ are the sizes of compressed files x and y. $C(xy)$ is the compressed size of concatenated x and y. This similarity measure is based on the information distance, which has been previously used in a wide range of other tasks. These include optical character recognition, fetal heart rate tracing, classification of books by the author, and even building an evolutionary tree from mitochondrial genomes. In these tasks, the parameter-free method has outperformed the traditional methods (Cilibrasi & Vitányi,

Table 1. Precision error rates for different distance measures in the query by example task

Distance measure	Precision error
HMM cross-likelihood ratio test (8 comp.)	4.8 %
GMM cross-likelihood ratio test (8 comp.)	5.3 %
KL-Goldberger, GMM (8 comp.)	4.8 %
Euclidean distance, GMM (8 comp.)	5.9 %
Mahalanobis distance	6.8 %

2005; Costa-Santos et al., 2006). In audio query by example task the results were also competitive against the parametric methods, but the real benefit is that explicit feature extraction can be avoided and therefore there is no need to choose the features to be used in the task.

One can argue about parametric freeness of such algorithms, since the compression algorithm has to be chosen. The aim here is however, the best approximation in the sense of Kolmogorof complexities and therefore the algorithm providing the highest compression ratio should be chosen.

Music Retrieval and Recommendation

Music information retrieval (MIR) is an important area of audio management. There is more music available nowadays than anyone can listen during his or her lifetime, but at the same time music is hard to find. Although Internet services like *Jogli*, *Songza*, and *Seeqpod* allow one to access and listen to virtually any artist or song the user can name, many people are not able to express their musical desires accurately outside the few popular artists they know. This has created the demand for more intelligent music retrieval and recommendation services which allow the user to discover new artists and songs.

Music signals are highly structured. Pitch relationships of the sounding notes are employed to build melodies and chords, timing relationships to create rhythms, and timbre of the sounding instruments to create meaningful contrasts. In music retrieval, acoustic features are extracted that cover all these perceptual dimensions of music.

Another characteristic of music signals is that they usually warrant a relatively large number of listeners. This is why *collaborative filtering* (CF) is an efficient technique for music retrieval and recommendation. CF is based on a user-item matrix, where the entries represent the rating of piece i by user j, or, in a simpler scenario, the number of times user j listened to piece i. Such a matrix can be used for several purposes. In music recommendation, a user's profile is compared with those of others and music items are recommended based on the ratings of like-minded users (Shardanand & Maes, 1995). The matrix also provides a basis for measuring the similarity of two music pieces: the ratings profile of a piece measures its acoustic characteristics, and in addition, also factors such as quality and usage which are difficult to measure from the audio signal directly (Slaney, 2007). In practice, a similarity measure can be derived for example by first reducing the matrix dimensions by singular value decomposition and then calculating cosine distance between the ratings vectors of two pieces. *Last.fm* (www.last.fm) is an example of a popular Internet radio that is mainly based on CF, although the service also supports collaborative tagging and other music community features.

Here the main emphasis is on audio-based MIR, as opposed to CF. Music retrieval based on CF alone has some inherent limitations that call for complementary methods. In particular, CF is not able to deal with items that are new or not popular enough to have many of listeners. Also, CF does not allow separating the various dimensions of similarity but these are all represented by the single ratings profile where all factors are mixed. Audio-based MIR, on the other hand, does not require usage data from other listeners. It also allows queries with specific content-based criteria, such as requesting pieces with certain singer vocal characteristics or slow tempo. *Pandora* (www.pandora.com) is an example of an audio-based MIR service, where users can name songs or artists that they like and the service responds by recommending new items that are musically similar. The service is based on metadata produced by human annotators.

Obviously, music annotation by human experts is costly and even collaborative tagging by the users of an on-line service is not effective for items that are not sufficiently popular. This creates the need for automatic content analysis tools. Indeed, music content analysis has been an active area of research in recent years and an annual evaluation contest on the various areas of music signal analysis has been organized since 2004 (Downey, 2008). In the following, tools for music content analysis are described. Two levels of difficulty are treated each in turn, first music classification and then "transcription-oriented" methods where some musically meaningful part of the signal, such as the melody line, is extracted and analyzed.

Music Classification

Music classification follows basically the same scheme as already described in the previous sections: frame-wise features are extracted and then passed on to a pattern classifier, such as a GMM, HMM, or a support vector machine. Most often the temporal order of the feature vectors is not taken into account, but a "bag of features" approach, such as the GMM classifier is used. The features employed can be categorized roughly according to the perceptual dimensions of sound: timbre-related features describe mainly the instrumentation, pitch-related features the harmonic content of music, and loudness variation over time the rhythm. Some of the most commonly used features are introduced below, for a comprehensive review see (Peeters, 2004) and (Lartillot & Toiviainen, 2007).

Starting from the most commonly used features, MFCCs and their time derivatives are used to measure the spectral energy distribution and its variation over time (Tokuda et al., 1994). These are often referred to as timbral features, since they are mainly affected by the timbre of the instruments involved in the piece of music. Since each musical genre (jazz, rock, etc.) usually has its characteristic instrumentation, timbral features are quite efficient for genre classification (Tzanetakis & Cook, 2002). Artist identification is another typical classification task (Berenzweig et al., 2002). More recently, work has emerged on automatic tagging of music with more diverse tags such as *emotional, danceable, electronica, male vocals, at party*, etc. (Torres et al., 2007).

Harmonic content of a music piece consists of its chord progression, tonality, and key (the basic note scale applied). These are effectively described by the chroma feature (Bartsch & Wakefield, 2001). In its simplest form, chroma is calculated by dividing the DFT spectrum into 1/12-octave regions, measuring the spectral power in each region, and then summing up the values across octaves to obtain a 12-dimensional chroma vector (for more sophisticated chroma calculation techniques, see (Ryynänen & Klapuri, 2008)). Because the harmonic content of music stems from the composition underlying a song, the chroma feature is effective in detecting so-called *cover songs* (Ellis & Poliner, 2007). These refer to a situation where different musicians perform the same underlying song or piece. Harmonic features have also been used for music *mood* classification, since a major or minor key affects the valence (happy/sad) of music. Chroma has also been used to analyze the internal structure of a music piece since it effectively reveals repeated sections within a piece (Paulus & Klapuri, 2008). The part which repeats most often is usually a good thumbnail to be presented as a query result to the user.

Rhythm in music is a longer-term concept and requires approximately 5-10 s long analysis window to measure it at any point of a song. A feature called *rhythmogram* is a relatively robust and straightforward way of describing the rhythm of music (Dixon et al., 2003; Jensen, 2007). It is calculated as follows. First, the amount of incoming spectral energy in the audio signal is measured, for example by calculating the difference between DFTs in successive time frames, setting negative values to zero, and then summing over frequency. The resulting signal is then subjected to autocorrelation function analysis (ACF) in successive 5-10 s time frames. In the resulting ACF, rhythmically meaningful lags in the range 0-2 s are retained, and optionally, some dimensionality reduction techniques such as the principal component analysis may be applied (Ellis & Arroyo, 2004). The rhythmogram can be used for music classification or for measuring the rhythmic similarity of two music pieces. In addition, rhythmic features have found use in analyzing the energy/intensity dimension of the mood of music (Liu & Zhang, 2006).

In query by example of music, it is possible to let the user control the features that are included in the similarity measurement. For example, imagine a situation where the piece "Bohemian Rhapsody" by the Queen is compared against a) London Symphony Orchestra's version of the same piece and b) against another piece by Queen. Which one is more similar? The riddle is solved by letting the user choose the features: if timbral features (e.g. MFCCs) are used, the two pieces performed by Queen are much more similar, if harmonic features (e.g. chroma) are used, the underlying composition is revealed and the two versions of Bohemian Rhapsody are likely to be more similar.

Transcription-Oriented Methods

Transcription-oriented music analysis methods attempt to extract some higher-level musical information from the audio signal. For example, the tempo of a piece can be estimated (McKinney et al., 2007) or the lead vocals separated from the rest and then used for feature extraction and similarity analysis. In singer identification, for example, extracting acoustic features from the separated vocals instead of the original audio has been shown to improve the results considerably (Fujihara & Goto, 2007; Mesaros et al., 2007). In order to measure the melodic similarity of two music pieces, it is first necessary to extract the melody pitch track from the two pieces. The pitch tracks can be compared by aligning them in time and then calculating the Euclidean distance (Ryynänen & Klapuri, 2008) or alternatively by calculating some statistical measures of the two pitch tracks. The bass line of a popular music piece can in principle be subjected to a similar analysis.

In order to review some techniques towards more advanced music analysis, let us reconsider the above problem of extracting the lead vocals from popular music. Some authors have approached this problem by first tracking the pitch of the main melody of the piece and then using the pitch information to select spectral components that are part of the singer's voice (Fujihara & Goto, 2007; Li & Wang, 2006; Mesaros et al., 2007). In another approach, instead of estimating the pitch, two timbre models are trained, one for the singing voice and one for the instrumental background, and these are then used to pull out the spectral components that correspond to the vocals (Ozerov et al., 2005). In a third alternative, stereo information is used to analyze the panning of different sound sources and to pick a sound source that most likely resembles the lead vocals (Barry et al., 2004). As this example demonstrates, there are many different approaches and integrating these is still underway.

In principle, vocals extraction also facilitates the analysis of lyrics in songs. Although lyrics recognition from realistic music pieces seems extremely difficult, some slightly easier tasks are already within reach. These include lyrics alignment to music (Wang et al., 2004), language identification, and perhaps keyword spotting in music.

Query by Humming

Query by humming is an application, where the user's humming or singing is used as a query. Such application becomes handy when user wants to find a certain song, but does not remember the song name or artist. Instead of these typical query data, the user is now able to hum the melody of the song into a microphone. There are typically two problems that have to be solved in a query by humming application. First, extracting the melody from the users humming and from the target music pieces, and second, finding similar melodies from the database. Ryynänen et al. (2008) solved the first problem by transcribing the query into notes and extracting pitch vectors from the notes. Similarly, melody notes were extracted from the target pieces. The second problem was solved by searching nearest melodic fragments, using Euclidean distance after tempo matching, for each query pitch vector, which was made efficiently using locality sensitive hashing (Datar et al., 2004).

There are applications available in the Internet which use melody search. Midomi (www.midomi.com) and Musicline (www.musicline.de) are commercial query by humming systems available for everyone. They have databases containing thousands of melodies and based on user's humming or singing they can retrieve the nearest matches. Musipedia (www.musipedia.org) also applies melody search but instead of humming, there are other ways to provide a melody to the system. The user can play the notes with the keyboard, give a melodic contour of the song, or draw notes in staff. Musipedia also provides a method to tap the rhythm of the song using the keyboard and search the song based on this rhythm.

Automatic Information Management Tools for Speech

Speech processing constitutes a rather independent subarea of information management. Speaker change detection is a natural starting point for speech segmentation. This can be accompanied with speaker recognition tools. Nowadays, the state-of-the-art speaker change detection algorithms are commonly based on the BIC (Chen & Gopalakrishnan, 1998). Speaker clustering can also be done efficiently based on the BIC measure (Vuorinen et al., 2008). If the identities of the persons speaking on the tape can be realistically assumed to be known, speaker recognition is a more powerful choice (Kinnunen, 2005). Conference call diarization systems, for example, can take advantage of proper speaker recognition. Most speaker recognition approaches, however, require much computational resources and pre-trained acoustic models. If speaker recognition is to be supported in personal audio content management framework, the best one can do is probably to train acoustic speaker models for the family members or for best friends or so. With the rest of the speakers, the speaker clustering can still cluster the data from one speaker although the identity of the speaker remains unknown. The problem with the clustering is that it can be efficiently performed on file level only. Similarity estimate between file level speaker clusters, if available, can be used to overcome the shortcoming (Lahti et al., 2008).

Speaker segmentation and clustering/recognition often provide a solid ground for further speech processing. For example, if the recorded speech is to be transcribed automatically, the results can be expected to be much better when performed for one speaker data at a time. If the speaker identity is known, speaker dependent acoustic models can be used and adapted resulting in considerably increased performance.

Automatic speech recognition (ASR) systems (Huang et al., 2001) are widely applied for voice dialing and voice UI purposes. Acoustic modeling based on HMMs has practically become a standard underlying technique. The performance of ASR systems has obtained already a rather mature level and Windows Vista, for example, has support for speech recognition. The Hidden Markov Model Toolkit (HTK) (Odell et al., 1995) is widely used for developing various speech recognition applications. HTK can support even very complex speech recognition applications.

Besides the tools, also various other resources are often required when developing a speech recognition application, which makes the work especially challenging. For example, large speech and text databases are needed in order to train acoustic models, text-to-phoneme mappings models (Jurafsky & Martin, 2000) etc. In multilingual speech recognition systems, the magnitude of the challenge is already enormous.

Also Text-To-Speech (TTS) synthesis systems have much to offer to automatic audio information management (e.g. www.cstr.ed.ac.uk/projects/festival and www.fon.hum.uva.nl/praat). TTS can provide an efficient solution for example for many UI problems with small portable device. Many disabled people benefit from TTS technology when they need computers in their everyday communication. For example, audio book kind of applications can read the textual material to the visually impaired people for their convenience but these applications can entertain other people as well. There are similar challenges in TTS development as with ASR mentioned above, but the availability of language specific TTS tools is considerable better.

Computational Issues and Indexing Techniques

When considering practical applications there are limitations in computational capacity. Especially when using mobile multimedia devices, the processors are relatively slow and users expect fast response from the algorithms. For example, query by example application has to calculate the distance between the example and all the samples in the database before retrieving the most similar samples. The computational complexity of such full search is too high for the large databases we have nowadays.

There are fundamentally two ways to reduce the computational complexity. The first is to make single distance calculation faster, which is typically done by reducing the dimensionality of the features (Kanth et al., 1998). The second is to reduce the number distance calculations during the search, which is our focus here. Both of these approaches naturally lead to a non-optimal retrieval result. However, the speed is usually more important than minor reduction in accuracy.

Clustering Techniques

An effective method to accelerate the search is to cluster the database prior to a query and then retrieve samples only within the most promising cluster. A problem in doing this is that the clustering would be really slow if we calculated the distances based on the feature vector pdfs of the samples. This is why it is practical to find a representation for which a simpler distance measure can be used and thus the clustering becomes faster.

An effective method to represent the samples, each initially represented by a series of feature vectors, is the key-sample transformation (Helen & Lahti, 2007). First, n reference points are chosen from the database, referred to as key-samples. Then, the distance from each database sample to these key-samples is calculated. After this, the distances from a database sample to the key-samples can be used as a feature vector in the clustering. For example k-means clustering and Euclidean distance can be used since the sample is represented using only a single feature vector of length n. The transformation can be written as

$$T(x, O, d) : \Gamma \to \Re^n,$$

where x is the original series of feature vectors, O is the set of n key-samples, d is the distance measure, Γ is the original feature space, and $\Re^n$ is the n-dimensional feature space where the ith element is the distance from x to i^{th} key-sample ($i=1,...,n$).

When choosing the number of key-samples, we again have to compromise between accuracy and speed. In Fig. 3, the left panel illustrates the effect of the amount of key-samples. As can be seen, that the higher the n, the more accurate the results. On the other hand, when the length of the feature vector increases, so does the computational cost. One can also observe that after the n value of 10, the increase in precision levels out, thus this is a justified choice for the number of key-samples.

The choice of the reference points is also an important factor in the key-sample transformation. Berenzweig & Ellis (2003) proposed using such a transformation in music classification and similarity measurements. They chose key samples (called anchors in their work) manually from different artists and from different musical genres. This approach is justified when the audio content is restricted for example to music. However, when performing generic query by example with no prior information about the content, this approach is questionable. Shapiro (1977) showed that in search application the reference points should be such that they are away from the cluster centers and from each other. Thus, it can be said that the keysamples should be in different parts of the feature space. This however, is not a trivial task since in the general case there is no prior information about where the samples will fall. This is why Helen & Lahti (2007) suggested choosing the key samples randomly from the existing database.

The accuracy of the clustering based search can be further improved by searching samples from several nearest clusters. In Fig. 3 the right panel illustrates the effect of searching from several nearest clusters and also the effect of the total number of clusters. The straight line is the reference, where search is extended to all clusters, corresponding to a full search. Already searching from the three nearest clusters gives precision very near to full search. Again, the computational cost is naturally higher when more similarity estimates have to be calculated.

Audio classification and query by example can also be combined in order to make the search more effective. Lahti et al. (2008) first classified the samples in the database into 4 predefined classes (speech, music, noise, and silence). Then, similar samples were only retrieved from within the same class as the query sample.

Figure 3. Left panel illustrates the effect of changing the number of key-samples. Right panel illustrates the effect of changing the number of clusters

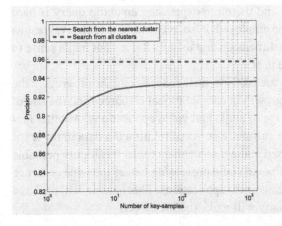
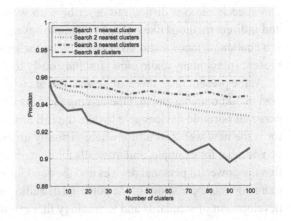

Locality Sensitive Hashing

Locality sensitive hashing (LSH) is a computationally efficient indexing technique which allows searching approximate nearest neighbors in large databases and in high-dimensional feature spaces (Datar et al., 2004). As already mentioned in the beginning of this section, there are two computational challenges involved: measuring the distance between each two feature vectors is heavy when the dimensionality of the feature vectors v_i is high (thousands of dimensions) and measuring the distance against all database items is out of the question when the number of items can be of the order of millions.

LSH is based on a couple of ideas that work towards solving the above two problems. The first observation is that a small collection of dot products $\langle c, v \rangle$ with random vectors c works as a *sketch* of feature vector v and can be used to estimate the norm of the vector, $\|v\|$. It is easy to see that the sketch is linearly decomposable: $\langle c, v_1 - v_2 \rangle = \langle c, v_1 \rangle - \langle c, v_2 \rangle$, where v_1 and v_2 are feature vectors representing two different audio samples. In LSH, the sketch is not used to estimate distances between vectors directly, but to assign hash values for them. Each hash maps feature vector v to an integer number, calculated as $\lfloor (\langle c, v \rangle + b) / r \rfloor$ where b is a real number chosen randomly form the range $[0, r]$ and $\lfloor \cdot \rfloor$ denotes rounding towards negative infinity. For a fixed parameter r, the probability that two feature vectors collide, that is, are hashed to a same "bucket", becomes higher when the distance between the vectors v_1 and v_2 is small. Finding approximate nearest neighbours, then, proceeds by hashing a query vector v_q with the same hash functions and investigating the vectors in the buckets where v_q was hashed to. By designing the hash functions carefully, LSH can be proven to find approximate nearest neighbors with high probability in bounded computation time (Datar et al., 2004). LSH has been used successfully in many problems, including query by humming of audio (Ryynänen & Klapuri, 2008).

FUTURE TRENDS

Despite the rapid progress in audio management tools during the last ten years, it is clear that retrieval and sorting operations for audio data are still far from being as flexible as they are for textual data. We still are experiencing an era that resembles "web pre-Google", as Celma and Lamere put it in their Music Recommendation Tutorial at the International Conference on Music Information Retrieval in 2007. There are several extremely interesting research challenges that are awaiting for creative solutions. Some of them are due to the inherent difficulties with presenting and describing audio information: non-speech audio is difficult to describe with words and therefore expressing an audio query is hard and indirect methods like query by example have to be employed. Also, presenting the retrieval results is a challenge, since audio takes place along the time dimension and usually it does not make sense to present (play) many audio clips simultaneously to the user.

At the present time, there are several factors which are likely to further accelerate the progress in the area of audio management. One driving factor is the growth in computational resources and the rise of personal portable devices able to take the full advantage of audio and video applications. Another factor is the new web 2.0 culture where virtually anyone can share personal multimedia data in the spirit of Youtube, for example, and this calls for content-based audio management tools. It is highly probable that the powerful personal devices and the need for personal audio processing makes the wide audience more and more conscious of the potential of audio management applications. This in turn, will push the development of standards and technology that eventually will make the life easier.

Some emerging research trends in this area are worth mentioning. One is the rapidly developing field of machine learning methods and particularly of unsupervised learning methods that have been proposed for finding structure in data automatically. The potential of this approach should not be underestimated at times when we have immeasurable amounts of (non-annotated) audio data available for developing such methods. Another trend is emerging due to the increased memory capacity of servers and the powerful indexing techniques. Imagine a situation where we have indexed, say, 10^{10} audio signals on a server, and given a query example, could retrieve perceptually the most similar clips in an instant. This leads to an approach, where we store examples instead of training a statistical model, which might have interesting implications for speech recognition and other fields. Provided that some contextual information about the stored signals would be available too, which is realistic if the data is collected with mobile devices, this would result in a large-scale audio recognition system.

Another, more cultural trend, is related to the production of data annotations that are usually needed for the development and evaluation of automatic content analysis tools. Some web communities, such as *Last.fm*, provide the users with tools for collaborative tagging of audio data, meaning that the users themselves manually tag the audio samples they hear. When the number of users grows to millions, this is a very effective way of getting metadata. Also, several game-based annotation applications such as Major Miner (www.majorminer.com) and Listen Game (www.listengame.com) have been proposed.

CONCLUSION

We have introduced state-of-the-art audio management tools used in both professional and personal content management. The described tools were concerned with audio segmentation and classification, query-by-example, music retrieval and recommendation, and speech management. In practical applications, processing speed is an essential factor and in large databases many of the management tools become too slow for practical use. In order to deal with this problem, we presented database indexing techniques and a key-sample transformation based clustering algorithm, which accelerate the search in large databases.

The future of audio information management seems promising. The research work has already reached a rather mature level in many areas, and the obstacles that caused trouble only a couple of years ago have started to disappear. Many components are available for application developers and therefore the developers do not necessarily need to be experts in audio processing any longer.

REFERENCES

Aaltonen, A. T. (2007). *Facilitating personal content management in smart phones*. PhD thesis, Proefschrift Rijksuniversiteit Groningen.

Barry, D., Coyle, E., & Lawlor, B. (2004). Real-time sound source separation using Azimuth discrimination and resynthesis. *117th Audio Engineering Society Convention*. San Francisco, CA, USA.

Bartsch, M. A., & Wakefield, G. H. (2001). To catch a chorus: using chroma-based representations for audiothumbnailing. *IEEE Workshop on Applications of Signal Processing to Audio and Acoustics*, (pp. 15-18). New Platz, NY, USA.

Berenzweig, A. L., Ellis, D. P., & Lawrence, S. (2002). Using voice segments to improve artist classification of music. *AES 22nd International Conference on Virtual, Synthetic, and Entertainment Audio.* Espoo, Finland.

Berenzweig, A., Ellis, D. P., & Lawrence, S. (2003). Anchor space for classification and similarity measurement of music. *IEEE International Conference on Multimedia and Expo (ICME 2003), 2*, pp. 29-32. Baltimore, Maryland, USA.

Cai, R., Lu, L., & Hanjalic, A. (2008). Co-clustering for auditory scene categorization. *IEEE Transactions on Multimedia , 10* (4), 596-606.

Chen, S. S., & Gopalakrishnan, P. S. (1998). Environment and channel change detection and clustering via the Bayesian information criterion. *DARPA Broadcast News Transcription and Understanding,* (pp. 127-132). Landsdowne, Virginia, USA.

Chen, S.-C., Shyu, M.-L., Zhang, C., Luo, L., & Chen, M. (2003). Detection of soccer goal shots using joint multimedia features and classification rules. *International Workshop on Multimedia Data Mining (MDM 2003),* (pp. 36-44). Washington, DC, USA.

Chu, W.-T., Cheng, W.-H., Hsu, J. Y.-J., & Wu, J.-L. (2005). Towards semantic indexing and retrieval using hierarchical audio models. *Multimedia Systems , 10* (6), 570-583.

Cilibrasi, R., & Vitányi, P. M. (2005). Clustering by compression. *IEEE Transactions on Information Theory , 51* (4), 1523-1545.

Cook, G. D., Kershaw, D. J., Christie, J. D., Seymour, C. W., & Waterhouse, S. R. (1997). Transcription of broadcast television and radio news: the 1996 ABBOT system. *IEEE International Conference on Acoustics, Speech, and Signal Processing, 2*, pp. 723-726. Munich, Germany.

Costa-Santos, C., Bernandes, J., Vitányi, P. M., & Antunes, L. (2006). Clustering fetal heart rate tracings by compression. *IEEE International Symposium on Computer-Based Medical Systems.* Salt Lake City, Utah, USA.

Datar, M., Immorlica, N., Indyk, P., & Mirrokni, V. S. (2004). Locality-sensitive hashing scheme based on p-stable distributions. *Twentieth Annual Symposium on Computational Geometry,* (pp. 253-262). Brooklyn, New York, USA.

Dixon, S., Pampalk, E., & Widmer, G. (2003). Classification of dance music by periodicity patterns. *4th International Conference on Music Information Retrieval,* (pp. 159-165). Baltimore, MD, USA.

Downey, J. S. (2008). The music retrieval evaluation exchange (2005-2007): A window into music information retrieval research. *Acoustic Science and Technology , 29* (4), 247-255.

Ellis, D. P., & Poliner, G. E. (2007). Identifying `cover songs' with chroma features and dynamic programming beat tracking. *IEEE International Conference on Acoustics, Speech, and Signal Processing,* (pp. 1429-1432). Honolulu, HI, USA.

Ellis, D., & Arroyo, J. (2004). Eigenrhythms: Drum pattern basis sets for classification and generation. *International Symposium on Music Information Retrieval,* (pp. 101-106). Barcelona, Spain.

Fujihara, H., & Goto, M. (2007). A music information retrieval system based on singing voice timbre. *International Conference on Music Information Retrieval*, (pp. 467-470). Vienna, Austria.

Gauvain, J.-L., Lamel, L., & Adda, G. (2002). The LIMSI broadcast news transcription system. *Speech Communication , 37* (1-2), 89-108.

Goldberger, J., Gordon, S., & Greenspan, H. (2003). An efficient image similarity measure based on approximations of KL-divergence between two Gaussian mixtures. *IEEE International Conference on Computer Vision*, (pp. 487-493). Nice, France.

Helén, M., & Lahti, T. (2007). Query by example large databases using key-sample distance transformation and clustering. *IEEE International Workshop on Multimedia Information Retrieval (MIPR 2007)*, (pp. 303-308). Taichung, Taiwan.

Helén, M., & Virtanen, T. (2007-1). A similarity of measure for audio signals query by example based on perceptual coding and compression. *International Conference on Digital Audio Effects (DAFx 2007)*, (pp. 173-176). Bordeaux, France.

Helén, M., & Virtanen, T. (2007-2). Query by example of audio signals using Euclidean distance between Gaussian mixture model. *IEEE International Conference on Acoustics, Speech, and Signal Processing (ICASSP 2007), 1*, pp. 225-228. Honolulu, Hawaii, USA.

Hershey, J. R., & Olsen, P. A. (2007). Approximating the Kullback Leibler divergence between Gaussian mixture models. *IEEE International Conference on Acoustics, Speech and Signal Processing, 4*, pp. 317-320. Honolulu, Hawaii, USA.

Huang, X., Acero, A., & Hon, H.-W. (2001). *Spoken language processing: a guide to theory, algorithm and system development*. Redmond, Washington, USA: Prentice Hall.

Jensen, K. (2007). Multiple scale music segmentation using rhythm, timbre, and harmony. *EURASIP Journal on Advances in Signal Processing , 2007*, 1-11.

Jurafsky, D., & Martin, J. H. (2000). *Speech and language processing: an introduction to natural language processing, computational linguistics, and speech recognition*. Upper Saddle River, NJ, USA: Prentice Hall PTR.

Kanth, R. K., Agrawal, D., & Singh, A. (1998). Dimensionality reduction for similarity searching in dynamic databases. *ACM SIGMOD International Conference on Management of Data, 27*, pp. 166-176. Seattle, Washington, USA.

Kapur, A., Benning, M., & Tzanetakis, G. (2004). Query-by-beat-boxing: Music retrieval for the DJ. *International Conference on Music Information Retrieval (ISMIR 2004)*. Barcelona, Spain.

Kashino, K., Kurozumi, T., & Murase, H. (2003). A quick search method for audio and video signals based on histogram pruning. *IEEE Transactions on Multimedia , 5* (3), 348-357.

Kinnunen, T. (2005). *Optimizing spectral feature based text-independent speaker recognition*. PhD thesis, Department of Computer Science, University of Joensuu.

Lahti, T., Helén, M., Vuorinen, O., Väyrynen, E., Partala, J., Peltola, J., et al. (2008). On enabling techniques for personal audio content management. *ACM International Conference on Multimedia Information Retrieval (MIR 2008).* Vancouver, Canada.

Lartillot, O., & Toiviainen, P. (2007). A Matlab toolbox for music information retrieval. *Annual Conference of the German Classification Society.* Freiburg.

Lehikoinen, J., Aaltonen, A., Huuskonen, P., & Salminen, I. (2007). *Personal content experience: managing digital life in the mobile age.* England: Wiley & Sons, Ltd.

Li, Y., & Wang, D. L. (2006). Singing voice separation from monaural recordings. *International Conference on Music Information Retrieval*, (pp. 176-179). Victoria, BC, Canada.

Liu, L. L., & Zhang, D. H.-J. (2006). Automatic mood detection and tracking of music audio signals. *IEEE Transactions on Audio, Speech, and Language Processing , 14* (1), 5-18.

Liu, S.-C., Bi, J., Jia, Z.-Q., Chen, R., Chen, J., & Zhou, M.-M. (2007). Automatic audio classification and speaker identification for video content analyses. *ACIS International Conference on Software Engineering, Artificial Intelligence, Networking, and Parallel/Distributed Computing (SNPD 2007), 2*, pp. 91-96. Beijing, China.

Lu, L., You, H., & Zhang, H.-J. (2001). A new approach to query by humming in music retrieval. *IEEE International Conference on Multimedia and Expo (ICME 2001).* (pp. 595-598). Tokyo, Japan.

Lu, L., Zhang, H.-J., & Jiang, H. (2002). Content analysis for audio classification and segmentation. *IEEE Transactions on Speech and Audio Processing , 10* (7), 504-516.

McKinney, M. F., Moelants, D., Davies, M. E., & Klapuri, A. (2007). Evaluation of audio beat tracking and music tempo extraction algorithms. *Journal of New Music Research , 36* (1), 1-16.

Mesaros, A., Virtanen, T., & Klapuri, A. (2007). Singer identification in polyphonic music using vocal separation and pattern recognition methods. *International Conference on Music Information Retrieval*, (pp. 375-378). Vienna, Austria.

Odell, J., Ollason, D., Woodland, P., Young, S., & Jansen, J. (1995). *The HTK book for HTK v2.0.* Cambridge, UK: Cambridge University Press.

Ozerov, A., Philippe, P., Gribonyal, R., & Bimbot, F. (2005). One microphone singing voice separation using source-adapted models. *IEEE Workshop on Applications of Signal Processing to Audio and Acoustics*, (pp. 90-93). Mohonk, NY, USA.

Paulus, J., & Klapuri, A. (2008). Acoustic Features for Music Piece Structure Analysis. *11th Conference on Digital Audio Effects.* Espoo, Finland.

Peeters, G. (2004). *A large set of audio features for sound description (similarity and classification) in the CUIDADO project.* Paris, France: CUIDADO I.S.T. Project report.

Ryynänen, M., & Klapuri, A. (2008). Automatic transcription of melody, bass line, and chords in polyphonic music. *Computer Music Journal , 32* (3).

Ryynänen, M., & Klapuri, A. (2008). Query by humming of MIDI and audio using locality sensitive hashing. *IEEE International Conference on Acoustics, Speech, and Signal Processing (ICASSP 2008)*, (pp. 2249-2252). Las Vegas, Nevada, USA.

Shapiro, M. (1977). The choice of reference points in best-match file searching. *Communications of the ACM , 20* (5), 339-343.

Shardanand, U., & Maes, P. (1995). Social information filtering: algorithms for automating "word to mouth". *SIGCHI Conference on Human Factors in Computing Systems*, (pp. 210-217). Dencer, Colorado, USA.

Slaney, M. (2007). Similarity based on rating data. *International Conference on Music Information Retrieval*, (pp. 479-484). Vienna, Austria.

Song, J., Bae, S.-Y., & Yoon, K. (2002). Query by humming: matching humming query to polyphonic audio. *IEEE International Conference on Multimedia and Expo (ICME 2002)*, (pp. 329- 332). Seoul, South Korea.

Tokuda, K., Kobayashi, T., Masuko, T., & Imai, S. (1994). Mel-generalized cepstral analysis - a unified approach to speech spectral estimation. *International Conference on Spoken Language Processing, 3*, pp. 1043-1046.

Torres, D., Turnbull, D., Barrington, L., & Lanckriet, G. (2007). Identifying words that are musically meaningful. *International Conference on Music Information Retrieval*, (pp. 405-410). Vienna, Austria.

Tzanetakis, G., & Cook, P. (2002). Musical genre classification of audio signals. *IEEE Transactions on Speech and Audio Processing , 10* (5), 293-302.

Wang, Y., Kan, M.-Y., New, T. L., Shenoy, A., & Yin, J. (2004). LyricAlly: automatic synchronization of acoustic musical signals and textual lyrics. *12th Annual ACM International Conference on Multimedia*, (pp. 212-219). New York, NY, USA.

Virtanen, T., & Helén, M. (2007). Probabilistic model based similarity measures for audio query-by-example. *IEEE Workshop on Applications of Signal Processing to Audio and Acoustics (WASPAA 2007)*, (pp. 82-85). New Paltz, New York, USA.

Vuorinen, O., Lahti, T., Mäkelä, S.-M., & Peltola, J. (2008). Light weight mobile device targeted speaker clustering algorithm. *IEEE Signal Processing Society, 2008 International Workshop on Multimedia Signal Processing.* Cairns, Queensland, Australia.

Zhou, B., & Hansen, J. H. (2000). Unsupervised audio stream segmentation and clustering via the Bayesian information criterion. *International Conference on Spoken Language Processing, 3*, pp. 714-717. Beijing, China.

Zwicker, E., & Fastl, H. (1999). *Psychoacoustics: facts and models.* Berlin-Heidelberg: Springer Verlag.

Chapter XII
PUM:
Personalized Ubiquitous Multimedia

Susmit Bagchi
Samsung India Software Operations, India

ABSTRACT

*Due to the advancement of hardware technologies and mobile communication systems, the mobile devices are transforming into multimedia devices capable of consuming multimedia data. The mobile multimedia devices having the **3G/4G mobile communication** interfaces have created the ubiquitous multimedia applications paradigm. The ubiquitous multimedia advocates that adaptable media contents should be available to users any time and any where. These ubiquitous multimedia applications have promising business potentials. The ubiquitous multimedia applications create an infrastructure for multimedia information management, where contents can be managed with interconnection and collaboration between users. The Personalized Ubiquitous Multimedia (**PUM**) is a subset of **ubiquitous multimedia applications**, where users can create, store, share and re-use the personalized heterogeneous media contents using mobile multimedia devices. Hence, PUM is an example of interconnected and collaborative multimedia content management system. This chapter illustrates the evolution of Computer-Phone and the concept of PUM. An integrated architecture is described aiming to deploy the PUM applications. The integrated architecture is composed of **Mobile Agent Systems** (MAS) and a specialized Mobile Distributed File System. A set of advantages of the integrated architecture is described.*

INTRODUCTION

The ubiquitous computing systems are composed of two main building blocks such as, mobile devices and the wireless communication systems, which form the network of mobile devices. The advancements in hardware technologies have enabled to realize miniaturized low-power electronic components, which paved the way towards the manufacturing of a variety of high-end mobile devices such as, PDA

(Personal Digital Assistant) and Smart-Phones. The 3rd Generation (3G) and 4th Generation (4G) wireless communication technologies have achieved high bandwidth and reliability of the communication link. For example, the bandwidth of 3G system is in the range from 384Kbps (urban outdoor) to 2048Kbps (indoor). The mobile devices equipped with 3G and 4G mobile communication systems have given birth of seamless ubiquitous computing. The present day mobile devices are equipped with inbuilt codec modules and thus, the mobile devices are transforming into the mobile multimedia devices capable to handle multimedia data stream. These newly evolved mobile multimedia devices offer internet services through WAP (Wireless Application Protocol) and are capable to adopt various video streaming technologies (Hartwig, 2000). The wireless-networked mobile multimedia devices have created a platform to deploy high-end ubiquitous computing applications. The set of high-end ubiquitous computing applications are comprised of the following examples (Plagemann, 1999; Bagchi, 2007):

- Mobile multimedia streaming or ubiquitous media
- Virtual enterprises or virtual organizations
- Distributed digital contents or e-briefcase

However, the ubiquitous computing paradigm has a set of resource limitations. The fundamental restriction of the ubiquitous computing paradigm is the energy limitation of the mobile devices, which limits the computing lifetime and the types of mobile applications. The set of limitations restricting the proliferation of ubiquitous computing can be summarized as (Adelstein, 2005), (a) limited battery power, (b) limited storage space, which is not enough to hold a large volume of data set, (c) intermittent wireless communication link, (d) limited computing resources available at mobile devices and (e) restricted physical size of the mobile devices.

On the other hand, there are four key technological developments, which have created the environment suitable for realizing ubiquitous computing including the mobile multimedia applications. These key developments are (Pereira, 2003; Barton, 2006), (a) increment of mobile communication bandwidth and reliability, (b) availability of higher amount of primary and secondary storage spaces at mobile devices, (c) the standardization of multimedia contents and (d) distribution of multimedia contents through the internet or WWW (World Wide Web). Due to the advancement of hardware technologies, the mobile devices are getting equipped with low-power electronic components such as, USB memory-stick, which can hold a large data volume as a secondary storage attached to the mobile devices. The availability of low-power CPU and USB memory-stick may transform the present day mobile phones into the personal computing devices in future (Barton, 2006). These personal computing devices have capability to support the ubiquitous and mobile multimedia applications. It is worth noting that, the ubiquitous multimedia applications have distinct commercial aspects and business potentials (Davidyuk, 2004; Madhavapeddy, 2005).

In this chapter, the concept and model of ubiquitous multimedia applications are illustrated, which follows the interconnected and collaborative information management architecture. The evolution of the new generation Computer-Phone (CP) is described. The CP is the new breed of mobile multimedia devices having multiple functionalities including mobile phone, codec and the personal computer. This chapter introduces the concept of PUM (**Personalized Ubiquitous Multimedia**), which is a class of ubiquitous multimedia applications. In the PUM application framework, the multimedia users can create, securely store, share and stream the personalized multimedia data in the interconnected and collaborative environment. The PUM application framework offers data security, location transparency, high availability and disconnected operations saving network bandwidth and cost. Finally, an integrated architecture is described realizing the PUM, where the integrated architecture is composed of two high-end technologies such as, mobile agents and a specialized mobile distributed file system. The advantages of the integrated architecture are outlined and the future technological trends are illustrated. In this chapter, the personalized media refers to the individualized heterogeneous media contents, whereas adaptation refers to the media rendering according to the configurations of the different mobile devices.

BACKGROUND STUDY

The resource-constrained mobile devices are getting rapidly transformed into high-end devices due to the availability of microscopic portable memory such as, USB memory-stick. Equipped with the enhanced storage and other low-power hardware resources, the mobile phones would become the devices having the computing as well as communication capabilities similar to the personal computers (Barton, 2006). The high-end mobile devices are embedded with multimedia codec modules. For example, a novel low-complexity video coding algorithm is designed and implemented in mobile devices (Wang, 2004). The algorithm considers the limitations of the computational resources and battery-power of the mobile devices. The high-end mobile devices equipped with codec are considered as the multimedia consumer devices (Hartwig, 2000). The examples of existing multimedia devices are PDA (Personal Digital Assistant), set-top-box and game consoles. The mobile phones equipped with codec solutions, mobile communication capabilities and enhanced resources are transformed into the mobile multimedia devices (Hartwig, 2000).

On the other hand, the traditional analogue multimedia broadcast systems are moving into digital domain (Madhavapeddy, 2005). However, the existing broadcast systems are not interactive to users and are not flexible. The push-model of broadcast media delivery needs to be modified to the interactive, flexible and adaptive media delivery system (Madhavapeddy, 2005). In this context, the users may consume and share multimedia contents using the media servers and the mobile multimedia devices. The concept of Universal Multimedia Access (UMA) advocates that, any multimedia content should be available to the mobile users any time, any where and the content delivery should be adaptive to the execution environment (Pereira, 2003). In addition, the **Universal Multimedia Experience** (UME) notion offers an equivalent and informative experience to the users any time and any where (Pereira, 2003). The provision of delivering the multimedia contents any time and any where has lead to the concept of ubiquitous multimedia or UbiMedia. In the direction of ubiquitous multimedia, researchers have proposed the delivery of media contents in the vehicle with special emphasis on DVB and GSM domains (Hartwig, 2000).

It is evident that the mobile multimedia devices have heterogeneous configurations in terms of the available resources at the mobile devices. Hence, the dynamically customized delivery of the media contents to the different devices is necessary. The $2K^Q$ is a dynamically customizable media delivery architecture involving different sets of service components (Xu, 2000). For each mobile client, the appropriate service component is chosen based on the instantaneous end-to-end resource availability. The Quality of Service (QoS) is an important measure to maintain a consistent user experience. The SMART is a self-reconfigurable and component-based middleware to maintain QoS of ubiquitous multimedia delivery system (Cui, 2001). The SMART middleware is an application-hinted adaptive system. Based on the SMART design architecture, the MobiMan multimedia service platform is constructed (Cui,

2001). Experimental results demonstrate that MobiMan keeps the overhead ratio of the middleware and application at a stable level for different types of resource configurations and component configurations. The CAPNET middleware architecture is designed to support mobile multimedia applications (Davidyuk, 2004). The CAPNET middleware offers service discovery, asynchronous messaging, event management and context-based adaptation of the media contents. The TV-like multimedia presentation by adapting the media to the user configurations is illustrated in (Lemlouma, 2003). The media is encoded by SMIL 2.0 and adapted to the user configurations on-the-fly (Lemlouma, 2003). The MPEG-based and offline media content adaptation is described in (Steiger, 2003).

The mobile agent system is a dynamic client/server architecture, which supports migration of mobile applications at remote servers (Kotz, 1999; Adelstein, 2005). The mobile agent systems can realize a wide set of high-end mobile applications such as, electronic commerce, mobile commerce and information retrieval from distributed databases (Adelstein, 2005). The advantages of using mobile agents are, saving wireless network bandwidth, cost and supporting disconnected operations between mobile clients and the remote servers. In addition, the mobile agent systems employ dynamic adaptation and ontological intelligence in the applications (Adelstein, 2005). The Mobile-C is a mobile agent platform, which is based on the interpreted C/C++ language (-ch-) helping the interaction of the mobile agents to the low-level system software (Chen, 2006). The other successful designs of agent systems are Agent TCL, ARA, Concordia, Mole, Tacoma and Voyager (Adnan, 2000). The Tacoma and Knowbot agent designs consider the operating systems support to implement agent migration in a network (Hylton, 1996; Johansen, 1997). The mobile agent systems are employed into the design of ubiquitous multimedia systems. An intelligent ubiquitous media agent based system is developed, which collects, indexes and sequences the multimedia contents depending upon the user preferences (Chen, 2001; Wenyin, 2001).

Apart from the ubiquitous multimedia systems, the intelligent agents are used for information retrieval in distributed and heterogeneous database systems (Yu, 2003). Hence, it may be concluded that, the ubiquitous multimedia system is a rapidly developing application area having market potentials and the mobile agent systems can be employed to take advantages of the intelligent agent based designs.

UBIQUITOUS MULTIMEDIA APPLICATIONS

The ubiquitous multimedia applications comprise a class of ubiquitous applications. Traditionally, there are three methods to deliver the multimedia contents such as, (a) cable based broadcast system, (b) wireless broadcast system and, (c) physical media for distribution viz. CD or DVD. However, in recent time, the internet or WWW has become another source for the distribution of multimedia contents. The research indicates that a potentially vertical market exists for the ubiquitous multimedia applications having business potentials (Davidyuk, 2004; Madhavapeddy, 2005) and thus, this class of applications has commercial viability. The developments in the embedded device design and multimedia content delivery model have enabled to realize UMA such as, integration of low-complexity codec solutions into the mobile devices and the change in the content delivery model from unidirectional broadcast to the interactive systems (Xu, 2000; Pereira, 2003; Madhavapeddy, 2005). The concept of UMA eventually leads to the ubiquitous multimedia systems. With the explosion of multimedia contents, the requirement for efficient description of multimedia contents by the use of metadata has become essential (Pereira, 2003). This metadata based description of large volume of multimedia data enables efficient content management, retrieval, sharing and data filtering.

The main challenges of ubiquitous multimedia applications are the applications adaptation to the users-need along with the changing computing environments. Although, the PersonalServer (Want, 2002) advocates the portability of large amount of data using mobile devices, however, this requires persistently reliable as well as high-bandwidth wireless communication link and higher computing power of the mobile devices in order to transcode and transfer the large data volume on demand (Madhavapeddy, 2005). In the context of multimedia content discovery and distribution, the peer-to-peer (P2P) model is widely used in the interactive ubiquitous multimedia applications. However, the server-centered as well as intelligent mobile agent based models provide enhanced user experiences and improved overall system performances (Pereira, 2003).

New Services and Requirements

The ubiquitous multimedia applications are designed based on mobile-client/stationary-server computing model. The mobile multimedia devices connected to the mobile communication systems have created the *personalized services* and *location-aware services* (Hartwig, 2000). For example, the mobile-commerce is a personalized service requiring user authentication for data security. The Global Positioning System (GPS) is an example of location-aware services. The PUM (Personalized Ubiquitous Multimedia) is a class of ubiquitous multimedia applications, which is a personalized and location-transparent service offered to the media users. The requirements of the ubiquitous multimedia applications are as followings (Pereira, 2003; Davidyuk, 2004; Madhavapeddy, 2005):

- **Adaptation to the user needs:** This means that the ubiquitous multimedia applications should be able to infer the user demands and act accordingly.
- **Context-awareness:** The context-aware ubiquitous multimedia applications consider the execution environment and adapt to the changes according to the context.
- **Flexible storage of large data volume:** This means that the large data volume associated to the multimedia contents should be stored at remote resource-fat servers (networked home-PC or web servers) and the stored media contents should be available any time (*highly available*) as well as any where (*location transparent*) on demand.
- **Security of data:** The multimedia contents of the different users stored at servers are personalized and hence, should be securely stored.

Ubiquitous Multimedia Applications Model

The ubiquitous multimedia applications are composed of three resources namely, (1) mobile-client-side local resources, (2) remote-server-side local resources and (3) end-to-end mobile/wireless network bandwidth and reliability. The details of these entities are summarized in Table 1.

The architectural model of the ubiquitous multimedia applications is comprised of the multimedia servers, mobile communication backbone and mobile clients. The architectural model deploying the ubiquitous multimedia applications is depicted in Figure 1.

The multimedia servers store the multimedia data or contents and are connected to the mobile communication backbone through high-bandwidth TCP/IP wired network. The mobile clients residing the cells of mobile communication infrastructure can access the multimedia contents any time and any where from the servers through the mobile communication interface. It is evident that, the server resources

Table 1. Required resources for ubiquitous multimedia applications

Mobile-client-side local resources	Remote-server-side local resources	End-to-end mobile network
CPU capacity, Primary memory space, Secondary Storage space, Battery power, High-resolution display	CPU capacity, Primary memory space, Disk array capacity	Available bandwidth, Reliability

Figure 1. Ubiquitous multimedia applications model

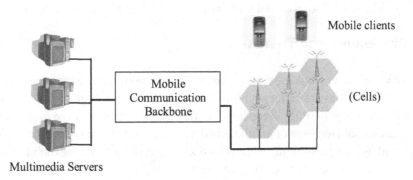

and the mobile communication bandwidth are two critical resources affecting the overall performance of the ubiquitous multimedia applications. The mobile clients, equipped with codec modules, consume the incoming multimedia data stream from the media servers.

PERSONALIZED UBIQUITOUS MULTIMEDIA (PUM)

The present day users create, consume and share a large volume of multimedia contents everyday (Hartwig, 2000; Xu, 2000; Madhavapeddy, 2005). The portable devices, such as camcorder and camera-phone, have enabled the users to exercise their artistic imaginations and the users of such devices create personalized multimedia contents. These multimedia contents created by the users are personal and heterogeneous in nature. The examples of such personalized multimedia contents are photo, audio clips and video clips created by the users. In addition, internet is the source of large volume of multimedia contents consumed by the users everyday (Lin, 2001). The multimedia users often download a large set of audio/video contents from internet (Lin, 2001). These created and downloaded multimedia contents form a large volume of **Personalized Multimedia Contents** (PMC). The common users would often want to store, re-use and share the PMC. Thus the **Personalized Multimedia Library** (PML) is formed by a set of PMCs and the volume of PML may be ever increasing as long as the users add the contents. The access to the contents of PMLs are authenticated meaning that, the PML of one user cannot be available to other users except specific access right issued by the owner of the PML concerned. Such access rights may be fine-grained in nature. For example, a user may grant some specific users the access right to view one of its photo albums present in his/her PML, but not to all the contents of the PML.

Hence, PUM is a ubiquitous multimedia application, where users create large volume of personalized multimedia library comprised of heterogeneous contents and store them on remote servers securely for future consumption and authenticated distribution. The schematic representation of PUM application scenario is illustrated in Figure 2.

In the Figure 2, the PUM servers securely store media library files of different users. The user 1 may create personalized as well as heterogeneous media contents and uploads the data to the PUM servers. This data volume is added within the existing media library of user 1. If user 2 is trusted to user 1 and a specific content sharing certificate is issued to user 2 by user 1, then user 2 may start viewing the content created by user 1 by down streaming the media data to the mobile multimedia device of user 2. The contents of PML, media sources and set of activities on the PML are depicted in Table 2.

Technical Challenges and Trends

The volume of PML of a user would be very high needing enormous storage space on the mobile devices. However, the mobile devices are battery-powered and have limited storage space as well as computing lifetime. Even the plug-n-play (PnP) secondary storage devices external to the mobile phones may not have enough space to hold terabyte of multimedia data of a personalized media library. The cost of the wireless bandwidth is high prohibiting continuous online streaming from one mobile device to another one for a long time. Although, the peer-to-peer multimedia content search and distribution model is dominant in present day, however, the server-centered delivery model is needed (Pereira, 2003). This would eliminate the storage space restrictions and the complexity of forming ad-hoc networks saving the overall cost. In addition, the use of mobile agents is increasingly becoming promising in order to

Figure 2. Schematic representation of PUM. (1) shooting a video/photo by user 1, (2) uploading the created media into media library of user 1 at remote servers, (3) down-streaming the video/photo to user 2 from media library of user 1.

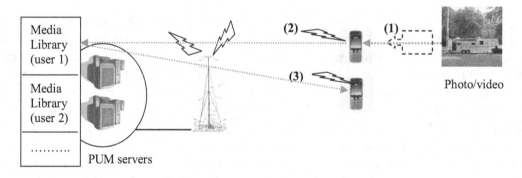

Table 2. Personalized media sources, contents and actions

PUM sources	PUM contents	Actions on PML
User creations, Internet.	Photo, audio, video.	Create, Store/upload, Delete, Index, Search, View/Stream, Share.

deploy resource-aware adaptive ubiquitous multimedia applications (Pereira, 2003). For example, web media agent is an agent based intelligent system, which automatically collects semantic descriptions of multimedia data on behalf of the users while accessing the internet media contents (Chen, 2001; Wenyin, 2001). In another application, the distributed database is designed based on intelligent agents (Yu, 2003). In majority of the mobile agent systems, the Operating System-Agent interaction appears as the technical challenge needing further research (Adnan, 2000). On the other hand, the trends in the manufacturing of the mobile devices indicate that in future the mobile devices will be transformed into the high-end Computer-Phones capable of creating and consuming multimedia data stream.

THE EVOLUTION OF COMPUTER-PHONE

Due to the continuous enhancement of hardware technologies and wireless communication systems, the future generation mobile phones may emerge as the personal computing devices having the PC-like capabilities (Barton, 2006). The following technological advances have envisioned the realization of the Computer-Phone (CP) supporting the mobile multimedia applications (Hartwig, 2000):

- **Wireless connectivity:** The reliability and high bandwidth of 3G/4G wireless communication systems help in creating new services based on mobile-client/stationary-server model.
- **Volatile and non-volatile storage:** The CP equipped with large volatile and non-volatile storage spaces allows offline computing through data caching and data processing model.
- **Processing power:** The new generation low-power CPU of the CP allows mobile computing and multimedia data processing.
- **Display:** The high-resolution colour monitor of the CP allows the display of the multimedia contents to the users along with suitably rendered special effects.

Hence, the Computer-Phone (CP) is the evolutionary product of the present day mobile phone. The CP is a mobile device, which has the following resources, (a) large secondary storage space, (b) a low-power CPU and sufficient RAM to allow computation, (c) multimedia codec module, (d) multimedia peripherals such as, camera and, (e) wireless internet connection and mobile communication capability. Hence, a CP is a mobile multimedia device, which can be viewed as the union of mobile iPhone and a portable minicomputer having wireless networking interface. The CP, as a mobile iPhone, communicates to the web servers through the intermediate mobile communication backbone as depicted in Figure 3. Along with the web servers, CP may communicate to the home-PC if the PC is connected to the internet.

Figure 3. Interaction of CP to Web servers and networked home-PC

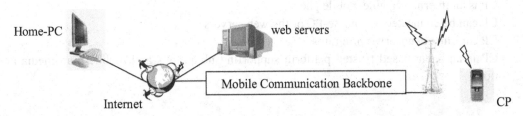

Figure 4. Layered software architecture of computer-phone

Mobile Applications	
Service Modules Interfaces	Mobile Agent Platform
Real-Time Operating Systems Platform	
CP Hardware	

Figure 5. Mobile agent based communication between CP and multimedia servers

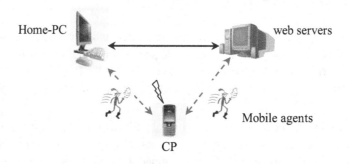

However, the CP is a mobile device and hence, maintaining a continuous wireless connection to the remote stationary server or internet is a rigid requirement and may not be economical. The CP uses mobile agents in order to perform ubiquitous computing and supporting mobile multimedia applications. Majority of the present day computers use some form of mobile code in everyday use. For example, the Java applets, Java scripts and web-browsers are the different forms of mobile codes. The mobile agents support the execution of mobile applications in the resource constrained environment (Adelstein, 2005). The mobile agent platform composes a middleware at CP, where mobile applications run with the support from the middleware as depicted in Figure 4.

Hence, the interaction between the CP, web servers and home-PC are based on the mobile agents. The mobile agents are composed at CP and are dispatched to the remote web servers or home-PC equipped with agent execution platform. The agents perform intended tasks at remote servers and return to the CP along with the results. The mobile agent based interaction model is depicted in Figure 5.

Hence, the characteristics of a CP can be summarized as:

- CP is an internet capable mobile phone.
- CP can be connected to a home-PC or the web servers.
- CP can run client/server programs.
- CP is an agent based trusted platform supporting ubiquitous and mobile multimedia applications.

The incorporation of the mobile agents in the CP as a middleware platform offers reduction of communication cost, enhanced reliability of the services and supporting disconnected operations between mobile multimedia devices (mobile clients) and the remote multimedia servers.

VMDFS AS MEDIA FILE STORE

The **Virtual memory based Mobile Distributed File System (VMDFS)** is a mobility-aware distributed file system layered on the remote servers stationed in the mobile communication infrastructure (Bagchi, 2007). The servers form Server-Group (SG) and elect a group leader as well as co-leader in order to manage the server resources. The schematic representation of VMDFS architecture is illustrated in Figure 6. The VMDFS stores the PML of the mobile clients as a set of structured files. The servers in a SG are connected by TCP/IP bus and are attached to the mobile communication backbone. The implementation of VMDFS targets the high-performance monolithic Linux kernel (Bagchi, 2007). The VMDFS is constructed in the kernel of the operating system of the individual servers in order to achieve better monitoring and utilization of available resources at servers and to establish faster inter-kernel communication system (Bagchi, 2007). The entire VMDFS architecture can be decomposed into two functional entities namely, VMDFS-client (VC) and VMDFS-server (VS). The VC residing in the user-space of a server machine acts as a server to the mobile clients. On the other hand, the same VC acts as a local client to its local VS residing in the kernel-space.

The VCs of a SG communicate through TCP/IP bus, whereas VSs of the SG communicate using a separate inter-kernel communication channel based on events. Hence, the <VC,VS> pairs of the server machines in SGs construct a distributed file system on top of the individual local disk file systems. The VC-VS interface is constructed using device file architecture of the monolithic Linux kernel. The VMDFS uses page-frame mapping technique along with selective page locking in order to reduce file access latency. In addition, based on the mobility of the CPs, the file sets are migrated from home location to the servers of the current location of the CPs with user-transparency in order to reduce network-distance between the clients and data. The internal components of VMDFS are illustrated in Figure 7.

Figure 6. The schematic representation of VMDFS architecture

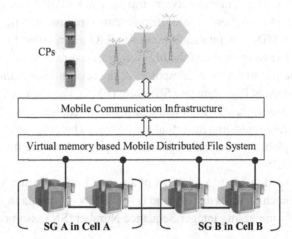

Figure 7. The VMDFS components at servers

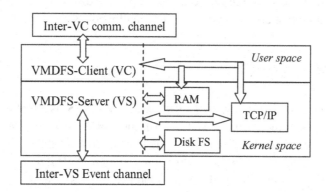

Figure 8. The VMDFS file system structure

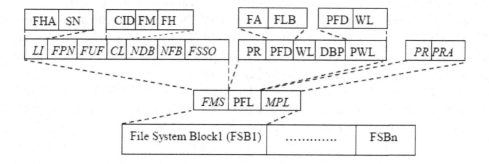

VMDFS: File System Structure and Consistency

The file system of VMDFS uses data-caching model based on page-level transfer (Bagchi, 2007). The advantage of such design is the reduction of network traffic. The VMDFS resides in the virtual memory pages of a server in a SG and is segmented into the metadata structure and the list of data blocks. The file metadata structure of VMDFS maintains file status and IO information for each CP along with the page update information. The components of the file system structure of VMDFS are depicted in Figure 8. At the bottom layer, the file structure is composed of the sequential stream of File System Blocks (FSB). Each FSB is comprised of File Metadata Structure (FMS), Page Frame List (PFL) and Migrated Page List (MPL). The FMS contains the file metadata information, whereas, the PFL contains the information related to page frames residing in virtual memory area holding the data blocks of multimedia files. The MPL holds the globally resolvable addresses of pages those are migrated to another server based on the mobility of a CP.

The List Index (LI) is used to locate a page list of an open media file at a VMDFS server in a SG. The LI of each open file at each server is distinct and is formed by concatenating the File Home Address (FHA) and a monotonically increasing integer Sequence Number (SN) assigned to the open files. The

File Path Name (FPN) gives the complete path and name of an open multimedia file. The File Update Flag (FUF) denotes the consistency states of the file in the file system, whereas, the mobile Client List (CL) denotes the list of CP-profiles accessing a file. The Number of Disk Blocks (NDB) of a file contains the file size as a multiple of page size and the Number of File Blocks (NFB) depicts the number of file blocks present in virtual memory at any time. The File Security and Sharing Option (FSSO) states the file sharing and security parameters as set by the owner of the corresponding file residing in the PML of the owner.

The Page Rank (PR $\geq$ 0) is a monotonically increasing integer associated to each page frame holding the media file data block and is immutable as long as the file blocks are memory resident. The Page Frame Descriptor (PFD) holds the mutable physical address of the page frame containing file data and the other information related to the page frame. The Write Limit (WL) of each page denotes the length of valid data in a frame from the starting address of the corresponding page frame. The Page Write Log (PWL) contains the updated data of a page in a newly attached page frame having null PR and results in the formation of a tree of page frames.

It is to be noted that the page frame in a PWL will have the PR equal to null until the update is merged. Update merging is done by simply readjusting the page frame addresses of the parent PFD and the PFD in PWL. This avoids the memory copy operation and facilitates the roll-back mechanism to recover from the failure. The tree of page frames containing the update log is depicted in Figure 9, where $PR_i < PR_j < ... < PR_n$. The file update mechanism can be simplified further by replacing the entire data blocks of the old media file stored on the disk by the new media file, when the corresponding media file is not in ongoing streaming mode. This is because, in general, a user may not want to update a media file byte-by-byte and rather, would replace the whole file.

The Disk Block Pointer (DBP) of each PFD contains the mutable disk block pointer of the underlying file system for the pages in PFD. Due to the mobility of CP users, the network-distance between a server in SG and a CP may increase. On the event of hand-off, a CP may cross the cell boundary entering in the domain of another SG. In order to reduce the network-cost and data-access latency, VMDFS servers employ inter-SG page migration while maintaining consistency of the data blocks. The MPL holds the PR and Page Remote Address (PRA) of the migrated pages where, PRA is a globally resolvable page address of a migrated page given as $\langle$Remote_Server_Address, LI$\rangle$. The CP accessing a file is denoted by individual CP identification (CID), File Mode (FM) of operations such as, read/write and, File Handle (FH) where, FH is given as $\langle$LI, PR, Offset$\rangle$. Each PFD contains the Frame Address (FA) giving the physical address of a page frame and the Frame Lock Bit (FLB) to control the locking of a

Figure 9. Page-oriented file update tree

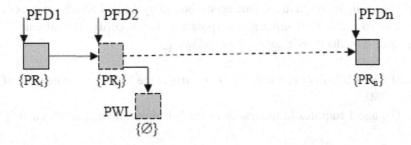

frame in the main memory. The page migration involves the transaction of ⟨FMS, PR, ⟨PFL-PFD, WL⟩, ⟨PWL-PFD, WL⟩⟩ between the source and destination VMDFS servers. The VMDFS incorporates page-based file IO using memory mapping approach. The duplicate data copy is avoided by mapping a set of memory-locked page frames into the address space of VC. The VMDFS employs dynamic page-set replication of the files among the servers of SGs based on the access pattern of the media files and the hand-off of the CPs. A complete file may get replicated dynamically if all the pages of that file are hot, while initiating a hand-off by a CP. Instead of employing directory-level lock granularity, the VMDFS design incorporates file-level lock granularity to maintain consistency. The VMDFS follows the concept of Pipeline RAM (PRAM) consistency model with memory coherence where, the write operations of a mobile client on pages are seen in a pipeline by all the other mobile clients accessing the file (Bagchi, 2007). However, the consistency model of VMDFS becomes simplified in case of PUM, because only the owner of a PML has write privilege on the media files contained within the corresponding PML. The properties of VMDFS model are as followings (Bagchi, 2007):

1. VMDFS servers dynamically construct the mobility graph of the mobile clients,
2. The pages of a media file in VMDFS may be distributed among a set of servers in different SGs,
3. Pages of a media file migrates based on location vector of the mobile clients i.e. CPs, and,
4. A file is replicated by convergent migration of page-set of that file at a server in a SG.

The mobile agents travel between the mobile devices and VMDFS servers enabling mobile devices to remotely execute the actions on PML and returning the results. Hence, establishment of persistent and high-bandwidth mobile network connection between mobile device and the VMDFS servers is not required.

AN INTEGRATED ARCHITECTURE FOR PUM

The integration of Mobile Agent Systems (MAS) and Virtual memory based Mobile Distributed File System creates the architecture suitable to deploy Personalized Ubiquitous Multimedia applications having mobile-client/static-remote-server computing model. The mobile agents support execution of mobile applications in the resource constrained environment (Adelstein, 2005). The mobile agents are integrated with the VC component of the VMDFS architecture establishing integrated system architecture suitable to deploy the PUM applications. The integrated architecture, composed of Agent Execution Engine (AEE) and VMDFS, is shown in Figure 10. The AEE is comprised of agent execution environment (AEX, which is an interpreter), agent security monitor and an inter-agent communication module. The AEX component of AEE interacts with VC to access media files of the users stored in VMDFS. The VC acts as a local media file server to the mobile agents hosted by AEE. There is no direct communication pathway between VS and AEE in order to incorporate system security. The simplified view of the set of actions performed by the mobile agents is as followings:

*   **Step 1.** At the mobile device, a user agent constructs the "task list" composed of selected set of actions on PML.
*   **Step 2.** The agent enquires to the leader of the SG of current cell about current location of the PML.

- **Step 3.** The agent migrates to the VMDFS servers containing the PML, authenticates and performs the operations (indexing, streaming etc.).
- **Step 4.** It returns to the mobile device with the results in the end.

The mobile agents are modeled with Belief, Desire and Intention (BDI model). An agent is comprised of the {mobile code, task list, rule base, PML-Index} representing tasks to be performed, the semantic expressions and the PML-Index representing the name and index of the user uniquely identifying the personalized multimedia library of that user stored in VMDFS. The Belief component of an agent contains the resource configurations (profile) of a CP user. This "profile" information is used by the agents to adapt the media contents according to the resource configurations of the CP device before streaming it to the CP. The schematic view of the mobile agent internals is illustrated in Figure 11.

The user agents are identified by Unique Agent ID (UAD) and one user agent cannot access the PML of another user agent. The UAD of an agent resident in a CP is same as the CP identification (CID) of the corresponding CP. Hence, the access to the PML of different users is authenticated based on UAD. The users can share the contents in PML by granting access rights to others. In this sharing model, fine-grained sharing of the content is possible; where one user may share one particular media file of his/her PML to another user, but not the whole PML. In addition, how many times a shared content can

Figure 10. The integrated architecture for PUM

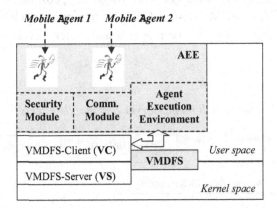

Figure 11. The mobile agent internals

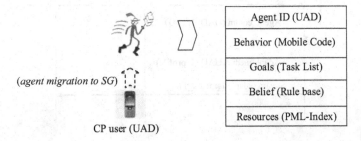

be viewed by others can be restricted by the content owner. The agents of different users can coordinate by communicating among each other using Agent Communication Language (**FIPA ACL**) and can initiate multimedia streaming to the designated CPs. The details of the interaction model between the PUM files server and different mobile agents are illustrated in Figure 12.

The personalized multimedia library contents of different users are stored in SG. On initiating a streaming request of media_1 by CP user having UAD_1 agent-identification, the corresponding agent migrates to the server in SG and adapts or renders media-1 content according to the profile of UAD_1 described in the Belief component of that agent. After adaptation, the agent starts streaming of the media to the designated CP user. It is assumed that UAD_1 is the owner of media_1 and before initiating media file retrieval and adaptation, the agent will perform the necessary security and file-access-right validations. At this point, if another user (UAD_2) requests the same media file (media_1), then agent from this second CP user migrates to the media file server. The access rights are determined through inter-agent communication mechanism. If the agent UAD_1 determines that UAD_2 is a trusted entity according to its Belief, then the second agent gains access to media_1. Next, the second agent (UAD_2) adapts the media_1 according to the profile of second user and starts streaming the adapted media contents.

Advantages

The advantages of this integrated architecture are contributed by the advantages of Mobile Agent Systems (MAS) and VMDFS. The MAS based ubiquitous computing offers a set of performance advantages such as (Kotz, 1999; Adelstein, 2005), saving network bandwidth, cost and supporting disconnected operations. Researchers have designed Mobile-C, which is an interpreted C/C++ language based mobile agent platform enabling the interactions between agents and system-level software modules (Chen,

Figure 12. Interaction model between multimedia server and mobile agents

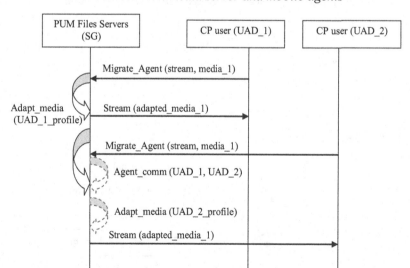

2006). On the other hand, the Virtual memory based Mobile Distributed File System (VMDFS) model establishes a high-performance file system deployed at remote servers residing within the cells of mobile communication infrastructure (Bagchi, 2007). The VMDFS model offers location transparency of the media files, scalability, high-availability of media contents and reduced file access latency (Bagchi, 2007). The combination of MAS and VMDFS establishes a reliable framework to deploy PUM applications supporting disconnected operations eliminating restrictions due to the computing resource constraints of the mobile devices.

FUTURE TRENDS

The present day mobile multimedia systems are primarily designed based on the available mobile communication bandwidth and the available mobile devices. Nowadays, the mobile phones are getting equipped with camera and the users can create the multimedia contents using these camera-phones. The most notable existing mobile multimedia applications are comprised of multimedia email, web browsing and music streaming involving camera-phones. However, the available storage space on the mobile phones and the mobile communication bandwidth are increasing. This is leading to the future generation of mobile multimedia applications. The future generation of mobile multimedia applications would be attractive and high-end such as, 3D games, real-time MP3 music downloads, mobile web-radio and mobile video streaming. Another attractive mobile multimedia application of future generation is DMB (Digital Media Broadcast) or Live-TV on mobile phones. The DMB services are deployed on trial basis in some countries in Europe and China. The DMB system can take two routs of content delivery such as, Satellite transmission (S-DMB) and Terrestrial transmission (T-DMB). The vision of DMB system is to deliver interactive Live-TV in automobiles and mobile phones in future. Apart from the mobile multimedia applications, the supporting technologies would attract research attention in future. The two major research challenges in supporting technologies are associated with high-resolution video coding, which should be efficient for mobile transmission and the delivery of mobile multimedia content to the mobile devices in the adaptive form. The device specific content adaptation should be fast and efficient having an acceptable level of end-user experiences. On the other hand, the transformation of mobile phones into video phones would give the possibility of mobile video telephony in future.

CONCLUSION

Due to the advent of high-end mobile devices equipped with 3G and higher mobile communication standards, the ubiquitous computing is becoming a reality. The mobile devices such as, mobile phones and PDA, are transforming into the mobile multimedia devices having higher computing resources and codec solutions embedded into the devices. In future, the handheld mobile multimedia devices having larger volume of primary as well as secondary storage capacities may act as Computer-Phone capable to consume multimedia data stream. The existing analogue media broadcast systems are moving into the digital media domain. The push-model of media broadcast needs to be changed to the adaptive, flexible and interactive multimedia delivery system. Along with the concept of Universal Multimedia Access (UMA), the ubiquitous multimedia applications are becoming a promising reality. The ubiquitous multimedia applications have the strong market potential. The Personalized Ubiquitous Multimedia (PUM) is a subset of ubiquitous media applications, where users can create, store, manage, stream and share the multimedia contents as a personal library. This chapter illustrates the evolution of ubiquitous multimedia and the Computer-Phone. The concept of PUM is introduced and a framework for designing and deploying the PUM applications is illustrated. The users can create their own multimedia contents from various sources such as, own creation (camcorder, digital camera, voice recorder) and downloaded media contents from the internet. The contents of the personalized multimedia library can be heterogeneous and may have high volume of data. This chapter illustrates that an integrated architecture comprised of mobile agents and Virtual memory based Mobile Distributed File System (VMDFS) creates a suitable platform for deployment of Personalized Ubiquitous Multimedia applications. The proposed framework considers the restrictions of ubiquitous computing paradigm and incorporates the possible solutions to realize the PUM applications. The integrated architecture incorporates the advantages of mobile agent systems and the specialized file system.

REFERENCES

Adelstein, F., Gupta, K. S. S., Richard III, G. G., & Schwiebert, L. (2005). *Fundamentals of Mobile and Pervasive Computing*, Chapter 6, Mc-Graw Hill, ISBN 0-07-141237-9.

Adnan, S., Datuin, J., & Yalamanchili, P. (2000). *A Survey of Mobile Agent Systems*, Project Report, CSE 221, University of California, San Diego.

Barton, J. J., Zhai, S., & Cousins, S. (2006). Mobile Phones Will Become The Primary Personal Computing Devices. *In the Proc. of the Seventh IEEE Workshop on Mobile Computing Systems & Applications (WMCSA'06)*. IEEE CS Press, USA.

Bagchi, S. (2007). VMDFS: Virtual Memory based Mobile Distributed File System. *International Journal of Multimedia and Ubiquitous Engineering, 2*(2), SERSC, South Korea.

Chen, B., Cheng, H., & Palen, J. (2006). Mobile-C: a mobile agent platform for mobile C/C++ agents. *Software – Practice and Experience, 36*, 1711-1733. John Wiley.

Chen, Z., Wenyin, L., Yang, R., Li, M., & Zhang, H. (2001). A Web Media Agent, *In the Proc. of 10th Annual Conference on World Wide Web Applications*, WWW Poster, Hong Kong.

Cui, Y., Xu, D., & Nahrstedt, K. (2001). SMART: A Scalable Middleware solution for Ubiquitous Multimedia Service Delivery. *2001 International Conference on Multimedia and Expo*, IEEE CS Press, Japan.

Davidyuk, O., Riekki, J., Rautio, V., & Sun, J. (2004). Context-aware Middleware for Mobile Multimedia Applications. *In Proc. of 3rd International Conference on Mobile and Ubiquitous Multimedia (MUM '04)*, ACM Press, Vol. 83, USA.

Hartwig, S., Luck, M., Aaltonen, J., Serafat, R., & Theimer, W. (2000). Mobile Multimedia – Challenges and Opportunities. *IEEE Transactions on Consumer Electronics, 46*(4), USA.

Hylton, J., Manheimer, K., & Drake, L. F. (1996). Knowbot programming: System Support for Mobile Agents. *In the Proc. of 5th International Workshop on Object Orientation in Operating Systems (IWOOOS '96)*, Washington, USA.

Johansen, D., & Renesse van, R., & Fred, B. S. (1997). *Operating System Support for Mobile Agents*, Readings in Agents, Morgan Kaufmann Publishers, ISBN 1-55860-495-2, USA.

Kotz, D., & Gray, R. S. (1999). Mobile Agents and the Future of the Internet. *ACM Operating Systems review, 33*(3).

Lemlouma, T., & Layaida, N. (2003). Encoding Multimedia Presentations for User Preferences and Limited Environments. *ICME Proceedings of the 2003 Inernational Conference on Multimedia and Expo, 1*, IEEE CS Press, USA.

Lin, F., Wenyin, L., Chen, Z., Zhang, H., & Long, T. (2001). User Modeling for Efficient Use of Multimedia Files. *In the Proc. of 2nd IEEE Pacific-Rim Conference on Multimedia, LNCS, 2195*. China: Springer-Verlag.

Madhavapeddy, A., & Ludlam, N. (2005). Ubiquitous Computing needs to catch up with Ubiquitous Media. *In the Proc. of PERVASIVE 2005 Workshop (UbiApp)*, Germany.

Pereira, F., & Burnett, I. (2003). Universal Multimedia Experience for Tomorrow. *IEEE Signal Processing Magazine, 20*(2), 2003.

Plagemann, T., Goebel, V., & Vorsen, P. H. (1999). Operating System support for Multimedia Systems, *Computer Communication Journal*, Elsevier Science, Special Issue on IDMS'98.

Steiger, O., Ebrahimi, T., & Sanjuan, D. M. (2003). MPEG-based Personalized Content Delivery. *ICIP proceedings of the 2003 International Conference on Image Processing*. Spain: IEEE CS Press.

Want, R., Pering, T., Danneels, G., Kumar, M., Sundar, M., & Light, J. (2002). The Personal Server: Changing the Way We Think about Ubiquitous Computing. *In Proc. of 4th International Conference on Ubiquitous Computing (UbiComp'02), 2498*. Springer-Verlag LNCS.

Wang, Y., Li, H., & Chen, C. W. (2004). A Novel Video Coding Scheme for Mobile Devices, *In Proc. of 3rd International Conference on Mobile and Ubiquitous Multimedia (MUM '04), 83*. USA: ACM Press.

Wenyin, L., Chen, Z., Lin, F., Yang, R., Li, M., & Zhang, H. (2001). Ubiquitous Media Agents for Managing Personal Multimedia Files. *In the Proc. of 9th ACM International Conference on Multimedia*. Canada: ACM DL.

Xu, D., Wichadakul, D., & Nahrstedt, K. (2000). Resource-Aware Configuration of Ubiquitous Multimedia Services, *In proc. of 2000 IEEE International Conference on Multimedia and Expo*, Vol. 2, USA.

Yu, H., Zhang, S., Yang, N., Ding, H., & Wang, X. (2003). Intelligent Agent-Based Distributed Heterogeneous Database System. *In the Proc. of 2nd International Conference on Machine Learning and Cybernetics*. China: IEEE CS Press.

Chapter XIII
Personalisation in Highly Dynamic Grid Services Environment

Edgar Jembere
University of Zululand, South Africa

Matthew O. Adigun
University of Zululand, South Africa

Sibusiso S. Xulu
University of Zululand, South Africa

ABSTRACT

Human Computer Interaction (HCI) challenges in highly dynamic computing environments can be solved by tailoring the access and use of services to user preferences. In this era of emerging standards for open and collaborative computing environments, the major challenge that is being addressed in this chapter is how personalisation information can be managed in order to support cross-service personalisation. The authors' investigation of state of the art work in personalisation and context-aware computing found that user preferences are assumed to be static across different context descriptions whilst in reality some user preferences are transient and vary with changes in context. Further more, the assumed preference models do not give an intuitive interpretation of a preference and lack user expressiveness. This chapter presents a user preference model for dynamic computing environments, based on an intuitive quantitative preference measure and a strict partial order preference representation, to address these issues. The authors present an approach for mining context-based user preferences and its evaluation in a synthetic m-commerce environment. This chapter also shows how the data needed for mining context-based preferences is gathered and managed in a Grid infrastructure for mobile devices.

INTRODUCTION

Given the accelerating pace of globalisation, liberalisation of market places, and the emergence of global e-market places, traditional boundaries no longer separate the vendor from the purchaser and competition has intensified. This makes it difficult for Small, Medium and Micro Enterprises (SMME) to survive competition from other well resourced enterprises, which can easily integrate state of the art IT solution in to their business operations. Neither adoption of enterprise-wide applications nor devising an enterprise-wide IT strategy has occurred for SMMEs in the world over. To remain in business, SMMEs must be able to identify the ICT infrastructures required to improve performance and global competitiveness. Unfortunately, most SMMEs lack the capacity to own ICT infrastructure and they are more conservative to adopt ICT infrastructure before they can be sure of the return on such investments.

Thus in summary, SMME ICT solution should be affordable, easy to use, bring fast Return On Investment (ROI), and require a short implementation cycle whilst giving them a competitive edge at minimum cost. Our core research niche area is aimed at providing just that through the Grid Utility Infrastructure for SMME Enabling Technologies (GUISET) (Migiro & Adigun, 2005), which employs a service oriented on-demand computing paradigm based on the utility Grid technology. In this technology SMMEs need not own the infrastructure but they can pay for what they use when they use it.

The emergence of the mobile telephony technology, with its affordability and ability to transfer data wirelessly is one of the key SMME enabling technologies that the GUISET infrastructure adopts to limit the hardware acquisition problem. Paradoxically, mobile computing presents both a dramatic step forward and a significant step backward from an information or service access standpoint. Mobile devices are hardly ideal information or services access devices owing to some constraints brought about by mobility. Context-awareness and personalisation have been adopted over the past decade as the solution to make mobile devices better computing devices. Context awareness involves the use of the context information to provide "relevant information and/or services to the user, where relevance depends on the user's task" (Dey & Abowd, 2000). Personalisation in our case involves tailoring the access and use of the web or grid services to user preferences. Unfortunately, user preferences in dynamic computing environments are heavily dependent on the dynamic user, environmental and application context (Gorgoglione et al, 2006). The major challenge to achieving advanced personalisation in this case is how we can make use of contextual information and exploit the change of context in the personalisation process, which most of the work on personalisation do not address. Attempts to address this problem from context-aware computing rather than from personalisation perspective, have led to the current mix-up between context and personalisation. Personalisation in mobile computing should contextually adapt content or services in order to enhance the quality of the user's interaction with the applications.

Traditionally, user preferences are captured in to the system explicitly from the users. However, given the fact that in dynamic computing environments, user preferences depend on the user, environment and application context, it will be a very cumbersome exercise for users to explicitly give their preferences for each and every context. Data mining is widely seen as the solution to this challenge. Over the past decade a lot of work has been done in the use of data mining techniques for automatically extracting user preferences from user session data. However, the mined user preferences are only as accurate as the preference model on ground. Data mining based preference models lack preference measures that give an intuitive measure and interpretation of a preference (Jung et al, 2005). Most user preference measures use scores or just distinguish liked and disliked items (Holland et al, 2003). Furthermore, most of the existing preferences models are found wanting when it comes to representing real user preferences because they lack user expressiveness, "I prefer A to B" semantics (Kiessling, 2002).

Despite the wide spread contribution by researchers towards development of infrastructures to support context-awareness and personalisation, context-aware and personalised applications are still not popular in the public domain. One of the key issues that have not been given much attention in this arena is the issue of management of the information that is needed to support the intelligence required for realisation of context-awareness and personalisation. The problem becomes more pronounced in grid environments where we have dynamic federation of service in an open computing environment. In this case sharing of personalisation information between different services (Cross-service personalisation) becomes a key requirement (Niederee et al, 2004). The major challenge is how personalisation information can be managed in such collaborative and open computing environment to support cross-service personalisation.

It is against this background that, in this chapter we are going to share our experiences in addressing the following issues in Grid Infrastructures for Mobile Devices:

1. Finding ways of representing user preferences that give *an intuitive interpretation of a preference* and *user expressiveness* to enhance advanced personalisation in the provision of m-Services,
2. Mining of context-based user preferences from user session data,
3. Representing user profiles as an integral part of advanced personalisation in the provision and access m-Service in collaborative Grid infrastructures for mobile devices, and
4. Information management for supporting mining of context-based user preferences and advanced personalisation for open and collaborative computing environments.

Thus the main objective of this chapter is to show how advanced personalisation, based on intuitive interpretation and representation of preferences, can be achieved in highly dynamic and open computing environments. The focus addresses the use of some data mining techniques to acquire context-based user preferences to be used in the personalisation process.

BACKGROUND

Classical recommender systems use historical data on user preferences to predict items the user might be interested in. The assumption is that user preferences are already captured into the system. However, in highly dynamic computing environments, getting user preferences is not an easy task. User preferences may have to be learned from the user session data.

Approaches for automatically learning user preferences from user session data can broadly be categorised as memory based, if they operate over the entire data to make predictions, and as model based if they use the historical data to build a model which will then be used for predictions (Zhang et al, 2002).

Automatically analysing user preference models, depending on how they represent preferences, can also be classified into the following three classes: Vector similarity, Probability, and Association rule based preference models (Jung et al, 2005). Vector similarity-based preference models use similarity between users and/or items to predict the active user's (the user for whom preference predictions are to be made) preferences.

Vector similarity based preference models can be broadly categorised into two groups and these are: Collaborative Filtering and Content-Based Filtering. Collaborative filtering refers to a set of methods that uses user prior preferences to predict new ones based on the preference similarities among users. A typical collaborative filtering algorithm has two stages: (i) find similarities between the active user and the users in the database, (ii) use the similarities found in (i) to predict the preferences of the active user. In content-based filtering each active user is assumed to operate independently. The user preference on an item is determined by the similarity between the contents/attributes of the items the user has selected before and the target items. As can be deduced from the definitions above, when preferences are represented as vector similarities, it is hard to get the intuitive interpretation about how much a user dislikes or likes an item and which items are preferred more than others.

Probability-based preference models determine the probability that a user selects an item from the historical user data and use this probability to predict which items users are likely to select. The problem with probability based approaches is that when preferences are represented as probability that a user selects an item, a preferred item with low frequency of selection or not so preferred items with high frequency of selection, is not measured correctly.

Association Rule-based preference models generate user preferences through scanning the database for some association rules that can be used to generate user preferences. These association rules can be between users and or between items. The concept of an association is different from that of a preference in that association deals with relations (relation in terms of occurring together) between item sets or relations between users rather than the intuitive interpretation of a given user's preference on an item. Apart from the lack of intuitiveness in the preference measure in association rule based preference models, the rules discovered can be spurious and irrelevant (Adomavicius and Tuzhlin, 2001) and one of the major problems which arises is how can these rules be validated without human intervention.

Against this background, researchers from both mathematics and computer science (e.g. Jung et al, 2005; Kiessling, 2002; Kiewera, 2005) have been working towards developing intuitive preference models. Our research work takes inspiration for user preference modelling from two frameworks: the Strict Partial Order preferences framework (Kiessling, 2002) and the feature preferences framework (Jung et al; 2002, 2005). The main weakness of the state of the art personalisation techniques for personalised web services is the usage of preference models with limited expressiveness. In a bid to address this problem, a very expressive and mathematically well founded framework for preferences was introduced in (Kiessling, 2002). In this framework, customer preferences are modelled as strict partial orders with "I prefer A to B" semantics. A preference P is defined as a strict partial order $P = (A, <p)$, where $A = (A_1, A_2, ...,A_k)$ denotes a set of attributes with corresponding domains (A_i). The domain of A is defined as the Cartesian product of the $dom(A_i)$, $preference(<p) \subseteq dom(A) \times dom(A)$ and $x <p y$ is interpreted "y is preferred to x".

A set of intuitive preference constructors for base preferences is defined. The constructors for base preferences on categorical domains are *POS(A, POS-set)*, *NEG(A, NEG-set)*, *POS/NEG(A, POS-set; NEG-set)*, *POS/POS(A, POS1-set; POS2-set)* and *EXP(A, E-graph)*. The *POS-set* $\subseteq dom(A)$ of a POS preference defines a set of items that are better than all other items of *dom(A)*. Analogously, the *NEG-set* of a NEG preference defines a set of items that are worse than all the other items in *dom(A)*, i.e. any other items which are not in the NEG-set are preferred to any of the items in the *NEG-set*. The *POS/NEG* preference is a combination of the previous preferences, where items in the *POS-set* are preferred to all the other items, items in the *NEG-set* are the least preferred and any other items neither in the *POS-set* nor the *NEG-set* are preferred to the items in the *NEG-set* and less preferred to the items in the *POS-set*. In *POS/POS* preference an optimal set of items (*POS1-set*) and an alternative set (*POS2-set*) can be specified. The items in *POS1-set* are the most preferred, followed by the items in the *POS2-set*.

All the items not in the *POS1-set* and *POS2-set* are less preferred. In an Explicit-graph (*E-graph*) of an EXPLICIT preference a user can specify any better-than relationships. An E-graph is a directed "better than" acyclic graph. All items in an acyclic graph are better than all other items in *dom(A)*.

For numerical domains, the preference constructors include *AROUND(A, z), BETWEEN(A, [low, up]), LOWEST(A)* and *HIGHEST(A)*. In an AROUND preference the desired value is *z*, but if it is not available values with nearest distance apart from *z* are best alternatives. For a BETWEEN preference values within [*low, up*] interval are optimal. For LOWEST (HIGHEST) preferences lower (higher) values are better.

The actual preferences will be predicted from the implicit preferences hidden in the user session data. To get these Holland et al (2003), building up from the strict partial order framework, introduced the concept of data driven preferences denoted by $P_D = (A, <_{PD})$

- For a categorical domain, *dom(A)*, a data-driven preference $P_D = (A, <_{PD})$ is defined as: $x <_{PD} y$ iff $freq_A(x) < freq_A(y)$ and

- For a numerical domain, *dom(A)*, a data driven preference $P_D = (A, <_{PD})$ is defined as $x <_{PD} y$ iff $\exists \varepsilon > 0$: $freq([x - \varepsilon, x + \varepsilon]) < freq([y - \varepsilon, y + \varepsilon])$

where $freq_A(x)$ is the frequency of selection of item *x* in domain *A*. Thus frequency of item selections in the user session is being used as a preference measure.

Frequency of selection, just like probability of selection, does not give an intuitive measure of preferences. The selection of an item by a given user is determined mainly by two factors: the user's preference on the item and the accessibility of the item (Jung et al, 2002). Although a user likes an item, the selection frequency can be low if the item is rarely distributed in that domain. Although a user does not like an item, the selection frequency can be high if the item appears very frequently in that domain. Thus frequencies can not be used as a preference measure.

To counter this problem our work adapts the idea proposed by Jung et al (2002, 2005). The work in (Jung et al, 2002) defines a preference as the concept to make a relationship between a person and a target item which contains several kinds of attributes (features). From this point of view a preference of an item is indirectly related to the preferences of the attributes contained by the item. This implies that the preference of an item can be represented by a combination of the preferences of the features of the same item. A preference is then mathematically represented as a function of item *x* and the user profile *G*. The user profile will be approximated by the User History *U*, i.e

$$Pref_A(X) = f(x, G) \approx f(x, U) \tag{1}$$

The user history is represented by a set of selected items $U = (x_1, x_2, x_3, x_4, ..., x_n)$. Each item has a set of several attributes denoted by *w*. Item *x* is then represented as a set of features, $x = (w_1, w_2, w_3, ..., w_m)$. The User Profile *G* is defined by the preference of each feature *w*, i.e. $G = \{pref_A(w_1), pref_A(w_2), pref_A(w_3), ..., pref(w_m)\}$.

The feature preference $Pref_A(w)$ is computed from the user history. Since the user profile *G* and the item *x* can be represented by common attributes, w_i's, they can be compared through these attributes. As a consequence, a preference of an item *x* is then represented as follows:

$$Pref_A(x) = \frac{1}{M(x)} \sum_{w \in x} Pref_A(w_i) \tag{2}$$

where *M(x)* is a normalisation term which is defined as the number of features in item x. Mutual information is used as a measure of a feature preference, $\text{Pref}_A(w) = I_A(X(w), U)$, where $X(w) = \{x \mid w \in x\}$, $I_A(X(w), U) \ln\{P_A(X(w); U/P_A(X(w))\}$. $P_A(X(w); U)$ is the feature selection probability given the user history and $P_A(X(w))$ is the unconditional feature probability, which gives a measure of the feature's accessibility.

CONTEXT-AWARENESS AND PERSONALISATION

Exploitation of context data in the personalisation process requires that these two concepts be well defined and distinguished from each other. This is because the bulk of the work in context-aware computing consider personalisation information as part of context information. This has led to a shift of focus in context-aware computing from the traditional object, the user, to the context around him (Jameson 2001). Though most people tacitly understand what context is, they find it hard to explain it and this makes it hard for application developers to determine what is context to the applications they are developing. This is because context is in itself contextual. In this section we give our working definitions of context and personalisation that will show how context can be distinguished from personalisation information. We will start by tracking the history of these two concepts and then give our criteria for distinguishing them.

Most of the early work on context-aware computing define context by giving an enumeration of examples or by choosing synonyms for context (Dey and Abowd, 2000). This, coupled with the fact that it was not clear whether context in relation to computing should refer to the user or application context, made it extremely difficult to apply context in practice. The lack of standardisation of the techniques which are emanating from the research in context-aware computing further complicates this challenge. Advances in the work on context-aware computing have led to more general definitions of context that include either, both the user and the application context, or the context of the interaction between the user and the computing environment. Out of this development came the most widely accepted definition of context given by Dey & Abowd (2000). They define context as:

any information that can be used to characterise the situation of an entity. An entity can be a person, an object or a place that is considered relevant in the interaction between an application and the user including the user and the application themselves (Dey & Abowd, 2000).

The above definition is more general and considers both the application and the user context. In this case the user, his/her profile, interests, behaviour and preferences become context to the application (or the interaction between the user and the computing environment). According to this definition an application is said to be context-aware if, it uses context, as defined above, to provide relevant information and/or services to the user ,where relevance depend on the user's task. This definition of context includes personalisation information as context information. This is evidenced by the fact that research efforts based on this definition e.g. (Riva, 2004), take user preferences, interests, user profile as context information. According to the above definition personalisation is taken as a subset of context-awareness.

The history of personalisation can be tracked as far back as the early user adaptive interfaces, personal assistants or agents, and adaptive information retrieval (Goker and Myrhaug, 2002). Most approaches originated from desktop computing with user's needs, preferences and expertise. Challenges to the field of HCI in mobile computing bring personalisation to a sharper focus, with much more emphasis on the user's preferences and their dependence on the dynamic user context. Ideally, for m-services, personalisation is supposed to be context-based and in principle it is regarded as system driven (Yang et al, 2006). Not much is available in literature on personalisation of m-services. One work closer to this goal is the work by Jostard (2006), but their view of personalisation does not consider the dynamic nature of user preferences in mobile computing environments and the need for semi-automation of the personalisation process. One of the major challenges for personalisation in dynamic computing environments is that the personalisation information relevant to the current context is not readily available. That is, personalisation in such environments should support semi-automatic gathering and management of the data needed for personalisation. Given this premise, the definition of personalisation in web services given by Bonett (2001) is closer to a practical definition personalisation in dynamic computing environments. Bonett defines personalisation of web services as; *"the process of gathering user information during interaction with the user, which is then used to deliver appropriate content and services tailor made to the user's needs and preferences"*.

From this perspective, we define personalisation information as; *any information that can be used to tailor or adapt the interaction of a user with a system or service to the needs and preferences of the user or user group.* And hence we define personalisation in m-services; as *the process of gathering personalisation information and the subsequent use of the gathered information to tailor/adapt the interaction of a user with a system or service to the needs and preferences of a specific user or user group.* According to this definition, personalisation refers to all processes that involve the gathering of data specific to a given user or user group and the subsequent tailoring of the interaction (based on this data or on the inferences drawn from this data) between the user and the computing environment to the user.

Our approach to distinguishing context-awareness from personalisation considers these concepts from the perspective of developing non-personalised context-aware services or applications. From this point of view and the definition of context given by (Dey and Abowd, 2000), we define context as *any information that can be used to characterise the situation of an entity that is not specific to the user or a user group. An entity is a person, place, or object that is considered important to the interaction between a user and an application, including the user and the application themselves.* This definition implies that when the interaction of the user and the computing environment is subjected to a certain context, the system must adapt itself in the same way for different users. If it adapts differently, it therefore means that the environment has been subjected to some personalisation some how. The distinction of context-awareness and personalisation reached at in this section formed the bases for the design for user preference mining framework for the GUISET architecture. It is also key to how context and personalisation information will be managed in the GUISET architecture.

THE GUISET ARCHITECTURE: PERSONALISATION ISSUES

The GUISET Architecture (Figure 1) consists of three layers: the resource layer, the middleware layer and the multimodal interface layer. The resource layer is a pool of all resources that are available for SMMEs ranching from computational resources, through knowledge resources to software and data services. All these resources are accessed as services through the utility broker in the middleware layer. The middleware layer handles all the resource and service brokering activities. The multimodal

Figure 1. The GUISET architecture (adapted from Migiro & Adigun, 2005)

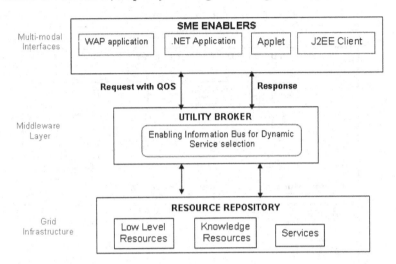

interface layer enables the users to access the GUISET infrastructure resources and services using the devices they have at hand.

In a bid to enable the GUISET architecture to handle context-awareness and personalisation, we developed the User Preference Centred Architecture for Mobile Services (UPCAMS) aimed at providing an infrastructure to support mining of context-based user preferences in Grid Infrastructures for Mobile Devices. The UPCAMS builds on the fact that in collaborative grid environments user preference can not only be mined from data produced through interaction with the applications/services, but they can also be mined from an overwhelming amount of data produced by grid operations to facilitate intelligent selection and composition of grid services and resources. This implies user preference mining and use can be done at two levels in the GUISET architecture and these are: within the services that are accessible as grid services (the Grid Services Layer) and in the grid middleware layer (Grid Middleware layer). The UPCAMS architecture is shown in Figure 2. Apart from handling context-based user preference mining, the UPCAMS also provides some components for managing the data to be used in the preference mining process. This data include the abstracted user context data and user session data. UPCAMS, as a technology meant to work in a collaborative environment, it also provides some means for managing and sharing of user preference profiles among similar application/services running on the same grid. In the next four (4) sections of this chapter, we are going to discuss how user preference modelling, user preference mining, and information management are handled in UPCAMS.

PREFERENCE MODELLING

Preferences are comparative in nature and are considered on a set of given options. It should be possible to identify preferences even amongst disliked items. Current user preference models do not capture this and they are thus said to lack user expressiveness. In a real life situation, a user is able to make prefer-

Figure 2. The UPCAMS infrastructure

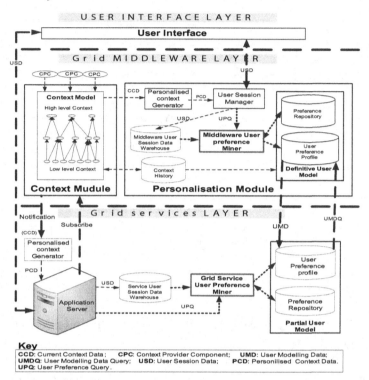

ence relationships even amongst a set of disliked items. That is, if a set of items available contains three disliked, items **a, b** and **c**, a user is still able to make a preference relationship on these items (e.g. I prefer **b** to **a** and **c**) even though he or she does not like any of them. So the challenge is to be able to represent these real life cases. To address this challenge, the strict partial order preference model is adopted and hence we define a user ***preference*** as a *strict partial order relation on a set of given items.*

A user prefers one item to the other because he or she likes it more than the other. In instances where the user explicitly gives his/her preferences, such preferences can be directly modelled by a qualitative modelling framework such as the Strict Partial order framework presented in (Kiessling, 2000). This cannot be directly done when preferences are being implicitly learnt from user session data without a quantitative measure of how much a user likes an item. So the challenge here is to define a measure of the degree to which a user likes an item. The most popularly used preference measures: *scores* and *frequencies* (or *probability*) of selection do not give an intuitive measure of a preference. Against this background, the discussion that follows illustrates how frequency (or probability) of selection fails to give an intuitive preference measure and subsequently define an intuitive preference measure.

Consider a universal set, ξ of all item occurrences for a given user in a given domain; the set, U of items selections (viewings) by the same user in the same domain; and occurrence sets X_1, X_2, X_3 and X_4, of items x_1, x_2, x_3 and x_4 in the universal set respectively. Refer to Figure 3.

Figure 3 depicts that the viewings (selections) of x_1 in the user session, $(X_1 \cap U)$ is less than that of x_2 in the user session, $(X_2 \cap U)$. Thus, if frequency (or probability) of selection is used as a preference measure on items x_1 and x_2, item x_2 will be taken as more preferred to item x_1. However, relative to the occurrence of the items x_1 and x_2 in the universal set, it can be deduced that x_1 was selected by the user almost half of the times it occurred and X_2 was selected far less than a third of the time it occurred. This implies that item x_1 is preferred to item x_2. It should be noted that x_1 was selected less often than x_2 because it is rarely distributed (not easily accessible) in the universal set. It is obvious that x_3 is the most preferred item since it was selected every time it was accessible and x_4 is the least preferred since in spite of its high occurrence the user never selects it.

From the foregoing discussion and the illustration in Figure 3, it is clear that an intuitive measure of a preference on a given set of items, in a given domain should consider the probability of the item being selected relative to the accessibility of the items in question (Jung et al, 2002, 2005). i.e.

$$pref(x) = \left(\frac{P(x;U)}{P(x)} \right) \qquad (3)$$

where $P(x;U)$ is the probability of item x being selected and $P(x)$ is the accessibility probability of item x. A fair preference measure on an item is calculated from the preferences of the item's attributes (Jung et al, 2002, Kiessling, 2002, Holland et al, 2003). The challenges that now arise are: (1) how can the item attribute value preferences be aggregated to deduce the user's preference on an item and (2) how the accessibility probability of an attribute value can be calculated. For the aggregation of the attribute value preferences, we assume equal weights on the item's preference and use Equation 2 to calculate the item preferences. To address the later challenge we use the Closed World Assumption (CWA) (Kiessiling, 2002). The Closed World Assumption (CWA) states that *the user knows of all possible values of all the choices that he or she can make.* In domains where the CWA holds, the accessibility probability of a feature, w, to a given user is given by the following equation:

$$P_A(x(w)) = \frac{n(A(w))}{n(A)} \qquad (4)$$

where $n(A(w))$ is the total number of items with feature w in domain A, and $n(A)$ is the total number of items in domain A. Equation 4 says the accessibility of a feature in the product catalogue or service

Figure 3. Item accessibility, probability of selection, and preferences (adapted from Jung et al, 2005)

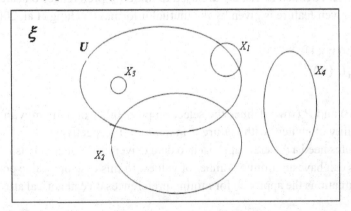

registry can be generalised to all the users since they are all aware of its existence. In domains where the CWA can not be assumed, the accessibility of an item to a given user is now dependent on whether the user is aware of its existence or not. In that case the accessibility of an item, and hence its features, differ for different users. Equation 5, below , estimates the accessibility probability of a feature, *w*, to a given user in domains where the Closed World Assumption does not hold.

$$P_A(x(w)) = \frac{freq_{A,R}(x(w);U)}{freq_{A,R}(U)} \tag{5}$$

where $freq_{A,R}(x(w); U)$ is the frequency of hits/logs/recommendations of items with feature *w* in domain *A* for a given user, *U*, and $freq_{A,R}(U)$ is the total number of item hits for a given user, *U*, in domain *A*.

Another important concept this work defines is the concept of a Strong Negative preference. An item is said to be a Strong Negative preference if the user is aware of its existence but he or she never selects it. In Table 1 we give definitions and notation of the parameters to be used in subsequent sections to get the preference measures to be used in this study.

USER PREFERENCE MINING

The actual user preferences will be predicted from implicit preferences hidden in the user session data. Data mining techniques will be used to extract the preferences from the user session data. The mining of the user preferences will involve three major stages. These are:

1. *Mining* of attribute value preferences from the user session data;
2. *Matching* items' features and the user's feature preferences to compute the user's preferences on an item, and
3. *Representation* of preferences as Strict Partial Order relations.

Mining of Attribute Value Preferences

Mining of attribute value preferences is divided in to two components, which are mining of attribute value preferences on numerical attributes and mining of attribute value preferences on categorical attributes. The parameters defined in Table 1 are used to mine for preferences on categorical attributes. The preference on a given feature is given by the mutual information (Jung et al, 2002, 2005).

$$pref_A(w) = \ln\left(\frac{P_A(x(w); U)}{P_A(x(w))}\right) \tag{6}$$

where the $P_A(x(w), U)$ and $P_A(x(w))$ defines the selection probability of an item with feature *w* and the accessibility probability of an item with feature *w* in *domain A* respectively.

Numerical attributes need a different approach to data driven preferences. This is because a domain for numerical values can have an infinite number of values. In this case one value occurs once or just a few times. In such situations the approach for mining preferences on categorical attributes is not appli-

Table 1. Notation and definitions: Observed parameter

Notation	Definition
$n(A(w))$	Number of items with feature w in domain A.
$n(A)$	Number of all items in domain A.
$freq_{A,R}(x,U)$	The frequency item x was recommended to a given user in domain A including cases were the user did not select it (i.e. number of hits on item x in domain A).
$freq_{A,S}(x,U)$	The frequency item x was selected by the user in domain A.
$freq_{A,R}(U)$	Total number of item recommendations to a given user in domain A.
$freq_{A,R}(x(w);U)$	Frequency of recommendation of items with feature w to a given user in domain A.
$freq_{A,S}(x(w);U)$	Frequency of selection of items with feature w by a given user in domain A.
$freq_{A,S}(U)$	Total number of item selections by a given user in domain A.
$P_A(x(w))$	$n(A(w))/n(A)$, measures accessibility probability of feature w in domain A, where the CWA can be assumed OR $freq_{A,R}(x(w);U)/freq_{A,R}(U)\sqrt{}$, measures the accessibility probability of a feature w in domain A, where the CWA can not be assumed
$P_A(x(w),U)$	$freq_{A,S}(x(w);U)/freq_{A,S}(U)$, measures the probability that a given user selects an item with feature w in domain A.
$pref_A(w)$	$\ln\left(\dfrac{P_A(x(w);\ U)}{P_A(x(w))}\right)$, measures the preference of feature w.
$pref_A(x)$	$\dfrac{1}{M(x)}\displaystyle\sum_{w_i \in x} pref_A(w_i)$, measures the user's preference on item x.

cable, since it assumes that attribute values are recurring. The distribution of continuous numeric values defines a probability density function $f(x)$. We can take advantage of this probability density function to descritise the data. The major challenge here is that the density function is not known a priori and, therefore, it has to be estimated. We use histograms to estimate the underlying density function. The distribution of the values in the items database within the estimated density function is used to estimate the accessibility of the attribute values. The selection probability will be estimated based on how attribute values in the log relation data are distributed within the estimated density function.

Mining Item Preferences

Item preferences are obtained by matching the items' features and the user's attribute value preferences (both for attributes in categorical and numerical domains) using Equation 2. Using the possible values of the item preference values as will be calculated from Equation 2, we define three classes of preferences on a bipolar preference scale as follows:

- An item x is a Strong Negative (STRONG_NEG) preference in domain A iff $freq_{A,R}(x, U) > freq_{A,R}(threshold)$ and $freq_{A,S}(x;U) = 0$
- An item x is a Soft-Negative (SOFT_NEG) preference in a given domain if $pref_A(x) < 0$.
- Item x is a Positive (POS) preference in domain A only if $pref_A(x) \geq 0$

where $freq_A(threshold)$ is threshold frequency item x must have been made available to the user for selection in $dom(A)$ for it to be considered to have been recommended sufficiently enough for the user to be aware of it. The pivot point of our bipolar preference scale is zero. Items with preference values less than zero represent the disliked items and those with preference values greater than or equal to zero represent the liked items. Bipolar preference scales are known for their effectiveness in reducing the number of false positive recommendations (Sicilia and Garcia, 2004). This is also very import in preference modelling since it allows representation of negatively preferred items as strict partial order relations.

Mining Strict Partial Order (SPO) Preferences (Preference Representation)

To represent the preference as strict partial orders we used the concept of Data Driven preferences, denoted by $P_D = (A, \prec_{PD})$ (Holland et al, 2003) (See Section 2). Using $pref_A(x)$ as a measure of a preference, we define a data driven preference on an item as follows:

- For $\forall x, y \in dom(A)$, a data-driven preference $P_D = (A, \prec_{PD})$ is defined as: $x, \prec_{PD} y$ iff $pref_A(x) < pref_A(y)$

The algorithm for our user preference mining framework is shown in the activity diagram in Figure 4.

Using our definition of a Data Driven preference and the definition of the preference classes we discussed in the previous subsection, some strict partial order preference representations shown in Figure 4 were defined. EXPLICIT preferences are represented in the form of a Directed Acyclic Graph (DAG), with the items in the DAG being more preferred to all the other items.

Our Preference Mining Algorithm

Our user preference mining algorithm consists of four parts namely: (i) Mining of item attribute value preferences; (ii) Matching items' features and the user's feature preferences to compute the user's preferences on an item; (iii) Mining of SPO categorical preferences, and (iv) Mining of explicit preferences within preference categories. This sub-section discusses the sub-algorithms involved in each of the aforementioned components of our preference mining algorithm.

The algorithm for mining attribute value preferences takes the userID, CID and the Domain of the items whose preference are to be mined as input. The user input is first used to compute the selection

Figure 4. Strict Partial order preference representation

1. There is a data-driven POS preference, iff $\forall x \in POS-set$, $\forall y \notin POS-set : y \prec_{PD} x$.
2. There is a data-driven STRONG_NEG preference, iff $\forall w \in STRONG\_NEG-set$, $\forall y \notin STRONG\_NEG-set$:
   $w \prec_{PD} y$.
3. There is a data-driven SOFT_NEG preference, iff
   $\forall x \in SOFT\_NEG-set$, $\forall w \in STRONG\_NEG-set$ $\forall z \notin (SOFT\_NEG-set \cup STRONG\_NEG-set) : x \prec_{PD} z$,
   $w \prec_{PD} x$.
4. There is a data-driven POS/POS preference, iff $\forall x \in POS1-set$, $\forall y \in POS2-set$, $\forall z \notin (POS1-set \cup POS2-set) : y \prec_{PD} x$, $z \prec_{PD} y$.
5. There is a data-driven SOFT_NEG/SOFT_NEG preference, iff $\forall x \in SOFT\_NEG1-set$,
   $\forall y \in SOFT\_NEG2-set$, $\forall w \in STRONG\_NEG-set$, $\forall z \notin (SOFT\_NEG1 \cup SOFT\_NEG2-set \cup STRONG\_NEG-set)$:
   $y \prec_{PD} x$, $x \prec_{PD} z$, $w \prec_{PD} y$.
6. There is a data-driven POS/SOFT_NEG preference, iff $\forall x \in POS-set$, $\forall y \in SOFT\_NEG-set$,
   $\forall w \in STRONG\_NEG-set$, $\forall z \notin (POS-set \cup SOFT\_NEG-set \cup STRONG\_NEG-set) : z \prec_{PD} x, y \prec_{PD} z, w \prec_{PD} y$.
7. There is a data-driven EXPLICIT_SOFT_NEG preference, iff $\forall y_1 \in CATEGORY_{SN}1-set$, $\forall y_2 \in CATEGORY_{SN}2-set \cdots \forall y_m \in CATEGORY_{SN}M-set$, $\forall w \in STRONG\_NEG-set : y_2 \prec_{PD} y_1, y_3 \prec_{PD} y_2 \cdots y_m \prec_{PD} y_{m-1}$ and $w \prec_{PD} y_m$.
8. There is a data-driven EXPLICIT_POS preference, iff $\forall x_1 \in CATEGORY_p1-set$, $\forall x_2 \in CATEGORY_p2-set \cdots \forall x_n \in CATEGORY_p n-set$, $\forall w \in STRONG\_NEG-set : y_2 \prec_{PD} y_1, y_3 \prec_{PD} y_2 \cdots y_m \prec_{PD} y_{m-1}$ and $w \prec_{PD} y_m$.
9. There is a data-driven POS/EXPLICIT_SOFT_NEG preference, iff $\forall x \in POS-set$, $\forall y_1 \in CATEGORY 1-set$, $\forall y_2 \in CATEGORY 2-set \cdots \forall y_n \in CATEGORYN-set$, $\forall w \in STRONG\_NEG-set : y_1 \prec_{PD} x, y_2 \prec_{PD} y_1, y_3 \prec_{PD} y_2 \cdots y_n \prec_{PD} y_{n-1}$, and $w \prec_{PD} y_n$.
10. There is a data-driven EXPLICITPOS/SOFT_NEG preference, iff $\forall y_1 \in CATEGORY 1-set$, $\forall y_2 \in CATEGORY 2-set \cdots \forall y_n \in CATEGORYN-set$, $\forall x \in POS-set$, $\forall w \in STRONG\_NEG-set : y_2 \prec_{PD} y_1, y_3 \prec_{PD} y_2 \cdots y_n \prec_{PD} y_{n-1}, x \prec_{PD} y_n$ and $w \prec_{PD} x$.
11. There is a data-driven EXPLICIT_POS/EXPLICIT_SOFT_NEG preference, iff $\forall x_1 \in CATEGORY_p1-set$, $\forall x_2 \in CATEGORY_p2-set \cdots \forall x_n \in CATEGORY_p n-set$, $\forall y_1 \in CATEGORY_{SN}1-set$, $\forall y_2 \in CATEGORY_{SN}2-set \cdots \forall y_m \in CATEGORY_{SN}m-set$, $\forall w \in STRONG\_NEG-set : x_2 \prec_{PD} x_1, x_3 \prec_{PD} x_2 \cdots x_n \prec_{PD} x_{n-1}, y_1 \prec_{PD} x_n, y_2 \prec_{PD} y_1, y_3 \prec_{PD} y_2 \cdots y_m \prec_{PD} y_{m-1}$ and $w \prec_{PD} y_m$.
12. Let $\prec_E$ a strict partial order on E represented by a DAG. A data-driven EXPLICIT preference holds, iff
    - $\forall x, y \in E$ with $x \prec_E y, x \prec_{PD} y$.
    - $\forall u \in E, \forall v \notin E : v \prec_{PD} u$

and accessibility probabilities for all item features in that Domain, both in discrete and continuous domains. These probabilities are then used to compute the user's preferences on each of the attribute values (features). This algorithm returns a vector of the user's attribute value preferences in a given domain (Domain) under a given context (CID). The algorithm is shown in Figure 5. This algorithm runs at the database layer.

The algorithm for matching the user's feature (attribute value) preferences and the items' features takes the vector of feature preferences from the attribute value preference mining algorithm and the item profiles as input (see Figure 6). The algorithm matches product's features to the attribute value preferences and compute the preferences on an item by summing the attribute value preferences of the features of an item and normalise them by dividing the 'sums' by the number of features the item has. This then gives the user's preference value on a given item. Equation 2 is used to compute the user's preference values for each and every item in a given domain. The algorithm outputs a vector of item preferences under the current context in a given domain.

The algorithm for mining Strict Partial Order categorical preferences on items (see Figure 7) takes the output from the matching algorithm. The algorithm first identifies the STRONG_NEGset and removes it from the set of items to be clustered. After removing the STRONG_NEGset the algorithm then invokes the clustering algorithm, first, to cluster the POS preferences and then second, to cluster the SOFT_NEG preferences. The POS and SOFT_NEG preferences are clustered separately to avoid cases where the clustering algorithm puts SOFT_NEGs and POSs in the same cluster. The algorithm outputs strict partial order data driven categorical preferences (Note that categorical preferences were defined in Figure 4). The k-means (Han & Kamber, 2006) clustering algorithm was used in this study. The silhouette technique (Holland, 2003) is adapted to determine the best possible clustering.

Within preference categories the user preferences will be represented as EXPLICT preferences (See definition in Figure 4) where applicable. The algorithm for mining explicit preferences (see Figure 8) takes as input the highest preference category from the SPO Categorical preference mining algorithm and some log relations *LR(LogID, UserID, ContextID, SessionID, ItemId, selected)* for the items in the

Figure 5. Algorithm for mining preferences on item features/attribute values

Input: UserID, CID, Domain.

1. get all the attributes in discrete domains under the current Domain
2. for a given UserID:
   a. compute the accessibility probability of each feature, w_i, under the current context (CID).
   b. compute the selection probability of each feature value, w_i, using the user history under the current context (CID).
3. get all the attributes in continuous domains under the current Domain
4. for each attribute estimate the density function using its attribute values in the current Domain.
5. For a given UserID:
   a. estimate the accessibility probability of each range of values, w_i, under the current context (CID) using the density function estimated by (4)
   b. estimate the selection probability of each range of values, w_i, under the current context (CID) based on the density function estimated by (4)
6. For a given UserID, and Domain under the current context (CID) compute the attribute value preferences, $pref_A(w_i)$, for attributes both in discrete and continuous domains

Output: User Preference Profile = { $pref_A(w_1)$, $pref_A(w_2)$, $pref_A(w_3)$, ..., $pref_A(w_m)$ }

Figure 6. Algorithm matching items' features to the users attribute value preferences

Input: User Preference Profile (Vector), item profiles (Vector)
for each item (x_i) in the item profiles (Vector) get its attributes and attribute values
    {
        1.   for each entry in the User Preference Profile
          {
              if the attribute value in the product profile is equal to attribute value in the User Profile
              {
                    $pref_A(x_i) = pref_A(x_i) +$ attribute value preference($pref_A(w_i)$)
              }
          }
        2.   Normalise $pref_A(x_i)$
    }
Output: ItemPrefValues $= \{pref_A(x_1), pref_A(x_2), pref_A(x_3), ... , pref_A(x_i)\}$

same preference category corresponding to a given user. For each instance the algorithm is invoked, it initialises an empty Directed Acyclic Graph (DAG). Then it does preference comparisons of each item in that category to each of the items in the same category with it. The comparison is done through checking that for all the sessions two items appeared together, which one was selected more than the other. If an item, x, is found to have being selected more times than item, y, then a relation (an edge from x to y) x is preferred to y is added to the DAG. Circular path are removed by removing all the edges to the item with the highest out degree in the cycle. The algorithm outputs EXPLICIT preferences represented in a DAG. In this case all the items in the highest preference category will be in the DAG and are thus detected to be more preferred to all the items in the lower categories, which fulfils the fact that all the items in the DAG are more preferred to all the items not in the DAG in the definition of EXPLICIT preference presented in Figure 4.

The logic behind the explicit preferences stems from the fact that since preferences are deduced from the features which are common to items in a given domain, items with almost similar features will have preference values close to each other and hence are most likely to be in the same preference category. To get which one is more preferred to the others, we need to compute relative preferences of each item to all the other items in the same preference category with it. The irreflexive, asymmetric and the transitive properties of strict partial order relations are used to get an explicit representation of the preferences of all the items in that category.

The overall algorithm for our user preference mining framework is shown in the activity diagram in Figure 9. $pref_A(w)$ as defined in Table 1 is used to compute attribute value (feature) preferences. The Attribute value preferences are stored in a User Preference Profile. The User Preference Profiles are meant to be shared amongst similar applications or services. If there is no enough data in the data warehouse to mine for a given user's preference in a given context and domain, the user preference miner invokes a web or grid service to look for the user preference profile from other similar applications. The feature preferences are input into a matching algorithm that will map them to the item features to compute the user's preference on the items ($pref_A(x_i)$). The k-means clustering algorithm is invoked to synthesis some Strict Partial Order (SPO) preference representation as defined in Figure 4. The SPO preferences are then stored in the Preference Repository. If the set of maximal values from a given SPO preference is

Figure 7. Algorithm for mining categorical preferences

Input: UserID, CID, domain, ItemPrefValues $=\{$ $pref_A(x_1)$, $pref_A(x_2)$, $pref_A(x_3)$, ... , $pref_A(x_i)$ $\}$.

1. For each x_i in a given domain, A, under the current context compute $freq_A(x;U)$ and $freq_A(x)$

2. Remove all x_i: $freq_A(x_i;U) = 0$ and $freq_A(x_i) \geq freq_A(threshold)$ from the item set. This is a set of Strong Negative (STRONG_NEG) preferences.

3. Extract the $pref_A(x)$ values for the remaining items

4. Compute a clustering of the x_i's with $Pref_A(x_i) \geq 0$ and that of the x_i's with $Pref_A(x_i) < 0$ separately, using a clustering technique.

   Depending on the clustering results compute data driven SPO preferences illustrated in Figure 4:

Output: The detected categorical preferences or no preference was found

Figure 8. Algorithm for mining explicit preferences (adapted from Holland et al, 2003)

Input: log data: LR(LogID, UserID, ContextID, SessionID, ItemId, selected) for a given preference category; highest preference category from the SPO preference mining algorithm.

1. Compute the k-occurring values $(x_1, x_2,..., x_k)$ in the log relation. Initialise the better than graph with $E - graph = \emptyset$

2. FOR $(i=1,...,k)$ and FOR $(j=i+1,....,k)$ DO:
   a. Consider the sessionIDs, whose according values contain x_i and x_j.
   b. Compute, s, the number of SessionIDs, where x_i was selected and x_j wasn't
   c. Compute, t, the number of SessionIDs , where x_j was selected and x_i wasn't
   d1. If $s > t$, set E-graph = $E - graph \cup (x_j,x_i)$.
   d2. If $s < t$, set E-graph = $E - graph \cup (x_i,x_j)$.
   d3. If $s=t$ do nothing.

3. Remove all circular paths by removing edges to the item with the highest out degree in the circular path.

Output: the detected EXPLICIT preferences represented in a DAG

greater than the maximum number of recommendations required, a DAG algorithm, which computes and represents item SPO preferences within preference categories is called in, to compute a sub-maximal set. If this sub-maximal set is still greater than the required maximal set, n (maximum number of recommendations) item with highest $pref_A(x)$ values will be recommended.

INFORMATION MANAGEMENT ISSUES

The implication of the foregoing discussion is that mining of context-based user preferences require management of the data to be mined and the knowledge extracted from the data through the mining process.

In the following three subsections, we will discuss how the data to be mined is handled and then discuss how the mined knowledge is managed in UPCAMS.

Managing the Context Data

We can group the data that is needed for context-based user preferences into three classes: context data, product details and the user session. Due to the fact that in a mobile computing scenario, the user might be involved in some other activities other than computing (e.g. driving, running, etc), the user's activity has to be considered to avoid recommendations that are irrelevant to the user's activity. Based on this consideration we came up with the context meta-model shown in Figure 10, in which a forth component, *activity* was added to *location, influences* and *time* considered in Holland and Kiessling (2004).

Considering the nitty-gritties of context each context occurs once or just a few times. This tends to discourage the whole idea of detecting context-based user preferences since it builds on the premise

Figure 9. User preference miner activity diagram

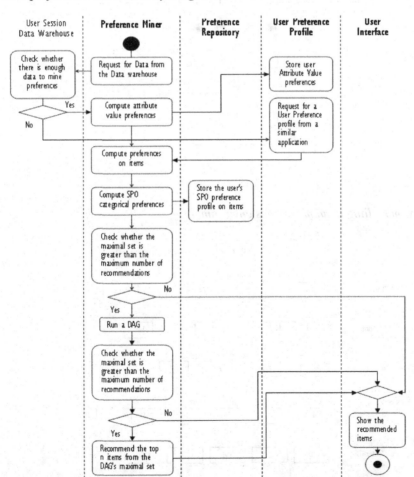

that user contexts are repeatable. Figure 11 shows our context model to support the mining and usage of context-based user preferences. Since we do not want each context description to be unique, context descriptions have to be clustered based on their similarities. An incremental clustering algorithm is used to cluster context first relative to time, then location, activity and lastly influences. A Context Identity (CID) is assigned to every leaf of the tree structure shown in Figure 11. The tree structure applies a breath first search for the CID, which any given context description is most similar to.

To get the CID most similar to the current context, the algorithm has to span at most N nodes for time, M nodes for location, K nodes for activity and L nodes for influences. This gives a linear $O(N+M+K+L)$

Figure 10. Context meta-model for m-services, an adaptation of the context meta-model from (adapted from Holland et al, 2004)

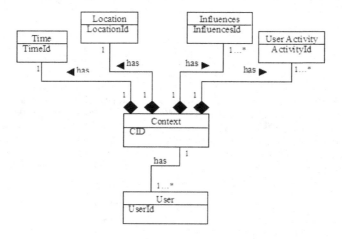

Figure 11. Context modelling in an m-services environment

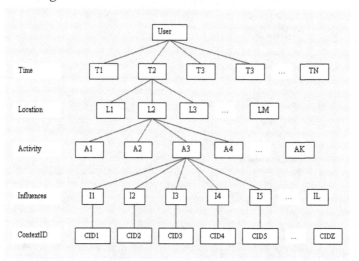

time complexity. The space complexity is also minimal since the algorithm only has to store only the node with the minimum distance from the current context description at each level.

Data Integration and Warehousing

To create a platform for the mining of the user preferences we define a structure of a User Session Data Warehouse model. The model defines a general structure for handling user session and item details data. Dimensional modelling is used to model the warehouse. Dimensional modelling is a logical design technique that seeks to present the data in the standard, intuitive framework that allows for high access performance. The data warehouse model is shown in Figure 12. In order to construct the data warehouse model, the following design principles were considered:

1. Data retrieval of UserID, DomainID, CID, and item attributes must be optimised, and
2. The warehouse should support retrieval of items at different levels of categorisation (e.g. domain, sub-domain, category and sub-category, e.t.c). To this effect we used domain modelling framework in designing the item details database.

Managing Context-Based User Preference Profiles

In collaborative and open grid environment such as the GUISET environment, some intermediate results of the preference model developed in this work can be shared among similar applications or services (cross-service personalisation). This is despite the seemingly obvious security, data custody and privacy issues, which still need to be addressed. The major question is now how can the user preference profiles be managed to allow them to be shared among similar applications. Figure 13 shows a sample of an XML repository for some intermediate results from our user preference mining framework. We named this repository *User Preference Profile*. The User Preference Profile holds each registered user's preferences on the attribute values for a given product domain under a given context. The attribute value preferences will then be used to compute the preferences on individual items using Equation 2. As long as the applications involved follow a standard way of defining items, the User Preference Profile generated from one application can be used in another similar application. The need to allow similar applications to share User Preferences Profiles makes XML the best option to implement the User Preferences profiles repositories.

EXPERIMENTS AND EVALUATION

The evaluation of the preference mining framework developed in this work is twofold: First, we evaluate the effectiveness of our user preference model in a simulated m-commerce environment. Second, we evaluate the performance of the algorithms developed in this work as components of our preference mining framework. Literature (e.g. Kobsa and Fink, 2003, Montgomery and Faloutos, 2000) has shown that *url* hits and viewings tend to follow a Zipf density function. To this end, we used the Zipf density function to simulate user session data.

Figure 12. The ERD for the data warehouse model

Evaluation of the Preference Model

The Preference miner was implemented using the JBuilder 2005 IDE for Java with JDK6. The underlying database used is the MS SQL server 2000 (using default settings). The preference miner was running on the same machine with the SQL server with a CPU with 2.8 ghz and a memory of 512 megabytes.

Preference profiles of 35 users were generated by passing log file data generated in Matlab 7.1 through the preference miner prototype developed in this work. Item selections were generated from a Zipf Probability Density Function (pdf) derived from the MATLAB 7.1's Generalised Pareto Probability Density Function (gppdf) with shape, scale and threshold parameters of 1.25, 1, and 0 respectively. The shape parameter for item selection was chosen basing on the observation made in (Montegomery, 2003) that the maximum likelihood estimate for the Zipf shape parameter of url viewings(selections) is 1.25. The average number of views per session in the data we simulated was 11 viewings per session.

The log data (all hits) was generated using a Zipf density function derived from Matlab 7.1's gppdf with a shape parameter 1.4, scale parameter 1 and threshold parameter 0. The shape parameter of the Zipf pdf for generating log data was chosen taking special care that the number of options available for a user to select was always greater than the number of selection made for each item.

Figure 13. User preference profile

```
<?xml version="1.0" encoding="UTF-8"?>
<!DOCTYPE UserProfile SYSTEM "UserProfile.dtd"[]>
<!--
  a repertoire of preferences that may occur in the DVDs application
-->
<UserProfile>
 <UserIdentifier Value="90000001">
   <UserProfileData Value="DVDs">
     <Context Value="10000001">
        <TimeStamp dateTime="2007-05-27T04:38:18"/>
        <Attribute Value="Genre">
          <AttributeValue Key="Action" Value="2.89"/>
          <AttributeValue Key="Comedy" Value="2.56"/>
          <AttributeValue Key="Adventure" Value="0.098"/>
          <AttributeValue Key="Classical" Value="-1.67"/>
        </Attribute>
        <Attribute Value="Actor">
          <AttributeValue Key="Mel Gibson" Value="1.67"/>
          <AttributeValue Key="Sylvester Stalone" Value="-3.89"/>
          <AttributeValue Key="Sharon Stone" Value="0.9"/>
                       .
                       .
                       .
          <AttributeValue Key="Tom Cruise" Value = "-0.67"
        </Attribute>
     </Context>
             .
             .
             .
   </UserProfileData>
             .
             .
             .
 </UserIdentifier>
          .
          .
          .
</UserProfile>
```

The resultant user profiles created from the process discussed above was then used to query the product database. A total 51990 logs were generated for all the users. The synthesised log data was then passed through the preference miner to investigate whether the preference miner would be able to return the original user profiles as illustrated in Figure 14. A comparison of the item preferences detected with the original item preferences was used to show the effectiveness of the developed preference mining framework. The following parameters (as defined in (Holland et al 2003)) were used to evaluate the effectiveness our preference model:

$$\Pr ecision = \frac{number\ of\ correctly\ \det ected\ item\ preferences\ of\ user\ i}{number\ of\ all\ \det ected\ item\ preferences\ of\ user\ i} \qquad (7)$$

$$\operatorname{Re} call = \frac{number\ of\ correctly\ \det ected\ item\ preferences\ of\ user\ i}{number\ of\ all\ item\ preferences\ of\ user\ i} \qquad (8)$$

Preference Recall was used to measure how good our preference model was in making sure that there were no missing relevant recommendations. Preference Precision measures how good the framework

Figure 14. Experimental setup for evaluating our user preference mining framework

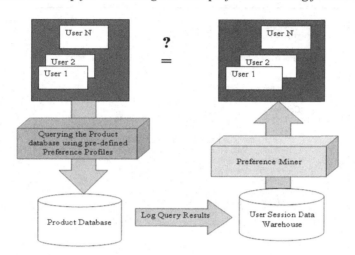

Figure 15. Preference recall and precision

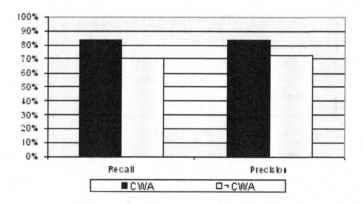

was, in reducing irrelevant recommendations. A good preference model is expected to optimise these two parameters.

Figure 15 shows the quality of our preference mining framework both in domains where the CWA held and where it did not hold. The framework was found to be more effective in domains where the CWA holds where it managed to return more than 80% of the original item preferences (recall) and more than 80% of the returned item preferences were relevant to the users (precision). In domains where the CWA does not hold our framework gave recall and precision values of about 71% and 73% respectively.

Evaluation of the Preference Mining Algorithms

For performance analysis, we ran preference miner with a silhouette value of at least 0.51 for the k-means algorithm. If the silhouette is less than 0.51 it was concluded that there was no reasonable structure

Table 2. Description of the evaluated sub-algorithms

Short Name	Algorithm Description
DBAccess	the process of accessing data from the user session data warehouse and computing the attribute values preferences.
Matching	algorithm for matching user's attribute value preferences to item features.
k-means	k-means clustering algorithm.
DAG	Algorithm for mining explicit preferences within categories.

Figure 16. Scalability of our preference mining framework (One clusters)

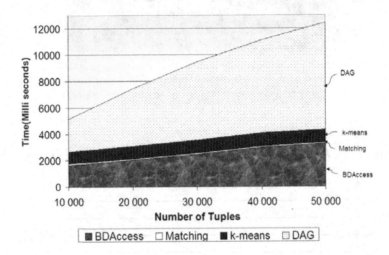

found and hence the clustering algorithm returned the unclustered data set. The silhouette was chosen based on the partitioning for evaluating quality of clustering used in (Holland, 2003). Using a minimum silhouette value of 0.71, which guaranteed detection of strong clustering structure, was found to be too restrictive on the clustering of the items, so much that it was only recognising the lower level preferences (i.e POS, SOFTNEG, and POSSOFTNEG). Table 2 shows the shortened nomenclature of the sub algorithms we discussed in Section "Our User Preference Mining Algorithm".

All the sub-algorithms to our user preferences mining algorithm were found to scale with increases in the tuples in the database (see Figure 16 and Figure 17). A comparison of Figure 16 and Figure 17 shows that instances of the preference miner where no reasonable cluster structure would have been found(which results in one cluster for all tuples thereby overloading on the DAG), became more computationally expensive with increasing number of tuples but not to the extent of causing serious scalability problems. This is because the computational complexity of the DAG algorithm would be a function of the database size compared to a case were a reasonable cluster structure have been found, where computational complexity is a function of the size of the maximal set of items from the clustering algorithm. Owing to this observation, instances of our user preference mining algorithm where the k-means algorithm returns a reasonable structure (which results in many clusters) made the DAG algorithm less computationally expensive (see Figure 17). Making sure that the k-means algorithm finds a reasonable structure in the data, solved the seeming DAG algorithm's scalability problem, and subsequently improved the performance of our preference mining framework as reflected by Figure 17.

Figure 17. Scalability of our user preference mining framework (many clusters)

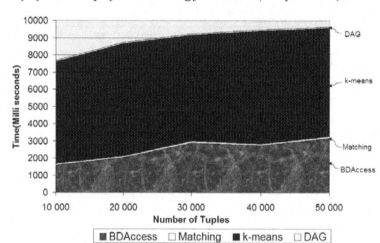

Figure 18. Scalability of the k-means algorithm with increase in the number of items to be clustered

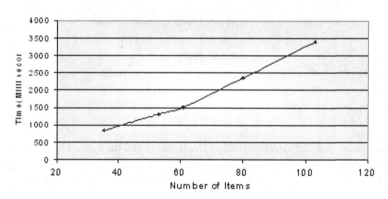

Figure 19. Scalability of the DAG algorithm with increases in the number of items to be represented

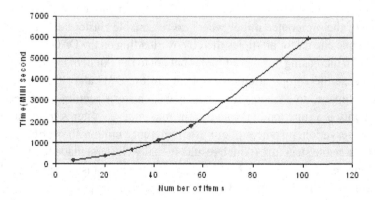

We also investigated how our preference mining framework would scale with increases in the number of items in the domain of concern. Figure 18 and Figure 19 show how the clustering algorithm and the DAG scale with increases in the number of item in a given domain. The k-means clustering algorithm scales linearly with increases in the number of items to be clustered, which is typical of the k-means algorithm (Han & Kamber, 2006). The DAG algorithm was adversely affected with the increases in the number of items it had to process. This is due to the fact that, given a maximal set of size, n, the DAG algorithm performs, $n-1$, pair-wise comparisons for each item in the maximal set. This results in an exponential time complexity of $O(n(n-1))$ for the DAG algorithm.

From the foregoing discussion of results, it was concluded that, for optimal performance of our preference mining algorithm, the clustering algorithm must find a well defined cluster structure. This implies that using a less restrictive silhouette value of 0.51 (compared to 0.71) would increase the performance of our preference mining algorithm.

FUTURE TRENDS

Grid computing is evolving from mere sharing of distributed resources for large computational tasks to the realisation of service-oriented architecture for transparent and reliable distributed system integration. Current research trends in grid computing can be viewed as a technology meant to complement the semantic web and web services by providing an infrastructure for handling large scale information systems.

Over the past eight years researchers who believe in the vision semantic web have been busy in trying to find ways in which the volumes of data and information available on the web can be effectively acquired, pre-processed, represented, integrated, and eventually converted into useful intelligence. This field of research has been coined Web Intelligence. Now, with the convergence of web services and grid services technology, all the efforts in the conversion of data and information on the grid in to useful intelligence are giving rise to a new field of research known as Grid intelligence.

In Grid intelligence, unlike in Web Intelligence, the challenge is not only conversion of data produced by the applications but it also involves conversion of an overwhelming amount of data produced by Grid operations into knowledge that can facilitate the intelligent use of grid services and resources. Quite a number of Grid-based data mining infrastructures, which include the DataMiningGrid (Stankovski et al, 2007), Knowledge Grid (Cannataro and Talia, 2003), GridMiner (Brezany et al, 2005), discovery Net (Curcin and Ghanem, 2001), etc, meant to cover key aspects of knowledge discovery and life cycle on the grid have been developed. These developments can be leveraged on to build some infrastructure for distributed cross-service personalisation in collaborative grid environments.

The use of grid-based technologies for this purpose is advantageous in three (3) major ways; (i) the Grid provides the capacity to run computationally intensive user preferences mining algorithms, (ii) the grid has the capacity of providing all the needed user preferences mining algorithms and enables applications to access the ones that are relevant to them at run time, (iii) the grid enables sharing and analysis of geographically distributed data among different applications. However, for us to be able to take advantage of these technologies, some challenges on how the distributed information resources and knowledge bases will be managed, represented and evolved as new information is added to the grid and new knowledge discovered needs to be addressed.

CONCLUSION

This chapter presented a framework for achieving advanced personalisation in highly dynamic computing environments such as Grid infrastructures for mobile devices. We showed how personalisation and context-awareness could be distinguished and how this distinction could be used to exploit the context data in the personalisation process. We presented a framework for mining context-based user preference that gives an intuitive preference measure and representation. The preference measure is adopted from the Feature preference model (Jung et al, 2002, 2005), and the preference representation is based on the strict partial preference mining framework (Kiessing, 2002). We also showed how information management issues needed to create a platform mining context-based preferences could be handled. An XML schema to support management and sharing of the mined preference was presented. Experiments carried with a prototype of our user preference mining framework in a simulated m-Commerce environment showed that our preference mining framework was promising in terms of its effectiveness. The framework was also found to scale relatively well with both increases in the number of tuples and number of items whose preferences were to be synthesised.

Apart from the lack of intuitive preference measures and user expressiveness, most of the approaches to preference mining algorithms did not scale with increases in the number of tuples in the underlying database, since they had to run on multidimensional data. Our preference mining framework first reduced the multi-dimensional structure to a single dimension, without losing any information, before applying computationally expensive algorithms. Thus the preference model developed in this chapter could be logically viewed as a model enhanced to give an intuitive measure of a preference, an intuitive representation of preferences, and to provide computational efficiency.

In reality users might be interested in one feature of an item than the other features. That is, in making choices, users prioritise some item features more than others. Our preference model was not able to capture this. It gave equal weights to all the features of the item in a given domain. Another potential point of weakness of our preference mining framework emanated from the fact that our framework assumed that the user's preferences on a set of items in a given domain were determined by the user's preferences on the domain's common attributes. In reality some items have some extra features, not possessed by other items in the same domain. It was possible that the user's preferences on a given set of items might be highly influenced by these extra features and hence our preference model would not be able capture this.

REFERENCES

Adomavicius, G., & Tuzhlin, A. (2001). Expert-Driven Validation of Rule-Based User Models for Personalisation Applications. *Data Mining and Knowledge Discovery 5*(1-2), 33-58.

Alvin, T. S., & Chuang, S. N. (2003). MobiPADS: A Reflective Middleware for Context- Aware Mobile Computing. *IEEE Transactions on Software Engineering, 29*(12), 1072-1085.

Barkhuus, L. (2005). *The Context Gap: An Essential Challenge to Context-Aware Computing.* Unpublished doctoral dissertation, The IT University of Copenhagen, Denmark. Retrieved on March 29, 2007, http://www.itu.dk/people/barkhuus/lou_ thesis05.pdf .

Bonett, M. (2001). Personalisation of Web Services: Opportunities and Challenges. *Ariadne, 28.* Retrieved April 24, 2006, from http://www.ariadne.ac.uk/issue28/personalization.

Coppola, P., Mea, V. D., Gaspero, L. D., Mizzaro, S., Scagnetto I., Selva A., Vassena L., & Rizio, P. Z. (2005). *MoBe: A Framework for Context-aware Mobile Applications.* Paper presented at the Workshop on Context-Aware Proactive Systems, Helsinki, Finland.

Dey A. K., & Abowd, G. D. (2000). *Towards Better Understanding of Context and Context-awareness.* Paper presented at the Workshop on The What, Who, Where, When, and How of Context-Awareness, Hague, Netherlands.

Fahy, P., & Clarke, S. (2004). *CASS-Middleware for Mobile Context-Aware Applications.* Paper presented in the Mobisys 2004 Workshop on Context Awareness. Boston, USA. Retrieved June 29, 2006, from www.sigmobile.org/mobisys/2004/context_awareness/papers/cass12f.pdf.

Gehlen, G., & Mavromatis, G. (2003). Mobile Web Services Based Middleware for Context-aware applications. In *proceedings of the 11th European Wireless Conference 2005 Volume 2* (pp 784-790).Nicosia, Cyprus. Retrieved June 29, 2002, from www.comnets.rwth-aachen.de/436+M5cc1c271ec8 .pdf.

Göker, A., & Myrhaug, H. I. (2002). *User Context and Personalisation.* Paper presented in the 6th European Conference/Workshop on Case-Based Reasoning (ECCBR 2002), Aberdeen, Scotland, UK. Retrieved March 29, 2007, from http://www.smartweb.rgu.ac.uk/papers/AGoker.pdf

Gorgoglione, M., Palmisano, C., & Tuzhilin, A. (2006). Personaliastion in Context: Does Context Matter When Building Personalised Customer Models, *In Proceedings of the sixth International Conference on Data Mining (ICDM'06)* (pp. 222-231). Hong Kong, China.

Gu, T., Pung, H. K., & Zhang D. Q. (2004). A Middleware for Building Context-Aware Mobile Services. *In Proceedings of the Vehicular Technology Conference, 2004 Volume 5* (pp 2656-2660). Univ. of Singapore, Singapore. Retrieved June 29, 2006, from www.comp.nus.edu.sg/~gutao/gutao_NUS /VTC2004 gutao.PDF

Han J., & Kamber M. (2006). *Data Mining Techniques and Concepts,* San Fransisco, CA, USA:Morgan Kaufmann Publishers.

Holland, S., Ester, M., & Kiessling, W. (2003). A Novel Approach on Mining User Preferences for Personalised Applications. *In Knowledge Discovery in Databases (PKDD 2003)* (pp 204-216). Dubrovnik, Croatia, Retrieved April 24, 2006, from http://www.cs.uoi.gr/~kstef/PreferenceMining.pdf

Holland, S., & Kiessiling, W. (2004). Situated Preferences and Preference Repositories for Personalised Database Applications. *In Proceedings of the 23rd International Conference on Conceptual Modelling* (pp 511-523). Shanghai, China Retrieved April 24, 2006, from http://www.cs.uoi.gr/~kstef/ 2004_hol_kie_er2004.pdf

Jameson, A. (2001). Modelling Both the Context and the User; *Personal and Ubiquitous Computing, 5(1),* 29-33. Retrieved April 24, 2006, from http://www.dfki.de/~jameson/pdf/pete01 .jameson.pdf

Jorstad, I., & Thanh, D. V. (2006). *Service Personalisation in Mobile Heterogenous Environments. In Proceedings of Advanced International Conference on Telecommunications (AICT2006)* (pp. 70-75), Washington DC, USA.

Jung, S. Y., Hong, J. H., & Kim, T. S. (2002). A Formal Model for Preference. *In proceedings of the 2002 IEEE international Conference on Data Mining (ICDM'02)* (pp 235-240). Maebashi TERRSA, Maebashi City, Japan

Jung, S. Y., Hong, J. H., & Kim, T. S. (2005). A Statistical Model for User Preferences. *IEEE Transaction on Knowledge and Data Engineering, 17*(6), 834-843.

Kiessling, W. (2002). Foundations of Preferences in Databases; *In: Proceedings 28th International Conference on Very Large Databases (VLDB 2002)* (pp. 311-322), Hong Kong, China. Retrieved April 24, 2006 from http://www.vldb.org/conf/2002/S09P04.pdf.

Kiewera, M. (2005). Iterative Discovering of User's Preferences Using Web Mining. *International Journal of Computer Science & Applications, 2*(2), 57-66.

Migiro, S. O and Adigun, M. O. (2005). ICTs, e_commerce and rural development: the case of arts and crafts SMEs in rural KwaZulu-Natal, *Commonwealth Youth and Development, 3(2)*, 65-83.

Montgomery, L. A., & Faloutos, C. (2000). *Trends and Patterns of WWW Browsing Behaviour.* Retrieved March 29, 2007, from http://www.andrew.cmu.edu/user/alm3/papers/web%20trends.pdf.

Niederee C. J., Stewart A., Mehta B., & Hemmje M. (2004). A multi-dimensional, unified user model for cross-system personalization. *In Proceedings of Advanced Visual Inter-faces International Working Conference (AVI 2004) - Workshop on Environments for Personalized Information Access*, Gallipoli, Italy.

Riva, O. (2004). *A Conceptual Model for Structuring Context-Aware Applications.* Paper presented at the Forth Berkeley-Helsinki student workshop on telecommunication Software architectures. University of Berkeley, USA.

Riva, O., & Flora, C. (2006). Controy: A Smart Phone Middleware Supporting Multiple Context Provisioning Strategies; *In proceedings of the 2nd International Workshop on Services and Infrastructure for the Ubiquitous and Mobile Internet (SIUMI'06), at the 26th International Conference on Distributed Computing Systems (ICDCS'06)* (pp. 68-74), Lisbon, Portugal. Retrieved June 29, 2006, from www.cs.helsinki.fi/u/riva/publications/riva siumi06 paper.pdf

Schmidt, A., Adoo K. A., Takaluoma, A., Tuomela, U., Laerhoven, K. V., & Velde, W. V. (1999). Advanced Interaction in Context. *Lecture Notes in Computer Science.* Retrieved April 24, 2006, from http://citeseer.ist.psu.edu/cache/papers/cs/12585/http:zSzzSzwww.teco.uni-karlsruhe.dezSz~albrechtzSzpublicationzSzhuc99zSzadvanced_interaction_context.pdf/schmidt99advanced.pdf.

Sicilia, M. A., & Garcia, E. (2004). On the Use of Bipolar Scales in Preference-Based Recommender Systems. *In Proceedings 5th International Conference on Electronic Commerce and Web Technologies (EC-Web 2004)* (pp. 268-276), Zaragoza, Spain, Retrieved June 12, 2006, from http://citeseer.ist.psu.edu/cache/papers/cs2/93/http:zSzzSzwww.cc.uah.eszSzmsiciliazSzpaperszSzSicilia_ECWEB_2004.pdf/sicilia04use.pdf.

Toivonen, S. (2004). Hybrid service provision model for mobile users: Prospects for the DYNAMOS project. *In Proceedings of the 11th Finnish Artificial Intelligence Conference (STeP 2004) Volume 2* (pp.

183-192), Vantaa, Finland, Retrieved March 29, 2007, from http://virtual.vtt.fi/virtual/proj2 /dynamos/ pubs/toivonendynamos.pdf.

Tseng, V. S. M., & Lin, K. W. C (2005). Mining sequential mobile access patterns efficiently in mobile Web systems. *In Proceedings of the 19ᵗʰ International Conference on Advanced Information Networking and Applications (AINA 2005) Volume 2* (pp 762-767). Taipei, Taiwan.

Yang, Y., Williams, H. M., Pooley, R., & Dewar, R. (2006). Context-Aware Personalization in Pervasive Communications. *In Proceedings of the IEEE International Conference on e-Business Engineering (ICEBE'06)* (pp. 663-669). Shanghai, China.

Zheng, T., & Iyengar, V. S. Recommender Systems Using Linear Classifiers. *Journal of Machine Learning, 2*, 313-334.

Chapter XIV
DYONIPOS:
Proactive Support of Knowledge Workers

Josef Makolm
Federal Ministry of Finance, Austria

Silke Weiß
Federal Ministry of Finance, Austria

Doris Ipsmiller
m2n Consulting and Development GMBH, Austria

ABSTRACT

Efficient and effective knowledge management plays an increasingly important role in knowledge intensive organizations. The research project DYONIPOS focuses on detecting the knowledge needs of knowledge workers and automatically providing this required knowledge just in time. The prototype DYONIPOS generates new knowledge out of artifacts, while avoiding additional work and violations of the knowledge worker's privacy. The knowledge is made accessible through semantic linkage of the relevant information from existing repositories. In addition DYONIPOS creates an individual and an organizational knowledge data base to achieve the knowledge. This chapter is structured as follows: the introduction section describes the current knowledge management approach and the new approach with use of the DYONIPOS prototype. The background section addresses the relation between the applied approach and the challenge in E-Government, summarizes the aims of the research project DYONIPOS and delivers also insight into the topic knowledge management by describing and criticizing the "SECI-model" according to Ikujiro Nonaka and Hirotaka Takeuchi. After this the research project DYONIPOS, the semantic and knowledge discovery technologies used are presented as well as the use case project DYONIPOS showing the results of the first and the second test and screenshots of the updated DYONIPOS application. The chapter concludes with presentation of the benefits and the technical advantages of the prototype DYONIPOS.

INTRODUCTION

Current Knowledge Management approach: a knowledge worker shortly wants to prepare an important topic but he neither knows where the according information is stored nor what colleagues he can ask for expertise. To get an overview about the topic, he normally proceeds in the following way: he successively searches in the available sources (server drive, own hard disk, internet, e-mail archive, specific applications, etc.) for important information with different "search tools". Therefore he has to run each query individually. In addition he must know the various functionalities of the different "search tools". Finally he has to screen the delivered search results if they adequately describe the relevant topic.

Knowledge Management with support of the DYONIPOS prototype: first of all the DYONIPOS knowledge worker has to start the DYONIPOS application manually because the automatical start is turned off due to privacy reasons. After activation of DYONIPOS, all keyboard entries and mouse moves are recorded as well as the reactions of the computer system. For instance, if the knowledge worker begins to create a power point presentation DYONIPOS is looking the knowledge worker over his shoulder. DYONIPOS calculates information needs to the entered words. The knowledge worker edits for example the title page for his presentation and writes "DYONIPOS (DYnamic ONtologybased Integrated Process OptimiSation): Effective and Efficient Knowledge Management science and research hand in hand". DYONIPOS detects the knowledge needs, e.g."DYONIPOS", „Knowledge Management" etc. In addition, DYONIPOS calculates so called "resources". These are corresponding documents, PDF-files, links to websites, electronic record management data (ELAK) which cover the information needs. The knowledge worker gets these resources indicated only by request. In fact, constantly local and global search results are delivered only if the button for this function is pressed. Apart from this associated concepts of the topic and the detected information need are indicated. These are for example individuals or organizations which deal with this topic. Besides the proactive support, DYONIPOS also offers active search for information.

This is done similar to conventional search tools via entering of a search item in a search window. Moreover DYONIPOS enriches the further handling and analysis of the indicated search results. For example important key words can be displayed which represent the content of the knowledge resource as well as association graphs that visualizes the relations of the associated concepts. DYONIPOS also classifies the detected resources and visualize them in topic landscapes. In these topic landscapes, thematically similar resources are mapped closer together. Trough the use of DYONIPOS knowledge workers get an impression of the content of search results without having ever read them. Furthermore, existing knowledge in an organization becomes available, transparent and semantically enriched.

BACKGROUND

"Knowledge is relevant information in context"; this is the underlying definition of the DYONIPOS project. Because of the transformation from the industrial to the information era, knowledge has grown up to an important production factor. This is classified by the part of the immaterial production (services, software, etc.) on the added value which increasingly exceeds the part of the material production. This became possible through electronic data processing. In public administration knowledge has always played a central role because the production of public services would not be possible without knowledge. As a matter of fact knowledge workers need more and more knowledge for processing their daily knowledge intensive work. Furthermore the ad hoc part of the processes increases steadily. Knowledge acquisition also becomes more complex because the amount of information increases continually and heterogeneous systems are used to obtain the needed knowledge. In addition the multitude of found information complicates the selection of the really needed knowledge. This leads to the fact that already existing knowledge gaps grow, respectively available information is not used. It is often not recognized that knowledge gaps exist or that information is available – even in the own organization – which could be used for streamlined processing or better results. Searching for knowledge in a growing number of various sources and accordingly formulating and deducing of search queries in a conventional way often is very complex and often does not deliver the desired results. Much irrelevant information is indicated which requires manual post processing of the search results. Often important information is missing. Implementing e-Government is intended to solve these problems not just by using information and communication technologies to exchange information with and to provide services for citizens and businesses. What is more, e-Government should also provide better and more efficient working conditions for civil servants in order to boost agility of public administration and quality of public services. Public administration work is knowledge work par excellence because information of governmental organizations is widely scattered and civil servants are confronted with an overload of information. Our opinion is that the knowledge of an organization can be classified into three kinds of information: public domain knowledge, partly available knowledge and tacit knowledge. Public domain knowledge is available for all knowledge workers. This knowledge is often stored online on the intranet or internet and accessible through search engines or knowledge databases. Partly available knowledge is only accessible for individual or specific groups of knowledge workers. This kind of knowledge is often stored on the employee's PC or the organization's server. The third kind of knowledge – tacit knowledge – is in the minds of employees and therefore only available for the owner of the knowledge. It is very time-consuming for a knowledge worker to find the adequate knowledge in the existing overload of information. If tacit knowledge is needed, the receipt of required resources is a matter of chance.

The research project DYONIPOS faces these challenges. Its aim is to provide personal, agile and proactive support for the knowledge worker by means of proactive, context sensitive knowledge delivery. DYONIPOS provides all kinds of knowledge that has been released for the organizational knowledge database, provided the user has the right to access this knowledge. In the case of tacit knowledge the name of the information owner will be supplied. Furthermore, DYONIPOS creates and continuously updates an individual as well as an organizational knowledge base. This knowledge base makes the organization's growing knowledge available. The DYONIPOS vision of knowledge management is that knowledge management works for people, not that people work for knowledge management. Additionally the system should adapt to peoples' wishes and not the other way round. The main idea is to release knowledge workers from additional work for knowledge management. For reaching the project visions, a completely new approach with technologies „on the leading edge" was used to develop the prototype DYONIPOS. Conventional search applications currently deliver only documents – DYONIPOS also delivers the knowledge stored in these documents.

The theory of knowledge creation is often referred to the SECI model of Ikujiro Nonaka and Hirotaka Takeuchi. With the help of this model they describe the knowledge creation in an organization. The main idea is that new knowledge is created through an interaction of tacit and explicit knowledge. SECI stands for socialization, externalization, combination and internalization which are the four different stages of knowledge transformation. The process model starts with socialization, meaning that individual tacit knowledge is shared through social interactions and experiences. In the second stage knowledge is made explicit through language, images, models etc and shared within a group. This externalization process is followed by the combination stage. In this step explicit knowledge (e.g. documents, ideas, information) is collected, shared and combined within an organization and between organizations – often with the use of IT. In a final stage, explicit knowledge is converted into tacit knowledge again. "Learning by doing" is a key statement in this process since explicit knowledge is applied and used in praxis. Nonaka and Takeuchi explain the dynamic interaction between the different stages of knowledge transformation on the basis of a knowledge spiral. Knowledge is transferred upwards from the individual to the group and finally to the organization. They use a spiral to illustrate this process.

New research results has led to an extension of the SECI model over the last years. For an effective interacting (rotating) in the spiral there is a need of enablers which motivate people and support interactions. Such enablers could be a vision, objectives or the environment. (Nonaka & Takeuchi, 1995), (Nonaka et al. 2008).

The self-acting system DYONIPOS – Dynamic Ontology based Integrated Process Optimization – goes in another direction. Knowledge is delivered automatically, proactive and just in time considering the knowledge needs. Therefore DYONIPOS produces no additional work effort. It is a premise of DYONIPOS that no additional work should be generated for the knowledge workers. Knowledge is extracted out of existing artifacts as produced by its users and the structuring is carried out automatically. The success or rather the acceptance of the DYONIPOS system is based on the motivation of the users like by the SECI model.

THE RESEARCH PROJECT DYONIPOS

The DYONIPOS research project started on January 2, 2006, and was completed by the end of the first quarter of 2008. The DYONIPOS research consortium consisted of m2n consulting and development gmbh (www.m2n.at), Know-Center Graz (en.know-center.at), the Institute for Information Systems and Computer Media (IICM) of the Graz University of Technology (www.iicm.tu-graz.ac.at) as well as HP Austria (welcome.hp.com/country/uk/en/welcome.html). Together they developed the prototype DYONIPOS. The DYONIPOS research project was financed by the "semantic systems" program within FIT-IT, an Austrian research program provided by the Federal Ministry of Transport, Innovation and Technology (BMVIT, www.bmvit.gv.at/en/index.htm). The proposal of the DYONIPOS project was awarded for best proposal of the regarding call.

DYONIPOS is based on automatic and semiautomatic knowledge management methods and technologies, e.g. knowledge discovery, semantic systems, knowledge flow analysis and the integration of heterogeneous knowledge sources. Semantic technologies enable handling structured as well as unstructured data from knowledge intensive processes (Kröll et al., 2006). All techniques are needed for learning of concepts through extraction of meta-knowledge, for context sensitive detection of "Information Needs" and for extraction of concepts and relations out of artifacts.

Knowledge Discovery Technologies

The identification of knowledge gaps, the just in time delivery of relevant information, the supply of associated concepts related to the corresponding topic and further analysis through filtering and evaluation of the delivered information are the major functions of DYONIPOS. To provide these functions

DYONIPOS captures the user's knowledge work, discovers inherent tasks, and supports the knowledge worker with information.

The first challenge is the observation of the knowledge worker's interactions with and reactions to the system and existing application data. This data is the so called low-level sensor data on the application and operating system level (Maier, 2005, p.443). The second challenge is to develop adequate techniques to discover work patterns and to automatically support users with appropriate information. The third challenge is to detect how knowledge workers can be effectively supported (Tochtermann, 2006).

In order to capture the worker's patterns a java tool called DYONIPOS Task Recognizer has been implemented (Rath, 2007). At first DYONIPOS records all interactions between the users and their computers; these are so called "events", e.g. mouse clicks or key strokes. Different sensors of the context observer module observe all interactions of the user with the desktop environment. DYONIPOS uses a key logger program to record and log all recognized events (Kröll et al., 2006; Rath et al., 2007). The observed events are stored in the so called event log. This monitored data is the basis for determining the work patterns. The next step is to reduce the immense quantity of data and to assign events to event blocks by filtering and relation analysis. This allows the elimination of irrelevant data, e.g. mouse movements. Owing to relation analysis a set of events can be bundled into an event block. At present, generic rules, application based rules and web browser based rules are applied for bundling events into event blocks (Rath, 2007). Generic rules are based on the title of the window currently opened by the user. A reason for the assignment of events to an existing event block is e.g. the title of the window currently opened. The implementation of further rules for assigning events to event blocks can easily be accomplished. The methods used for learning task assignments are k-nearest neighbor classification, Support Vector Machines based on graph kernels (Rath et al., 2007). Additionally there is the possibility to train the classifier, i.e. the above mentioned bundling agent, by means of task assignments is done by the user. A method for detecting tasks, which is the next level of semantic enrichment, is clustering based on similarity between content and structural features and the scatter/gather approach. During the first test phase the assignment was initially performed by the key-user but in the second test phase the classification of features and tasks worked automatically and had only to be controlled by the key-user. Currently – in the third test phase – the assignment works fully automated.

Semantic Technologies

DYONIPOS is a modern information system which supports users by proactive delivery of contextual information (resources) while knowledge workers are doing their daily work. The application of ontologies is useful in such a system, because they ensure interoperability and the development of "new" knowledge. Furthermore, ontologies are used for the learning process of the user context. Not only the structure but also the recognition of context is based on ontologies. The knowledge base and also the internal program flow are based on ontologies. In addition ontologies can be used for the unambiguous description of information resources. As a consequence, Resource Description Framework (RDF) is a key technology of DYONIPOS. RDF is an ontology and a formal language used to encode ontologies. All events, event blocks and tasks described in section 3.1 are represented and stored by RDF-Triples (Kröll et al, 2006). This means all data extracted from metadata, documents, presentations, e-mails etc. will be saved in a structured manner. For example, the DYONIPOS ontology consists of the concepts "Person", "Organization", "Document" and "Topic". An example for a specific "Person" may be employee John Q. Public. John Q. Public works at the Federal Ministry of Finance and wrote some articles about semantic technologies. The circumstance described above results in the following specific classifications: John Q. Public is an object of the concept "Person", the Federal Ministry of Finance is an object of the concept "Organization", all written articles are objects of the concept "Document", and the identified "Topic" is a semantic technology. The following relationships exist between the objects: John Q. Public is employed by the Federal Ministry of Finance. John Q. Public is the author of some articles. John Q. Public deals with the topic of semantic technology. More conclusions drawn are the following: John Q. Public is an expert in the topic of semantic technology and the Federal Ministry of Finance deals with the topic of semantic technologies. The newly learned knowledge – e.g. that John Q. Public is an expert in the topic of semantic technology – is a recognized resource of DYONIPOS. It should be mentioned that for privacy reasons only knowledge related persons that are registered DYONIPOS participants will be stored and supplied.

THE USE-CASE PROJECT DYONIPOS

Parallel to the research project DYONIPOS the use-case project DYONIPOS is implemented in the Directorate General for Information Technology (DG-IT) of the Federal Ministry of Finance, Austria. In order to handle their daily work, knowledge workers in public administration need the following additional knowledge:

- Where is the relevant information stored?
- How can this information be found?
- How relevant is the delivered information?

The challenge is to provide administrative employees automatically with information they need. Consequently the above mentioned additional know-how is made available by DYONIPOS. Other objectives are to support the employees of the DG-IT without creation of additional work by means of knowledge management and to ensure privacy of the knowledge workers. DYONIPOS contribute to the resolution of these challenges by an efficiently and an effectively support of the daily work of the individual employees in the DG-IT. The DYONIPOS Task Recognizer provides employees with the necessary knowledge produced by semantic cross-linking of the relevant information from the existing repositories and processes. Additionally, DYONIPOS independently develops new relations between sources of knowledge. This explains why the DYONIPOS Task Recognizer at the one hand supports the user by visualization of existing documents, files or websites etc. and on the other hand displays the new generated information such as the name of the person who has the specific know-how. The ministry or rather fifteen employees support the research consortium. Together they work on the realization of the research results and they ensure the transformation of current scientific results into an easily useable software solution. The staff of the ministry shares its domain specific know-how with the research consortium, by supporting the development of DYONIPOS base technologies.

Initial interviews with employees were carried out to get both, an impression of the kind of work and how this work is done. The results of these interviews provided information which sensors should be developed and which events the sensors should observe. The researchers found out that employees work mainly with standard applications such as Microsoft Office tools, Internet Explorer and the e-mail system Novell GroupWise. That is why a first research step was to develop sensors to observe events of these applications. In addition to the observation of these standard applications the final DYONIPOS prototype records all electronic artifacts from the electronic record management system (ELAK), the file-system on the servers, the Livelink-system (a system to store office documents in a specific server environment) as well as the specific application KOMPASS, a system to administrate persons, resources and authorizations.

The implementation of the use-case is structured in three evaluation phases. These tests serve as basis for improving the functions of DYONIPOS e.g. by a continuous refinement of the rules to assign events to event blocks. In the first test phase of the pilot software ten key-users took part to support the work of the researchers. The test lasted for a period of five weeks from April to May 2007. Main objective of the first test was to gather detailed information about the key-users. The preliminary data collection included user input and work content. Further objectives were testing and evaluating the recording and analysis module of the DYONIPOS proactive assistant. Besides to the test and the evaluation the key-users also had the possibility to express specific requests concerning the functionality and graphical user interface of DYONIPOS. Therefore the key-users had the chance to take actively part in the design process of the system. At this stage the prototype DYONIPOS was stored and implemented on the local hard disc of each personal computer of the participating key-users. A central storage on the server was not established. The employees were introduced in the software handling and had to manual assign event blocks to tasks. The collected information served as training basis for the DYONIPOS Task Recognizer. Furthermore the key-users had the possibility to evaluate the functions and to document suggestions for improvements. Outcomes of this first test were stored in log files and documented in test protocols and questionnaires.

The Results of the First and Second Test Phase

Through evaluation of the log files, questionnaires and the analysis of the first and the second test the following information and operating figures about the key-user and the DYONIPOS Task Recognizer were derived. A basic result of the evaluation of the first test was that key-users always worked on several tasks at the same time. This information represented a challenge for DYONIPOS, because it is an objective of DYONIPOS to provide just in time information based on the context. Furthermore we found out that a key-user used different searching tools and searched in very heterogeneous sources. Another objective of DYONIPOS is to support the work of the user by proactive and context sensitive information delivery. DYONIPOS therefore searches for information in different repositories and implements the function of a searching tool. Moreover it creates cross-links between the context of different repositories in order to deliver existing and new generated information. By using DYONIPOS knowledge workers receive transparency over the existing sources of information.

DYONIPOS gives additional references about the relevance of the found search results which include all currently available information. The parallel implementation of the funded research project and the use-case project made it possible to exchange ideas between research and practice constantly; this was useful for both projects. Furthermore the inclusion of all stakeholders (Makolm & Orthofer, 2007, p.391) such as researchers, users, IT experts and also the staff council – in the development process assures that the results of the research project DYONIPOS can and will be transformed optimally and in real time into a practical application.

The second test phase was started in January 2008 and took approximately two months. A fundamentally improved version of the prototype DYONIPOS was released. It established an organizational knowledge base with new functionalities and also included artifacts stored on the server. Apart from this electronic records were proven by 13 key-users. In the second test the former manual assignment of event blocks to tasks worked automatically. The key-user just observed this assignment. Nevertheless he was able to give feedback by doing corrections of wrongly assigned event blocks and by confirmations of correctly assigned event blocks. Results of the second test phase were the following suggestions from the key-users: Firstly, for a knowledge worker more detailed context information of an information resource was desired. Secondly the opening of search results directly in the operational application could improve the continued processing and would save also time. Thirdly, the analyzing of individual search results could be beneficial. Finally, on the one hand the training of the tasks was too time-consuming; on the other hand, the detection of tasks was absolutely sufficient to support the knowledge worker with the appropriate knowledge.

Figure 1. DYONIPOS enables the display of information in topic landscapes (© 2008, Doris Ipsmiller. Used with permission.)

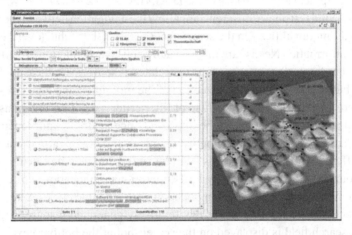

Figure 2. The graphical user interface of DYONIPOS. (© 2008, Doris Ipsmiller. Used with permission.).

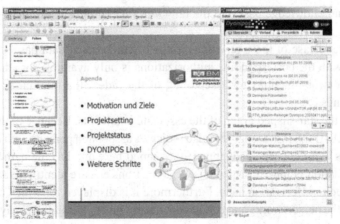

Therefore the third prototype enables the classification of detected resources and the visualisation of topic landscapes (see Figure 1). In the topic landscape, thematically similar resources are mapped to close regions. Moreover, the selection of different resources and the display "how similar they are" is possible. In addition, DYONIPOS allows the selection of artifacts according to sources e.g. file system, KOMPASS, ELAK and Web.

Figure 2 shows the DYONIPOS user interface. When the task recognizer is started, all mouse clicks and tasks are registered. Information needs for a certain topic are recognized. On demand the user is provided with information that he searches for or that is related to the content of his work. If the user works for example on a power point presentation concerning the topic DYONIPOS, the task recognizer shows all web resources, presentation, word documents etc. related connected to this topic in the "global search results". To every newly entered word or sentence, DYONIPOS searches for information or concepts in the personal and organizational database which could be useful for the knowledge worker. While the user is working on a particular topic, the DYONIPOS task recognizer is always shown in the right front of the desktop. As a consequence ,information found by the application appears permanently. If this is not wished the task recognizer can be minimized.

Figure 3 shows the graphical user interface of the DYONIPOS Task Recognizer window for the third test phase. Like in the second test phase, different tabs allow the navigation between the various delivered supplied resources and functionalities. On the screenshot the tab "Übersicht" (overview) is opened. On this tab the so called "Information Needs" are mapped at the top. The deduction of "Information Needs" occurs automatically, but for performance reasons the related resources are measured only after clicking on the activating button. Afterwards the detection of the individual and global resources related to the "Information Need" gets started. With the help of filter criteria e.g. filtering on associated persons or organization, the located search results can be improved once again. In addition also the associated concepts such as the name of experts, terms, application areas and organizations corresponding to the particular topic are offered. "Information Needs" will be stored and may be calculated again at a later date. All located resources are opened directly in its operational application. For example, a located e-mail can be opened in the associated e-mail application with a double click . A key-user has also the possibility to search actively for information in the iteratively generated resource repository by using the search field. This search field is displayed on the screenshot at the bottom next to the magnifying glass. On the left side of the screenshot an association graph is opened. This graph shows different associated concepts regarding a selected resource. On the tab "Persönlich" (individual) the adjustment of personal DYONIPOS functionalities can be carried out, e.g. the deletion of knowledge, which is stored at the organizational knowledge base. On the tab "Verlauf" (progress) all finally opened resources is displayed.

Furthermore the release of these resources to the organizational data base is possible on this tab. The tab "Admin" with the corresponding authorizations is only available for administrators. This tab contains diverse control functions for assembling of the index, the internal system procedures, the KOMPASS-mappings etc.

Figure 4 shows the star-shaped graph of the associated concepts. Because of the identified information needs, the DYONIPOS task recognizer also indicates associated persons with certain concepts. The graph which shows these concepts is mapped star-shaped here and has the name of the person in the centre. In the association graph, those persons, organizations etc. are identified that are connected with several topics linked to information need. Furthermore it is displayed for which company respectively which department the person works and contact details are given. In the same way the graph points out,

Figure 3. Screenshot of the DYONIPOS Task Recognizer (© 2008, Doris Ipsmiller. Used with permission.)

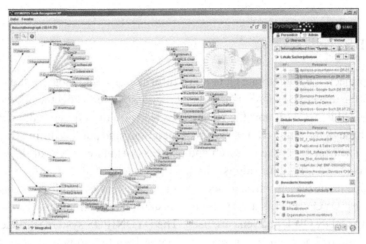

Figure 4. Screenshot of the DYONIPOS star shaped association graph (© 2008, Doris Ipsmiller. Used with permission.)

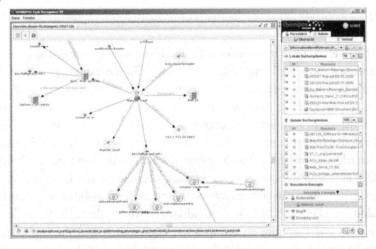

for which other projects the person works or rather with which concepts he or she is identified. Consequently links to further information are available by clicking on a symbol. For example if the person is responsible for semantic technologies, information about "semantic technologies" can be received.

Finally the third test phase starts in November 2008. The requirements of the users and the research results from the first and the second test phase were successfully implemented in the system. In the third testing phase the key-users will also test the whole functionalities of DYONIPOS. This third test will be closed with an evaluation and documentation of the use-case results in a final project report. Starting in the end of 2008 the whole DG-IT or rather all 180 employees will take part in a final test of the prototype DYONIPOS. The final evaluation will be done after one year of practical experience. The documentation and evaluation of this final test provides the basis for the decision whether DYONIPOS will be used in the DG-IT further on. In the same way the decision will be made whether DYONIPOS should be proceeded as a commercial tool or not.

FUTURE TRENDS

In the DYONIPOS project, the Directorate General of Information Technology of the Federal Ministry of Finance is innovation driver and solution provider at the same time. Altogether 15 key-user from different areas and selected experts support the research consortium directly with the implementation of the pilot software. Through the joint venture of science, economy and public administration good results could be generated. The transfer of the research and use-case results was part of the project objective. DYONIPOS supports above all organizations which collect knowledge in a written form, which do a high part of knowledge intensive activities, which are active in a very dynamic environment and implement ad-hoc processes. DYONIPOS is a very flexible system. For the implementation of DYONIPOS open standards such as RDF, OWL and Jena are used. The DYONIPOS system is model-based and can be individually configured. The connector principle enables the integration in different IT-landscapes. The scale and the performance allocation can also be individually adapted.

CONCLUSION

The use of DYONIPOS leads to an increase of the effectiveness of the knowledge organization. This is because not only the own individual knowledge is available for the handling of the daily work but also the global organizational knowledge is supplied proactively. Likewise, more knowledge can increase the quality of products since important information can be considered for the creation of products. DYONIPOS can also contribute to a reduction of double work because similar work that is already done is automatically indicated to the present topic. Due to the fact that work can (partly) be used again valuable work time can be saved and consistency can be assured which ends up in a more efficient work method. Furthermore DYONIPOS improves the individual work situation of single knowledge workers. Workers of a knowledge organization can concentrate on their core responsibilities as bureaucratic activities are reduced. In addition, DYONIPOS links individual employees through the indication of potential conversational partners and therefore encourages the cooperation and the exchange of information in a company. Newest leading edge technologies are tested in the DYONIPOS research and use-case project. It can be concluded that the joint venture between research, economy and administration was successful.

REFERENCES

Kröll, M., Rath A., Weber, N., Lindstaedt, S., & Granitzer M. (2007, August). *Task Instance Classification via Graph Kernel.* Paper presented at Mining and Learning with Graphs 07, Florence, Italy.

Kröll, M., Rath, A., Granitzer, M., Lindstaedt, S., & Tochtermann, K. (2006, October). *Contextual Retrieval in Knowledge Intensive Business Environments.* Paper presented at Workshop Information Retrieval 2006, Hildesheim, Germany.

Nonaka, I., & Takeuchi, H. (1995). *The Knowledge-Creating Company: How Japanese Companies Create the Dynamics of Innovation.* Oxford University Press.

Nonaka, I., Toyama, R., & Hirata, T. (2008). Managing Flow: A Process Theory of the Knowledge-Based Firm. Palgrave Macmillan.

Maier, R. (2005). Modelling Knowledge Work for the Design of Knowledge Infrastructures. *Journal of Universal Computer Science, 4,* 11, 429-451.

Makolm, J., & Orthofer, G. (2007). Holistic Approach, Stakeholder Integration and Transorganizational Processes: Success Factors of FinanzOnline. In J. Makolm & G. Orthofer (Eds.), *E-Taxation: State & Perspectives, E-Government in the Field of Taxation: Scientific Basis, Implementation Strategies, Good Practice Examples*, (pp. 389-402). Linz: Trauner Verlag.

Rath, A., Kröll, M., Andrews, K., Lindstaedt, S., Granitzer, M., & Tochtermann, K. (2006). Synergizing Standard and Ad-Hoc Processes. *Proceedings of the 6th International Conference on Practical Aspects of Knowledge Management* (pp. 267-278). Heidelberg: Springer Berlin.

Rath, A., Kröll M., Lindstaedt, S., & Granitzer, M. (2007). Low-Level Event Relationship Discovery for Knowledge Work Support, In N. Gronau (Ed.), *Proc. of the 4th Conference on Professional Knowledge Management* (pp. 227-234), Potsdam: GITO-Verlag.

Rath, A. (2007). A Low-Level Based Task And Process Support Approach for Knowledge-Intensive Business Environments. *Proceedings of the 5th International Conference on Enterprise Information System Doctoral Consortium DCEIS 2007* (pp. 35-42), Madeira, Portugal.

Tochtermann, K., Reisinger, D., Granitzer, M., & Lindstaedt, S. (2006). Integrating Ad Hoc Processes and Standard Processes in Public Administrations. *Knowledge transfer across Europe, 4th Eastern European eGov Days and 5th eGov Days, 203.* Vienna: OCG Serie.

Chapter XV
User Culture, User–System Relation and Trust:
The Case of Finnish Wikipedia

Juhana Kokkonen
University of Art and Design Helsinki, Finland

ABSTRACT

In this chapter the open-source based collaboration model of Finnish Wikipedia is examined from the perspective of user culture, which is the fundamental basis of Wikipedia's project management. The concept of user culture in a mediated collaboration project is introduced and the user culture of Finnish Wikipedia is analyzed in terms of this concept. Also the concept of user-system-relation is presented and the relation between users and the socio-technical system of Wikipedia is examined. This analysis considers the crucial factors in the process of building a trusting relation between the user and the Wikipedia system. From the perspective of user-system-relation, the relationship of trust between the user and the system is much more important than the trust relations between individual users. This article explains the role of user culture and user culture design in a collaborative Web community and considers the nature of a trusting user-system-relation. Examination of one functional example of open information management gives understanding of management tools for open peer-collaboration in general.

INTRODUCTION

The social uses of information and communication technology (ICT) have rapidly developed in recent years. More and more people are using the Internet as a social tool. A large number of collaborative web communities have emerged, and peer-modification and horizontal networking have become part of our everyday life.

A new kind of collaboration model emerged as a consequence of the pervasiveness of ICT. This collaboration model was first used in software development, but has since been adopted in content production as well. Wikipedia, for example, uses the same kind of operation model as technology-oriented open-source projects (e.g. Linux development). In these kinds of projects, development is based on voluntary peer-collaboration and peer-review. In order to keep the project thriving in changing circumstances, the peer-developers must have possibilities to modify and redesign the operational structure and the goals of the whole project. Thus in open-source projects the parallel development of the activity must be enabled. In Wikipedia this has been made possible by emphasizing the importance of cultural codes and rules. I will argue that not only the technological development and the user interface design, but also the user cultures and their design and management should be taken into account. For this reason I use the concepts of *user culture* and *user culture design*. Along with the new collaboration model we also have the pivotal trust relationship, which is no longer a relationship between persons, but between the whole enabling infrastructure and the individual user. The concept of *user-system-relation* is developed to explain this trust relationship.

Wikipedia's management model is very open. This article examines it as a functional example of open information management. Examination of one working management model gives understanding of open peer-collaboration management tools in general.

BACKGROUND

User-System-Relation and Trust in the Social Media

In a collaboration-oriented Web community, users do not necessarily know the other participants. There can be thousands of members in such a community, so a new user may not recognize any individuals at the beginning. For example, in Wikipedia the outcome of collaboration is often displayed anonymously (or at least the user's individual share is not emphasized), so the process of becoming acquainted with other users takes time. It is obvious that there are also social bonds and interpersonal relations within the Wikipedia community, but the relation between the user and the whole socio-technical system is more crucial.[a] I call this relation the User-System-Relation (USR). In mediated voluntary-based collaboration the user's trust in the fairness and functionality of the socio-technical system is the precondition for a successful co-project. Various things affect the USR. I will explicate these factors in the case of Finnish Wikipedia and draw wider conclusions about the relationship of trust in mediated collaboration communities. If the user sees benefits in participating and does not question the expressed goals of a socio-technical system, her motivation, commitment and initiative become deeper. In this way he or she can consider becoming intensely committed to the project.

The Concept of User Culture

We find user cultures in relation to any use of technology, but in mediated collaboration projects using the logic of the open-source production model there is an absolute necessity to design and manage these user cultures. For most normal Web services restrictions on the use of the service can be put in place using technical means or user interface design, but in projects where participant action orientation is rather freely organized, limitations cannot be very strict. In these cases the role of the user culture and its design is remarkably important.

Implicit and Explicit User Culture

User culture consists of all the types of activities, which are developed in a user community by

1. the possibilities and restrictions of the socio-technical system,
2. design actions, and
3. the consequences of users' ways of thinking and acting.

The user culture can be implicit or explicit. The implicit user culture contains all the ways of thinking and acting which are not made visible (i.e. all the ways of thinking and acting that are not tangibly shared with the user community). To this category also belong all the tacit ways of thinking and acting that result from the restrictions set by the technical system and its design (including user interfaces).

The explicit user culture consists of all those ways of thinking and practicing which are written down and which the user community has accepted. Explicit user culture includes rules, bylaws, norms, documented practices, and shared explicated values. Explicit user culture can develop from implicit user culture during the activity processes.

User Culture as a Boundary

I will examine the user culture as a boundary between the user and the whole socio-technical system. The bi-directional activity on this boundary has a fundamental role in the development of an intentional and successful USR. In order to examine this culture, one user is detached from the socio-technical system to which he or she belongs. From this point of view all activities (i.e. interaction, communication, and operation) between the user and the system are included in the domain of user culture (see Figure 1). This explanatory model has been developed on the basis of Etienne Wenger's (1998) theory of communities of practice.

The theory of communities of practice explains the functionality of informal social groups. The main idea is that the members take part in the everyday actions of the community and therefore learn the habits, norms, beliefs and truths of that specified group. The community of practice consists of three different dimensions. *First*, the group must have a joint enterprise (i.e. a member must have some kind of orientation or goal that is shared with the group*); second,* the group must have mutually committed themselves to their enterprise; and *third*, the group must have a shared repertoire of tools, concepts, artifacts and discourses which serve as the foundation for their cooperation (Wenger 1998, 73).

The vitality and activity of a community of practice depend on the interplay of two aspects of practice: participation and reification.[b] For membership to be meaningful, a member must have the right to interact and have discourse with the group (i.e. participation), and he or she must also have access to the shared repertoire of the group's documents, projections, instruments and points of focus (i.e. reification). There cannot be participation without reification, and vice versa. Participation in community practices transforms the reifications, and reifications are the foundation of effective participation (Wenger 1998, 63).

The concept of communities of practice is also a suitable theoretical tool for analyzing mediated collaborative communities. The primary ideas of (1) joint enterprise, mutual engagement and shared repertoire, and (2) the interplay between participation and reification, can be readily found in Internet communities. First, Internet communities usually have a single clear goal or focus; the member's shared interests commit them to the more or less shared goal; and all Internet communities are based on technology and software, so the community always shares some kind of instrumental repertoire.

Second, because of the instrumental repertoire, Internet communities necessarily possess reification of a sort, and there are always possibilities to participate in the community's practices (e.g. discussion forums, commenting on features, collaborative moderation), even if the intensity of participation varies. Thus, the concept of communities of practice appears to be a suitable theoretical framework for the analysis of the Wikipedia community. In fact, it has been used, e.g., in Susan L. Bryant, Andrea Forte and Amy Bruckman's (2005) work about Wikipedia users' process of transformation from novice users to expert ones.

Activities in the Domain of User Culture

I have divided the activities of user culture according to Wenger's theory. The essential elements of the user culture in open-source-based projects appear to be

1. sharing of the activity tools by the socio-technical system,
2. activities by the user,
3. guidance of activities by the socio-technical system, and
4. further development of activity tools by the user (see Figure 1).

The activity tools consist of the technology and its interfaces; tools for specified tasks; types of structuring information; and helpful terms and concepts for communication, collaboration and deeper comprehension. By using these tools, the users contribute to the socio-technical system. The activities differ in various projects and thus take multiple forms. In order to guide the user, the socio-technical

Figure 1. User culture and the activities between a user and a socio-technical system in an open-source-based project

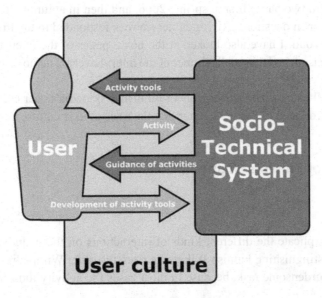

system must give support, feedback and guidance for his or her actions. These three elements can be found in every mediated collaboration project. The last one is a vital part, at least in the open-source projects. In these projects users can potentially develop the activity tools. This signifies the open-source projects' need to be profoundly open to far-reaching contributions by users. This bi-directional exchange of practices forms the 'turbine' which keeps the project thriving.

THE USER CULTURE AND THE USER-SYSTEM-RELATION IN FINNISH WIKIPEDIA

Research Questions, Material and Methods

In this article I will analyze

1. the user culture of Finnish Wikipedia (including activity tools, activities, guidance of activities and development of activities inside Finnish Wikipedia) and
2. how the trusting USR is formed between the socio-technical system of Wikipedia and the individual user (i.e. what are the critical factors in the trust formation process).

I also consider what can be said about the user culture design of Finnish Wikipedia in general and what are the challenges and possibities of it. The research material for the analysis has been gathered from the Finnish Wikipedia web site, other Wikipedias and a small scale e-mail survey; involving qualitative interviews with nine active Finnish Wikipedia users. In the section of Future Trends I make some general suggestions about open peer-collaboration management.

The analysis is based on Christine Hine's method of *virtual ethnography* (2000). This approach includes participatory observation, close reading of the web content, and e-mail interviews with users. Because most of the material is in text form, the method is quite close to discourse analysis (Hine 2000, 142–143). For approximately 1½ years I have observed the activities of Finnish Wikipedia. The interviews were conducted in two parts; first in spring, 2006, and then in autumn, 2006. These interviews consisted primarily of open questions. All nine interviewees responded to the first part of the survey; eight of them to the second. I have also looked at the home-pages of the interviewees as part of my analysis, and for that reason, and the small number of the interviewees, I do not separate the individuals to guarantee their anonymity.

In the analysis I will categorize the elements of Finnish Wikipedia's user culture according to the types of interaction introduced in Figure 1. After that the roles of user culture design and USR will be examined.

The User Culture of Finnish Wikipedia

Activity Tools

In this section I will explicate the different kinds of interactions on the boundary of user culture in Finnish Wikipedia. Distinguishing Finnish Wikipedia from the other Wikipedias, especially from the English version, is a burdensome task, because in most cases the activity tools and practices used in

Finnish Wikipedia are reproductions of other language editions, or they are taken from MetaWiki – a Wiki dedicated to the development and the management of all of the Wikimedia Foundation's projects.[c] Next I will introduce the common activity tools of Wikipedia, focusing on the tools used in the Finnish edition.

1. *Technology and user interfaces.* The obvious activity tools provided by the Finnish Wikipedia socio-technical system are technological tools and user interfaces. The system is based on a Wiki called MediaWiki, which is an open-source product developed independently alongside of Wikipedia. The Wikimedia Foundation also administers the MediaWiki project. To a great extent the core functions and user interfaces of the system have been developed in the MediaWiki project. But there are also possibilities to manage these features inside Wikipedia. User interfaces of articles can be modified though the normal editing interface with HTML. Also the meaning of the functions can be varied. Templates, explained later, are an example of this kind of function.

2. *The essential goal of the project.* In the case of Wikipedia the ultimate goal is to be an open, free, multilingual, and inclusive encyclopedia. This gigantic intention is the very ground of whole project and steers the participation of all users. The goal is used frequently in discussions as a justification for the user's opinion or guidance.

3. *The copyright licenses.* Because it has been determined to keep the use of Wikipedia open and free, users must accept loosened copyrights for their contributions. Wikipedia uses the *GNU Free Documentation Licence* (GFDL), whereupon the content produced by anybody can be revised, copied and translated.

4. *Categories.* Because of the Wikipedia's database structure, there is not any kind of given hierarchy between the individual articles or pages. The categories are mentioned to build up the information architecture for the content. New categories can be made easily and they can be also modified, merged or even deleted later.

5. *Templates.* Compared to categories, the usage of templates is more versatile. A template is a fast and easy way to mark some features of an article in a controlled way. With a template, a user can mark an article, e.g., as a 'stub' (i.e. short and incomplete articles), as an official policy of Wikipedia, or as an article that might violate some copyrights. There are also lots of templates designed for users' personal homepages – e.g., templates to inform others about one's language skills (Babel templates) and templates that tell about the person's competences and interests (user boxes). There is also a variety of motivational templates users can give to each other by way of their user pages. In Finnish Wikipedia there is, e.g., a mark called the *papukaijamerkki* ('parrot mark') which a user can give to another as a sign of respect for exemplary activity. As with categories, templates are also somewhat indefinite; they can be edited, revised or deleted.

6. *Explicated collaboration types.* Wikipedia's user culture has generated different collaboration models; on Finnish Wikipedia we find at least two explicated types of collaboration: the collaboration article of the week and Wikiprojects.[d] These have been designed as ways of collaborating and building new links between members. It is a different kind of way to contribute to Wikipedia. One interviewee said that the meaningfulness of contributing develops through initiating a new, interesting project.

7. *Concepts and terms.* Concepts and terms used within the Wikipedia community are also important grounds for activities. The concept of neutral point of view (NPOV) is the salient one. The NPOV is a rule about how to write to Wikipedia. The rule signifies that users should not write from a

one single viewpoint; on the contrary they should represent all the different but significant ways of thinking about the article at issue. Most of the users interviewed in this study mentioned NPOV as a ground rule in Finnish Wikipedia.

There are lots of other concepts and terms which have developed over the course of time. For example different kinds of Wikipedian philosophies have been specified, which are seen in distinct editing policies. Whereas an *immedialist* believes that the quality of the Wikipedia content could be improved by the immediate deletion of substandard articles, an *eventualist* thinks that Wikipedia's quality will develop little by little, and she wants to give more time to the improvement process than an *immedialist*.ᵉ Even though some of the users interviewed consider the debate over the Wikipedian philosophies insignificant, the appearance of these kinds of terms is a fine example of the process of reification through participation. One other noteworthy matter is that for the most part these concepts are copied and translated from the English Wikipedia or from MetaWiki. The user culture of Finnish Wikipedia is, as a whole, a local adaptation of English Wikipedia's and MetaWiki's practices and ways of thinking. The English Wikipedia, MetaWiki, and Jimmy Wales – the founder of Wikipedia – are often mentioned as justifiable authorities in users' own statements concerning user culture design discussions on Finnish Wikipedia.

8. *Guidelines for users.* Finnish Wikipedia's guidelines for users is the main location for explicated user culture. It includes three categories: First, *general information,* contains facts about Wikipedia, general instructions on how to write and edit articles, and facts about members and the community (i.e. lists of registered users and administrators and advice about various communication channels). Second, *the style guide* gives instructions about naming articles, structure policies, grammatical hints and technical guidance in generating specific types of content (e.g. tables, pictures, and mathematical formulas).

    Third, the *practices* section introduces a substantial part of Finnish Wikipedia's user culture. With these explicated practices, users are continuously justifying their own opinions and actions, so their existence is a crucial factor in keeping the project focused. In Finnish Wikipedia the practices guide can be subdivided in four sections: *key-practices*, the *code of conduct*, *writing guidelines* and *other practices*.

The key-practices section covers policies of NPOV, copyright issues and the openness of content issue mentioned above. The code of conduct introduces a collection of behavioral rules that users should follow, e.g. For not making personal attacks on other people. There should not be usernames which are against the rules, user pages with inappropriate content, or secret use of several usernames. Users should avoid edit wars (i.e. quarrelling users reverting repeatedly to different versions of an article), and they should never disrupt Wikipedia to illustrate a point. The writing guidelines refer to a style guide and the NPOV rule. They also present encouragement to be bold in editing articles. This be-bold-rule is a great example of how Wikipedia makes an attempt to embolden the users, especially the newcomers, to contribute. Besides things mentioned above, the writing guideline prohibits, e.g., including original research in these articles (i.e. users should not form new theories or concepts inside an article), and underlines the importance of proper ways of citing information sources. The other practices section covers, e.g., administrative practices (including practices of blocking users, deleting and reverting articles, and protecting pages) and guidelines for voting.

User Activities

Because Wikipedia users' action orientations are freely organized, there is a rich variety of activities for them. At least following common activities can been found on Finnish Wikipedia:

1. *Reading.* Everybody who uses Wikipedia reads articles, but also user pages, discussions, the recent changes lists, etc.
2. *Article writing.* All of the active users interviewed have written articles. Many of them said that they wanted write more than what they were able to at the moment. Most of those interviewed have taken on administrative responsibilities and thus they have less time for article writing.
3. *Editing.* One of the key-features of Wikipedia is the possibility to edit articles instantly. A user can correct punctuation or rectify factual errors in a minute. Editing is also at the core of collaborative writing. Everyone can contribute as much they want and the final edits of articles (if there can be such a thing) are built from massive quantities of micro-contributions (i.e. small-scaled, easy and agile contributions).[f]
4. *Moderation.* For the active users of Wikipedia moderating is one salient job description. The Wikipedia system records all changes in the recent changes log, and some users have taken the log monitoring as their special job. One interviewee had volunteered to observe especially new articles listed on the *recent changes* log. The moderation includes all kinds of tasks, e.g. revising older versions and marking articles (e.g. marking new but irrelevant articles as 'trash'). Another user had specialized in paying attention to copyright issues regarding media material.
5. *Translating articles from other Wikipedias.* There are also users who translate articles of good quality from other Wikipedias. Generally the source of translations is the English Wikipedia, but others, e.g. the German version, are used as well. Because of the GFDL this is possible and actually desirable.
6. *Discussion.* All extensive changes and new arrangements are based on conversations. For every single article there is a discussion page attached. A typical discussion page for an article consists of debates regarding viewpoints, choices of words, the textual structure, the policy for naming the article, and comments about other's attitudes. Also all new practices are produced through discussions and arguments. As Wenger mentions, the reification processes and the shared repertoire of useful tools are developed in the discourses and negotiations of meaning (Wenger 1998, 52). This kind of chain of development also can be seen in discussions in the Finnish Wikipedia.
7. *Voting.* There is a lot of voting in Finnish Wikipedia. Some interviewees thought that voting is more common than in other Wikipedias. This is possible perhaps because the Finnish Wikipedia community is considerably smaller than, e.g., the English one. In bigger communities voting is a burdensome procedure because of the amount of users, voters, revisions and opinions.
8. *Designing media material.* In addition to the textual material there are large number of other types of informational material, e.g. pictures, figures, charts, maps and audio. Some members have profiled themselves as producers of a specific sort of media material. There is an international database for this kind of material called *Wikimedia Commons*, and there is an on-going attempt to upload most of the media material used to this site.
9. *Designing information architecture tools and templates.* In Wikipedia there is a category system to make it easier to search for and manage information. The information architecture is growing and changing all the time. Some people try to standardize the information structure by modifying the

categories of single articles. This can lead to bitter debates about the best information structure. Different kinds of templates have been designed and used to standardize the different kinds of messages used in the collaboration. For messages between users, most interviewees found the Babel templates quite useful and the user boxes pointless since, e.g., anyone can add any kind of competence template to their own page without any kind of verification. Also some described the designing of user boxes as a school kids' hassle. In Finnish Wikipedia, as well as in the English version, the user boxes should contain only information that is useful and an integral part of the activities of the project. The parrot mark and other recognition templates polarize the opinions of interviewees. Some find these irrelevant and others see them as a convenient way to give a positive response.

10. *Designing and participating in collaborative projects.* Users can start up and participate in collaborative projects on different topics. In Finnish Wikipedia there are over 50 different such projects. The content varies from collaborative writing about Egyptology or football to managing and developing user boxes or illustrations for articles. One interviewee said that designing and participating in collaborative projects is a meaningful way to contribute. Besides topic-based collaboration, there is also a rotating collaborative article of a week.

11. *Higher level administrative activities.* Active users can be voted into the position of administrators with extended rights of use. Administrators can delete and protect pages, restore deleted pages and ban the participation of a disruptive user. Normally administrators are active users who have credibility inside the community. There has also been a discussion about the permanence of administrative status, since many administrators have not participated for a long time but their extended rights continue to exist anyway. Administrators participate actively in all kinds of developmental discussions and debates. Every administrator contributes from their own perspective and have their own vision for Wikipedia's developmental process. Because of this there can be bitter differences of opinions over the administrators who independently make more radical moderations and decisions. Some users even accuse the administrators of despotic behavior. Some users also think of the whole core group as arrogant and despotic and feel themselves to be outsiders.

12. *Participating in other Wikimedia Projects.* In the domain of the Wikimedia Foundation there are other projects than just Wikipedia. For example, there is a dictionary called Wiktionary, a project for collecting free content textbooks called Wikibooks and collection of quotations called Wikiquote. New Wikimedia Projects can be suggested in MetaWiki.

13. *'Hanging around'.* The majority of those interviewed mentioned the active and tight community as a key factor in the success of Finnish Wikipedia. Naturally this is a subjective interpretation, but it is evident that active users also tend to 'hang around' in the Wikipedia community; it has an IRC channel, the Coffee Room, for freer and more general discussions. These kinds of activities can lead to social bonding and friendship building.

Guidance for Activities

In this section I will analyze the guidance methods for activities inside Finnish Wikipedia. I will examine this guidance especially from new user's point of view.

1. *Feedback.* In Wikipedia in general there is a strong emphasis on the importance of positive feedback. The parrot mark is an example of a positive feedback convention in the Finnish edition. Beyond

that, consensual collaborative writing itself is a form of positive feedback. But besides the positive feedback orientation, there are a number of acts that can be specified as negative feedback. Returning an article to an older version is a clear comment on the quality of newest revision, and deleting a whole article as trash indicates the attitudes of an administrator about the desirable content. In developmental discussions there can be many openings where no response at all is received. This silence can also be also understood as a negative feedback. Generally it seems that the positive feedback belongs more in the explicit domain of and the negative in the implicit user culture.

2. *Encouraging new users.* The formal goal is to assume the good faith of every user. This means that moderators should gently advise newcomers as to the right kind of behavior and assume that all the irrelevant or even harmful contributions are because of a mistake, not because of malevolence. There is also an official rule of *Please do not bite the newcomers*, which illustrates the same thinking of good faith from a little bit different perspective. In practice newcomers are treated in a variety of the different ways, ranging from real encouragement to rude devaluation.

3. *Guidelines and rules.* As mentioned above, there is a rich variety of help pages in Finnish Wikipedia. In these pages there are guidelines and rules for several specific activities. Users are often directed to read these guidelines. They are also helpful in conflict situations, where the written rules and codes of conduct can be used as a justification for one's own opinions or administrative decision-making.

4. *Introduction of working methods.* With the collection of positive and negative feedback, acts of encouragement and the guidelines and rules, new users are socialized into the user culture of the community. New users can also ask about proper procedures on the administrator's personal discussion pages or on general discussion pages.

Development of Activity Tools

In this section the user-centered development of activity tools will be examined. The activity tools mentioned above are studied from the perspective of on-going development.

1. *Technology and user interfaces.* The MediaWiki platform is an open-source project, so anyone willing can take part in it. The interfaces designed within Wikipedia projects are often chosen after a discussion or vote. In the case of Finnish Wikipedia, the main page has been one of the most actively developed pages; its interface having been transformed several times.

2. *The essential goal of the project.* There is a rule that *Wikipedia does have firm rules*, but it is hard to imagine that the ultimate goal would change radically. As community design researcher Jenny Preece argues, a community designer can carry out some fundamental design acts and leave everything else to the forming community to decide. The central design acts Preece mentions are the main idea of the community and its by-laws (Preece 2000, 81, 95–96). Because these kinds of things are the foundation of the project, they are very hard to modify later, but in principle it would be possible in Wikipedia, if a mutual understanding of a new kind of goal emerged.

3. *The copyright licenses.* If you choose to contribute Wikipedia, you must accept that your material is published using the GFDL. There have been several discussions about the functionality of this license, and some users have adopted a so-called dual license system, where they license their own work with both GFDL and some chosen Creative Commons license.

4. *Categories.* Because of the cumulative nature of Wikipedia, the category system is continually developing. Normally changes in category structure are subject to discussion, especially in cases where a user has made significant revisions, and other views arise as a result. Normally these disagreements can be settled in discussions.

5. *Templates.* Like categories, Wikipedia templates are also cumulative and constantly evolving subsystem. Anyone can make new templates or edit existing ones.

6. *Explicated Collaboration Types.* All users can take part in existing collaborations and develop them further. Users can also launch new collaborations that interest them.

7. *Concepts and terms.* Wenger argues that in communities of practice new concepts and terms either emerge through discussions and negotiations inside the group or they come from outside the group but their real meaning develops within the community (Wenger 1998, 53). This sort of pattern can certainly be seen in Finnish Wikipedia. Some parts are borrowed and translated from other Wikipedias and some are developed in discussions within the Finnish community.

8. *Guidelines for users.* Because of the centrality of the guidelines in the orientation of newcomers and in settling disputes, users are keen to improve the Wikipedia help pages. As with normal articles, anyone can modify these pages as well. From the discussion pages we find that new ideas for guidelines arise from situations where users discover some implicit habit or new kind of problem, and then decide to write an explicit guide concerning it.

User-System-Relation in Finnish Wikipedia

As mentioned above, the trusting relationship between the user and the socio-technical system is a critical factor in keeping open, mediated collaboration thriving. Different kinds of trust issues are linked

Figure 2. Summary of the user culture in Finnish Wikipedia

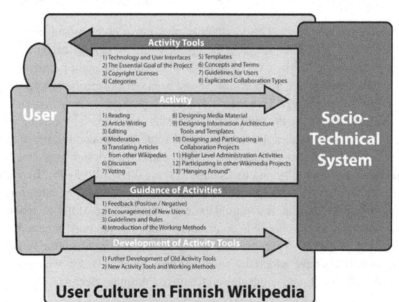

to the activities of users. There are the reliability considerations of existing content, but also the user must form a trust relationship with the socio-technical system. This takes time and involves number of different stages. It seems that this relationship, like in any strong system of mutual collaboration, is formed bit by bit (see Tuomela 2000, 30–33). The trust between the user and the system builds on several elements.

1. *Ideology.* The ideological underpinning of the system should be reflected in everything it does. In the case of Wikipedia, the central ideological issue is the altruistic free sharing of information, including the collaborative compilation of information as a method. Because the original idea was not to edit the content inside a Wiki, the main idea was to offer a universal and free encyclopedia.[g] Therefore the primary ideology of Wikipedia is the belief that all information should be freely distributed and used. This ideology should be in harmony with all components of the system; otherwise users will not consider the system to be credible. The congruence of users' and the system's philosophical thinking bridges the relation between them. For example, because of the altruistic goal of the project, interviewees said that they somehow felt duty-bound to participate. They did not question the Wikimedia Foundation's stated goals, i.e. they did not suspect the Foundation of having some kind of ulterior motives.
2. *Idea of the system.* In the formation the USR, the idea of the system must be attractive and understandable. As said, the main idea is to offer a free and global encyclopedia. The compilation method derives from the main functionality of Wiki. This combination is the core of the whole project, and the idea coheres with the ideology.
3. *Organizational design.* Organizational decisions also affect the USR. Most of the users interviewed thought that it is quite important for the Wikipedia project to be foundation-based. The Wikimedia Foundation follows an extremely open communications policy and is donation-based. Almost everyone there participates voluntarily; with only a handful of hired workers. The selected copyright license strengthens this impression and also enables straightforward collaboration. Also Jimmy Wales, as the personification of Wikipedia, has a certain role in the trust building. The founder is a typical front man and role model for an open-source project.
4. *Technological design and user interfaces.* The decision to use and develop open-source software as a platform adds to the impression of the system having altruistic purposes. The possibility to produce simple interface solutions instantly makes parallel development paths possible in very simple and thus powerful ways. Because of the possibility to micro-contribute, all newcomers can try their hand at editing and see instant results. Because of this rapid possibility to participate, it is relatively easy to 'hook up' on Wikipedia. The first experiences of participation do not take more than a couple of minutes.
5. *Benefits.* To be motivated to participate, users must believe that they receive sufficient benefits. For example many of those interviewed said that they use Wikipedia as their own learning platform. They were motivated to write about topics of personal interest to them or subjects they were studying. Also if a user uses Wikipedia as an information source, he or she can feel duty bound to contribute something for others in return. From the system's point of view a user's participation must be in someway valuable. In the case of Wikipedia the growing number of articles and the improved quality of the content are direct benefits for the system. Also, for example, users' pedagogical use of Wikipedia means that the users are willing to invest quite much of their time in participation. These kinds of active and strongly motivated users are a remarkably important driving force.

6.   *Existing user culture.* The existing user culture and its implications are one major factor in user trust building. The activeness of the peer-production and the large user community demonstrate the success of the system. The previous activity reverberates in users' decisions to take part. Fast growing projects can achieve a snowball effect, where the number of users explodes. In Finnish Wikipedia trust in the system is partly built upon the popularity of English Wikipedia. Even if the active users interviewed see various problems in the functionality of the English user community, the fact that there are 2.5 million articles there is a strong evidence of efficiency of a Wiki-based encyclopedia and the power of normal people. Also the vast number of editions in other languages elevates the credibility of the project.

The formation of trust relationships between the individual user and the socio-technical system does not mean that there are no differences of opinion or confrontations. In fact vibrant discussion and debate are a key-factor in tying users into the community and its dynamic user culture.

Future Challenges of Finnish Wikipedia

All interested users can suggest changes in Wikipedia's activities and ways of working. Because of the acquired user culture, including the large numbers of discussions and votes taken, the success of rapid and large-scale modifications is unlikely. In general, developmental acts are either small-scale improvements on older activity tools or minor new additions to the pool of cultural rules. At the same time the cultural emphasis in project management enables parallel lines of development, but it can also frustrate development-oriented users because the user culture is based so much on discussions and debate.[h]

The Finnish Wikipedia community has thus far been growing continuously. Users must thus reconsider the functionality of collaboration all the time. At some point a growing number of users tends to polarize a community into subgroups, and this kind of trend can be seen inside the Finnish Wikipe-

Figure 3. Summary of building materials for the user-system-relation in Finnish Wikipedia

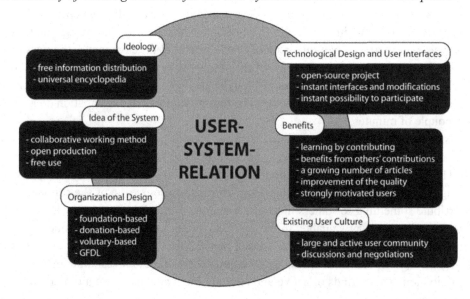

dia community as well. More than one of the interviewee was concerned about the future of Finnish Wikipedia and the problems of an expansive user community. Some of the users said that they hope the Finnish Wikipedia community can avoid the growth problems they have personally witnessed in English and Swedish Wikipedias.

Because the Wikipedia user culture is radically open, the design and management are also community-based and participatory. The individual's voice can thus be lost in the mass of contributions and opinions. There are, however, a couple of persons who have influenced to the user culture considerably. Besides Jimmy Wales, the importance of Larry Sanger, another founder of Wikipedia, can be highlighted. In his own writing, Sanger points out that in the early days of Wikipedia there were hardly any rules or conventions. Sanger strongly advocated strict rules and tighter moderation policies than most other members wanted. Because of this he was forced to leave the development community, but it can still be argued that his influence on the development of the user culture has been at least as important as Jimmy Wales's (see Sanger 2006). This kind of counter role for the user culture designer could be one possible working method for an external user culture designer in general.

Another crucial element in the success of Wikipedia is its acceptance of diversity and different kinds of thoughts on a fundamental level. On the fundamental level the openness of the system and its 'radical trust' in users has lead to a user culture where users have possibilities to make real adjustments, even if the users' position in the hierarchy of the community has a strong effect on the acceptance their acts by others.

For a novice the amount of written rules and conventions can be overwhelming. Because the technical system enables a rich variety of content, there are lots of guides and help pages which can give new users a sense of information overload. This is one reason for the strong emphasis on encouraging newcomers. The Finnish Wikipedia user community has also become aware of the need for well-designed and user-friendly training material for new users. From the old users' perspective continuous alteration can also be seen as a threat, in that new rules or user cultural adjustments may alter established habits. They may see the changes in the user community structure as risks. The growth of community can lead to new problems but existing positions inside the community can also change in response to newcomers. Because of these different perspectives among new and old users, there is a fistful of rules which are ensconced as fundamental guidelines of Wikipedia, referred to in the English version as the *Five Pillars of Wikipedia*.[i] These pillars are the foundation of Wikipedia's user culture and the basis of vibrant user culture design, partially due to the rule that *Wikipedia does have firm rules*.

The challenges of Finnish Wikipedia's user culture design are controllable through explicit discussion. Expressed understanding of the open-source based collaboration and its cultural possibilities and the challenges gives a solid ground for the growing community.

FUTURE TRENDS

In the future the use of open peer-collaboration is going to be growing. In the light of the analysis of Finnish Wikipedia it seems that the trusting USR could be a crucial factor in open-source based or voluntary based collaboration in general. The development of a trusting relationship must be in central role in the forward planning and in the starting process of a peer-collaboration service. Here are some suggestions to designers and facilitators.

The ideology of the service should be analyzed and considered explicitly. In voluntary based collaboration projects there must be a possibility to feel some kind of duty-bound to participate. The central idea of the service should be very simple and it must be attractive for some user group or groups. Because of this the designer or facilitator should locate the essential user groups. These are the groups that can benefit most of the service. These user segments can most likely feel duty-bound to contribute.

The users should be informed about the background of the service. That means the organizational design and structure should be transparent. The used technology should enable parallel development paths and micro-contribution. These features are the starting point that makes the process of evolutionary user culture design possible.

The idea of user culture design must be shared with the whole community. The importance of the guidance of activities and the development of activity tools must be emphasized. These two factors of user culture design are the most vital for the success of open peer-collaboration project. If the community as a whole understands the significance of the bi-directional exchange of practices and explicitly debate on these subjects, there is a strong possibility that there also develops a feel of ownership.

The user interfaces of peer-collaboration tools should be under further development. In the Wikipedia community the lack of instant understanding of the processes, especially for the newcomers, suggests that the user interfaces of showing the history of changes in a wiki is a little bit hard to perceive. This problem could be solved, for example, with figures or diagrams of the development process in a single page or in whole service.

CONCLUSION

On the one hand, the development of the user culture in Finnish Wikipedia is strongly based on the creativity of individual users; on the other hand, it strongly depends on discussion and negotiation. This enables expeditious response to occasional problems without giving too much power to any one individual, since in the long run the majority within the community decides the direction of user culture. These discussions and debates keep the project in transition and keep the user culture lively.

First impressions are a crucial factor in forming a trusting USR. The versatility of the articles, the number of users, the ease of making first contributions and the unconventional openness of Wikipedia tend to give new users a comfortable feeling about the system. Another important factor in the formation of a trusting USR is the flexibility of the existing user culture, which enables an individual to contribute as much or as little as she pleases. The possibility to make quick micro-contributions is also an important feature, because through these small acts a user is transformed from being a content consumer to being a peer-editor almost without noticing it. Little by little the most enthusiastic users get hooked up and take on more and more voluntary responsibility (see Bryant et.al. 2005).

It is evident that the open-source project model of Wikipedia is successful. It can offer a solid operational ground for other content-focused collaboration projects as well. The concepts of user culture, user culture design and user-system-relation also appear to be useful in analyzing and developing social media projects. The user culture perspective could offer helpful tools for social media designers to develop. First we should study the specific methods a designer might use to participate in the user culture design process of a project. Second, we can look at the different kinds of design acts by means of which users can be encouraged to trust and motivated to participate in a project. In the light of this research we can then take the harmony between the different designer methods and design acts in a project to be the source of a trusting USR. From there we can go on to study the different alternatives for harmonious project structures, since Wikipedia represents only one type – albeit an exceptional type – of project structure design for social media.

REFERENCES

Bryant, S. L., Forte, A., & Bruckman, A. (2005). Becoming Wikipedian: Transformation of Participation in a Collaborative Online Encyclopedia. *Proceedings of the 2005 international ACM SIGGROUP conference on Supporting group work. SESSION: Net communities* (pp. 1-10). Sanibel Island, FL: ACM. Retrieved February 1, 2007, from http://portal.acm.org/citation.cfm?id=1099203.1099205

Hine, C. (2000). *Virtual Ethnography.* London: Sage.

Preece, J. (2000). *Online Communities - Designing Usability, Supporting Sociability.* Chichester: Wiley.

Sanger, L. (2006). The Early History of Nupedia and Wikipedia: A Memoir. In C. DiBona, D. Cooper, & M. Stone (Eds.), *Open Source 2.0.* (pp. 307–338). Sebastopol, CA: O'Reilly.

Tuomela, R. (2000). Cooperation. A Philosophical Study. *Philosophical Studies Series, 82.* Dordrecht: Springer.

Wanger, C. (2005). Breaking the Knowledge Acquisition Bottleneck through Conversational Knowledge Management. *Information Resources Management Journal, 19*(1), 70–83.

Wenger, E. (1998). *Communities of Practice. Learning, Meaning, and Identity.* Cambridge: Cambridge.

ENDNOTES

[a]   In my definition the socio-technical system of an open-source-based project includes the technology used and its interfaces, the user community and its members, legal issues (e.g. the copyright licenses), and the background organization of the project.

[b]   I use concept of reification similarly than Wenger (1998, 59). Reification is a process where people in a group develop new kind of concepts or tools for themselves. The reification makes the activity more understandable and effective for the community of practice.

[c]   The Wikimedia Foundation is the background organization behind all different language versions of Wikipedia and other similar projects.

[d]   By the term *Wikiproject* I mean a content producing project within Wikipedia. There are also other projects of Wikimedia Foudation (e.g. Wikitionary, Wikiversity, and Wikispecies), which I refer to as *Wikimedia projects.*

[e]   In Finnish Wikipedia *deletionism* (i.e. users who want to delete not only poor-quality articles, but also articles about marginal issues), *exclusionism* (i.e. users which try to improve the usefulness of articles by deleting all excessive information), *fakkism* (i.e. users which believe the segmentation of the Wikipedia user community is a natural and desirable thing), *inclusionism* (i.e. users

which think that the accuracy of facts is the crown jewel of Wikipedia and want to restore articles about marginal issues), *indifferentism* (i.e. users who do not concern themselves about other users' thoughts and categorizations about her), *mergism* (i.e. users who believe that short or marginal articles should be merged into other articles), and *vandalism* (i.e. users who want to aggravate the development of Wikipedia for some reason) are also mentioned.

[f]   I have borrowed the term micro-contribution from Petri Kola, a researcher in Helsinki University of Art and Design.

[g]   For more about the history of Wikipedia, and its predecessor Nupedia, see Sanger 2006.

[h]   Christian Wanger (2005) writes about the possibilities of conversation-based knowledge management within a Wiki. This same kind of conversational method can be generalized to cover many other aspects of collaborative user culture design as well.

[i]   These pillars do not have a clear counterpart in Finnish Wikipedia for some reason.

Chapter XVI
P2P-Based Management of Collaboration Communication Infrastructures

Cristina Melchiors
Federal University of Rio Grande do Sul, Brazil

Lisandro Zambenedetti Granville
Federal University of Rio Grande do Sul, Brazil

Liane Margarida Rockenbach Tarouco
Federal University of Rio Grande do Sul, Brazil

ABSTRACT

The use of information management tools in open and unbounded operational environments demands an efficient and robust communication infrastructure in order to allow the appropriate transmission of large amount of information and the collaboration among several humans located in geographically distant places, in different organizations, and usually involving several network administrative domains. In order to provide such efficient communication infrastructure, mechanisms for data network management must be used. However, traditional network management models do not provide the required support to the management of such networks. In this context, an alternative distributed network management model must be employed to the efficient management of the communication infrastructure required to support these information management tools. This chapter presents the use of peer-to-peer (P2P) technologies as support for the management of such networks. It presents a P2P-based distributed network management model and a network management environment that follows this model. The functionalities required for the environment are discussed, including its features, potentialities, and drawbacks.

INTRODUCTION

The current information management paradigms present limitations when applied to domains where the operational environment is open and unbounded, such as in human collaboration domain or in complex activities. A new approach to information management that focuses on these requirements and provides tools for them is Open Information Management (Yli-Hietanen & Niiranen, 2008).

The use of information management tools that deal with open operational environments demands an efficient and robust communication infrastructure in order to allow the appropriate transmission of large amount of information and the collaboration among several humans located in geographically distant places, in different organizations, and usually involving several network administrative domains. In order to provide such efficient communication infrastructure, mechanisms for data network management (Clemm, 2007; Commer, 2006; Hegering, Abeck, & Neumair, 1999; Leiwand & Conroy, 1996; Udupa, 1996) must be used.

However, traditional network management models used in current days do not provide the required support to the management of such networks that encompasses several administrative domains. In this context, an alternative distributed network management model must be employed to the efficient management of the communication infrastructure required to support that information management tools.

A promising alternative for these needs is the use of peer-to-peer (P2P) technology (Androutsellis-Theotokis & Spinellis, 2004; Lua, Pias, Sharma, & Lim, 2005), as investigated by Granville et al. (2005) and Panisson, Melchiors, Granville, Almeida, and Tarouco (2006). This chapter will cover the use of P2P as supporting technology for the management of such networks. It will present a P2P-based distributed network management model and a management environment that follows this model. When compared to traditional management environments, the use of this new environment allows the management of networks with several administrative domains, provides better fault tolerance and scalability as well as support for collaboration among human administrators belonging to different network administrative domains. In addition, it provides data and experience sharing among the different entities involved in network management and allows the simplified maintenance of the management environment.

The main objective of this chapter is twofold. First, it presents the limitations of current network management models to managing the communication infrastructure required to support information management tools in open and unbounded operational environments. Second, it presents the distributed network management model and environment based on P2P technology, explaining why such model is suitable for the management of this communication infrastructure and how a management environment based on such model is conceived.

This chapter is organized in five main sections. The *Background* section provides a definition about terminology, network management and P2P technology. The *Current Issues and Problems* subsection of *P2P-Based Distributed Network Management* section discusses the limitations of the current network management models to manage the data communication networks required to support information management tools such as previously discussed. The following subsections of this section present the P2P-based distributed network management model, the network management environment that materializes this model and the services and applications of the environment. *Future Trends* section discusses emerging tendencies. Finally, the *Conclusion* section presents the concluding remarks.

BACKGROUND

This section provides broad definitions to improve the understanding of this chapter. The first subsection discusses the terminology used in the chapter. The second one describes the FCAPS reference model that organizes the network management activities in five functional areas. The third subsection presents the network management paradigms. The forth introduces the P2P technology. Finally, the last one discusses the application of P2P technology to network management.

Terminology

In Computer area, some commonly used terms are employed in a non-strict way, and frequently the same term is used to express different concepts according to its specific context. In order to improve the reading of this chapter, this subsection presents a definition of some terms used through this chapter that can be misunderstood.

There is a lot of confusion between the terms "**paradigm**" and "**model**" when discussing network management approaches. In this chapter, "**paradigm**" will be employed to define in a very higher level the approach used to structure conceptually the network management operations. Here, it will be used for the presentation of *centralized, weakly distributed, strongly distributed and cooperative network management paradigms* (Martin-Flatin, Znaty, & Hubaux, 1999) (see *Network Management Paradigms* subsection).

On the other hand, "**model**" will be used to define a lower level conceptual view of the entities that compose a network management structure and how these entities are organized. A model represents one of the possible ways to employ a paradigm in direction to real world using some domain existent solution, frequently attached to one or more specific technologies. In this chapter, the term model will be used, for instance, when explaining the *manager-agent model* (see *Network Management Paradigms* subsection), when presenting the *computation model* used by P2P systems (see *P2P Technology* subsection) and when discussing the *P2P-based distributed network management model* (see *The P2P-Based Distributed Network Management Model* subsection).

Finally, the term "**environment**" will be employed to discuss how to materialize a model in real world. In this chapter, it is used to define how to apply the presented *P2P-based distributed management model* to a real network management (see *The Management Environment* subsection).

"**Agent**" is used with different purposes in the several Computer areas. When used to network management, this term is applied in almost all cases to name an actor of the *manager-agent model* (see *Network Management Paradigms* section). This is the case, for example, of agents that follows the Simple Network Management Protocol (SNMP) (Harrington, Presuhn, & Wijnen, 2002), usually referred as *SNMP agents*. However, "agent" is also used in Computer domain to define *mobile agents* (Bieszczad, Pagurek & White, 1998; Fuggetta, Picco & Vigna, 1998), a mobile code approach which is characterized by an execution unit that migrates its code and some intermediate results from a node to another. Finally, another use of the term "agent" is related to *intelligent agents* (Cheikhrouhou, Conti, Labetoulle, & Marcus, 1999), an approach originated from Distributed Artificial Intelligence (DAI) and Multi-Agent Systems (MAS) domains. In this chapter, when "agent" appears in an isolated way, it will be used to agents in the context of *manager-agent model*. When applied to a different purpose, "agent" will be used with its additional terms, such as *mobile agent* and *intelligent agent*.

FCAPS Reference Model

Network management involves a set of functionalities related to the operation, administration, maintenance and provisioning of network devices and systems (Clemm, 2007). The functional reference model more established is known as *Fault, Configuration, Accounting, Performance, Security* (FCAPS). It is part of the *Telecommunications Management Network* (TMN) reference model (International Telecommunication Union, 2000a; International Telecommunication Union, 2000b; International Telecommunication Union, 2000c), which provides a set of standards of International Telecommunications Union (ITU). According to FCAPS model, the network management can be organized in five functional areas (Clemm, 2007; Commer, 2006; Leinwand & Conroy, 1996):

- **Fault management:** Involves monitoring the network in order to make sure that everything is happening in a correct way and react when a problem situation is found. Its mainly functionalities are: network monitoring, fault diagnosis, proactive fault management and trouble ticketing. The network monitoring includes collecting network information and measures in order to check if the network is working in a proper way, maintaining the record of the current status of the network and visualizing this status. Two ways are used to collect network information: polling and event notifications including alarms, sent by the managed resources.
- **Configuration management:** Includes several functionalities, such as: to configure managed resources, including the deployment of the initial configuration and its updates through the time; to maintain what is installed and configured in the network; to maintain and restore backups of network configuration; to keep track of the software images installed in the network devices and to provide ways to install new images when they were released by network equipment vendors.
- **Accounting management:** Allows to obtain information about the utilization of the network resources and to keep track of it; to set usage quotas and control them; and to bill users by the utilization of the network resources.
- **Performance management:** Its goal is to monitor network performance and maximizes it. It involves obtaining snapshots of the performance in the network, collecting performance information and analyzing it in order to identify changes in historical values and trends.
- **Security management:** It involves making sure that the access to operation management and managed resources is restricted only to authorized people, keeping security auditing trails that register management operations realized, and monitoring network traffic in order to detect intrusion attempts.

The FCAPS model is used since the nineties, having influenced several researches in network management area. It constitutes a simplification, because some management functionalities are, in fact, executed with several goals and fits several functional areas. However, FCAPS model provides a simple conceptual framework that provides a common terminology. Besides, it allows structuring the network management functionalities, allowing the identification of the several activities that network management should execute in order to manage a network in a complete and effective way.

Network Management Paradigms

Network management is usually accomplished through the **manager-agent model**, in which the manager is responsible to contact agents and to obtain a set of management objects. These objects represent a resource of managed information, hiding from the manager the implementation details to manipulate this information. Besides responding requests from managers, the agents can also send asynchronous messages to managers reporting the occurrence of some event. An example of an architecture that follows this model is Simple Network Management Protocol (SNMP) (Harrington et al., 2002).

The manager-agent model can also be extended to define other more elaborated architectures. An example is the introduction of entities that play the manager and agent roles at the same time. These entities can be used as intermediate managers in order to allow the implementation of hierarchical paradigms.

Several taxonomies have been used to describe the network management paradigms, where one of the most used criteria is organization structure (Martin-Flatin et al., 1999). Using this criterion to classification, the network management paradigms can be grouped in four categories:

- **Centralized paradigm:** The oldest one. It is characterized by the presence of only one manager, that concentrates all management processing and intelligence, and a large set of agents limited to the role of simple data collectors. This paradigm is represented by technologies such as Simple Network Management Protocol version 1 (SNMPv1) (Case, Fedeor, Schoffstall, & Davin, 1990; Rose & McCloghrie, 1991, Rose & McCloghrie, 1990) and Community-based Simple Network Management Protocol version 2 (SNMPv2c) (Case, McCloghrie, Rose, & Waldbusser, 1996; McCloghrie, Perkins, & Schönwälder, 1999; Presuhn, Case, McCloghrie, Rose, & Waldbusser, 2002).
- **Weakly distributed hierarchical paradigm:** In this paradigm, the management system is spread across some entities. There is the presence of a single main manager and a small group of intermediate managers, with one or two magnitude orders between the number of intelligent entities and the number of simple data collector entities involved in the management. This paradigm is followed by technologies such as Remote Network Monitoring (RMON) (Waldbusser, 1997, 2000).
- **Strongly distributed hierarchical paradigm:** In this paradigm, the management processing is decentralized to managers and agents. Now, management tasks are attributed also to agents. Managers and agents are organized in a hierarchical way, with a large number of intermediate managers in relation to the total number of entities. This paradigm if followed by technologies such as mobile agents (Bieszczad et al., 1998) and CORBA (Common Object Request Broker Architecture) (Object Management Group, 2004).
- **Strongly distributed cooperative paradigm**: in this paradigm, the processing is decentralized to managers and agents. It is represented by intelligent agents, originated from Distributed Artificial Intelligence (Martin-Flatin et al., 1999).

P2P Technology

Popularized in the beginning by its utilization in file sharing systems such as Napster and Kazaa, the P2P technology (Androutsellis-Theotokis & Spinellis, 2004; Lua et al., 2005; Milojicic et al., 2003) has

Figure 1. Client-server (a) and P2P (b) models

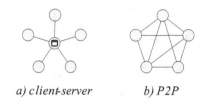

a) client-server   b) P2P

now been largely used for the development of decentralized systems. The P2P operation is based on a virtual computer network and links among its nodes, called **P2P network**. This overlay network is created upon a physical computer network, typically a TCP/IP network. It is composed of software nodes (**peers**) that can act as clients and servers simultaneously, sending requests to other peers and responding requests received. The computational model adopted by P2P systems contrasts with the one adopted in client-server systems, where a small number of servers, usually with big computation capacity, attends a large number of clients. In figure 1, the left schema *(a)* presents a client-server system example where a server attends simultaneously requests from five clients; the right schema *(b)* presents a P2P system with five peers that can play client and server roles simultaneously.

Several characteristics are attributed to P2P networks, including decentralization, scalability, auto-organization, application transparency, resource sharing and collaboration facilities. These characteristics make P2P technology very promising to be used as support to distributed network management. Using such technology the management environment can deal with very large networks, constant inclusion of new technologies and collaborative management of networks with several distinct administrative domains, as will be discussed in following sections.

P2P Technology Applied to Network Management

The use of P2P technology to network management has been investigated in some researches. State and Festor (2003) propose a network management framework using Java Management Extensions (JMX) technology (Sun Microsystems, 2006) and JXTA infrastructure (Gong, 2001; Traversat et al., 2003). The devices and service agents are structured using JMX and the JXTA service search mechanisms and communication channels are used as base. Service dependencies are treated through an extension of JXTA announcement services.

Another work that deals with use of P2P networks to network management is presented by Binzenhöfer, Tutschku, Graben, Fiedler, and Arlos (2006). This work proposes a framework to network management project for Quality of Service (QoS) tests and monitoring. Its architecture is based on homogeneous agents that makes a management overlay based on a distributed hash table (DHT). It represents an independent distributed application that provides support for a central management station.

With a different approach, some researches analyze the use of overlay networks to aggregation functions with network management purpose. Dam and Stadler (2005) propose a protocol called GAP that calculates device variables aggregated values in a continuous way. The protocol is based on a distributed algorithm that constructs and maintains a network tree graph, using this tree to propagate aggregated values to the root node. An extension of this protocol is presented by Pietro and Stadler (2007), called A-GAP. This protocol uses a filter schema to message propagation, sending aggregation messages only when a minimum difference between the current value and the last update value was reached.

In a previous work (Granville et al., 2005), we have presented an initial model to distributed network management based on P2P and have discussed some example of facilities provided by the use of this model. The present document extends this, discussing several new aspects. An improved model is now showed. A management environment that materializes this model is also presented and discussed, analyzing a complete view of the main services and applications of the functional areas of network management, including the characteristics, potentialities, benefits and difficulties to the deployment of each service.

Finally, the document from Panisson et al. (2006) presents a framework for implementation of peers that materialize a management entity. It discusses the components of a management peer and implementation details of such components, focusing on how to implement a network management peer using JXTA (Gong, 2001; Traversat et al., 2003).

According to the knowledge of the authors of this chapter, there is not a document in Computer literature that compiles in an integrated way the topics and aspects discussed in this work.

P2P-BASED DISTRIBUTED NETWORK MANAGEMENT

As previously discussed, information management tools that deal with open operation environments involve the transmission of large amount of information and the collaboration among humans located in geographically distant places, usually in several network administrative domains. In order to provide the robust and efficient communication infrastructure required for the utilization of these tools, data network management mechanisms should be used.

This section presents a data network management approach for the management of such communication infrastructure. The first subsection discusses the issues and problems of current data network management approaches when applied to the management of communication infrastructure like this one. The following subsections present the use of P2P technologies as support for the management of such data networks.

Current Issues and Problems

In domains where the information has not well-defined limits and evolves constantly, such as in Medicine and Life Sciences areas, the current existent information management approaches have limitations. It happens because the use of pre-designed and static structures to content is not appropriate and adaptable to collaboration requirements. In such domains, tools based on dynamic structures are required both to allow the collaboration of the involved humans and to evolve with their own use, as presented by Yli-Hietanen and Niiranen (2008). These tools allow, in an iterative and collective way, to handle large amount of information and to get correlations among them, identifying individual meanings for particular cases.

In virtue of their iterative, collective and collaborative use, such tools demand continuous and broadly available communication support, in order to provide system access at any time, in any place. At the same time, because the collaboration frequently involves the interaction of remote groups, the communication support should offer means for the tools to be used by groups localized in different and distant organizations. The support to remote access should even allow these tools to handle, in an efficient and robust way, large amounts of information localized remotely. This way, such new information management tools have communication and support requirements that demand a robust, efficient and pervasive communication infrastructure, providing high availability and performance.

Providing a communication infrastructure with these characteristics and high quality requirements is only possible through the appropriate management of the data networks involved in the communication, through efficient and novel network management mechanisms. At the same time, such mechanisms should support the management of different network administrative domains, because remote groups localized in different organizations and, presumably, in different network administrative domains, should interact in an appropriate way through the information management tools.

The current network management models do not provide the required support to the management of networks with the requirements listed above; especially with regards to the management of networks that encompasses several administrative domains. Models that follow the *centralized and weakly distributed hierarchical network management paradigms* (Martin-Flatin et al., 1999) present several limitations of scalability and fault tolerance (Schönwälder, Quittek, & Kappler, 2000). The *centralized network management paradigm* concentrates the management traffic and processing in a unique network management station. It generates serious scalability problems and represents a unique point of failure. The *weakly distributed hierarchical network management paradigm* distributes the management in some stations in the network. However, although it distributes the actions in the network, the management processing is still concentrated in very few stations, also generating scalability limitations. Besides, in case of failure in the communication between the manager station and the agents, these agents have no other ways to make corrective actions.

Network management models that follow the *strongly distributed hierarchical network management paradigm* (Martin-Flatin et al., 1999) also present limitations. In this paradigm, the management processing is decentralized to managers and agents, involving a large number of network elements. This way, this paradigm offers scalability and fault tolerance requirements. Nonetheless, it does not solve the requirements for interaction and collaboration among several administrative domains because the hierarchical structure of this paradigm demands a central point of decision. Besides, although several network management models following this paradigm have been proposed based on technologies such as mobile agents, CORBA, etc; these models have seldom been applied in real networks. That is so in virtue of their limitations such as the complexity involved in designing, developing and maintaining such environments, the processing power required to operate such environments, etc. Finally, although the *cooperative network management paradigm* (Martin-Flatin et al.) seems to be appropriate to the requirements of such networks, few network management models following this paradigm have been proposed and real examples of their use are rarely found.

In this context, an alternative distributed network management model must be employed to the efficient management of the communication infrastructure required to support these information management tools. In this section, we will present a model and environment to the management of such complex modern networks.

The P2P-Based Distributed Network Management Model

The P2P-based distributed network management model aggregates to traditional management models the functionalities provided by the utilization of an infrastructure composed by a P2P network. So, P2P network characteristics, such as decentralization, auto-organization, transparency to applications, file sharing and collaboration facilities can now be used by the distributed management model, bringing several potentialities to the management facilities supported by the model.

In the P2P-based distributed network management model (Granville et al., 2005), each peer in P2P network represents a management entity, responsible by some functionalities. The set of peers composes the management system and this system is responsible to lead and maintain the managed network in an appropriate status. The peers that compose the management system can play different roles, each one with a distinct function, representing a specific management entity. This way, the P2P-based management model is composed by four entities:

- *Network administrator interface entity*, that provides applications and tools directly to human network administrator. The peer represented by this entity, reacting to requests from human administrator, communicates to other peers to perform a management task;
- *Managed resource control entity*, responsible by the communication with the agents of the managed resources, executing management activities over such resources. The peer represented by this entity retrieves managed devices information and reports the status of such devices. This peer has no contact with human users;
- *Management service entity*, that provides management functionalities to the environment. This peer has no contact with human users, it interacts only with other peers in the network;
- *P2P network connectivity entity*, that provides connectivity functionalities to P2P network. The peer represented by this entity reacts to other peer requests and has no contact with human users.

The peers represented by the first three entities simultaneously execute management activities and communicate with other peers in the network. The peers represented by the forth entity also communicates with other peers, improving the network connectivity. Figure 2 presents the schema of the model.

Figure 2. P2P-based network management

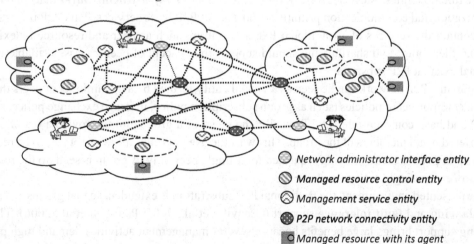

○ Network administrator interface entity
○ Managed resource control entity
○ Management service entity
● P2P network connectivity entity
□ Managed resource with its agent

Figure 3. Managed resource view

In the model, the *managed resource control entity* can be seen in a unified way with the management software of the real resource, as composed by two distinct parts: the first one represented by the real managed resource, its services and its native management software; the second, represented by the peer responsible for the management of the resource. In this way, the native management support existent in several network devices, usually rigid and limited, can be extended by the inclusion of the peer responsible by the management of the resource. Figure 3 shows the unified view of a managed resource.

The Management Environment

The network management model discussed in the previous subsection represents a conceptual view of the main entities present in the P2P-based network management and how these entities are organized. This model is applied in real network management through a network management environment that materializes the defined model. This subsection presents this environment, discusses its requirements, its architecture and its service, as well as its application categories. The following subsections describe in detail its services and applications.

A management environment that materializes the P2P-based distributed network management model should support functionalities that allow the effective management of the network, attending both the requirements already identified in traditional network management models (that are also needed in this new model) and the new ones that have arisen with the complex modern networks. Several functionalities categories should be offered in order to make operational the management environment, including *environment infrastructural services category* and *network management services category*.

These functionalities categories were developed above a ***P2P infrastructure layer*** that contains a set of organization and communication primitives and a set of P2P basic services. This P2P infrastructure should contain the services of a traditional P2P substratum, such as peer and resource indexing and searching; file storage and sharing; and should support the concept of peer groups, available in some traditional existent P2P substrata.

A group in a P2P network can be seen as a virtual entity formed by a dynamic set of peers that have defined a common set of policies (such as group subscription police, message exchange police, security policies) and have common interests. Typically, the peers of a group aim to provide a list of services that is offered by all members of the group. This way, the use of groups allows a service to be requested for a group of peers instead of being requested for a single peer only. A group is seen, to the rest of the P2P network, as a single entity.

In the presented environment, the traditional P2P substratum is extended, so that groups can provide **load balancing** and **fault tolerance** support (Granville et al., 2005; Panisson et al., 2006). The **load balancing** support brings large benefits because several management activities demand high processing power. With load balancing, the management activities can be distributed transparently among all the peers of a group, in a balanced way, and be seen as attributed to a single entity. Groups can also be used to provide better **fault tolerance** in service availability. It is done by implementing mechanisms in groups so that even when peers join and leave the groups dynamically, at least one peer always is member of the group. It can be provided through a service of the group itself that monitors periodically the active peers in that group, activating other peers if necessary, or it can be provided through a P2P network service responsible for monitoring active groups membership.

Figure 4 presents the schema of the *integrated distributed environment structure*, showing the *services categories* and *P2P infrastructure* that makes part of the environment. The structure represents the integrated environment, composed by the union of all the peers included in the management environment. The *infrastructural* and *network management services categories* are, in fact, distributed among several peers. A service or application can be spread through one or more peers, according the specific service or application provided. Finally, the P2P infrastructure is distributed among all the peers that compose the environment.

The **environment infrastructure services category** (or just **infrastructural services**) comprehends the basic services useful to any distributed environment. Such services can be used by network management services and applications and by other infrastructural services. This category includes structural and environment maintenance services. One of the main services of this category is the notification service. This service provides the propagation of notifications indicating events occurred in network managed resources. Such service is responsible to disseminate and to publish critical network information through the network. It involves one of the most important activities of network management and it is part of network monitoring activity. The notification service is also used in several other contexts by several other client services such as performance services (sending alarms indicating threshold crossing values in performance data collection) and configuration services (sending notifications reporting new software versions).

Other services of this category are related to facilities that the P2P-based distributed environment makes available to the maintenance of the environment itself, such as services to automatically install software components in peers when necessary and services to update the software component versions

Figure 4. Integrated distributed environment structure

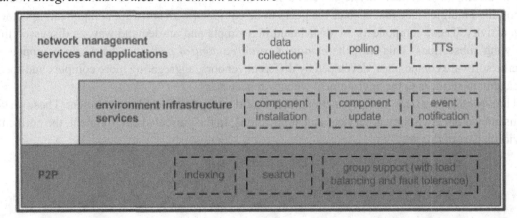

when a new software version is available. In management environments, especially in complex modern networks, the presence and efficiency of such maintenance services are very relevant because there are a large number of entities involved in management, with a large heterogeneity of managed resources and high update rate. It is crucial that the management environment can be updated in a simplified way to support new types of devices, new functionalities, and so on. In the presented environment, the utilization of a P2P infrastructure brings large benefits to these services through its file sharing support and its inherent mechanisms that facilitates the localization of resources in the network.

Finally, the ***network management services and applications category*** comprehends the facilities used in network management. This category includes (*i*) facilities already present in traditional network management environments that are also necessary in this new environment and (*ii*) facilities that are available only because of the potentialities of the P2P-based distributed environment. In the first set (*i*), even if it has already been implemented in traditional management environments, several services and applications can be remodeled to obtain benefits of the characteristics and potentialities of the new P2P-based distributed environment in order to attend for scalability, fault tolerance, heterogeneity support, multiple administrative domain collaboration and high update rates of complex modern networks. Examples of such services and applications include polling service, performance data collection service and trouble ticket applications. The second set (*ii*) includes services and applications that are now possible thanks to the use of P2P-based distributed environment. This set attends requirements of the new complex modern networks. Examples include tools designed to improve the interaction and collaboration among human administrators of different administrative domains; the sharing and reutilization of management parameters and configuration tools; and mechanisms to facilitate the distribution of software images to the managed devices.

The following sections present the several facilities that compose the P2P-based distributed management environment, their characteristics and potentialities.

Environment Infrastructure Services

The *environment infrastructure services* include *environment maintenance and structural services* useful to any distributed environment. The *environment maintenance services* involve functionalities that make it possible to deploy and to maintain the management environment. It includes, for instance, services such as installing new software components in the existent management entities and keeping software components updated. The presented environment, thanks to the P2P infrastructure, benefits a simplified maintenance that enables the peers to be equipped with software components specific for each activity. These components are distributed in a simple and on-demand way, as discussed in the following subsections. This way, the *managed resource control peers* can be easily equipped with specific software components, developed by different vendors, aggregating more complex and specific management services to the environment whenever necessary.

The *structural services* involve functionalities useful to any distributed environment. These services are used by other environment services and applications. In the presented environment, the notification service is part of this set.

On-Demand Software Component Auto-Installation Service

Through time, new resources, including new devices and services, are installed in the networks. In complex modern networks, this characteristic is still more stressed thanks to the large heterogeneity of existent technologies and the constant new demands presented by users. That way, several entities involved in management have to be updated frequently in order to provide an effective network management.

In the presented environment, this update is easier because of the resource search and file sharing support provided by P2P infrastructure. So, when a peer wants to provide a service but the respective software component has not yet been installed, it searches through the network whose peers have the software component, chooses one of these peers and download it automatically from the chosen one, without requiring any human administrator interaction. This auto-installation functionality can be used, for instance, when a *managed resource control peer* finds a new device that it is not able to deal with, or when a human administrator designates that a specific activity be executed by a specific peer and this peer is still not equipped with the software components required to execute this activity.

Software Components Update Service

The P2P infrastructure of the management environment can also be used to update software component versions in the peers. This task, usually laborious in a traditional environment, can be easier in the P2P-based environment by the inclusion of mechanisms that uses the distributed environment and the file sharing along with the resource search of P2P infrastructure.

When a new management software version is received, the human administrator (via an application in a *network administrator interface entity*) indicates the availability of a new software component management version. The application uses resource search mechanisms of P2P infrastructure to identify the peers that have that software component installed and notifies them about the availability of a new version. The interested peers download the new version and install it automatically.

Notification Service

One of the main tasks of fault management is network monitoring that includes event notification propagation from managed resources to interested management applications. Initially, for instance in SNMP-based management platforms, this interaction was done, usually, by the configuration of one or more manager IP addresses in the SNMP agents. In these platforms, when an event is generated, the SNMP agent sends SNMP traps directly to the manger IP addresses configured.

However, this mechanism is not appropriate to the management of the complex modern networks composed by a large number of managed resources. Besides, the utilization of a distributed management model as the one presented demands the utilization of a communication approach that allows decoupling among the managed entities and the manager role entities. An appropriated approach for this context that has been largely used to notification propagation in distributed environments is a notification service based on publish-subscribe paradigm (Behnel, Fiege, & Mühl, 2006; Eugster, Felber, Guerraoui, & Kermarrec, 2003; Mahambre, Kumar, & Bellur, 2007).

In this communication paradigm, **subscribers** inform their interest in receiving certain events through a **subscription**. When these events occur, they are published in publish-subscribe infrastructure by the **publishers** and the related subscribers are notified of their occurrence. The paradigm is based on a notification service that mediates the communication between publishers and subscribers, providing the subscription management with an efficient delivery of the events.

One of the main advantages of publish-subscribe utilization is the provided decoupling of space, time and synchronization (Eugster et al., 2003), that enhance the systems scalability. Subscribers and publishers do not have to know each other. When an event occurs, publishers publish this event through the notification service, without worrying about the interested subscribers. Besides, subscribers and publishers do not have to actively participate in communication. According the quality of service provided by the publish-subscribe infrastructure, publishers can publish events when subscribers are not connected to the network: when the subscribers join the network again, they receive the previous published notifications. Finally, when publishers publish a notification, they do not need to block while the interested subscribers receive the message. The notification is done asynchronously because the event publication by the publisher and the event receipt by the subscribers do not occur in the main control flow. The decoupling of such systems also allows that publishers and subscribers do not know the publish-subscribe network organization and size: the network can be composed by a single broker or by a set of them, organized in different architectures.

The utilization of a publish-subscribe infrastructure in a network management environment should allow the transmission of notifications according the characteristics and the quality of service (QoS) demanded in such environment. At the same time, it should consider the characteristics of the P2P network under the management environment.

The **message model** of the notification service should support the three types of messages: advertisements, subscriptions and notifications. **Advertisement** messages are used *by managed resource control entities* to inform the network about the properties of the notifications that they are able to publish, according the resources managed by these entities. **Subscription** messages are used by subscribers to inform to the infrastructure which events they want to receive. Typically, the subscription messages are sent by *network administrator interface entities* and *management service entities*. Finally, **notification messages** are used typically by *managed resource control entities* to inform the occurrence of an event that was previously advertised.

The **subscription schema** supported by the model should be flexible to allow dealing with new events in the management network. It should also provide support to events with variable characteristics because the management network has a large resource heterogeneity that results in different types of events, originated from several protocols, with different attributes.

The **architecture** of the infrastructure can be distributed or intermediate. A centralized architecture, implemented by a single broker, is not viable for this model because it has a single point of failure. It results in high traffic in the links next to the broker and it demands large processing power in single equipment.

The **dissemination** of the notifications should be done by taking care of the several characteristics of the network management environment. The scalability must be observed because in a computer network there is a large number of managed resources. In addition, in situations where a fault occurs in a managed resource, it is common to generate a large number of events in a very short time, emitted by the fault resource itself and by the other resources affected by the fault. It gets worse in situations which the fault results in a reduction of the available network links bandwidth, since a large number of notifications is generated in an environment where the bandwidth is reduced. Fault tolerance requirements must also be considered in the way used to notification dissemination, in order for important events never to be lost in the management network.

The support provided by P2P networks has been largely used for notification dissemination in publish-subscribe (Choi & Park, 2005; Courtenage & Williams, 2006; Gupta, Sahin, Agrawal, & Abbadi, 2004; Koubarakis, Tryfonopoulos, Idreos, & Drougas, 2003). In the presented environment, this utilization is easier because P2P infrastructure integrates the management model. The P2P infrastructure can be used in different ways, for different mechanisms. The notification sending mechanisms can, for instance, locate the subscriptions (therefore, the subscribers) using a distributed hash table (DHT) (Choi & Park; Gupta et al.); can also identify the subscribers through super-peers (Koubarakis et al.); or even access the subscribers directly via communication channels previously initialized. Hybrid mechanisms can be used as well, as the one proposed by Courtenage and Williams, that uses a structured P2P network for infrastructure configuration and JXTA framework to provide event routing. P2P network functionalities that provide physical topology awareness can be used as well besides being useful in event dissemination. They can consider network features such as bandwidth, fault tolerance of the involved links, physical distance between the nodes, administrative domain which the node is part of, and so on.

Regarding **quality of service (QoS) guarantees** in publish-subscribe systems (Behnel et al., 2006; Eugster et al., 2003; Mahambre et al., 2007), two big groups exist: *global infrastructure level guarantees* and *subscription and notification level guarantees*. These guarantees will be discussed bellow.

Global Infrastructure Level QoS Guarantees

In environments that use P2P support to disseminate the notifications, the *global infrastructure level QoS guarantees* are heavy related to the provided P2P infrastructure. Besides, the adoption of publish-subscribe paradigm in a management environment demands a careful look at certain QoS guarantees. Some examples are bandwidth and delivery guarantees.

The **bandwidth** consumed by the publish-subscribe infrastructure is related to its architecture and the way used to notification dissemination. The bandwidth requirement to the execution of the publish-subscribe infrastructure is an important feature because the management should cause the minor possible impact in the real physical network. It is important, therefore, to make possible for the publishers to include in their advertisements which is the traffic limit that their events generate. Besides, it should be possible for the subscriptions to delimitate what the maximum bandwidth is that the publish-subscribe infrastructure is allowed to use when attending the subscription. This bandwidth control need is more important if management entities in mobile nodes are present, because such nodes have severe resource limitations and a higher traffic can cause them energy consumption they do not support.

The *event composition* can be an alternative to reduce bandwidth. It happens because by using it, only one message is generated and delivered by the publish-subscribe infrastructure in substitution for delivering several published messages that follow certain sequence or pattern, in a way that the generated message represents the several original published messages. This composition can be done in subscription level, as proposed by Courtenage and Williams (2006). The support to event composition, however; elevates the complexity level of the other infrastructure aspects such as subscription schema, architecture, event dissemination, and so on. The proximity of concepts in event composition and *network management event correlation* – topic very discussed in network management area (Commer, 2006) – suggests a unified analysis of both techniques in order to allow the integration of network management event correlation in publish-subscribe model.

The **delivery guarantees** demanded in the management environment are related to the characteristics of the generated events and their severity. In a general analysis, in alarm notification, the notification reception must be done because it is through this notification that the management environment will be able to detect the occurrence of a fault in a managed resource. With the elimination of the network monitoring via polling, this requirement receives more importance because the reception of the notification is now the only way for the management system to identify the fault occurrence.

The **duplication delivery** of a notification can cause problems to certain subscribers, according to the goals of the applications used by them. In applications which the goal is only to show the last status of a resource, the occurrence of a duplicated notification message does not cause a problem because the application will show consistent results. However, in applications where the ones that present a list of events occurred in the network, the presence of duplicated messages can cause incorrect interpretations if no way to eliminate them is provided. The same occurs for alarm correlation, because the occurrence of identical sequential alarms can cause the generation of a specific correlated alarm.

So, in an environment like the one presented, it is convenient that the subscriptions indicate the guarantees required by the subscribers. This indication can be used also in advertisements and notifications: publishers could indicate default requirements to the notification and these requirements could be overwritten by the subscribers. The possibility of publishers indicating the required guarantees is important when dealing with new events without needing to configure the subscriber applications.

The **message persistence** is another important guarantee in network management environments, varying according to the subscriber goals. For instance, applications in mobile nodes that need to show the last resource status can substitute persistence by a refreshing mechanism when the node is connected to the network again. When analyzing the need for persistence in each subscriber, it should be considered for which time the notifications will remain valid. In a general analysis, the support for notification persistence is important because any fault in a physical network link can cause interruption in the P2P network channels, blocking the alarm sending even from those resources not involved in the fault.

Subscription and Notification Level QoS Guarantees

As previously presented, the second group of QoS guarantees in publish-subscribe systems is related to the semantics of subscription and notifications (Behnel et al., 2006; Eugster et al., 2003; Mahambre et al., 2007).

The **notification order** in network management can be relevant to some kind of notifications in some subscribers because sometimes the occurrence of one event after another one is relevant to identify the root of the fault. As this guarantee is not demanded by all subscribers, this requirement should be configured in subscription.

Another important guarantee is the **interval validity** of notification. It can be expressed in a time unity or through the reception of a more recent notification. This guarantee, especially in situations where the notification validity is identified by the reception of another more recent notification, is related to order and delivery guarantees. The use of **redundant sources** for the same event is not relevant for network management environments given it generates large traffic volume without providing real guarantees for the delivery of the notification.

The **sporadic or periodic delivery** indicates if the notification can be received periodically, reporting the status of the information at the moment, or sporadically, reporting only changes in the status of the information based on the comparison of the current information value with the previous value using pre-configured thresholds. This guarantee is not necessary in a basic publish-subscribe system applied to a management environment. However, it can be used in a more elaborated infrastructure to implement several management tasks. For instance, this guarantee can proportionate the filtering of duplicated alarms that are generated repeatedly to indicate the same fault situation, or it can be extended to eliminate oscillating alarms, where the same fault situation causes repeatedly alarm sequences.

The **subscription selectivity** in network management environment should allow for the subscription to define event filter features such as managed resource type, information type, event information content, and so on. Because of the large number of managed resources in a network and the performance requirements usually present in such environments, the matching schema among the published notifications and the subscriptions emitted by the subscribers should enable a small number of false positives and should be done, if possible, next to the publishers.

Some management environments can also demand **authentication** requirements for subscribers and publishers. This can be necessary in order to avoid that not authorized subscribers and publishers receive and publish events. Finally, the **confidentiality** of the notifications can be necessary in management environments such as the ones in corporative networks, military networks, and so on. In these contexts, cryptography can be used over the P2P networks.

Publish-Subscribe Service in Management Environment

The deployment of a publish-subscribe notification service in a network management environment results in benefits for several services and applications in the environment, that can now use a scalable, efficient and flexible mechanism for the sending of notifications of any type. The use of a P2P network in publish-subscribe infrastructure has been studied, as previously discussed, in several systems (Choi & Park, 2005; Courtenage & Williams, 2006; Gupta et al., 2004; Koubarakis et al., 2003). It has been used in these systems to locate subscriptions and to route notifications for the interested subscribers through its communication and search mechanisms. In the presented environment, the notification service execution is realized using the peers of the environment themselves. *Network administrator interface peers*, *managed resource control peers* and *management service peers* can take over the role of subscriber. Typically, the role of publishers is performed by *managed resource control peers* and *management service peers*. However, *network administrator interface peers* can also publish notifications (for instance, when reporting a user action in an application, like with the inclusion of a resource in a map that controls the devices to be monitored). The notification service itself is implemented over all peers that compose the environment, making use, according to the used architecture, of the P2P infrastructure to communicate among publishers and subscribers.

In a network management environment the main management service that uses this structural service is the sending of events, including alarms, from the managed resources to the management applications and services. However, other services can also use the notification service. Examples include the service of installing new software images and the service of generating performance alarms. These functionalities will be detailed in the next sections.

Network Management Services and Applications

The *network management services and applications* include the environment facilities that perform the management of the network devices. Some of these facilities have already been used in traditional management environments, but their transposition to a P2P-based distributed environment should be analyzed in order to identify how to design each facility in the new environment, as well as the potentials and drawbacks of their utilization in this new context. Other management facilities are new in management environments. These facilities are now offered thanks to features of this new environment, such as the use of a distributed environment and the collaboration and file sharing support provided by the P2P infrastructure. In the next sections, the main network management facilities of the proposed environment will be discussed and detailed.

Sending/Receiving Event Notifications from Managed Resources

In a traditional management environment, there are a small number of intelligent entities involved in management and a large number of entities only responsible for reporting the device status. Nonetheless, this traditional approach is not adequate for the management of complex modern networks that are composed by a large number of resources, since the management processing is concentrated in only few entities. In virtue of that, in the proposed environment, the management operations are distributed to several peers of the network. In this new approach, the *managed resource control peers* are responsible for identifying the notifications generated by the resources, converting these notifications into the P2P network information model and publishing the notifications in the publish-subscribe notification service discussed in the previous section. The peers interested in receiving event notifications from any managed resource send a subscription message to the notification service and this service is responsible for transmitting the notifications through the publish-subscribe infrastructure.

Polling

The use of polling operation for network monitoring is not an appropriate approach in complex modern networks because it causes a large amount of traffic in the network links and it demands high processing power at the application management station. Because of that, the polling task has been avoided whenever possible and has been replaced by event and alarm notification reception.

However, the polling task can be necessary in some situations. It happens, for instance, when a management application needs to monitor the status of device information that does not generate events. Another example is when the event delivery is not guaranteed, like with managed resources that support only SNMPv1 traps. In these situations, a distributed architecture can be employed in such a way that the information request is executed by network entities topologically close to the devices. These entities are responsible for generating and publishing event and alarm notifications that indicate the occurrence of anomalous situations.

In the presented management environment, the polling task can be implemented by a service provided by a group of *managed resource control peers*. This service is responsible for the generation and publication of alarms when an undesirable situation is identified. It can be done equipping these peers with software components prepared to effectively manage each particular resource. These components do not need to be present in the original peer configuration: they can be obtained using P2P network support, as discussed in previous section *On-Demand Software Component Auto-Installation Service*. This way, when the peer identifies device information such as device type, version and vendor, the peer sends a message requesting which other peers own the desired component. When the peer receives the responses, it contacts one of the peers, downloads the software component, activates the component in itself and starts managing the device.

When compared to polling of traditional environments, the polling operation in the presented management environment has the advantage of distributing the management tasks to a large number of nodes, improving the processing power and link traffic distribution. This is different of traditional environments, in which the polling task is usually designed for a very small number of machines. Besides, in the presented environment several facilities are provided by the use of groups, such as fault tolerance and possibility of distributing polling among all the peer members of the group according to parameters such as processing power and memory capacity of each peer, peer reliability, network distance between the peer and the managed resource, link traffic utilization in the links between the peer and the managed resource.

Performance Data Collection

The performance data collection from the managed resources is one of the management tasks that can cause larger traffic volume in network links when realized in a traditional way, with few entities with manager role responsible for the data collection. So, alternative ways to perform this task need to be evaluated in a management environment that aims at providing scalability.

Two main approaches can be used to improve data collection and solve these problems. If the managed resource has support to be configured to perform the data collection itself from its managed data, the resource should do that and store the collected data locally. In so doing, a manager entity can request the collected data periodically, for instance, once a day, during the night. However, this facility is not supported by most of the managed resources and a second approach has to be used. In these situations, *managed resource control peers* are designated to perform data collection. This is done through group service, in which a group service provided by some peers collects data from a set of resources, in a similar way as discussed in the polling task. This data collection approach, as well as in polling, is improved thanks to the features provided by the P2P network group support, that allows developing mechanisms to select which peer in the group will execute a specific activity according load balancing, network proximity between the peer and the managed resource, etc, besides providing better fault tolerance.

Fault Management Facilities to Improve Interaction among Human Administrators

Fault management tasks can benefit from the inclusion of functionalities that provide higher human administrators interaction, especially in tasks usually demanding the presence of human administrators to be executed, such as fault diagnosis. The support in cooperating, inherent to P2P environment, makes it easier for the development of managing tools to provide human collaboration, inclusive for humans located in different administrative domains. These tools could, for instance, perform execution tests in a link that crosses several administrative domains and demands the interaction of the several administrative domains involved.

Instant message, voice and file sharing tools are the examples more common of facilities that can be employed to provide higher interaction among human administrators. Besides these, other more specific for network management can be implemented, such as tools to execute and monitor tests through several administrative domains, tools to construct network topology maps, tools to share views for network monitoring, etc.

Distributed Trouble Ticket Systems

Trouble ticket systems (Clemm, 2007) are tools used by network administrator to manage the faults occurred in the network, helping monitor the problems occurred, keeping a record of their life cycle and storing the historical memory of the network faults. These systems are traditionally used to register problems of a single domain, being used uniquely by the team responsible for the management of that domain. However, when transposed to a P2P-based distributed management environment, these systems can be enhanced by using file sharing and collaboration facilities of P2P infrastructure. That way, the systems can perform trouble ticket sharing among the several administrative domains. It allows for the historical memory of a domain to be used for increasing the knowledge of the other network administrative domains.

Some trouble ticket systems were improved in the past in order to use an Artificial Intelligence technique called Case-Based Reasoning (CBR) (Bartsch-Sporl, Lenz, & Hubner, 1999; Kolodner, 1993; McBurney & Parsons, 2005) for fault diagnosis. These systems propose solutions for current problems using the trouble tickets from previous situations (cases), like Dumbo system (Melchiors & Tarouco, 2000). These systems, initially designed for a traditional management environment, can now also be improved through their transposition to the new P2P-based distributed environment. The file sharing support of the P2P infrastructure helps the use of distributed case bases, allowing the integration of case bases in different administrative domains. Besides, the search support provided P2P infrastructure can be adapted to the retrieval of similar cases. It brings performance improvements in the similar case retrievals and, at the same time, allows the search to be performed in a paralyzed way since the case similarity calculation can be distributed along the whole network, being realized in the peers where the cases are stored, in a similar way to the one proposed by Berkovsky, Kuflik, and Ricci (2005).

The support to collaboration of P2P infrastructure can also be integrated to the existent trouble ticket systems with CBR through the improvement of their cases and their adaptation mechanism. So, after the case retrieval mechanism that retrieves trouble tickets stored in several administrative domains, the system can use information present in the cases to perform automatic tasks, such as starting the execution of cooperation and communication tools to the human administrators involved in the fault (through network administrator interface peers), proposing or activating integrated tests execution (through *managed resource control peers*), and so on.

Facilities for Sharing and Reusing of Management and Configuration Parameters

The support provided by P2P networks for data sharing can also be employed to improve or automate management tasks by the use of data already present in other network entities. An example is the network device monitoring through *managed resource control peers*. In this situation, the monitoring of two similar devices will have similar monitoring configuration parameters. Therefore, a human administrator can reuse the configuration parameters from one device to the others making only small changes when necessary. That way, a tool to improve the configuration of the device monitoring can be employed. This tool uses the P2P infrastructure search and data sharing support to search for similar contexts in other peers in the network, retrieve the files with configuration parameters from these peers and present these parameters to the human administrator for confirmation. The search can consider characteristics from the device such as device type, version and management protocol used, device functionality, administrative domain, etc. The tool can also contain mechanisms to automatically configure these parameters according the policies established by human administrator.

Similarly, tools to configure the devices themselves can use configuration data from other devices. Human administrators can use these tools to obtain and reuse information present in the other entities of network even from different administrative domains. Additional goals of these tools include sharing and reusing of event reception subscriptions as well as performance data collection configuration parameters.

Artificial Intelligence techniques like CBR can be employed to improve the process of identify similar contexts, too. This way, the subscription and configuration parameter files are seen as cases and each peer that contains these files is seen as a case base. The search and matching mechanisms of the CBR retrieval process use case bases distributed over the several peers, providing the use of enhanced techniques to identify similar data in the other peers in the network.

The sharing and reusing information tools can also be combined with tools for collaboration among the several administrative domains. It is useful, for example, in a situation where it is necessary to configure devices in more than one administrative domain, like the configuration of a link that crosses several administrative domains. These tools can provide the cooperation among the domains and, simultaneously, share information among them and apply this configuration in a semi-automatic way. These tools are still more relevant in complex modern networks because they manage functionalities that need to be configured in several administrative domains synchronizedly, like in bandwidth reservation of network links.

Distribution of New Software Images to Managed Devices

One of the configuration management tasks is the maintenance of software images installed in the managed devices. In the management environment presented, this task can be made easier by the inclusion of mechanisms that uses the distributed environment and the file sharing and resource search support of the P2P infrastructure.

Thus, when the human administrator receives a new software version of a certain device type, he informs a tool (at a *network administrator interface peer*) which are the characteristics of the new image, such as device type, version, update demand (critical, recommended, optional) and effects of its installation (none execution interruption, temporary interruption without reset the device, reset of the device). Two approaches can then be employed to update the image.

In the first approach, the peer searches the network requesting which devices are of that type and which *managed resource control peers* are responsible by these devices. Using pre-configured policies, the tool identifies which devices should be updated and which should not (like when device cannot be interrupted at that time). The tool presents the list of devices to be updated to the human administrator and he changes it if necessary. The administrator confirms the list and the tool sends the *managed resource control peers* the new software image. These peers can install the new image using a management protocol or other mechanism of the device. The tool can also allow that the human administrator or network policies to indicate at what time the images not marked for installation should be further installed. This schedule is informed to the *managed resource control peers* and they install the image at the appropriated time.

This approach concentrates a lot of control in the *network administrator interface peer*, allowing the human intervention in several steps. It also demands that the *managed resource control peers* be equipped with a software component that updates the software image, but this component has a simplified function, being responsible only for the image installation itself.

In the second approach to image update, more control is transferred to the *managed resource control peers* that are equipped with a more elaborated software management component. After the human administrator informing the new image characteristics, the tool in the *network administrator interface peer* announces the management environment the presence of the new image. This announcing can be done, for instance, via a notification service. So, when a *managed resource control peer* starts to manage a device, it subscribes to receive new image version events from this device type. When a new version is made available by the human administrator, the tool publishes an event with this information in the notification service and this service transmits it to the subscriber peers. When these peers receive the notification, they consult pre-configured policies and decide if they should perform the image update. If yes, they download the new image from the *network administrator interface peer* and install it in the device.

Other Network Management Tasks

In virtue of its distribution and P2P infrastructure, the presented environment provides also benefits for several other network management tasks. The configuration management, for instance, involves tasks of maintenance of the devices and services that are in the network besides their configuration. In the presented environment, the existence of *managed resource control peers* makes it easier for this task because these peers can be located physically closer to the managed resources. These peers, thanks to P2P infrastructure support, can be easily equipped with software components specific for managing each device and these components can audit the device configuration and identify when configuration alterations were done. The audited information can be stored in the *managed resource control peers* themselves, reducing the traffic volume generated by this control in traditional environments such as weakly distributed management environments. At the same time, the P2P infrastructure support allows for an easier distributing storage of information.

The tasks on network security management can also be improved when transposed to the presented environment. Tools for network security can be adapted to make use of the content and collaboration support provided by P2P infrastructure, sharing security information among the several administrative domains managed by the environment. For instance, tools that use CBR for intrusion detection as the one proposed by Locatelli, Gaspary, Melchiors, Lohmann, and Dillenburg (2004) can be adapted to retrieve similar cases stored in case bases of similar tools present in other nodes of the network, including nodes from other administrative domains. This way, lists of suspect nodes detected by the security tools can be shared with the other domains. The several lists can also be compared to increase the matching weights when a node is present in more than one list, for example.

Management Environment Security

The security of the management involves guaranteeing that the management operations are safe (Clemm, 2007). It includes several functions, such as ensuring that the access to management applications and resource management interfaces be done only by people with the appropriated access privileges; ensuring the security of the management network to avoid the interruption of management tasks; keeping auditing security trails that register the management operations realized.

The utilization of a P2P infrastructure in an environment like the presented brings some difficulties for the security of the management. P2P networks are susceptible to security breaches of malicious peers (DePaoli & Mariani, 2004; Gaspary, Barcellos, Detsch, & Antunes, 2007; Lua et al., 2005), which can act as clients or servers in the network. These peers can cause several types of attacks in the network, such as Denial-of-Service attacks (Daswani, Garcia-Molina, & Yang, 2003); routing attacks, like Eclipse attack (Singh, Castro, Druschel, & Rowstron, 2004) where a group of malicious peers hide correct neighbor nodes by discarding or rerouting messages addressed to them; inventing multiple identities, like in Sybil attack (Douceur, 2002). Thus, given the network management environment controls all devices and services managed in the network, the use of a P2P infrastructure to this environment has to consider several security requirements. In the presented environment, these requirements are still more relevant because the presence of multiple administrative domains in the environment results in more difficulties to ensure the presence of only trusted nodes (Ahmed, Limam, Xiao, Iraqui, & Boutaba, 2007).

The more important and necessary security requirements include the peers' authentication and integrity mechanisms to make sure that the messages between the peers were not changed. In a lower degree, as the management messages can contain sensible corporative information like the number of faults in some specific devices or services, mechanisms of confidentiality are also indicated in order to avoid that messages captured by malicious nodes can be deciphered.

Additionally, in the presented environment, an authorization mechanism that relates the peers involved and the users realizing management operation through these peers is necessary. This mechanism should provide facilities that allow attributing different access levels to the managed resources and management environment facilities, considering the team in which the user is part and the administrative domain where the peer is located. The storage of the information used to access control of each managed resource must be done inside the administrative domain that contains it, in order to ensure the security of the information.

Management Environment Integrated View

The previous sections presented the several services and applications of a P2P-based distributed network management environment, discussing the environment structure, the environment infrastructure services, the network management services as well as applications and the environment security. As previously discussed, the main benefits of such environment are:

- Providing better fault tolerance than traditional network management environments. It happens because the P2P-based presented environment does not have a single point of failure and management tasks can be assigned to a entity group, instead of being assigned to a single entity only;
- Providing larger scalability, because the management tasks processing can be distributed among all the environment entities. Besides, the management tasks can be assigned to an entity group, allowing load balancing among them;
- Providing lower network traffic in network links. The distribution of management tasks to all environment entities allows these tasks to be executed closer to managed resources, reducing the traffic in the other links in the network;
- Providing the collaboration among the human network administrators of the several network administrative domains, through collaboration and data sharing facilities inherent to P2P systems;
- Providing the data and experience sharing among the several entities involved in network management, including entities in different network administrative domains;

- Providing larger scalability in event notifications transmission from managed resources to management entities. It happens thanks to the use of a publish-subscribe notification service that uses the P2P infrastructure;
- Providing support to ease distribution of new vendor image software versions to managed resources;
- Providing simplified maintenance of the management environment, because this environment introduces facilities for the distribution of new management software component versions to the several entities and offers support to these entities find and retrieve software components that they are not equipped with.

As previously discussed, the several environment services and applications are used in an integrated way in order to provide the complete management of the network. An integrated view of the presented management environment with the presence of some management services is presented in figure 5.

In the first level of the figure 5, the physical view of the network resources is presented. The second level illustrates a P2P network over these network resources. The third level shows the environment infrastructure services. In this level, a notification service is represented. Finally, the upper level exemplifies some management services. At the upper level left side, a *managed resource control peer group* is presented. This group is responsible for monitoring some network resources, providing event reception service, polling service and performance data collection service. Other groups are represented in the central region and right side of the figure. Besides these groups, two peers follow network administrator interface role. In one of these peers a tool for visualization of the events occurred in the resource in real time is been executed, while the other peer accesses the trouble ticket CBR tool. In addition, both peers execute collaborative tests of execution tools.

The presented environment can be implemented using several P2P frameworks. An example of a management framework developed following the P2P-based distributed management model is ManP2P (Panisson et al., 2006). ManP2P is based on JXTA P2P framework (Gong, 2001; Traversat et al., 2003), a Java P2P framework hybrid architecture based on super-peers. Besides ManP2P and JXTA, other P2P frameworks with support to peer groups can be employed for the development of such environment, using either hybrid or structured architectures.

FUTURE TRENDS

P2P-based management enables, at different levels, features that current traditional management systems do not provide. Application-level routing, management load distribution, and human-centered cooperation are some examples. Still, the management processes, using or not P2P technologies, are mastered by network specialists that not always may understand the peculiarities of the services that use the managed infrastructure. In such situation, user needs can become transparent for the network operators, which is not adequate because: (*i*) users and associated applications expect the network to provide the adequate services, and when that does not happen users try to "solve" the situation at the application level, because this level in fact is orchestrated and controlled by the users; and (*ii*) knowing the users' necessities, network administrators can not only deliver better services, but they can also optimize the managed network to fulfill the needs of a larger population of users.

Figure 5. Management environment integrated view

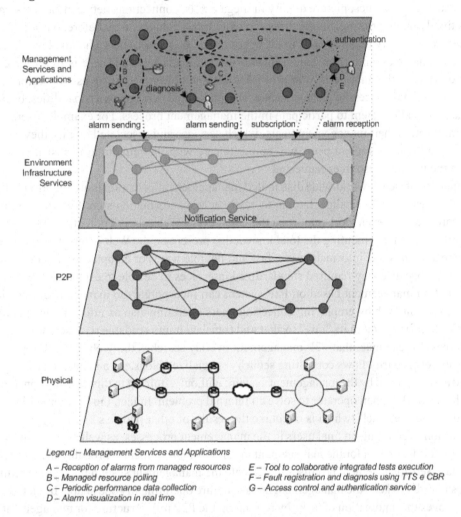

Legend – Management Services and Applications

A – Reception of alarms from managed resources
B – Managed resource polling
C – Periodic performance data collection
D – Alarm visualization in real time

E – Tool to collaborative integrated tests execution
F – Fault registration and diagnosis using TTS e CBR
G – Access control and authentication service

The biggest challenge regarding the later is how to establish the human connection between the necessities of users and the decisions taken by the operators. Two approaches can be employed: (*i*) improve the communication between users and operators via common interfaces; or (*ii*) delegate management power to users. Common interfaces to improve the communication among humans have been already investigated and developed in several areas of computer science, and information management is not an exception. The delegation of management power to users, however, is something less often, and P2P technologies will play a key role in such a process.

Power delegation in computer processes usually raises the questions that the delegation itself is accompanied by an increase complexity for the interested users. On the other hand, some users may be willing to deal with increased complexity if that allows them to achieve their goals. Take the example of digital photography. In the recent past, users took pictures with analog cameras and delivered films to be developed at specialized photo shops. Nowadays, however, users need to deal with memory cards, different storage capacities, picture quality in mega pixels, connections between cameras and computers, and finally photo printing. Surely the complexity today is higher than before, but still users seem to prefer such complexity to going back to the times of analog pictures being handled by photo shops.

P2P can enable a similar movement in information management. There is trend for counting on users' expertise in the management of processes without always requiring user/operator communications. Users will have access to management peer with limited management capabilities, but sufficiently sophisticated to allow them to participate in the management process. For example, users will be able to inform, through their management peers, which services and associated quality they need from the network, and the management peers will communicate with the remaining infrastructure in order to negotiate the network resources requested.

Acquisition of richer, world-wide distributed management information is another trend. The Internet and popular search engines allow human to easily access information stored in different parts of the globe. Moreover, and even more important than that, every Web user is a potential author and creator of further information, augmenting the total knowledge present on the Web. Users, through the Web, can thus create and consume information in a fast and flexible way. For computing systems, however, that is not so easy because they required standardized interfaces to be able to exchange such knowledge.

Information management based on P2P system can incorporate the management knowledge present on the current Web by employing collecting peers operating also as information adaptors, able to retrieve Web information in its "raw" format and translate it into readable representation in a machine. This enables, for example, that P2P management overlay searches the Web using these adaptor peers to discover new security flaws consulting security specialized blogs. As a result, security solutions are retrieved and employed by the management system, without requiring in this case the constant intervention of the network human operator to solve an internal problem. In fact, the solution will be potentially provided by the Web itself (which is of course the results of other people's knowledge).

In addition to counting on final users in the management processes, as well as using the Web knowledge as input information for the management tasks, self-management is probably the more preeminent trend today. Self-management promises to delegate the management system the responsibility of taken decisions in order to keep the management infrastructure operating in good shape. In fact, self-management improves the automation of tasks by relying on the P2P infrastructure for management decisions. The most utopist scenario is the one where no human intervention is required at all, and in fact is even unperceivable from a human point of view. In a more realistic situation, however; human operators will be still responsible for defining general operating policy rules (e.g., deciding which applications should get higher priority because they are mission critical for a specific business), but the P2P infrastructure should be sufficiently clever to interpret such policies and translate them to lower lever, device specific configuration action, thus freeing the administrators of dealing with too low details so as to then focus on the management policies themselves.

CONCLUSION

As previously discussed, the development of the new information management tools that deals with open and unbounded operational environments requires an efficient and robust communication infrastructure that supports complex and modern features such as: collaboration among humans located in geographically distant places, in different network administrative domains, as well as the transmission of large amounts of information among these domains. This communication infrastructure can only be provided through the use of mechanisms for data network management able to deal with these complex and modern requirements.

However, traditional network management models used in current days do not provide the required support for the management of such complex modern networks. In this context, this chapter presented an alternative distributed network management model based on P2P technologies. It presented a P2P-based distributed network management model. Next, it discussed a network management environment that materializes this model, analyzing the characteristics, benefits, drawbacks and potentialities of the main network management and environment infrastructure services and applications, such as: on-demand software components auto-installation service, software components update service, publish-subscribe notification service, polling service, performance data collection service, fault management facilities to improve interaction among human administrators, etc. Finally, the chapter commented on management security and presented an integrated view of the management environment, followed by a discussion of the future trends in domain.

The environment analysis presented, discussing the several management and maintenance services along with applications, provides a view of the benefits and potentialities of the utilization of a P2P-based distributed network management model. Its analysis shows that a management environment based on this model can be used for the complete, efficient and integrated management of complex modern networks, attending the requirements of the discussed information management tools.

REFERENCES

Ahmed, L., Limam, N., Xiao, J., Iraqui, Y., & Boutaba, R. (2007). Resource and Service Discovery in Large-Scale Multi-Domain Networks. *IEEE Communication Surveys, 9*(4), 2-30.

Androutsellis-Theotokis, S., & Spinellis, D. (2004). A Survey of Peer-to-Peer Content Distribution Technologies. *ACM Computing Surveys, 36* (4), 335-371.

Bartsch-Sporl, B., Lenz, M., & Hubner, A. (1999). Case-Based Reasoning: Survey and Future Directions. In: F. Puppe (Ed.), *Proceedings of the 5th Biannual German Conference on Knowledge-Based Systems XPS-99 LNAI 1570* (pp. 67-89). Berlin: Springer.

Behnel, S., Fiege, L., & Mühl, G. (2006). On Quality-of-Service and Publish-Subscribe. In: *Proceedings of the 26th IEEE International Conference on Distributed Computing Systems Workshops ICDCS 2006* (pp. 20-25). Washington: IEEE Computer Society.

Berkovsky, S., Kuflik, T., & Ricci, F. (2005). P2P Case Retrieval with an Unspecified Ontology. In: *Case-Based Reasoning Research and Development: Proceedings of 6th International Conference on Case-Based Reasoning ICCBR 2005 LNAI 3620* (pp. 91-105). Berlin: Springer.

Bieszczad, A., Pagurek, B., & White, T. (1998). Mobile Agents for Network Management. *IEEE Communications Surveys and Tutorials, 1*(1).

Binzenhöfer, A., Tutschku, K., Graben, B., Fiedler, M., & Arlos, P. (2006). A P2P-Based Framework for Distributed Network Management. In M. Cesana. & L. Fratta (Eds.), *Wireless Systems and Network*

Architectures in Next Generation Internet: Second International Workshop of the EURO-NGI Network of Excellence LNCS 3883 (pp. 198-210). New York: Springer.

Case, J. D., Fedeor, M., Schoffstall, M. L., & Davin, J. (1990). *Simple Network Management Protocol (SNMP), RFC 1157, STD 15.* IETF.

Case, J., McCloghrie, K., Rose, M., & Waldbusser, S. (1996). *Introduction to Community-based SNMPv2, RFC 1901.* IETF.

Cheikhrouhou, M.; Conti, P., Labetoulle, J., & Marcus, K. (1999). Intelligent agents for network management: a fault detection experiment. In: M. Sloman, S. Mazumdar, E. Lupu (Eds.), *Distributed Management for the Networked Millennium: Proceedings of the Sixth IFIP/IEEE International Symposium on Integrated Network Management* (pp. 595-609). Boston: IEEE.

Choi, Y., & Park, D. (2005). Mirinae: A Peer-to-Peer Overlay Network for Large-Scale Content-Based Publish/Subscribe Systems. In: *Proceedings of the International Workshop on Network and Operating Systems Support For Digital Audio and Video* (pp. 105-110). New York: ACM.

Clemm, A. (2007). *Network Management Fundamentals.* Indianapolis: Cisco Press.

Comer, D. E., (2006). *Automated Network Management Systems: Current and Future Capabilities.* Pearson Prentice Hall.

Courtenage, S., & Williams, S. (2006). The Design and Implementation of a P2P-Based Composite Event Notification System. In: *Proceedings of the 20th international Conference on Advanced information Networking and Applications - Volume 1 (Aina'06) - Volume 01* (pp. 701-706). Washington: IEEE Computer Society.

Dam, M., & Stadler, R. (2005). A Generic Protocol for Network State Aggregation. *Radiovetenskap och Kommunication (RVK)*, Sweden, 2005.

Daswani, N., Garcia-Molina, H., & Yang, B. (2003). Open Problems in Data-Sharing Peer-to-Peer Systems. In: D. Calvanese, M. Lenzerini & R. Motwani (Eds.), *Proceedings of 9th International Conference on Database Theory ICDT 2003, LNCS 2572* (pp. 1-15). Springer.

DePaoli, F., & Mariani, L. (2004). Dependability in Peer-to-Peer Systems. *IEEE Internet Computing, 8*(4), 54-61.

Douceur, J. (2002). The Sybil Attack. In: *Revised Papers from the First International Workshop on Peer-to-Peer Systems, LNCS 2429* (pp. 251-260). Springer.

Eugster, P., Felber, P., Guerraoui, R., & Kermarrec, A. (2003). The Many Faces of Publish/Subscribe. *ACM Computing Surveys, 35*(2), 114-131.

Fuggetta, A., Picco, G. P., & Vigna, G. (1998). Understanding Code Mobility. *IEEE Transactions on Software Engineering, 24*(5), 342-361.

Gaspary, L., Barcellos, M. P., Detsch, A., & Antunes, R. S. (2007). Flexible security in peer-to-peer applications. *Computer Networks, 51*, 4795-4815.

Gong, L. (2001). JXTA: A network programming environmen. *IEEE Internet Computing, 5*(3), 88-95.

Granville, L., Rosa, D., Panisson, A., Melchiors, C., Almeida, M., & Tarouco, L. (2005). Managing Computer Networks Using Peer-to-Peer Technologies. *IEEE Communications Magazine, 43*(10), 62-68.

Gupta, A., Sahin, O. D., Agrawal, D., & Abbadi, A. E.. (2004). Meghdoot: Content-Based Publish/Subscribe over P2P Networks. *Proceedings of the 5th ACM/IFIP/USENIX international Conference on Middleware, LNCS 3231* (pp. 254-273). New York: Springer.

Harrington, D., Presuhn, R., & Wijnen, B. (2002). *An Architecture for Describing Simple Network Management Protocol (SNMP) Management Frameworks, RFC 3411, STD 62,* 2002. IETF.

Hegering, H., Abeck, S., & Neumair, B. (1999). *Integratd Management of Networked Systems.* San Francisco: Morgan Kaufmann.

International Telecommunication Union. (2000a). *ITU-T Recommendation M.3000: Overview of TMN Recommendations.* International Telecommunication Union.

International Telecommunication Union. (2000b). *ITU-T Recommendation M.3010: Principles for a Telecommunications Management Network.* International Telecommunication Union.

International Telecommunication Union. (2000c). *ITU-T Recommendation M.3400: TMN Management Functions.* International Telecommunication Union.

Kolodner, J. (1993). Case-Based Reasoning. Morgan Kaufmann.

Koubarakis, M., Tryfonopoulos, C., Idreos, S., & Drougas, Y. (2003). Selective Information Dissemination in P2P Networks: Problems and Solutions. *SIGMOD Record, 32*(3), 71-76.

Leinwand, A., & Conroy, K. F. (1996). *Network Management: A Practical Perspective.* Reading: Addison-Wesley.

Locatelli, F., Gaspary, L., Melchiors, C., Lohmann, S., & Dillenburg, F. (2004). Spotting Intrusion Scenarios from Firewall Logs Through a Case-Based Reasoning Approach. In: *Utility Computing: Proceedings of 15th IFIP/IEEE International Workshop on Distributed Systems: Operations and Management DSOM 2004 LNCS 3278* (pp. 196-207). Berlin: Springer.

Lua, E., Pias, M., Sharma, R., & Lim, S. (2005). A Survey and Comparison of Peer-to-Peer Overlay Network Schemes. *IEEE Communications Surveys & Tutorials, 7*(2), 72-93.

Mahambre, S. P., Kumar, S. D. M., & Bellur, U. (2007). A Taxonomy of QoS-Aware, Adaptive Event-Dissemination Middleware. *IEEE Internet Computing, 11*(4), 35-44.

Martin-Flatin, J., Znaty S., & Hubaux, J. (1999). A Survey of Distributed Enterprise Network and Systems Management Paradigms. *Journal of Network and Systems Management, 7*(1), 9-26.

McBurney, P., & Parsons, S. (2005) *The Knowledge Engineering Review, 20*(3).

McCloghrie, K, Perkins, D., & Schönwälder, J. (1999). *Structure of Management Information Version 2 (SMv2), RFC 2578.* IETF.

Melchiors, C., & Tarouco, L. M. R. (2000). Troubleshooting network faults using past experience. In: *Proceedings of 2000 IEEE/IFIP Network Operations and Management Symposium 'The Networked Planet: Management Beyond 2000' NOMS 2000* (pp. 549-562). IEEE.

Milojicic, D. S., Kalogeraki, V., Lukose, R., Nagaraja, K., Pruyne, J., Richard, B., Rollins, S., & Xu, Z. (2003). *Peer-to-Peer Computing* (Tech. Rep. HPL-2002-57). Palo Alto: HP Laboratories Palo Alto.

Ng, W., Lam, W., & Cheng, J. (2006). Comparative Analysis of XML Compression Technologies. *World Wide Web*, 9(1), 5-33.

Object Management Group. (2004). *Common Object Request Broker Architecture: Core Specification Version 3.0.3*. Needham: OMG.

Panisson, A. (2007). A*plicação de técnicas de distribuição de carga em sistemas de gerenciamento de redes baseados em P2P*. Unpublished master dissertation, Federal University of Rio Grande do Sul, Rio Grande do Sul, Brazil.

Panisson, A., Melchiors, C., Granville, L. Z., Almeida, M. J. B., & Tarouco, L. M. R. (2006). Designing the Architecture of P2P-Based Network Management Systems. In: P. Bellavista, C. Chen, A. Corradi, M. Daneshmand (Eds.), *Proceedings of the 11th IEEE Symposium on Computers and Communications ISCC 2006* (pp. 69-75). IEEE Computer Society.

Pietro, A. G., & Stadler, R. (2007). A-GAP: An Adaptative Protocol for Continuous Network Monitoring with Accuracy Objectives. *IEEE Transactions on Network. and Service. Management.*, 4(1), 2-12.

Presuhn, R., Case, J., McCloghrie, K., Rose, M., & Waldbusser, S. (2002). *Version 2 of the Protocol Operations for the Simple Network Management Protocol (SNMP), RFC 3416, STD 062*. IETF.

Rose, M., & McCloghrie, K. (1990). *Structure and Identification of Management Information for TCP/IP-based internets, RFC 1155, STD 16*. IETF.

Rose, M., & McCloghrie, K. (1991). *Concise MIB Definitions, RFC 1212, STD 16*. IETF,

Schönwälder, J., Quittek, J., & Kappler, C. (2000). Building Distributed Management Applications with the IETF Script MIB. *IEEE Journal on Selected Areas in Communications*, 18(5), 702-714.

Singh, A., Castro, M., Druschel, P., & Rowstron, A. (2004). Defending against eclipse attacks on overlay networks. In: *Proceedings of the 11th Workshop on ACM SIGOPS European Workshop* (pp. 21-26). New York: ACM.

State, R., & Festor, O. (2003). A management platform over a peer to peer service infrastructure. In: *Proceedings of 10th International Conference on Telecommunications ICT 2003* (pp. 124-131). IEEE.

Sun Microsystems. (2006). *Java Management Extensions (JMX) Specification version 1.4*. Santa Clara, CA: Sun Microsystems.

Traversat, B., Arora, A., Abdelaziz, M., Duigou, M., Haiwwod, C., Hugly, J., Pouyoul, E., & Yeager, B. (2003). *Project JXTA 2.0 Super-Peer Virtual Network*. Sun Microsystems.

Udupa, D. K. (1996). *Network Management Systems Essentials*. New York: Mc-Graw-Hill.

Waldbusser, S. (1997). *Remote Network Monitoring Management Information Base Version 2 using SMIv2, RFC 2021.*

Waldbusser, S. (2000). *Remote Network Monitoring Management Information Base, RFC 2819.*

Yli-Hietanen, J., & Niiranen, S. (2008). Towards Open Information Management in Health Care. *The Open Medical Informatics Journal, 2*(1), 42-48.

Chapter XVII
A Framework for Semi–Autonomous Servers in the Wireless Network Environment

John Tsiligaridis
Heritage University, USA

ABSTRACT

The problem of server performance in a contemporary, rapidly developed and multi-discipline environment is examined. Multiple requests in a very short period of time increase the number of connections and push the server to the limit. Nowadays servers' ability to work semi autonomously, in regards to the decision of the appropriate query plan and the provision of the effective data location, plays a significant role for the query and network performance. For autonomous server operations many of the offered services need to be self-managed. Data sources' administration during the execution of the query plan becomes of primary interest especially for the starting query server. The proposed server grouping process, server's scale up capabilities and the application of Data Mining concepts in a wireless environment can contribute a lot to the optimization of the query plan and also increase server independence. Various methods of distributed data exploration and exploitation that support server's semi-autonomous operational behavior are developed. Simulation results are provided. This chapter covers a significant part of cooperative domains in the area of information management and can offer integrated solutions very attractive to the mobile users.

INTRODUCTION

The number of mobile and wired users has rapidly increased over the last few years. This large user base is playing a significant role on server available resources for internet services. A mobile-client/server model is developed. Servers in various network sites usually have a heavy workload to execute. In (Menasce, & Kephart, 2007) the need of building a large-scale fully autonomic computing, comprised of multiple components that work together to satisfy high-level business goals, is imperative. A more effective organization of data distribution and acquisition across the internet could mediate the server workload. Future database systems will need to optimize queries of much higher complexity than the current ones.

For some problems new solutions can be considered under more thorough elaboration. Our focus is the problem of query optimization considering also two additional factors: the group and query mobility and the dependency of servers. These two new factors play a significant role in the development of the query design. Moreover the new network infrastructure and the scale up capabilities of the servers can support this framework. The issue addressed in this study is to minimize the total cost of the queries and to discover, for at least some of them, a new less delayed solution in order to reduce the dependency of servers. In the context of information management and the rapid growth of wireless data applications, the study of the multidimensional problem for server autonomicity provides an innovative solution for the query performance. There are two servers that play a significant role for any query in our study; the starting server, from where the query starts the execution, and the last server where the data are produced.

The data have to follow the users' moves. This is accomplished by sending the results directly to the last server (or to the mobile user cache) in advance evading the round-trip delay of data requests. This *pairing* between the starting and the last server, for the most popular group and query paths, facilitates bandwidth reservation across the path, and replicates the data in advance whenever needed. Moreover, the Base Station (BS) is the key part of the wireless network infrastructure and it is responsible for sending and receiving data to and from a wireless host that is associated with that base station. A cell is the geographical area covered by a BS.

This work focuses on discovering periodical events (e.g., football match) over long time periods utilizing the most popular group route (critical routes). The predictive policy aids the service of hand off calls and shortens the query response time. The techniques for distributed database design are based on allocation, replication and fragmentation. Each database can be broken up into logical units called fragments which may be assigned for storage at the various sites. Each fragment (or each copy of a fragment) must be assigned to a particular site in the distributed system. This process is called data allocation. Data from a relation can also be stored in various sites. This is called data replication. Replication is useful in improving the availability of data (Silberschatz, Korth, & Sudarshan, 2006). The mobile environment needs dynamic replication schemes that will replicate the data when and where needed (Tang, & Chanson, 2004). For some queries the result is taken after the cooperation of servers.

The servers' dependency, based on the transferring of messages, data or subqueries, finally attenuates the network performance especially with the increasing number of the mobile and wired users' requests that might create congestion conditions. In order to avoid these undesirable network situations, we should reduce the *spread* of query part executions over various sites and minimize the query execution time. In this way the better allocation of services (messages, files, databases etc) can help the servers work with restricted *dependency*. We use Data Mining methods twice. First, to discover the group and query mobility via the Merge Itemsets Algorithm (MIA) and second to measure the server dependency, providing new metrics and analytical results. Finally, since the starting server knows in advance the distribution of data and the last server, where the user (or group) will be at the end of the transaction, it can prepare an *optimal* query plan (less response time) in order to send the results directly to the last cell location. In order to examine the server dependency we have created groups of servers to facilitate either the replication or the new data organization so that the execution query cost is minimized. In this way, we minimize the transmission costs, the control messages (which to a large extent dependent on the mechanisms provided by the servers) and the response time while we increase the system availability. The latter is easier now to achieve utilizing the server enhanced capabilities (CPU, main memory utilization, I/O operations, scale up). For the distributed databases the transaction manager (DTM) (or the coordinator) has to make the final commit or abort decision. A server is multi dependent on many other servers for a variety of services. We use the decomposition method in order to simplify and analyze the dependency among servers for a variety of services. Matrices for each service of a group of servers have been created. A set of rules is introduced so that the *server dependency for each service (SSD)* is examined.

Some of the servers are specific services oriented. This server characteristic provides the same query path for the particular service. Based on this fact the independent service algorithm (ISA) investigates the service tables and defines an order in order to eliminate the servers' dependency using a set of methods (such as Hot Data Replication, -HDR- etc) of the semi-autonomous processing algorithm (SSPA). This work can also be considered as a moving location query (MQ) on static objects (Gedik, & Liu, 2006). The results of an MQ consist of objects that are covered by the query spatial region and satisfy the query filter. In (Gedik & Liu, 2006) the user is moving to any direction in an area according to the naïve approach or the central velocity approach and is assumed it operates under a central processing scheme. Our work provides a prediction scheme based on predefined next cell moves according to Data Mining techniques.

The starting server (or the site of the origin of the transaction) must know in advance the distribution of data, the execution plan and the last server where the user (or group) will be at the end of the transaction, in order to send the results directly and avoid the cost. Data Mining with its association rules is ideal for this purpose. Additionally, a reduction of the uplink streams (from mobile users to a server) can be achieved with the "prefect" operation using Data Mining methods.

With this in mind, a framework with a set of algorithms considering the user mobility is proposed. A prediction scheme for Group and Query Mobility (GQM) based on the Merge Itemset Algorithm (MIA) discovers the most popular group and query path. In addition, it provides the users with the "prefetch" operation depending on their mobility so that their data are waiting for them in the next appropriate cell. In this work we are focusing on the group mobility.

The chapter is organized as follows. First, the model description is presented. Second, the Merge Itemsets Algorithm (MIA) is described. Third, the General Server Dependency approach with the Decomposition method is described. Fourth, the Service Operation Approach with ISA is developed. Fifth, the Query Processing Methods, SSPA with some rules for Service Server Dependency are described. Finally, simulation results are included.

BACKGROUND

An innovative framework for the management of server services at various sites across a communication network is presented. It provides better organization of the queries' plan and data allocation considering group and query mobility along with the dependency of servers. Nowadays servers' ability to work semi autonomously, in regards to the decision on the appropriate query plan and the provision of the effective data location, can seriously affect the query and network performance.

In this work we address, the servers' autonomic operation at their sites and associate it with the problem of distributed query optimization trying to provide solutions for local and global mobile users. The goal is to minimize the total cost of the queries and to discover, for at least some of them, a solution exhibiting less delay. In the distributed system we have to examine several techniques for choosing a strategy to process a query that minimizes the amount of time it takes to get the answer. The cost of data transmission over the network and the delay, play the most significant role in the distributed query processing (Silberschatz, Korth, & Sudarshan, 2006).

The self management of queries by the starting server (the server from where the query starts) is vital and is achieved via Data Mining methods. Depending on the type of the query a different approach is taken.

There are three query execution policies: data shipping, query shipping, and hybrid shipping (Franklin, Jonson , & Kossmann, 1996), (Kossmann, 2004). Query optimization is an expensive process primarily because the number of alternative access plans grows at least exponentially with the number of relations participating in the query (Ioannidis, & Kang, 1990). In (Feng, & Chen, 2003), data allocation schemes have been presented in various scenarios using the incremental Data Mining technique, but with no consideration of the time domain. Thus, there is no accurate design for the prediction of that point of time at which a user would most probably be found in the subsequent cell to receive updated data. Details for the query processing path and its discrimination from the mobile path have not been developed. In the kangaroo transaction model (Dunham, Helal, & Balakrishnam, 1997) it is basically considered that the query and mobility paths follow the same cells and BSs. On the other hand, we consider different paths and we focus on the query results being sent directly to the new mobile position. With the consideration of those kinds of paths we can achieve good prediction, since the time and the location of the starting and last server is predefined. Finally, the server sends the query results directly to the last server (last server approach) instead of having them sent back to the starting server and have them eventually reach the last server (naïve approach) after following the group path.

MODEL DESCRIPTION

Our model is based on the collaboration among Wireless Network (GSM, IS-41, UMTS), Data Mining, Distributed Databases, and Query Processing techniques. A user resides in a cell and communicates with one Base Station (BS). The BS is responsible for forwarding data between mobile users and the wired network.

Data Mining

A Data Mining method is developed in order to predict mobility patterns by utilizing their previous history. Here is some introductory information. Let $I_m = \{ i_1, i_2, i_3, \dots, i_m \}$ be a set of literals called items. *An itemset containing k items is called a k-itemset* ($I_k = \{i_1, i_2, i_3, \dots, i_k\}$, where k≤m). For the 2-itemset the representation is as: $I_2 = \{i_1, i_2\}$. Let X is a set of items. A transaction, named T, is said to contain X if and only if $X \subseteq T$ (Silberschatz, Korth, & Sudarshan, 2006). An *association rule* implies the form X=> Y, where $X \subseteq I$, $Y \subseteq I$, and $X \cap Y = \emptyset$.

For the association rules there are two basic measures, the *support* and the *confidence*. *Support (sup)* of an itemset (string) stands for the number of times an itemset or sub-itemset appears in the database. The task of mining association rules is essential to discover strong associations' rules in large databases. The *prediction* results are used to reserve bandwidth in advance of a connection with, eventually, adjacent cells.

For our group mobility we use the 2-itemsets. *Each item represents a cell.* The cell is the geographical area covered by a BS. For example, item A represents cell A. A mobile resides in a cell *and* communicates with its current BS. The path is an *itemset or a large itemset (l-itemset)* that is a set of items (numbers or letters). In a user/group path there is a *branch* when a user/group moves to various adjacent cells after following a common subpath. *Common subpath (cos)* is the common part of the branch paths. The cos of "abcde" and "abcdef" is the subpath "abcd" and "e", "f" are the two branches. *Restricted Support* is the support given by the first same items that compose the cos. *Extensive support* is given by extension of the support operation beyond the first cos. The confidence (conf) of the rule is computed as the quotient of the supports for the itemsets conf = sup(A,B,C,D) / sup(A,B,C). Strong association rules are rules with a confidence value, conf, above a given threshold (Hand, Smith, & Manilla, 2000).

Distributed Query Processing

The principal problem for the evaluation of a query on distributed databases appears when two relations must be joined while they reside in various sites. For the join operation one relation from the one site must be shipped to the other site. Since communication cost is the principal cost for the distributed databases minimizing the amount of shipped data is of primary interest. Of course, it is not possible to eliminate the communication costs completely but it is possible to *minimize it significantly.* There are two main methods for querying processing. The first is when we have local processing with all the restrictions applied and the second is when we use join or semi-join (Silberschatz, Korth, & Sudarshan, 2006). Our purpose is to minimize the transmission cost (SDD-1) (Silberschatz, Korth, & Sudarshan, 2006) by applying semi-joins to reduce for reducing the cardinality (reducers) and the delay. It is likely to have a chain of semi-joins (one after the other) at the same or various sites.

For the query optimization plan the site(s) selection is the most important factor because it provides information on when and where the query should be submitted, and which part of the data should be optimized (Kossmann, 2004). In order to effectively optimize queries in a distributed environment it is necessary to have a reasonably accurate cost model. The *response time* of a query is defined to be the elapsed time from the initiation of query execution until the time the last tuple of the query result is displayed at the client. The total cost is identical to the response time if all the operators of a plan are executed sequentially.

The Description of the Group and Query Mobility (GQM)

We use a collaborative system (cell-BS-server-node(or high level servers)) with the *composition* approach, in order to take the mobility trend at special congestion times (periodical events) *without taking into account the user's mobility profile.* The GQM based on the *groups' mo*ve, can guarantee the acceleration of the query execution. The operations of the GQM components are described bellow:

The *cell* works as follows: (1) When a mobile user moves from cell i (c_i) into a cell j (c_j) area, a message (*uplink* stream) is sent directly from cj to its BS with the tuple: "arrival time, id cells (previous, target), #channel, duration previous cell". The itemset of this tuple has a *pair* of items (2-itemset), (2) this process continues to every subsequent cell until the end of the path for all the mobile users. The *indication of congestion (IC),* under the symbol c (congestion), can be added at the end of the tuple.

The *BS* creates the *preprocessing* phase. (1) It gathers the tuples according to their arrival time and distributes them in a predefined time period (dt), (2) it sorts them according their time period, (3) additionally, it gathers information for the query execution path (time, sites, etc from Fig 1), (4) periodically, or at the end of the day it goes through the phase of sorting and transferring the tuples (with support>ms, (Hand, Smith, & Manilla, 2000) to the nodes for processing. The aggregate tuple *replaces* all the analytical ones.

The *server* of each query path (including the last one) also sends the time and the support of the requested data to the node (or upper level server).

The *node* works in two phases. In the *first phase*, it gathers the information of the group and query mobility (in tables), finds the paths in each BS first and among adjacent BSs afterwards. This way, it creates the *most popular group path*. This information is sent to the BSs. In the *second phase* it elaborates with the query optimization performance (replication of data, compression path etc), prepares the new query path, and informs analogous servers(especially the last ones) about the time and the location the group's results need to be sent to. According to the new query path the local servers (along with the BSs) regulate the data replication on the corresponding sites before the execution of the query.

THE MERGE ITEMSET ALGORITHM (MIA)

There are more than one ways to connect the subpaths of two or more routing tables of the BSs. In this work we develop the Merge Itemset Algorithm (MIA). *Connectivity* is the possibility to connect 2-itemsets and this happens when for two 2-itemsets: the 2-itemset$_i$ (item$_{1i}$, item$_{2i}$) and the 2-itemsetj (item$_{1j}$, item$_{2j}$) we have: item$_{2i}$ = item$_{1j}$. We define also the internal connectivity when the user moves inside the BSi (all the items or cells belong to the same BS$_i$) and *external* connectivity if the item$_{2j}$ $\in$ BSj. The steps for MIA are:

For each BS: (1) Find the internal connectivity, (increasing time period) ending up to external connections. Create a group of a series of internal itemsets followed by external itemsets. From Figure 1 we take the group of items: "abd", where: "ab" is the internal connection and "bd" the external. (2) Find the confidence for each 2-itemset$_i$, and sort them according to that confidence (only when we have increasing or decreasing trend of moves). After we finish this process for each BS we continue with the pair process.

For a pair of BSs: Find the external connections for any itemset of the 1st BS with any itemset of 2nd BS. From Figure 1 we can see the external connectivity is d->j for BS2.

The BS information (the popular group paths) is sent to the servers in order to take control of the group and query process. The pseudocode of MIA is in Example A.

For the design of the wireless network the access layer (lower level including the BS) and the service layer (higher level including server) along with the transport and control layers between them are needed. For the two steps of MIA the service orchestration would be implemented as follows: Step 1 can be implemented in the access layer while step 2 in the service layer using a Northbound Interface (NBI),on the top of the application server, allowing to gather data (popular group paths) from heterogeneous and multivendor access providers. The NBI typically manages the disparate network elements from multiple vendors and can pose significant technical and operational challenges for business solutions' convenience. It monitors equipment, collects traffic statistics. It also enables provisioning services, report inventories, and alarm propagation. Finally, it can offer web services (XML).

THE GENERAL SERVER DEPENDENCY APPROACH

Definition 1: The cell from where the user asks for execution of a query is named *starting query cell* (sqc).

Definition 2: A *query execution path (qep)* is the sequence of (complementary) servers that this query has to follow at various sites using the join or semi-join operation. The *size of qep (s_qep)* is determined by the number of the servers of a qep.

Definition 3: Starting server (ss) is the server from which the user starts the query. This information is also held by the initial (for query) BS and is transferred to the ss. *Users moving to the next cell send a message first to the initial BS and then to the corresponding ss.* Hence, the ss holds all the history of the query moves for individual and group users.

Definition 4: Last server (ls) is the server where the query results are finally ready. All the others between ss and ls are called intermediated server(s) (is). (e.g., for the qep ="BEG", ss="B", ls = "G", is= "E").

Example A.

```
Input:   SI_i : set of 2_itemsets for BS_i, min_sup: is predefined
Output: internal and external connectivity
print internal connectivity
for each B S_i
    for each  2_itemset_i (item_{1i}, item_{2i}) ∈ SI_i , with sup_i > min_sup)
        for each  k_itemsetj (item1j, item2j, ...., itemkj  where k?2 and i≠j)
            if item_{ki} = item_{1j}
                (k+1)_itemset_i = k_itemset_i ∪ {item_{kj}}
                    SI_i ← (k+1)_itemset
            end if
        end for
    end for
end for
print external connectivity
for each k_itemset ∈ SI_i
    for each m_itemset  ∈ SI_j , j≠I, k.m ∈ I
        if (item_{ki} = item_{1j})
            (k+m)_itemset
        end if
    end for
end for
```

Figure 1. The structure of node finding the group trend with the query processing

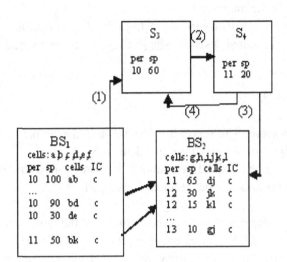

Example 1: A user is *moving* across the path "ABCD". While being at cell B, sends a query which cannot be answered locally (from the local server) and the data are sent to other cells not included in the user path. The path that the data follow is: "BEG". After the integration of the query execution, the results are sent back to cell B, from where the updated data are sent to the new user location (cell D) according to the user's mobility.

Thus, in this case the data cannot be *prefetched* by the updated user location. To minimize the data delay the ls has to send them *directly* to the new user location. It would be very helpful for the query and for any hybrid shipping operation if the data were not spread out to many sites. An effort is made to diminish the number of sites for data tuples or relations by *replicating* the data from the one site to the other before the execution of the query. Our purpose is to increase the self-management ability of servers. To this direction we have to examine the server dependence.

Definition 5: *Internal* query is when there is no qep or when the ss is also the last one (ls). *External* query is created when a server i is weak to provide direct response and asks for the execution of a part or the entire query to be performed from servers in various sites. This comes from the starting server (ss) of a qep.

Definition 6: For a set of n servers the *dependency table (dt)* is given by:

$$dt=[a_{ij}]= \begin{array}{c} a_1 \\ a_2 \\ \ldots \ldots \\ a_n \end{array} = \begin{array}{l} a_{11} \ a_{12} \ a_{13} .. \ a_{1n} \\ a_{21} \ a_{22} \ a_{23} .. \ a_{2n} \\ \ldots \ldots \\ a_{n1} \ a_{n2} \ a_{n3} .. \ a_{nn} \end{array} \qquad (1)$$

The diagonal elements are the independence elements (a_{ii}) and we have : $a_{ii} + \sum a_{ij} = 1$ ($i \neq j$). The dependency table is a *stochastic* matrix.

Generally a server i is *dependent* on server j if from the *decomposition* of a query into subqueries (r) some of them need to be executed at server site j. The qep can be divided into a set of paths. This means that:

$$qep_i = p_1 + p_2 + ... + p_r = \sum_{n=1}^{r} (p_n),$$

where: p_i is the $path_i$,(from server S_i to server S_{i+1}). An illustrated example is presented in Table 1 with the *Server Query Table (SQT)* of S_1 which is dependent on S_2.

The values of Table 1 can be obtained by counting the number of users' calls that send queries to the server. The time period is also calculated for each user call.

Definition 7: In a set S of n dependent servers the elements of the table S_i *(a_{ij})* is the percentage of internal, external support of S_i shared by all n servers (j $\in$ S, j$\neq$i, i+j =n). For a server i the elements of a line from (1), is given from the vector a_i: $a_i = [\ a_{i1} \quad a_{i2} \quad a_{i3} \ . \quad a_{ii} ... \ a_{in}\ ]$.

Definition 8: The independence ratio (ir) of a S_i is the ratio of internal support of S_i to the total support of S_i. For S_i the independent ratio is standing for by ir_i. It is obvious that $ir_i = a_{ii}$.

Definition 9: The *dependence ratio (dr)* for S_i (dr_i) is given by $dr_i = (ext\_sup_i / tot\_supp_i)$ and can be analyzed into a set of dependence (non diagonal) elements which represent the percentage of external support for the S_i dependent servers. Hence, for n dependent servers of S_i the dr_i is given from the first line of (1) by:

$$dr_i = \sum_{j=1, j \neq i}^{n} a_{ij}$$

Definition 10: From (1) server i is *external oriented or dependent server (sd)* on a set of n servers when: $sd_i = ir_i / \sum a_{ij}$ (j=1,...,n, j $\neq$i) $= ir_i / dr_i < min\_thr_1$ (predefined value) or the a_{ii} terms (or ir_i) take very low values that drop below a predefined threshold (<min_thr). On the other hand, for the *internal oriented servers* the dc_{ii} terms take higher values, above a predefined

Table 1. The server query table SQT_1

Query name	type	next server	shipment	time period	sup
Q1	internal	S1		2	10
Q2	internal	S1		3	20
Q3	external	S2	data	12	10
Q4	external	S2	data	14	20
Q5	external	S2	query	14	15
Q5	external	S2	hybrid	14	5

threshold (>max_thr). The values of min_thr, and max_thr are defined from the system. Further examination is needed for the external oriented server in order the case of dependency of S_i from a particular server to be discovered.

Example 2: From Table 1, S_1 has tot_sup= 80, ir_i = 30/80 = 0.375, dr_i = 5/8=0.625 and $ir_i + dr_i$ =1, with max_tht =0.5. Since dr_i > max_thr , S_1 is externally oriented and it needs further study.

Definition 11: The *maximum* value of the a_{ij} of S_i for a group of n servers is given by: a_{ik} = max(a_{ij})= max(a_{i1}, a_{i2}, a_{i3},...,a_{in}) and S_k is the server with that value. The S_k is the *central server (cs) of* S_i if and only if : a_{ik} > max_thr *(predefined value, central server property -csp-)*. The cs holds the *hot* data for S_i.

Definition 12: Vertical dependency of server i for a set of n servers is when the max (a_{ij}) for all the rows of the dt lies on the same column j. The vertical dependency can create a *group* of n servers having the server j as the cs. In the *vertical partial dependency* only some of the servers of the group have server j as the cs.

Definition 13: Servers i, j, k have a *serial dependency* (not in the same line or column) when S_i is dependent on Sj, Sj is dependent on S_k (Si = dep. on Sj)

Definition 14: A server i is considered *strongly dependent server(sds)* on server k if (a) S_i is dependent and (b) max(a_i) = a_{ik} > max_thr. The S_i is considered as *weakly dependent server (wds)* on S_m if (a) S_i is dependent and (b) min(a_i) = a_{im} < min_thr$_2$ (predefined value).

Definition 15: N servers can create a *group* if they have strong dependency and they have the same cs (vertical dependency).

Definition 16: From a set of n servers a *partial group* can be created with any m (m<n) strongly dependent servers. Then we have again the cs *but only* for the m servers.

The cs can be reached to the limit for some time due to the large number of connections from internal and external users. Diminishing the server dependency can provide a solution for managing the network traffic while also providing better server and query performance. Data from the cs will be sent in advance to the dependent servers. This step leads to the server independence which in extend provides the autonomic behavior.

Example 3: Let us consider the dependent servers S_1, S_2, S_3, S_4 with max_thr =0.3. The dt$_1$ is as follows:

	s1	s2	s3	s4
	0.3	**0.4**	0.1	0.2
dt$_1$ =	0.1	**0.7**	0.1	0.1
	0.2	**0.4**	0.3	0.1
	0.2	**0.5**	0.1	0.2

The second column holds the maximum values since max (a_{i2}) , $\forall i=1,...,4$, = [0.4, 0.7,0.4, 0.5], and all these values are greater than the max_thr = 0.3. The servers S_1, S_3, and S_4 are strongly dependent on S_2. Hence S_2 is the cs for all the other servers and holds the hot data. The group is: G= $\{S_1, S_2, S_3, S_4\}$. This dependency table can also be represented by a flow diagram.

The flow diagram becomes more complicated when more servers are involved in the group and the study of their behavior becomes more difficult. Additionally, some services are offered only by certain servers making it easier to trace and apply any method to them. For this reason a different approximation is needed. In addition, the kind of services that servers offer must be considered further.

THE DECOMPOSITION METHOD

It is evident that it is not so easy to find solutions when concentrating on a set of services. For any server the dt cover information for all services offered, without including details for each one. The flow diagram of the general server dependency can be analyzed now into n flow diagrams for n services provided by the servers respectively. But this is not only too difficult but also a waste of time. There are many kinds of services that a server has to provide in a short time and some of the methods used are different from each other. The responses to the user requests must be current, accurate and offered without delay. Some servers specialize to a specific kind of services (weather, sports, flights arrivals and departures etc) also needed by other servers that belong to the same group. The *categorization* of services provides a new and easier way of discovering the servers' dependency according to their services.

For this purpose a *decomposition method* is developed so that the *service server dependency* is derived from the server dependency. The service oriented dependency can also be obtained by gathering only the queries related to a *specific* service. All the terms developed in the general server dependency approach will be used in relation with the offered services. As an example, a server i is strongly dependent on server j with the service k.

THE SERVICE OPERATION APPROACH

The general approach of server dependency is referred to a set of services offered by the server. The server works differently for each service. This discrimination of the server(s) behavior gives a new dimension to the server dependency problem. Working with each service separately it is easier to apply the methods and examine the results instead of following the general approach. In this regard more information on the service operation is needed. The services are considered independent of each other (service$_i$ ∧service$_j$ =∅). All the definitions of the general approach related to the servers, can be used with the *service extension* as well. Hence, the serial servers' dependency can be considered now as serial servers' dependency for service i.

For a group of servers, each kind of service has its own *service table* (ST$_i$, where i =1,2,..n, services). The server operations can be considered as a set of provided services (serv$_i$, i=1,2,..). Server S$_i$ is dependent on server S$_j$, for service k and the symbol is S$_{ijk}$. A server S$_i$ can provide a set of services to the users. A ST for a group of servers that has greater values in the diagonal elements is called *independent*. On the other edge a *dependent* ST, has the lower values in the diagonal elements. The process of moving from the dependent ST to an independent one is called *transition process (TP)* or *independency service process (ISP).* It is important to know the server dependency for various services including the creation of grouping. For this reason, ISP using the *independence service algorithm (ISA)*, can provide less dependency among servers working with a set of service tables (one for each service). Our goal is, after finding the STs for a group of servers, to apply ISA (for maximum column work) and then extend that to the other columns using methods from the SSPA. Therefore, some *useful concepts* are developed. The sum of the diagonal values of the tables (DV) shows whether a set of servers is working independently or not for each service. The service with the maximum value of DV is the one that is less dependent and is named as *main service* (MS). Starting from the MS, the ISA finds the next service that has the less distance using the Euclidean Distance norm. In this way we follow an (increasing) order of distance values for the ST process which needs decreasing *transition work* for achieving the independence. By transition work we mean the use of a set of methods for query processing that will enable the server work independently. The ST that has lower distance from MS needs more *transition work* to be done for the independency operation. The direction is from the service that needs more work (that is, the ST has less distance from MS), to the service that needs less work (the corresponding ST has more distance from MS). The central server (if there is any) can be tracked by using the L_1 form of each table. Finding the cs the HDR method from the SSPA can be applied directly to all the other servers of the group. A combination of all the other methods from SSPA can also be applied. The servers's efficiency can be enhanced by applying the SSMP methods. We can find dependency by either flow diagrams or ISA. ISA uses the *two phases method;* the *first phase* for finding the strong dependency server(s) (the hot data server) and the *second phase* for finding the weak dependency servers. Finally, at the end of the process, new ST_i are produced which make a group of servers work more independently minimizing the communication cost and providing faster services.

THE ISA

The phases of ISA and the pseudocode are in Example B.

Example 4: Let us consider three STs:

$$
\begin{array}{ccc}
\begin{array}{ccc} S_1 & S_2 & S_3 \\ 0.1 & 0.4 & 0.5 \\ A=0.2 & 0.3 & 0.5 \\ 0.2 & 0.3 & 0.6 \end{array} &
\begin{array}{ccc} S_1 & S_2 & S_3 \\ 0.1 & 0.2 & 0.7 \\ B=0.3 & 0.3 & 0.4 \\ 0.1 & 0.2 & 0.7 \end{array} &
\begin{array}{ccc} S_1 & S_2 & S_3 \\ 0.3 & 0.5 & 0.2 \\ C=0.4 & 0.3 & 0.3 \\ 0.3 & 0.5 & 0.2 \end{array}
\end{array}
$$

a. MS= B, since ST_{max} = max(sum(a_{ii}), sum (b_{ij}), sum (c_{ij})) = max(1.0, 1.1, 0.8) = 1.1, MS = B
b. S_1 is sds from server S_3 (because of the value 0.7).
c. MS=B, distance2d(A,B) = 0.4243, distance2d(B,C)= 0.8718. The transition work will follow the order: B → A → C.
d. Considering B as the main service we have to find the sender and the receiver server.

Example B.

```
ISA: Input: ST_i, i=1,....,k, k=#of service table, n: is the dimension of ST_i (or the # of servers)
Output: change ST_i using methods, for independent servers
A. find the MS (the ST_i with the maximum diagonal elements)
    read ST_j(a_ii), ∀ i,j ∈ I, i is the # of servers, j is the # of services (or STs)
    MS= ST_max = max_j [sum( a_ii)]
B. find the Euclidean distance of ST_i from MS (or ST_max), i≠max
    ST_k = | a_ij|, k≠max, i=1,...,n , i≠max
```

$$D_{max,k} = \sqrt{\sum_{i=1}^{n}\sum_{j=1}^{n}(a_{ij} - b_{ij})^2},$$

```
C. create an increasing order of the ST (according to their distance)
    print D_max,1 <...<D_m,k<...<D_m,1 .....<D_m,n (1,...k,..1,..,n ≠max)
    print ST_1, ....., ST_k,.....,ST_1,.... ST_n (the corresponding order)
    so that trans_work (ST_i)> trans_work (ST_i+1)
    tran_arr= [MS, ST_1, ..,ST_i, ST_i+1,..ST_n]
D. find: strong dependency, sender server, receiver server (1^st Phase)
    for each ST ∈ trans_arr
```

$$\|ST\|_1 = b_j = \max\left(\sum_{i=1}^{n}a_{i1}, \sum_{i=1}^{n}a_{i2}, ..., \sum_{i=1}^{n}a_{in}\right), \text{ for } j=1,..,n,$$

```
        max_col= ||ST||_1, sender server= S_max_col
        row_line=i= max(a_imax_col) ,where: i=1,...,n
        receiver server = S_rec_row
        if ( a_row_line max_col > max_thr)
            sender sever is cs , apply HDR
        end if
    end for
```

From $\|B\|_1$ we find the sender server with max_col =3 and row_line=1 at the following: $\|B\|_1 = \max(|0.1|+|0.3|+|0.1|, |0.2|+|0.3|+|0.2|, |0.7|+|0.4|+|0.7|)= \max(0.5, 0.7, 1.8)= 1.8$, max_col= 3, row_line = 1,sender server = S_3. The receiver server is S_1. The arrow in B illustrates the sender and receiver servers. According to Phase 1, since $a_{rec_row\,max_col} > $ max_thr (≥ 0.5) the HDR is applied and data are transferred from S_3 (cs) to S_1. Additionally, data from S_3 (with percentage 0.4) for row_line 2 are transferred to S1 (with percentage 0.3) as well (Phase 2).

THE QUERY PROCESSING METHODS

The query can be described as a sequence of operators (f.e. join) executed at various sites. Analytically: q= (cost_ex(q_i), cost_ex(q_{i+1}), cost_ex(q_{i+1}), ..., cost_ex (q_n)) where: cost_ex(q_i) is considered as the cost of execution of an operator of query q at site i. Moreover we have: cost_ex(q_i)=load(tab_i)+ex_oper(o_i)+transfer_time(of the results to server i+1) (2) where: load(tab_i) is the total loading cost of a table on server i, ex_oper (o_i) is the cost to execute the operator on the table of server i, and transfer_time is the time to transfer the results to the next server i+1 which of course is analogous to the amount of data to be transferred. It is assumed that there are no data   loaded from any server yet (*cold server*). The methods applied are as follows:

Method 1: (Local processing of Application - LOA) Achieving local processing is one of the major goals of the distributed databases. The data distribution in the sites characterizes the locality or the remoteness of the process. Application with complete locality (ss =ls) provides the best execution time with zero transmission cost and delay. Hence the optimization of a distributed query is composed of two parts: The distribution of access methods among sites, which can be achieved only by transmissions, and the determination of local access methods using methods of centralized databases). LOA is applied on any kind of dependency.

Method 2: (Operation improvement using Semi-Join - OISJ) For the optimization algorithms the consideration of the semi-join operation as a new perspective could be proved very profitable. An intuitive explanation is given by an example. A simple traditional semi-join example is presented (Figure 2) between two sites (S_1, S2) with the relations (A, B) respectively without an attempt of optimization. Project B from S_1 and send the results to site S_2 (*1*). The semi-join is performed in S_2 and the results are sent back to S_1(*2*). After that the join is performed at time t at site S_1 while the user is at S_3. Finally, the results will be sent to user location S_3.

We notice that relation A appears twice and this approach needs improvement. Additionally, the user location has not been taken into consideration. Obviously a better solution could be one of the following (Figure 2): (a) both the results in S_2 and S1 to be sent directly to S_3 (*3*, *4*) for local processing or (b) Data from S_2 to be sent (in advance) (*2*) to S_1 and after the processing the new results to be sent directly to S_3(*3*). In this way the cost optimization is achieved (2). This can be achieved with the use of Data Mining. The server examining the user and query paths in comparison with the corresponding paths of the *dependent* servers can define the most probable popular path, the time and the ls where the results have to be sent. Then it *decides* how to design the query plan so that it avoids duplicates and *unnecessary paths.*

Method 3: (Hot Data Replication-HDR) From dt, when there are values $>$ max_thr analytical work has to be performed in order to discover the most dependent server and create the group of servers. Data have to be sent from cs to the members of the groups or to some of them *(partial group)* in advance so that the transmission costs and control messages be eliminated. The balance of the hot data can be achieved when the communication is cheap (i.e. high bandwidth, low delay) by replication.

Method 4: (compress the qep-CQEP) When qep is above a certain bound ($\leq$3 hops) it is better to shorten the path by condensing the subpath with *support* $<$ *min_support*. With this process we avoid the additional intermediate times (load, execute operator on a table, transmission time to the next server). *This can be applied for the serial dependency servers.*

Other methods such as Balance Data Distribution, partition, protocols etc are not developed here. Moreover, our developed methods can provide the self-healing, self-managing and self-protecting characteristics of autonomic computing. *Self-healing* capabilities detect failing components (replication process from site to site) and take the necessary recovery steps. *Self-managing* can be offered with HDR, so that hot data can be replicated to the dependent servers. *Self-protecting* is also achieved since with CQEP the qep is shortened to avoid the intermediate subpaths, and minimize the attack risk, promising shortly integrated security process. The new servers' infrastructure can enable dynamic resource additions and changes, implement in the lowest layers of hardware, operating systems and network and finally, promises the use of the automatic allocation of computing resources "on the fly", as business conditions change.

Example 5. From example 4, the dt of service B is considered. From a_{13} (=0.7) it seems that S_3 is a "hot" server for S_1. Using all the sets of queries that belong to the value of 0.7 in order to minimize the total query cost we can apply the HDR method and have the data sent to S_1 before the process starts. The results are taken directly from S_1 (where the transaction process takes place) with a smaller number of control messages and without the transmission cost of the big size results. Since the application is running locally, the response time is reduced by the additional time required for communication between the two sites considering also the time to set up the query at the S_3 site as well as the network delay. For 10 query groups the reduction of the response time (or total delay) of the results' transfer (R=10KB) from S_3 to S_1 (distance 5 km) using Ethernet (10Mbps) with propagation speed: 177.000 km/sec, is as: Total delay (for 1query group) = transmission delay + propagation delay = R/ L + d / s = (10.000 * 8 (bits) / 10.000 (bits/sec)) + (5 km / 177.000 km/sec)= 8 + 0.00000282 =8.0000282sec. The total delay for the 10 query groups is about 80 sec. This is the additional cost (without considering the round trip time , RTT) when there is no network delay (because of congestion) and no consideration of the intermediate servers (or routers) between S_1 and S_3 as well as the handoff problems.

THE SEMI-AUTONOMOUS SERVER PROCESSING ALGORITHM (SSPA)

From all the above the process to create a semi autonomous server using Data Mining methods is essential. The SSPA includes a set of methods (including HDR) that facilitate the change of the stage of a dependent server to an efficient one depending on the service. The pseudocode of SSPA is as follows in Example C.

Illustrative examples are given below:

Figure 2. The semi-join example

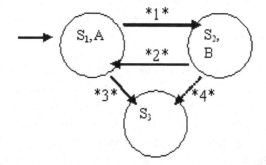

LOA: Let us consider: the qep=$\{p_1,p_2,p_3\}$ with the servers S_1,S_2,S_3,S_4 , and ss=S_1 and ls =S_4. Since ss is different from ls, replication of data from $S_4 \rightarrow S_3 \rightarrow S_2 \rightarrow S_1$ will be realized until ls = ss. The query execution will take place at the ls.

OISJ: Let us consider: qep==$\{p_1,p_2\}$ with servers S_k,S_m,S_n where (S_k and S_m) are mutually dependent and ss=S_k and ls=S_n. To avoid the delay of moving results and data from Sk to Sm , it would be better to replicate the data of S_k, S_m directly to the ls (S_n) where the query execution will be hold.

RULES OF SERVER DEPENDENCY FOR EACH SERVICE (SSD)

Some *rules* that can be applied to the service server dependency are the following:

1. If S_1 is dependent on S_2 and S_3, for service 1 (S_1 = dep_serv$_1$(S_2,S_3) then the $S_1,S_2,S_3 \in$ group G for serv$_1$ (or G $_{serv1}$ = $\{S_1,S_2,S_3\}$).
2. If (S_1, S_2) $\in$ G $_{serv1}$ and (S_2, S_3) $\in$ G $_{serv1}$ => (S_1, S_2, S_3) $\in$ G $_{serv1}$
3. If (S_1, S_2) $\in$ G $_{serv1}$ and (S_2, S_3) $\in$ G $_{serv2}$ => two groups of servers have to be used with S_2 being a common server for both services.
4. In the vertical dependency, if the value of an element of a column > max_thr (a threshold that is predefined) certain methods (HDR) can be applied for the independent server operation from SSPA
5. If there is serial dependency then LOA or CQEP (for longer size of query paths) are more suitable of SSPA for the independency.

These rules are used in order to create the groups of services and the independence process.

The *optimum case* for independence is when all servers work independently and this can be represented with the identity matrix for each service.

SIMULATION

Setup

A sampling method is used so that bandwidth can be reserved for a user at a specific time. For our experiments, we assume the uniform mobility behavior of the users. This means that a user follows a cyclic pattern within one day period. We use time sub-periods during a day, for several weeks, (in order to find periodical events) and examine the mobility of each user. There are two processes: the group and the query one. Simulation is held in two phases; the initial and the main. The *initial* phase contains the path generation, and the discovery of the favorite group and query path. There are five steps:

1. *Creation of group and query paths.* The group path is generated as follows: (a) select two nodes in the graph, randomly, as original and destination nodes (b) whenever the mobile user leaves the current cell, moves to a neighboring cell which is closest to the destination.
2. *Apply MIA for finding the favorite paths.* The favorite group path (a table) is selected for each BS according to MIA. Some of the query paths do not follow exactly the group paths, depending

on the way the data for the queries are allocated on the servers, partitions and the query plan. For convenience, it is considered that for each group path there is a query execution path. For our simulation it is assumed that the resources (bandwidth) are offered to the users in FIFO mode. For each favorite group and query path the initial cell k (belong to a BS_i) from a group path and the lc cell that belong to the BS_i or BSj ($j \neq i$) are selected. These paths, as large itemsets (1-itemsets),

Example C.

```
SSPA Input: S={S₁,S₂,...,Sₙ} a set of servers
max_thr, serial dependency: S₁ dep on S₂, S₂ dep on Sₙ etc.
set E=(p₁, p₂, p₃,...,pₙ)={S₁S₂,S₂S₃,S₃S₄,...,Sₙ₋₁Sₙ}
ss= starting server, ls= last server
Output: set E'=(p₁, p₂, p₃,...,pₖ), where k<n
if there is serial dependency
   for each STᵢ
     apply HDR, LOA, CQEP, OISJ
   end for
endif


HDR
A1: vertical, partial strong dependency (1ˢᵗ Phase)
        mes= "vert. dependency", mes1="partial dependency"
        mes2="no strong dependency"
        for each a ᵢₘₐₓ_col (i≠ rec_row)
          if a ᵢₘₐₓ_col > max_thr
             if a ᵢᵣₒw_line < a ᵢₘₐₓ_col
                sender server: S ₘₐₓ_col , receiver server: Sᵢ,
                print mes
             else print mes1
             endif
           else print mes2
           end if
           end for
A2: weak dependency   (2ⁿᵈ Phase)
         for each a ᵢₘₐₓ_col (i≠ rec_row)
           if a ᵢᵣₒw_line < a ᵢₘₐₓ_col
               sender server is S ₘₐₓ_col, receiver server Sᵢ,
           endif
           end for
 LOA:
    for each qep ∈ E
    for each pᵢ(i= n,...,1) , pᵢ=Sᵢ,Sᵢ₊₁
       ss=S₁
       while (ss!=ls)
         if ( Sᵢ != ss)
            replicate data from Sᵢ₊₁ to Sᵢ
            ls = Sᵢ
         else ls=ss
         endif
       end while
    end for
    end for
```

Example C. continued

```
OISJ:
    if((Sₖ is dep on Sₘ) && (Sₘ is dep on Sₖ)
        && (ss= Sₖ) && (Sₘ next of Sₖ) && (1s=Sₙ))
        replicate data from Sₘ and Sₖ to Sₙ
        local processing at Sₙ
    end if


CQEP:
        for each q∈ E
            for each pᵢ (i=1,...,n)
                if sup(pᵢ) <min_sup
                    replicate data from Sᵢ₊₁ to Sᵢ
                end if
            end for
        end for
```

are used in the simulation. From this assumption the ss knows, in advance, the lc and there is no need to have "prefetched" data at wrong time and place.

3. *From SQTs create the DTs.* After the creation of the group and query mobility from the SQTs, we have the creation of the DT. The DT_i is computed by calculating the percentage of the total support of the internal and external queries of S_k the most favorite group and query path,

4. *Preparation for services and many servers, using ISA.* After finding the STs for a set of servers and applying ISA an order for the ST process is created.

5. *SSPA application.* We focus on the study of a service using various methods from SSPA.

Depending on the frequency, data are requested by a site and the execution order of the different parts of a query at various sites. The SSPA reduces the data route, the communication messages, the response time of later access and provides the ability of sending the results from the ls to the new mobile location, lc, directly. It works independently of the type of the network (tree or some other structure) and the type of shipping (query or data). The application of methods of SSPA can provide us with a data replication scheme according to their qeps and can also minimize the communication cost by moving copies of part (or all) of the data to servers that are located near the users that are likely to use those data. *SSPA is estimated by the nodes and it can cooperate with any server query processing plan finding optimal solutions. This is the final technique applied to ensure the server's independent work.*

The *main* phase contains the simulation of the arrival and service process of users. The table of the favorite group paths (l-itemsets) contains the cells and the time that a user will visit. A clock is activated offering the necessary time information. We consider a coverage area that consists of 20 base stations, each having 6 neighbors on average with 20 servers (one server for each one base station). When the query can not be answered by the local server, the query (or subquery) is sent to the server that can respond. The one-to-one correspondence between BS and server speed up the searching and can provide the same query and group subpaths to some extend. This may be applied to periodical events (after or before the event) covering queries for location and event information (requests such as: hotel location, path destination, other next time event, the distance, road congestion etc). After the collection of data and the application of MIA the users follow their group paths and it is not necessary to send again messages to the initial server for their new position (naïve approach). The second approach is to have the results sent to the ls. Therefore, the servers and BSs will operate free of any handoff problems.

The average distance between two BSs is 1 mile. Call duration is the same for all calls and exponentially distributed with mean value of 120s. Call requests are generated according to a Poisson process with rate λ (calls/cell/s) and exponential service time for any cell of the group and query path. Two cases of mobility are considered: low user mobility (0- 40 miles/hour); and high user mobility, (40-70 miles/hour). Each cell can service a limited number of users according to the number of available channels. The range of support (e.g., "abc" –restricted- or "abcd" –extensive-) defines the number of items of the most popular group paths (l-itemsets) that their bandwidth will be reserved. The rest of the simulation parameters with their values are listed in Table 2.

We consider the following users categories: users with branches and restricted support, users with branches and extensive support, and all the kinds of users. The meaning of branches is that the users, after a following the same subpath, separate their moves following different subpaths. We have conducted the experiments for the previous kinds of users in the form of input of new l-itemsets, support tables, producing various delay times. The *probability of excess of the predefined response time* (*pert*) is defined as the ratio of the number of queries that had a delay over the pred_resp, divided by the total number of the queries. The users have some tolerance to delay and this can be obtained by the pert. The base station sends the data with a moderate downlink speed of 200MB/sec. The performance of the proposed algorithms is examined for various group and queries mobility patterns and various scenaria are considered.

Experiments

The scenaria are the following:

1. *The naïve and last server approach (scenario 1).* A set of queries (3 sets) for three servers is considered. Better response time is provided with the last server approach since the results are sent

Table 2. Parameters used in the simulation

Parameter	Value
#groups	50 paths
#queries	50 paths
# of groups	5
query size	512bytes
result size	10Kbytes
# servers	20
base station down link speed	200Mb/s
data base size	20, 80,100Kbytes
ethernet	10Mbps
λ	0.7

there is no dependency, we have LOA and there is no delay. (b) In Figure 5, the partial dependency provides slightly worse results than Figure 4, because HDR can be applied only for some servers. (c) Queries with data in 1,2 or 3 servers are considered. The pred_resp = 10 sec. The upper positioned curve refers to the case before any SSPA method be applied. At first CQEP diminishes some paths in order to avoid the minimum support and provides a better approach. The minimum

Figure 3. The response time for set of queries with two approaches

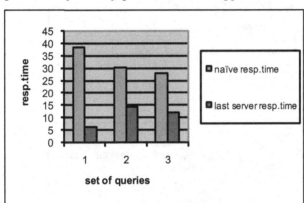

Figure 4. The pert with vertical dependency

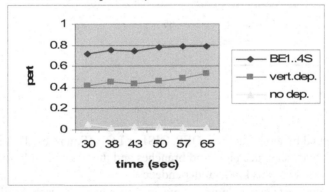

directly to the last server instead of following the naïve approach (from the start server to the last). For set 1 there is a big difference between the two approaches because in the naïve approach the results have to be sent back (to the start server) and then again forwarded to the last server (the end node of the group path). For the other two sets the last server is an intermediate node of the group path.

2. *All kinds of users (scenario 2).(a)* Queries with data in four servers are considered (Figure 5). The pred_resp=10 sec (*tight* response time condition). The term BE means before the application of any execution method. Using HDR with the vertical dependency we take better results. When

Figure 5. The pert with partial dependency for all kinds of users

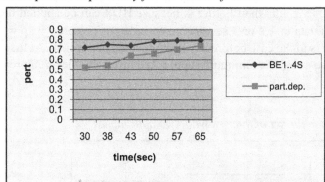

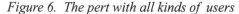

Figure 6. The pert with all kinds of users

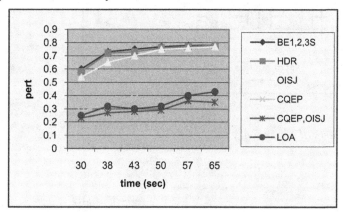

value of pert is achieved by applying the CQEP, OISJ or LOA (Figure 6). This is due to the fact that there are queries with sequence parts and branches and there are not a lot of "hot data". The next scenaria are based on various kinds of dependency.

3. *Users with branches and restricted support (scenario 2).* A new set of user mobility patterns with more branches, with a variety of sets of group queries, pred_resp =10sec, and data shared in four servers are considered. The upper curve refers to the case before the SSPA methods' use. Because of the small size of the restricted support paths, LOA offers better results than the OISJ (Figure 7). The HDR cannot be applied since there is no strong server dependency. The CQEP cannot provide better results because it is activated for serial dependency (>=3hops) and not for queries with restricted support.

4. *Users with branches and extensive support (scenario 3).* The same parameters are used as in Figure 7, except for 10 servers. The values of pert are a little higher than those of Figure 7 because of the greater size of the path. By contrast with the restricted support paths, here it is more possible for the user to move at a far away location, which adds an additional time to the response query time.

Figure 7. The pert for restricted support (any kind of dependency)

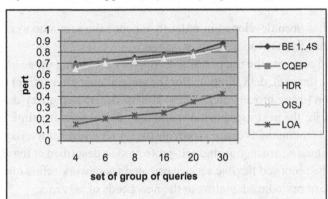

Figure 8. Pert with extensive support (any kind of dependency)

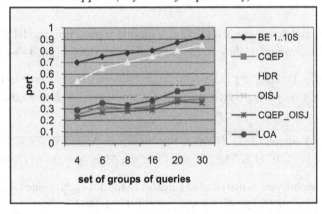

LOA cannot provide the best results since data are spread to many sites and it is basically useful for restricted support queries. It works only for the first common subpaths without caring about the rest of the servers of the query that have extensive support. The CQEP provides better results because it is activated for the extensive support queries and covers all the common subpaths that belong to extensive support paths. Increased the number of groups leads to increased values of pert before and after the application of any method. Additionally, the combination of CQEP_OISJ provides better results.

FUTURE WORK

The new wireless generation of devices armed with location capabilities and the next generation servers with scale up possibilities, tools etc can enhance the servers self-sufficiency. More methods in a dependent services environment will be examined in the near future.

CONCLUSION

A server grouping process has been developed in order to enhance the semiautonomous servers with better performance and reduce the network resources' usage.

Considering the proposed concepts the use of SSPA seems very promising especially when we have query shipping (for a middle tier site), data shipping (for the general query execution) or any economic model for resource allocation (using brokers etc). A new kind of distributed query design plan can be created using the prediction for the next user positions and their correspond ing time in order to avoid basically the round trip cost. Our methods can also provide the server with characteristics of autonomic computing such as self-healing, self-managing and self-protection as described at the above query processing methods section. The proposed flexible service oriented framework offers query optimization utilizing its flexible scheme of periodic adaptation to the new needs of services.

REFERENCES

Dunham, M., & Helal, A.& Balakrishnam, S. (1997). A mobile transaction model that captures both data and movement behavior. *Journal Mobile Networks and Applications* (pp. 149-162).

Feng, W., & Chen, M. (2003). Developing Data Allocation Schemes by Incremental Mining of User Moving Patterns in a Mobile Computing System. *IEEE Transactions on Knowledge and Data Engineering, 15*(1), 70-85.

Franklin, M., Jonson, B. & Kossmann, D. (1996). Performance Tradeoffs for Client-Server Query Processing. *Proceedings of 1996 ACM SIGMOD Int. Conf. on Management of Data* (pp.149-160)

Gedik, B., & Liu, L.(2006). MobiEyes: A distributed Location Monitoring Service Using Moving Location Queries, *IEEE Transaction on Mobile Computing, 5*(10), 1384-1402.

Hand, D., Smith, P., & Manilla, H. (2000). *Principles of Data Mining.* Boston: MIT Press

Ioannidis, Y., & Kang, Y. (1990). Randomized Algorithms for optimizing Large Join Queries. *Proceedings of 1990 ACM SIGMOD Int. Conf. on Management of Data* (pp. 312-331)

Kossmann, D. (2004). The State of the Art in Distributed Query Processing. *ACM Computing Surveys, 32*(4), 422-469.

Menasce, D., & Kephart, J. (2007). Autonomic Computing, *IEEE Internet Computing* (pp. 18-21)

Silberschatz, A., Korth, H., & Sudarshan, S. (2006) . *Database System Concepts*, 5^t edition, Boston: McGraw Hill.

Tang, X., & Chanson S. (2004). Minimal cost Replication of Dynamic Web Contents under Fault Update Delivery. *IEEE Transactions on Parallel and Distributed Systems, 15*(5), 431-439.

Chapter XVIII
Open Information Management in User–Driven Healthcare

Rakesh Biswas
People's College of Medical Sciences, India

Ankur Joshi
People's College of Medical Sciences, India

Kevin Smith
National Digital Research Centre, Ireland

Vinod Narkhede
People's College of Medical Sciences, India

Carmel M. Martin
Northern Ontario School of Medicine, Canada

Jitendra Jain
People's College of Medical Sciences, India

Joachim P. Sturmberg
Monash University, Australia & The University of Newcastle, Australia

ABSTRACT

This chapter discusses the role of open health information management in the the development of a novel, adaptable mixed-platform for supporting health care informational needs. This platform enables clients (patient users) requiring healthcare to enter an unstructured but detailed account of their day-to-day health information requirements that may be structured into a lifetime electronic health record. It illustrates the discussion with an operational model and a pilot project in order to begin to explore the potential of a collaborative network of patient and health professional users to support the provision of health care services, and helping to effectively engage patient users with their own healthcare. Such a solution has the potential to allow both patient and health professional users to produce useful materials, to contribute to improved social health outcomes in terms of health education and primary disease prevention, and to address both pre-treatment and post-treatment phases of illness that are often neglected in the context of overburdened support services.

INTRODUCTION

Managing chronic medical illnesses in the community is a universal challenge. The traditional patient and health professional clinical encounter has evolved into a series of fragmented exchanges of information, often between several professionals. The information exchange between professionals mostly excludes the patient and is usually limited to a synthesized 'factual' written account – often referred to as 'the clinical (integrated) medical record'. The synthesized 'factual' written account however fails to convey much of the subtlety gained through the information exchanges in the encounter (which would have built a more valuable knowledge base about a patient) (Sturmberg, 2007). The clinical encounter has the potential to actually evolve into an informational collaborative process, i.e. ongoing learning persistent in virtual space and time. A persistent clinical encounter has immense potential advantages for the patient as well as her health professionals.

Medicine is a collaborative effort in problem solving between individual patients and their health professionals. The collaborations also involve others who are directly or indirectly related to the patient and health professional (for example, the patient's relatives, the practice staff, other members of the physicians' institutions etc) who provide the necessary support to the two main actors.

We suggest viewing such an integrated approach to health care as 'User driven health care' that may be defined as, "Improved health care achieved with concerted collaborative learning between multiple users and stakeholders, primarily patients, health professionals and other actors in the care giving collaborative network across a web interface." (Biswas et al., 2008 a) It needs to be differentiated from the current ubiquitous 'Consumer driven health care' model, which is essentially a strategy for users/consumers to decide how they may pay for their own health care through multiple stakeholders like employers who provide the money and insurance companies who receive the premiums (Tan, 2005).

OPEN INFORMATION MANAGEMENT AND HEALTH 2.0

Patient user generated and suitably anonymous informational content initially confined to email boxes or web based individual health record vaults can be further invested in online web pages linked to what is loosely termed as Web 2.0 technologies. That may provide opportunities for linking common experiences in order to generate improved patient and caregiver learning

In web sites using this technology user-generated tags would allow the site to evolve, enabling individual users to conduct more precise searches, make additional associations, and explore a diverse undercurrent of themes to synthesize for learning purposes.

Health 2.0 in realtion to health care has been described to be all about Patient Empowered Healthcare whereby patients have the information they need to be able to make rational healthcare decisions (transparency of information) based on value (outcomes over price).

The Four Cornerstones (Connectivity, Price, Quality, and Incentives) of the Value Driven Healthcare movement begin to create a virtuous cycle of innovation and reform. Transparency serves as a key catalyst in this process by creating positive sum competition that can deliver better outcomes at a lower cost...

As more information becomes available as a result of increased transparency, there will be a wave of innovation at all points along the full cycle of care, which includes phases where health care professionals Educate, Prevent, Diagnose, Prepare, Intervene, Recover, Monitor, and Manage the various disease states (Health 2.0 Definition, 2007).

Each and every human has the capacity for and likelihood of performing both roles of caregiver and care seeker (patient) in their lifetimes. The illness experience posts would automatically generate related posts depending on the keyword-tags they use to represent their posts and this would enable every user posting his/her individual experience, to access similar relevant lived experiences of other individuals. This would be a tool delivered remotely, often anonymously, and yet may foster a sense of belonging and intimacy. In this way any individual user feeding input into the net can receive automatic feedback that can grow as individual users keep updating their own data in this Web-based solution. This may function purely on the power of human collaborative intelligence rather than artificial intelligence and yet may prove to be much more efficient.

Each and every individual is the author of his/her own destiny (as well as his/her own web log) that reflects their experiential life processes and decisions that can shape their future. User driven health care is an attempt to help make those decisions. It is a grassroots activity to document valuable individual experiences of patients, physicians, allied health professionals and medical students which have to-date usually gone undocumented and have been a loss to the medical literature (Biswas 2008a some text in this section has been reused with permission).

OPEN HEALTH INFORMATION MANAGEMENT AND SELF ORGANIZATION

Self-organization is the property of well functioning complex adaptive systems that allows the natural relationships among individuals and groups to shape the nature of an evolving knowledge base (Martin & Kaufman, 2007).

The organizational complexity of an individual's interactions with his/her environment defines the level of his functionality. The more the connections an individual is able to develop and the greater the diversity of his network the more it may reflect his/her vitality (Biswas 2003). This is even witnessed at a micro-level inside the human body where there is a demonstrable withering of neuronal connections and complexity with senescence and a resultant loss of neuronal functionality reflected in overall loss of functionality of aging. (Lipsitz & Goldberger, 1992). Quite a few studies demonstrate the relationship between intimacy and health, and how disease survivors who report positive family relationships or access to support groups consistently live longer than those without them. The challenge for us ahead is coupling our traditional focus on monitoring efficiencies with providing deeper human connections to promote sustainable behavior change (Darsee, 2007).

The inscrutably enduring power of the anecdote itself is what incites all our most fearsome defences. The irony in our growing intolerance of the anecdote is that storytelling is full of lessons in imagination and invention so beneficial to the creative investigator. (Campo, 2006). If only all our daily processes were documented along with the anecdotes generated from them they may yet be a valuable form of evidence. It may not be an impossible dream in this electronic information age. Web-based sharing of individual patient and health professional experiences based on individual user needs through fixed and mobile information technology interfaces, would make for better E-learning in health care. This would enable all learners to integrate information and knowledge and manage health and medicine with additional wisdom. (Sturmberg, 2007).

James Surowiecki in his book "The Wisdom of Crowds," mentions four key qualities that make for collective wisdom. It needs to be diverse, so that people are bringing different pieces of information to the table. It needs to be decentralized, so that no one at the top is dictating the crowd's answer. It needs a way of summarizing people's opinions into one collective verdict. And the people in the crowd need to be independent, so that they pay attention mostly to their own information, and not worrying about what everyone around them thinks (Surowiecki, 2004).

As a word of caution it is possible to imagine highly profitable and very destructive feedback platforms based on servers in unscrupulous jurisdictions that are driven by advertising, from personal litigation lawyers to purveyors of therapeutic snake oil. Avoiding this and achieving the best for citizens will require vision, balance and coordinated effort between all those concerned for the individual user in this new age of democratized voice (Hodgkin & Munro, 2007).

User driven health care applying multidimensional approaches of persistent clinical encounters and wisdom of crowds has the potential to be transformational in challenging the complex, high cost, institutional approach that typifies health care delivery systems today. The health care industry desperately needs ideas that offer lower costs, higher quality and greater convenience and accessibility. Also relaxing central control will make local trust and strategic health workers feel more engaged in the project (Kmietowicz, 2007). While dominant players are focused on preserving business models of expensive care and technology arsenals, user driven innovations promise cheaper and simpler access to virtual clinical encounters thus meeting learning needs of the vast majority of patients who may otherwise suffer simply due to lack of information (Biswas 2008a some text in this section has been reused with permission).

CREATING PERSISTENT CLINICAL ENCOUNTERS THROUGH OPEN HEALTH INFORMATION MANAGEMENT

At present most of our chronic disease population is managed in hospitals and clinics (both in the public and private sector). The average appointment time a patient is reviewed in the hospital may arrive at 2-3 monthly intervals. This discontinuity in patient monitoring may be due to patient related factors for example if a daily wage earner has to spend hours attending a hospital outpatient department during working hours it may mean no income for that particular day. A farmer may not be able to come for follow up during sowing and harvesting. Similarly a busy executive or business man may find it difficult to address his/her healthcare needs in terms of maintaining continuity which is vital to improve health outcomes.

In the interval between the physician visits, the patient (for example a diabetic) on his/her own is expected to continue a judicious diabetic diet, maintain an optimal exercise schedule and dutifully consume all his/her medicines on time (and presumably also have an understanding of correct dosage). Any confusion or queries on the patient's part would be solved on the next visit unless it can be prescheduled (which is not easy due to the patient related factors mentioned previously).

Apart from these usual information needs that are compromised there may be other emotional information needs that would otherwise go unexpressed.

The gap between the paucity of what is proved to be effective for selected groups of patients versus the infinitely complex clinical decisions required for individual patients has been recently recognized and termed the 'inferential gap.' The breadth of the inferential gap varies according to available knowledge, its relevance to clinical decisions, access to the knowledge (that is, what the physician actually knows at the time of a clinical decision), the variable ways in which knowledge is interpreted and translated into a decision, the patient's needs and preferences, and a host of other factors. Clinicians are required to fill in where their knowledge (or knowledge itself) falls short. (Stewart, Shah & Selna, 2007), and where their patients look for answers outside of the prevailing knowledge frameworks (Shaughnessy, Slawson & Becker, 1998).

As this need for information remains unaddressed, there may be a gradual build up of patient dissatisfaction unrelated to the worsening of the disease. Timely answering of question and concerns would have resulted in a better-educated patient and may have prevented this. Patient education has long been a recognized as a positive factor in successful management of illness and a good education may result from problem based experiential learning that begins with addressing patient's information needs

At present most patient data exist either in their own or their physician's memories as well as in very brief unstructured paper notes or records that are difficult to preserve and update. As a result there is considerable duplication as well as attrition of a single patient's data at multiple entry points as s/he shifts from one health professional to another across various healthcare facilities.

Often patients do not remember all the minute, but sometimes significant details in their illness history even on careful questioning – on each occasion we have to reconstruct our stories anew in light of our current understanding. (Greenhalgh, 2006). This may however be preserved in regular daily/weekly or even monthly inputs made by the patient her/himself that is stored and summarized into a readily retrievable electronic health record, creating a persistent clinical encounter (Figure 1) (Biswas 2008b some text and Figure 1 in this section has been reused with permission).

KEY ATTRIBUTES OF THE PROPOSED OPEN INFORMATION MANAGEMENT SOLUTION PLATFORM IN INDIA

The solution will consist of a patient information input point into a system that would produce content in the form of a dynamic electronic health record that evolves with time and is complemented by a web interface with interactive inputs from health professionals for structuring and interacting with this content in between intervals of face-to-face sessions.

The entry point for patient data would be in strategically located internet kiosks that would contain a desktop with broadband access and would be managed by a person from the same community who would type patient verbal data into the desktop portal in Hindi using English fonts or alternatively record the patient's conversation onto a voice mail.

Figure 1. From current limited clinical encounter to an ideal persistent clinical encounter

Patient Input Data Capture and Storage

A typical case scenario would consist of a patient user who may visit the Internet kiosk at the end of a working day and pour out his/her physical/mental troubles experienced over the course of the day/week/month all of which may be recorded verbatim into an e-mail with a gmail address (for example userdrivenhealth@gmail.com). This would be done by the person managing the desktop at the rural/urban health kiosk and s/he would simultaneously mail the same unstructured data to the primary care physician project participant who would then structure the data to the best of his/her abilities and if necessary forward it to other health professionals in the collaborative online network best suited to tackle the particular patient problem.

Patient data may be recorded by the village health kiosk data entry operator simply on video or a voice mail that can be stored online inside multiple gmail boxes beginning with the internet kiosk gmail account (for example userdrivenhealth@gmail.com), the patient's own gmail account to which this data could be mailed, the gmail account of the Hindi medical transcriptionist who would convert this raw patient unstructured conversational voice data to text using Hindi and English fonts, to the gmail account of the language translator who would translate this into English and finally to the primary caregiver in charge of the patient. Other than voice and text, images (still and video) taken by patients, their relatives or caregivers with direct or indirect bearing on their disease (with due care to preserve privacy) may be easily stored in their gmail boxes (individual health record vaults).

Patient Confidentiality and Privacy

This user driven solution will encourage patient users to avoid entering any identifying information, which they may feel uncomfortable divulging or associating themselves with. The most important identifying information that would need to be omitted is patient names, addresses and names of others that may have been associated with them in the course of their illness history. Patients may only identify themselves using self assigned 10 digit numbers (one suggestion would be to use the patient's mobile phone number). There is a common assumption that a patient may not be easily identified in general through his/her mobile phone number although in reality they may still be easily identified if someone who knows their mobile number specifically looks for them. To circumvent this problem we propose giving patient's the option of using a separate Subscriber Identity Module (SIM) in a separate mobile handset solely for interacting with our healthcare network.

Patients maybe expected to have issues regarding safety of using emails (especially gmail) but as long as they utilize usernames which they can suitably make anonymous and feel comfortable with and stick to not entering any identifying information their privacy and confidentiality would be preserved.

Patient Input Data Sharing and Feedback

Patients will need regular feedback on their informational inputs particularly to address their informational requirements; their disease based queries and its myriad diagnostic and management uncertainties. This can be done by the primary physician in charge of the patient (patients may be given the option of choosing their own primary physicians). The primary physician in charge can make use of online empirical or experiential evidence to engage in persistent conversational learning with the patient all of which would be stored in the electronic health record (EHR). The physician could also ask opinion of other experts on the collaborative network (through email) again all conversations of which would be recorded on the electronic health record.

Healthcare professionals may enter their feedback onto gmail and mail it to the email addresses of the individual patient concerned as well as the gmail address where all patient electronic health records would be stored (as a central place to collate and further process the data for example userdrivenhealth@gmail.com). Putting all this patient data together on the gmail box can enable searching for similar patient experiences by simply typing a few matching keywords on to the gmail search engine and checking out matching patient records stored in the gmail box. This is one important aspect of the solution that is expected to grow with time as more and more patient data is stored in the gmail box (which also has an adaptable storage capacity to match user needs).

Other than this, patients can be transmitted limited feedback utilizing existing web-based services that allow free short messaging services (SMSes) to be sent (although limited to 80 characters as opposed to the standard 160 characters available in a basic mobile).

In rural as well as urban India there exists a large digital divide. In recent times a number of attempts have been made to bridge this gap by utilizing mobile phone technology.

These web based services could be effectively utilized by the primary physicians and other healthcare professionals in our collaborative network to provide essential informational feedback to each individual patient tailored to their informational requirements. In this manner the solution could develop a sustained conversation between patient and healthcare professional users. The best return on investment for the patient (who invests her time into this) would be in the form of health professional and other patient informational feedback that eventually helps let him/her gain favorable outcomes. For health professionals investing their time into this the biggest driver would be the insights gained into their patient's lives.

For all actors in this collaborative venture learning would be the common driver.

All this learning for the health professional could be organized into health professional E-portfolios linking the health professional with his/her patient records. A patient could look up the range of cases his/her health professional has come across corroborated and validated by the network and decide if this particular health professional has handled a similar case with a similar initial illness trajectory (which could be a new approach to selecting a health professional rather than go by the not so well informed referrals from other health professionals).

FUTURE TRENDS

In the simplified solution, with the platform discussed in this chapter, a detailed Personal Health Record (PHR) shall be accessible to the patient only on the web and a very truncated version of the above may be sent through SMS on demand from the registered user. Once the present basic mobile phone version is phased out in the near future and the PDA (personal digital assistant) mobile phone becomes the basic model along with ubiquitous WiMAX (Worldwide Interoperability for Microwave Access) connectivity, larger PHRs such as these could be easily accessed by patients into their device directly from the Internet.

On completion of the test phase this web-based solution to integrate healthcare E-learning needs can be opened to the world in a simple forum model, already in use at present in various web sites using what is loosely termed as web 2.0 technology. Regular experiential informational input may be posted on to the forum along with a copy to the individual user's password protected web account that would function as an E-portfolio if s/he were posting as a caregiver and a personal health record if s/he is posting as a patient. The individual user could even do this through email and every post made by mail could easily open a new post on to the forum. Most PC users in recent times spend most of their internet time in their mailbox and integrating this solution into the mailbox would target this population (Biswas et al., 2008b).

CONCLUSION

This is an operational model of user driven health care developed in an attempt to optimally answer multidimensional needs, in individual patients and health professionals to cater to an urban-rural Indian community. It is hypothesized that this may allow them to achieve better health outcomes through inter-individual collaboration between multiple stakeholders in the care giving and care seeking collaborative network.

Overall, the project will help to explore the potential of a collaborative network of patient and health professional users to support the provision of health care services, helping to effectively engage patient users with their own healthcare. Such a solution has the potential to allow both patient and health professional users to produce useful materials, to contribute towards improved social health outcomes in terms of health education and primary disease prevention, and to address both pre-treatment and post-treatment phases of illness that are often neglected in the context of overburdened support services.

This operational prototype, which still continues to evolve, has been shared with other future stakeholders particularly in the healthcare system. We look forward to the beginning of the validation process along with a future positive collaborative venture in user driven healthcare with multiple stakeholders in the public and private sectors.

ACKNOWLEDGMENT

Professor GC Dixit, Dean, People's College of Medical Sciences, Bhopal, India, Mr Arun Gurtu, Director of Research, People's College of Medical Sciences, Bhopal, India and Captain Ruchi Vijaywarghia, Director, HR and IT, People's College of Medical Sciences, Bhopal, India for their continued support.

REFERENCES

Biswas, R., Martin, M., Sturmberg, J., Shankar, R., Umakanth, S., Shanker, & Kasthuri A. S. (2008a). User driven health care - Answering multidimensional information needs in individual patients utilizing post EBM approaches: A conceptual model. *Journal of Evaluation in Clinical Practice.*

Biswas, R., Maniam, J., Lee, E. W. H., Das, P. G., Umakanth, S., Dahiya, S., & Ahmed, S. (2008b). User driven health care- Answering multidimensional information needs in individual patients utilizing post EBM approaches: An operational model. *Journal of Evaluation in Clinical Practice.*

Biswas, R. (2003). *Patient networks and their level of complexity as an outcome measure in clinical intervention.* Retrieved December 16, 2007, from http://www.bmj.com/cgi/eletters/324/7329/63

Campo, R. (2006). Anecdotal evidence: Why narratives matter to medical practice. *PLoS Medicine, 3*(10), e423 doi:10.1371/journal.pmed.0030423. Retrieved July 25, 2008, from http://medicine.plosjournals.org/perlserv/?request=get-document&doi=10.1371/journal.pmed.0030423

Darsee, J. (2007). *Creating healing communities through telemedicine.* Retrieved December 16, 2007, from http://www.hhnmostwired.com/hhnmostwired_app/jsp/articledisplay.jsp?dcrpath=HHNMOSTWIRED/PubsNewsArticleMostWired/data/07Summer/070905MW_online_Darsee&domain=HHNMOSTWIRED

Greenhalgh, T. (2006). *What seems to be the trouble? Stories in illness and healthcare.* Oxford: Radcliffe Publishing.

Hodgkin, P., & Munro, J. (2007). The long tale: public services and Web 2.0. *Consumer Policy Review, 17*(2), 84-88.

Kmietowicz, Z. (2007). MPs "dismayed" at confusion about electronic patient records. *British Medical Journal, 335*(7620), 581.

Lipsitz, L. A., & Goldberger, A. L. (1992). Loss of 'complexity' and aging. Potential applications of fractals and chaos theory to senescence. *Journal of the American Medical Association, 267*(13), 1806-1809.

Martin, C. M., & Kaufman, T. (2007). *Glossary of Terms in New Orientations, a Shared Framework: A Way Forward to Adaptive Primary Health Care Systems Across Canada: A Discussion Monograph.* Commissioned by the Canadian Association of Community Health Centre Associations and the Association of Ontario Health Centers.

Shaughnessy, A. F., Slawson, D. C., & Becker, L. (1998). Clinical jazz: harmonizing clinical experience and evidence-based medicine. *Journal of Family Practice, 47*(6), 425-428.

Health 2.0 Definition. (n.d.). Retrieved December 16, 2007, from http://health20.org/wiki/Health_2.0_Definition

Stewart, W. F., Shah N. R., & Selna M. J. (2007). Bridging the inferential gap: The electronic health record and clinical evidence. *Health Affairs, 26*(2), w181-w191.

Sturmberg, J. P. (2007). *The foundations of primary care.* Oxford: Radcliffe Publishing

Surowiecki, J. (2004). *The wisdom of crowds.* New York: Random House

Tan, J. (Ed.). (2005). *E-health care information systems.* Jossey-Bass: Wiley Imprint

Chapter XIX
Open Information Management:
Jurisdictional, Legal and Ethical Factors

Michael Losavio
University of Louisville, USA

Adel Elmaghraby
University of Louisville, USA

Deborah Keeling
University of Louisville, USA

ABSTRACT

The global interconnected information space offers unprecedented ways of accessing and analyzing information. New infringements of the rights of individuals to privacy, personality and personal autonomy may be a consequence presenting possible legal and ethical issues for developers and users of open information systems. Awareness of these issues will assist the use, engineering and regulation of open information systems with minimal infringement of those rights. We examine

- *National, international and transnational jurisdictional issues affecting open information management*
- *Privacy and personal autonomy*
- *intellectual property concerns*

Consideration of these issues will minimize risks of problems developing from the implementation and use of open information systems.

INTRODUCTION

General Perspective

The evolution of open information systems has advanced the sharing of data, information and knowledge. Yet this comes in cultures where "practical obscurity" (Stevens, 1989) of information has had value as to privacy and security. As open information management and use infringes on the privacy and security of objects, people and their rights, conflicts will develop in law and ethics. The conflicts may be national or transnational and range from private, individual issues to issues of sovereign state power to regulate, analyze and use information.

Chapter Objectives

The objectives of this chapter are to list some immediate or potential conflict areas and suggest a framework by which developers and researchers in open information management may anticipate, and possibly remediate, these conflicts. This chapter establishes for the reader some of the potential legal and ethical issues that may be impacted by open information management, particularly in an interconnected and collaborative environment. It should serve as a practical-level reference outline to guide the reader toward solutions in open information systems design and use that are legal and ethical.

BACKGROUND

Open information management has been of extraordinary benefit for the free exchange of information and ideas in domains ranging from commerce to science to politics. The development of Standard General Markup Language (SGML), for example, has opened information to expanded processing across multiple platforms.

The system of Hyper Text Markup Language (HTML), a subset of SGML, as implemented over the World Wide Web component of the Internet, has revolutionized information exchange. The United States Supreme Court, in rejecting a government effort to limit certain content over this open system, noted the Internet is "the most participatory form of mass speech yet developed.", …"serving to foster an exchange of information or opinion on a particular topic running the gamut from, say, the music of Wagner to Balkan politics to AIDS prevention to the Chicago Bulls" … "It is "no exaggeration to conclude that the content on the Internet is as diverse as human thought." Id. [n.7]" (Stevens 1995)

Yet it is precisely the potential injuries due to open information misuse that raises legal and ethical issues for OIM systems. Open information systems should anticipate these issues as part of design and commentary.

Definitions and Key Concepts

The scope of these issues is seen in the core terms for this subject.

- **Open information management:** ""Open Information Management" (OIM) means managing information so that it is open to processing and use by any program, not just the program that created it. That extends even to application programs not conceived of at the time the information was created." (from the introduction to the Charles F. Goldfarb Series on Open Information Management)

- **Jurisdiction:** Jurisdiction is the authority and power of a political entity, real or asserted, to control a person and her actions. Jurisdiction most often seen as power over people and acts occurring with the physical jurisdiction of a sovereign state, e.g., within the borders of the Republic of Finland or the U.S. Naval Base at Guantanamo Bay, Cuba. Jurisdiction may extend to a state's citizens when in another state. And jurisdiction may extend to people and acts in a foreign state that have an impact on people in another state; this transnational issue of jurisdiction has grown in importance due to Internet activity and globalization.

- **Privacy:** Privacy was defined by the great American jurist Louis Brandeis as "the right to be left alone." More broadly, privacy has developed into a regime relating to personal autonomy and the extent to which a person may restrict the knowledge or intervention of others in his or her life. Legal notions of privacy have developed under both common law and civil law traditions. Given the extreme conservatism of common-law protections of privacy, most of the current evolution of law regarding privacy occurs within state statutes.

- **Security and information security:** Security generally refers to the safety of individuals and the services needed for protection. Information security as a discipline is a security subset that addresses the protection of information. One suggested set of categories for information security defines it as assuring the confidentiality, integrity and availability of information. Compromise of any one of these categories is a breach of information security that may potentially injure individuals. A breach of confidentiality may infringe on the privacy of the person. The damage to the integrity of information, such as a medical database, may lead to a physical injury through incorrect treatment based on erroneous information. Interference with the availability of information renders it of no use or value.

- **Intellectual property:** Intellectual property is a broad regime designed to reward creative endeavor. It creates a regime that is in some ways analogous to that of traditional property by giving a creator certain rights in their creation. Copyright, patent and trade secret are all areas of intellectual property with special relevance to data, information and their expression.

- **Criminal and civil liability and injury to others:** All states proscribe and prohibit actions that are deemed injurious to others. That conduct may be injury to their persons or injury to their property, or may be conduct deemed injurious to "the State." Civil liability may require the acting party to make whole the parties injured, usually through the payment of money. Criminal liability, which may be deemed an offense against the state, may require punishment of the acting party by incarceration, the payment of financial fines, the submission to state oversight or other forms of penalties.

- **Consent and waiver:** Consent is the knowing and voluntary agreement by a person to a proposition, such as the open and transparent exchange of personal information. Waiver is the surrender of a right or protection; it may be given by consent or agreement or by a failure to assert that right.

- **Ethics:** Ethics serve as standards of conduct that may exist separately from any legal regime and guide personal and group decisions as to the propriety of activities. Punishment for ethical violations may range from opprobrium to professional debarment to penal sanction.

Literature Review

Consideration of issues relating to the legal and ethical consequences of information systems is a part of information studies. But there is relatively little that specifically focuses on these issues in relation to open information management. Rather, the literature in this area broadly covers legal and ethical issues in computing and information science.

For example, Tavani provides a survey of ethical and legal analysis across the computing domain. (2007) The survey ranges from initial introductions to cyberethics to review of problems with privacy, security, crime and intellectual property in cyberspace. Similarly, Pfleeger & Pfleeger survey information security with a focus on the scientific and technical foundations for information security. (2007) They specifically address the legal and ethical issues within this discipline as a separate chapter touching on the protection of programs and data (intellectual property) and civil and criminal liability for information breaches, among other topics. Lastly, McQuade directly addresses misconduct involving information and computing systems under a cybercrime classification. (2006) Much of this book's discussion focuses on abuses relating to the fabrication, manipulation and transmission of information. These books are emblematic of the expanded focus across the computing of information disciplines with legal and ethical issues. The controversies surrounding legal and ethical use of computing and information systems can be seen in current events. State regulation of the Internet's information exchange capabilities, such as those detailed in the U.S. Supreme Court case *ACLU v. Reno,* are efforts to bar transmission of certain kinds of information content. (Stevens, 1997) This led to a challenge to the legality of government prohibitions on certain types of open information exchange, prohibitions enacted by majority vote of the federal legislative body of the United States, to control and limit the open exchange of information. That prohibition was as to "indecent" material, a broad category that could include accurate images of the Venus de Milo and methods of controlling sexually transmitted diseases.

Challenges and objections to open information exchange relating to the Internet cover a broad range, including encryption technology, decryption technology, infrastructure, culture, and politics. (Diffie & Landau 1998) This is also magnified by what is perceived as Internet customary practices or norms which in some scenarios have legal implication as discussed by Polanski. (2005). Similarly, the evolution of open information management in proprietary databases has also enriched the information assets of businesses and governments, permitting new, more efficient use and exchange of data resources. But this has led to challenges and objections as to threats to privacy and security, engendering national and transnational laws in response. Cross-aggregation of databases may threaten to reveal previously private aspects of the personal lives of citizens. (see, e.g., Privacy Act of 1970 (U.S)). Collection and disclosure of non-public data on persons may be illegal and a source of public unease with privacy corrosion. (Selis· Ramasastry· Kim· Smith 2002) Cross-border exchanges of data on individuals may similarly infringe privacy in unintended ways, including the perpetuation of erroneous data. (see, Organization for Economic Cooperation and Development (1980)).

LEGAL AND ETHICAL CHALLENGES

Issues, Controversies, Problems

Open information systems facilitate free exchanges of information for private speech and increase business efficiency. But the same technology could be used inadvertently or maliciously with criminal intent to cause injury to others. Types of injuries might include violating privacy rights or infringing on intellectual property rights. Jurisdiction for prosecuting perpetrators of such violations is more complex in a world with distributed Internet where servers and users are spread over geographical, political, cultural, and legal boundaries. The complexities arising from such a complex graph requires ongoing attention to many issues.

The initial issues confronted are:

1. The application of regulatory power of states over such systems,
2. The impact on personal autonomy of such systems (privacy, free expression), and
3. The impact on "intellectual" property rights of such systems.

These may manifest themselves as ethical breaches, civil liability or criminal sanctions. And it is not enough to excuse conduct as being that of a remote user of an OIM system. Ethical opprobrium or legal liability may attach simply by making available a system for misuse by others. And this may attach whether or not a developer or researcher had knowledge of the risk of the injury resulting from the misuse. Figure 1 depicts these issues as integral parts for consideration in OIM.

The issues raised by research, development, implementation and use of open information systems are of concern for three reasons. The first is to avoid any legal or ethical problems in research and development. This may be the least likely risk to a researcher or developer, but it is one needing attention. Second, a researcher or developer should be prepared for any questions raised as to legal or ethical problems in research and development. This avoids distractions and challenges that may be collateral to OIM efforts but which may divert attention, time and resources unnecessarily as those challenges are addressed. Lastly, under principles of contributory liability, a researcher or developer may be held responsible along with any downstream users of OIM systems for the injuries done to others. A researcher or developer can better assure adoption and use of their work won't be impeded by such

Figure 1. Issues for OIM consideration

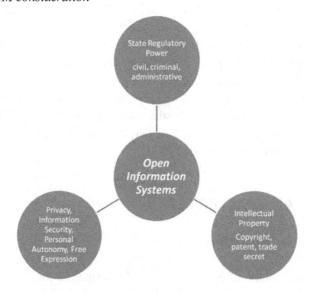

problems and they, whether legally liable or not, have minimized the risk of harm to others through the misuse of their work. This may present the greatest issue in the implementation of OIM systems in the current massively aggregated, interconnected environment.

Jurisdiction and State Power

Because of the great, global interconnectivity of information systems, data exchanges may easily become the focus of the laws of multiple nations.

Unfortunately, these laws may be contradictory in terms of the prohibitions and sanctions they place on system use. For example, United States and the European Union have different laws regarding data exchanges across borders. This led to a serious dispute over the types of airline passenger name record data (PNR) to be exchanged for passengers flying to the United States from Europe, bringing European privacy laws into a conflict with U.S. national security concerns that was resolved only by a European Union – US-DHS agreement specifying the privacy protections for PNR. (European Union, 2007)

International/transnational treaties and conventions may facilitate prosecutions across borders. And even without treaties the impact of globalization extends the practical reach of jurisdiction. In one example, a computer engineer in Russia decrypted a security measure on a U.S. software product, a legal act in Russia, but was arrested and detained by federal agents in the U.S. while attending a conference.

The Las Vegas, Nevada arrest of visiting Dmitri Sklyarov of Moscow-based ElcomSoft for allegedly violating U.S. law while working (legally) in Moscow highlights how states may assert jurisdiction world-wide; Sklyarov programmed a circumvention of Adobe E-book security that led to Adobe's complaint against him. (Bennett, 2001) (Sklyarov was later released and the charges dropped after months of protests.) Anyone developing and deploying open information systems should be aware that they may be subject to the regulations of jurisdictions other than that of their home nation/jurisdiction depending on how the system is deployed, particularly where activity involving wide area networks such as the Internet is involved.

This regulatory jurisdiction goes beyond compliance to the power of another jurisdiction to act against a person it deems in violation of its regulations. This may range from asserting that a particular person may be held to account before the courts of the jurisdiction up to asserting the right of that jurisdiction to seize, arrest and incarcerate a person, as seen in the Sklyarov affair.

These transnational issues have grown with the expansion of Internet-based criminal activity involving multiple states (Allan, 2005; Sietz, 2004), leading to such efforts as the Council of Europe's Convention on Cybercrime. (Council of Europe 2001)

An OIM a researcher or developer must additionally be concerned with issues of jurisdiction and the regulatory regime under which their work is governed, particularly when the research and development involves individuals and organizations in more than one country. This is equally true with the implementation of OIM technology or its use in all more than one country, particularly in situations where there are trans-border transmissions of data; situations involving the trans-border transmission of data on individuals will be especially scrutinized.

Personal Autonomy and Security

As OIM makes it easier to process and exchange data, it may also make it more difficult to preserve the traditional privacy and security of isolation and obscurity. This may come in several forms. The ease with which multiple data bases and data collections may be aggregated and analyzed permits unprecedented correlations and profiles of individuals. The ease with which even the individual data sets may now be used, regardless of a particular processing platform or tool, changes the focus of data security and efforts to prevent unauthorized or malicious access to such data sets. OIM facilitates this data processing and exchange and, as information security is seen to be contrary to information usability, it can be argued the ease of the use that OIM seeks runs counter to the goals of information security. One commentator has noted the irony of discussing security in the context of open information management. (Slade 1999)

Some jurisdictions, such as the European Union, have coherent, universal policies for data privacy. Others, like the United States, use a piecemeal approach that develops privacy policies for specific areas, such as medical and financial data, that may limit disclosure to third-parties of data but require disclosure to persons of the data collected on them and the purposes for which it will be used. (Gramm-Leach-Bliley Act, 1999 (US); Health Insurance Portability and Accountability Act (HIPAA) (US)). As privacy concerns grow globally, individual states create new privacy laws or expand existing ones. Data analysis involving open information systems may be permissible in one jurisdiction but barred or limited by privacy statutes in another. (Privacy Protection Act of 1980 (US); Council of Europe 1998)

The risks regarding the violations of statutory privacy rights may be significant. These include criminal penalties for unauthorized disclosures of information. (See, e.g., Fair Credit Reporting Act ("FCRA") (US)). Similarly, states may respond with their own legislation regarding systems for information security. For example, the Federal Republic of Germany has passed legislation impacting the use of some security testing technologies.

OIM must be prepared to respond to these concerns. OIM systems must be able to incorporate and comply with growing and changing requirements on the protection and security of data and data privacy. These requirements may, at a minimum, require that an OIM technology address issues of access and access control to data, particularly data on individuals. Review of access control must also incorporate controls and validation techniques as to data integrity, particularly for data that may affect an individual.

A parallel issue relates to data and information attribution. The authentication and identification of particular individuals within an OIM environment can have many ramifications. False attribution, whether negligent or through an intentional malicious act, can injure individuals through a false and untruthful portrayal of them or their beliefs. A positive attribution in the context of open, anonymous speech on political forums and weblogs may put individuals in danger of retribution, whether by hostile individuals or states. Some consideration should be given to protecting these rights to personal political autonomy in the face of risks of retribution.

Intellectual Property

In facilitating the exchange, analysis and the transformation of data, OIM may facilitate infringements of rights in information, rights sometimes called "intellectual property." And even where there is no legal infringement of intellectual property rights, there may be ethical or moral implications from the use of the intellectual creations of others, such as through plagiarism.

Rights in information come in a variety of forms. The most common is the regime of copyright, whereby states grant a bundle of rights in information, such as copying, distribution, and preparation of derivative works, to a particular holder of those rights. Other traditional regimes include trade secret and patent. Newer regimes of property interests and rights in information are possible, such as *sui generis* rights in database information that may not otherwise be protected.

In some ways this is another aspect of information security concerns for OIM. Precisely because OIM makes exchange and use of information far easier than in the past, it makes it easier to violate the proprietary rights in such information. Common examples are the "pirating" of books and music over the Internet.

Liability for the violation of such "intellectual property" rights is not confined to those who directly infringe those rights. Legal doctrines and legislation have evolved that may hold third parties responsible for "assisting" those responsible for direct violations of intellectual property rights, such as notions of contributory and vicarious copyright infringement. In the United States, the Digital Millennium Copyright Act places significant restrictions on any technologies that may be used to circumvent systems for the protection of copyrighted material. Use of the intellectual creations of others is not necessarily infringement of intellectual property rights. Creative content is built on the work of others and copyright laws permit fair and transformative uses that promote advancements in knowledge.

There may be still other ethical or moral considerations. Plagiarism, the unattributed use of the work of others, may be legal in some cases but is always viewed negatively as to the honesty and ethics of the user. (Gajadhar 1998) Such unattributed use may not be intentional but still may damage reputations. Just as open information exchange may increase the possibilities for unattributed use it also makes possible automated systems for discovering such misuse.

OIM issues with intellectual property parallel, in some ways, those with the protection of privacy in personal autonomy. An OIM technology should be evaluated as to any risks it creates for uncontrolled access to data objects. This may include an evaluation as to direct or collateral circumvention of access control systems to such data objects or the ability of a particular OIM technology to incorporate and implement access controls to data.

Personal Injury and Criminal Liability

With evolving law and perceptions relating to privacy, security and rights in information, states may exercise their power (jurisdiction) to regulate in areas where information and its use or misuse cause injury to their citizens. As noted above, OIM systems may impact information use in its effect on people in several areas.

How such regulation manifests itself will depend on the particular legal tradition of a state. In common-law jurisdictions, it is possible that civil liability for the injury to others will first manifests itself through court decisions prior to any legislation. For businesses, this is an inherent risk as evolving standards of civil liability may be difficult to predict. In civil law jurisdictions civil liability for information injuries will usually be predicated on legislation, giving better prior notice of the possible liability for also subjecting the area regulated to unintended consequences of the legislation.

Criminal liability in both civil law and modern common-law jurisdictions is only predicated on express legislation making conduct criminal. Again, this should give better prior notice of the possibility of criminal liability. But liability for personal injury and criminal misconduct may not be solely predicated on intentional conduct through the development and implementation of OIM systems. States may define liability for lesser levels of culpability. The most common area of liability for unintentional injury to a person is that of noncriminal, financial liability for failing to act with proper care as to others to whom a duty is owed. But states may have the power to even establish strict criminal liability regardless of the level of culpability by a particular act or period. While this very severe legal regime is relatively rare, it remains a possibility in many areas to state regulation.

It is particularly important to review OIM systems as to the risks of harm to individuals. The most significant of such risks would be the risks of physical injury. This may seem inapplicable to OIM systems, but consider how the systems may be used by others. For example, in OIM system may facilitate access to information used to stalk and injure a user's object of the possession. While the benefits of that OIM system may help allay the risks of such misconduct, awareness of those risks may lead to solutions for the mitigation of the risk to others.

The risk of harm may also relate to property interests of individuals. Consideration of potential infringement of intellectual property rights or interests is merited. Indeed, any kind of injury or infringement on the rights, perceived rights or interests of others, including sovereign states, warrants an evaluation as a potential conflict with the laws of those states.

Consent and Waiver

One factor that may complicate state regulatory power, organizational interests in open information management and rights in personal autonomy is that of personal consent. Personal consent may act as a waiver to state regulation and legal protections regarding the transmittal and use of information. "Person" may include organizations as well as individuals. For example, in the United States there is a matrix of statutory regulations that limit the disclosure of stored electronic communications transactional and content data.(18 U.S.C. 2510, et. Seq. and 18 U.S.C. 2701, et seq.) Similarly there are statutory limits on the disclosure of financial data of customers by financial institutions. (FCRA)

In both of these cases, however, an individual may consent to the release of that information. That consent may be a term and condition of the initial agreement for using the services of a particular organization, an agreement for disclosure without which a person may not be allowed to use that service. Or it may be through an "opt out" provision by which an individual must positively assert it does not wish disclosure and transmittal of private information, or otherwise take action to preserve privacy. (E.g., N.Y. Comp. Codes 2001; Gramm-Leach-Bliley Act 1999) Failure to take a required action to assert a right to privacy or restrictions on data transfers may waive that right and have the same effect as consent use on that data.

The use of personal consent or waiver to remove limitations on information exchange, including consent extracted through exercise of market power, may be subject to strict construction. Where consent or waiver applies to one type of disclosure for one type of data, any other disclosures of any other data may exceed the consent or waiver. This, in turn, may subject the disclosing party to sanctions. (e.g., FRCA) Further, states may limit the ability of organizations to use personal consent or waiver to avoid use and disclosure limitations. Thus even when an individual may consent, state regulation may void the effectiveness of that consent or place requirements on the data holder to verify that the consent is truly knowing and voluntary.

Ethics

Information ethics is an evolving field beginning first with ethics in library science and coming to touch upon the fields of "computer ethics" and "media ethics." (Froehlich 2004) At its core information ethics looks at the harm that can be done in the use or misuse of information and the obligations of particular individuals to avoid or mitigate that harm. Similarly, ethics is viewed as a core competency of computer science education (ABET 2007)

The *European Commission Action Plan: Science and Society* highlights the risk of ethical breach in the implementation of research activities:

The level of awareness among researchers of the ethical dimension of their activities is rather uneven in Europe. Actions to raise awareness of good scientific practices, including the ethical dimension, research integrity and the key elements of European legislation, conventions and codes of conduct should be encouraged. The development and the implementation of codes of conduct will be encouraged in various areas. These actions should take full account of cultural differences. (European Commission 2001)

OIM is intertwined with this evolution of information ethics and the development of professional ethics in computer engineering and information studies which may offer some aid to researchers and developers with OIM. For example, the Association for Computing Machinery (ACM), the Institute of Electrical and Electronics Engineers (IEEE), the Council of European Professional Informatics Societies (CEPIS), South East Asia Regional Computer Confederation (SEARCC) and Centro de la Informática, Telemática y Medios Afines (CITMA) have ethical/professional codes for member conduct in computational and informatics engineering. (ACM 1992; IEEE 2006; IEEE 1999; CEPIS; SEARCC; CITMA)

These statements of professional conduct all promote the key issue in applied ethics: anticipating and avoiding harm to others. The European Commission encourages examination of codes of ethics and arguments for their application in science and research. (Evers, 2003) IEEE encourages its members to be aware of the ethical implications of their work at all times. (IEEE 2004) Similarly, Fallis argues that for the information professionals in the discipline of libraries, study of information ethics is essential as a supplement to professional ethics to avoid harm. (2007)

Ethical awareness has the benefit of calling upon our knowledge of right conduct in the world and applying it to the tasks before us. For OIM researchers and developers this awareness simply asks us to consider what all the outcomes from our work may be in multiple domains. As is inevitable in this work with information, knowledge and wisdom there will be both benefits and detriments.

An ethics early warning system can take many forms. Perhaps overly simplistic, some ethical discussions begin with the "Mom" test, to wit, would your mother approve of the outcome of your work? This approach invokes a person's immediate experiences with proper conduct under the aegis of a near-universal authority figure. This may be expanded to ask how would your friends, coworkers and professional colleagues evaluate your conduct? Another approach is to analyze the benefits against the risks, including professional and reputational damage to the research themselves. Yet another asks if the particular conduct treats the subjects of that conduct with respect due them.

At the core of an analysis is that you have, in fact, considered the outcomes and impact on others of your work. Without such an analysis you may not be able to judge any potential ethical problems.

Certainly any potential legal issues that were discussed above can serve as potential alerts to ethical problems. Most legal problems in world legal regimes reflect concern over harm to others. Even where analysis finds no potential legal problems and delays the issue of whether the conduct is appropriate ethically to the individual one which may be subject to the solution permitting the conduct or providing for ways to mitigate and reduce potential ethical problems.

SOLUTIONS AND RECOMMENDATIONS

Forewarned is forearmed. Consideration of system impact on the lives of others can help address possible legal or ethical issues. Adding full-time legal scholars to OIM research and development projects is not a recommended solution as those resources may be better spent directly on OIM studies.

The most salient recommendation is to be aware of the potential impact of OIM systems and how they may pose any risk of harm. The simple awareness as documented for particular applications can serve as an alert to those implementing OIM projects of potential risks to be addressed. This is particularly true for risks to personal autonomy, privacy, security and infringement of intellectual property.

Awareness of risks also serves to engage the primary researchers and developers in at least postulating their concerns and possible solutions to potential problems and issues. As primary researchers and developers they are in the best position to appreciate solutions that will remediate risks created by the systems.

Using this awareness may be as simple and straightforward as reviewing a short checklist of concerns, such as how much the system impact information privacy, information security, the protection of intellectual property or otherwise potentially increase the risk of harm to others. Again, our own innate sense of ethical conduct can help alert us to potential issues so that we would to flag these matters for later in review and consideration, including by legal professionals.

One crucial recommendation is that OIM researchers and developers continue to consider and discuss these issues with each other, particularly in the context of their professional and scientific associations. These discussions will be essential for continuing appropriate awareness and addressing new issues and risks associated with information, its processing and exchange. This will be vital as the OIM community must itself be actively involved in the process by which state regulations are designed and passed into law, as discussed below in the section on Future Trends.

One intermediate solution is possible for some of the wide-open jurisdictional problems is the use of licensing agreements whereby a choice of law and a choice of location for the resolution of disputes is specified as a condition for the use of a particular technology. This licensing agreement solution is commonly seen in End User Licensing Agreements (EULA). This solution is effective for many types of civil liability unless the law of a jurisdiction prohibits the use of this solution. This solution is not as effective when dealing with issues of criminal liability in the assertion of a jurisdiction of its police power.

Another intermediate solution is a simple checklist of items to consider that touch on the concerns discussed here. Although quite broad, discussion and consideration of these matters by a researcher or developer may help elicit potential problems for further review. Table 1 below is an example of such a checklist for OIM developers.

CHECKLIST

This is a preliminary checklist for factors that should alert a researcher or developer to potential legal or ethical issues that should be considered.

A "yes" answer to any of these questions indicates further review may be warranted.

Table 1. OIM checklist

Issue	Characteristics Of Conduct	No	Yes
Jurisdiction			
	Does the research and development in OIM involve individuals in more than one country?		
	Does the implementation of OIM technology involve conduct in more than one country?		
	Will the use of OIM technology involve cross-border transmissions of data?		
Privacy, personal autonomy, and security			
	Does the use of the OIM technology risk uncontrolled access to data on individuals?		
	Does the implementation of the OIM technology risk violations of data integrity as to information on individuals?		
	Does the use of the OIM technology carry a risk of attribution and identity to a user, including false attribution and curtailment of anonymous speech?		
Intellectual property			
	Does the use of the OIM technology risk uncontrolled access to data objects?		
	Does the use of the OIM technology risk circumvention of access control systems to data objects?		
	May the OIM technology implement secure access control systems for data objects?		
Civil and criminal liability			
	Does the use of the OIM technology create a risk of personal harm to individuals?		
	Does the use of OIM technology create a risk of infringement of intellectual property rights or interests of others?		
	Does the use of OIM technology create a risk of injury or any infringement on the rights or perceived rights and interests of others, including sovereign states?		
Consent and waiver			
	Is there documented consent by a person regarding use of their personal data or intellectual property by an OIM technology?		
	Is there a documented waiver by a person regarding use of their personal data or intellectual property by an OIM technology?		
	Does the use of a person's personal data or intellectual property exceed the scope of the consent or waiver by that person?		
Ethics			
	Did you answer "yes" to any of the above questions?		
	Have you not yet done a thorough evaluation of the impact of your OIM work on people?		
	Would you want your mother to be a user or a subject of your OIM technology?		

FUTURE TRENDS

State laws will continue to evolve to address the uses of information in world society, as will application of ethical principles to new information systems. OIM systems will be subject to these evolving rules and may, in fact, be specific subjects of those regulations. How those laws develop may depend on the engagement of the OIM community in the legislative process. Often, through narrow self-interest or simply ignorance of the particular technologies and the scope of laws, unintended consequences can result.

The evolution of laws relating to copyrighted information, encryption systems and information security, as with most laws, reflects both concerns for the public good as well as the influence of particular groups seeking to protect their interests. In the United States copyright law has become progressively more onerous for those seeking free exchange of information, granting longer and longer copyright periods to the holders and delaying the passing of copyrighted information into the public domain for new uses.

Similarly, some encryption research has increasingly faced legal hurdles under the Digital Millennium Copyright Act (US), which prohibits the distribution of technologies that may circumvent methods of controlling access to copyrighted digital objects. The burden of the DMCA is such that any encryption researcher whose work may run afoul of the DMCA, or any similarly complex statute, should consult legal counsel.

OIM is subject to these same trends in regulation. Whether on a research, development or implementation level, participation by OIM specialists in legislative process may be necessary to prevent unintended and ill advised restrictions on OIM technologies.

CONCLUSION

Open information management has been a boon for knowledge and innovation in most every way. As it has been integrated into global, broad-based information technologies, its benefits may now be perverted by those with malicious intent. OIM researchers and developers should be aware of potential legal and ethical obligations to address possible harms resulting from the misuse of information from OIM systems. Being aware of those possibilities, these researchers and developers can act to alert downstream users to potential risks and themselves begin the process of protection from those risks.

Increased awareness of legal and ethical issues should also bring the OIM community into engagement with state authorities over regulation of information practices. By informing legislative bodies and participating in creating that regulation, the OIM community can assure effective regulation. This will result in the protection of people while avoiding unnecessary or ill advised and harmful regulation that could harm OIM research and development and limit its benefits for the spread of knowledge throughout the world.

REFERENCES

ABET (2007). *ABET Criteria for Accrediting Engineering Programs, Effective for Evaluations During the 2007-2008 Accreditation Cycle, Curriculum Standard IV-17.* http://www.abet.org/forms.shtml, last visited August 24, 2008

ACM Code of Ethics and Professional Conduct, (1992). adopted 10.16.1992, http://www.acm.org/about/code-of-ethics, last visited August 24, 2008

Allan, G. (2005). *Responding to Cybercrime: A Delicate Blend of the Orthodox and the Alternative,* 2 NZ Law Review 149 (2005)]

Benner, J, (2001). Russian Hacker Has a Party. *Wired,* 12/19/01, http://www.wired.com/politics/law/news/2001/12/49272, last visited August 10, 2008

Bennett, A. (2001). Protestors call for release of Russian programmer. *ITWorld,* July 23, 2001, http://www.itworld.com/IDG010723arrest, last visited August 24, 2008

CEPIS, Council of European Professional Informatics Societies, European Informatics Skills Structure (EISS - CEPIS) *Constitution, http://www.ecdl.org/cepis/index.jsp* last visited August 24, 2008

CITMA, Centro de la Informática, Telemática y Medios Afines , *Standards Of Computer Science Deontology Of C.I.T.E.M.A.*, http://ethics.iit.edu/codes/coe/centro.informatica.telematica.medios.afines. code.html, last visited August 24, 2008

Council of Europe (1998). ETS No. 005, as amended. *Convention for the Protection of Human Rights and Fundamental Freedoms, Article 8*, http://conventions.coe.int/Treaty/en/Treaties/Html/005.htm, last visited August 24, 2008

Council of Europe (2001) CETS No. 185 Convention on Cybercrime, *opened for* signature Nov. 23, 2001, http://conventions.coe.int/Treaty/en/Treaties/Html/185.htm, last visited August 24, 2008

European Commission (2001) Communication from the Commission to the Council, the European Parliament, the Economic and Social Committee and the Committee of the Regions, *Science and Society – Action plan*, COM(2001) 714., Item 31 at pg 22

European Union (2007) AGREEMENT between the European Union and the United States of America on the processing and transfer of passenger name record (PNR) data by air carriers to the United States Department of Homeland Security (DHS), Adopted by the Council of Europe August, 2007, http://epic. org/privacy/pdf/pnr-agmt-2007.pdf, last visited October 11, 2008

Evers, K. (2003). *Codes of Conduct: Standards for Ethics in Research,* European Commission Report, Brussels, 2003, http://ec.europa.eu/research/science-society/pdf/codes_conduct_en.pdf, last visited August 24, 2008

Fair Credit Reporting Act (15 USC §1681 et seq.) (US)

Fallis, D. (2007) *Information Ethics for 21st Century Library Professionals*, http://dlist.sir.arizona. edu/1820/, last visited August 24, 2008

Froehlich, T. (2004), *A Brief History Of Information Ethics*, Textos Universitaris De Biblioteconomia I Documentació, http://www.ub.es/bid/13froel2.htm, last visited August 24, 2008

Gajadhar, J. (1998). *Issues in Plagiarism for the New Millennium: An Assessment Odyssey.* The Open Polytechnic of New Zealand, UltiBASE, December, http://ultibase.rmit.edu.au/Articles/dec98/gajad1. htm, last visited October 15, 2008

Gramm-Leach-Bliley (1999). The Financial Modernization Act of 1999 (the Gramm-Leach-Bliley Act) (US)

IEEE Code of Ethics (2006). adopted February, 2006, http://www.ieee.org/web/aboutus/ethics/code. html, last visited August 24, 2008

McQuade, S. C. (2006). *Understanding and Managing Cybercrime.* Boston, MA, Allyn and Bacon.

N.Y. Comp., Codes R., & Regs. tit. 11, §§ 420.0-420.24 (2001), entitled "Privacy of Consumer Financial and Health Information."

Organization for Economic Cooperation and Development, *OECD Guidelines on the Protection of Privacy and Transborder Flows of Personal Data* (1980)

Pfleeger, C. P., & Pfleeger, S. L. (2007). *Security in Computing.* 4th Ed., Upper Saddle River, New Jersey, Pearson Education, Inc.

Privacy Protection Act of 1980, 42 USC §2000aa (U.S.)

SEARCC, South East Asia Regional Computer Confederation Code of Ethics, http://courses.cs.vt. edu/~cs3604/lib/WorldCodes/SEARCC.Code.html, last visited August 24, 2008

Selis, P., Ramasastry, A., & Smith, K. S. (2002). Office of the Attorney General, State of Washington, USA, *Cameron, Consumer Privacy and Data Protection: Protecting Personal Information Through Commercial Best Practices.* http://www.atg.wa.gov/uploadedFiles/Home/News/Press_Releases/2002/ PrivacyPolicy1.doc last visited October 11, 2008

Sietz, N. (2004). Transborder Search: A New Perspective on Law Enforcement? *9 Int'l J. Comm. L. & Pol'y 2* (Fall 2004)

Slade, R. (1999). Review: Top Secret Intranet. http://www.landfield.com/isn/mail-archive/1999/Feb/0074. html, last visited August 24, 2008

Software Engineering Code of Ethics and Professional Practice, Version 5.2, adopted 1999 by the IEEE Computer Society and the ACM, see http://www.open.hr/etika/en_code.pdf, last visited August 24, 2008

Stevens, J. (1997). *Reno v. ACLU* 521 U.S. 844

Stevens, J. (1989). *United States Department Of Justice Et Al. V. Reporters Committee For Freedom Of The Press.* 489 U.S. 749

Tavani, H. T. (2007). *Ethics & Technology: Ethical Issues in an Age of Information and Communication Technology.* Hoboken, New Jersey: John Wiley & Sons, Inc.

Diffie, W., & Landau, S. (1998). *Privacy on the Line: The Politics of Wiretapping and Encryption*, Boston, MA: The MIT Press.

Polanski P. (2005). *Common Practices in the Electronic Commerce and Their Legal Significance.* 18th Bled e Conference eIntegration in Action

Bled, Slovenia, June 6 - 8, 2005 (available online).

Compilation of References

Aaltonen, A. T. (2007). *Facilitating personal content management in smart phones*. PhD thesis, Proefschrift Rijksuniversiteit Groningen.

Aaron, C., Cristopher, M., & Newman, M. (May 2008), Hierarchical structure and the prediction of missing links in networks. *Nature, 453*, 98-101.

ABET (2007). *ABET Criteria for Accrediting Engineering Programs, Effective for Evaluations During the 2007-2008 Accreditation Cycle, Curriculum Standard IV-17*. http://www.abet.org/forms.shtml, last visited August 24, 2008

Abney, S. (1996). Partial parsing via finite-state cascades. *Natural Language Engineering, 2*(4), 337–344.

Abrams, D., Baecker, R., & Chignell, M. (1998). Information archiving with bookmarks: personal web space construction and organization. *Proceedings of the SIGCHI Conference on Human Factors in Computing Systems* (pp. 41-48). ACM Press/Addison-Wesley Publishing Co., New York, NY, USA.

ACM Code of Ethics and Professional Conduct, (1992). adopted 10.16.1992, http://www.acm.org/about/code-of-ethics, last visited August 24, 2008

Adelstein, F., Gupta, K. S. S., Richard III, G. G., & Schwiebert, L. (2005). *Fundamentals of Mobile and Pervasive Computing*, Chapter 6, Mc-Graw Hill, ISBN 0-07-141237-9.

Adnan, S., Datuin, J., & Yalamanchili, P. (2000). *A Survey of Mobile Agent Systems*, Project Report, CSE 221, University of California, San Diego.

Adomavicius, G., & Tuzhlin, A. (2001). Expert-Driven Validation of Rule-Based User Models for Personalisation Applications. *Data Mining and Knowledge Discovery 5*(1-2), 33-58.

Aggarwal, S., Hung, F., & Weiyi, M. (25-28 August 1998). WIRE-a WWW-based information retrieval and extraction system. *Proceedings of Ninth International Workshop on Database and Expert Systems Applications,* (pp. 887 - 892).

Ahmed, L., Limam, N., Xiao, J., Iraqui, Y., & Boutaba, R. (2007). Resource and Service Discovery in Large-Scale Multi-Domain Networks. *IEEE Communication Surveys, 9*(4), 2-30.

Aho, A. V., & Ullman, J. D. (1972). *The Theory of Parsing, Translation, and Compiling, Vol. 1*. Englewood Cliffs, NJ: Prentice-Hall.

Aho, A. V., Sethi, R., & Ullman, J. D. (2006). *Compilers: Principles, Techniques, and Tools*. New York. Addison Wesley, 2nd edition.

Aho, A., Lam, M., Sethi, R., & Ullman, J. (2008). *Compilers – principles, techniques, & tools*. (2nd ed.). Boston, Massachusetts: Addison Wesley.

Ajiferuke, L., Burrel, Q., & Tague, J. (1988). Collaborative Coefficient: A Single Measure of the Degree of Collaboration in Research. *Scientometrics, 14*, 421-433.

Alberts, D., Garstka, J. Hayes, R., & Signori, D. (2001). *Understanding Information Age Warfare*. Command and Control Research Program. Washington DC.

Aldana-Gonzalez, M., Coppersmith, S., & Kadanoff, L.P. (2003). Boolean dynamics with random couplings. In E. Kaplan, J. E. Marsden, & K. R. Sreenivasan (Eds.), *Perspectives and Problems in Nonlinear Science*. New York: Springer.

Alexiev, V., Breu, M., Bruijn, J., Fensel, D., Lara, R., & Lausen, H. (2005). *Information integration with ontologies*. Hoboken, New Jersey: John Wiley.

ALICE. (2005). Artificial Intelligence Markup Language (AIML) Version 1.0.1, *AI Foundation*. Retrieved August 23, 2008, from http://alicebot.org/TR/2005/WD-aiml.

Allan, G. (2005). *Responding to Cybercrime: A Delicate Blend of the Orthodox and the Alternative*, 2 NZ Law Review 149 (2005)]

Allanna, J., Tullahoma, M., Robert, M., & Craig, T. (March 27-31, 1989). A hierarchical data structure representation for fusing multi-sensor information. *SPIE Technical symposia on Aerospace Sensing* Orlando, FA.

Allen, J. F., Byron, D. K., *Dzikovska*, M., Ferguson G., *Galescu, L.,* & Stent, A. (2001). Toward conversational human-computer interaction. *AI Magazine*, (22) 4, (pp. 27-37).

Almendral, A., López, L., Mendes, F., & Sanjuán, F. (2003). Modeling Of Complex Systems: Seventh Granada Lectures. *AIP Conference Proceedings, 661*, 253-253.

Alpert, J., & Hajaj, N. We knew the web was big. *The Official Google Blog*. Retrieved August 10, 2008, from http://googleblog.blogspot.com/2008/07/we-knew-web-was-big.html

Alvin, T. S., & Chuang, S. N. (2003). MobiPADS: A Reflective Middleware for Context- Aware Mobile Computing. *IEEE Transactions on Software Engineering, 29*(12), 1072-1085.

Amgoud, L., & Cayrol, C. (2002). A reasoning model based on the production of acceptable arguments. *Annals of Mathematics and Artifcial Intelligence, 34*(1.3), 197-215.

Ancona, D., & David, C. (1990), Information Technology and Work Groups: The Case of New Product Teams. *Intellectual Teamwork: social and technological foundations of cooperative work,* (pp. 173-190).

Andrecut, M. (2005). Mean field dynamics of random Boolean networks. *Journal of Statistical Mechanics, P02003*.

Andrecut, M., & Ali, K. (2001). Chaos in a simple Boolean network. *International Journal of Modern Physics B, 15*(1), 17–23.

Andriessen, & Erik, J. (2003). *Working with groupware: understanding and evaluating collaboration technology*. London: Springer.

Androutsellis-Theotokis, S., & Spinellis, D. (2004). A Survey of Peer-to-Peer Content Distribution Technologies. *ACM Computing Surveys, 36* (4), 335-371.

Anne S. (2008). *Collaboration for Victims'. National Victim Assistance Academy Textbook*. Retrieved 5 November 2008 from http://www.ojp.usdoj.gov/ovc/assist/nvaa2000/academy/chap19.htm

Annie I. (1996). Goal-Based Requirements Analysis. *IEEE Proceedings of ICRE* '96 (pp. 136-144).

Anticlue (2006). *Information Distribution*. Retrieved 5 November 2008 from http://www.anticlue.net/archives/000804.htm

Argamon, S., Dagan, I., & Krymolowski, Y. (1998). A memory-based approach to learning shallow natural language patterns. In *COLING/ACL-98* (pp. 67–73). Montreal: ACL.

Arkin, A., Ross, J., & McAdams, H. H. (1998). Stochastic Kinetic Analysis of Developmental Pathway Bifurcation in Phage λ -infected *Escheria Coli* Cells. *Genetics, 149*, 1633-1648.

Arrow, K. J. (1963). *Social Choice and Individual Values*. 2nd ed. New Haven: Yale University Press. Original edition, (1951), New York: John Wiley & Sons.

Asahi, T., Turo, D., & Shneiderman, B.i, T., Turo, D., & Shneiderman, B. (December 1995). Using treemaps to visualize the analytic hierarchy process. *Information Systems Research, 6*(4), 357-375.

Attewell, P., & Rule, J. (1984). Computing and Organizations: What We Know and What We Don't Know. *Communications of the ACM, 27*(12), 128-136. 4.

Awerbuch, B., Du Y., & Shavittb, Y. (2000). The effect of network hierarchy structure on performance of ATM PNNI hierarchical routing. *Computer Communications, 23*(10), 980-986.

Bagchi, S. (2007). VMDFS: Virtual Memory based Mobile Distributed File System. *International Journal of Multimedia and Ubiquitous Engineering, 2*(2), SERSC, South Korea.

Bagrow, J., & Bollt, E. (2005). Local method for detecting communities. *Physical Review E, 72,* 046108.

Bailey, R. W. (1989). *Human Performance Engineering Using Human Factors/Ergonomics to Achieve Computer System Usability.* New Jersey, USA: AT&T Bell Laboratories.

Baker, M. (2003). *The Atoms of Language: The Mind's Hidden Rules of Grammar.* New York: Basic Books.

Baker, W., & Faulkner, R. (1993). The social organization of a conspiracy. *American Sociological Review, 58*(6), 837-860.

Barabási, A-.L., & Albert, R. (1999). Emergence of Scaling in Random Networks. *Science, 286,* 509-512.

Barker, J. Invisible Web: What it is, Why it exists, How to find it, and Its inherent ambiguity *UC Berkeley - Teaching Library Internet Workshops.* Retrieved August 10, 2008 from http://www.lib.berkeley.edu/TeachingLib/Guides/Internet/InvisibleWeb.html

Barkhuus, L. (2005). *The Context Gap: An Essential Challenge to Context-Aware Computing.* Unpublished doctoral dissertation, The IT University of Copenhagen, Denmark. Retrieved on March 29, 2007, http://www.itu.dk/people/barkhuus/lou_ thesis05.pdf .

Barreau, D. (1995). Context as a Factor in Personal Information Management Systems. *Journal of the American Society for Information Science, 46*(5), 327-339.

Barrick, M. R., et al. (1998). Relating Member Ability and Personality to Work-Team Processes and Team Effectiveness, *Journal of Applied Psychology,* (3), 377-391.

Barry, D., Coyle, E., & Lawlor, B. (2004). Real-time sound source separation using Azimuth discrimination and resynthesis. *117th Audio Engineering Society Convention.* San Francisco, CA, USA.

Bartlett, R. O. (1991). *An Evaluation of Participative Management: Effects of Group Decision Making on Productivity and Job Satisfaction in a Satellite Ground Station.* Doctoral dissertation, George Washington University.

Barton, J. J., Zhai, S., & Cousins, S. (2006). Mobile Phones Will Become The Primary Personal Computing Devices. *In the Proc. of the Seventh IEEE Workshop on Mobile Computing Systems & Applications (WMCSA '06).* IEEE CS Press, USA.

Barton, Jr., G. E., Berwick, R. C., and Ristad, E. S. (1987). *Computational Complexity and Natural Language.* Cambridge, MA: MIT Press.

Bartsch, M. A., & Wakefield, G. H. (2001). To catch a chorus: using chroma-based representations for audio-thumbnailing. *IEEE Workshop on Applications of Signal Processing to Audio and Acoustics,* (pp. 15-18). New Platz, NY, USA.

Bartsch-Sporl, B., Lenz, M., & Hubner, A. (1999). Case-Based Reasoning: Survey and Future Directions. In: F. Puppe (Ed.), *Proceedings of the 5th Biannual German Conference on Knowledge-Based Systems XPS-99 LNAI 1570* (pp. 67-89). Berlin: Springer.

Bates, E., & Elman, J. (1996). Learning rediscovered. *Science, 274,* 1849-50.

Behnel, S., Fiege, L., & Mühl, G. (2006). On Quality-of-Service and Publish-Subscribe. In: *Proceedings of the 26th IEEE International Conference on Distributed Computing Systems Workshops ICDCS 2006* (pp. 20-25). Washington: IEEE Computer Society.

Benahmed, Y., & Selouani, S. A. (2006). Robust Self-Training System for Spoken Query Information retrieval using Pitch Range Variations. *Proceedings of IEEE*

Canadian Conference on Electrical and Computer Engineering (pp. 949-952). Ottawa, Canada.

Bench-Capon T. J. M., & Dunne P. E. (2007). Argumentation in Artificial Intelligence. *Artificial Intelligence*, *171*(10–15), 619-641.

Benner, J, (2001). Russian Hacker Has a Party. *Wired*, 12/19/01, http://www.wired.com/politics/law/news/2001/12/49272, last visited August 10, 2008

Bennett, A. (2001). Protestors call for release of Russian programmer. *ITWorld*, July 23, 2001, http://www.itworld.com/IDG010723arrest, last visited August 24, 2008

Bennett, C. H. (1988). Logical depth and physical complexity. In R. Herken (Ed.), *The Universal Turing Machine; A Half-Century Survey*. Oxford: Oxford University Press.

Bennett, C. H., Gacs, P., Li, M., Vitanyi, P. M. B., & Zurek, W. (1998). Information distance. *IEEE Transactions on Information Theory*, *44*(4), 1407–1423.

Benz, B., & Durant, J. (2003). *XML programming*. New York, New York: Wiley.

Berenzweig, A. L., Ellis, D. P., & Lawrence, S. (2002). Using voice segments to improve artist classification of music. *AES 22nd International Conference on Virtual, Synthetic, and Entertainment Audio*. Espoo, Finland.

Berenzweig, A., Ellis, D. P., & Lawrence, S. (2003). Anchor space for classification and similarity measurement of music. *IEEE International Conference on Multimedia and Expo (ICME 2003)*, *2*, pp. 29-32. Baltimore, Maryland, USA.

Bergman, O., Beyth-Marom, R., & Nachmias, R. (2006). The Project Fragmentation Problem in Personal Information Management. *In Proceedings of the SIGCHT conference on human factors in computing systems*, (pp. 271-274).

Berkovsky, S., Kuflik, T., & Ricci, F. (2005). P2P Case Retrieval with an Unspecified Ontology. In: *Case-Based Reasoning Research and Development: Proceedings of 6th International Conference on Case-Based Reasoning ICCBR 2005 LNAI 3620* (pp. 91-105). Berlin: Springer.

Bernasconi, A. (1998). *Mathematical Techniques for the Analysis of Boolean Functions*. PhD thesis, University of Pisa.

Bettenhausen, K., & Murnighan, J. K. (1985). The Emergence of Norms in Competitive Decision-Making Groups, *Administrative Science Quarterly*, (30), 350-372.

Bickerton, D. (1990). *Language & Species*. Chicago: University of Chicago Press.

Bickerton, D. (1995). *Language and Human Behavior*. Seattle: Washington University Press.

Bieszczad, A., Pagurek, B., & White, T. (1998). Mobile Agents for Network Management. *IEEE Communications Surveys and Tutorials*, *1*(1).

Bilek, J., & Hartmann, D. (2003). Development of an Agent-based Workbench supporting Collaborative Structural Design. *Proc. of the 20th CIB W78 Conference on Information Technology in Construction* (pp. 39-46).Waiheke Island, New Zealand.

Bill, D. (March 31st 2008). *IBM predicts demise of traditional offices*. Retrieved 24 August 2008 form http://blogs.techrepublic.com.com/wireless/?p=222

Binzenhöfer, A., Tutschku, K., Graben, B., Fiedler, M., & Arlos, P. (2006). A P2P-Based Framework for Distributed Network Management. In M. Cesana. & L. Fratta (Eds.), *Wireless Systems and Network Architectures in Next Generation Internet: Second International Workshop of the EURO-NGI Network* of Excellence LNCS 3883 (pp. 198-210). New York: Springer.

Biswas, R. (2003). *Patient networks and their level of complexity as an outcome measure in clinical intervention*. Retrieved December 16, 2007, from http://www.bmj.com/cgi/eletters/324/7329/63

Biswas, R., Maniam, J., Lee, E. W. H., Das, P. G., Umakanth, S., Dahiya, S., & Ahmed, S. (2008b). User driven health care- Answering multidimensional information needs in individual patients utilizing post EBM approaches: An operational model. *Journal of Evaluation in Clinical Practice,* (in press).

Biswas, R., Martin, M., Sturmberg, J., Shankar, R., Umakanth, S., Shanker, & Kasthuri A. S. (2008a). User driven health care - Answering multidimensional information needs in individual patients utilizing post EBM approaches: A conceptual model. *Journal of Evaluation in Clinical Practice,* (in press).

Blake, M., & Cabri, G. (June 2003). Agent-based Computing for Enterprise Collaboration. What Agents Can Learn from Human Collaboration? *Proceedings of the WETICE2003: The 2003 Workshops on Enabling Technologies: Infrastructure for Collaborative Enterprises,* (pp. 21-23). IEEE Press.

Blouin, A., & Beaudoux, O. (2007). In P. King & S. Simske (Ed.), *Proceedings of the 2007 ACM Symposium on Document Engineering Conference* (pp. 219-221). New York, New York: ACM.

Boardman, R., Spence, R., & Sasse, M. (2003). Too Many Hierarchies? The Daily Struggle for Control of the Workspace. *In Proceedings of HCI international,* (pp. 16-620)11.

Boland, R., Schwartz, G., & Tenkasi, R. (November 1992). Sharing perspectives in distributed decision making. *In Proceedings of CSCW '92,* Toronto Canada, ACM Press, (pp. 306-313).

Bolstad, C., & Endsley, R. (2005). Choosing Team Collaboration Tools: Lessons from Disaster Recovery Efforts. *Ergonomics in Design, 13,* 7-14.

Bonett, M. (2001). Personalisation of Web Services: Opportunities and Challenges. *Ariadne, 28.* Retrieved April 24, 2006, from http://www.ariadne.ac.uk/issue28/personalization.

Borgman, C., Bates M., Cloonan, M., Efthimiadis, E., Gilliland-Swetland, Kafai, A., Leazer, Y. G. L. & Maddox, A. (1996). Social Aspects of Digital Libraries. Final Report to the National Science Foundation; Computer. Information Science, and Engineering Directorate; Division of Information, Robotics, and Intelligent Systems; Information Technology and Organizations Program. Retrieved July 15, 2008, from http://is. gseis.ucla.edu/research/dl/indexhtml.

Bouchet, J., & Nigay, L. (2004). ICARE: A Component-Based Approach for the Design and Development of

Multimodal Interfaces. *Extended Abstracts of International conference for human-computer interaction* (pp. 1325-1328). CHI2004: Vienna, Austria.

Boukottaya, A., & Vanoirbeek, C. (2005). Schema matching for transforming structured documents. In P. King (Ed.), *Proceedings of the 2005 ACM Symposium on Document Engineering Conference* (pp. 101-110). New York, New York: ACM.

Bouthillier, F., & Shearer, K. (2003). Assessing Collaborative Tools from an Information-Processing Perspective: Identification of Value-Added Processes. *Proceedings of the Twelfth IEEE International Workshops on Enabling Technologies: Infrastructure for Collaborative Enterprises (WETICE'03)*

Branscombe, N., Ellemers, N., Spears, R., & Doosje, B. (1999). The context and content of social identity threat. In N. Ellemers, R. Spears, & B. Doosje (Eds.), *Social identity: Context, commitment,content* (pp. 35-58). Oxford, UK: Blackwell Science.

Brattico, P. (2008). Shallow reductionism and the problem of complexity in psychology. *Theory & Psychology, 18,* 483-504.

Brian, J., & Shneiderman, B. (22-25 October 1991). Tree-maps: a space-filling approach to the visualization of hierarchical information structures (pp. 284-291). *Proceedings of IEEE Conference on Visualization Publication*

British Columbia Province (10 October 2003). Records Management in the system development life cycle. Retrieved 2 November 2008, from http://*www.cio.gov. bc.ca/other/daf/recmgmt_sdlc_v1-6.pdf*

Brownell, D. (2002). *SAX2.* Sebastopol, California: O'reilly.

Bryant, S. L., Forte, A., & Bruckman, A. (2005). Becoming Wikipedian: Transformation of Participation in a Collaborative Online Encyclopedia. *Proceedings of the 2005 international ACM SIGGROUP conference on Supporting group work. SESSION: Net communities* (pp. 1-10). Sanibel Island, FL: ACM. Retrieved

February 1, 2007, from http://portal.acm.org/citation.
cfm?id=1099203.1099205

Burt, R. (1992). *Structural Holes*. Cambridge, MA:
Harvard Press.

Butcher, D., & Rowley, J. (1998). The 7'Rs of Information
Management. *Managing information, 5*(2), 5-7.

Caelen, J. (2003). Strategies of Dialogue. *Speech Tech-
nology and Human-Computer Dialogue Conference,
Editura Academiei Romane* (pp. 27-42). Bucharest,
Romania.

Cai, R., Lu, L., & Hanjalic, A. (2008). Co-clustering for
auditory scene categorization. *IEEE Transactions on
Multimedia , 10* (4), 596-606.

Caldarelli, G. (2007). *Scale-Free Networks: Complex
Webs in Nature and Technology*. New York, NY. Oxford
University Press.

Campo, R. (2006). Anecdotal evidence: Why narratives matter to medical practice. *PLoS Medicine, 3*(10),
e423 doi:10.1371/journal.pmed.0030423. Retrieved
July 25, 2008, from http://medicine.plosjournals.org/
perlserv/?request=get-document&doi=10.1371/journal.
pmed.0030423

Case, D. O. (2006). Information Behaviour. *Annual
Review of Information Science and Technology, 40*,
293-327.

Case, J. D., Fedeor, M., Schoffstall, M. L., & Davin, J.
(1990). *Simple Network Management Protocol (SNMP),
RFC 1157, STD 15*. IETF.

Case, J., McCloghrie, K., Rose, M., & Waldbusser, S.
(1996). *Introduction to Community-based SNMPv2,
RFC 1901*. IETF.

Casillas J., Cordòn O., Herrera F., & Magdalena L.
(2003). Interpretability issues in fuzzy modeling. Vol.
128, *Studies in fuzziness and soft computing*, Springer,
Berlin Heidelberg NewYork.

Castineyra, I., Chiappa, J., & Steenstrup, M. (February
1996). The nimrod routing architecture, Internet Draft,
Nimrod Working Group.

Castore, C. H., & Murnighan, J. K. (1978). Determinants
of Support for Group Decisions, *Organizational Behavior
and Human Performance*, (22), 75-92.

CEPIS, Council of European Professional Informatics
Societies, European Informatics Skills Structure (EISS
- CEPIS) *Constitution, http://www.ecdl.org/cepis/index.
jsp* last visited August 24, 2008

CERN. The website of the world's first-ever web server.
Retrieved August 10, 2008, from http://info.cern.ch/

Chaib-draa, B., Naudet, N., Labrie, M.-A., Bergeron, M.,
& Pasquier, P. (2006). *DIAGAL: An Agent Communication Language Based on Dialogue Games and Sustained
by Social Commitments. Journal of Autonomous Agents
and Multi-Agent Systems, 13*(1), 61-93.

Chaitin, G. J. (1969). On the length of programs for computing finite binary sequences: Statistical considerations.
*Journal of the Association of Computer Machinery,
16*(1), 145–159.

Chappell, H. W., Jr., McGregor, R., & Vermilyea, T.
(2004). Majority Rule, Consensus Building, and the
Power of the Chairman: Arthur Burns and the FOMC.
Journal of Money, Credit & Banking, 36, 407-422.

Charmaz, K. (2006). *Constructing Grounded Theory. A
practical Guide Through Qualitative Analysis*. Wiltshire,
GB: Sage Publications.

Chattopadhyay, P. (1999). Beyond direct and symmetrical
effects: The influence of demographic dissimilarity on
organizational citizenship behavior. *Academy of Management Journal, 42*, 273-287.

Cheikhrouhou, M.; Conti, P., Labetoulle, J., & Marcus,
K. (1999). Intelligent agents for network management: a
fault detection experiment. In: M. Sloman, S. Mazum-
dar, E. Lupu (Eds.), *Distributed Management for the
Networked Millennium: Proceedings of the Sixth IFIP/
IEEE International Symposium on Integrated Network
Management* (pp. 595-609). Boston: IEEE.

Chen, B., Cheng, H., & Palen, J. (2006). Mobile-C: a
mobile agent platform for mobile C/C++ agents. *Software
– Practice and Experience, 36*, 1711-1733. John Wiley.

Chen, H., & Tompa, F. (2003). Set-at-a-time access to XML through DOM. In C. Roisin, E. Munson, & C. Vanoirbrrk (Ed.), *Proceedings of the 2003 ACM Symposium on Document Engineering Conference* (pp. 171-174). New York, New York: ACM.

Chen, J., Wolfe, S., & Wragg, S. (2000). A Distributed Multi-Agent System for Collaborative Information Management and Sharing. *In 9th International Conference on Information and Knowledge Management (CIKM-00)* MacLean, VA.

Chen, J.R., Shawn, R.W., Wragg, S. D. (2000)A Distributed Multi-Agent System for Collaborative Information Management and Sharing. *Proceedings of the ninth international conference of information and knowledge management* (pp. 382-388). Nov. 06-11, Virginia, USA.

Chen, S. S., & Gopalakrishnan, P. S. (1998). Environment and channel change detection and clustering via the Bayesian information criterion. *DARPA Broadcast News Transcription and Understanding,* (pp. 127-132). Landsdowne, Virginia, USA.

Chen, S.-C., Shyu, M.-L., Zhang, C., Luo, L., & Chen, M. (2003). Detection of soccer goal shots using joint multimedia features and classification rules. *International Workshop on Multimedia Data Mining (MDM 2003),* (pp. 36-44). Washington, DC, USA.

Chen, Z., Wenyin, L., Yang, R., Li, M., & Zhang, H. (2001). A Web Media Agent, *In the Proc. of 10th Annual Conference on World Wide Web Applications,* WWW Poster, Hong Kong.

Cheng, J. (2006). *Open document format published as ISO standard.* Retrieved July 10, 2008, from http://arstechnica.com/news.ars/post/20061204-8349.html

Choi, Y., & Park, D. (2005). Mirinae: A Peer-to-Peer Overlay Network for Large-Scale Content-Based Publish/Subscribe Systems. In: *Proceedings of the International Workshop on Network and Operating Systems Support For Digital Audio and Video* (pp. 105-110). New York: ACM.

Chomsky, N. (1959). Review of Verbal Behavior by B.F. Skinner. *Language, 35,* 26-57.

Chomsky, N. (1969). *Aspects of the theory of syntax.* Cambridge, MA: MIT Press.

Chomsky, N. (1975). *Reflections on Language.* New York: Pantheon.

Chomsky, N. (1981). *Lectures on Government and Binding. The Pisa Lectures.* The Hague: Mouton.

Chomsky, N. (1988). *Language and Problems of Knowledge. The Managua Lectures.* Cambridge, MA: MIT Press.

Chomsky, N. (1995). *The Minimalist Program.* Cambridge, MA: MIT Press.

Chomsky, N. (2000). *The Architecture of Language.* Oxford: Oxford University Press.

Chomsky, N. (2001). Derivation by Phase. In M. Kenstowicz (Ed.), *Ken Hale: A Life in Language* (pp. 1-52). Cambridge, MA: MIT Press.

Chomsky, N. (2005). Three factors in language design. *Linguistic Inquiry, 36,* 1-22.

Chomsky, N. (2007). Approaching UG from below, ms, MIT.

Chomsky, N. (2008). On Phases. In R. Freidin, C. P. Otero & M. L. Zubizarreta (Eds.), *Foundational Issues in Linguistic Theory. Essays in Honor of Jean-Roger Vergnaud.* Cambridge, MA: MIT Press.

Christopher, W., William, M., Paulo, S., Deborah, L., David, F., & Richard, F. (2005). Tracking Information Extraction from Intelligence Documents. *International Conference on Intelligence Analysis,* McLean, VA.

Chu, W.-T., Cheng, W.-H., Hsu, J. Y.-J., & Wu, J.-L. (2005). Towards semantic indexing and retrieval using hierarchical audio models. *Multimedia Systems , 10* (6), 570-583.

Chuang, T. R., & Lin, J. L. (2004). On modular transformation of structural content. In Jean-Yves Vlon-Dury (Ed.), *Proceedings of the 2004 ACM Symposium on*

Document Engineering Conference (pp. 201-210). New York, New York: ACM.

Cilibrasi, R., & Vitanyi, P. (2005). Clustering by compression. *IEEE Transactions on Information Theory, 51*(4), 1523–1545.

Cilibrasi, R., & Vitányi, P. M. (2005). Clustering by compression. *IEEE Transactions on Information Theory , 51* (4), 1523-1545.

CipherOptics (2008). Secure information sharing. Retrieved 13 November 2008 from http://www.cipheroptics. com/securitysolutions/secure-information-sharing. html

CITMA, Centro de la Informática, Telemática y Medios Afines , *Standards Of Computer Science Deontology Of C.I.T.E.M.A.*, http://ethics.iit.edu/codes/coe/centro. informatica.telematica.medios.afines.code.html, last visited August 24, 2008

Clemm, A. (2007). *Network Management Fundamentals.* Indianopolis: Cisco Press.

Clemons, E., Reddi, S., & Row, M. (1993). The impact of information technology on the organization of economic activity: The "move to the middle" hypothesis. *Journal of Management Information Systems: Jmis, 10*(2), 9-35.

Cohen, S. G., & Bailey, D. E. (1997). What Makes Teams Work: Group Effectiveness Research from the Shop Floor to the Executive Suite. *Journal of Management*, (3), 239-290.

COLLOQUIS INC. (2006). Comparing Automated Service Agent (ASA) Systems to Browse-and Search Search-Based Self-Service Solutions, Maximize Self-Service ROI through Savings and Sales. Retrieved August 23, 2008, from http://download.microsoft.com/download/5/8/c/58c709a8-921f-4ae4-ac48-05020a9186c0/ ASAvsSearch.pdf

Comer, D. E., (2006). *Automated Network Management Systems: Current and Future Capabilities.* Pearson Prentice Hall.

Comrie, B. (2001). Languages of the World. In M. Aronoff & J. Rees-Miller (Eds.), *The Handbook of Linguistics.* Cornwall: Blackwell.

Cook, G. D., Kershaw, D. J., Christie, J. D., Seymour, C. W., & Waterhouse, S. R. (1997). Transcription of broadcast television and radio news: the 1996 ABBOT system. *IEEE International Conference on Acoustics, Speech, and Signal Processing, 2*, pp. 723-726. Munich, Germany.

Cooke, N. (January 2005). *Measuring collaborative cognition.* Collaboration and knowledge management workshop proceedings, San Diego, CA.

Coppola, P., Mea, V. D., Gaspero, L. D., Mizzaro, S., Scagnetto I., Selva A., Vassena L., & Rizio, P. Z. (2005). *MoBe: A Framework for Context-aware Mobile Applications.* Paper presented at the Workshop on Context-Aware Proactive Systems, Helsinki, Finland.

Corbett, J. (2003). *Size Trees: augmenting hierarchies to aid size comparisons between categories and individuals.* Retrieved 25 July, 2008, from http://www.pictographer.com/sizetree/index.html

Costa-Santos, C., Bernandes, J., Vitányi, P. M., & Antunes, L. (2006). Clustering fetal heart rate tracings by compression. *IEEE International Symposium on Computer-Based Medical Systems.* Salt Lake City, Utah, USA.

Council of Europe (1998). ETS No. 005, as amended. *Convention for the Protection of Human Rights and Fundamental Freedoms, Article 8*, http://conventions. coe.int/Treaty/en/Treaties/Html/005.htm, last visited August 24, 2008

Council of Europe (2001) CETS No. 185 Convention on Cybercrime, *opened for* signature Nov. 23, 2001, http://conventions.coe.int/Treaty/en/Treaties/Html/185. htm, last visited August 24, 2008

Courtenage, S., & Williams, S. (2006). The Design and Implementation of a P2P-Based Composite Event Notification System. In: *Proceedings of the 20th international Conference on Advanced information Networking and Applications - Volume 1 (Aina'06) - Volume 01* (pp. 701-706). Washington: IEEE Computer Society.

Cover, T. M., & Thomas, J. A. (1991). *Elements of Information Theory.* Hoboken, New Jersey: Wiley-Interscience.

Crain, S., & Lillo-Martin, D. (1999). *An Introduction to Linguistic Theory and Language Acquisition.* Oxford: Blackwell.

Crow, K. A. (1994). *Building Effective Product Development Teams / Integrated Product Teams.* Palos Verdes, CA: DRM Associates. Retrieved November 10, 2001, from http://www.npd-solutions.com/pdt.html.

Cui, Y., Xu, D., & Nahrstedt, K. (2001). SMART: A Scalable Middleware solution for Ubiquitous Multimedia Service Delivery. *2001 International Conference on Multimedia and Expo*, IEEE CS Press, Japan.

CURT (2004). *Collaboration, Integrated Information, and the Project Lifecycle in Building Design, Construction and Operation.* Retrieved 6 November 2004 from *www.eua.com/pdf/resources/integrated_project/Construction_Users_Round_Table.pdf*

Dam, M., & Stadler, R. (2005). A Generic Protocol for Network State Aggregation. *Radiovetenskap och Kommunication (RVK)*, Sweden, 2005.

Danon, L., Duch, J., Diaz-Guilera, A., & Arenas, A. (2005). Comparing community structure identification. *Journal of Statistical Mechanics: Theory and Experiment,* 09, P09008.

Darsee, J. (2007). *Creating healing communities through telemedicine.* Retrieved December 16, 2007, from http://www.hhnmostwired.com/hhnmostwired_app/jsp/articledisplay.jsp?dcrpath=HHNMOSTWIRED/PubsNewsArticleMostWired/data/07Summer/070905MW_online_Darsee&domain=HHNMOSTWIRED

Daswani, N., Garcia-Molina, H., & Yang, B. (2003). Open Problems in Data-Sharing Peer-to-Peer Systems. In: D. Calvanese, M. Lenzerini & R. Motwani (Eds.), *Proceedings of 9th International Conference on Database Theory ICDT 2003, LNCS 2572* (pp. 1-15). Springer.

Datar, M., Immorlica, N., Indyk, P., & Mirrokni, V. S. (2004). Locality-sensitive hashing scheme based on p-stable distributions. *Twentieth Annual Symposium on Computational Geometry,* (pp. 253-262). Brooklyn, New York, USA.

David N. (2002). *A Cognitive Description of Collaboration and Coordination to Help Teams Identify and Fix Problems.* Retreived 13 November 2008 from http://www.stormingmedia.us/authors/Noble__David.html

Davidow, W. H, & Malone, M. S. (1992). *The virtual Corporation: Structuring and Revitalizing the Corporation for the 21st Century.* New York, Harper Collins.

Davidyuk, O., Riekki, J., Rautio, V., & Sun, J. (2004). Context-aware Middleware for Mobile Multimedia Applications. *In Proc. of 3rd International Conference on Mobile and Ubiquitous Multimedia (MUM '04)*, ACM Press, Vol. 83, USA.

Deacon, T. (1997). *Symbolic Species. The Co-evolution of Language and the Brain.* New York & London: Norton.

Deng, L., & Huang, X. (2004). Challenges in adopting speech recognition. *Communications of the ACM, 47*(1), 69-75.

DePaoli, F., & Mariani, L. (2004). Dependability in Peer-to-Peer Systems. *IEEE Internet Computing, 8*(4), 54-61.

Derrida, B., & Pomeau, Y. (1986). Random networks of automata: a simple annealed approximation. *Europhysics Letters, 1,* 45–49.

Derrida, B., & Stauffer, D. (1986). Phase transitions in two dimensional Kauffman cellular automata. *Europhysics Letters, 2,* 739–745.

Dey A. K., & Abowd, G. D. (2000). *Towards Better Understanding of Context and Context-awareness.* Paper presented at the Workshop on The What, Who, Where, When, and How of Context-Awareness, Hague, Netherlands.

Dhillon, I. S. (2001). Co-clustering documents and words using bipartite spectral graph partitioning. In *Proceedings of the seventh ACM SIGKDD international conference on Knowledge discovery and data mining* (pp. 269-274). ACM, New York.

Diaper, D., & Sanger, C. (2006). Tasks for and tasks in human-computer interaction. *Interacting with Computers, 18*(1), 117–138.

Dias, C. (2001). Corporate Portals: A Literature Review of a new Concept information Management. *International Journal of Information Management, 21,* 269-287.

Dias, W. P. S. (1990). Circular Organizational Structure for Project Teams, *Journal of Management in Engineering, 6*(4), 471-478.

Dickinson, T., & McIntyre, R. (1997). A conceptual framework for teamwork measurement. In M. T. Brannick, E. Salas, & C. Prince (Eds.), *Team performance assessment and measurement: theory, methods and applications,* (pp. 19-44), Hillsdale, NJ:Erlbaum.

Diffie, W., & Landau, S. (1998). *Privacy on the Line: The Politics of Wiretapping and Encryption,* Boston, MA: The MIT Press.

Ding, C., Zhang, Y., Li, T., & Holbrook, S. R. (2006). Biclustering Protein Complex Interactions with a Biclique Finding Algorithm. In *Proceedings of the Sixth IEEE International Conference on Data Mining* (p. 178-187). IEEE Computer Society Washington, DC, USA.

Dixon, S., Pampalk, E., & Widmer, G. (2003). Classification of dance music by periodicity patterns. *4th International Conference on Music Information Retrieval,* (pp. 159-165). Baltimore, MD, USA.

DOM. (2000). Document Object Model (DOM) Level 2 Core Specification. W3C Recommendation. Retrieved October 4, 2008, from http://www.w3.org/TR/2000/REC-DOM-Level-2-Core-20001113/DOM2-Core.pdf

Dorogovtsev, S. N., Goltsev, A. V. & Mendes, J. F. F. (in press). Critical phenomena in complex networks. *Reviews of Modern Physics.*

Douceur, J. (2002). The Sybil Attack. In: *Revised Papers from the First International Workshop on Peer-to-Peer Systems, LNCS 2429* (pp. 251-260). Springer.

Dourish, P., & Bellotti, V. (November 1992). Awareness and coordination in shared workspace. In *Proceedings of CSCW '92* (pp. 107-114), Toronto Canada: ACM Press.

Dourish, P., Edwards, W., LaMarca, A., & Salisbury, M. (1999). Presto: An Experimental Architecture for Fluid Interactive Document Spaces. *ACM Transactions on Computer-Human Interaction, 6*(2), 133-161).

Downey, J. S. (2008). The music retrieval evaluation exchange (2005-2007): A window into music information retrieval research. *Acoustic Science and Technology , 29* (4), 247-255.

Driskell, J. E., & Salas E. (1991). Group Decision Making Under Stress. *Journal of Applied Psychology, 76*(3), 473-478.

Druckman, D., Singer, J. E., & Cott, H. V. (Eds.). (1997). *Enhancing Organizational Performance.* Washington, D.C.: National Academy Press.

Dunham, M., & Helal, A.& Balakrishnam, S. (1997). A mobile transaction model that captures both data and movement behavior. *Journal Mobile Networks and Applications* (pp. 149-162).

Earley, J. (1970). An efficient context-free parsing algorithm. *Communications of the ACM, 6*(8), 451-455.

ECMA International: Office Open XML Overview (2008). Retrieved September 1, 2008, from http://www.ecma-international.org/news/TC45_current_work/OpenXML%20White%20Paper.pdf

Education Limited.

Egmont Group (2001). *Principles for Information Exchange between Financial Intelligence Units for Money Laundering and Terrorism Financing Case.* Retrieved July 25, 2008, from http://www.egmontgroup.org/princ_info_exchange.pdf .

Ellis, D. P., & Poliner, G. E. (2007). Identifying 'cover songs' with chroma features and dynamic programming beat tracking. *IEEE International Conference on Acoustics, Speech, and Signal Processing,* (pp. 1429-1432). Honolulu, HI, USA.

Ellis, D., & Arroyo, J. (2004). Eigenrhythms: Drum pattern basis sets for classification and generation. *International Symposium on Music Information Retrieval,* (pp. 101-106). Barcelona, Spain.

Enrique, J., Duarte M., & Mingyan L. (15 November 2003). Data-gathering wireless sensor networks: organization and capacity. *Computer Networks 43*(4), 519-537.

Eugster, P., Felber, P., Guerraoui, R., & Kermarrec, A. (2003). The Many Faces of Publish/Subscribe. *ACM Computing Surveys, 35*(2), 114-131.

European Commission (2001) Communication from the Commission to the Council, the European Parliament, the Economic and Social Committee and the Committee of the Regions, *Science and Society – Action plan*, COM(2001) 714., Item 31 at pg 22

European Union (2007) AGREEMENT between the European Union and the United States of America on the processing and transfer of passenger name record (PNR) data by air carriers to the United States Department of Homeland Security (DHS), Adopted by the Council of Europe August, 2007, http://epic.org/privacy/pdf/pnr-agmt-2007.pdf, last visited October 11, 2008

Evers, K. (2003). *Codes of Conduct: Standards for Ethics in Research,* European Commission Report, Brussels, 2003, http://ec.europa.eu/research/science-society/pdf/codes_conduct_en.pdf, last visited August 24, 2008

Eylon, B., & Reif, F. (April 8-12, 1979). *Effects of Internal Knowledge Organization on Task Performance.* Paper presented at the Annual Meeting of the American Educational Research Association 63rd, San Francisco, California.

Fahy, P., & Clarke, S. (2004). *CASS-Middleware for Mobile Context-Aware Applications.* Paper presented in the Mobisys 2004 Workshop on Context Awareness. Boston, USA. Retrieved June 29, 2006, from www.sigmobile.org/mobisys/2004/context_awareness/papers/cass12f.pdf.

Fair Credit Reporting Act (15 USC §1681 et seq.) (US)

Fallis, D. (2007) *Information Ethics for 21st Century Library Professionals*, http://dlist.sir.arizona.edu/1820/, last visited August 24, 2008

Fandert, H., Fischer, K., & Kämper, J. (1992). The open document architecture: from standardization to the market. *IBM Systems Journal, 31*(4), 728-754.

Farris, D. R., & Sage, A. P. (1975). Introduction and Survey of Group Decision Making with Applications to Worth Assessment. *IEEE Transactions on Systems, Man, and Cybernetics, SMC-5(*3), 346-358.

Feng, W., & Chen, M. (2003). Developing Data Allocation Schemes by Incremental Mining of User Moving Patterns in a Mobile Computing System. *IEEE Transactions on Knowledge and Data Engineering, 15*(1), 70-85.

Fensel, D. (2005). *Ontologies: a silver bullet for knowledge management and electronic commerce.* New York, New York: Springer.

Ferber, J. (1995). *Les systèmes Multi-Agents Vers une intelligence collective.* Paris: Edition InterEditions.

Fischer, K., Muller, J. P., & Pischel, M. (1996). A pragmatic BDI architecture. In M. Wooldridge, J. P. Muller, & M. Tambe, (Ed.), *Intelligent Agents II: Agent Theories, Architectures and Languages, LNAI 1037.* Berlin: Springer.

Flyvbjerg, H. (1988). An order parameter for networks of automata. *Journal of Physics A: Mathematical and General, 21*(19), L955–L960.

Fodor, J. (1983). *The Modularity of the Mind.* Cambridge, MA: MIT Press.

Fodor, J. (2000). *The mind doesn't work that way: The scope and limits of computational psychology.* Cambridge, MA: MIT Press.

Fodor, J., & Pylyshyn, Z. (1988). Connectionism and cognitive architecture. *Cognition, 28*(1-2), 3-71.

Ford, C. W., Chiang, C.-C., Wu, H., Chilka, R. R., & Talburt, J. (2004). Confidence on approximate query in large datasets. In P. K. Srimani (Ed.), *Proceedings of the IEEE International Conference on Information Technology Coding and Computing* (pp. 480-484). Los Alamitos, California: IEEE.

Ford, C. W., Chiang, C.-C., Wu, H., Chilka, R. R., & Talburt, J. (2005). Text data mining: a case study. In H. S. Selvaraj & P. K. Srimani (Ed.), *Proceedings of the IEEE International Conference on Information Technology Coding and Computing* (pp. 122-127). Los Alamitos, California: IEEE.

Fortunato, S., & Castellano, C. (in press). Community Structure in Graphs. *Encyclopedia of Complexity and Systems Science*.

Forward, A., & Lethbridge, T. (2002). The relevance of software documentation, tools and technologies: a survey. In E. Munson, R. Furuta, & J. Maletic (Ed.), *Proceedings of the 2002 ACM Symposium on Document Engineering Conference* (pp. 26-33). New York, New York: ACM.

Foster, J. (2006). Collaborative Information Seeking and Retrieval. *Annual Review of Information Science and Technology, 40*, 329-356.

Fountain, J. (August 2007). Challenges to Organizational Change:Multi-Level Integrated Information Structures (MIIS). *Paper presented at the annual meeting of the American Political Science Association, Hyatt Regency Chicago and the Sheraton Chicago Hotel and Towers, Chicago, IL* Online <APPLICATION/PDF> Retrieved 15 August 2008 from http://www.allacademic.com/meta/p210129_index.html

Fox, M., & Faver, C. (1984). Independence and cooperation in research. *Journal of Higher Education, 55*(3), 347-359.

Franklin, M., Jonson, B. & Kossmann, D. (1996). Performance Tradeoffs for Client-Server Query Processing. *Proceedings of 1996 ACM SIGMOD Int. Conf. on Management of Data* (pp.149-160)

Fred, F. (2006). *An Ontology-Driven Model for the Efficient Use of Provenance Information*. Retrieved 15 July, 2008, from http://www.personal.psu.edu/facultv/f/u/fuf1/publications/fonseca NCSA.pdf.

Frey, B.J. & Dueck, D. (2007). Clustering by Passing Messages between Data Points. *Science, 315*, 972-976.

Froehlich, T. (2004), *A Brief History Of Information Ethics*, Textos Universitaris DeBiblioteconomia I Documentació, http:/www.ub.es/bid/13froel2.htm, last visited August 24, 2008

Fuggetta, A., Picco, G. P., & Vigna, G. (1998). Understanding Code Mobility. *IEEE Transactions on Software Engineering, 24*(5), 342-361.

Fujihara, H., & Goto, M. (2007). A music information retrieval system based on singing voice timbre. *International Conference on Music Information Retrieval*, (pp. 467-470). Vienna, Austria.

Fukuda, K., Takayasu, H., & Takayasu, M. (2000). Origin of critical behavior in Ethernet traffic. *Physica A, 287*, 289–301.

Fussell, S., Kraut, R., Lerch, F., Scherlis, W., McNally, M., & Cadiz, J. (November 1998). Coordination, overload and team performance: Effects of team communication strategies. *In Proceedings of CSC W '98* (pp. 275-284). Seattle, WA: ACM Press.

Gajadhar, J. (1998). *Issues in Plagiarism for the New Millennium: An Assessment Odyssey.* The Open Polytechnic of New Zealand, UltiBASE, December, http://ultibase.rmit.edu.au/Articles/dec98/gajad1.htm, last visited October 15, 2008

Gançarski, A., & Henriques, P. (2003). Interactive information retrieval from XML documents represented by attribute grammars. In C. Roisin, E. Munson, & C. Vanoirbrrk (Ed.), *Proceedings of the 2003 ACM Symposium on Document Engineering Conference* (pp. 171-174). New York, New York: ACM.

Garvin, D. A., & Roberto, M. A. (2003). What You Don't Know About Making Decisions. *IEEE Engineering Management Review, 31*(2), 3-9.

Gaspary, L., Barcellos, M. P., Detsch, A., & Antunes, R. S. (2007). Flexible security in peer-to-peer applications. *Computer Networks, 51*, 4795-4815.

Gauvain, J.-L., Lamel, L., & Adda, G. (2002). The LIMSI broadcast news transcription system. *Speech Communication , 37* (1-2), 89-108.

Gedik, B., & Liu, L.(2006). MobiEyes: A distributed Location Monitoring Service Using Moving Location

Queries, *IEEE Transaction on Mobile Computing, 5*(10), 1384-1402.

Gehlen, G., & Mavromatis, G. (2003). Mobile Web Services Based Middleware for Context-aware applications. In *proceedings of the 11ᵗʰ European Wireless Conference 2005 Volume 2* (pp 784-790).Nicosia, Cyprus. Retrieved June 29, 2002, from www.comnets.rwth-aachen.de/436+M5cc1c271ec8 .pdf.

Geman, S., Bienenstock, E., & Doursat, R. (1992). Neural networks and the bias/variance dilemma. *Neural Computation, 4*, 1-58.

Gemmell, J., Bell, G., Lueder, R., Drucker, S., & Wong, C. (2002). MyLifeBits: Fulfilling the Memex Vision. *In Proceedings of the 10ᵗʰ ACM international conference on multimedia* (pp. 235-238).

Gemmy, A. (2002). *Supervision.* Retrieved 6 October 2008 from http://ollie.dcccd.edu/MGMT1374/book_intro.html

George, W. (1986). Generalized fisheye views *In Pro-Factors in Computing Systems, Visualizing Complex Information Spaces*, (pp. 16-23).

Gerhard, W., Matthias, N., Michael, R., & Felix, F. (2004). Specifying the Intertwining of Cooperation and Autonomy in Agent-based Systems. *International Journal of Computer and Information Science, 5*(2):73-88.

Gibson, E. (1991). *A computational theory of human language processing: Memory, limitations and processing breakdown.* Doctoral dissertation, Carnegie Mellon University, Pittsburgh, PA.

Gibson, E. (1998). Linguistic complexity: Locality of syntactic dependencies. *Cognition, 68*, 1-76.

Gifford, D., Jouvelot, P., Sheldon, M., & OToole, J. (1991). Semantic File Systems. *In Proceedings of the 13th ACM symposium on operating systems principles,* (pp. 16-25).

Glass, A., & Grosz, B. J. (2003). Socially Conscious Decision-Making. In *Journal of Autonomous Agents and Multi-Agent Systems*, Special Issue. The Netherlands: Springer.

Glushko, R., & McGrath T. (2005). *Document engineering: analyzing and designing documents for business informatics & Web services.* Cambridge, Massachusetts: The MIT Press.

Goebel Group: Desktop Search Tools Matrix (2008). Retrieved September 1, 2008, from http://www.goebelgroup.com/desktopmatrix.htm

Göker, A., & Myrhaug, H. I. (2002). *User Context and Personalisation.* Paper presented in the 6ᵗʰ European Conference/Workshop on Case-Based Reasoning (EC-CBR 2002), Aberdeen, Scotland, UK. Retrieved March 29, 2007, from http://www.smartweb.rgu.ac.uk/papers/AGoker.pdf

Gold, E. M. (1967). Language identification in the limit. *Information and Control, 10*, 447-474.

Goldberger, J., Gordon, S., & Greenspan, H. (2003). An efficient image similarity measure based on approximations of KL-divergence between two Gaussian mixtures. *IEEE International Conference on Computer Vision*, (pp. 487-493). Nice, France.

Gollmann, D. (1999). *Computer Security.* Chichester, England: John Wiley & Sons.

Gomez-Perez, A., Corcho, O., & Fernandez-Lopez, M. (2004). *Ontological engineering.* New York, New York: Springer.

Gong, L. (2001). JXTA: A network programming environmen. *IEEE Internet Computing, 5*(3), 88-95.

Goodman, N. (1955). *Fact, Fiction, and Forecast.* Cambridge, MA: Harvard University Press.

GOOGLE Inc. (2006). Google Voice Search. *US patent No 7027987,* Mountain View, CA. available at http://patft.uspto.gov/

google. (2008). In Merriam-Webster Online Dictionary. Retrieved September 1, 2008, from http://www.merriam-webster.com/dictionary/google

Gopal, B., & Manber, U. (1999). Integrating Content-Based Access Mechanisms with Hierarchical File Systems. *In Proceedings of the 3rd symposium on operating systems design and implementation* (pp.265-278).

Gorgoglione, M., Palmisano, C., & Tuzhilin, A. (2006). Personaliastion in Context: Does Context Matter When Building Personalised Customer Models, *In Proceedings of the sixth International Conference on Data Mining (ICDM'06)* (pp. 222-231). Hong Kong, China.

Gorrell, P. (1995). *Syntax and parsing.* Cambridge: Cambridge University Press.

Graffi, F. (2001). *Two Hundred Years of Syntax: A Critical Survey.* Amsterdam: Benjamins.

Gramm-Leach-Bliley (1999). The Financial Modernization Act of 1999 (the Gramm-Leach-Bliley Act) (US)

Grant, J. (2000). Proactive behavior in organization. *Journal of management, 26*(3), 435-462.

Granville, L., Rosa, D., Panisson, A., Melchiors, C., Almeida, M., & Tarouco, L. (2005). Managing Computer Networks Using Peer-to-Peer Technologies. *IEEE Communications Magazine, 43*(10), 62-68.

Greenberg, J. H. (Ed.). (1963). *Universals of Language.* Cambridge, MA: MIT Press.

Greenhalgh, T. (2006). *What seems to be the trouble? Stories in illness and healthcare.* Oxford: Radcliffe Publishing

Gross, R. L., & Brodt, S. E. (2001). How Assumptions of Consensus Undermine Decision-Making. *Sloan Management Review, 42*(2), 86-94.

Grossman, S. (1997). Turning Technical Groups into High-Performance Teams. *IEEE Engineering Management Review, 25*(4), 32-34.

Gruenfeld, D. H., et al. (1996). Group Composition and Decision Making: How Member Familiarity and Information Distribution Affect Process and Performance. *Organizational Behavior and Human Decision Processes, 67*(1), 1-15.

Gu, T., Pung, H. K., & Zhang D. Q. (2004). A Middleware for Building Context-Aware Mobile Services. *In Proceedings of the Vehicular Technology Conference, 2004 Volume 5* (pp 2656-2660). Univ. of Singapore, Singapore. Retrieved June 29, 2006, from www.comp.nus.edu.sg/~gutao/gutao_NUS /VTC2004 gutao.PDF

Guasti, M. T. (2002). *Language Acquisition: The Growth of Grammar.* Cambridge, MA: MIT Press.

Gupta, A., Sahin, O. D., Agrawal, D., & Abbadi, A. E.. (2004). Meghdoot: Content-Based Publish/Subscribe over P2P Networks. *Proceedings of the 5th ACM/IFIP/ USENIX international Conference on Middleware, LNCS 3231* (pp. 254-273). New York: Springer.

Gutwin, C., & Greenberg, S. (June 14-16 2000). The Mechanics of Collaboration: developing low cost usability evaluation methods for shared workspaces. *IEEE 9th international workshop on enabling technologies: infrastructure for collaborative enterprises*, NIST, Gaithersburg, MD USA.

Hackman, J. R. (Ed.). (1990). *Groups That Work (and Those That Don't).* San Francisco: Jossey-Bass.

Hackman, J. R., & Morris, C. G. (1975). *Group Tasks, Group Interaction Process, and Group Performance Effectiveness: A Review and Proposed Integration.* (US Office of Naval Research, Organizational Effectiveness Research Program, Contract No. N00014-67A-0097-0026, photocopy), (pp.45-95).

Haiying, T., Jeffrey, A., Satnam, S., Krishna, R., & Peter, W. (November 2006). Information Integration via Hierarchical and Hybrid Bayesian Networks, Systems, Man and Cybernetics, Part A. *IEEE Transactions on 36*(6), 1257-1268.

Hakia Search Engine Beta (2008). Retrieved September 1, 2008, from http://hakia.com/

Hammond, T., Hannay, T., Lund, B., & Scott, J. (April 2005). Social book marking tools (I) – A General Review. *D-Lib Magazine 11*(4).

Han J., & Kamber M. (2006). *Data Mining Techniques and Concepts*, San Fransisco, CA, USA:Morgan Kaufmann Publishers.

Hand, D., Smith, P., & Manilla, H. (2000). *Principles of Data Mining.* Boston: MIT Press

Hansen, K. L., & Tatum, C.B. (1996). How Strategies Happen: A Decision-Making Framework. *Journal of Management in Engineering, 12*(1), 40-48.

Hansen, P., & Jaervelin, K. (2005). Collaborative Information Retrieval in an Information-intensive Domain. *Information Processing and Management, 41,* 1 1 0 1 - 1119.

Hardy, M. (2007). The Mars project – PDF in XML. In Peter King & Steven Simske (Ed.), *Proceedings of the 2007 ACM Symposium on Document Engineering Conference* (pp. 161-170). New York, New York: ACM.

Hardy, M., & Brailsford, D. (2002). Mapping and displaying structural transformations between XML and PDF. In E. Munson, R. Furuta, & J. Maletic (Ed.), *Proceedings of the 2002 ACM Symposium on Document Engineering Conference* (pp. 95-102). New York, New York: ACM.

Harrington, D., Presuhn, R., & Wijnen, B. (2002). *An Architecture for Describing Simple Network Management Protocol (SNMP) Management Frameworks, RFC 3411, STD 62,* 2002. IETF.

Hartwig, S., Luck, M., Aaltonen, J., Serafat, R., & Theimer, W. (2000). Mobile Multimedia – Challenges and Opportunities. *IEEE Transactions on Consumer Electronics, 46*(4), USA.

Health 2.0 Definition. (n.d.). Retrieved December 16, 2007, from http://health20.org/wiki/Health_2.0_Definition

Hector, S. (to appear). Biotic Feedback: Priority and supremacy in Nature, science and Society. *Part of the series Bios and the Cybernetics of creative system, special issue for cybernetics and semiotics edited by Hector Sabelli.*

Hegering, H., Abeck, S., & Neumair, B. (1999). *Integratd Management of Networked Systems.* San Francisco: Morgan Kaufmann.

Heinzelman, W., Chandrakasan, A., & Balakrishnan, H. (2000). Energy-efficient communication protocol for wireless microsensor network. *In Hawaii International Conference on System Sciences* (HICCS), Maui, HI.

Helén, M., & Lahti, T. (2007). Query by example large databases using key-sample distance transformation and clustering. *IEEE International Workshop on Multimedia Information Retrieval (MIPR 2007),* (pp. 303-308). Taichung, Taiwan.

Helén, M., & Virtanen, T. (2007-1). A similarity of measure for audio signals query by example based on perceptual coding and compression. *International Conference on Digital Audio Effects (DAFx 2007),* (pp. 173-176). Bordeaux, France.

Helén, M., & Virtanen, T. (2007-2). Query by example of audio signals using Euclidean distance between Gaussian mixture model. *IEEE International Conference on Acoustics, Speech, and Signal Processing (ICASSP 2007), 1,* pp. 225-228. Honolulu, Hawaii, USA.

Herbst, P. (1976). *Alternatives to Hierarchies.* Leiden, the Netherlands: H. E. Stenfer Kroese.

Herman, M. (2002). Making Teamwork Work. Retrieved 6 November 2008 from *www.hermanmiller.com/hm/content/research_summaries/pdfs/wp_Collaborative_Settings.pdf*

Herrera-Viedma, E., Herrera, F., & Chiclana, F. (2002). A Consensus Model for Multiperson Decision Making With Different Preference Structures. *IEEE Transactions on Systems, Man and Cybernetics—Part A: Systems and Humans, 32*(3), 394-402.

Hershey, J. R., & Olsen, P. A. (2007). Approximating the Kullback Leibler divergence between Gaussian mixture models. *IEEE International Conference on Acoustics, Speech and Signal Processing, 4,* pp. 317-320. Honolulu, Hawaii, USA.

Hine, C. (2000). *Virtual Ethnography.* London: Sage.

Hinsz, V., Tindale, R., & Vollrath, D. (1997). The emerging conceptualization of groups as information processors. *Psychological Bulletin, 121*(1), 43-64.

Hinton-Walker, P., Botelho, R., & Suchman, A., (1998). Partnerships, power and process: An introduction. In A. Suchman, R. Botelho & P. Hinton-Walker (Eds.), *Partnerships in healthcare: Transforming relationship process,* (pp. 3-9). Rochester, NY: University of Rochester Press.

Hirsch, H.-G., Dobler, S., Kiessling, A., & Schleifer, R. (2006). Speech recognition by a portable terminal for voice dialing. *European Patent* EP1617635.

Hodgkin, P., & Munro, J. (2007). The long tale: public services and Web 2.0. *Consumer Policy Review, 17*(2), 84-88.

Hofman, J. M., & Wiggins, C. H. (2008). A Bayesian Approach to Network Modularity. *Physical Review Letters, 100*, 258701.

Hofmann, T. (1999). Probabilistic latent semantic indexing. In *Proceedings of the 22nd Annual ACM SIGIR Conference on Research and Development in Information Retrieval*, (pp. 50-57). New York: ACM.

Hogg, M. A., & Vaughan, G. M. (2005) *Social Psychology*. Gosport, UK: Pearson

Holland, S., & Kiessiling, W. (2004). Situated Preferences and Preference Repositories for Personalised Database Applications. *In Proceedings of the 23rd International Conference on Conceptual Modelling* (pp 511-523). Shanghai, China Retrieved April 24, 2006, from http://www.cs.uoi.gr/~kstef/ 2004_hol_kie_er2004.pdf

Holland, S., Ester, M., & Kiessling, W. (2003). A Novel Approach on Mining User Preferences for Personalised Applications. *In Knowledge Discovery in Databases (PKDD 2003)* (pp 204-216). Dubrovnik, Croatia, Retrieved April 24, 2006, from http://www.cs.uoi.gr/~kstef/PreferenceMining.pdf

Hollenbeck, J. R., et al. (1995). Multilevel Theory of Team Decision Making: Decision Performance in Teams Incorporating Distributed Expertise. *Journal of Applied Psychology, 80*(2), 292-316.

Holohan, A. (2005). Collaboration Online: The Example of Distributed Computing. *Journal of Computer-Mediated Communication*.

Hood, L., & Galas, D. (2003). The digital code of DNA. Nature, *421*, 444-448.

Hornsby, J. S., Smith, B. N., & Gupta, J. N. D. (1994). The Impact of Decision-making methods on Job Evaluation Outcomes: A Look at Three Consensus Approaches. *Group & Organization Management, 19*(1), 112-128.

Hsairi, L, Ghédira, K., Alimi, M. A., & Ben Abdelhafid, A. (2006, October), *Resolution of Conflicts via Argument Based Negotiation: Extended Enterprise Case*. Paper presented In: IEEE/SSSM06, (pp. 828-833), Université de Technologie de Troyes, IEEE Press, France.

Hsairi, L, Ghédira, K., Alimi, M. A., & Ben Abdelhafid, A. (2008, September). *R²-IBN: Argumentation Based Negotiation Framework for the Extended Enterprise*. Paper presented In HAIS'08, 3rd International workshop on Hybrid Artificial Intelligence systems, LNAI 5271, (pp. 533-542), Springer-Verlag Berlin Heidelberg, Burgos, Espagne.

http://www.israel21c.org/bin/en.jsp?enZone=Technology&enDisplay=view&enPage=BlankPage&enDispWhat=object&enDispWho=Articles%5El1000http://www.israel21c.org

Huang, X., Acero, A., & Hon, H.-W. (2001). *Spoken language processing: a guide to theory, algorithm and system development*. Redmond, Washington, USA: Prentice Hall.

Hudlicka, E. (1996). Requirements elicitation with indirect knowledge elicitation techniques: comparison of three methods (15-18 April 1996). *Proceedings of the Second International Conference on Requirements Engineering*, (pp. 4-11).

Huffman, D. A. (1952). A method for the construction of minimum-redundancy codes. *Proceedings of the Institute of Radio Engineers, 40*, 1098–1102.

Hughes, T., Marton, M., Jones, A., Robers, C., Stoughton, R., Armour, C. et al. (2000). Functional discovery via a compendium of expression profiles. *Cell, 102*, 109–126.

Hyldegard, J., & Ingwersen, P. (2007). Task Complexity and Information Behaviour in Group Based Problem Solving. *Information Research, 12*(4), Retrieved May 21, 2008, from http://InformationR.net/ir/12-4/colis/colis27.html.

Hylton, J., Manheimer, K., & Drake, L. F. (1996). Knowbot programming: System Support for Mobile Agents. *In the Proc. of 5th International Workshop on Object Orientation in Operating Systems (IWOOOS '96)*, Washington, USA.

Ickes, W., & Gonzalez, R. (1994). Social cognition and social cognition: From the subjective to the inter-subjective. *Small Group Research, 25*, 294-315.

IEEE Code of Ethics (2006). adopted February, 2006, http://www.ieee.org/web/aboutus/ethics/code.html, last visited August 24, 2008

IEEE. 2008. Overview on IEEE wireless standards. Retrieved October 8, 2008, from http://standards.ieee.org/wireless/overview.html

Imad, S., Souren P., Peter Jr., & Priya S. (2003). The Collaborative Conflict Management Style and Cultural Diversity in DGSS Supported Fuzzy Tasks: An Experimental Investigation. *Proceedings of the 36th Hawaii y International Conference on System Sciences (HICSS'03).*

Indratmo, & Julita V. (2008). A Review of Organizational Structures of Personal Information Management. *Journal of Digital Information, 9*(26).

Ingwersen, P. (1996). Cognitive Perspectives of Information Retrieval Interaction: Elements of a Cognitive IR Theory. *Journal of Documentation, 12*(1), 1-18.

Integrated Product Teams (IPT). (n.d.). Retrieved November 10, 2001 from http://www.dsmc.dsm.mil/jdam/contents/ipt.htm.

Interacting with Computers, 17(3), 251–264.

International Telecommunication Union. (2000a). *ITU-T Recommendation M.3000: Overview of TMN Recommendations*. International Telecommunication Union.

International Telecommunication Union. (2000b). *ITU-T Recommendation M.3010: Principles for a Telecommunications Management Network*. International Telecommunication Union.

International Telecommunication Union. (2000c). *ITU-T Recommendation M.3400: TMN Management Functions*. International Telecommunication Union.

Ioannidis, Y., & Kang, Y. (1990). Randomized Algorithms for optimizing Large Join Queries. *Proceedings of 1990 ACM SIGMOD Int. Conf. on Management of Data* (pp. 312-331)

ISO, (2006). *Information technology − open document format for office applications (OpenDocument) v1.0. ISO/IEC 26300:2006*, Retrieved July 10, 2008, from http://www.iso.org/iso/iso_catalogue/catalogue_tc/catalogue_detail.htm?csnumber=43485

Iyengar R. K., & Malyankar, R. M. (2002). A method for automating text markup. In *Proceedings of the 2002 Annual National Conference on Digital Government Research* (pp. 1-6). New York, New York: ACM.

Jackson, S., Brett, J., Sessa, V., Cooper, D., Julin, J., & Peyronnin, K. (1991). Some differences make a difference: Individual dissimilarity and group heterogeneity as correlates of recruitment, promotions, and turnover. *Journal of Applied Psychology, 76*, 675-689.

James, W. (2007). Defection and Hierarchy in International Intelligence Sharing. *Journal of Public. Policy., 27*, 151-181.

Jameson, A. (2001). Modelling Both the Context and the User; *Personal and Ubiquitous Computing, 5*(1), 29-33. Retrieved April 24, 2006, from http://www.dfki.de/~jameson/pdf/pete01 .jameson.pdf

Jang, J. (1997). IN P. Hall (Ed.), *Neuro-Fuzzy and Soft Computing.*

Jared, F., & Kathleen, P. (June 17-19, 2003). Collaborative Critical Thinking. *8th International Command and Control Research and Technology Symposium*. National Defense University, Washington, DC.

Jennings N. R., Faratin P., Lomuscio A. R., Parsons S., Sierra C., & Wooldridge M. J. (2001). Automated negotiation: prospects, methods and challenges. *IJG of Decision and Negotiation, 10*, 199-215.

Jensen, K. (2007). Multiple scale music segmentation using rhythm, timbre, and harmony. *EURASIP Journal on Advances in Signal Processing , 2007*, 1-11.

Jie, L., Guangquan, Z., & Fengjie, W. (January, 2008). Team Situation Awareness Using Web Based Fuzzy Group Decision Support Systems. *International Journal of Computational Intelligence Systems, 1*(1) 50-59.

JISC Infonet Service (2007). *Manage the information lifecycle.* Retrieved 5 November 2008 from www.jiscinfonet.ac.uk/infokits/information-lifecycle

Joan, M., Leandro N., & Thanasis, D. (2004). Extending the Scope of Asynchronous Collaboration: a Matter of Being Autonomous and Self-sufficient. *Proceedings of the 13th IEEE International Workshops on Enabling Technologies: Infrastructure for Collaborative Enterprises (WET ICE'04).*

Johansen, D., & Renesse van, R., & Fred, B. S. (1997). *Operating System Support for Mobile Agents*, Readings in Agents, Morgan Kaufmann Publishers, ISBN 1-55860-495-2, USA.

Johnson-Laird, P. (1983). *Mental models: toward a cognitive science of language, inference, and consciousness.* Harvard University Press, Cambridge, MA.

Jones, W., Phuwanartnilrak, A., Gill, R., & Bruce, H. (2005). Don't Take My Folders Away! Organizing Personal Information to Get Things Done. *In CHI '05 extended abstracts on human factors in computing systems*, (pp. 1505-1508).

Jørgensen, A. H., & Myers, B. A. (2008). User interface history. *In Proceedings of ACM CHI 2008 Conference on Human Factors in Computing Systems* (pp. 2415-2418). Florence, Italy.

Jorstad, I., & Thanh, D. V. (2006). *Service Personalisation in Mobile Heterogenous Environments. In Proceedings of Advanced International Conference on Telecommunications (AICT2006)* (pp. 70-75), Washington DC, USA.

Judd, J. S. (1990). *Neural network design and the complexity of learning.* Cambridge, MA: MIT Press.

Judd, S. J. (1996). Complexity of learning. In P. Smolensky, M. C. Mozer & D. E. Rumelhart (Eds.), *Mathematical perspectives on neural networks.* New Jersey: Erlbaum.

Jung, S. Y., Hong, J. H., & Kim, T. S. (2002). A Formal Model for Preference. *In proceedings of the 2002 IEEE international Conference on Data Mining (ICDM'02)* (pp 235-240). Maebashi TERRSA, Maebashi City, Japan

Jung, S. Y., Hong, J. H., & Kim, T. S. (2005). A Statistical Model for User Preferences. *IEEE Transaction on Knowledge and Data Engineering, 17*(6), 834-843.

Jurafsky, D. (1996). A probabilistic model of lexical and syntactic access and disambiguation. *Cognitive Science, 20*, 137-194.

Jurafsky, D., & Martin, J. H. (2000). *Speech and language processing: an introduction to natural language processing, computational linguistics, and speech recognition.* Upper Saddle River, NJ, USA: Prentice Hall PTR.

Kanehisa, M., & Goto, S. (2000). KEGG: Kyoto encyclopedia of genes and genomes. *Nucleic Acids Research, 28*(1), 27–30.

Kanth, R. K., Agrawal, D., & Singh, A. (1998). Dimensionality reduction for similarity searching in dynamic databases. *ACM SIGMOD International Conference on Management of Data, 27*, pp. 166-176. Seattle, Washington, USA.

Kaplan, R. M. (1973). A general syntactic processor. In E. Rustin (Ed.), *Natural Language Processing* (pp. 193-241). New York: Algorithmics Press.

Kaptelinin, V. (2003). UMEA: Translating Interaction Histories into Project Contexts. *In Proceedings of the SIGCHI conference on human factors in computing systems*, (pp. 353-360).

Kapur, A., Benning, M., & Tzanetakis, G. (2004). Query-by-beat-boxing: Music retrieval for the DJ. *International Conference on Music Information Retrieval (ISMIR 2004).* Barcelona, Spain.

Karamuftuoglu, M. (1998). Collaborative information retrieval: towards a social informatics view of IR interaction. *Journal of American Society for Information Sciences, 49*(12), 1070-1080.

Karger, D., & Jones, W. (2006). Data Unification in Personal Information Management. *Communications of the ACM, 49*(1), 77-82.

Karger, D., & Quan, D. (2004). Collections: Flexible, Essential Tools for Information Management. In CHI '04 extended abstracts on human factors in computing systems, (pp. 1159-1162).

Kashino, K., Kurozumi, T., & Murase, H. (2003). A quick search method for audio and video signals based on histogram pruning. *IEEE Transactions on Multimedia , 5* (3), 348-357.

Katzenbach, J. R., & Smith, D. K. (1999). *The Wisdom of Teams.* New York: HarperCollins.

Kauffman, S. A. (1969). Metabolic stability and epigenesis in randomly constructed genetic nets. *Journal of Theoretical Biology, 22,* 437–467.

Kauffman, S. A. (1993). The Origins of Order: Self-organization and selection in evolution. New York: Oxford University Press.

Kay, M. (1986). Algorithm schemata and data structures in syntactic processing. In B. J. Grosz, K. S. Jones & B. L. Webber (Eds.), *Readings in natural language processing* (pp. 35–70). San Francisco, CA: Morgan Kaufmann Publishers.

Keim, D. (January - March 2002). Information Visualization and Visual Data Mining. *IEEE Transactions on Visualization and Computer Graphics, 7*(1), 100-107.

Kelly, G. A. (1955). *The Psychology of Personal Constructs.* NY: Norton.

Kelly, G. A. (1991). *The Psychology of Personal Constructs.* London: Routledge.

Kepner, C. H., & Tregoe, B. B. (1997). *The New Rational Manager: an updated edition for a new world.* Princeton: Princeton Research Press.

Kesseli, J., Rämö, P., & Yli-Harja, O. (2005). Tracking perturbation in Boolean networks with spectral methods. *Physical Review E, 72,* 026137.

Kesseli, J., Rämö, P., & Yli-Harja, O. (2006). Iterated maps for annealed Boolean networks. *Physical Review E, 74,* 046104.

Keyes, E., Krull, R. (1992). User Information Processing and Online Visual Structure. *Proceedings of the 10th annual international conference on System Documentation.* (pp.121-128), Ontario, USA.

Kidd, A. (1994). The Marks are on the Knowledge Worker. *In Proceedings of the SIGCHI conference on human factors in computing systems,* (pp. 186-191).

Kiessling, W. (2002). Foundations of Preferences in Databases; *In: Proceedings 28th International Conference on Very Large Databases (VLDB 2002)* (pp. 311-322), Hong Kong, China. Retrieved April 24, 2006 from http://www.vldb.org/conf/2002/S09P04.pdf.

Kiewera, M. (2005). Iterative Discovering of User's Preferences Using Web Mining. *International Journal of Computer Science & Applications, 2*(2), 57-66.

Kim, J., Brian, C., & Robert, C. (1987). Assaying and isolating individual differences in searching a hierarchical file system. Human, Factors, 29(3),(pp.349-359).

Kinnunen, T. (2005). *Optimizing spectral feature based text-independent speaker recognition.* PhD thesis, Department of Computer Science, University of Joensuu.

Kitahara, H. (1997). *Elementary Operations and Optimal Derivations.* Cambridge, MA: MIT Press.

Klein, G. (1999). *Sources of Power: How People Make Decisions.* Cambridge: The MIT Press.

Kmietowicz, Z. (2007). MPs "dismayed" at confusion about electronic patient records. *British Medical Journal, 335*(7620), 581.

Kocher, M., Strauß, S., & Sutter, M. (2004). Individual or team decision-making – Causes and consequences of self-selection. In *Discussion Papers on Strategic Interaction.* Jena, Germany: Max Planck Institute of Economics.

Kolmogorov, A. N. (1965). Three approaches to the quantitative definition of information. *Problems in Information Transmission, 1*(1), 1–7.

Kolodner, J. (1993). Case-Based Reasoning. Morgan Kaufmann.

Komarova, N. L., & Nowak, M. A. (2003). Language, Learning and Evolution. In M. H. Christiansen & S. Kirby (Eds.), *Language Evolution*. Oxford: Oxford University Press.

Kossmann, D. (2004). The State of the Art in Distributed Query Processing. *ACM Computing Surveys, 32*(4), 422-469.

Kotz, D., & Gray, R. S. (1999). Mobile Agents and the Future of the Internet. *ACM Operating Systems review, 33*(3).

Koubarakis, M., Tryfonopoulos, C., Idreos, S., & Drougas, Y. (2003). Selective Information Dissemination in P2P Networks: Problems and Solutions. *SIGMOD Record, 32*(3), 71-76.

Kovac, G. L., & Paganelli, P. (2003). A planning and management infrastructure for large, complex, distributed projects—beyond ERP and SCM. *Computer in Industry, 51*, 165-183.

Kraus, S., Sycara, K., & Evenchik, A. (1998). Reaching agreements through argumentation: A logical model and implementation. *Artificial Intelligence, 104*, 1-69.

Krawitz, P., & Shmulevich, I. (2007a). Basin Entropy in Boolean Network Ensembles. *Physical Review Letters, 98*(15), 158701.

Krawitz, P., & Shmulevich, I. (2007b). Entropy of complex relevant components in Boolean networks. *Physical Review E, 76*, 036115.

Kröll, M., Rath A., Weber, N., Lindstaedt, S., & Granitzer M. (2007, August). *Task Instance Classification via Graph Kernel*. Paper presented at Mining and Learning with Graphs 07, Florence, Italy.

Kröll, M., Rath, A., Granitzer, M., Lindstaedt, S., & Tochtermann, K. (2006, October). *Contextual Retrieval in Knowledge Intensive Business Environments*. Paper presented at Workshop Information Retrieval 2006, Hildesheim, Germany

Kuhl, J., & Atkinson, J. W. (1986). *Motivation, Thought, and Action*. NY: Praeger Publishers.

Kuhlthau, C. (1991). Inside the Search Process: Information Seeking from the User's Perspective. *Journal of American Society for Information Sciences, 42*(5), 361-371.

Kuikka, E., Leinonen, P., & Penttonen, M. (2002). Towards automating of document structure transformations. In E. Munson, R. Furuta, & J. Maletic (Ed.), *Proceedings of the 2002 ACM Symposium on Document Engineering Conference* (pp. 103-110). New York, New York: ACM.

Kunis, R. Rünger, G., & Schwind M. (2007). A Model for Document Management in e-Government Systems Based on Hierarchical Process Folders. *The Electronic Journal of e-Government, 5*(2), 191 – 204.

Kuo, Y. S., Shih, N. C., Tseng, L., & Hu, H.-C. (2005). In P. King (Ed.), *Proceedings of the 2005 ACM Symposium on Document Engineering Conference* (pp. 58-60). New York, New York: ACM.

Kuo, Y. S., Wang, J., & Shih, N. C. (2003). In C. Roisin, E. Munson & C. Vanoirbrrk (Ed.), *Proceedings of the 2003 ACM Symposium on Document Engineering Conference* (pp. 222-224). New York, New York: ACM.

Kurtev, I., & Berg, K. (2003). Model driven architecture based XML processing. In C. Roisin, E. Munson & C. Vanoirbrrk (Ed.), *Proceedings of the 2003 ACM Symposium on Document Engineering Conference* (pp. 246-248). New York, New York: ACM.

Kwasnik, B. (1989). How a Personal Document's Intended Use or Purpose Affects Its Classification in an Office. *In Proceedings of the 12th annual international ACM SIGIR conference on research and development in information retrieval,* (pp. 207-,210).

Kwasnik, B. (1991). The Importance of Factors that are not Document Attributes in the Organisation of Personal Documents. *Journal of Documentation, 47*(4), 389-398.

Lahti, T., Helén, M., Vuorinen, O., Väyrynen, E., Partala, J., Peltola, J., et al. (2008). On enabling techniques for personal audio content management. *ACM International Conference on Multimedia Information Retrieval (MIR 2008).* Vancouver, Canada.

Lambiotte, R., & Ausloos, M. (2005). Uncovering collective listening habits and music genres in bipartite networks. *Physical Review E, 72,* 066107.

Lansdale, M. (1988). The Psychology of Personal Information Management. *Applied Ergonomics, 19*(1), 55-66

Laplant, B., Trewin, S., Zimmermann, G., & Vanderheiden, G. (2004). The Universal Remote Console: a universal access bus for pervasive computing. *Pervasive Computing, IEEE, 3*(1), 76–80.

Larson, J., & Christensen, C. (1993). Groups a problem-solving units: Toward a new, meaning of social cognition. *British Journal of Social Psychology,* (pp. 5-30).

Lartillot, O., & Toiviainen, P. (2007). A Matlab toolbox for music information retrieval. *Annual Conference of the German Classification Society.* Freiburg.

Laufer, A., Woodward, H., & Howell, G. (1999). Managing the Decision-Making Process During Project Planning. *Journal of Management in Engineering, 15*(2), 79-84.

Leavitt, H., & Whisler, T. (1958). Management in the 1980s. *Harvard Business Review, 36,* 41-48.

Lehikoinen, J., Aaltonen, A., Huuskonen, P., & Salminen, I. (2007). *Personal content experience: managing digital life in the mobile age.* England: Wiley & Sons, Ltd.

Lehmann, S., Schwartz, M., & Hansen, L. K. *BCfinder.* Retrieved December 12, 2007 from http://www2.imm. dtu.dk/~mhs/bcfinder/

Lehmann, S., Schwartz, M., & Hansen, L.K. (2008). Biclique communities. *Physical Review E, 78,* 016108.

Leinwand, A., & Conroy, K. F. (1996). *Network Management: A Practical Perspective.* Reading: Addison-Wesley.

Lemlouma, T., & Layaida, N. (2003). Encoding Multimedia Presentations for User Preferences and Limited Environments. *ICME Proceedings of the 2003 Inernational Conference on Multimedia and Expo, 1,* IEEE CS Press, USA.

Lexxe Search Engine (2008). Retrieved September 1, 2008, from http://www.lexxe.com

Li, M., & Vitanyi, P. (1997). *An Introduction to Kolmogorov Complexity and Its Applications.* New York: Springer-Verlag., 2nd edition.

Li, M., Chen, X., Li, X., Ma, B., & Vitanyi, P. (2004). The similarity metric. *IEEE Transactions on Information Theory, 50*(12), 3250–3264.

Li, Y., & Wang, D. L. (2006). Singing voice separation from monaural recordings. *International Conference on Music Information Retrieval,* (pp. 176-179). Victoria, BC, Canada.

Li, Y., Zhang, C., & Swan, J. (2000). An Information Filtering Model on the Web and its Application in Job Agent. *Knowledge-Based Systems, 13*(5), 285-296.

Libby, R., Trotman, K. T., & Zimmer, I. (1987). Member Variation, Recognition of Expertise, and Group Performance. *Journal of Applied Psychology, 72*(1), 81-87.

Lin, D. (1993). Principle-based Parsing without Overgeneration. *Proceedings of ACL 93. Columbus, Ohio* (pp. 11-120).

Lin, D. (1994). PRINCIPAR: An Efficient, Broad-coverage, Principle-based Parser. *Proceedings of COLING 94. Kyoto, Japan* (pp. 482-488).

Lin, D. (2001). LaTaT: Language and Text Analysis Tools. *Proceedings of the Human Language Technology Conference.*

Lin, F., Wenyin, L., Chen, Z., Zhang, H., & Long, T. (2001). User Modeling for Efficient Use of Multimedia Files. *In the Proc. of 2nd IEEE Pacific-Rim Conference on Multimedia, LNCS, 2195.* China: Springer-Verlag.

Lipsitz, L. A., & Goldberger, A. L. (1992). Loss of 'complexity' and aging. Potential applications of fractals and chaos theory to senescence. *Journal of the American Medical Association, 267*(13), 1806-1809.

Liu, L. L., & Zhang, D. H.-J. (2006). Automatic mood detection and tracking of music audio signals. *IEEE Transactions on Audio, Speech, and Language Processing, 14* (1), 5-18.

Liu, S.-C., Bi, J., Jia, Z.-Q., Chen, R., Chen, J., & Zhou, M.-M. (2007). Automatic audio classification and speaker identification for video content analyses. *ACIS International Conference on Software Engineering, Artificial Intelligence, Networking, and Parallel/Distributed Computing (SNPD 2007), 2,* pp. 91-96. Beijing, China.

Locatelli, F., Gaspary, L., Melchiors, C., Lohmann, S., & Dillenburg, F. (2004). Spotting Intrusion Scenarios from Firewall Logs Through a Case-Based Reasoning Approach. In: *Utility Computing: Proceedings of 15th IFIP/IEEE International Workshop on Distributed Systems: Operations and Management DSOM 2004 LNCS 3278* (pp. 196-207). Berlin: Springer.

Lopez, L., Jose, F., & Miguel, A. (15 December 2002). Hierarchical social networks and information flow. *Physica A: Statistical Mechanics and its Applications, 316*(1-4), 695-708.

Lu, L., You, H., & Zhang, H.-J. (2001). A new approach to query by humming in music retrieval. *IEEE International Conference on Multimedia and Expo (ICME 2001).* (pp. 595-598). Tokyo, Japan.

Lu, L., Zhang, H.-J., & Jiang, H. (2002). Content analysis for audio classification and segmentation. *IEEE Transactions on Speech and Audio Processing, 10* (7), 504-516.

Lua, E., Pias, M., Sharma, R., & Lim, S. (2005). A Survey and Comparison of Peer-to-Peer Overlay Network Schemes. *IEEE Communications Surveys & Tutorials, 7*(2), 72-93.

Luce, R. D., & Raiffa, H. (1957). *Games and Decisions.* New York: John Wiley & Sons.

Luque, B., & Sole, R. V. (2000). Lyapunov exponents in random Boolean networks. *Physica A, 284*(1-4), 33–45.

Lyons, K., Skeels, C., Starner T., Snoeck, C. M., Wong, B. A., & Ashbrook, D. (2004). Augmenting conversations using dual-purpose speech. *Proceedings of the 17th annual ACM symposium on User Interface Software and Technology* (pp. 237-246). Santa Fe, USA.

Ma, H.-W., & Zeng, A.-P. (2003). Reconstruction of metabolic networks from genome data and analysis of their global structure for various organisms. *Bioinformatics, 19*(2), 270–277.

MacDonald, M. E., Pearlmutter, N., & Seidenberg, M. (1994). The lexical nature of syntactic ambiguity resolution. *Psychological Review, 101,* 678-703.

Madhavapeddy, A., & Ludlam, N. (2005). Ubiquitous Computing needs to catch up with Ubiquitous Media. *In the Proc. of PERVASIVE 2005 Workshop (UbiApp),* Germany.

Mahambre, S. P., Kumar, S. D. M., & Bellur, U. (2007). A Taxonomy of QoS-Aware, Adaptive Event-Dissemination Middleware. *IEEE Internet Computing, 11*(4), 35-44.

Maier, R. (2005). Modelling Knowledge Work for the Design of Knowledge Infrastructures. *Journal of Universal Computer Science, 4,* 11, 429-451.

Makolm, J., & Orthofer, G. (2007). Holistic Approach, Stakeholder Integration and Transorganizational Processes: Success Factors of FinanzOnline. In J. Makolm & G. Orthofer (Eds.), *E-Taxation: State & Perspectives, E-Government in the Field of Taxation: Scientific Basis, Implementation Strategies, Good Practice Examples,* (pp. 389-402). Linz: Trauner Verlag.

Malone, T. W., & Crowston, K. (1994). The interdisciplinary study of coordination. *ACM Computing Surveys, 26*(1),87-118.

Malone, T., Yates, W., & Benjamin, R. (1987). Electronic Markets and Electronic Hierarchies. *Communications of the ACM, 30*(6), 484-497.

Malyankar, R. (2002). Vocabulary development for markup languages – a case study with maritime information. *Proceedings of the 11th International Conference on World Wide Web* (pp. 674-685). New York, New York: ACM.

Mander, R., Salomon, G., & Wong, Y. (1992). A 'Pile' .Metaphor for Supporting Casual Organization of Information. In Proceedings of the SIGCHI conference on human factors in computing systems, (pp. 627-634).

Manjeshwar A., & Agrawal, D. (2001). Teen: a routing protocol for enhanced efficiency in wireless sensor networks. *International Workshop on Parallel and Distributed Computing Issues in Wireless Networks and Mobile Computing in Conjunction with the International Parallel and Distributed Processing Symposium* (IPDPS), San Francisco, CA.

March, J., & Simon, H. (1958). *Organizations*. New York: Wiley.

Marcus, G. F. (1993). Negative evidence in language acquisition. *Cognition, 46*, 53-83.

Martin, C. M., & Kaufman, T. (2007). *Glossary of Terms in New Orientations, a Shared Framework: A Way Forward to Adaptive Primary Health Care Systems Across Canada: A Discussion Monograph*. Commissioned by the Canadian Association of Community Health Centre Associations and the Association of Ontario Health Centers. (in press)

Martinez, M. T., Fouletier, P., Park, K. H., & Favrel, J. (2001). Virtual enterprise-organisation, evolution and control. *International Journal of production economics, 74*, 225-238.

Martin-Flatin, J., Znaty S., & Hubaux, J. (1999). A Survey of Distributed Enterprise Network and Systems Management Paradigms. *Journal of Network and Systems Management, 7*(1), 9-26.

Mary, R. (2007). Collective Team Identification in Temporary Teams. *Proceedings of the 40th Hawaii International Conference on System Sciences.*

Maryland Coalition for Inclusive Education (1999). Collaborative Teams Structures for Success. Retrieved on 11 November http://www.mcie.org/docs/publications/Collaborative%20teams.doc

Maslov, S. & Sneppen, K., & Zaliznyak, A. (2004). Detection of topological patterns in complex networks: correlation profile of the internet. *Physica A, 333*, 529.

Maslov, S., & Sneppen, K. (2002). Specificity and Stability in Topology of Protein Networks. *Science, 296*, 910-913.

Matache, M., & Heidel, J. (2004). A random Boolean network model exhibiting deterministic chaos. *Physical Review E, 69*, 056214.

Matsuura, N., Fujino, G., Okada, K., & Matsushita, Y. (1996). A tele- communication environment to support awareness for informal interaction. In D. Shapiro, M. Tauber & R. Traunmuller (Eds.), *The Design of Computer Supported Cooperative Work and Groupware Systems*. Amesterdam: Elsevier Science B.V.

Matthews, G., Davies D. R., Westerman, S. J., & Stammers, R. B. (2004). *Human*

McBurney, P., & Parsons, S. (2005) *The Knowledge Engineering Review, 20*(3).

McBurney, P., Parsons S., Van Eijk, R., & Amgoud, L. (2002). A dialogue-game protocol for agent purchase negotiations. *Journal of Autonomous Agents and Multi-Agent Systems.*

McCloghrie, K, Perkins, D., & Schönwälder, J. (1999). *Structure of Management Information Version 2 (SMv2), RFC 2578.* IETF.

McGrath, S. (2000). *XML processing with Python.* Prentice Hall.

McGregor, D. (1957, April 9). The Human Side of Enterprise. *Proceedings of the Fifth Anniversary Convocation of the School of Industrial Management.*

McIntyre, R., & Salas, E. (1995). Measuring and managing for team performance: emerging principles from complex environments. In R. Guzzo and E. Salas, (Eds.), *Team effectiveness and decision making in organizations* (pp. 149-203). San Francisco: Jossey-Bass.

McKinney, M. F., Moelants, D., Davies, M. E., & Klapuri, A. (2007). Evaluation of audio beat tracking and music tempo extraction algorithms. *Journal of New Music Research , 36* (1), 1-16.

McNeese, M., Rentsch, J., & Perusich, K. (2000). Modeling, Measuring and Mediating Teamwork: The Use of Fuzzy Cognitive Maps and Team Member Schema Similarity to Enhance BMC3I Decision Making. *IEEE International Conference on Systems, Man and Cybernetics,* (pp. 1081-1086). NY: Institute of Electrical and Electronic Engineers.

McQuade, S. C. (2006). *Understanding and Managing Cybercrime.* Boston, MA, Allyn and Bacon.

Meisel, J. M. (2000). Parameters in Acquisition. In P. Fletcher (Ed.), *The handbook of child language* (pp. 10-35). Oxford: Blackwell.

Melchiors, C., & Tarouco, L. M. R. (2000). Troubleshooting network faults using past experience. In: *Proceedings of 2000 IEEE/IFIP Network Operations and Management Symposium `The Networked Planet: Management Beyond 2000' NOMS 2000* (pp. 549-562). IEEE.

Menasce, D., & Kephart, J. (2007). Autonomic Computing, *IEEE Internet Computing* (pp. 18-21)

Mesaros, A., Virtanen, T., & Klapuri, A. (2007). Singer identification in polyphonic music using vocal separation and pattern recognition methods. *International Conference on Music Information Retrieval,* (pp. 375-378). Vienna, Austria.

Michael B., & Robert A. (2005). Improving Collaboration in Command and Control Environments: Creating and Exchanging Iconic Tags of Key Information. *CCRTS 2005.* Retrieved 6 November from www.dodccrp.org/events/10th_ICCRTS/CD/papers/057.pdf

Michael, B. (Sept. 1997). What is a 'document'? *Journal of the American Society for Information Science, 48*(9), 804-809.

Migiro, S. O and Adigun, M. O. (2005). ICTs, e_commerce and rural development: the case of arts and crafts SMEs in rural KwaZulu-Natal, *Commonwealth Youth and Development, 3(2),* 65-83.

Milo, R., Shen-Orr, S., Itzkovitz, S., Kashtan, N., Chklovskii, D., & Alon, U. (2002) Network Motifs: Simple Building Blocks of Complex Networks. *Science, 298,* 824-827.

Milojicic, D. S., Kalogeraki, V., Lukose, R., Nagaraja, K., Pruyne, J., Richard, B., Rollins, S., & Xu, Z. (2003). *Peer-to-Peer Computing* (Tech. Rep. HPL-2002-57). Palo Alto: HP Laboratories Palo Alto.

MindTools (2008). *Information Gathering.* Retrieved 6 November 2008 from http://www.mindtools.com/pages/article/newLDR_03.htm

Mitchell, R., Day, D., & Hirschman, L. (1995). Fishing for information on the internet. *Proc. IEEE Information Visualisation '95,* (pp. 105-111).

Montgomery, L. A., & Faloutos, C. (2000). *Trends and Patterns of WWW Browsing Behaviour.* Retrieved March 29, 2007, from http://www.andrew.cmu.edu/user/alm3/papers/web%20trends.pdf

Moreira, A., & Amaral, L. (2005). Canalizing Kauffman networks: Non-ergodicity and its effect on their critical behavior. *Physical Review Letters, 94,* 218702.

Moro, A. (2008). *The Boundaries of Babel: The brain and the enigma of impossible languages.* Cambridge, MA: MIT Press.

Mowshowitz, A. (1986). Social dimensions of office automation. *Advances in Computers, 25,* 335-404.

Mukherjea, S., Foley, J., & Hudson, S., (1995), Visualizing complex hypermedia networks through multiple hierarchical views. *Proc. ACM CHI95 Conference: Human Factors in Computing Systems,* (pp. 331-335) + color plate.

Mulders, I. (2002). *Transparent parsing: head-driven processing of verb-final structures.* Doctoral dissertation, Utrecht University, LOT dissertation series.

Myers, B. A. (2005). Using handhelds for wireless remote control of PCs and appliances.

N.Y. Comp., Codes R., & Regs. tit. 11, §§ 420.0-420.24 (2001), entitled "Privacy of Consumer Financial and Health Information."

Nahavandi, A., & Aranda, E. (1994). Restructuring Teams for the Re-engineered Organization. *Academy of Management Executive, 8*(4), 58-68.

Nation, D., Plaisant, C., Marchionini, G., Komlodi, A. (June 12, 1997). Visualizing Websites Using A Hierarchical Table Of Contents Browser: WebToc, *Proceedings of Designing for the Web: Practices and Reflections*, (13 pages). Denver.

Nau, D., Au, T., Ilghami, O., Kuter, U., Murdoek, J., Wu, D., & Yaman F. (2003): *SHOP2: An HTN Planning System. J. Artifical intelligence Research, 20*(12), 379-404.

Ned, F. (2008). *Encyclopedia of E-collaboration.* Published by Idea Group (IGI).

Newman, M. E. J. (2001a). Scientific collaboration networks. I. Network construction and fundamental results. *Physical Review E, 64*, 016131.

Newman, M. E. J. (2006). Modularity and community structure in networks. *Proceedings of the National Academy of Sciences, 103*, 8577-8582,

Newman, M. E. J., & Girvan, M. (2004). Finding and evaluating community structure in networks. *Physical Review E, 69*, 026113.

Newman, M. E. J., Barabasi, A.-L., & Watts, D. J. (2006). *The Structure and Dynamics of Networks: (Princeton Studies in Complexity).* Princeton, NJ. Princeton University Press.

Newman, M.E.J. (2001b). Scientific collaboration networks. II. Shortest paths, weighted networks, and centrality. *Physical Review E, 64*, 016132.

Ng, W., Lam, W., & Cheng, J. (2006). Comparative Analysis of XML Compression Technologies. *World Wide Web, 9*(1), 5-33.

Nguyen, H., & Caelen, J. (2004). Multi-session Management in Spoken Dialogue System. *Advances in Artificial Intelligence*, IBERAMIA 2004, Springer editors. (pp. 266-274).

Nichols, J., Chau, D. H., & Myers, B. A. (2007). Demonstrating the viability of automatically generated user interfaces. *Proceedings of the SIGCHI conference on Human factors in computing systems* (pp. 1283-1292).

Niederee C. J., Stewart A., Mehta B., & Hemmje M. (2004). A multi-dimensional, unified user model for cross-system personalization. *In Proceedings of Advanced Visual Inter-faces International Working Conference (AVI 2004) - Workshop on Environments for Personalized Information Access*, Gallipoli, Italy.

Nonaka, I., & Takeuchi, H. (1995). *The Knowledge-Creating Company: How Japanese Companies Create the Dynamics of Innovation.* Oxford University Press.

Nonaka, I., Toyama, R., & Hirata, T. (2008). Managing Flow: A Process Theory of the Knowledge-Based Firm. Palgrave Macmillan.

Nowak, M. A., Komarova, N. L., & Niyogi, P. (2001). Evolution of Universal Grammar. *Science, 291*, 114–118.

Nowak, M. A., Komarova, N. L., & Niyogi, P. (2002). Computational and evolutionary aspects of language. *Nature, 417*, 611–617.

Nykter, M., Price, N. D., Aldana, M., Ramsey, S., Kauffman, S. A., Hood, L., et al. (2008). Gene expression dynamics in the macrophage exhibit criticality. *Proceedings of the National Academy of Sciences USA, 105*(6), 1897–1900.

Object Management Group. (2004). *Common Object Request Broker Architecture: Core Specification Version 3.0.3.* Needham: OMG.

OCLC (1993). *Electronic Dewey.* Dublin OH, 1 Forrest Press.

Odell, J., Ollason, D., Woodland, P., Young, S., & Jansen, J. (1995). *The HTK book for HTK v2.0.* Cambridge, UK: Cambridge University Press.

Offermann, L. R., & Spiros, R. K. (2001). The Science and Practice of Team Development: Improving the Lin. *Academy of Management Journal, 44*(2), 1-17.

Office of Naval Research (2008). Human Performance: Collaboration and Knowledge Interoperability. Retrieved 5 November 2008 from http://www.onr.navy.mil/sci_tech/34/341/hp_ckm.asp

Openformats.org: Open vs. proprietary formats (2008). Retrieved September 1, 2008, from http://www.open-formats.org/

OPERA Software ASA. (2006). Opera Browser. Retrieved August 23, 2008, from http://www.opera.com/voice.

Orasanu, J., & Salas, E. (1992). Team Decision Making in Complex Environments. In G. Klein, J. Orasanu, & R. Calderwood (Eds.), *Decision Making in Action: Models and Methods.* Norwood, NJ: Ablex Publishing Corp.

O'Reilly, C., Caldwell, D., & Barnett, W. (1989). Work group demography, social integration, and turnover. *Administrative Science Quarterly, 34,* 21-37.

Organization for Economic Cooperation and Development, *OECD Guidelines on the Protection of Privacy and Transborder Flows of Personal Data* (1980)

Ozerov, A., Philippe, P., Gribonyal, R., & Bimbot, F. (2005). One microphone singing voice separation using source-adapted models. *IEEE Workshop on Applications of Signal Processing to Audio and Acoustics,* (pp. 90-93). Mohonk, NY, USA.

Paek, T., & Chickering, D. (2007). Improving command and control speech recognition: Using predictive user models for language modeling. *User Modeling and User-Adapted Interaction Journal, 17*(1), 93-117.

Palazzolo, E., & Clark, M. (2007). Knowledge Interdependence and Information Retrieval Affects on Performance Satisfaction in Transactive Memory Teams. *Paper presented at the annual meeting of the International Communication Association, TBA, San Francisco, CA* Online <APPLICATION/PDF> Retrieved 20 August 2008 from http://www.allacademic.com/meta/p172543_index.html

Palla, G., Derényi, I., Farkas, I., & Vicsek, T. (2005). Uncovering the overlapping community structure of complex networks in nature and society. *Nature, 435,* 814-818.

Panisson, A. (2007). *Aplicação de técnicas de distribuição de carga em sistemas de gerenciamento de redes baseados em P2P.* Unpublished master dissertation, Federal University of Rio Grande do Sul, Rio Grande do Sul, Brazil.

Panisson, A., Melchiors, C., Granville, L. Z., Almeida, M. J. B., & Tarouco, L. M. R. (2006). Designing the Architecture of P2P-Based Network Management Systems. In: P. Bellavista, C. Chen, A. Corradi, M. Daneshmand (Eds.), *Proceedings of the 11th IEEE Symposium on Computers and Communications ISCC 2006* (pp. 69-75). IEEE Computer Society.

Parsons S., Sierra C., & Jennings N. (1998). Agents that reason and negotiate by arguing. *Journal of Logic and Computation, 8*(3), 261-292.

Paul, G., Kam, S., & Gregory, K (May 1998). Tharp. Mars Pathfinder mission Internet-based operations using WITS. *In Proceedings IEEE International Conference on Robotics and Automation,* Leuven, Belgium (pp. 284-291).

Paulus, J., & Klapuri, A. (2008). Acoustic Features for Music Piece Structure Analysis. *11th Conference on Digital Audio Effects.* Espoo, Finland.

Peeters, G. (2004). *A large set of audio features for sound description (similarity and classification) in the CUIDADO project.* Paris, France: CUIDADO I.S.T. Project report.

Pereira, F., & Burnett, I. (2003). Universal Multimedia Experience for Tomorrow. *IEEE Signal Processing Magazine, 20*(2), 2003.

Performance, Cognition, Stress and individual differences. NY: Psychology Press.

perspective. Sheffield: University of Sheffield Department of Information Studies.

Pfleeger, C. P., & Pfleeger, S. L. (2007). *Security in Computing.* 4th Ed., Upper Saddle River, New Jersey, Pearson Education, Inc.

Phillips, C. (1996). *Order and structure.* Doctoral dissertation, MIT.

Pietquin, O. (2004). *A Framework for Unsupervised Learning of Dialogue Strategies*. Doctoral dissertation, Presses Universitaires de Louvain, SIMILAR Collection, ISBN 2-930344-63-6.

Pietro, A. G., & Stadler, R. (2007). A-GAP: An Adaptative Protocol for Continuous Network Monitoring with Accuracy Objectives. *IEEE Transactions on Network. and Service. Management.*, *4*(1), 2-12.

Pinker, S. (1994). *The Language Instinct*. London: Penguin Books.

Pinker, S., & Prince, A. (1988). On language and connectionism: Analysis of a Parallel Distributed Processing model of language acquisition. *Cognition, 28*, 73-193.

Piolle, G., Demazeau, Y., & Caelen, J. (2006). Privacy Management in User-Centred Multi-agent Systems. *In Engineering Societies in the Agent World (ESAW 2006)*, (pp. 354-367). Dublin, Ireland.

Plagemann, T., Goebel, V., & Vorsen, P. H. (1999). Operating System support for Multimedia Systems, *Computer Communication Journal*, Elsevier Science, Special Issue on IDMS'98.

Podani, J., Oltvai, Z. N., Jeong, H., Tombor, B., Barabási, A.-L., & Szathmáry, E. (2001). Comparable system-level organization of archaea and eukaryotes. *Nature Genetics, 29*(1)5, 4–56.

Podolny, J., & Baron, J. (1997). Resources and relationships. *American Sociological Review, 62*(5), 673-693.

Polanski P. (2005). *Common Practices in the Electronic Commerce and Their Legal Significance*. 18th Bled e Conference eIntegration in Action Bled, Slovenia, June 6 - 8, 2005 (available online).

Popick, P. R., & Sheard, S. A. (1996). *Ten Lessons Learned from Implementing Integrated Product Teams*. Retrieved November 9, 2001 from http://www.stsc.hill. af.mil/crosstalk/frames.asp?uri=1996/07/tenlesso.asp.

Preece, J. (2000). *Online Communities - Designing Usability, Supporting Sociability*. Chichester: Wiley.

Presuhn, R., Case, J., McCloghrie, K., Rose, M., & Waldbusser, S. (2002). *Version 2 of the Protocol Operations for the Simple Network Management Protocol (SNMP), RFC 3416, STD 062*. IETF.

Prinz, W., Rodden, T., Syri, A., & Trevor, J. (1996). Cooperative work settings with active workspaces. In D. Shapiro, M. Tauber, & R. Traunmuller (Eds.), *The Design of Computer Supported Cooperative Work and Groupware System*. Amsterdam, The Netherlands: Elsevier Science B. V.

Pritchett, B. (1992). *Grammatical competence and parsing preference*. Cambridge, MA: MIT Press.

Privacy Protection Act of 1980, 42 USC §2000aa (U.S.)

Pugin, C., & Ingold, R. (2007). Combination of transformation and schema languages described by a complete formal semantics. In P. King & S. Simske (Ed.), *Proceedings of the 2007 ACM Symposium on Document Engineering Conference* (pp. 222-224). New York, New York: ACM.

Pylyshyn, Z. (Ed.). (1986). *The robot's dilemma: the frame problem in artificial intelligence*. Norwood: Ablex.

Qiao B., & Zhu J. (1999). *Agent-Based Intelligent Manufacturing System for the 21st Century*. From www. shaping-thefuture.de/pdf_www/152_paper.pdf.

Qiuming, Z., Stuart, L., & Tomas, N. (July 2007). Hierarchical Collective Agent Network (HCAN) for efficient fusion and management of multiple networked sensors. *Information Fusion* 8(3), 266-280.

Rahwan I., Sonenberg L., & Dignum F. (2004). On interest-based negotiation. *Advances in Agent Communication, vol. 2922 of LNAI*, (pp. 383-401). Springer Verlag, Germany.

Rahwan, I. (2004). *Interest-based Negotiation in Multi-Agent Systems*. Unpublished doctoral dissertation, Department of Information Systems, University of Melbourne, Melbourne, Australia.

Rahwan, I., Pasquier, P., Sonenberg, L., & Dignum, F. (2007). *On the Benefits of Exploiting Underlying Goals in Argument-based Negotiation*. Paper presented In:

Proceedings of 22nd Conference on Artificial Intelligence (AAAI). AAAI Press, California, USA.

Rajeev R., Snehasis M., Michael B., & Nila P. (9-12 September 1997). D-SIFTER: A Collaborative Information Classifier. *International Conference on Information, Communications and Signal Processing (ICICS '97)* Singapore.

Ramchurn S., Jennings N. R., & Sierra C. (2003). *Persuasive negotiation for autonomous agents: a rhetorical approach.* Paper presented in IJCAI Workshop on Computational Models of Natural Argument, pp. 9-17. AAAI Press.

Rämö, P., Kesseli, J., & Yli-Harja, O. (2005). Stability of functions in gene regulatory networks. *Chaos, 15,* 034101.

Rämö, P., Kesseli, J., & Yli-Harja, O. (2006). Perturbation avalanches and criticality in gene regulatory networks. *Journal of Theoretical Biology, 242,* 164–170.

Ramshaw, L. A., & Marcus, M. P. (1995). Text chunking using transformation-based learning. In *Proceedings of the Third Annual Workshop on Very Large Corpora* (pp. 82–94).

Raphael, K., Gudula, R., & Michael, S. (2007). A Model for Document Management in e-Government Systems Based on Hierarchical Process Folders. *Electronic Journal of e-Government, 5*(2), 191-204.

Rath, A. (2007). A Low-Level Based Task And Process Support Approach for Knowledge-Intensive Business Environments. *Proceedings of the 5th International Conference on Enterprise Information System Doctoral Consortium DCEIS 2007* (pp. 35-42), Madeira, Portugal

Rath, A., Kröll M., Lindstaedt, S., & Granitzer, M. (2007). Low-Level Event Relationship Discovery for Knowledge Work Support, In N. Gronau (Ed.), *Proc. of the 4th Conference on Professional Knowledge Management* (pp. 227-234), Potsdam: GITO-Verlag.

Rath, A., Kröll, M., Andrews, K., Lindstaedt, S., Granitzer, M., & Tochtermann, K. (2006). Synergizing

Standard and Ad-Hoc Processes. *Proceedings of the 6th International Conference on Practical Aspects of Knowledge Management* (pp. 267-278). Heidelberg: Springer Berlin.

Raux, A., Langner, B., Black, A., & Eskenazi, M. (2003). *LET'S GO: Improving Spoken Dialog Systems for the Elderly and Non-natives, Eurospeech 2003* (pp. 753-756). Geneva, Switzerland.

Ravasio, P., Schar, S., & Krueger, H. (2004). In Pursuit of Desktop Evolution: User Problems and Practices with Modern Desktop Systems. *ACM Transactions on Computer-Human Interaction, 11*(2), 156-180.

Ray, R., Chiang, C.-C., & Melescue, J. (2005). Text extraction on Windows-based documents. *Proceedings of the IEEE Eighteenth International Conference on Systems Engineering* (pp. 205-210). Los Alamitos, California: IEEE.

Reddy, M. C., & Jansen, B. J. (2008). A Model for Understanding Collaborative Information Behaviour in Context: A Study of Two Healthcare Teams. *Information Processing and Management, 44,* 256-273.

Redwood Center for Theoretical Neuroscience (2007). *Hierarchical Organization, feedback and generative models.* Retrieved July 18, 2008, from http://redwwod. berkely.edu/wiki/Mission_Research.

Reinhart, T. (2006). *Interface Strategies: Optimal and Costly Computations.* Cambridge, MA: MIT Press.

Reiss, D. J., Baliga, N. S., & Bonneau, R. (2006). Integrated biclustering of heterogeneous genome-wide datasets for the inference of global regulatory networks. *BMC Bioinformatics, 7,* 280.

Re'mi, C. (2002). Treemaps for Search-Tree Visualization. *The seventh Computer Olympiad Computer-Games Workshop Proceedings* Uiterwijk, J.W.h.M., Maastrich.

Renear, A., Dubin, D., Sperberg-McQueen, C. M., & Huitfeldt, C. (2002). In E. Munson, R. Furuta, & J. Maletic (Ed.), *Proceedings of the 2002 ACM Symposium on*

Document Engineering Conference (pp. 119-126). New York, New York: ACM.

Ribeiro, A. S., Este, R. A., Lloyd-Price, J., & Kauffman, S. A. (2006). Measuring information propagation and retention in Boolean networks and its implications to a model of human organizations. *WSEAS Trans. on Systems, 12*(5), 2935.

Ribeiro, A. S., Kauffman, S. A., Lloyd-Price, J., Samuelsson, B., & Socolar, J. (2008). Mutual information in Random Boolean models of regulatory networks. *Physical Review E, 77*(1), 011901.

Ribeiro, A. S., Zhu, R., & Kauffman, S. A. (2006). A General Model for Gene Regulatory Networks with Stochastic Dynamics. *Journal of Computational Biology, 13*(9), 1630-1639.

Rissanen, J., & Langdon, G.G. (1979). Arithmetic coding. *IBM Journal of Research and Development, 23*, 149–162.

Riva, O. (2004). *A Conceptual Model for Structuring Context-Aware Applications*. Paper presented at the Forth Berkeley-Helsinki student workshop on telecommunication Software architectures. University of Berkeley, USA.

Riva, O., & Flora, C. (2006). Controy: A Smart Phone Middleware Supporting Multiple Context Provisioning Strategies; *In proceedings of the 2nd International Workshop on Services and Infrastructure for the Ubiquitous and Mobile Internet (SIUMI'06), at the 26th International Conference on Distributed Computing Systems (ICDCS'06)* (pp. 68-74), Lisbon, Portugal. Retrieved June 29, 2006, from www.cs.helsinki.fi/u/riva/publications/riva siumi06 paper.pdf

Robert, A. (2007). *Implicit & Explicit communication*. Retrieved 6 November 2008 from http://ezinearticles.com/?Implicit-and-Explicit-Communication&id=464406

Robert, B. (1994). *Navigating and Searching in Hierarchical Digital Library Catalogs Information Filtering*. Retrieved 5 November 2008 from *www.csdl.tamu.edu/DL94/paper/allen.html*

Robin, L., & Theodosios, P. (January 1997). Fuzzy Decision Tree Algorithms. *IEEE Transaction on Systems, Man, & Cybernetics, SMC-7*(1), 28-35.

Roderick, I., Tom, P., Peter, N., Marius, H., & Adrie, CM. (Summer 2002). Multiparty Negotiation Support: The Role of Visualization's Influence on the Development of Shared Mental Models. *Journal of Management Information Systems, 19*(1), 129-150.

Roger R., Gareth F., & David S. (2006). *Data Lifecycles: Managing Data for Strategic Advantage*. Wiley Publishing

Rose, M., & McCloghrie, K. (1990). *Structure and Identification of Management Information for TCP/IP-based internets, RFC 1155, STD 16*. IETF.

Rose, M., & McCloghrie, K. (1991). *Concise MIB Definitions, RFC 1212, STD 16*. IETF,

Rosvall, M., & Bergstrom, C. T. (2007). An information-theoretic framework for resolving community structure in complex networks. *Proceedings of the National Academy of Sciences, 104*, 7327-7331.

Rothschild-Whitt, J. (1979). The collectivist organization. *American Sociological Review, 44*(4), 509-527.

Russo, J. E., & Schoemaker, P. J. (1990). Decision *Traps: the ten barriers to brilliant decision-making and how to overcome them*. New York: Simon & Schuster, Fireside.

Ryynänen, M., & Klapuri, A. (2008). Automatic transcription of melody, bass line, and chords in polyphonic music. *Computer Music Journal, 32* (3).

Ryynänen, M., & Klapuri, A. (2008). Query by humming of MIDI and audio using locality sensitive hashing. *IEEE International Conference on Acoustics, Speech, and Signal Processing (ICASSP 2008)*, (pp. 2249-2252). Las Vegas, Nevada, USA.

Sadeh-Leicht, O. (2007). *The Psychological Reality of Grammar: The Theta Principle in Parsing Performance*. Doctoral dissertation, Utrecht University, LOT dissertation series.

Sadri F., Toni F., & Torroni P. (2001). Dialogue for negotiation: agent varieties and dialogue sequences. In John-Jules Meyer & Milind Tambe, (Ed.), *Intelligent Agent Series VIII: Proceedings of the 8th International Workshop on Agent Theories, Architectures, and Languages.*

Saffran, J. R., Aslin, R. N., & Newport, E. L. (1996). Statistical learning by 8-month old infants. *Science, 274,* 1926-1928.

Safoutin, M. J., & Thurston, D. L. (1993). A Communications-based Technique for Interdisciplinary Design Team Management. *IEEE Transactions on Engineering Management, 40*(4), 360-372.

Samuelsson, B., & Socolar, J. (2006). Exhaustive percolation on random networks. *Physical Review E, 74,* 036113.

Sanger, L. (2006). The Early History of Nupedia and Wikipedia: A Memoir. In C. DiBona, D. Cooper, & M. Stone (Eds.), *Open Source 2.0.* (pp. 307–338). Sebastopol, CA: O'Reilly.

Sattler, L., & Sohoni, V. (1999). Participative Management: An Empirical Study of the Semiconductor Manufacturing Industry. *IEEE Transactions on Engineering Management, 46*(4), 387-396.

Schmidt, A., Adoo K. A., Takaluoma, A., Tuomela, U., Laerhoven, K. V., & Velde, W. V. (1999). Advanced Interaction in Context. *Lecture Notes in Computer Science.* Retrieved April 24, 2006, from http://citeseer.ist.psu.edu/cache/papers/cs/12585/http:zSzzSzwww.teco.uni-karlsruhe.dezSz~albrechtzSzpublicationzSzhuc99zSzadvanced_interaction_context.pdf/schmidt99advanced.pdf.

Schönwälder, J., Quittek, J., & Kappler, C. (2000). Building Distributed Management Applications with the IETF Script MIB. *IEEE Journal on Selected Areas in Communications, 18*(5), 702-714.

Schrage, M. (1995). No More Teams! *Mastering the Dynamics of Creative collaboration,* Doubleday, as cited in P.A. Dargan.

Schuler, D. (1994) Social computing, *Communications of the ACM, 37*(1), 28–29.

Schweiger, D. M., William, W. R., & Ragan, J. W. (1986). Group Approaches for Improving Strategic Decision Making: a comparative analysis of dialectical inquiry, devil's advocacy, and consensus. *Academy of Management Journal, 29*(1), 51-71.

Scime, A. (2004). *Web Mining: Applications and Techniques.* Idea Group Publishing.

Scott, A. Mark, B., Xiao Qi, C., & Geoffrey, J. (2008). Human-Robot Collaboration: A Literature Review and Augmented Reality Approach in Design. *International Journal of Advanced Robotic Systems, 5*(1), 1-18.

SEARCC, South East Asia Regional Computer Confederation Code of Ethics, http://courses.cs.vt.edu/~cs3604/lib/WorldCodes/SEARCC.Code.html, last visited August 24, 2008

Search Engine History (2008). Retrieved September 1, 2008, from http://www.searchenginehistory.com/

Selis, P., Ramasastry, A., & Smith, K. S. (2002). Office of the Attorney General, State of Washington, USA, *Cameron, Consumer Privacy and Data Protection: Protecting Personal Information Through Commercial Best Practices.* http://www.atg.wa.gov/uploadedFiles/Home/News/Press_Releases/2002/PrivacyPolicy1.doc last visited October 11, 2008

Selouani, S. A., Tang-Hô, L., Benahmed, Y., & O'Shaughnessy, D. (2008). Speech-enabled tools for augmented Interaction in e-learning applications. *Special issue of International Journal of Distance Education Technologies, 6*(2), 1-20. IGI publishing.

Serra, R., Villani, M., & Semeria, A. (2004). Genetic networks models and statistical properties of gene extression data in knock-out experiments. *Journal of Theoretical Biology, 227,* 149–157.

Shah, S. A. A, Ul Asar, A., & Shah, S. W. (2007). Interactive Voice Response with Pattern Recognition Based on Artificial Neural Network Approach. *International conference on Emerging Technologies,* (pp. 249-252). IEEE.

Shannon, C.E. (1948). A mathematical theory of communication. *Bell System Technical Journal,* 27:379–423.

Shapiro, M. (1977). The choice of reference points in best-match file searching. *Communications of the ACM, 20* (5), 339-343.

Shardanand, U., & Maes, P. (1995). Social information filtering: algorithms for automating "word to mouth". *SIGCHI Conference on Human Factors in Computing Systems*, (pp. 210-217). Dencer, Colorado, USA.

Shaughnessy, A. F., Slawson, D. C., & Becker, L. (1998). Clinical jazz: harmonizing clinical experience and evidence-based medicine. *Journal of Family Practice, 47*(6), 425-428.

Shmulevich, I., & Kauffman, S.A. (2004). Activities and sensitivities in Boolean network models. *Physical Review Letters, 93*(4), 048701(1–4).

Shmulevich, I., Kauffman, S. A., & Aldana, M. (2005). Eukaryotic cells are dynamically ordered or critical but not chaotic. *Proceedings of the National Academy of Sciences of the USA, 102*(38), 13439–13444.

Shouman, M., Abou-Ali, G., & Mostafa, A. (2008). A Hybrid Model for Knowledge Acquisition Using Hierarchical Cluster Analysis. *International Arab* Conference of e-Technology.

Shrideep, P., Geoffrey, F., & Harshawardhan, G. (to appear). On the Secure Creation, Organization and Discovery of topics in Distributed Publish/Subscribe Systems. *International Journal of High Performance Computing and Networking (IJHPCN)*. Special issue of extended versions of the six best papers at the ACM/IEEE GRID Workshop in Seattle, W.A.

Sicilia, M. A., & Garcia, E. (2004). On the Use of Bipolar Scales in Preference-Based Recommender Systems. *In Proceedings 5th International Conference on Electronic Commerce and Web Technologies (EC-Web 2004)* (pp. 268-276), Zaragoza, Spain, Retrieved June 12, 2006, from http://citeseer.ist.psu.edu/cache/papers/cs2/93/http: zSzzSzwww.cc.uah.eszSzmsiciliazSzpaperszSzSicilia_ECWEB_2004.pdf/sicilia04use.pdf.

Sidi-Yacoub, M., Selouani, S. A., O'Shaughnessy, D. (2008). Improving Dysarthric Speech Intelligibility through Re-synthesized and Grafted Units. *21ˢᵗ IEEE-Canadian Conference on Electrical and Computer Engineering* (pp. 1523-1526).

Sietz, N. (2004). Transborder Search: A New Perspective on Law Enforcement? *9 Int'l J. Comm. L. & Pol'y 2* (Fall 2004)

Silberschatz, A., Korth, H., & Sudarshan, S. (2006) . *Database System Concepts*, 5ᵗ edition, Boston: McGraw Hill.

Simnett, R. (1996). The Effect of Information Selection, Information Processing and Task Complexity on Predictive Accuracy of Auditors. *Accounting, Organizations and Society. 21*(7/8), 699-719.

Simoff, S., & Maher, M. (1998). Ontology-based multi media data mining for design information retrieval. *In Proceedings of Computing in Civil Engineering* ASCE, Reston, VA, (pp. 212-223).

Sing, G. O., Wong, K. W., Fung, C. C., & Depickere, A. (2006). Towards a more natural and intelligent interface with embodied conversation agent. *Proceedings of international conference on Game research and development* (pp. 177-183), Perth, Australia.

Singh, A., Castro, M., Druschel, P., & Rowstron, A. (2004). Defending against eclipse attacks on overlay networks. In: *Proceedings of the 11th Workshop on ACM SIGOPS European Workshop* (pp. 21-26). New York: ACM.

Slade, R. (1999). Review: Top Secret Intranet. http://www.landfield.com/isn/mail-archive/1999/Feb/0074.html, last visited August 24, 2008

Slaney, M. (2007). Similarity based on rating data. *International Conference on Music Information Retrieval*, (pp. 479-484). Vienna, Austria.

Software Engineering Code of Ethics and Professional Practice, Version 5.2, adopted 1999 by the IEEE Computer Society and the ACM, see http://www.open.hr/etika/en_code.pdf, last visited August 24, 2008

Soh, L., & Li, X. (2004). *Adaptive, Confidence-based Mult-iagent Negotiation Strategy*. Paper presented in: AAMAS'04, New York, USA.

Sokol, L. (2002). Creating knowledge from heterogeneous data stove pipes. *Proceedings of the Fifth International Conference on Information Fusion 2*, 1162 - 1167

Solomonoff, R. (1964). A formal theory of inductive inference. *Information and Control, 7*, 1–22.

Sommer A. K. (2005). Israeli research introduces the 'Maestro' - voice-only Internet system for drivers. Retrieved August 23, 2008 from:

Song, J., Bae, S.-Y., & Yoon, K. (2002). Query by humming: matching humming query to polyphonic audio. *IEEE International Conference on Multimedia and Expo (ICME 2002)*, (pp. 329- 332). Seoul, South Korea.

Sosa, M. E., et al. (2002). Factors That Influence Technical Communication in Distributed Product Development: An Empirical Study in the Telecommunications Industry. *IEEE Transactions on Engineering Management, 49*(1), 45-58.

Soules, C., & Ganger, G. (2003). Why Can't I Find My Files? New Methods for Automating Attribute Assignment. *In Proceedings of the 9th workshop on hot topics in operating systems*, (pp.115-120).

Speech Group. (2006). The HTK Book (Version 3.4), Cambridge University. Retrieved August 23, 2008, from http://htk.eng.cam.ac.uk/docs/docs.shtml.

Sphinx Project. (2008). *The CMU Sphinx Group Open Source Speech Recognition Engines*. Retrieved August 23, 2008 from (http://cmusphinx.sourceforge.net/).

Spink, A. (1997). Study of Interactive Feedback during Mediated Information   Retrieval. *Journal of the American Society for information science, 48*(5), 382-394.

Stasser, G., & Titus, W. (1985). Pooling of Unshared Information in Group Decision Making: Biased Information Sampling During Discussion. *Journal of Personality and Social Psychology, 48*(6), 1467-1478.

State, R., & Festor, O. (2003). A management platform over a peer to peer service infrastructure. In: *Proceedings*

of 10th International Conference on Telecommunications ICT 2003 (pp. 124-131). IEEE.

Steiger, O., Ebrahimi, T., & Sanjuan, D. M. (2003). MPEG-based Personalized Content Delivery. *ICIP proceedings of the 2003 International Conference on Image Processing*. Spain: IEEE CS Press.

Stelluto, G. C. (2002). Continuous Learning - Get the Jump on Getting a Job. *The Institute, 26*(4), 1.

Stevens, J. (1989). *United States Department Of Justice Et Al. V. Reporters Committee For Freedom Of The Press*. 489 U.S. 749

Stevens, J. (1997). *Reno v. ACLU* 521 U.S. 844

Stewart, W. F., Shah N. R., & Selna M. J. (2007). Bridging the inferential gap: The electronic health record and clinical evidence. *Health Affairs, 26*(2), w181-w191.

Strauss, A., & Corbin, J. (1998). *Basics of Qualitative Research. Techniques and Procedures for Developing Grounded Theory*. California, USA: Sage Publications.

Sturmberg, J. P. (2007). *The foundations of primary care*. Oxford: Radcliffe Publishing

Subramanian, L., & Katz, R. (2000). An architecture for building self-configurable systems. *In IEEE/ACM Workshop on Mobile Ad Hoc Networking and Computing (MobiHoc)*, Boston, MA.

Sun Microsystems. (2006). *Java Management Extensions (JMX) Specification version 1.4*. Santa Clara, CA: Sun Microsystems.

Surowiecki, J. (2004). *The wisdom of crowds*. New York: Random House

Suzuki, Y., Matsumoto, N., & Sai, K. (29-30 January 2004). Collaborative visualization for supporting joint researches. *In ITBL project Creating, Connecting and Collaborating through Computing*, (187).

Talja, S. (2002). Information Sharing in Academic Communities: Types and Levels of Collaboration in Information Seeking and Use. *New Review of Information Behaviour Research. 3(3)*, 143-160.

Tan, J. (Ed.). (2005). *E-health care information systems*. Jossey-Bass: Wiley Imprint

Tang, X., & Chanson S. (2004). Minimal cost Replication of Dynamic Web Contents under Fault Update Delivery. *IEEE Transactions on Parallel and Distributed Systems, 15*(5), 431-439.

Tavani, H. T. (2007). *Ethics & Technology: Ethical Issues in an Age of Information and Communication Technology*. Hoboken, New Jersey: John Wiley & Sons, Inc.

Taylor, A., & Farrell, S. (1992). Information Management in Context. *Aslib Proceedings, 44*(9), 319-322.

The Open Directory Project (2008). Retrieved September 1, 2008, from http://www.dmoz.org

Tiehua, Z., Gruver, W., & Smith, M. (1999). Team scheduling by genetic search. *Proceedings of the Second International Conference on Intelligent Processing and Manufacturing of Materials (IPMM apos, 99), 2*, 839 – 844.

Tochtermann, K., Reisinger, D., Granitzer, M., & Lindstaedt, S. (2006). Integrating Ad Hoc Processes and Standard Processes in Public Administrations. *Knowledge transfer across Europe, 4th Eastern European eGov Days and 5th eGov Days, 203*. Vienna: OCG Serie.

Toivonen, S. (2004). Hybrid service provision model for mobile users: Prospects for the DYNAMOS project. *In Proceedings of the 11ᵗʰ Finnish Artificial Intelligence Conference (STeP 2004) Volume 2* (pp. 183-192), Vantaa, Finland, Retrieved March 29, 2007, from http://virtual.vtt.fi/virtual/proj2 /dynamos/pubs/toivonendynamos.pdf.

Tokuda, K., Kobayashi, T., Masuko, T., & Imai, S. (1994). Mel-generalized cepstral analysis - a unified approach to speech spectral estimation. *International Conference on Spoken Language Processing, 3*, pp. 1043-1046.

Tollervey, N. H. (2006). Program# - An AIML Chatterbot in C#. Retrieved August 23, 2008 from http://ntoll.org/article/project-an-aiml-chatterbot-in-c. Northamptonshire, United Kingdom.

Tollmar, K., Sandor, O., & Schemer, A. (November 1996). Supporting social awareness Work: Design and experience. *In Proceedings of CSCW'96* (pp. 298-307). Cambridge MA: ACM Press.

Tomasello, M. (2003). *Constructing a language: A Usage-Based Theory of Language Acquisition*. Cambridge, MA: Harvard University Press.

Torres, D., Turnbull, D., Barrington, L., & Lanckriet, G. (2007). Identifying words that are musically meaningful. *International Conference on Music Information Retrieval*, (pp. 405-410). Vienna, Austria.

Traversat, B., Arora, A., Abdelaziz, M., Duigou, M., Haiwwod, C., Hugly, J., Pouyoul, E., & Yeager, B. (2003). *Project JXTA 2.0 Super-Peer Virtual Network*. Sun Microsystems.

Trueswell, J. C., & Tanenhaus, M. (1994). Towards a lexicalist framework for constraint based syntactic ambiguity resolution. In C. Clifton, L. Frazier & K. Rayner (Eds.), *Perspectives on sentence processing*. Hillsdale, NJ: Lawrence Erlbaum.

Tseng, V. S. M., & Lin, K. W. C (2005). Mining sequential mobile access patterns efficiently in mobile Web systems. *In Proceedings of the 19ᵗʰ International Conference on Advanced Information Networking and Applications (AINA 2005) Volume 2* (pp 762-767). Taipei, Taiwan.

Tsui, A., Egan, T., & O'Reilly, C. (1992). Being different: Relational demography and organizational attachment. *Administrative Science Quraterly, 37*, 549-579.

Tsung-Yi, C. (2008). Knowledge sharing in virtual enterprises via an ontology-based access control approach. *Computer in industry, 59*, 502-519.

Tuomela, R. (2000). Cooperation. A Philosophical Study. *Philosophical Studies Series, 82*. Dordrecht: Springer.

Tyson, R., & Scott, E. (May 1990). *Viewing large graphs*. (Tech. Rep. No. 90). University of Arizona.

Tzanetakis, G., & Cook, P. (2002). Musical genre classification of audio signals. *IEEE Transactions on Speech and Audio Processing , 10* (5), 293-302.

Udupa, D. K. (1996). *Network Management Systems Essentials*. New York: Mc-Graw-Hill.

Vainikka, A. (1989). *Deriving Syntactic Representations in Finnish*. Doctoral dissertation, University of Massachusetts, Amherst.

Vakkari, P. (1999). Task Complexity, Problem Structure and Information Action: Integrating Studies of Information Seeking and Retrieval. *Information Processing and Management, 35*, 819-837.

Valian, V. (1990). Logical and psychological constraints on the acquisition of syntax. In L. Frazier & J. De Villiers (Eds.), *Language Processing and Language Acquisition* (pp. 119-145). Dordrecht: Kluwer Academic Publishers.

Valiant, L. G. (1984). A theory of learnable. *Communications of the ACM, 27*, 1134-1142.

Valverde, S., & Sole, R. V. (2002). Self-organized critical traffic in parallel computer networks. *Physica A, 312*, 636–648.

Vance, M., & William, K. (June 1997). Collaborative Virtual Prototyping. *Joint Avionics Weapon Software Support and Simulation Conference Proceedings*.

Vapnik, V. (1995). *The Nature of Statistical Learning Theory*. Berlin: Springer.

Vilkuna, M. (1989). *Free word order in Finnish. Its syntax and discourse functions*. Helsinki: SKS.

Vilkuna, M. (2000). *Suomen lauseopin perusteet*. Helsinki: Edita.

Virtanen, T., & Helén, M. (2007). Probabilistic model based similarity measures for audio query-by-example. *IEEE Workshop on Applications of Signal Processing to Audio and Acoustics (WASPAA 2007)*, (pp. 82-85). New Paltz, New York, USA.

Von Neumann, J., & Morgenstern, O. (1944). The Theory of Games and Economic Behaviour. *Princeton University Press*.

Vuorinen, O., Lahti, T., Mäkelä, S.-M., & Peltola, J. (2008). Light weight mobile device targeted speaker clustering algorithm. *IEEE Signal Processing Society, 2008 International Workshop on Multimedia Signal Processing*. Cairns, Queensland, Australia.

Waldbusser, S. (1997). *Remote Network Monitoring Management Information Base Version 2 using SMIv2, RFC 2021*.

Waldbusser, S. (2000). *Remote Network Monitoring Management Information Base, RFC 2819*.

Walsh, J., & Maloney, N. (2007). Collaboration Structure, Communication Media and Problems in Scientific Work Teams. *Journal of Computer Mediated Communication, 12*(2), 19.

Wang, Y., Kan, M.-Y., New, T. L., Shenoy, A., & Yin, J. (2004). LyricAlly: automatic synchronization of acoustic musical signals and textual lyrics. *12th Annual ACM International Conference on Multimedia*, (pp. 212-219). New York, NY, USA.

Wang, Y., Li, H., & Chen, C. W. (2004). A Novel Video Coding Scheme for Mobile Devices, *In Proc. of 3rd International Conference on Mobile and Ubiquitous Multimedia (MUM '04), 83*. USA: ACM Press.

Wanger, C. (2005). Breaking the Knowledge Acquisition Bottleneck through Conversational Knowledge Management. *Information Resources Management Journal, 19*(1), 70–83.

Want, R., Pering, T., Danneels, G., Kumar, M., Sundar, M., & Light, J. (2002). The Personal Server: Changing the Way We Think about Ubiquitous Computing. *In Proc. of 4th International Conference on Ubiquitous Computing (UbiComp'02), 2498*. Springer-Verlag LNCS.

Warner, N., Letsky, M., & Cowen, M. (November 2004). *Structural Model of Team Collaboration, Office of Naval Research, Human Systems Department*, Arlington, VA. Retrieved on 5 November 2006 from *www.au.af.mil/au/awc/awcgate/navy/model_of_team_collab.doc*

Warner, N., Letsky, M., & Cowen, M. (September 2005). *Cognitive model of team collaboration: macro-cognitive focus*. Paper presented at the 49th Annual Meeting of the Human Factors and Ergonomics Society. Orlando.

Warner, N., Wroblewski, W., & Elizabeth, M. (January 2004). *Achieving Collaborative Knowledge in Asynchronous Collaboration. Collaboration and knowledge*

Management Workshop Proceedings. Office of Naval Research, Human Systems Department, Arlington, VA.

Warwick, C., Colin, W., & Julie, W. (18-19 June 2001). Archiving the Web: The Pandora Archive at the National Library Of Australia. *Preserving the Present for the Future Web Archiving Conference*. Copenhagen.

Watson, W., Michaelsen, L. K., & Sharp, W. (1991). Member Competence, Group Interaction, and Group Decision-making: A Longitudinal Study. *Journal of Applied Psychology, 76*(6), 803-809.

Watts, D. J., & Strogatz, S. H. (1998). Collective dynamics of "small-world" networks. *Nature, 393*, 440.

Weaver, R., & Farrell, J. (1997). *Managers as facilitators*. San Francisco: Barrett-Koehler.

Wegner, D. (1987). Transactive memory: A contemporary analysis of the group mind. In B. Mullen & G. R. Goethals (Eds.), *Theories of group behavior* (pp. 185-208). New York: Springer – Verlag,.

Wegner, D. (1995). A computer network model of human transactive memory. *Social Cognition, 13*, 319-339.

Weinberg, A. (1999). A Minimalist Theory of Human Sentence Processing. In S. D. Epstein & N. Hornstein (Eds.), *Working Minimalism* (pp. 283-316). Cambridge, MA: MIT Press.

Weiss, S. M., Indurkhya, N., Zhang, T., & Damerau, F. J. (2005). *Text mining: predictive methods for analyzing unstructured information*. New York, New York: Springer.

Wenger, E. (1998). *Communities of Practice. Learning, Meaning, and Identity*. Cambridge: Cambridge.

Wensheng, Z., Vellaikal, A., & Son D. (2001). Cooperative content analysis agents for online multimedia indexing and filtering. *The Proceedings of the Third International Symposium on Cooperative Database Systems for Advanced Applications, CODAS 2001*, (pp. 118 – 122).

Wenyin, L., Chen, Z., Lin, F., Yang, R., Li, M., & Zhang, H. (2001). Ubiquitous Media Agents for Managing Personal Multimedia Files. *In the Proc. of 9ᵗʰ ACM International Conference on Multimedia*. Canada: ACM DL.

Wexler, K., & Culicover, P. (1980). *Formal Principles of Language Acquisition*. Cambridge, MA: MIT Press.

Whittaker, S., & Sidner, C. (1996). Email Overload: Exploring Personal Information Management of Email. *In Proceedings of the SIGCHI Conference on Human Factors in Computing Systems*, (pp. 276-283).

William, K. (1997). Put a Virtual Prototype on Your Desktop. *Program Manager Magazine*, (pp. 94-99).

William, K. (2003). *Distributed Collaborative Environments for Decision Support*. Retrieved 5 July 2008, from http://www.modelingandsimulation.org/text/McQuay.html

Williamson, O. (1985). *The Economic Implications of Capitalism: Firms, Markets, and Relational Contracting*. New York: Free Press.

Wilson, T. D. (1981). On User Studies and Information Needs. *Journal of Documentation, 37*(1), 3-15.

Wilson, T. D. (1999). Models in Information Behaviour Research. *Journal of Documentation. 55*(3), 249-270.

Wilson, T. D., & Walsh C. (1996). *Information behaviour: an interdisciplinary*

Wu, G., Huang, Y., Shian-Shyong, T., & Zhang, F. (1999). A knowledge sharing and collaboration system model based on Internet. *IEEE International Conference on Systems, Man, and Cybernetics, 2*, 148-152.

Xie, H. I. (2000). Shifts of Interactive Intentions and Information-Seeking Strategies in Interactive Information Retrieval. *Journal of American Society for Information Science. 51*(9), 841-857.

Xing-kai, Y., & Yan-zhang, W. (2006). A New Information Exchange Model Based on the Multi-agent. *Proceedings of the 2006 IEEE/WIC/ACM International Conference on Web Intelligence and Intelligent Agent Technology*.

Xiong, N., & Svensson, P. (June 2002). Multi-sensor management for information fusion: issues and approaches. *Information Fusion, 3*(2), 163-186.

XLMiner (2007). *Classification Tree*. Retrieved on 23 November 2008, from http://www.resample.com/xlminer/help/Ctree/ClassificationTree_intro.htm.

XML. (2008). Extensible Markup Language (XML) 1.0, 4th Ed., World Wide Web Consortium. W3C Recommendation. Retrieved June 18, 2008, from http://www.w3.org/TR/REC-xml

Xu, D., Wichadakul, D., & Nahrstedt, K. (2000). Resource-Aware Configuration of Ubiquitous Multimedia Services, *In proc. of 2000 IEEE International Conference on Multimedia and Expo*, Vol. 2, USA.

Yager, R. R. (2001). Penalizing Strategic Preference Manipulation in Multi-Agent Decision Making. *IEEE Transactions on Fuzzy Systems, 9*(3), 393-403.

Yang, C. (2002). *Knowledge and Learning in Natural Learning*. Oxford: Oxford University Press.

Yang, Y., Williams, H. M., Pooley, R., & Dewar, R. (2006). Context-Aware Personalization in Pervasive Communications. *In Proceedings of the IEEE International Conference on e-Business Engineering (ICEBE'06)* (pp. 663-669). Shanghai, China.

Yeaple, R. N. (1992). Why Are Small R&D Organizations More Productive? *IEEE Transactions on Engineering Management, 39*(4), 332-346.

Yeatts, D. E., & Hyten, C. (1998). *High-Performing Self-Managed Work Teams: A Comparison of Theory to Practice*. Thousand Oaks, CA: Sage Publications.

Yli-Hietanen, J., & Niiranen, S. (2008). Towards Open Information Management in Health Care. *The Open Medical Informatics Journal, 2*(1), 42-48.

Younger, D. H. (1967). Recognition and parsing of context-free languages in time n^3. *Information and Control, 10*, 189–208.

Yu, H., Zhang, S., Yang, N., Ding, H., & Wang, X. (2003). Intelligent Agent-Based Distributed Heterogeneous Database System. *In the Proc. of 2nd International Conference on Machine Learning and Cybernetics*. China: IEEE CS Press.

Zadeh, L. A. (1965). Fuzzy sets. *Inform Control, 8*, 338-358.

Zeigler B. P., & Hammonds P. E. (2007). *Modeling and simulation-based data engineering*. Boston, Massachusetts: Elsevier Academic Press.

Zhao, F., Shin J., & Reich J., (March 2002). Information-driven dynamic sensor collaboration for tracking applications. *IEEE Signal Processing Magazine, 19*(2), pp.61-72.

Zheng, T., & Iyengar, V. S. Recommender Systems Using Linear Classifiers. *Journal of Machine Learning, 2*, 313-334.

Zhou, B., & Hansen, J. H. (2000). Unsupervised audio stream segmentation and clustering via the Bayesian information criterion. *International Conference on Spoken Language Processing, 3*, pp. 714-717. Beijing, China.

Zhou, L. (2007). Research of Data Processing in Mine Safty Monitoring System Based on Multisensor Information Fusion. *The Eighth International Conference on Electronic Measurement and Instruments ICEMI'2007*

Ziv, J., & Lempel, A. (1977). A universal algorithm for sequential data compression. *IEEE Transactions on Information Theory, 23*(3), 337–343.

Zuboff, S. (1988). *In the Age of the Smart Machine: The Future of Work and Power*. New York: Basic Books.

Zwicker, E., & Fastl, H. (1999). *Psychoacoustics: facts and models*. Berlin-Heidelberg: Springer Verlag.

About the Contributors

Samuli Niiranen received his MSc (Tech.) and DSc (Tech.) degrees in biomedical engineering and signal processing from the Tampere University of Technology (Tampere, Finland) in 2001 and 2005, respectively. He is currently with the Department of Signal Processing of the Tampere University of Technology where his research focus is on open information management with an emphasis on health care applications. His previous research areas include use of information technology in chronic disease management as well as broadcasting multimedia. Apart from his work in academia, Dr. Niiranen has participated in a number of commercial ventures in the field of chronic disease information management and hospital information systems. He is the author or co-author of more than 30 scientific publications in health informatics and multimedia and is the co-author of a textbook on broadcasting multimedia. He was a visiting faculty member at the Decision Systems Group, Brigham and Women's Hospital, Harvard Medical School (Boston, Massachusetts, USA) from 2006 to 2007. Dr. Niiranen has received, among others, the Nokia Corporation Educational Award. He was a member of a consortium selected as a finalist for the eEurope Awards for eHealth 2003 organized by the European Commission.

Jari Yli-Hietanen received an MSc (Tech.) degree in signal processing from the Tampere University of Technology, Tampere, Finland, in 1995. He is currently with the Department of Signal Processing at the Tampere University of Technology. His current research focus is on open information management with an emphasis on natural language methods.

Artur Lugmayr describes himself as a creative thinker and his scientific work is situated between art and science. His vision can be expressed as to create media experiences on future emerging media technology platforms. He is the head and founder of the New AMbient MUltimedia (NAMU) research group at the Tampere University of Technology (Finland) which is part of the Finnish Academy Centre of Excellence of Signal Processing from 2006 to 2011 (http://namu.cs.tut.fi). He is holding a Dr.-Techn. degree from the Tampere University of Technology (TUT, Finland), and is currently engaged in Dr.-Arts studies at the School of Motion Pictures, TV and Production Design (UIAH, Helsinki). He chaired the ISO/IEC ad-hoc group "MPEG-21 in broadcasting"; won the NOKIA Award of 2003 with the text book "Digital interactive TV and Metadata" published by Springer-Verlag in 2004; representative of the Swan Lake Moving Image & Music Award board member of MindTrek, EU project proposal reviewer; invited key-note speaker for conferences; organizer and reviewer of several conferences; and has contributed one book chapter and written over 25 scientific publications. His passion in private life is to be a notorious digital film-maker. He is founder of the production company LugYmedia Inc.

* * *

Abdellatif BenAbdelhafid received the postgraduate certificate in Automatic from the University of Havre, France, the PhD degree in Automatic from the University of Havre, France and the HdR degree in Computer Science from the University of Havre, France. He is the Director of the research unit Integrated Logistic System (ILS) of CERENE Laboratory. His research interests include logistic, integrated logistic system, computational intelligence: fuzzy systems, genetic and evolutionary algorithms, multi-agent systems, parallel and distributed architectures, Prof. ABDELLATIF is an IEEE Member and member of several committees of program related to various conferences, revues and journals.

Matthew O. Adigun recieved his PhD in Computer Science at Obafemi Awolowo University, Nigeria. He is currently the Professor and Head of the Department of Computer Science, University of Zululand, South Africa, a position he has held since 1989. His research interests are in Software Engineering and Architecting of Mobile and Pervasive Systems. He has presented papers at national and international conferences in his and related areas of research interests. As a principal investigator, he has led research sponsored by the National Research Foundation under the Research Niche Area titled *Software Infrastructure for E-Commerce and E-Business* with a group of CS, IS and Business Management researchers from inside and outside of the University of Zululand, South Africa.

Adel M. Alimi received the engineer degree in Electrical Engineering from the National School of Engineers, University of Sfax, Tunisia, the PhD degree in Electrical Engineering from Polytechnique Schools of Montréal, Canada and the HdR degree in Electrical Engineering (Computer Engineering) from the National School of Engineers, Tunisia. He is currently a Professor and Director of the National School of Engineers, Tunisia. He is the Founder and Director of the Laboratory REGIM (Research Group on Intelligent Machines) and the Associate Editor for the international journal « Pattern Recognition Letters ». His research interests include computational intelligence: neural systems, fuzzy systems, genetic and evolutionary algorithms, learning, artificial intelligence, multi-agent systems, parallel and distributed architectures, VLSI implementation, pattern recognition, document analysis, PDA handwriting GU, multimedia information analysis. Prof. ALIMI is an IEEE Senior Member and member of several committees of program related to various conferences, revues and journals.

Susmit Bagchi received BSc(Honours) from Calcutta University in the year of 1993. He received BE (Electronics Engg.) and ME (Electronics & Telecom. Engg.) from Nagpur University and Bengal Engineering and Science University (BESU), Shibpur in 1997 and 1999 respectively. He completed PhD in Computer Science from BESU, Shibpur in the year of 2008. Currently he is holding Technical Lead position in ATD, Samsung Electronics Ltd. (SISO) at Bangalore. His domains of research interests are in Operating Systems, Distributed Algorithms and Systems and Mobile Computing.

Yacine Benahmed received his BSc degree in computer science in 2005 and MS degree in 2008 in electrical engineering both from the Université de Moncton. He worked as a research assistant at the Human-Machine Interaction Lab. at the Université de Moncton, Campus de Shippagan since 2005. In 2007, the Université de Moncton granted him a performance scholarship for his outstanding results. His main research interests involve distributed interactive systems, dialogue systems on mobile telecommunications, intelligent agents and pervasive technologies.

Rakesh Biswas is a professor of medicine in People's college of Medical Sciences, Bhopal, India. He is actively involved in patient centred learning with an aim to create a learning network between patients, health professionals and other actors in a care giving collaborative process that has been termed 'user driven health care'.

Pauli Brattico currently works as a senior assistant at the department of Computer Science and Information Systems, University of Jyväskylä, Finland. He obtained his PhD degree in 2004 from the University of Helsinki, and his research interests include biolinguistics, syntax, semantics and complexity.

Chia-Chu Chiang is an associate professor in the Department of Computer Science at University of Arkansas at Little Rock (UALR). Dr. Chiang earned his PhD degree in Computer Science from Arizona State University, Arizona, USA in 1995. He has published more than 90 referred research papers in IEEE, ACM, and international journals and conferences with his collaborators, colleagues, and students. Dr. Chiang has obtained external funding from ETRI, Syntel™ LLC., Acxiom, CognitiveDATA, DOD (US Department of Defense), and NSF (National Science Foundation). He is involved in many professional service activities including advisory board members, conference chairs, program committee members, reviewers, and journal editors. His research areas include formal methods, reverse engineering, reengineering, program analysis, component-based software development, middleware, heterogeneous distributed parallel programming, and text extraction from various file formats. Dr. Chiang is a member of ABET, ACM, and IEEE.

Adel S. Elmaghraby is professor and Chair of the Computer Engineering and Computer Science Department at the University of Louisville. He has also held appointments at the SEI - CMU, and the University of Wisconsin-Madison. His research is in Network Performance and Security Analysis, Intelligent Multimedia Systems, Neural Networks, PDCS, Visualization, and Simulation with applications to biomedical computing, automation, and military wargames. He is a Senior Member of the IEEE and active in editorial boards, and conference organization. He has been recognized for his achievements by several professional organizations including a Golden Core Membership Award by the IEEE Computer Society.

Khaled Ghedira received the engineer degree in Hydraulics from the Superior National School of Electrotechnic, Electronic, Data Processing, Hydraulic and Telecommunication, France, the specialization engineer degree in Computer Science and Applied Mathematic from the ENSIMAG, France, the PhD degree in Computer Science from Paris Graduate School of Economic, Statistics and Finance, France, and the HdR degree in Computer Science from the National School of Computer Science, University of Manouba, Tunisia. He is currently a Professor in the Higher Institute of Management, Tunisia. He is the Founder and Director of the Laboratory LI3 (Laboratory of Intelligent Computer Engineering, Ex-SOIE) and the Director of ATIA (Tunisian Association of Artificial Intelligence). His research interests include: multi-agent systems, Constraint Satisfaction Problems, artificial intelligence, optimization combinatorial by metaheuristics, scheduling problem and transportation, fuzzy systems, genetic and evolutionary algorithms, learning, parallel and distributed architecture, logistic. Prof. Ghedira is a member of several committees of program related to various conferences, revues and journals.

Christine B. Glaser (c.glaser@surrey.ac.uk) is a PhD student at the University of Surrey. She studied Media and Communication at the University of Vienna, Austria and graduated in April 2005. The focus of her PhD is the investigation of distributed synchronous collaboration, human-computer interaction and human-human interaction. She is particularly interested in the technical and social features of collaborative interfaces required to support distributed synchronous collaboration by means of qualitative content analysis, grounded theory, hermeneutics and activity theory.

Lisandro Zambenedetti Granville is an associate professor at the Institute of Informatics of the Federal University of Rio Grande do Sul (UFRGS), Brazil. He received his MSc and PhD degrees, both in computer science, from UFRGS in 1998 and 2001, respectively. He has served as a TPC member (2003-2008), General Co-Chair (2004), and Steering Committee member (2005-2008) for the Brazilian Symposium on Computer Networks (SBC/LARC SBRC). Currently, he is member of the Brazilian Internet Committee (CBG.br). He has served as a TPC member for IFIP/IEEE IM 2005, NOMS 2006, IM 2007, NOMS 2008 and IFIP/IEEE DSOM 2005, DSOM 2006, DSOM 2007 (TPC Co-Chair), DSOM 2008. His main areas of interest include policy-based network management, management using/of Web services, network monitoring and configuration, and P2P-based services and applications.

Habib Hamam obtained the Diploma of Engineering in information processing from the Technical University of Munich, Germany, 1992, and the PhD degree in telecommunications from Université de Rennes I conjointly with France Telecom Graduate School, France 1995. He also obtained a postdoctoral diploma, "Accreditation to Supervise Research in Signal Processing and Telecommunications", from Université de Rennes I in 2004, based on research work in France Telecom, University of Montreal, University of Moncton and Laval University. He is currently a full Professor in the Department of Electrical Engineering at University of Moncton, a Canada Research Chair holder in "Optics in Information and Communication Technologies", the Director of the Research Center of the Canadian University of Dubai and its acting Vice-President in charge of Academic Affairs. He is expert in accreditation for engineering programs (North-American and UAE criteria). He is an IEEE senior member and a registered professional engineer in New-Brunswick. He is among others associate editor of the IEEE Canadian Review, member of the editorial boards of Wireless Communications and Mobile Computing - John Wiley & Sons - and of Journal of Computer Systems, Networking, and Communications - Hindawi Publishing Corporation. He is also member of a national committee of the NSERC (Canada). His research interests are in optical telecommunications, Human-Computer Interaction, Optical/Wireless hybrid systems, Electromagnetics applied to health, RFID systems and e-Learning.

Marko Helén, born 1977, received his MSc degree from Tampere University of Technology, Tampere, Finland, in 2001. He is currently a researcher at the Department of Signal Processing, Tampere University of Technology, where he is part of the audio research group. His research interests include multimedia information retrieval, sound source separation, and object based coding. He is finalizing his PhD thesis on similarity measures in audio retrieval applications. He has authored a number scientific papers on audio signal processing, especially on audio retrieval.

Lobna Hsairi received the university degree in Computer Science from Faculty of Economic Sciences and Management of Sfax, University of Sfax, Tunisia, the postgraduate certificate in Information Systems and new Technologies from Faculty of Economic Sciences and Management of Sfax, Tunisia.

She is currently PhD Student on Computing System Engineering, in National School of Engineers, Tunisia. She is an assistant in Computer Sciences Department at the Faculty of Economic Sciences and Management of Sfax, Tunisia. She is member of three research laboratories: LI3 Ex-SOIE, REGIM, ILS-CERENE. Her research interests include computational intelligence: artificial intelligence, multi-agent systems, argumentation, negotiation, argumentation based negotiation, fuzzy systems, parallel and distributed architectures, enterprise, extended enterprise, logistic, scheduling problem and transportation. Dr. Hsairi is an IEEE graduate student, and a member of ATIA (Tunisian association of Artificial Intelligence).

Doris Ipsmiller is CEO of the innovation and development company m2n – consulting and development ltd. She founded the m2n in 1999 while being staff member of the Johannes Kepler University in Linz. Apart from widespread project experience, primarily in the public and industry sector, Doris Ipsmiller has lectured on the topics of knowledge management and knowledge organisation in diverse academic institutions like the Johannes Kepler University Linz, the Danube University Krems, the Fachhochschule Hagenberg and the University of Applied Sciences, Berlin. She has held speeches at various events and conferences like the I-KNOW, the IRIS, International Legal Informatics Symposium or the symposium "Medienzeitreise" in Berlin and has published numerous titles on topics concerning agile business process development, applied ontology management, ontology based application development and rule based engineering. She is currently leader auf numerous projects like the DYONIPOS Pilotproject at the Ministry of Finance.

Jitendra Jain is an assistant professor of Medicine in People's College of Medical Sciences with a special interest in non invasive cardiology, medical education and health administration.

Edgar Jembere is a PhD student in the Centre for Mobile Services for Development at the University of Zululand. His research interests include data mining, knowledge engineering, service-oriented computing and mobile computing. Edgar Jembere received a BSc (Hons) degree in Statistics from the University of Zimbabwe and an MSc in Computer Science from the University of Zululand.

Ankur Joshi perused his graduation in Medicine and masters in Community Medicine from Gandhi Medical College, Bhopal, respectively at 2004 and 2008. His area of interest is infectious disease epidemiology (more specifically T.B., HIV and related issues) and health policy analysis. He has been involved in some community oriented studies during his residency period several of which were funded by reputed internal organization and Govt of India. He presented several papers in national and international conferences. His thesis topic in post gratuation was addressed to issue of nonadherence in Tuberculosis. He believes that User Driven Health -care may be an appropriate, acceptable and affordable as well as sustainable response to meager resources in a developing country set up.

Deborah G. Keeling has a PhD in Sociology from Purdue University. She is currently a professor and Chair of the Department of Justice Administration and responsible for oversight of academic programs in Justice Administration and the Southern Police Institute and the National Crime Prevention Institute. Dr. Keeling serves on a number of university and professional boards including the Victim Assistance Committee of the International Association of Chiefs of Police, Metro Louisville Police Accountability Commission, Board of Directors of the Kentucky Regional Computer Forensics Laboratory, Member of the Advisory Board for the Turkish Institute for Security and Democracy and Kentucky PROTECT the Secret Service Cybercrimes partnership. Most recently, Dr. Keeling has been completing a federally funded $2.9 million project in partnership with the FBI. As a result of this project, the first FBI Regional Computer Forensics Lab to be directly located on a university campus in partnership with the institution has been established at the University of Louisville. Through this federal funding and an additional $701,000 recently acquired, Dr. Keeling in partnership with university faculty, the FBI, Kentucky Attorney General and Kentucky Bar Association has been working to provide digital forensics training to the full range of criminal justice practitioners within the Commonwealth. Dr. Keeling has also worked extensively on international projects related to the democratization of policing and cessation of domestic violence in China, Hungary, Romania, Slovakia and Panama. Dr. Keeling has extensive experience in applied research within criminal justice agencies. She has conducted research and consultation for various federal, state, and local organizations including the Federal Bureau of Justice Statistics, New York State Police, Kentucky Department of Corrections, Kentucky Justice Cabinet, Metro Criminal Justice Council, and Louisville Metro Police Department. She is the author or co-author of numerous publications on various topics within criminal justice and law enforcement. She is or has been actively involved in the analysis of crime victim and citizen attitude surveys for a number of local and state police agencies. She has received the Melvin Shein Award of the Kentucky Law Enforcement Council for contributions to law enforcement training, the Mayor's Award for distinguished service, Business and Professional Women's Award for "Woman of Achievement", Hungarian National Police Award for contributions to democratization and Slovakia Ministry of the Interior award for contributions to police education.

Juha Kesseli was born in Riihimäki, Finland, in 1979. He received his MSc and Dr.Tech degrees from the Department of Information Technology, Tampere University of Technology (TUT), Finland, in 2001 and 2007, respectively. His PhD thesis is entitled "*Annealed approximation and Boolean network dynamics*", and it has been awarded the Tampere science foundation award for the best thesis of TUT in 2007. The work for the thesis was done in the group of Computational Systems Biology of Prof. Olli Yli-Harja at the Institute of Signal Processing. Dr. Kesseli has co-authored 7 articles in international scientific journals. Starting from September 1st, 2008, he has been working as a post-doctoral researcher in the Group for Neural Theory at Ecole Normale Supérieure, Paris, France.

Anssi Klapuri received his PhD degree from Tampere University of Technology (TUT), Tampere, Finland, in 2004. In 2005, he spent six months at the Ecole Centrale de Lille, Lille, France, working on music signal processing. In 2006, he spent three months visiting the Signal Processing Laboratory of Cambridge Univerisity, Cambridge, UK. He is currently a Professor at the Department of Signal Processing, TUT, where he leads the audio research group. His research interests include speech and audio signal processing, auditory modeling, and information retrieval. He has co-edited the book "*Signal processing methods for music transcription*" and authored a number of scientific papers on audio signal processing.

Juhana Kokkonen is senior lecturer in Helsinki Metropolia University of Applied Sciences. He has been project manager and researcher in numerous R&D-projects, where the focus is in social media applications and products. Kokkonen is also a PhD student in University of Art and Design Helsinki's

Media Lab. The subject of his doctoral thesis is organizational development and management using transparent social media.

Ahmet M. Kondoz (a.kondoz@surrey.ac.uk) was born in Cyprus. He studied BSc (Hons.) degree in engineering, and MSc degree in telematics in 1983 and 1984, respectively, before receiving his PhD degree in communication in 1986. He became a Lecturer in 1988, a Reader in 1995, and then in 1996, a Professor in Multimedia Communication Systems and deputy director of Center for Communication Systems Research (CCSR), University of Surrey, Guildford, U.K. He has over 250 publications, including two books on low-bit-rate speech coding and several book chapters, and seven patents. He has graduated more than 50 PhD students in the areas of speech/image and signal processing and wireless multimedia communications, and has been a consultant for major wireless media terminal developers and manufacturers. Prof. Kondoz has been awarded several prizes, the most significant of which are The Royal Television Societies Communications Innovation Award and The IEEE Benefactors Premium Award. Prof. Kondoz is also a director of Mulsys Ltd. a University of Surrey spin-off company marketing worlds first secure GSM communication system through the GSM voice channel.

Tommi Lahti, born 1973, Professor Lihti finished his masters and licentiate theses in mathematics in 2000 and 2005, respectively. While working first for Technical university of Tampere (TUT), he moved to Nokia research center in 2001. He is currently a senior research scientist. The research topics include automatic speech recognition, audio content analysis and multimedia content analysis research more in general. Tommi Lahti is an author of more than 10 conference publications. He has also lead multimedia collaboration projects with various research institutes. Currently he is finalizing his PhD thesis on low complexity automatic speech techniques and automatic audio content analysis.

Sune Lehmann is currently a postdoc at Center for Complex Network Research at Northeastern University and a Research Fellow at the Center for Cancer Systems Biology, Dana Farber Cancer Institute, Harvard University. His work focuses on understanding the structural and dynamical aspects of complex network topology, seen from a statistical standpoint. He is currently working to understand how the temporal dynamics of network edges influence the modular structure found in many social networks. Previous work has foucused on understanding the type of correlations that scientific authors and collaborations impose on the (citation) links between the publications. Sune is a graduate of the Niels Bohr Institute (MSc, 2004) and the Technical University of Denmark (PhD, 2007).

Michael Losavio is an attorney working on issues of law, ethics and society and information security in the computer engineering and justice administration disciplines He works with the Department of Justice Administration and the Department of Computer Engineering and Computer Science at the University of Louisville in teaching and training in these areas. He teaches and has published on the synthesis of legal/ethical precepts and social science data with computer engineering, digital forensics and computing's impact on judicial and legal practice. Mr. Losavio also works on curriculum development for conferences, courses and seminars on the impact of information and computing systems in a variety of disciplines. He holds a JD from Louisiana State University Law School, and a BS in Mathematics, also from Louisiana State University, USA.

Mikko Määttä (M.A.) is a researcher interested in several aspects of natural languages including parsing and language acquisition. He is working at the Department of Psychology (Cognitive Science Unit) of the University of Helsinki, Finland. He is currently employed in a project to develop a parser for the Finnish language implementing ideas from a recent research program in linguistics called Minimalism. Mikko Määttä is currently located at the Institute of Cognitive Science at the University of Osnabrück, Germany, as part of the researcher exchange program of the project. He has previously worked in several research institutions including the Helsinki school of economics Center for knowledge and innovation research (CKIR).

Josef Makolm is head of IT-Audit in the Directorate General for Information Technology at the Austrian Federal Ministry of Finance. He has over 30 years of experience in research, consulting and managing projects. His main activities and responsibilities are topics in e-Government, e-Taxation, e-Participation, e-Procurement, Knowledge Management, Interoperability and Multiple Use. He has published articles and books on these topics. He is member of the board of the Austrian Computer Society, co-leader of the Forum e-Government, head of workgroups in the Forum e-Government and the Austrian BLSG-Cooperation and lecturer at Danube University Krems. At present, he is project manager of the research and of the awarded use case project DYONIPOS and the program leader of the Austrian part of the EU project PEPPOL (Pan European Public Procurement Online). He is responsible for the Workpackage 2 "Virtual Company Dossier" - a project for borderless collection of business certificates and attestations.

Carmel M. Martin is an associate professor of Family Medicine at the Northern Ontario School of Medicine. She is a health services researcher with a special interest in Primary Health Care systems in Canada, Australia, the UK and internationally. Her research themes include complex adaptive chronic care, equity and health disparities.

Cristina Melchiors is a PhD student in Computer Science at the Institute of Informatics of the Federal University of Rio Grande do Sul (UFRGS), Brazil. She currently works on cooperative and distributed network management using P2P technologies. She received a BSc degree in Informatics from the Pontifical Catholic University of Rio Grande do Sul (PUCRS) in 1995, and a MSc degree in Computer Science from Federal University of Rio Grande do Sul (UFRGS) in 1999. Her main areas of interest include cooperative network management, distributed network management, fault management, artificial intelligence applied to network management, case-based reasoning and P2P computing.

Khaled Ahmed Nagaty is an associate professor at The British University in Egypt, Computer Science Department, Cairo, Egypt. Khaled is currently an associate professor of Computer Science at the British University in Egypt, an Egyptian University in partnership with Loughborough University in UK. He is an associate professor at the Faculty of Informatics and Computer Science, Computer Science department. Khaled was graduated from Cairo University in Egypt with a bachelor's degree in Statistics in 1982, and a masters' degree in computer science in 1990. He completed his doctorate in pattern recognition in 1999 in Cairo University. Khaled started teaching at the information sciences institute in Egypt in 1985 and became involved with systems analysis and design for many governmental departments at the Egyptian Ministry of Interior. He worked as an Assistant Professor of computer science at Ain-Shams University in 2000 in Cairo and in 2003 he worked as a visiting assistant professor at Amman University in Jordan. From 2006 until 2008 he worked as a visiting associate professor in Saudi Arabia at Taibah University. His research interests include biometrics, statistical pattern recognition and image processing.

Vinod Narkhede is an assistant professor of Community medicine with a special interest in community based applied nutrition and health informatics.

Matti Nykter was born in Finland, October 12, 1978. From 1999 to 2002 he was a MSc student and research assistant, in the Department of Information Technology, Tampere University of Technology, Finland. He received his Master of Science in Technology (with distinction), Tampere University of Technology with the thesis: *"Localization of a Sound Source Using Acoustic Vector Sensors"*. His major was in Signal processing methods. From 2003 to 2006 he was a post-graduate student in Department of Information Technology, Tampere University of technology, Finland. His supervisor was Prof. Olli Yli-Harja. In 2006 he became a Doctor of Science in Technology, Tampere University of Technology. Thesis title was: *"Signal Processing Methods and Information Approach to Systems Biology"*. From 2002 to 2006 he was a researcher and project manager at institute of digital and computer systems, Tampere University of technology. From 2006 to 2007 he was a Senior Researcher at institute of signal processing, Tampere University of Technology. Since 2007 he has been a post-doctoral fellow at Institute for Systems Biology; also associated with the Institute of Signal Processing, Tampere University of Technology.

Andre Sanches Ribeiro was born in March 8, 1976, Luanda, Angola, and is of Portuguese nationality. He graduated in Physics, Faculdade de Ciências, University of Lisbon, Portugal (1999). He received his PhD degree in Physics Engineering at Instituto Superior Técnico, University Tecnica of Lisbon, Portugal, in July, 2004, under the supervision of Prof. F. Carvalho Rodrigues. From 2004 to 2007 he was a Post-Doctoral fellow in Institute for Biocomplexity and Informatics and Department of Physics & Astronomy, University of Calgary, Canada. He was supervised by Stuart A. Kauffman, MD. Since November 2007, he is a Senior Researcher, at the Computational systems biology research group, Institute of Signal Processing, Tampere University of Technology, Finland.

Dwayne Rosenburgh is a senior research scientist & engineer at the Laboratory for Telecommunications Sciences (US DoD). He is also a member of the adjunct faculties at the University of Maryland, and Howard Community College. His research interests include wireless networking & communications, decision theory, and the design & management of technical organizations. He received his D.Sc. and MSc in engineering from the George Washington University; and the BSc in physics from Morgan State University. Dr. Rosenburgh is listed in Marquis' Who's Who in America, and Who's Who in Science & Engineering. He is a member of Mensa, and a senior member of the IEEE.

Teemu Saarelainen has studied information technology at Tampere University of Technology (TUT) and worked as a researcher at the signal processing laboratory for a few years during the late 1990's. In the early 2000 he began working as a software engineer and researcher for a reverse vending machine manufacturer, but at the same time he also continued his post graduate studies at TUT. From 2004 onwards Mr. Saarelainen has worked at Kymenlaakso University of Applied Sciences, where he has acted as a research manager and part-time lecturer at the software engineering study programme.

Nowadays, Mr. Saarelainen is responsible for the information technology study programme and holds the position of a senior lecturer with teaching activities in the fields of software engineering, programming, algorithms and technical mathematics.

Sid-Ahmed Selouani received his B.Eng. degree in 1987 and his MS degree in 1991 both in electronic engineering from the Algiers University of Technology (U.S.T.H.B). He joined the Communication Langagière et Interaction Personne-Système (CLIPS) Laboratory of Université Joseph Fourier of Grenoble taking part in the Algerian-French double degree program and then he got a Docteur d'État degree in the field of signal processing and artificial intelligence in 2000. From 2000 to 2002 he held a post-doctoral fellowship in the Multimedia Group at the Institut National de Recherche Scientifique (INRS-Télécommunications) in Montréal. He is currently full Professor and responsible of the Human-Machine Interaction Laboratory at the Université de Moncton, Campus de Shippagan. He is also an invited Professor at INRS-Télécommunications. His main areas of research involve speech and signal processing, e-services, information management, data mining, ubiquitous systems and assistive technologies for the elderly.

Kevin Smith is translational research leader with National digital research centre, Ireland and a Scientific Advisor on collaborative medical education to the Northern Ontario School of Medicine. In 1977 he received an MPhil in pure mathematics from Murdoch University in Western Australia and then spent 10 years at the University of London working on the application of massively parallel computing to a wide range of applications from lattice gauge simulations to medical image processing. He returned to Australia in 1990 and joined CSIRO - the Australian Government's main R&D agency. There he set up the joint Australian National University - CSIRO Virtual Environments Laboratory that pioneered the development and application of collaborative hapto-visual environments to surgical training. In 2001, he was the founding Director of the Western Australian Interactive Virtual Environments Centre before moving to Canada in 2003 to be a Strategic Advisor to the National Institute for Nanotechnology.

Joachim P. Sturmberg is an associate proffessor of General Practice at Monash University Melbourne and The University of Newcastle, Australia. He has a longstanding involvement in under- and post-graduate teaching in General Practice. His main research interest relates to the complex adaptive nature of health service structures and their impact on patient care.

Amy Tan (a.tan@surrey.ac.uk) is a human factors researcher and participates across several research communities such as Simulation, Architectural Computing, Transport Research, Wireless World Research Forum, Spatial Cognition and Computation. Her research expertise is in the user experience of a virtual collaboration system and evaluations of such systems with a combination of lifecycle, ethnographic, and usability engineering methods. This includes exploring ways to understand user needs and to incorporate them in new future collaborative technologies and how such new technologies impacts on the socio-technical organisational structures and vice versa.. She is particularly interested in cross cultural distributed teams and in longitudinal case studies that produces qualitative results on an extended use of a system to understand technology adoption and acceptability issues.

Liane Margarida Rockenbach Tarouco has a PhD Electrical Eng. (USP-Brazil) Full Professor at Federal University of Rio Grande do Sul in Porto Alegre, Brazil. Vice-Director at Interdisciplinary

Center for Studies on Technology in Education. Researcher at Graduate Program in Computer Science at UFRGS. Author of book Computer Networks published by McGraw Hill (in Portuguese).

John Tsiligaridis obtained his most recent PhD in Computer Science and Engineering from The State University of New York at Buffalo, USA, in Sept 2003.Before that he got a MPhil by research in Computation/Data Mining from the University of Manchester, UK. He also holds a PhD in Computer Networks from the National Technical University of Athens, and a MSc in Informatics and Operational Research from the University of Athens, Greece. His BSc have been in Mathematics and Economics. He has worked for more than 10 years in Software Engineering positions and developed a variety of projects and applications. He is currently working as Assistant Professor in the Mathematics and Computer Science Department of Heritage University in Toppenish, WA. Before that he worked as Research Faculty Fellow at the Pacific Northwest National Laboratory in Richland, WA. He has published extensively and his current research interests include Distributed Systems, Networking, Scheduling, Mobile Databases, Wireless Communications, Data Mining, Text Mining, and Bioinformatics.

Silke Weiß studied "Diplom Informationswirtschaft" at the University of Karlsruhe. Currently she is consultant at the Federal Computing Center of Austria and she works for the Federal Ministry of Finance. In addition she is co-leader of the working group "Organisation" within the Forum e-Government of the Austrian Computer Society. For two years she has been working in the field of e-Government. Her research interests are in the fields of e-Government, e-Participation (especially Stakeholder Involvement at new e-Government Projects), Knowledge Management, Semantic Technologies and Orchestration of Business Processes. On this topics and especially on DYONIPOS she has published several articles. At present, she is consultant at the research and use case project DYONIPOS and also involved in the Austrian part of the EU project PEPPOL.

Sibusiso S. Xulu received his PhD in Applied Mathematics at University of Zululand, South Africa. He has been attached to Computer Science department, University of Zululand, as a Senior Lecturer since 2001. He currently leads a research project funded by the South African National Research Foundation (2008-2010) titled *Context management and personalization Issues*. His research interests are in Mobile Computing, and in General Relativity.

Index

Symbols

A

B